THE EARLY CHRISTIAN CHURCH

VOLUME I

THE FIRST CHRISTIAN CENTURY

THE EARLY CHRISTIAN CHURCH

BY

PHILIP CARRINGTON
ARCHBISHOP OF QUEBEC

VOLUME I
THE FIRST CHRISTIAN CENTURY

CAMBRIDGE
AT THE UNIVERSITY PRESS
1957

PUBLISHED BY
THE SYNDICS OF THE CAMBRIDGE UNIVERSITY PRESS

Bentley House, 200 Euston Road, London, N.W.1
American Branch: 32 East 57th Street, New York 22, N.Y.

Printed in Great Britain at the University Press, Cambridge
(Brooke Crutchley, University Printer)

To

FREDERICK CLIFTON GRANT

Professor of Biblical Theology at the
Union Theological Seminary
New York

CONTENTS

List of Illustrations . . . . *page* ix
List of Maps and Tables xii
The Sources xiii
Introduction xvii
Chapter 1 The Hellenistic Period 1
2 Galilee and Jerusalem 24
3 Caesarea 47
4 Antioch and Galatia 66
5 Conference in Jerusalem 87
6 Macedonia and Achaia 108
7 Ephesus 125
8 Pilgrimage to Jerusalem 148
9 Paul in Rome 166
10 The Martyrdoms 186
11 The Tradition of Peter 205
12 The Fall of Jerusalem 221
13 Jewish Christianity 238
14 The Pauline Successors 256
15 Christian Literature under Vespasian 273
16 The Elders in Asia Minor 290
17 The Syrian Gospel 312
18 The Tyranny of Domitian 332
19 The Ephesian Gospel 350
20 Corinth and Rome 370
21 Hermas and his Angel 391

CONTENTS

Chapter 22 Oriental Christianity . . . . . *page* 410
23 The Wars of Trajan 428
24 Ignatius the Martyr 445
25 Apostolic Tradition 464
26 Catechism and Sacrament 481

Bibliography 502

Index 507

LIST OF ILLUSTRATIONS

1 Seleucid monarchs of the Hellenistic period . . *facing page* 16
(*a*) Seleuchus I (*c*) Antiochus III
(*b*) Antiochus I (*d*) Antiochus IV

Coin portraits from Rostovtzeff, *Social and Economic History of the Hellenistic World*, by permission of the Clarendon Press

2 A portion of Isaiah; a scroll in Hebrew from the Dead Sea 17

By courtesy of the American Schools of Oriental Research

3 Alexandria. A symbolic representation of the city in mosaic, signed by Sophilus and found at Thmuis 32

By courtesy of the Museum of Alexandria

4 (i) Jerusalem from the Mount of Olives. The Temple area and the Dome of the Rock are in the foreground . . . 33

Photograph, Paul Popper

(iii) The Temple area and the Dome of the Rock, which is supposed to stand on the original site of the Altar of Burnt Offerings in Solomon's Temple 33

Copyright, The American Colony, Jerusalem

5 (i) The Mount of Olives, showing the garden of Gethsemane and the recently completed Basilica 64

By courtesy of the Rev. J. N. Schofield

(ii) The Valley of Jehoshaphat, between the wall of the Temple area and the Jewish cemetery on the lower slopes of the Mount of Olives 64

By courtesy of Professor J. van der Ploeg

6 The Inscription of Theodotus in the Synagogue of Ophel, Jerusalem 65

From Sukenik, *Ancient Synagogues in Palestine and Greece*, by courtesy of the British Academy and the Department of Archaeology in the Hebrew University of Jerusalem

7 The Tyche of Antioch. This 'fortune' or city-goddess is a symbolic representation first devised (according to Pausanias) by the sculptor Eutychides. It is reproduced on coins, silver

ornaments and this marble statuette in the Vatican. The goddess rests on the rock, while the river Orontes, a young man, swims out from beneath her feet . . . . . . *facing page* 80
Photograph, Anderson

8 Caligula 81
From the bust in the Glyptotek, Copenhagen

9 The Cilician Gates, a mountain pass between Tarsus and Iconium. It was in all probability through this pass that Paul and Silas travelled in their visit to the 'Galatian' cities . . 112
Photograph, Paul Popper

10 (i) Athens: the Areopagus, showing the steps leading to the summit 113

(ii) Corinth: the 'Bema' on which in Byzantine times a church was built dedicated to St Peter and St Paul. This Bema is assumed to be the tribune on which Gallio stood when he heard the complaint of the Jews against Paul 113
Photographs, American Schools of Classical Studies, Athens

11 (i) Corinth: Ruins of the Temple 128
Photograph, Dorien Leigh

(ii) Ephesus: The Temple of Diana 128
From the reconstruction in Dinsmoor, *Architecture of Ancient Greece*, by permission of the Royal Institute of Architects

12 A Roman Ship: from a relief at Sidon 129
From Rostovtzeff, *Social and Economic History of the Ancient World* by permission of the Clarendon Press

13 Portrait of the Emperor Nero. From the bust in the Museo Nazionale, Rome 160
Photograph, Anderson

14 Christian burials near Jerusalem, showing Christian symbols . 161
Reproduced from an article by the late Professor Sukenik in the *American Journal of Archaeology*, by permission of the Department of Archaeology, the Hebrew University, Jerusalem

15 The sign of the cross in a Roman house at Herculaneum, possibly a Christian symbol 176

16 Writing materials of the imperial period: a papyrus roll, ink-wells, pens and styli . . . . *facing page* 177
British Museum

17 A scribe writing on his knee; he is in fact a census official . 208
From the Altar of Ahenobarbus in the Louvre. Archives photographiques, Paris

18 The Appian Way, an ancient road leading from Capua to Rome 209
Photograph, Anderson

19 The Arch of Titus at Rome, erected to commemorate the victory over the Jews in A.D. 70 224
Photograph, Anderson

20 The Arch of Titus: detail showing sacred ornaments captured by the Romans 225
Photograph, Alinari

21 Portrait of the Emperor Domitian. From the bust in the Museo Capitolino, Rome 336
Photograph, Alinari

22 A gallery in the Cemetery of Domitilla 337
Photograph by courtesy of the Benedictine Sisters of the Catacombs of Priscilla, Rome

23 (i) The Jewish Synagogue at Capernaum 352
From *Light from the Ancient Past* (Princeton University Press) by permission of the author, Mr J. Finegan

(ii) The Jewish Synagogue at Capernaum, the north-west corner 352
From Sukenik, *Ancient Synagogues*, by courtesy of the British Academy and the Department of Archaeology, Hebrew University of Jerusalem

24 Portrait of the Emperor Trajan. From the bust in the Museo Vaticano, Rome 353
Photograph, Alinari

25 The Colosseum, or Flavian Amphitheatre 384
Photograph, Anderson

26 (i) The Cathedra or Chair of Moses in a Synagogue . . 385
From Sukenik, *Ancient Synagogues*

(ii) Mosaic on a Synagogue floor 385
Ibid.

27 A Roman house: the atrium of the casa del Tramezzo di Legno at Herculaneum . . . . *facing page* 400
Photograph, Soprintendente alle Antichita della Campania, Naples

28 Catacomb paintings: (i) a baptism, a fisherman, the eucharist; (ii) a fisherman, a baptism 401
Photographs supplied by the Benedictine Sisters of the Catacombs of Priscilla

29 Catacomb paintings: (i) Eucharistic symbols; (ii) birds and fruit 416
Photographs supplied by the Benedictine Sisters of the Catacombs of Priscilla

30 Gnosticism: Vibia enters into the Sabazian Paradise . . 417
Photograph supplied by Professor Carlo Cechelli of Rome, and reproduced by his permission and that of the Istituto di Archaeologia Cristiana

31 A Sabazian Hand, a characteristic symbol from the syncretist Sabazian cult, contemporary with early Christianity . . 432
British Museum

LIST OF MAPS AND TABLES

Map 1 Palestine 48
2 The Christian Dispersion prior to A.D. 50 . . . 68
3 The new Pauline missions, A.D. 49–50 . . . 110
4 Asia, showing St Paul's churches A.D. 60 . . . 168
5 The Seven Churches of Asia 292
6 The journey of Ignatius 446
7 The Roman empire under Trajan . . . . *at end*

Chronological Tables:
The Oriental empires 1
The Maccabaean kingdoms 21
The Hasmonaean rulers 23
The first Christian generation A.D. 30–70 125

Genealogical Tables:
The descendants of Herod the Great 25
Family connexions of Jesus 31

List of High Priests in Jerusalem from 4 B.C. 186

THE SOURCES

SELECTED LIST OF ANCIENT AUTHORS FREQUENTLY QUOTED, MAINLY CHRISTIAN

(1) Period from A.D. 50 to 60

An asterisk * is used when alternative dates are given for a New Testament book. The Authorized version is used, except where the author has made his own translation.

For further information see similar list at the beginning of Volume II.

(*a*) PAUL. The *Epistles of Paul* provide the oldest literary sources which have come down to us intact. They were written between about A.D. 50 and about A.D. 65. The first group consists of *Galatians in 49, Thessalonians in 50, Corinthians in 54, and Romans in 54–55 (or *Galatians in 54); the second group, which was written from Rome, consists of *Ephesians, Colossians, Philippians, and Philemon. (For the Pastorals see below.)

(*b*) LUKE. The *Journals of Luke* belong to exactly the same period, and are incorporated into the Acts. They concern the evangelization of Greece by Paul and Silas in 49–50, and the foundation of the church at *Corinth*; the evangelization of Asia by Paul with Timothy and others in 52, and the foundation of the church at *Ephesus*. Then comes the pilgrimage to Jerusalem in 55 or 56, and *two years' residence at Caesarea* during 55–57.

This is succeeded by the voyage to *Rome* and *two years' residence* there between 58 and 61. Here the Journals come to an end; there is no sign in the Acts of any later sources, or any reference to later events or conditions.

(*c*) EARLIER SOURCES USED IN ACTS. The Journals of Luke belonged to a class of literature which dealt with the expansion of the gospel through apostolic persons, and the foundation of important churches which became centres of further evangelization. Luke possessed written sources describing the evangelization of Palestine, 'beginning from *Jerusalem*', through the preaching of Peter (with John); these also describe the evangelization of Samaria and the coast towns through the preaching of Philip, and the foundation of the church at *Caesarea* through the preaching of Peter. Another source described the evangelization of Syria, beginning with the foundation of the church at *Antioch*, from which the evangelization of eastern Phrygia took place through the preaching of 'Barnabas and Saul' in 47 or 48.

This material, in the form in which it appears in Acts, ends with the *Jerusalem Council* in 49. It leaves James in charge of the Jerusalem church.

The connecting link with the Journals of Luke is the prominence in both of the Jerusalem-Caesarea tradition, and the name of Philip.

(*d*) OTHER AVAILABLE SOURCES. The Acts and Epistles have embedded in them older material which took form in the apostolic mission, such as *kerugmata* (gospel preachings), catechisms, and apocalypses; also 'testimonies' or collections of prophetic passages from the Old Testament. These were probably still mainly oral in character and not fixed in form.

The material from which the written gospels were composed was also originally oral and was being taught by disciples of Jesus. A good deal of this may have been written down, and scholars assign to this period *the gospel document called Q*.

(2) PERIOD A.D. 60–70

(*a*) The *PASTORAL EPISTLES were ostensibly written before and during the Neronian persecution of 64; they contain material from letters of Paul written at this time to Timothy and Titus in Asia, and to Timothy from Rome, probably with some degree of editing.

(*b*) PETER. The **First Epistle of Peter* was written from Rome 'through Silvanus' (Silas), and included a salutation from Mark. (There is a theory that it is a 'pseudonymous' work of a later date.)

(*c*) MARK. The *Gospel of Mark*, written in Rome between 64 and 70, is based on the gospel tradition of Peter. Doubtless it was not the only attempt in this period to write down the gospel tradition. The document called Q is assigned to a slightly earlier date; and there is a tradition to the effect that Matthew wrote down some form of the gospel tradition in Aramaic.

(*d*) JOHN. The *Revelation of John* contains a number of prophecies which were composed in Jerusalem prior to its destruction in 70. (Some scholars think that they were not necessarily written by the prophet who composed the complete book.)

(3) PERIOD AFTER A.D. 70

(*a*) The *PASTORAL EPISTLES quite possibly received their present form in this period; some scholars place them in the nineties or later.

(*b*) LUKE AND ACTS. The *Acts of the Apostles* comes to an end in the year 60, but a great number of scholars think that it received its present form in this period. The *Gospel of Luke* makes use of Mark, which is assigned to about 67. (Some scholars place Luke-Acts in the nineties, and assign it to a later author, who made use of Luke's Journals with the other sources mentioned above, which could themselves then be placed later.)

(*c*) HEBREWS was written in this period, probably to Rome. (*Ephesians and *I Peter are placed in this period by those scholars who regard them as 'pseudonymous' writings composed in the apostolic schools. James and Jude are often included in this classification.)

(*d*) JOSEPHUS. The *Wars of the Jews* gives an account of the Jewish Wars, concluding with the war of 66–70.

(4) END OF THE CENTURY

(*a*) MATTHEW. This *Gospel* was produced in a Hellenistic church in Syria. It makes use of Mark and Q and Jewish-Christian material, possibly the Aramaic Matthew. The author did not know the work of Luke.

(*b*) JOSEPHUS. The *Antiquities of the Jews* traces the history of the Jews from the beginning down to 66.

(*c*) JOHN. The *Gospel* and *First Epistle*, and the *Revelation*, which are assigned by many scholars to different authors. There are also two small epistles.

(*d*) CLEMENT. A Roman writer in the succession of Peter and Paul wrote an *Epistle to the Corinthians* for the Roman church known as I Clement, A.D. 96.

(*e*) HERMAS. The *Visions* of Hermas; about 97–100 in Rome.

(5) EARLY SECOND CENTURY

(*a*) HERMAS. The *Commandments* and *Parables*, between 100 and 140; combined with the *Visions* to form the *Shepherd* or *Pastor*.

(*b*) IGNATIUS, bishop of Antioch, wrote seven *Epistles*, 110 to 115.

(*c*) POLYCARP, bishop of Smyrna, a pupil of John, wrote an *Epistle to the Philippians*, 110 to 115; died as a martyr 155 or 156.

(*d*) The so-called *Epistle of Barnabas* about 125, perhaps in Alexandria; and the *Didache* or *Teaching of the Twelve Apostles*, probably in Syria, 120 to 150.

(*e*) PAPIAS, bishop of Hierapolis (and the 'elders' of his period). Papias collected the sayings of Philip, John, and other disciples of the Lord, from the oral tradition and by personal intercourse, and used them to illustrate his *Interpretations of the Oracles of the Lord.* The book has not survived, but was quoted by Irenaeus, Eusebius, and others.

(*f*) *Latin Authors*. Tacitus, Pliny, Suetonius.

(6) Mid Second Century

(*a*) Justin was a contemporary of Papias and Polycarp during his early period as a Christian in Asia, about 125–135; began work in Rome about 145–150; died as a martyr about 165.

(*b*) Irenaeus was a pupil of Polycarp and the elders; quoted from Papias and Polycarp traditions of John; wrote his *Refutation* (or *Against Heresies*) about 185. Worked in Asia, Rome, and Gaul.

(*c*) Hegesippus, a Palestinian scholar, arrived in Rome about 160, with information about the Jewish-Christian traditions of James, and the family of the Lord, and the older Jewish sects; wrote his *Note-books* about 180. The book has not survived, but was used by Irenaeus, quoted by Eusebius, and also used by Epiphanius.

(*d*) The Mishnah. Traditions of the Jewish Rabbis of the first century were written down in the second century and incorporated in the Mishnah, 180–220, and in other Jewish literature.

(*e*) The Muratorian Fragment is a Latin translation of a Roman list of apostolic books originally composed in Greek between 180 and 200; ancient *Prologues* to New Testament books are found in some manuscripts.

(*f*) Hippolytus, a Roman Bishop, 200–235, preserved second-century traditions and information; e.g. he used lost works of Justin, and gives a transcript or summary of the prophet *Elkhasai* about 100.

(7) Church Historians

(*a*) Eusebius, the *Ecclesiastical History*, fourth century, quotes Papias, Hegesippus and numerous other early writers. Abbreviated as *E.H.*

(*b*) Epiphanius, the *Panarion*, and *Weights and Measures*, quotes good second-century sources which include Hegesippus.

INTRODUCTION

The primary object of this history is to provide an introduction to the story of the Christian church during the first two centuries, in narrative form, with sufficient detail and a sufficient use of original sources to make it a useful reference book for the persons and events of the period. The attempt to arrange so much material in chronological order and to relate it to the current of general history is no easy one, and decisions have had to be made on many points which are under debate among the leading scholars. It has not been possible to argue these points in detail, but it has been possible to indicate where serious differences of opinion exist, and to allow for alternative reconstructions of the history.

The foundation of history is a close study of the sources on which it is based. The knowledge of the sources must precede and support every other form of reading. An attempt has been made to present these sources, to give some account of each, and to let them speak for themselves. This is a book about sources as well as about events and persons.

It is probable that this history will be regarded as a 'conservative' one. The author is one of those who believe that the process of theoretical reconstruction has gone far enough, and that the time has come to review and consolidate the work. Nevertheless, it can hardly be denied that some reconstructions of a hypothetical character have been included. It is hoped that their hypothetical or suggestive character has always been clearly indicated.

The valuations which are placed upon the documents of the period today are by no means the same as were generally accepted a century ago. These new valuations should be accepted wherever it can be established that they are based upon sound literary or historical criticism; and this is where opinions are bound to differ. An element of personal judgement enters into the making of these decisions which no author can avoid. It often happens that a novel 'critical' valuation appeals to a scholar because it supports his own understanding of Christian history, or even some theoretical reconstruction to which he is committed; and this is equally true of 'conservative' and 'radical' scholars. No scholar can be confident that he is quite free from this tendency.

The 'tendency' in this history is to trust the evidence, and the tradition of the church in which it was produced and preserved; and to tell the story as the evidence presents it after it has been fairly examined and criticized. Those who desire to go further along the road of radical reconstruction can do so; and it is advantageous, even in this case, to begin with the story which the documents actually tell, and allow them to make their own impression.

In a few instances, however, a suggestion is made or an interpretation of the evidence is adopted which has an individual touch, or at any rate is not that of a majority of scholars. When this occurs it is clearly indicated, and it is hoped that such suggestions may prove to be of value as a contribution to the great work in which all are engaged.

The author does not, for instance, accept the undue emphasis upon apocalyptic or eschatology, very literally interpreted, which is common in modern scholarship; he regards it as a species of poetry. He does not accept the low estimate of the Revelation of St John which is common among scholars of the eschatological school; he regards it as a work of genius of the same order as the *Divine Comedy* of Dante or the *Paradise Lost* of Milton. He shares with many scholars the interest in liturgy as the historical medium in which the gospel expressed itself, and the importance of taking into account the Jewish antecedents in this and similar fields. Liturgy and apocalypse and gnosis seem to have been interrelated modes of thought which were congenial to the gospel as a Jewish movement of that particular period.

The gospel of Jesus Christ was of course the creative and determinative factor in the whole historical process. Doctrine is a legitimate development of the gospel in the course of interpretation and communication; but this history does not claim to be an introduction to Christian doctrine. It traces the emergence of the early theological schools from their beginnings in the creative evangelical period; it indicates their character; but that is as far as it goes. Its interest is primarily in the human beings who were the actors in the drama; the apostles, prophets, teachers, bishops, deacons, elders, martyrs, widows, virgins, and confessors; and even more the men and women and children who formed the rank and file of the church.

The author was led to the present study by a period of intensive research into the history of his own diocese. The first Bishop of Quebec was consecrated in 1793, and his journeys were far greater in extent than those of St Peter and St Paul; indeed, the journeys of the present bishop are not much less, though infinitely easier physically. It was an interesting experience, once this work had been done, to compare the analysis of the documentary records with the statements which were made by church people out of the local personal tradition. It is worth recording some of the results.

Fifty years is as nothing; there are always people who clearly remember the important facts; at one anniversary we had present with us the clergyman and one warden who had held office fifty years before. Statements about eighty years ago are reliable; false statements made at a church gathering would be promptly corrected. In connexion with the origins of a church, some facts from a hundred years ago are faithfully transmitted. The names of bishops or leading clergy and laity could easily be obtained without recourse to written documents. The sixth bishop of Quebec is still living at the age of ninety-six, and has told me about long conversations which he used to have with an old man who had clear memories of the first bishop. These two memories cover a hundred and forty years of time, being securely dated by a reference to the battle of Waterloo.

The author is therefore prepared to take seriously similar statements made by equally responsible church leaders in the church of the first or second century, out of the personal and official tradition, and all the more because oral tradition was then an organized means of communication. It does not seem right to brush aside such evidence, as some scholars do.

Such perhaps are the points on which the reader should be warned. If he disagrees with the author on these points, it will be no great difficulty for him to make the necessary adjustments. The constant reference to the sources makes such adjustment possible; and the sources themselves should be consulted as the final court of inquiry, and allowed to have the last word.

The author owes much to the kindness and patience of many friends who have helped and encouraged him; more than all, as he realizes now, to his father, who was a pupil of B. F. Westcott; to the various institutions of learning in many parts of the world in which he has studied, and particularly the Universities of New Zealand and Cambridge; to Laval University, Quebec, the oldest collegiate institution in North America, for library facilities; to his friend Canon R. K. Naylor of

Montreal, a master of theological learning; to Canon W. K. Lowther Clarke of Chichester, who kindly read through the first volume and made many stimulating suggestions; to his brother, Professor C. E. Carrington of the Royal Institute of International Affairs, for his advice and active assistance; and above all to Professor F. C. Grant of the Union Theological Seminary, New York, whose fabulous learning, kindly advice, and unfailing friendship it has been his privilege to enjoy for over a quarter of a century.

He also thanks Dr H. P. van Dusen, President of the Union Seminary, and other members of the staff for their great generosity in welcoming him into their midst, and allowing him the use of their magnificent library and other resources; and of course the Syndics and officials of the Cambridge University Press for encouraging him to undertake the task, and criticizing and supplementing his work. In connexion with the illustrations he desires to express his appreciation for the help given by Professor J. M. C. Toynbee, Dr W. H. Frend, the Rev. J. N. Schofield, Professor D. W. Thomas and others who have helped to supply photographs. Naturally none of these persons should be held responsible for any errors or omissions which may still persist, or for such personal views on the subject of 'The Early Church' as may not generally commend themselves.

PHILIP QUEBEC

New York
Feast of the Annunciation, 1955

CHAPTER 1

THE HELLENISTIC PERIOD

Alexander the Great, *p.* 2. Syrian Hellenism, *p.* 4. Oriental Faiths, *p.* 5. Egyptian Hellenism, *p.* 7. The Septuagint, *p.* 8. Jewish Hellenism, *p.* 10. The Hasmonaeans, *p.* 12. The Pharisees and Sadducees, *p.* 13. The Influence of Hellenism, *p.* 14. The Maccabaean Literature, *p.* 15. Hebrew or Aramaic Literature, *p.* 16. The Literature of Jewish Hellenism, *p.* 17. The Sibyl, *p.* 18. King Solomon's Wisdom, *p.* 19. Philo Judaeus, p. 20. The Times of Jesus, *p.* 20.

THE ORIENTAL EMPIRES

B.C.

THE ASSYRIAN EMPIRE

701 Sennacherib besieges Jerusalem.
Period of Isaiah.

THE BABYLONIAN EMPIRE

597 Nebuchadnezzar captures Jerusalem.
Period of Jeremiah.
586 Destruction of Jerusalem.
Period of Ezekiel.
Jewish leaders taken into exile in Babylon.
Other Jews take refuge in Egypt.

THE PERSIAN EMPIRE

550 Cyrus the Persian conquers the Medes.
538 Cyrus captures Babylon.
c. 520 Return of exiles to Jerusalem.
Period of Haggai and Zechariah.
c. 444? Nehemiah visits Jerusalem and builds walls.
c. 397? Ezra promulgates the Law in Jerusalem.

(*Note.* The dates of Nehemiah and Ezra are disputed; Nehemiah has been placed under Artaxerxes I and Ezra under Artaxerxes II; Ezra is not likely to be under the first; it is *possible* to place Nehemiah under the second.)

THE CONQUESTS OF ALEXANDER THE GREAT

332 Alexander conquers Palestine.
323 Death of Alexander.

B.C.

323–281 WARS OF THE DIADOCHI (successors of Alexander)

312 Battle of Gaza.

301 Battle of Ipsus.

SUCCESSORS OF ALEXANDER IN THE EAST

In Syria. Seleucus I, founder of Antioch, gave privileges to Jews.

312 Accession.

280 Antiochus I, settled Jews in Lydia and Phrygia.

In Egypt. Ptolemy I (Alexandria), gave privileges to Jews.

305 Accession.

285 Ptolemy II, under whom the Hebrew Bible was translated into Greek (Septuagint).

Development of Hellenistic Judaism.

(*Notes.* The four empires mentioned in Daniel vii are the Babylonians, *Medes*, Persians, and Greeks. The Median empire is non-historical. There was no Median empire with its capital in Babylon as in Dan. vi. 1.

The Greek kings who succeed Seleucus in Antioch are called Seleucids; they counted their years from 312 (the Seleucid era), and began the year in September according to the Macedonian calendar. The old Babylonian year had begun in March-April. This difference of calculation creates an ambiguity of one year in many dates of this period. See Oesterley and Robinson, *History of Israel*, vol. II, pp. 23 f.

In New Testament times the oriental empire was known as Parthia, and was ruled by the Arsacid kings, who had Persian blood and followed the Persian (Magian) religion.)

ALEXANDER THE GREAT

It is a fact of common observation that the gospel of Jesus Christ, in becoming the religion of the European world, took up the inheritance of Greek philosophy and culture, to a greater or lesser extent, just as it took up the inheritance of Roman social and administrative order. It identified itself with the civilization which it overcame. How far, may it be asked, did the gospel yield ground in the process? How far was foreign matter taken up into the Christian movement? Was the Christian church 'secularized' in the process? When, and by what steps, did the process occur?

In studying these questions it is well to remember that Christianity originated as a form of Judaism, and Judaism had already been subjected to the influence of Hellenism. The influence was therefore pre-natal.

There were Jews who had fallen under the spell of Hellenism even before the time of Alexander the Great, who died in 323 B.C. Hecataeus of Abdera, who wrote a century before this date, stated that the Jews had abandoned many of their national customs, and Aristotle mentions a Jew of Asia Minor who was 'Hellenic' not only in speech but even in mentality. The conquests of Alexander, who was a pupil of Aristotle, spread the language, philosophy, politics, music, science, architecture and religion of the Greeks far and wide; and this expansion of Hellenic culture was eagerly welcomed and absorbed. Wherever it went there was an access of power in the cultural and intellectual life, and a number of new Hellenic, or more properly Hellenistic, forms of culture came into existence. There was a Persian Hellenism, a Babylonian Hellenism, a Syrian Hellenism and even an Indian Hellenism; there were also, in due course, a Jewish Hellenism, an Egyptian Hellenism and a Roman Hellenism; and this area of Hellenistic culture indicates at once the field of expansion of the gospel in the first two centuries of its existence. It was by no means conterminous with the Roman empire.

Nothing could prevent the free intercourse of ideas between these various forms of Hellenism, once they had all adopted the Greek language and literary tradition. It was an age of 'syncretism' or mixing. Yet this syncretism was not a new thing. It existed already on an Aramaic or Syrian basis.

The Persian empire, which Alexander and his successors had taken over, was itself the successor of the old oriental empire of the Babylonian and Assyrian monarchs. The Persians had been friendly to the old cults and systems of learning; they had been obliged to accept in part the Semitic culture which they found in possession; and they had carried on the government in the prevailing language, a west-Semitic form of speech known as Aramaic or 'Chaldee'. The Jews, who lived fairly happily under this empire, adopted the Aramaic language. It was a change which had enduring consequences; for it meant that the people could no longer understand the old Hebrew scriptures which were read to them in the synagogues, and required the services of an interpreter. The old Hebrew gradually became a sacred and learned language, which was known only to the priests and the scribes; on the other hand, the

Aramaic language linked them with the culture of the other provinces of the Persian empire, and so they were strongly influenced by 'Babylonian' and Persian ideas, which reached them, no doubt, in the form of a Perso-Babylonian 'syncretism'.

SYRIAN HELLENISM

After the death of Alexander, wars broke out between his leading generals. The old oriental empire of Babylon and Assyria, with its border states in Asia Minor, was reconstituted by Seleucus, who founded the city of Antioch on the Orontes River, and became the first of a line of kings, who are known by his name as the Seleucids. This city guarded the main highway of trade and warfare between east and west, a highway which becomes, in our period, the lifeline of the gospel. The era of the Seleucids began in September 312 B.C., and the Jews counted their years from this date, as we see in the Books of the Maccabees. It is an interesting coincidence that the Roman emperors, who were their conquerors and successors, dated their regnal years from September.

The world-wide dispersion of the Jewish race had already begun. There were colonies of Jews south of the Caspian Sea, who had been placed there by Shalmaneser and Nebuchadnezzar, though no trace of their descendants remains in recorded history. They are often referred to as the 'lost ten tribes'. The Seleucids encouraged Jews to settle throughout their wide dominions. Seleucus I, 'the Conqueror', made them citizens of those cities which he founded, or refounded, in Asia Minor and Lower Syria, and in his metropolis of Antioch; in fact he gave them privileges equal to those of the Macedonians and Greeks; and Josephus, the Jewish historian, claims that these privileges were confirmed and continued by the Romans. Antiochus I, the successor of Seleucus, removed two thousand Jewish families from Mesopotamia and Babylon, and settled them in Lydia and Phrygia. The way was thus prepared, three hundred years beforehand, for the expansion of the gospel through Antioch into Asia Minor. Christianity had begun to express itself in terms of Syrian Hellenism before it invaded the Greco-Roman world.

These Jews must have gone through many changes before St Paul visited them with the gospel. There were orthodox and conservative communities, like the circle in Tarsus in which he grew up himself; but in other cases there was a mixture with the local population which produced mixed cults like that of Sabazius in Apamea, a god who united some of the features of Jehovah with some of the features of a local deity who rather resembled the Greek god Dionysus. The resultant cult was connected with the story of Noah, and the community placed the emblems of this 'syncretist' cult on their coins. This is a most instructive example of what could and did happen outside the rigid enforcement of the Law of Moses. The cult of Sabazius spread to Rome and appears there side by side with Christianity in the evidence of the catacombs.

In many Jewish colonies, it may be, the Aramaic language prevailed, as it did in Palestine and the East. In others it gave way to Greek, and this must have occurred in Antioch itself. There must have been well-organized synagogues there, in which the Bible was read and the prayers offered in the Greek tongue. There was, in short, a Jewish Hellenism in Antioch, though our information about it is defective. We should expect that it would reflect in some degree the Syrian Hellenism of the Seleucid empire, which was the tutor of imperial Rome in the realms of Greek literature and philosophy; for Stoic philosophy, with its feeling for monotheism, and its ethic of self-discipline, may be looked on as in some degree the offspring of Syrianism.

ORIENTAL FAITHS

The Hellenism of the Seleucid empire was probably little more than a screen behind which the old religions of the east continued their very lively existence. Antioch was nominally a Greek city with a Syrian substratum; but farther north and east there were little Syrian principalities in which Syriac or Aramaic was the native tongue, though the Greek culture would be welcomed and adopted as a civilizing influence. Among these were Commagene with its capital at Samosata; Osrhoene with its capital at Edessa across the Euphrates; and Adiabene with its capital at Arbela across the Tigris. There were cities like Nisibis and Nehardea in the old Assyrian country; and Seleucia and Ctesiphon farther south, not far from the ancient city of Babylon. Ctesiphon was the capital city of the Parthian monarch who was the principal rival of the Roman emperor. These cities and kingdoms were all more or less

Hellenized, and they all had their Jewish colonies. The rabbinic schools of 'Babylon' were said to be more learned and conservative than those of Judaea. They had produced the authorized version of the Law of Moses, and sent it to Jerusalem by the hand of Ezra the scribe. In the reign of Herod the Great they provided Jerusalem with a high priest in the person of Hananel, and a great scholar and teacher in the person of Hillel the Elder, who became the founder of the new Pharisaism.

The native Syrian religion seems to have been a worship of the forces of nature; the spirits who haunted the holy rocks or wells and mountains; or the spirit which animated the palm or the vine or the growing grain. The latter assumed mythical form in the legend of Tammuz, or Adonis, whose death was lamented at the time of harvest; and Ishtar, the wife of his youth, who descended into hell and rescued him from the goddess of the underworld. These local, agricultural, or mythical spirits could readily be incorporated into some sort of relation with a universal spirit or deity.

The old Persian empire had supplied such a deity in the high God of Zoroastrianism, who was thought of as eternal light and power, in ceaseless conflict with the forces of darkness and evil. Out of his eternal being proceeded various spiritual emanations which could assume mythical form. Among these was Mithras, the god of radiant light; and below them were the daevas or spirits. The 'Magian' religion of the Persian empire could thus find room for the polytheism which its prophet had denied.

Among the cults with which it could come to terms was 'Chaldaism', the old Babylonian worship of the heavenly luminaries, especially the seven planets, revolving round the earth in their invisible spheres, and controlling the lives of men and nations. They too could be incorporated into a tolerant spiritual monotheism. The Persian sole God could be elevated far beyond space or time, to allow for this inclusiveness. When the Greeks took over the Persian empire, Zarvan, or endless time, was identified with Zeus or Apollo (whose symbol was the sun), and the Seleucid monarchs could become his earthly manifestation—*Theos epiphanes*, 'God made manifest'.

Or Judaism could be worked into the Syro-Hellenistic system, which was what Antiochus IV wanted to do. Jehovah could be the high God of endless time; the Ancient of Days; he who was and is and is to come. Or alternatively he could be the chief of the seven planetary deities who ruled over this unsatisfactory universe. A syncretism of this kind was effected and appears historically in the Christian gnosticism of the second century.

A priest from Babylon named Berosus, or Berossus, taught the Greeks about the motions of the heavenly bodies; and with this knowledge astrology or astral determinism began its long history in the west. Chaldean or Magian priests cast up horoscopes. The seven-day week was universally adopted, each day being assigned to a planet—the Sun, the Moon, Mars, Mercury, Jupiter, Venus, Saturn.

Greek philosophy had its own monotheism, of course, of which Socrates was the principal personal exponent. In Plato and Aristotle the deity was an eternal immaterial being, rather apart from the universe; Aristotle made him external to the planetary spheres of the Babylonian astronomy; Stoicism brought him back into the cosmos. He was the soul of the world; the breath which nourished it from within; the mind that moved the whole mass; the reason which made itself known in the human breast. This line of thought was not worked out without help from the East.

The empire of Seleucus was eventually divided between the Parthians and the Romans, the Parthian kings patronizing the Magian priesthood with its predominantly Persian faith, the Roman emperors patronizing the Greek philosophers with their Stoic 'theology'. Judaism developed in this world of syncretism and rivalry, but it belonged to the oriental half of it rather than to the Hellenistic; though it had an oriental half which was mainly Aramaic-speaking, and a western half which was mainly Greek-speaking.

EGYPTIAN HELLENISM

Another of Alexander's generals, Ptolemy by name, made himself master of Egypt. Alexandria, the new city on the Nile delta, had been built by Alexander himself, and called by his name; his body was buried there. Like Antioch, it became a great centre of trade, since Egypt had ports on the Red Sea from which ships sailed to the eastern coasts, including India and Ceylon. Under the Ptolemies, the ancient civilization of the Pharaohs came into touch with the newest Greek science and criticism, to form an Egyptian Hellenism which far outshone that of Antioch, or even that of Athens itself, in this formative period of our civilization. The tradition of Aristotle was carried on there, with its emphasis on exact knowledge and precise thinking; and we are not surprised to find that the savants of Alexandria led the world in mathematics, astronomy, and scientific discovery generally. They owed a great deal, however, to their Babylonian and Egyptian predecessors.

The Egyptian character persisted in Alexandrian Hellenism, just as the Syrian character persisted in the Antiochene. The old religious and mystical traditions were civilized, and entered into the new world-culture in their Hellenized forms. This Egyptian tradition was more devoted to the abstract and the ideal than to the local or the historical, and it therefore proposed for worship the universalized and allegorized gods such as Serapis and Isis; the Syrian, with its more human touch, and its sentimental quality, turned the old myth of Adonis into an emotional and poetic romance with a more popular appeal. The Greeks in Greece had transformed their own cults in their own way, producing the dramatic forms known as the Eleusinian and Dionysian mysteries. The 'mystery religion', with its secret lore and its sacramental rites, soon spread throughout the Hellenistic world, including the cities of Asia Minor, taking in eventually the Persian Mithras, the lord of light and truth and glory. Would this movement be strong enough to engulf Judaism too? It would appear from the records that this very nearly happened.

THE SEPTUAGINT

It was Ptolemy I (305–285 B.C.) who founded the 'Museum' (or institute of the Muses) in Alexandria. His son Ptolemy II (285–246 B.C.) greatly enlarged it. It was said that his aim was to provide a home for the literature of the world. Egypt was the principal source of the supply of papyrus, which was the most suitable writing material of the period, and consequently it was the main centre of book production. The king of Pergamum in Asia Minor encouraged the production of parchment (*pergamena*) for the purpose, but papyrus continued to be the favourite material of the sort in the Hellenistic world. The literature and history of the older civilizations was not neglected in the Museum. Berosus, the priest of Babylon, wrote the history of that ancient empire, where sacred texts were still being produced on clay tablets. Manetho and others did the same for Egypt. The chronicles of Phoenicia were recorded by Menander of Ephesus or Pergamum. Their books, with numerous others, were in use among scholars for three or four centuries, though they are no longer extant. We have to be content with a few extracts preserved in Jewish or Christian writers.

Among the older literatures which are said to have been preserved in this library was the literature of the Jews. The production of the Greek Bible is thought to have been undertaken, piece by piece, for synagogue purposes, in accordance with the needs of the Jewish population. There had been Jewish settlements in Egypt from at least the times of Jeremiah, six centuries before the time of Christ. The papyrus fragments discovered at Assouan are dated about a hundred and fifty years later (408 B.C.), and show that the Jewish colonists of that period, who were auxiliary troops in the Egyptian army, still spoke Aramaic, and practised a form of their religion which had never been purified and disciplined by the Law and the prophets. There were other gods, and even goddesses, worshipped in association with Jehovah. They had a temple of a sort, and corresponded with the priesthood in Jerusalem.

This would hardly be the case with the numerous settlers, many of them army veterans, who were encouraged by Ptolemy I and Ptolemy II to settle in Alexandria in the third century, and were given equal privileges with the Macedonians and the Greeks. On the other hand, their children and grandchildren would soon lose the use of Aramaic; Greek would be their daily speech, for they do not seem to have been at all interested in the native people, and looked down on their very archaic religion, with its worship of cats and crocodiles. The production of Greek texts for synagogue purposes would become a necessity. The use of interpreters in the service, if it was ever tried, would appear to have been found inadequate.

According to tradition, the production of the official authorized version was sponsored by Ptolemy II; and this is not at all impossible, since Palestine was part of his dominions. At a later date the Greek Bible was accompanied by a document called the *Letter of Aristeas*, just as the English Bible is accompanied by a letter addressed to King James I. The *Letter of Aristeas* is a romantic fiction, written about A.D. 100, but it may be based on a true historic tradition. It states that King Ptolemy II sent to Jerusalem for a copy of the Jewish Law, which was provided for him by the high priest Eleazar, written no doubt, according to the Jewish custom, on prepared skins. Seventy-two 'elders'[1] were also sent to Egypt, who completed the work of translation in seventy-two days; it is interesting that these elders from Jerusalem should have been thought of as bilingual. In later forms of the story the seventy-two elders appear as seventy; and marvellous features are added to the story. They do their work in separate cells, and yet, when they are compared, the various versions exactly agree. Such stories were intended to enhance the divine inspiration of the translation, which was known as the Version of the Seventy or *Septuaginta*.

The *Letter of Aristeas* is only concerned with the translation of the Law, that is to say the first five books of the Bible. The collection known as the Prophets (which includes what we call the historical books) was probably not completed in Hebrew in the reign of Ptolemy II; but it was translated into Greek, probably piecemeal, the process being completed within another hundred years. Interesting variations in the text show that the process of editing was continuing during the period of translation. As for the other books of the Bible, the Psalms, the Proverbs, Daniel, and others, there was no authoritative list till after the time of Christ, and the Septuagint comprised many more books than were included in the Hebrew canon. This larger Bible constituted the original Bible of the Christian church, and a number of the extra books have been retained in the Apocrypha. We owe a great debt to Alexandrian Judaism for the preservation of this literature.

As Greek prose or poetry the Septuagint has few merits. It abounds in 'barbarous' words and constructions and figures of speech. It can only have been intended in the first place for use among Jews. Yet it carries into the Greek tongue something of the majesty and charm of the Hebrew originals. It may be said to have created a new form of Greek, which contributed to the formation of the idiom in which the gospel was preached, and the New Testament written, and the oldest Christian liturgy and theology worked out. The New Testament is a supplement to the Septuagint, not to the Hebrew Bible.

JEWISH HELLENISM

During the period from the death of Alexander to about 170 B.C. the Jewish state, which consisted only of the territory round Jerusalem, continued to be governed by the high priest, who was chosen from the

[1] A tradition in the Mishnah says five elders.

descendants of Solomon's high priest, Zadok, and was also acceptable to the Seleucid king in Antioch, to whose dominions Jerusalem belonged. Towards the beginning of the second century B.C. his suzerainty was challenged by the king of Egypt. In the year 169 B.C., the Syrian monarch, Antiochus IV, called Epiphanes, or '[God] made manifest', invaded Egypt, captured King Ptolemy VI, and asserted his authority. On his return journey to Antioch, he entered Jerusalem and plundered the Temple. In 168 he again invaded Egypt and was repulsed by the Romans. In 167 he again entered Jerusalem, and on this occasion he set up the worship of Olympian Zeus (which doubtless meant the universal God of Syrian Hellenism) in place of the worship of Jehovah. An altar of the Greek type was superimposed on the great altar of burnt-offering, and sacrifices of a pagan type were offered there on the twenty-fifth day of the ninth month (Kislev). It is a very important date. The action was followed by an organized campaign to force a Hellenized form of religion upon the Jews; they were compelled, on pain of death, to surrender their copies of the Law, to abandon the customs of their race, and to sacrifice to the new universal deity, whose earthly representative was the king himself.

A close critical study of the documents shows that this was no act of foreign aggression. Antiochus was supported by the high priest Menahem, or Menelaus as he called himself, and also by other leading men. For a century or more the Greek influence had been at work in Jerusalem. Greek customs had been accepted; the young men had adopted the Greek dress; circumcision was unfashionable; a 'gymnasium' had been established. The time seemed fully ripe to bring this backward city into line with the rest.

There was a political background, too, which cannot be fully explained; for Menahem-Menelaus had evicted Jesus-Jeshua (also called Jason) from the priesthood, and he in his turn had ejected the legitimate high priest, Onias III, son of the great Simon who is glorified at the end of Ecclesiasticus as the model high priest. Onias had fled to Antioch, where he was murdered. His son, Onias IV, fled to Egypt and was given a grant of land at Leontopolis, where he built a temple which endured till A.D. 73. So Egyptian Jews had an actual temple, with what claimed to be the legitimate priesthood.

THE HASMONAEANS

Jerusalem had come under the control of a family or group of families in the high-priestly line, who had felt the fascination and pressure of Syrian Hellenism, and relaxed their devotion to the Law sufficiently to enter into union with it. On the other hand, their temporary success only served to prove that there were parties in Israel who held to the Law with a devotion and tenacity unknown in Israel before. They found a leader in a village priest named Mattathias, 'the son of Simon, the son of Asmonaeus', whose five sons proved themselves remarkable generals and diplomats, the most famous of them being Judas, who was called Maccabaeus or 'the Hammer'. They were supported by groups of religious enthusiasts known as the Hasidim or pious. There were martyrdoms, heroic sufferings, desperate acts of courage, and devious political intrigues; but the worship of the God of Israel was restored in his Temple on the twenty-fifth day of Kislev in 164 B.C., the third anniversary of the profanation of the altar. The day became a festival in Israel, almost equal in importance to the sacred festivals of the Law of Moses; it is the feast of *Hanukkah*, the Renewal or Rededication, a midwinter festival.

There were further disastrous turns in the fighting, the danger reaching its worst point when the Syrian authorities appointed a new high priest, Jakin (or Alkimus), from the recognized priestly family, and some of the Hasidim joined his forces; but a sufficiently strong body among the loyalists was so dissatisfied with the old high priesthood that they decided to settle the succession in the family of Mattathias, though it was not descended from Zadok. Judas was dead, so that Jonathan was the first to receive this honour, and he was succeeded after his own death in battle by his brother Simon. This dynasty was known as the Hasmonaeans, after the grandfather of Mattathias, or more often the Maccabaeans, after the title given to Judas. In time they received the recognition of the successors of Antiochus, who found them valuable auxiliaries. They extended their power over the whole of Palestine, as the unfortunate Syrian empire succumbed to its inward dissensions and to the warlike pressure of Parthia and Rome. They devastated Samaria and destroyed the Samaritan temple at Shechem, which also had a legitimate Zadokite priesthood. They forcibly converted Galilee to Judaism.

It is not necessary to go into the intricacies of the Maccabaean succession, and tell of the orthodox John Hyrcanus (Hyrcanus I) who was priest and prophet and all but king; or his less orthodox successor Alexander Jannaeus (Jonathan) who reigned and warred after the manner of the Gentiles, and put on a royal 'diadem' which would seem to have been a Persian royal emblem, connected possibly with the sun-god. The widow of Alexander Jannaeus, Alexandra Salome (called in the Mishnah *Shĕlōm Zion*), restored orthodoxy with the help of the Pharisee party. It is enough to say that the influence of Hellenistic culture and religion, which had been courageously resisted in the hour of crisis, had been felt by all, even by those who had resisted it; and though the national tradition was established and even extended, nevertheless there was more than one way of interpreting it.

THE PHARISEES AND SADDUCEES

The numerous sects into which the Jewish race was divided were probably all descended from this period of conflict, and were probably political in character as well as theological. There was the diehard devotion to the Law of the Hasidim, who are little more than a name; there was the ascetic communism of the Essenes, whose affiliation with some Zadokite group may be progressively clarified as we learn more from the 'Dead Sea Scrolls'; there were the Pharisees who were an offshoot from the Hasidim, and produced a rather artificial pedigree of teachers which seems to stem from the old high priest Simon III, who was the father of Onias III (or perhaps from an earlier Simon called Zaddik—the Just); and there were the Sadducees, the high priestly party of the time of Christ, whose name seems to show that they too claimed succession or descent from Zadok. But the significance of these names is still obscure.

We would like to have more information than we actually possess about these divisions in Israel; for the traditions preserved in the Talmud see everything through the eyes of the rabbinism of the second century A.D.; and the remarks of Josephus are singularly unconvincing. We know next to nothing of the Sadducees, whose theology was so archaic as not to have accepted the prophetic writings as fully canonical; like the Samaritans they based their faith on the Law of Moses only, to which the Samaritans added the book of Joshua; they rejected the Pharisee doctrines of the resurrection of the dead and the existence of angels. The Sadducees were the aristocrats; the Pharisees were the popular party; they had at times resisted the Hasmonaean rulers, and later on they resisted King Herod. The meaning of their name is disputed. It is said by some to come from the Hebrew word *parash* which means 'to separate'; but from whom they separated themselves is not known. It could simply be a popular nickname for a party which practised a strict piety based on laws of 'clean and unclean'; or it could be derived from some political cleavage.

It has been observed that the Pharisees were not immune from the Babylonian and Persian influences which had come in prior to the Greek period. They believed in a life to come and an angelic world of good and evil spirits, which the Sadducees rejected. We find too what is called an 'eschatology', an imaginatively conceived panorama of history, culminating in a divine judgement, and the coming of God, or of his Anointed, or of a 'Son of Man', with retribution for the evil and rewards for the good in a new phase of existence—ideas which are strange in Judaism before the Maccabaean period. It has been suggested that Persian influence has something to do with this type of thought. It has even been suggested that the name Pharisee really means 'Persian' (*Fharsi* or *Parsee*).

THE INFLUENCE OF HELLENISM

The national tradition could not escape the Greek influence, at least in its external and social life. The Hebrew speech of the learned Pharisee tradition, even in its Mishnaic form, was enriched with a number of Greek loan-words, such as the word 'sanhedrin', which is simply the Greek word *sunhedrion* ('a sit-together'), and was adopted for the supreme council of seventy priests and elders which met in Jerusalem under the presidency of the *ab-beth-din* ('father of the house of justice') or of the high priest; thus making seventy-two in all. The great number of these Greek loan-words (and later on of Latin loan-words), is sufficient to prove the existence of a continuous Hellenistic pressure in the very heart of Judaism, to which it could not help yielding. It appears, too, in such everyday matters as clothes and meals.

'The dress of the Jew', says Dr Albright, 'consisted essentially of the same garments, including tunic and mantle, shoes or sandals, and a hat or cap of some kind to protect the head, that were worn by contemporary Greeks.' It is erroneous, therefore, to portray the twelve apostles in the costume of modern Arabs, as is so constantly done. In the same way, the custom of reclining at meals, which was done even at the Passover, was in accordance with the Greek, not with the old Jewish custom. Ordinary daily life, we gather, especially in the towns, was assimilated to the universal culture of the day.

It has even been suggested that the calendar and round of festivals which governed the religious life had been influenced by foreign customs too. The Persian and Babylonian influence can hardly be doubted; it comes out clearly as early as Ezekiel and Zechariah, and culminates in the eschatological literature; and eschatological ideas were prominent in the Feast of Tabernacles, which was the climax of the whole ritual and agricultural year. It has been suggested that the processions at this festival, with songs and branches of trees, were adopted from Greek ceremonies like the revels of Dionysus, which took place at the same autumnal season, and were also vintage rites. The theory of Greek influence is more probable in the case of the new festival of the Dedication, which took place on Kislev 25 (November or December), and commemorated the very day on which Antiochus had established the Greek ritual in the Temple. The Maccabaeans may have been forced to substitute something for the attractive Greek ceremonies, and to continue such Greek rituals as the kindling of lights before the doors of the houses, which very likely gave it the name of the Feast of Lights which we find in Josephus.

THE MACCABAEAN LITERATURE

The greatest document of the Maccabaean period is, of course, the Book of Daniel, in which the terrors of an age of war and persecution are mirrored in the stories of the den of lions and the burning fiery furnace. Its picture of the Ancient of Days, his angelic attendants, his fiery streams, and his heavenly assessor 'like a son of man', has a distinctly Persian look. It is a product of an Aramaic-speaking Judaism, which was acquainted with a Babylonian syncretism; its hero surpasses all the Chaldeans in their own art. It was written in Aramaic, and was adapted for use in the synagogue by translating its opening and closing passages into Hebrew.

The First Book of the Maccabees was originally written in Aramaic or Hebrew, from older sources, not long after the death of John Hyrcanus in 104/3 B.C. We possess it in a Greek translation which was included in the Septuagint; a history of the high-priesthood of John Hyrcanus himself has failed to survive. The Second Book of the Maccabees had a rather different origin. Not long after the wars, a Jew of Cyrene, called Jason, wrote a history of them in the Greek style in five volumes; and what we have is an abridged form of Jason. Two letters addressed from Jerusalem to Alexandria were added to it at a later date; they urge the Alexandrians to keep the Feast of the Dedication.

We can distinguish three stages in the production of a Greek literature by the Jews. The first was the translation of Hebrew classics, or recent compositions in Hebrew or Aramaic; the second was the production of Greek books in the style established by these translations; the third was the production of Greek books in the Greek style. II Maccabees belongs to the second class, just as the gospels do. The same is true of III Maccabees, a weak production, which relates an imaginary, or largely imaginary, story of persecution in Egypt, for use on a festal occasion. IV Maccabees attempts to capture the style and spirit of Greek philosophy and rhetoric. It is a eulogy of the martyrs of the Maccabaean period, for use at the Feast of the Dedication, when such heroes seem to have been remembered; it describes the sufferings of a certain Eleazar, and of a mother who died on behalf of the Law, with her seven sons; it is lauded in the Stoic manner as a triumph of reason over passion. It is a precursor of the literary forms which were adopted by the Christians for what are called the Acts of the Martyrs.

Christians even took over the mother with her seven sons in the legends of St Symphorosa and St Felicitas. A commemoration of the Maccabees themselves remains in the Roman Breviary.

HEBREW OR ARAMAIC LITERATURE

It would not be possible to give an account of all the Hebrew or Aramaic literature of this period, so far as it still survives in Greek translation. It would include such tales as Esther, Tobit, and Judith. But there is a group of books dating from the Maccabaean period, to which reference must be made. These are the Book of Enoch, the Book of Jubilees, and the Testaments of the Twelve Patriarchs.

These books are amplifications of the Old Testament tradition with special ends in view, and doubtless a rather broader-than-average theology. Enoch reveals the secrets of the world above, narrates the

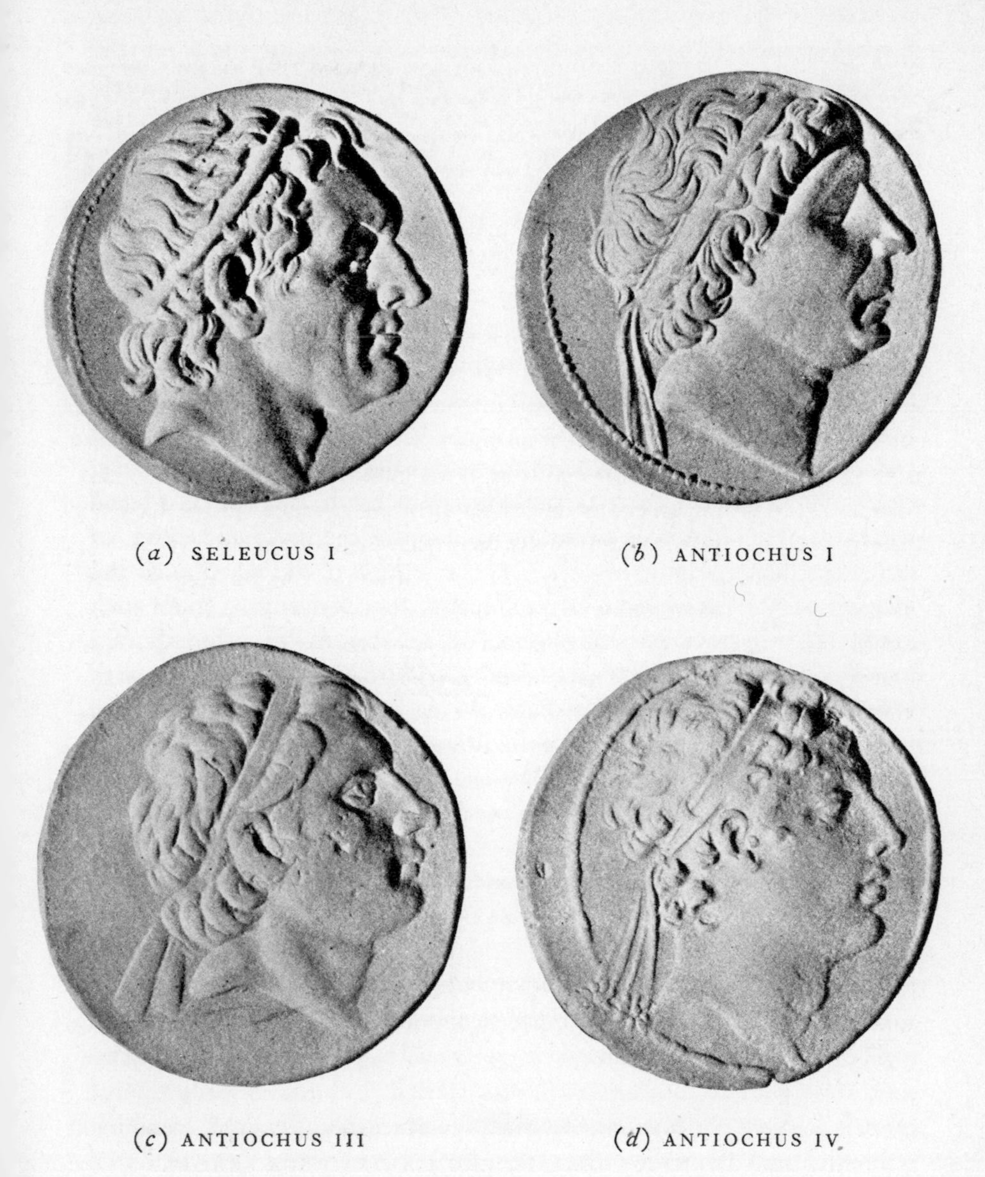

(*a*) SELEUCUS I (*b*) ANTIOCHUS I

(*c*) ANTIOCHUS III (*d*) ANTIOCHUS IV

I. SELEUCID MONARCHS

2. FRAGMENT OF ISAIAH, FROM A DEAD SEA SCROLL

story of the fallen angels, and surveys the history of this world, which is to end with the appearance of a divine saviour or judge from heaven, who is called the Elect One, or Son of Man. It is an amalgamation of texts from different sources, and quotes a still earlier Book of Noah, which has not survived; its place of origin may have been in Galilee. Jubilees recounts the history of Israel from Abraham to Moses, arranging it in accordance with a revised calendar, which would simplify the calculation of the liturgical year. This new calendar and its basis in astronomical theory are also outlined in Enoch. In Patriarchs, each of the sons of Jacob gives ethical teaching to his descendants, foretelling what will happen in the last times. While Joseph is the pattern of perfect conduct and Judah is awarded the kingship, Levi is given the supremacy over the others as the inheritor of the priesthood.

The original text of these books has disappeared, but they were translated into Greek, and so passed into the library of the Christian church. Patriarchs, which had passed through several editings, was edited again for Christian use in the second century after Christ, and a number of Christian passages were inserted into it.

THE LITERATURE OF JEWISH HELLENISM

Before the time of the Maccabees, and not long after Berosus and Manetho, a Jewish writer who called himself Demetrius occupied himself with the chronology of the sacred books. No doubt he was a pioneer of the school of thought which tried to convince the Greeks that the Hebrew literature was the oldest in the world, a claim which was also made by Aristeas. This point of view was further developed in the writings of the Jewish philosopher Aristobulus, who addressed his works to King Ptolemy VI, and therefore flourished during the Maccabaean wars. He was a disciple of Aristotle and the Stoics, but he maintained that the Greek philosophers and poets derived their teaching from Moses, adding that the substance of the Law had been translated into Greek before the production of the Septuagint. Eupolemus, who was his contemporary, wrote a history, in which he asserted that Moses was the first of the sages, and that he had delivered the art of writing to the Jews, from whom it passed to the Phoenicians, who gave it to the Greeks. Other historians who cannot be dated with exactness were Artapanus, a second Aristeas, and Cleodemus (also called

Malchus). Artapanus carried the notion of Moses as the original source of pagan culture so far as to claim that he was the inaugurator of the Egyptian religion. In the Book of Jubilees a rather similar claim is made for Abraham, who is said to have passed on to the Gentile nations the art of writing and the science of astronomy.

The existence of a genuine Hellenistic literature shows that there were actual reading circles or academic institutes among the Greek-speaking Jews; for Greek literature was intended to be read aloud. No doubt sympathetic Greeks were invited to these séances. There were poets, too, in this tradition; for Philo the Elder wrote a poem on Jerusalem, and Theodotus, who must have been a Samaritan, wrote a poem on Shechem. Did a Hasmonaean monarch like Alexander Jannaeus enjoy listening to the recital of the historical glories of Israel, as Ahasuerus, in the Book of Esther, listened to the reading of his own warlike exploits? There was also a theatre; for a certain Ezekiel composed a number of tragedies in Greek verse, including one on the Exodus, of which considerable fragments survive. King Herod built a theatre in Jerusalem, close to the Temple, and we may conjecture that such works were performed in it.

We would have little notion of this literary activity but for a Greek writer named Alexander Polyhistor, who flourished about 80–40 B.C., and copied a number of extracts from these authors into his book *Concerning the Jews*. The book is lost, but it was used by Josephus, Clement of Alexandria, and Eusebius of Caesarea, to whom we owe our knowledge of it.

In addition to this, there were Jews who composed verses in the style of Sophocles and other Greek poets, and these turn up in Christian writers, who believed that they were genuine. There is a long poem, ascribed to the sixth-century gnomic poet Phocylides, a good part of which is a versification of the nineteenth chapter of Leviticus, a chapter which gives instruction in the elements of Jewish piety, and formed the basis of Judaeo-Christian catechisms.

THE SIBYL

The most important piece of imitative literature, however, was the Jewish 'Sibylline Oracles'. The Sibyl was a well-known figure in the Greek literary tradition. She was an imaginary prophetess of a legendary character, who had uttered dooms on the nations in Homeric hexameters. Actually the verses which circulated in her name had been composed in various times and places; and this resulted in the theory of a Babylonian Sibyl, a Persian Sibyl, and so forth. As early as the Maccabaean period, perhaps about 145 B.C., some of the prophecies which are now contained in Book III of the Oracles were composed and circulated. Their Jewish material seems to be grafted on to a 'Babylonian' stock. They proclaim a pure monotheism; they denounce ungodliness and idolatry; they utter dooms upon the nations, referring particularly to the Seleucid monarch at Antioch; and they foretell a judgement upon the world.

We shall hear more of the Sibylline Oracles, which continued to be produced for four or five centuries by Jews and Christians alike.

KING SOLOMON'S WISDOM

We have found some traces of Greek philosophy in the *Letter of Aristeas*, the writings of Aristobulus, and IV Maccabees; but the influence was wider than that. It is doubtful whether it extended to the Book of Proverbs; but it is quite clear in Ecclesiastes. The figure of Solomon was beginning to be exalted as the exponent of a wisdom which was superior to that of the wise men of the East; and possibly even of the West; and a number of books were composed and circulated in his name. Just as all the Law appeared under the name of Moses, who was its originator, and all the Psalms under the name of David, so all the traditional wisdom was collected under the name of Solomon.

One of the most daring of these works of art was the Wisdom of Solomon, which was composed in Greek in Alexandria, not long before or after the birth of Christ. Its poetic beauty secured it a place in close proximity to the Greek Bible, into which it was admitted, at least by the Christians. It dramatized the Word of God as a warrior figure, leaping from his throne, and penetrating into this dark world. It dramatized his Wisdom as a female figure who co-operated in creation, preserved the righteous, and illuminated the wise. She was a pure spirit, poured out upon all creation, entering into holy souls, and making them friends of God and prophets. It was a view which had been anticipated by Aristobulus; indeed, it had been anticipated in the Book of Proverbs. Her mode of speech has been compared in some respects with the contemporary treatment of the Egyptian goddess Isis. It is interesting that this personified picture of God and his Word and his Wisdom should appear in Egypt, where Jehovah had once been worshipped with a goddess by his side.

PHILO JUDAEUS

The emphasis on the need for personal illumination by the divine spirit is also to be found in the Alexandrian Jewish writer Philo, who was contemporary with Jesus of Nazareth, and outlived him by one or two decades. This remarkable man came from a powerful and wealthy family. He read copiously in the Greek philosophers as well as in the Hebrew scriptures and the Jewish Hellenistic writers. He made great use of the accepted Alexandrian principle of allegorism, which was certainly not without precedent in Judaism. In this way he made the characters in Genesis into 'types' or patterns of general ideas or principles; and by this means Moses was found to be at one with the philosophers.

Philo is not only the climax of the long and rich story of Jewish Hellenism, he is an important figure in the general history of Western philosophy, because he is the forerunner of that revival of Platonism which became apparent in the second century after Christ, and gathered strength in the third. We shall see that Christian teachers, after making some use of Stoic philosophy in Athens and Rome, eventually adopted the new Platonism in its oriental form, as the best medium in which to interpret the gospel to the Hellenistic world; but this new Platonism had departed from the intellectualism of the master, in admitting more fully the doctrine of personal illumination by the universal deity or by a spiritual power proceeding from him.

THE TIMES OF JESUS

The evidence given could easily be added to, but it is sufficient to show that the transition of the Jewish faith to the world of the Hellenistic culture had been accomplished, so far as it was possible, before ever the gospel appeared upon the scene of history. A worldwide Hellenistic Judaism, if not a Jewish Hellenism, everywhere existed, in intimate relation to the oriental world to which it historically belonged. This

Hellenistic Judaism had its synagogues, its Bible, its liturgy, its catechisms, its learned literature, and even its philosophy of history. It stood ready, like others, to enter into its inheritance as a world-religion. Why then did it not do so?

The answer is very simple and instructive. It was the Pharisees, and later on the Zealots, with their political exclusiveness and their insistence on every detail of the Law, both oral and written, who were responsible. Every Greek synagogue with any pretensions to culture would have its circle of Gentile enquirers who were attracted by the life and worship, and almost persuaded by the propaganda. Even Capernaum in Galilee provides an example. What they could not accept was the national Law with its demand for circumcision, the keeping of Sabbaths, and so forth. The substitution of the gospel of Jesus Christ for the law of Moses as the supreme authority within Judaism broke down what St Paul called the middle wall of partition, and the fusion was immediate.

Is it true to say that this period of cosmopolitan Hellenism was stirred by a feeling of expectation that a Saviour was to come who would bring peace to the world? It was certainly so in Judaism itself, and it may have communicated itself to other races; but the religious feeling of the age seems to have expressed itself more characteristically in the temple inscriptions which give thanks for the Roman peace which had been brought by that efficient deity, the Emperor Augustus. At any rate, what expectations there were, even among the Jews, were strikingly different from what actually happened.

THE MACCABAEAN KINGDOM IN JERUSALEM

B.C.

199 Battle of Panion; Antiochus III (the Great) takes Palestine from Ptolemy VI of Egypt.

175 Accession of Antiochus IV (Epiphanes—the Glorious) who attempts to Hellenize the Jewish state.

Deposition of the legitimate high priest Onias III, whose son Onias IV built the temple at Leontopolis in Egypt; two successive high priests 'Jason' and 'Menelaus', in conflict.

169 First Egyptian campaign of Antiochus, who plunders the Temple on his return journey.

B.C.

168 Second Egyptian campaign of Antiochus, who desecrates the Temple on his return journey, perhaps in 167. Altar for Olympian Zeus built on top of the old Temple altar; the 'abomination of desolation' as it was called by Daniel and others. Greek (Dionysiac?) worship introduced probably on 15 or 25 Kislev (November-December).

166/5 Revolt of law-observing Jews led by the priest Mattathias of Modin, and his five sons, called the Maccabees. Death of Mattathias; Judas the eldest son takes command.

164 Jerusalem under control of Judas; purification and 'rededication' of the Temple on Kislev 25. Feast of Hanukkah instituted.

163 Death of Antiochus III; confusion in Syrian Kingdom.

161 Alkimus high priest; Judas sends an embassy to Rome.

160 Death of Judas; succeeded by his brother Jonathan.

159 Death of Alkimus; vacancy in the position of high priest.

152 Jonathan made high priest by popular acclamation; killed 143.

142/1 Simon high priest and chief of government.

139 First reference to Jews in Rome.

134/3 John Hyrcanus high priest and chief of government (king?).

108 Wars of Hyrcanus; destroys Samaria.

103/2 Aristobulus I high priest and king (son of Hyrcanus).

102/1 Alexander Jannaeus (Jannai) high priest and king (son of Hyrcanus).

75/4 Alexandra Salome (widow of above) becomes queen with Hyrcanus II (her son) as high priest.

67/6 Death of Alexandra.

66/5 Aristobulus II (younger brother of Hyrcanus II) seizes power; high priest and king.

63 Aristobulus deposed by Pompey; Roman rule begins; Hyrcanus II restored as high priest; Antipater of Edom in charge of army.

40 Antigonus (son of Aristobulus) seizes Jerusalem with the aid of the Parthians; becomes high priest and king.

37 Roman armies in alliance with Herod (son of Antipater) seize Jerusalem. Herod (the Great) becomes king and appoints a new succession of high priests, none of whom held office very long.

Notes. The years from 169 to 152 are approximate and fluctuate within a margin of one year; they are based on Oesterley and Robinson, *History of Israel* (1932). In addition to the uncertainty in the period after 170 there is the ambiguity due to the differences in the calendar, the old Babylonian year beginning in the spring, and the Seleucid in the autumn.

According to I Maccabees iv. 54, Kislev 25 was the anniversary of the desecration (after three years); but Daniel xii. 11 implies three and a half years.

The title 'Maccabaeus' (the hammer) is properly speaking the title of Judas only.

THE HASMONAEAN RULERS

Judas Maccabaeus, 165–160.
Jonathan (high priest), 160–142.
Simon (high priest), 142–135.
John Hyrcanus I (high priest and king), 134–104.
Aristobulus I (high priest and king), 103.
Alexander Jannaeus, (high priest and king), 102–76.
Alexandra Salome, 75–67.
Hyrcanus II (high priest), 75–66 and 63–40.
Aristobulus II (high priest and king), 66–63.
Antigonus (high priest and king), 40–37.
Herod the Great (king), 37–4.

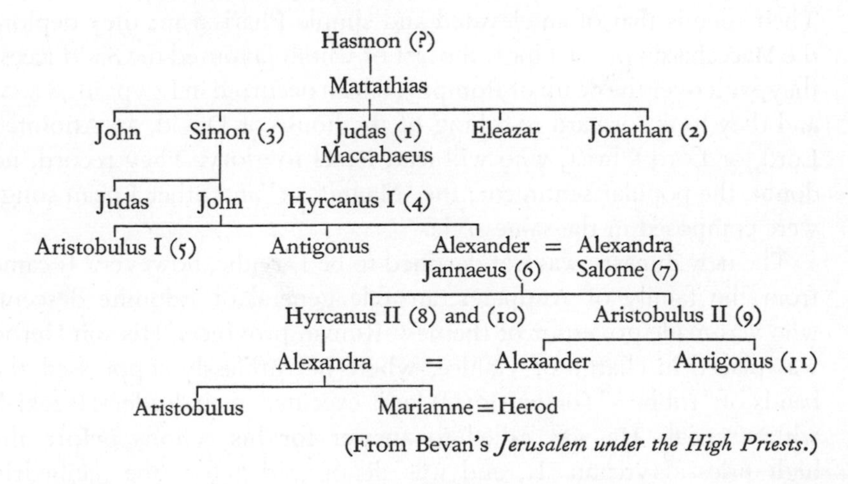

(From Bevan's *Jerusalem under the High Priests*.)

CHAPTER 2

GALILEE AND JERUSALEM

Herod the Great, *p.* 24. Judas the Galilean, *p.* 26. Pontius Pilate, *p.* 27. John the Baptist, *p.* 28. Jesus of Nazareth, *p.* 29. The Kingdom of God, *p.* 30. The Twelve Apostles, *p.* 33. The Passover in Jerusalem, *p.* 34. The Day of Pentecost, *p.* 37. The *Kerugma* of the Gospel, *p.* 38. The Jerusalem Church, *p.* 39. Houses and families, *p.* 41. Persecution, *p.* 42. Stephen and his companions, *p.* 43. The Twelve Apostles, their names and order, *p.* 45.

HEROD THE GREAT

The Parthian empire succeeded to the dominions of the Seleucids in Mesopotamia and the East; the Roman empire to those in Asia Minor and western Syria. Palestine was annexed in 63 B.C. when Pompey the Great entered the holy city, took the Temple by force, and made his way into the holy of holies, where he was amazed to find no image or object of worship whatever. This outrage is the burden of a number of songs which were collected under the name of the 'Psalms of Solomon'. Their tone is that of an elevated and simple Pharisaism; they deplore the Maccabaean priest-kings, the last of whom favoured the Sadducees; they exult over the death of Pompey, which occurred in Egypt in 48 B.C.; and they look forward to a king of the house of David, an Anointed Lord, or Lord Christ, who will lead Israel to glory. They record, no doubt, the popular sentiment; the 'Magnificat' and other Lucan songs were composed in the same style.

The new dynasty was not destined to be Davidic, however. It came from the family of Antipater, an able general of Edomite descent, who was made governor of the new Roman province. His son Herod was placed in charge of Galilee, where he ruthlessly suppressed the bands of 'robbers' (or patriots?), and executed their leader Hezekiah without trial. He was called to answer for his actions before the high priest Hyrcanus II, and was denounced before the Sanhedrin by the two Pharisee leaders, Pollio and Sameas, who appear in the rabbinic tradition as Abtalion and Shemaiah; but he had the support of the Roman authority, and withdrew to Galilee. It is said, however, that he showed a great respect for the Pharisees; and it was the Pharisees who opened the gates of the city to him and his armies in 37 B.C.

In 40 B.C. Antigonus II, the last of the Maccabaean line to reign in Jerusalem, captured Jerusalem with the help of a Parthian army, and reigned there for three years. The Roman senate decided to bestow the crown on Herod, who captured Jerusalem and became king in 37 B.C. He proved himself an efficient agent and ally of the Roman empire. The story of his reign is a mixture of splendour and horror. He was an able general and a strong administrator. He held the country down by force, he amassed wealth, he built cities. He entirely rebuilt the Jerusalem Temple in the most magnificent style, and provided it with new high priests, who claimed descent from the family of Zadok; but none of them lasted very long. He had one from Babylon, one from Egypt, and one even from Jerusalem. All were subservient to his will.

DESCENDANTS OF HEROD THE GREAT

(IN PART)

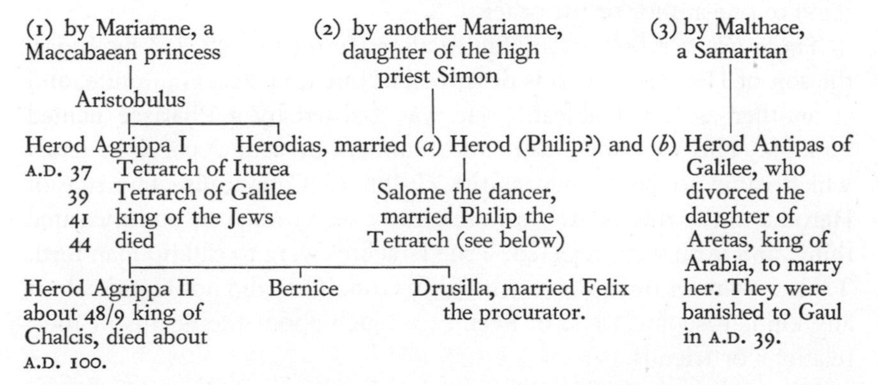

Notes. (1) In 4 B.C. Herod the Great died and his son Archelaus (another son of Malthace) became tetrarch of Judaea until 2 B.C. when he was banished to Gaul.

(2) Herod Philip, whose mother was named Cleopatra (not identical with the Herod (Philip?) mentioned above—see Mark vi. 17), became tetrarch of Iturea and Trachonitis (east of the Sea of Galilee) from 4 B.C. to A.D. 37 when he died.

(3) The Herod Antipas mentioned above received his tetrarchy of Galilee in the same year, 4 B.C.

He had ten wives, the second of whom was a Maccabaean princess named Mariamne, whom he murdered in a fit of jealousy. As he grew older the vendettas between his various families made his life miserable. The tale of intrigue and murder is told in some detail by Josephus. Not long before his death there were devious plots in which his sister Salome and his brother Pheroras were implicated; three of his sons were put to death. There was some sort of resistance at this time from six thousand armed Pharisees who refused to swear an oath of allegiance to the Roman emperor and to Herod's government, and the leaders of this movement were executed. The story in Josephus is obscure, and the whole facts are not given.

It was during these last years, according to Luke, that a census was ordered by Augustus, the master of the Roman world; Joseph and Mary went up from Galilee to Judaea to be enrolled, and Jesus was born in Bethlehem, the city of David.

JUDAS THE GALILEAN

Josephus has no reference to this 'first census' as Luke calls it, but he gives an account of a census which took place during the disturbances after the death of Herod in 4 B.C. There may be some confusion in the mind of one author or the other.

There was a rebellion in Galilee after Herod's death, led by Judas, the son of Hezekiah, who is described at one time as a Gaulonite, and at another as 'the Galilean'. He was assisted by a Pharisee named Zadduk. The two men were the founders of a new party in Israel which came to be known as the Zealots or Cananeans. The rule of Herod and the rule of Rome were clearly seen to be one and the same thing, and both were rejected. True Israelites were to call no man lord. Their only ruler or lord was Almighty God. They did not fear death of any kind, Josephus says, or even care much about the deaths of their relations or friends.

We think of the 'robber' Hezekiah, who was the father of Judas; of more than one delegation, sent to Rome, praying that the nation might be relieved of kings altogether; of the six thousand Pharisees who would not take the oath of loyalty; of the obvious liaison between the Pharisees in Jerusalem and the insurgents in Galilee; and we realize that there was a nationalist movement of considerable magnitude behind these events. There were fanatics who would stop at nothing to establish a theocratic state on the ruins of the Herodian and Roman dominion. This party grew in power until it was able to wage the war which led to the ruin of the Israelite state in A.D. 70.

Strangely enough Josephus does not tell us how the rebellion of Judas was put down, though he mentions the suppression of other rebellions which broke out at the same time; but Rabbi Gamaliel, in a speech which is reported in the Acts, says that his revolt was suppressed and came to nothing. He also mentions a certain Theudas, who headed a revolt prior to Judas; but there may be some confusion here with a later Theudas. It is possible that the report of his speech in Acts is confused.

PONTIUS PILATE

On the death of King Herod his surviving sons competed for the throne, but the Romans did not continue the kingdom. The country was partitioned. Judaea was assigned to Archelaus, Galilee and Peraea to Antipas, and the country east of the Lake of Galilee to Philip. They were given the title of 'tetrarch', a Greek word which meant originally the ruler of the quarter of a country; but what it meant by now was that they were governors of small principalities, not kings.

Archelaus mismanaged his tetrarchy, and was banished by the emperor to Vienne in Gaul. Judaea and Samaria were placed under a Roman governor, with the title of 'procurator', or agent of the emperor. His capital city was Caesarea, a northern coast town where old Herod had built a magnificent harbour. The procurator, in his turn, may have been subject to the legate in Antioch. Jerusalem, with its surrounding country, was administered by the high-priestly families, who reckoned their descent from Zadok and Aaron. It was the name of Zadok, apparently, that gave their supporters the title of Sadducees. One of their number occupied from time to time the ancient position of high priest, and was the titular head of the Jewish state; but their power was subordinate to that of the procurator, who followed the Herodian example in deposing them from time to time.

Among these shadowy figures there are two names of some importance in Christian history; the first is Annas, or Ananus, who saw five of his sons enjoy the high priesthood; the second is Caiaphas, who was his son-in-law. They were what we would call puppet rulers. They were as much agents of Rome as Herod himself had been, and their popularity was no greater than his. Their power was limited by the Sanhedrin, a council of seventy priests and elders, on which their enemies the Pharisees had a majority.

In the year A.D. 26 Pontius Pilate succeeded Valerius Gratus, the fourth procurator. He owes his fame to the fact that he happened to be the minor official who had to deal with the appearance of another Galilean movement, under another Galilean leader, Jesus of Nazareth. He was a man of no particular distinction, ruthless in action on occasion, and yet afraid to provoke the Jewish people too far, in case a complaint to Caesar might result in his recall in disgrace; and that is exactly what happened to him after eleven years.

JOHN THE BAPTIST

Under these unhappy conditions, a great religious revival occurred among the Jews, and laid hold upon the common people who belonged to no sect or party. It was about A.D. 26 or 27 that John the Baptist was living the life of a hermit in the desert of Judaea among the wild mountains which slope down to the Jordan River. He spoke of a judgement of God upon the nation, for which he was to prepare the way; and he administered a baptism of repentance. Another was coming after him who would baptize in fire and in the spirit. According to Matthew he announced the coming of a 'kingdom of heaven'.

Asceticism was not a new factor in Israelite life, and we have a striking example of it in the Essene community on the shores of the Dead Sea. The Pharisees had taken into their strict and holy legalism certain ideas of Babylonian and Persian origin; the Essenes appear to have been open to further influences from the religious philosophies of Syria, Persia, or even India. They practised communism, monastic discipline, holy immersions, holy meals, celibacy, and even, it would appear, sun-worship. They knew the names of angels. There was a military element in their tradition and history, and doubtless a political one too; but they abstained from the national life, and even from the Temple sacrifices; they thought their numerous ablutions were more effective spiritually. They revered the Law of Moses, but they must have interpreted it in a peculiar manner. We shall know more about them after more extended study of the 'Dead Sea Scrolls'.

John should not be confused with these sectarians. His asceticism was that of the Old Testament prophets and 'nazirites', which was still practised in Israel, though only as a rule for limited periods. It was associated, as a rule, with a special vow. Devotees of this sort drank no wine, ate no flesh, and let their hair grow. They were set apart for a while for the service of the God of Israel, and received the Spirit in special strength. John came in the succession of Elijah and the old prophets of his type, who recalled Israel to her allegiance to the true God.

There is no sign, in what we are told about John, of the eschatological fancies which appear in some of the contemporary Jewish literature. Many creative movements in religion, and in art or literature too, are inspired by a return to a 'primitive' or less sophisticated period. Elijah's own message had been of this kind; it had protested against the corrupted civilization of the day. John and his successors in the Christian church returned to the fountains of inspiration of a simpler time. He spoke of wrath and fire, of the axe laid to the root of the tree, and of one coming to judgement stronger than he.

John was a preacher as well as a recluse. His appeal was so powerful that numbers came to his baptism from the surrounding country, and even from Jerusalem itself. His influence extended throughout the Jewish world, for we know of a group of his followers in Ephesus some twenty years later. We are told in the fourth gospel that he baptized in Transjordania and in Samaria; and there were strange sects in both regions. Hellenistic 'mystery' ideas, usually with a Syrian religious base, were popular in Samaria. Simon Magus, the reputed father of Christian heresy, flourished there, and later legend said that he was a disciple of John; and so was his partner and rival Dositheus. Doubtless the religious revival which was stirred up by John was productive of strange and varied developments throughout Palestine.

We mention these points, since it is essential to remember that Christianity, from its earliest beginnings, was accompanied and followed by strange sects which had some affinity with it and were often an embarrassment or even a danger. The Judaism of this period was not always the well-regulated Judaism of the Mishnah.

JESUS OF NAZARETH

Among the disciples of John there was a group from Galilee which included Jesus of Nazareth. We are told in the gospels that when he was baptized in the Jordan River, he saw the heavens torn apart, and the Spirit descending into him, like a dove. There was a voice from the heavens which said 'Thou art my beloved Son in whom I delight'.

This is an example of the visionary experience and language in which the new movement expressed itself; for the gospel appeared within the old Hebrew tradition, in an atmosphere of spiritual fervour in which such experiences were perfectly natural.

Many scholars suggest that this was a 'subjective' experience of Jesus alone; but the fourth Gospel asserts that John too recognized the descent of the Spirit, which designated Jesus as the one coming after him who would baptize in Holy Spirit. Furthermore the gospel, as it was preached in the Petrine School (according to Mark and Acts), took the baptism of Jesus as its historical starting-point. In Acts and John, the discipleship of the first followers is said to date from this event, which marked out Jesus as the 'Anointed' and 'Son of God' and bearer of the Holy Spirit.

There seems to have been a period of unknown duration, perhaps between the years 27 and 28, during which Jesus remained in Judaea, in close touch with the Baptist. Certain traditions which are preserved in the fourth Gospel refer to this period in his life; and it is clear from the evidence of all the Gospels that he was a well-known figure in Jerusalem. This period was brought to an end when the Baptist was arrested by Herod Antipas of Galilee, and imprisoned in the fortress of Machaerus on the eastern side of the Dead Sea. According to Josephus, Herod feared his influence with the people; according to Mark, he had reproved Herod for his marriage with his brother's wife, a fact which Josephus also records.

The imprisonment of John, and his subsequent murder, came as a great shock to the people generally, Josephus says, and forms the background of the campaign of Jesus in Galilee.

THE KINGDOM OF GOD

The attempt to fit the events of this Galilean campaign into a single year can hardly be regarded as successful. Two years, or at any rate parts of two years, seem to be required. If we suppose that Jesus went into Galilee early in 28, this would give the summer of this year for his announcement of the coming of God's kingdom, the call of his first five disciples, his teaching in the local synagogues, his acts of healing, his fame and popularity over a wide area, and his first controversies with the scribes and Pharisees.

SOME FAMILY CONNEXIONS OF JESUS

(A) Family of Mary: possibly of the tribe of Levi

Elizabeth (a kinswoman) m. to Zacharias the priest.
- *John the Baptist*, who was put to death by Herod Antipas c. A.D. 29.

Salome (a sister?) m. to Zebedee, a master fisherman.
- Jacob (or *James*) and *John*, the apostles. (James put to death by Herod Agrippa before A.D. 44. John lived till about A.D. 100.)

Mary was who espoused to *Joseph* the Carpenter.
- Jesus crucified c. A.D. 30 under Pontius Pilate.

(B) Family of Joseph: of the tribe of Judah and house of David

Eli, or *Jacob* (James)

Joseph the Carpenter.
- *Jacob* (or James) 'brother of the Lord', first bishop of Jerusalem. Martyred A.D. 62.
- *Judas*
  - ?
    - grandsons who were accused before Emperor Domitian, 81–96.

Clopas (Cleopas) (Alphaeus?)
- *Symeon*, the second bishop of Jerusalem. Martyred c. 104–7.

Notes. The inference that Salome was a sister of the Virgin Mary is based on a comparison of John xix. 25, Matthew xxvii. 56, and Mark xv. 40. According to John xix. 26-7, Jesus left his mother in the care of the apostle John, which implies a close connexion.

Joseph the carpenter had two other sons, Simon and Joses, and at least two daughters.

The name Clopas may be identified with the Aramaic Halphai (Alphaeus), and Cleopas may be regarded as a Greek substitute for it. The wife of Alphaeus was named Mary. There was a Levi and another James, who were called sons of Alphaeus.

The relationship of Clopas and Symeon to Jesus is vouched for in the old Jewish Christian tradition preserved by Hegesippus.

Jesus announced the coming of 'the Kingdom of God', one of his simple phrases which no theology can adequately expound. It cannot be dissociated, of course, from the 'eschatological' or adventist expectations of the time, which were linked with a special view of world history. The long story of Israel was coming to a climax; God's kingdom was to come; indeed it was here already in the personality and ministry of Jesus himself.

He called himself the Son of Man, a mysterious title with a long history in the tradition of Israel. In Daniel and Enoch the Son of Man is a divine figure through whom God acts or reveals himself on earth. He shares the throne of God or comes with the clouds of heaven; but in the language of Jesus he appears on this earth in poverty and humility to suffer and die and give his life a ransom for many. This dramatic picture which culminates in the cross and in the Resurrection has been discussed at length by modern scholars without adding greatly to its own inherent grandeur and pathos. It can be illuminated by relating it to various theologies, but this is not the place to discuss them. We will not attempt in this short chapter to do anything more than present some of the external historical features which gave form and shape to primitive Christianity.

The principal creative factor in the making of Christianity was the personality of the founder. The point which everybody remarked about him and his mission was that it was a conductor of spiritual power in the existent situation. He spoke of greater 'glory' in the future, but the immediate effect was one of extraordinary 'power' or 'authority' on earth now in a person-to-person relationship. The source of the power was within the personality of Jesus; in his words of course, but also in his acts of forgiveness and healing, and in his voice and hands and eyes. He had an extraordinary power over crowds. They came to him from Galilee and Judaea, Mark says, and from Decapolis and Tyre and Sidon. He became the centre of a mass movement on a large scale.

His gospel of the kingdom and his ministry of forgiveness brought him into happy intimate relations with common people; but it made for deadly conflict with the religious authorities, and especially with the more legalistic form of Pharisaism, which was beginning to direct and dominate the religious life in Israel. Delegations of learned men from Jerusalem weighed him in the balance and found him wanting. It was an evil spirit in him that cast out the devils, they said; he was a magician

3. ALEXANDRIA

4. (i) JERUSALEM FROM THE MOUNT OF OLIVES

4. (ii) THE TEMPLE AREA

who deceived the people, we read in the Mishnah. The antagonism was so acute as to cause a break with the synagogue, in which so far his announcing and healing had taken place. He withdrew to the Sea of Galilee; he made use of a boat for preaching and travel; he frequented the mountains; he met his followers in desert places. He built up an organization which he referred to as his household or family. He was the 'master of the house', or 'the Rabbi'. Rabbinic schools were so called; we read of the 'house' of Hillel or the 'house' of Shammai.

THE TWELVE APOSTLES

According to the records he selected twelve men from among his disciples to be with him and receive authority from him. They were the trusted servants in his house, as he called them in parabolic language; he sent them out to preach and to visit and to heal. They came to be called apostles; but their oldest designation was simply 'the Twelve'. The number twelve was chosen to mark the household as the nucleus of a new Israel. The part they actually played in the later history of the church, as a group of twelve, cannot be fully reconstructed now, but their names were delivered and recorded wherever the gospel took written form.

Their leader was Simon of Bethsaida, and Jesus conferred upon him the name of Kephas (or Peter) which means 'the Rock'. Next came James and John, on whom he conferred the name Boanerges which is said to mean 'Sons of Thunder'; or in some lists Andrew the brother of Simon comes second, and the Sons of Thunder come third and fourth. They were the four fishermen who were first chosen, and were therefore senior to the rest. The fifth to be called was Levi the publican (or tax-collector), who was given the name of Matthew or 'Gift of God', as we infer from the Matthaean Gospel. The lowest names were those of Simon the Zealot and Judas Iscariot; the Zealots were the nationalist party for which Galilee was famous; Iscariot may mean 'Sicarius', the dagger-man or assassin.[1] Another explanation is 'Man of Kerioth', a village in Judaea.

During the early stages of these developments the news came that John the Baptist had been beheaded, probably in the spring of 29. At

[1] These may be later appellations. Zealots and Sicarii took the lead in the rebellion of the sixties.

Passover time of that year there was a convocation of some five thousand followers of Jesus at 'the mountain', and we are told in one gospel that disciples of John were also present. Jesus was the natural successor to John as the leader of the popular religious movement which John had initiated. It is even said in one gospel that the crowds wanted to have Jesus as their king. The scene on the mountain, with Jesus looking up into heaven and breaking the bread among the five thousand, was indelibly imprinted upon their minds at this high moment of crisis and revelation. As the Judaeans had gone out into the desert to receive from John the baptism of repentance, so the Galileans went out into the desert to receive from Jesus the broken bread.

It was the beginning of a period of more intense faith, in which the Twelve and others came to see in him something more than an ordinary prophet. He had called himself the Son of Man; they now saluted him as the Messiah or Anointed of the Lord; and even under the conditions of his earthly life, they came to have a vision of his more-than-earthly glory; for such would seem to be the significance of the mystical vision of the Transfiguration. That glory would be more fully displayed in the future, he said; he was thinking of his approaching death and Resurrection in Jerusalem, of the judgement which was to befall the city, and of his own coming in the glory of his Father with the holy angels.

Such was the outline of the Galilean tradition, as it came into existence at this time, and was handed down in the tradition of Peter, and recorded by Mark in his Gospel, and in other forms in other documents no doubt. The tradition has been critized and interpreted in a variety of ways in modern times; but it seems best to give it here as it appears in the evidence.

THE PASSOVER IN JERUSALEM

The Gospels are pertectly agreed on the question of the day of the week on which Jesus was crucified; it was a Friday. They are less sure about the day of the month. We shall follow John, who places it on Nisan 14, the day when the Passover lamb was slain and eaten; the other evangelists place it on Nisan 15, thus allowing Jesus and his disciples to keep the Passover the evening before. Perhaps this divergence may be due to differences of liturgical custom in the churches,[1] for the story of the Passion seems to have been repeated or recited or read or recalled on the Passover day as it came round each year. As Paul says:

> Christ our Passover is sacrificed for us;
> Therefore let us keep the Feast.

Scholars regard 29 or 30 as the most probable year for the Passion; and the indications are rather in favour of 30. Accepting 30 for the Passion, we place in the autumn of 29 the visit of Jesus to Jerusalem for the Feast of Tabernacles. This allows about six months for teaching in the Temple courts, and in and round Jerusalem.

It was not until the Passover of 30, according to this computation, that he came to Jerusalem, with his Galilean followers, to make his final appeal. On Sunday Nisan 9 (possibly April 3), according to John, who dates the day precisely, he was saluted by crowds of enthusiastic followers with palms and branches of trees and refrains from the Psalms. Their acclamations implied that they accepted him as the Messiah or king of David's line. It was on the following day, according to the arrangement of Mark, that he assumed command of the Temple enclosure and made his protest against the commercialization of the religious life of the nation by clearing out the merchants and the money-changers; but John places this episode as much as two years earlier. On such points we cannot have certainty. The evangelists were indifferent to them.

Jesus spoke daily in the Temple courts, and the popular support was so strong that the authorities did not dare interfere. He did not spare the rulers of the people. Scholars debate what the significance of his words and actions may have been, and especially what his attitude was to the Temple worship, with its ceaseless succession of animal sacrifices. It is enough to realize that his message was in line with that of the older prophets who warned the people of judgement to come. The Temple itself would not escape destruction; its place would be taken by a structure 'not made with hands', his enemies accused him of saying. Interwoven with this was his consciousness of his personal mission as Messiah or Son of God, though he did not support his public message

[1] Outside Palestine the Jews kept the Passover on two successive days in case there was an error in their computation. This duplication of the day must have been very confusing.

by using these words. He came to them in the name of the Lord, in succession to John the Baptist, and his message was one of coming judgement.

On the Wednesday night, Nisan 12, Judas Iscariot went to the Temple authorities, and agreed to betray him in such a way that they could arrest him apart from the crowd.

On Thursday, Nisan 13, the day before the Passover (if John is correct), Jesus found his way unobtrusively into the city by night. He sat down with the Twelve at the Last Supper, and gave them the sacrament of the broken bread, adding the cup of blessing, as a covenant of love which would be stronger than death. He went out into the garden of Gethsemane, where he was betrayed by Judas, arrested by an armed force from the high priest, and deserted by his disciples.

During the preliminary inquiry, which was held at a conference of sanhedrin members, the question of his attitude to the Temple was brought up, but the evidence was conflicting. He made no reply to these accusations. Then the high priest addressed him: 'Are you the Messiah', he said, 'the Son of the Blessed?' Jesus answered by saying, 'I am [or 'Thou sayest']; and from now you will see the Son of Man seated at the right hand of power and coming with the clouds of heaven.' These words are taken from the language of vision and psalmody. They imply that the Kingdom or Judgement or Glory of God would be revealed for all men to see in his own person; indeed they imply that this revelation was beginning as he spoke; his reign on earth began with his suffering and crucifixion. They were all horrified, and he was condemned to death. It was during this inquiry that Peter, who had followed him into the palace where the inquiry was held, denied having any knowledge of him.

The sanhedrin had no power to order the death sentence; and at dawn on Friday, Nisan 14, which was the Passover day, they brought him before the Roman governor, Pontius Pilate, after holding a brief official meeting to confirm their action of the previous night. They now accused him of attempting to make himself king, and there had been grounds for this accusation, in his actions during the week, and in the words which he had spoken to the high priest. Pilate vacillated a little. The great festivals with their excited crowds had often produced similar problems. He listened to the priests; he temporized with the mob; he thought upon the emperor, Tiberius Caesar, who would expect rebellions to be promptly suppressed; and he condemned Jesus to be crucified.

The story of the Crucifixion is shortly told. That evening the body lay in the tomb, with the stone rolled to the door. The twenty-four-hour period which began with the Last Supper was over. The burial of Jesus seems to have concluded the Passion narrative as it was recited or told in the church.

THE DAY OF PENTECOST

No doubt the authorities thought that the popular movement, which was now deprived of its great leader, would crumble; but the organization which had been framed in Galilee held together. Judas had proved a traitor; but Simon Peter, in spite of his denial, rallied the other men, and stood firm. We must credit him with considerable powers of leadership and organization. John the son of Zebedee was closely associated with him. An unexpected accession was James, the brother of Jesus, who was not one of the Twelve. There is no connected account of this critical period, and the reconstructions of learned theologians, whether they believe in the Resurrection or otherwise, all suffer from the disconnected nature of the evidence. It is conceded, however, that the devoted men, who preserved the tradition of Jesus and organized the church and launched the gospel upon the world, were convinced that they had seen him risen from the dead. It is not just a question of so much verbal evidence, oral or written, though this is more than sufficient in itself; it is a question of lives laid down and testimony sealed in blood. It gave a new word to the vocabulary of the world, the word 'martyr', whose original meaning was simply 'a witness'.

According to the Acts of the Apostles, it was fifty days later, at the Feast of Pentecost, on Sunday Siwan 6, perhaps May 22, that the apostles attracted attention in Jerusalem by affirming that they had seen their master risen from the dead; that he was even now exalted to the right hand of God, and that he had sent upon them the gift of the Holy Spirit of which John the Baptist had spoken, so that the Baptist was vindicated too.

We depend entirely upon the second chapter of the Acts for this narrative; but the reception of the Holy Spirit as a personal gift after the Resurrection was another of the primary facts of Christian experience. The central article in the creed of the first Christians was the death and Resurrection of Jesus, followed by the exaltation into heaven, and the hope of his coming again in glory; and this faith was associated with the reception of the Holy Spirit as a fact of evangelical experience. From this encounter with the risen Lord with the gift of the Holy Spirit came the gospel, the apostolate, the sacraments, the observance of Sunday as the Lord's day, and the whole world-wide expansion which is the subject of our study.

THE 'KERUGMA' OF THE GOSPEL

The Greek word *kerussein*, which is translated as 'preach', means literally to proclaim like a herald, *kerux*. The word *kerugma* means 'a proclamation'. The 'preaching' of the apostles was of this kind. They were the heralds or ambassadors of Jesus to the Jewish people, and after that to the whole world. Their proclamations were delivered under intense spiritual tension, and often fell into rhythmical or poetic form; they were preserved in the church as customary oral forms. We find a number of them in the first chapters of the Acts, as speeches of Peter, and there seems to be no good reason to doubt that the author received them from excellent Palestinian sources. They proclaim Jesus as the Messiah, or Anointed of the Lord, who was foretold in the prophets and the Psalms of David, but greater than David, as is proved by his resurrection and exaltation. The word 'king' is carefully avoided.

Similar formulas of a shorter character may be traced in the remaining New Testament literature. The most interesting of these is the gospel formula which was delivered by Paul to the Corinthians about twenty years after the crucifixion. He had received it himself in the same manner, presumably at his baptism; 'I also received it', he says.

> That the Anointed died for our sins according to the scriptures,
> And that he was buried,
> And that he rose again according to the scriptures...
>
> (I Corinthians xv. 3)

The references to the scriptures, which mean the Old Testament of course, will be dealt with in the next chapter; it suffices to say here that the preachings of Peter in the Acts are supported by many references to the prophets and the Psalms.

This primitive creed-form is followed by a list of witnesses, which is a part of the formula as a whole. The witnesses seem to divide into three classes. First there was Peter, then the Twelve, and then a group of five hundred brethren of whom the majority were still living when Paul wrote. Secondly there was James, who seems to be associated somehow with 'all the apostles'. Thirdly there was Paul himself, who received his appearance of the Lord 'like one born out of due order'.

Since there were only eleven of the Galilean apostles left, the use of the word Twelve at this point shows how securely established this designation was. The reference to 'all the apostles' seems to show that the word 'apostle' could include others.

THE JERUSALEM CHURCH

The importance of this list of witnesses is obvious. It proves the existence of a variety of traditions in the church from the beginning. First, of course, there was the Galilean apostolate of Peter and the Twelve, which had been built up by Jesus; then there was the family of Jesus, whose leading figure was Jacob (or James, as we say in English). Then there was Paul himself, whose position, in some way, was different from that of the others. He was conscious that there were differences of opinion in these groups, and that is why he emphasizes the fact that there was no difference with regard to the gospel which they proclaimed; 'Whether it be I or they,' he says, 'so we proclaim, and so you believed.' We shall find that the inner relations of this triple tradition are the key to our study of church history for the first century or even longer. It is a significant fact that these names had to be solemnly delivered to the Corinthian converts twenty years later, just as the names of the twelve Galilean apostles and of the brothers of Jesus were delivered to the Romans in the tradition which Mark drew upon.

We need not, for our purposes, enter into the discussion whether these brothers were sons of Mary or not;[1] it is sufficient for our purposes to accept them as sons of Joseph the carpenter, who was Mary's husband, so that the descent from David could be claimed for them too. It is only in the second century that it is claimed for her. There were four of these brothers, James, Joses, Judah and Simon, as well as a

[1] It is believed by many that they were sons of Joseph by a previous wife; or even cousins.

number of sisters. It seems that Joseph the carpenter had died before the commencement of the gospel story; but he left a brother named Clopas, who had a son named Symeon who was therefore a first cousin of Jesus; the identification of this Clopas with Cleopas, or even with Alphaeus, is a very reasonable conjecture. The importance of the family of Jesus in the tradition is proved by the fact that James became the first bishop of the Jerusalem church, and that he was succeeded by Symeon, who is said to have presided over the fortunes of the original Jerusalem community till after A.D. 100.

James may have been the head of a distinct group from the beginning; he is said to have belonged to the ascetic tradition like John the Baptist. It may be that men of this type, who were dubious during the Galilean period, came into the fold at this point.

Paul, or Saul as he was then called, was not yet a believer; but he was almost certainly in Jerusalem, where he attended the school of the Pharisee Rabbi Gamaliel, and then rose to a position of some responsibility under the high-priestly government. He was well known in Pharisee circles, or, as he said himself, 'far advanced in Judaism'. We should also include among the conversions of this quite early period the names of Andronicus and Junia (or Junias) who were 'kinsmen' of Paul, and may have ranked as apostles; where they were converted, we do not know, but their conversion preceded that of Paul. They worked as evangelists, and resided in Rome at a later date.

The recital of these names, and the perusal of the stories related by Luke, and even the enumeration of the credal points of crucifixion, resurrection, advent, and Holy Spirit, are quite inadequate to give any idea of the power and purpose which was pent up in the original Church of Christ. We can only judge it by its effects, and those communicated themselves to every part of the known world, and have never ceased to vibrate in the human heart. Every student of primitive Christian history has to make his own valuation of this incommensurable factor.

The personality of Peter must have been the decisive factor in those early days. According to the narrative of Acts, the Jerusalem church accepted the leadership of Peter and the Twelve, who made up their number by the inclusion of Matthias, who had been closely associated with them since the 'baptism of John', which was regarded as the starting point for the preaching of the Gospel. The believers continued in the apostles' teaching and fellowship, and in the breaking of the bread, and in the prayers. Their numbers soon rose from about three thousand to about five thousand. They held public meetings in the Temple courts as Jesus had done, and met in houses for the breaking of the bread. Such is the picture given by Luke in Acts.

HOUSES AND FAMILIES

The family was an important constituent unit in Judaism and in the primitive church order. Family relationships are carefully indicated, and references to houses and families occur with great frequency in the Gospels. When the apostles were sent out on tour by Jesus, they selected the house of a prominent believer, and made it their permanent residence when they were in that city; they were not to change from house to house. We may see in these references, perhaps, an anticipation of the part played by the house of the prominent believer in the expansion of the gospel—in Corinth for instance, twenty years later.

There was a house in Jerusalem which had an upper room available for Jesus at the Passover, and its owner knew him as 'the Rabbi', the name he was called by in his lifetime. The account of the day of Pentecost in Acts shows that the apostles had the use of a house in which they resided; it had an upper room spacious enough for an assembly of a hundred and twenty persons. Whether it was the same house we do not know, though the supposed site has been pointed out in Jerusalem for many centuries under the name of the Cenaculum. As the numbers grow, however, the picture becomes rather clearer and we read that the sacrament of the breaking of the bread was carried on 'by houses'. The 'house-church' comes into view.

Two wealthy believers of the Jerusalem church are mentioned in Acts, one for praise and the other for reprobation. The first was Joseph called Barnabas, a Levite from Cyprus, who later on ranked as an apostle; the other was Ananias. The name Barnabas was given to Joseph by the apostles, and is explained as meaning 'Son of Consolation', though this seems only to be a rough equivalent. It reminds one of the names given by Jesus to some of the Twelve. We are told that Joseph Barnabas sold his property, and laid the proceeds of the sale at the feet of the apostles; and it may be that this splendid gift, with others of the same sort, did much to help the young church through its early financial difficulties. We are not told, however, that he placed his house at the disposal of the church, if he had one in the city; but this seems to have been done by Mary, who was the mother of his cousin Mark. He was considerably older than Mark.

We have now introduced most of the leaders of the church in the first generation, and it is interesting to find them all within the confines of one city at the same time, and in some cases members of a family or family group; for Peter and Andrew were brothers, and so were James and John, whose mother Salome would appear to have been a sister of the Virgin Mary. She too was living in Jerusalem, as we learn from the Acts; the fourth Gospel informs us that she resided in the house of her nephew John. James and his brothers formed another group of the same sort.

The fellowship within the church was thus very closely knit. It even presented the appearance of communism; but that was only on the surface. There was a common fund, but there was no compulsion to pay into it, as plainly appears in the story of Ananias; and we are not told that Barnabas parted with everything he had. Contributions were voluntary, but they were so spontaneous and generous as to justify the saying that no one looked on anything he possessed as his own. It would appear that the apostles had to support themselves out of this common fund, and also do what we call social service, especially among the widows, who constitute a serious problem in countries where divorce is easy and child-marriage common. 'They divided out to all according to their need', we are told. They also looked after the sick, if we may presume that the healing miracles recorded in Acts are evidences of a practical concern for the sick.

PERSECUTION

Luke preserves two stories about persecution, which some scholars regard as independent accounts of one persecution. Attempts were made by the Sadducee priesthood to suppress the preaching and healing that went on in the new sect, which came to be called the Nazarenes, or Nazareans; but the Pharisees, who were strongly represented on the sanhedrin, used their influence to discourage this policy. This seems a strange reversal of the picture which is given us in the Gospels; but the narrow-minded self-important observant of the Law who is portrayed there was not the only type of Pharisee. The best of the Pharisees were great men, and it is possible that such leaders as Gamaliel I had not approved of the crucifixion of Jesus, or had come to regret it. They also had some traditional sympathy with popular movements in Galilee, as we have seen. They were still the popular party, Josephus says, and were likely to oppose the Sadducees, whom they hated.

It is not surprising, therefore, that a liberal-minded Pharisee like Gamaliel should use his influence on the sanhedrin against a policy of persecution, which seemed to be fruitless and unnecessary. He was the grandson of Hillel, and the recognized head of his 'house' or academy. The apostle Paul had received some training in this institution, and his leading pupil, Johanan ben Zakkai, was a broad-minded man like himself. His policy of toleration was enunciated by him in a speech before the sanhedrin, which is included in the narrative of the Acts; but, like other speeches in that book, it may owe its present literary form to the art of the author.

STEPHEN AND HIS COMPANIONS

In this way matters went on for a year or two, the energies of the church being concentrated on the maintenance of its existence in Jerusalem and Judaea, and no doubt in Galilee too, though we get no more information about the fortunes of the gospel there. The narratives given by Luke in Acts are lacking in chronological data. They are excellent narratives, but he has not got sufficient first-hand information to weld them together into a connected history.

A different note appears in the story of Stephen, which opens up a new chapter. There were numbers of Jews living in Jerusalem, such as Barnabas and Saul, who had been born and grown up overseas, in the 'Diaspora', as it was called. They spoke the Greek language and had some degree of Hellenistic culture. As the church grew, it made progress among these Hellenists. Presently the task of administering the common fund became too much for the Twelve, and it was among the Hellenistic brethren that complaints were heard; their widows were being overlooked in the daily ministrations, they said. The solution of the problem was a simple one, though it must have added to the overhead cost. Seven men were nominated by the church to take over this kind of work, and so set the Twelve free for the ministry of preaching and prayer. They were ordained for this work by the Twelve with the laying on of hands, an old Hebrew rite called the *semikah*, which was used in conferring authority for a sacred office or in blessing.

The Seven are not given any specific title in the Acts, but they are usually called the 'Seven Deacons', since the work they did was similar to that which was done by the deacons not very much later; and the verbal form *diakonein*, meaning 'to serve' or 'minister', is actually used of them. They seem to have done the work which was later on done by a bishop and a staff of deacons. They all had Greek names, and one of them, Nicholas of Antioch, was a convert from paganism. The first two names on the list are those of Stephen and Philip. It is interesting that this new departure in church order, within the primitive Jerusalem church, should have been formed on a Hellenist basis.

The Greek-speaking Jews had a synagogue of their own in Jerusalem—or it might be synagogues, for the meaning of the passage is not perfectly clear. It was the synagogue of the 'freed-men', that is ex-slaves,[1] of the Cyrenians (from North Africa), of the Alexandrians (from Egypt), of the Cilicians (from Paul's country) and of the Asians (from the neighbourhood of Ephesus). Luke does not give these names accidentally; they establish connexions of which we hear more later on. They take back the basis of Gentile expansion into the very earliest period. In this synagogue, Stephen argued with great brilliance, and nobody could stand up to him. He was a radical, and the cry went round that he was speaking 'words of blasphemy against Moses and against God'. He was brought before the sanhedrin, we are told, where he was accused by 'false witnesses' of speaking 'against this holy place and against the Law'; he was also charged with saying that 'this Jesus of Nazareth' would destroy 'this place' and change the customs which Moses delivered.

There is a clear connexion here with the charges which were framed against Jesus himself. They border on sedition and blasphemy. Stephen made a strong defence, but it was defiant in tone, and only served to enrage those who heard it. As the hostility of the crowd became more apparent, he passed into a state of spiritual exaltation in which the sense of vision came to him. 'I see heaven opened', he cried out, 'and the Son of Man standing on the right hand of God.' The scene ends in uproar and confusion; they rush upon him and stone him to death, crushing his body, that is, under great stones which they piled upon

[1] Or possibly Libyans, reading '*libustikon*' for *libertinon*.

him. When this began, he knelt down and said, 'Lord Jesus, lay not this sin to their charge'; and when he had said this, he fell asleep.

So ends the earliest example of what is known as the Acts of a martyr.

THE TWELVE APOSTLES (their names and order)

FIRST STAGE: CHOICE OF THE FOUR FISHERMEN

(1) Simon who was called Kephas or *Petros* (the stone); and his brother *Andrew*, who is fourth on the list in Mark but second in Matthew and Luke. They were sons of Jonah or John.

(2) Jacob (the English *James*) and *John*. They were the sons of Zebedee, a master fisherman, and his wife Salome who may have been a sister of the Virgin Mary.

SECOND STAGE: CHOICE OF THE 'PUBLICAN'

The word publican means a person engaged in the collection of taxes. The publican is called *Levi* the son of Alphaeus in Mark and Luke; but no Levi occurs in their lists of the Twelve. In Matthew he is called *Matthew* and identified with the apostle of that name, who comes seventh in the lists of the Twelve.

THIRD STAGE: CHOICE OF THE TWELVE

1–4. The four fishermen who were first called.

5–9. Five more names which are the same in all our sources: *Philip*, *Bartholomew*, *Matthew*, *Thomas* and *James* the son of Alphaeus, so called no doubt to distinguish him from James the son of Zebedee. The name Thomas means a twin; and the fourth gospel calls him Didymus which is the Greek word for twin.

10–11. A little uncertainty meets us in the tenth and eleventh places. In Mark the tenth place goes to *Thaddaeus* (Theudas), a name which is simply another form of the name Judas; he seems to be the 'Judas not Iscariot' of the fourth Gospel and the '*Judas of James*' who occupies the eleventh place in Luke.

The eleventh place in Mark and Matthew goes to *Simon the Zealot* (or Cananean) who occupies the tenth place in Luke.

12. *Judas Iscariot*, 'who also betrayed him'. Iscariot is often explained as Ish Keriot or Kariot, the 'man' or leading person of Kerioth, a village in Judaea; others connect it with the Latin word Sicarius meaning an assassin, the name of a revolutionary party closely allied with the Zealots.

ADDITIONAL NAMES

The title of apostle is given to a few others in apparently the same manner as it is given to the Twelve; to *Matthias* who was co-opted into the number of the Twelve to fill the place of Judas; to *Paul* who received a special appearance of the risen Lord; and apparently to *Barnabas* and *Silas*, companions of Paul.

Note. In some manuscripts belonging to what is called the Western text of the Gospels, the name *Lebbaeus* occurs in the place of Thaddaeus in Matthew and Mark; Origen speaks of *Lebes*; some scholars think that this was an attempt to work in the name Levi.

THE 'DEAD SEA SCROLLS'

Since the writing of this book, the manuscripts discovered at Qumran have attracted a good deal of attention, and a note on their historical value seems desirable.

They will greatly enrich our knowledge of Judaism and its political and religious divisions, illuminating such literature as Enoch and Patriarchs and Jubilees on the one hand, and such sects as the Essenes on the other. They will shed light on the text of the Old Testament, and will help us to understand the Jewish background of Christianity, which originated as a Jewish sect. In so doing, they confirm the principle of Judaeo-Christian continuity which is emphasized in this history; for the Qumran sect expressed itself in the same liturgical media; the Hebrew scriptures, prophecies, apocalyptic, covenant language, catechism, baptisms, eucharistic meals and so forth. Even the ministry and order were not unlike. Now this is exactly what we would expect; the same Jewish liturgical tradition is reproduced in both.

The holy meal of the Qumran community was associated with a 'messiah' (or two messiahs?); that is to say, an 'anointed', who in their case, was an anointed high priest; but the significance of this association is not clear at all.

The frame is very much the same; it is the picture in the frame that is different. Mishnaic Judaism provides another example of the same pattern.

CHAPTER 3

CAESAREA

Hellenism in Jerusalem, *p.* 47. The earliest literary forms, *p.* 51. The 'Books of Testimonies', *p.* 52. The theology of Stephen, *p.* 53. The Gospel in Samaria, *p.* 54. Simon Magus, *p.* 55. The church in Caesarea, *p.* 56. Saul of Tarsus, *p.* 57. Damascus, *p.* 59. Saul in Jerusalem, *p.* 60. Political events in Palestine, A.D. 36–37, *p.* 61. Peter in Caesarea, *p.* 62. The controversy in Jerusalem, *p.* 64.

HELLENISM IN JERUSALEM

The existence of a Hellenistic community in Jerusalem, and a Greek-speaking synagogue for Jews from overseas, is no surprise for those who have considered the available evidence. It comes as a shock only to those who think of the Jews in Palestine as a unilingual minority of little political importance, cut off from the civilization of the day, and shut up within a backward and racially pure Judaism. When Pilate wrote out the inscription which was to be placed over the head of Jesus on the cross, he did it in three languages; Aramaic for such native Jews as knew no other tongue, Latin for the soldiers and officials, and Greek for all those who used the universal language of the day. A few years ago R. Weill discovered in the ruins of Ophel or Mount Zion, the part of the old city which lay south of the Temple, the remains of a synagogue of our period, and a stone which bears the following inscription in Greek:

> Theodotus, son of Vettenus, priest and synagogue-ruler, son of a synagogue-ruler, grandson of a synagogue-ruler, built the synagogue for the reading of the Law and for the teaching of the commandments; furthermore the guest-house and the rooms and the water-installation for the lodging of needy strangers; the foundation had been laid by his father and the elders and Simonides.

This was quite possibly the actual synagogue in which Stephen preached.

There is also a burial inscription in which the Greek name Theodotion, in Aramaic characters, is followed by the Greek word *didaskalos* (teacher) in Greek characters. It is interesting, too, that the name of Jesus in a recently discovered funerary inscription (prior to A.D. 70) is in Greek characters.

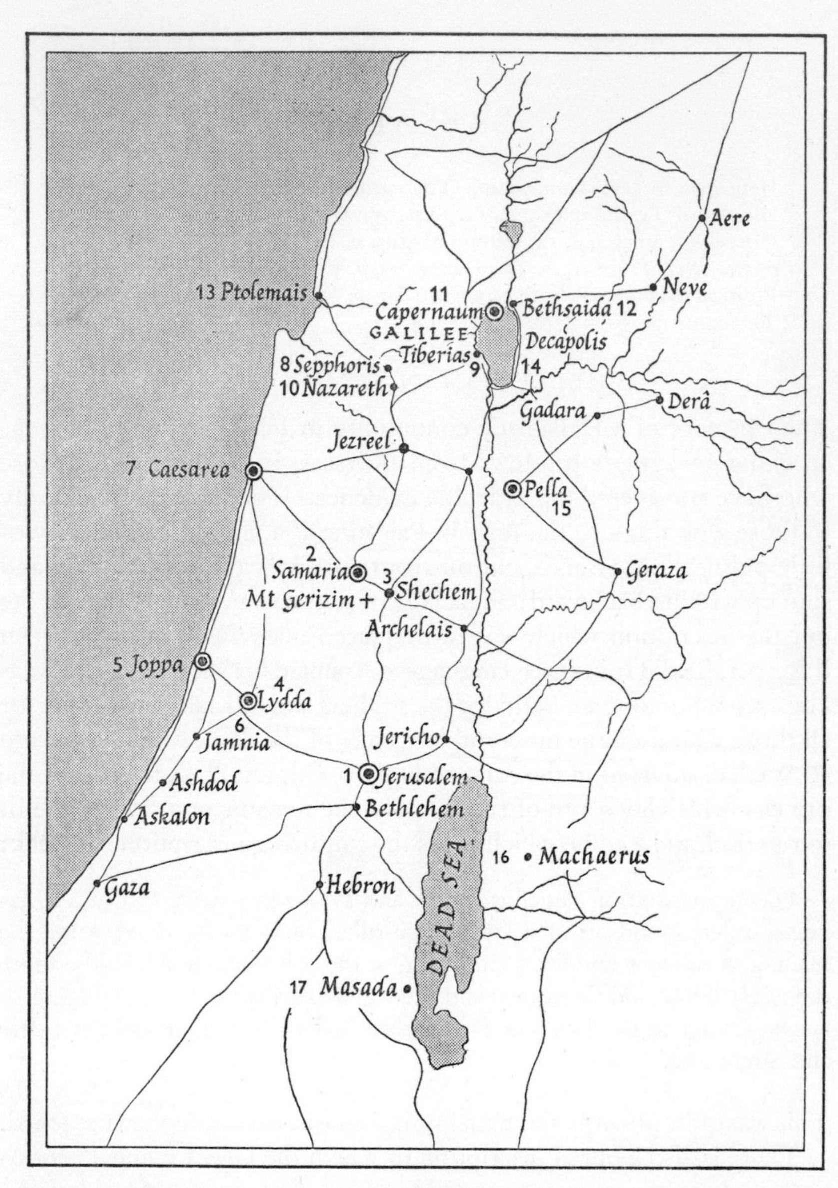

Map 1. Palestine.

NOTES TO MAP 1

(1) *Jerusalem and Mount Zion*, the old capital city of David, and the site of the Temple. Here Jesus was crucified. Here a migration from Galilee founded the first church under the twelve apostles.

(2) *Samaria*, north from Jerusalem, a Greek city founded by Alexander. Here Philip, 'the deacon', fled after the martyrdom of Stephen. Here Simon Magus, traditionally a disciple of John the Baptist, developed his mystery cult in competition with Peter and the apostles.

(3) South of Samaria, the old sites of *Shechem* and *Mount Gerizim*, older by far in Jewish history than Jerusalem. The Samaritan temple on Mount Gerizim competed with the Jewish Temple on Mount Zion.

(4–6) Philip also evangelized the sea-coast towns, passing south along the road that led to Gaza. Peter found a church at *Lydda* (4) and another at *Joppa* (Jaffa) (5). After the fall of Jerusalem in A.D. 70 rabbinic academies flourished in these towns, the most authoritative being the one at *Jamnia* (6).

(7) It was a day's journey from Jerusalem to Joppa, and a second day from Joppa to *Caesarea*, the seat of the procurator or Roman governor, who ruled over Samaria and Judaea. Here Peter founded a church in the house of the Roman officer Cornelius. Here Philip and his family settled. Paul and Luke came to know it well.

(8–13) The Acts speaks of the church in Judaea, Samaria, and Galilee, as enjoying peace, and Peter as travelling about in all parts. It is not specifically said that he visited Galilee; but it is natural to suppose that his own country was included in his peregrinations. Herod Antipas was still the tetrarch of Galilee. His principal cities were *Sepphoris* (8) and *Tiberias* (9). Other well-known places in Galilee were: (10) *Nazareth*, the hometown of Jesus; (11) *Capernaum*, the centre of his preaching and church organization; (12) *Bethsaida*, the town from which Peter and Andrew had come to take up fishing in Capernaum; Philip also came from Bethsaida; (13) *Ptolemais* (Acre), the seaport of Galilee.

(14) *Decapolis*, the 'Ten Cities' was the name given to the country east of the Sea of Galilee. It was in the tetrarchy of Philip the brother of Antipas. The 'Ten Cities' were mainly non-Jewish.

(15) South of the Sea of Galilee, on the eastern side of the Jordan, was *Pella*, a Greek city, to which the Christians from Jerusalem fled for refuge during the siege of 66 to 70. Here they established a church-in-exile under the leadership of members of the family of Jesus.

(16) *Machaerus*, a fortress belonging to Herod Antipas, in which he imprisoned John the Baptist, and (17) *Masada*, another Herodian fortress.

We learn from Josephus indeed that 'among us they do not welcome those who learn the language of many nations, and adorn their speeches with polished phrases, because this accomplishment was common to various sorts of free men, and even to those who desired it among slaves'. The training in elaborate Greek was available, therefore, though it was despised in the Pharisaic or priestly circles in which Josephus grew up. It should not be considered impossible, therefore, or unnatural, that men like Simon Peter or James the brother of the Lord, should be able to speak and write Greek, or command the services of those who were proficient in it, or even make use of a Greek Bible. Jerusalem was a city with cosmopolitan connexions. It was the centre of a world-wide dispersion, and the sanhedrin received taxes from every synagogue in the empire or out of it. It could not have carried on its ordinary business or government for a day without the use of the universal language.

Among the leading Christians in the holy city, Barnabas came from Cyprus and Paul from Cilicia, and both were bilingual. The 'speech' of Stephen shows points of contact with the Alexandrian Philo and with the tradition of the Samaritans. The Twelve came from 'Galilee of the Gentiles', where important Greek cities were located, and Greek influence was strong. The family of Jesus had connexions with Egypt, according to Matthew and the tradition in the Mishnah. Mark is a Roman name; Clopas, the uncle of Jesus, seems also to have been known as Cleopas, which is a man's name corresponding with that of Cleopatra; and Mark Antony and Cleopatra had once played a part in Jewish politics. The seven deacons all had Greek names, and one of them was a convert from paganism.

We must assume, therefore, that by sheer force of circumstances, the earliest preaching and teaching went on simultaneously in Aramaic and Greek. This is a point which deprives the literary research into hypothetical Aramaic originals of some of its value. The 'Aramaisms' of some New Testament texts may be the Aramaisms of some popular Palestinian Greek such as must have existed on certain levels of culture in a bilingual society. Only where retranslation into Aramaic provides an explanation for some incomprehensible phrase, can we begin to be sure that we are dealing with a later translation from an Aramaic document; and the experts are often divided on these points.

THE EARLIEST LITERARY FORMS

It is considered unlikely that the earliest forms of preaching and teaching were literary in the strict sense of the word. The indications are that the oldest forms were delivered orally in accordance with the custom of the rabbinic schools. Jesus had adopted the style and methods of the rabbis. He was saluted as a rabbi, even by his enemies. Indeed, the application of this title to Jesus is the first clear historical instance of this form of address. We may take it for granted, therefore, that his disciples continued to operate his teaching in oral form and in Aramaic; but it would be necessary to have Greek translations at once.

Other forms, which originated orally, were the 'kerugmata', or proclamations of the risen Jesus as Lord, or Anointed, or Child of God, or Prince of Life. The Aramaic quality in the kerugmata of Peter is very evident, so much so that many scholars think they may safely be regarded as translations.

These primitive Christian traditions are inseparable from the Jewish liturgical tradition. They cannot be understood apart from the Law, the Prophets, the psalms, the services of the Temple and synagogue, and so forth. It would appear that, so far as all these things went, the sect of the Nazareans was unimpeachably orthodox; but they had received from their master, within his household, a faith in God, and a way of living, and a liberating Spirit, which must have transformed the old liturgical order; for the prayers and the blessings and the thanksgivings and the sacraments would be 'all in the name of the Lord Jesus', and the Spirit would give them a certain largeness and freedom of utterance. Indeed the Jewish liturgical prayers themselves were not altogether fixed at this period.

Those scholars who talk about the church of this period as simply another Jewish sect, with the added doctrine that Jesus of Nazareth was the (Jewish) Messiah who was to come shortly in glory, forget the creative factor which Jesus himself contributed. His appearance on earth, his creative personality and teaching, his death and Resurrection, and his gift to the saints of the Holy Spirit, were acts of Almighty God in their midst, which were bound to outshine and transform and even supersede the old revelation of God.

THE 'BOOKS OF TESTIMONIES'

There was a Nazarean scholarship which was at work on the text of the Law, the Prophets, and the psalms, examining them from this point of view. In the defence and confirmation of the gospel, and above all in controversy with other Jews, it was necessary to meet the opposition of the scribes with apt quotations from Holy Writ, and even to develop a new interpretation of it. Luke insists that the new insight into the old Bible was one of the greatest gifts of the risen Jesus to his church.

There were three theological problems with which they had to grapple in order to win their battle of wits. First they had to show that Jesus was the promised Messiah; secondly they had to show that it had been indicated in the scriptures that this Messiah was destined to die, and to rise from the dead; and thirdly they had to explain how it came about that the chosen people had been so blind as to reject their heavenly leader when he came to them. According to the Gospels, Jesus had anticipated these points to some extent; but the scriptures were now searched for new texts, and at some early date collections of these were made for the use of teachers and evangelists. A theory has been advanced that the first book to be produced in the early church was a transcript of these texts. This theory seems to be too precise, but such collections of prophetic extracts were made very soon, and we shall allude to them as the *Book* or *Books of Testimonies*, not of course accepting thereby any particular theory of their character or contents. We prefer indeed to think of a school of oral study and a variety of partial transcripts.

This early Christian work on the Old Testament was of a very different character from the work of modern scholars; but it grasped the important principle that, while on the one hand there was a body of law and ritual in Israel which had attained a fixed and static form, there was also a forward-looking tradition in the canonical prophets, which could not find complete satisfaction therein, and dreamed of future acts and revelations of God that would transform the older Judaism into a religion of the spirit. On the other hand, the work on the *Testimonies* bears witness that there was no thought of founding a new religion apart from Judaism.

THE THEOLOGY OF STEPHEN

It is a favourite thesis of the literary critics that the various 'speeches' which we find in the Acts were composed by the author, and put into the mouths of his characters, with the object of clarifying their outlook and motives. This was a regular element in the literary technique of the Greek historians, and took the place of those analyses of purposes and policies which modern historians make on their own account and give as their own contributions to the history. Josephus, the Jewish historian, adopted this literary convention, and it would not be very astonishing if Luke had done the same; but the hypothesis is not perfectly satisfactory. The so-called speeches are of such different types. The kerugmata of Peter, for instance, do not look a bit as if they were freely composed by Luke; they look as if he found them in the sources which he used; they would appear to be Palestinian in origin, and Aramaic in character. The speech of Stephen, on the other hand, seems too long and elaborate to have been delivered on the spur of the moment at a trial which seems to have been hasty and irregular; indeed, it has been suggested that it was no trial at all, but simply an act of violence by the crowd, which was connived at by the authorities. Of course it is astonishing what an accomplished controversialist can do under extreme pressure; but it looks rather as if it were a summary of Stephen's theology which had been combined with the Acts of his martyrdom in order to clarify the causes for which the martyr gave his life.

It is a very distinctive piece of work, containing a highly original theology, which Luke obviously regarded as important. It dealt with the Old Testament from a novel point of view. The people of Israel, so far from being specially receptive of the truth, had always been rebellious and antagonistic to it; they had resisted all the messengers and ordinances of God, beginning with Moses himself. The Holy Land, which they regarded as sacred above all others, had not been the scene of his greatest revelations; he had revealed himself to the patriarchs in Syria and Egypt and Arabia. A simple quotation from Isaiah disposed of the great claims made for the Temple: 'Heaven is my throne; earth is my footstool; where is the house ye will build unto me? For all these things hath mine hand made, saith the Lord.'

This powerful theology shows that there was dynamite in the new sect. It was by no means a group of pious observants with a private devotional tradition. A leading spokesman was capable of visualizing a larger Judaism on a grander scale than had yet been achieved, though the ancient prophets of the race had suggested it; a Judaism which was not dependent upon temples or sacrifices or holy places.

THE GOSPEL IN SAMARIA

The sudden persecution of Greek-speaking Christians in Jerusalem scattered them far and wide; and the loss of these men may be one of the causes which led to the development of a more conservative and legalistic form of Christianity in the city. It certainly served to spread abroad the more liberal or radical type of Jewish Christianity. Philip, who was next to Stephen on the list of the Seven, fled to Samaria, where he preached with marked success. The city of Samaria was a Greek city which had been founded by Alexander and restored by Herod the Great; the people of the little country were mixed in nationality and hospitable to foreign cults; those who claimed to be Israelites differed from the Jews of Judaea and Galilee mainly in their refusal to accept Jerusalem as the central sanctuary spoken of in the Law of Moses. This opinion made it impossible for them to accept the writings of the prophets. Their scriptures consisted of the five books of Moses, together with the book of Joshua, his stalwart successor, who had occupied the part of the country they lived in long before the southern Israelites, under David, had taken possession of Jerusalem. Their temple was situated on Mount Gerizim near to the ancient city of Shechem, where Abraham had erected his first altar. Their priesthood claimed to possess legitimate Zadokite descent. Their sacred rites have continued there uninterruptedly down to modern times.

Many Samaritans believed and were baptized, Samaritans of Israelite descent, we may suppose. It was within the competence of Philip to administer this sacrament; but it was felt that his converts had not received the Holy Spirit which was the mark of the new Christian's 'justification' or acceptance by God. The news of conversions in Samaria was received with joy in Jerusalem, where the apostles had remained, untouched apparently by the persecution which had broken upon the Hellenists. They sent Peter and John to Samaria, who assembled the newly baptized, prayed for them, and laid their hands upon them, after which they too received the Holy Spirit. This interesting narrative is our first record of the apostles being sent out from Jerusalem on evangelistic work, and it is also our first record of the laying-on of hands with prayer as the sacramental completion of baptism, and the mode by which the new believers received the Holy Spirit.[1] It also introduces the enigmatic and sinister figure of Simon Magus, who offered the apostles money in return for the right or power of conferring the Holy Spirit in this way.

SIMON MAGUS

The 'magus' was a well-known figure in the ancient world, the religious adventurer. The original magus was a priest of Median origin, who was regarded as having the power of reading the stars and divining the future. The word was soon applied to any enchanter or magician. It suggested some acquaintance with astrology and occult lore. The man who practised these arts did not hesitate to attribute his marvels to the assistance of unseen spirits of a higher order than man; and Simon claimed that such a power was embodied in himself, 'the power of God which is called great', as Luke said.

Simon had a long and successful career. His triumph in Samaria was remarkably complete. Justin Martyr, who was born there about sixty years later, says that almost all the Samaritans in his time believed in him. He adds that he paid a visit to Rome in the reign of Claudius, and dazzled the metropolis by his displays of the magic art. He became a great figure in the Christian literature and myth of the second century, and was regarded as the father of all the gnostic heresies. He must have been a man of enormous force of character, and we see him now at the beginning of his career. The story of his visit to Rome has been doubted by modern historians, but the arrival there of Simon, or some form of Simonianism, would explain why Luke thought it necessary to devote so much space to him in the Acts.

It has been observed that many of the stories in the first part of the Acts have assumed the character of popular tales, and Luke loves to tell them in this spirit. It is obvious that he glorifies the apostles and evangelists; he enjoys the element of the supernatural; and he tends to idealize the early church. He does this simply and innocently,

[1] Naturally there are other explanations of this apostolic action. See, for instance, *The Apostolic Age* by G. B. Caird (1955), pp. 59 ff.

however, and the historical value of his sources is proved by their almost unconscious admissions. In this case the narrative admits that Simon was at one time a believer, if not a colleague. (Later legend makes him a disciple of John the Baptist.) Peter rebukes him because he offers money in order to buy his way into the apostolate. This recalls the rebuke of Ananias, who had attempted to deceive Peter in the matter of a money offering. In that case the rebuke had gone home; Ananias died. In the case of Simon Magus nothing happened; there is a perfunctory submission by Simon, but the story is robbed of its dramatic conclusion. Strictly speaking it has no end. Of the two Simons it might be said, 'And so we measured swords—and parted.' This is history, not fable, even though it may be told after the manner of the popular tale.

THE CHURCH IN CAESAREA

We are entering now upon the first of three sequences of narratives in the Acts, each of which comes to a close at Caesarea. Shorter stories are threaded together to form these sequences, but each sequence is a unity. There is good reason for supposing that they took form in Caesarea, and that the author of Acts obtained them there.

They are tales which have been told many times, and improved in the telling; for evangelism thrives on 'human interest' anecdotes which illustrate its own spiritual power and effectiveness. It was useless to bring the gospel in word only, St Paul said; it had to come in power and in the Holy Spirit and in much fulfilment. In the course of telling, the tales go through a process of adaptation. Minor detail which seems to be superfluous falls away; the wonder or the beauty or the pathos is heightened; there can be exaggeration even; but the story retains its spiritual power and dramatic effect. From the evangelical point of view, its essential truth may be intensified; for all great art works its miracles by the process of elimination, selection, and emphasis.

These stories are distinctly less Judaistic than the Jerusalem stories, and they enable us to see the nature of the evangelistic mission which established itself in Caesarea. It was a movement of the Spirit which expressed itself in the marvellous; in visions, voices, conversions, healings, and so forth. It was still Jewish in the heart of it, but it was a Judaism which had come to terms with Syrian Hellenism. It delighted in romantic narratives and visual images. At some dramatic moments it speaks of the Angel of the Lord in preference to the Spirit of the Lord; the words are practically interchangeable terms; but it is possible to visualize an Angel.[1] Philip lives in perpetual dependence upon the invisible world. The Angel of the Lord bids him journey to the south; the Spirit commands him to leap into the chariot of the Ethiopian chancellor; he baptizes him at a moment's notice, and the Spirit whirls him away. He is 'found' at Azotus. He preaches his way to Caesarea.

Caesarea was the most important city in Palestine after Jerusalem. It was the centre of the Roman government in the country, and Pontius Pilate was still residing there in the praetorium, when Philip first arrived. Jews and Greeks were supposed to have equal rights, but there was continual friction between the two races. Here the Hellenistic form of Jewish Christianity was able to develop more freely than it had done in Jerusalem. It did not yet address itself to Gentiles, but it was a borderline church where the original Jewish Christianity could develop along Hellenistic lines.

Philip was what modern scholars call a 'pneumatic'; a man guided and controlled by the Spirit. He was neither an apostle nor a prophet; but the spiritual ferment in which he lived was the kind of substance out of which Christian prophecy developed. It is an interesting point that it is not Philip, but his daughters, who are said to have prophesied. He came in time to be called an evangelist. In any case he was a great figure in the church, and became the head of a new missionary district, in a city of strategic importance.

SAUL OF TARSUS

The second sequence of Caesarean stories turns back to Jerusalem, and picks up the figure of Saul, a 'young man' who had taken an official part in the stoning of Stephen. He was a Hellenist from Tarsus in Cilicia, which was a home of Stoic philosophy, and he was proud of his city; but he was prouder still of his Israelite ancestry. He was a Hebrew of the Hebrews, he said, a Pharisee of the Pharisees; he was a devotee of the Law and of the traditions handed down from the fathers; and he tried to find what was mysteriously called 'justification' in the

[1] This poetic visualization of spiritual forces is found in the writings of the Roman prophet Hermas.

precepts of that law. He speaks in veiled terms of a period in his life when he lived apart from the Law. He fled to the Law to find redemption from the power of his passions; but while it brought illumination and discipline, it only increased his sense of inward conflict; it dealt him a mortal blow.

He was enrolled in the classes of the wise Gamaliel, but can have had little in common with that master of moderation. He remained unhappy and frustrated; and he hated men like Stephen, because they were a threat to the system of Law which was now his sole spiritual hope, though it had brought him, as yet, no peace or satisfaction.

It was this violent and unhappy man who led the persecution in Jerusalem which followed the death of Stephen, a persecution which may have been directed only against those Christians who shared the radical views of the martyr. He broke into their homes, he put them in chains, he threw them into prison, he had them punished in the synagogues, he forced them to 'blaspheme the name'. Such are the details which we gather from various references in the Acts. It was all done in the cause of righteousness, but it only added to his sense of guilt.

The story of his conversion is told three times in the Acts, and there are some allusions to it in his own writings. Armed with letters of commendation from the high priest, the same Caiaphas who had handed over Jesus to the Romans, he set out for Damascus to take action against the devotees of 'the way' in that city. It was a journey of something under two hundred miles, and, in all probability, he took the road through Galilee, where Jesus had preached two or three years before. The road skirted the western side of the Lake and then ran east of Mount Hermon with its range of lofty peaks, on one of which, it seems probable, Peter had been given the vision of his master 'transfigured'. As Saul entered on the last stage of his journey, the conflicting passions from which he suffered reached a degree of intensity which was too much for him to endure. His conversion occurred; the only sudden conversion of this type in the New Testament records. He saw a light brighter than the noon-day sun; he was thrown to the earth blinded with its glory; he heard a voice which called him by his name; 'What are you persecuting me for?' it said.

Much has been written about St Paul's physical constitution. He was a man of immense nervous energy, and he suffered from some psychological or bodily malady which caused him profound humiliation; but we do not know what it was. It has been possible perhaps to work out some of the psychological connexions by which this instantaneous release came to him; but even so, little has been explained. It may rightly be called a conversion, because it was the occasion on which every motive and conviction in his mind was radically reversed; but he spoke of it himself as a resurrection-appearance of the Son of God, similar to the appearances which had come to those who were apostles before him; and they in turn recognized this by admitting him to their company. It was always, for Paul, an intervention in his life by the risen Lord, who had thereby given him 'grace' and apostleship.

As a conversion, however, it abolished once and for all the moral and spiritual conflicts in his soul; the contention of Law and sin ceased to exist. His old life came to an end; the 'body of sin' (that is to say, his sinful self) was destroyed; a 'new man' was created in him. He was a creature full of grace and power. He was 'justified'; he was right with God; a 'righteousness' which he had never earned was conferred upon him.

There was an intellectual change, too. The system of Law which had been given to Israel through Moses ceased to be the dominant thought in his religious life; it retreated into the background before the new vision of the Son of God, who had been crucified for him, and raised from the dead by the power of God. This does not mean that the moral and religious law ceased to exist, or was no longer true or valid. It was still an expression of the will of God; but it was not his last word. His last word was Jesus Christ. A new revelation of God's righteousness had been given.

DAMASCUS

The gospel had reached Damascus and was sufficiently strong there to attract the attention of the authorities in Jerusalem. It is not very far from Galilee, and ranked as one of the cities of Decapolis, a territory in which Jesus had preached and ministered. Its condition at the time of Saul's conversion is uncertain. There had been a war between Aretas, king of Arabia, and Herod Antipas of Galilee, who had divorced the daughter of Aretas in order to marry Herodias. Herod had got the worst of it, and the Jews regarded his defeat as a judgement upon him for the murder of John the Baptist. The Roman legate in Antioch had come to his assistance, but we do not know whether peace had been made or on what terms. Aretas appears to have had some interest in Damascus, since coins of his are found there.

The leading Christian in Damascus was a certain Ananias, who was a model of Hebrew piety. He debated in his prayers whether he should visit Saul or not, but was convinced by a dream that it was his mission to do so. He prayed with him and laid his hands upon him, after which he recovered his sight; he received baptism and began to preach in the synagogues. He went away into Arabia, but it is not known what he did there. What we do know is that when he got back to Damascus the local representative of Aretas was on the watch for him. He escaped from the city by being lowered over the wall in a basket. He arrived in Jerusalem again 'after three years', which means after two years in our idiom.

By working out the notes of time which Paul gives in Galatians, and comparing them with the indications which we find in the Gospels and the Acts, we arrive at the following chronology which may be regarded as approximately correct.

A.D. 30. The Crucifixion and Resurrection.
A.D. 32–33. Martyrdom of Stephen: conversion of St Paul.
A.D. 35–36. St Paul returns to Jerusalem.

It is sometimes suggested that this gives too little time for all the developments which have taken place; but events move fast in a period of high spiritual tension.

SAUL IN JERUSALEM

In Jerusalem the brethren were scared of Paul, and unwilling to trust him, Luke says in the Acts; but Barnabas took him and introduced him to the apostles. Paul himself gives an account of the matter in Galatians ii, in which he does not mention Barnabas. He says that he went to Jerusalem to see Peter, and stayed only a fortnight; 'but I saw no other of the apostles except James the brother of the Lord'; an expression which does not necessarily imply in the Greek idiom that James ranked as an apostle. It would seem that the brother of the Lord had a spiritual position of great eminence which was not quite classified.

Paul says that he was unknown by face to the churches of Judaea; but Luke says that he spoke boldly in the name of the Lord Jesus, and disputed with the Hellenists. These encounters probably took place in the synagogue.

Minor discrepancies between excellent sources are inevitable in all human evidence. They are a sign that we are dealing with independent witnesses. Luke seems to be writing out of his own knowledge here, rather than from a special source; Paul is quite capable of stating his case rather too absolutely; and in his Epistle to the Romans (xv. 19) he does regard his career as an evangelist as having begun in Jerusalem. However this may be, both writers agree that his witness was cut short, if indeed it was ever seriously begun. Luke says that there was a plot against his life, and that the brethren took him down to Caesarea, and sent him away on a mission to Tarsus; and in one of Paul's speeches, as recorded in Acts, there is a reference to a vision which he had in the Temple, which convinced him that his life's work would be among the Gentiles. This mission of Paul to the regions of Syria and Cilicia is confirmed in Galatians. The course of events is clearly established, and the narrative of the Acts has again returned to Caesarea.

POLITICAL EVENTS IN PALESTINE, A.D. 36–37

The third sequence of Caesarean narratives begins with the statement that the whole church throughout Judaea, Galilee, and Samaria had peace and was 'built up', or as we would say, organized. It then speaks of Peter as passing round through all places. It is our first glimpse of him as a supervising and travelling apostle, and our only reference to the church in Galilee subsequent to the ministry of Jesus. However, it is natural to suppose that Peter did visit his native country from time to time; and though the Twelve are said to have taken up residence in Jerusalem, there is no need to suppose that they never left it on evangelistic journeys. Indeed, our view of the Twelve is rather dim subsequent to the events of the day of Pentecost, and they do not appear in the records any more as the Twelve. We constantly read of 'the apostles', but we cannot be sure that it does not refer to a larger body.

In the year 36 there was a disturbance in Samaria. A prophet arose who claimed that he knew where Moses had concealed the sacred vessels of the tabernacle on Mount Gerizim; he collected a considerable following, and Pilate sent soldiers from Caesarea who attacked them and killed a number of them. The Samaritans were not without friends in Rome, however, and Pilate was recalled, arriving in Rome shortly after the death of the Emperor Tiberius on 16 March 37. This synchronism supplies us with the date of the event. Nothing whatever is known of the further history of Pilate.

Vitellius, the legate of Syria, who had intervened in the emergency, appointed a temporary procurator, Marcellus, who took Pilate's place, until the new procurator, Marullus, arrived. Vitellius, who was the father of the emperor of that name, visited Jerusalem for the Passover of 37, and won the good opinion of the Jews. He deposed Caiaphas, the high priest who had condemned Jesus, and appointed his brother-in-law Jonathan; but Jonathan did not last long; he was deposed and succeeded by his brother Theophilus, the administration remaining throughout in the same family. These changes removed from the scene two of the sinister figures of the gospel narrative, and may be responsible for the period of peace for the church to which Luke alludes. The travels of Peter may have occurred between 37 and 39.

PETER IN CAESAREA

Luke is making use of a source which tells of a missionary journey to the sea-coast during which Peter visited the towns of Lydda and Joppa, where healing miracles are recorded.

We would gather from the gospel record that Peter was no Pharisee. He appears to have been a pious Jew of a simple, old-fashioned type, who kept the Law as he understood it, even if he did not observe all the fasts, or practise the ablutions before meals. He had kept the food laws, however, and had never eaten anything which was common or unclean. His eyes were now to be opened. As he prayed and fasted on the flat roof of Simon the tanner at Joppa, in sight of the blue water of the Mediterranean, he passed into a trance and had a curious dream. 'A vessel', he said, 'like a great sheet', was let down from heaven by its four corners, full of living creatures of all kinds; and a voice said to him, 'Get up, Peter, and kill and eat.' When Peter protested that he had never eaten anything common or unclean, the voice rebuked him, 'What God has cleansed', it said, 'do not *you* make common or unclean' —a theology as radical as that of Stephen.

The dream had the vague and elusive quality which dreams have, but its message of liberation and release was as clear as that which had come to Paul on the road to Damascus. No doubt it was the climax of great searchings of heart; and there were older declarations which seem to have contributed, in a rather confused way, to this revelation. When God created the world, he had said that it was all good. When Jesus was in Galilee, he had said that nothing which entered into a man could make him common or unclean. And yet the Law said that certain foods *were* common or unclean, and defiled a man if he ate them.

Peter woke, and while he was waiting to have a meal, he heard men knocking at the door. They were messengers from Cornelius, a Roman officer who had a house in Caesarea, a Gentile adherent of the synagogue. This man presented a new problem. The synagogues in the Gentile world had attracted many adherents of this kind, who accepted the piety and the moral commandments and the worship of the One God, but were never circumcised, and did not observe the outward forms of the Law. They were Gentiles still. They accepted Judaism, but they had not taken the step which made them Israelites in all respects. Cornelius was pious and devout; he fasted and prayed, he gave alms, he received visions. An angel had appeared to him and told him to send for Peter; but how could Peter accept such an invitation? It was contrary to every Jewish instinct, it was an irreligious act, to accept the hospitality of a Gentile, and eat and drink in his house; but Peter was caught between two visions, and he surrendered. The Spirit spoke in his ear and told him to go. God had taught him to call nothing common or unclean.

We have to make the best we can of these stories; for this was the atmosphere of primitive Christianity. Life was lived in accordance with impulses from another world. Indeed, the surprising thing would be if the records did not contain such stories.

Peter went to Cornelius in accordance with his dream, which had by now become a spiritual certainty in his mind; and when he saw the company of Gentiles all waiting for him in faith, he summed up the significance of the occasion in a sentence from the Hebrew scriptures which was filled now with a new significance, 'Of a truth I see that God is no respecter of persons.'

He announced his doctrine of the absolute equality of all human beings in the sight of heaven. He uttered his third great 'kerugma', his declaration of the gospel for the Gentiles, without any quotations from the Hebrew scripture, as it happens. So soon as this was done, there were manifest signs of an outpouring of the Holy Spirit. Without hesitation, he administered the sacrament of baptism; he accepted their hospitality; he ate and drank with them; a new church was born.

Such is the story of this very interesting document, which concludes the series connected with Caesarea. We have it, no doubt, in the form in which it was accepted in the Caesarean church, when Luke stayed there with Philip about twenty years later. The motive for its preservation there is obvious; it formed the credentials of the Gentile church in Caesarea. But it was a greater thing than this; it was a glimpse of a wider Judaism without distinctions of race or ritual purity.

THE CONTROVERSY IN JERUSALEM

Peter went back to Jerusalem without fully realizing, perhaps, all the consequences of his action. His mind was not like that of Paul; for Paul was able to visualize things rapidly in their relation to one another, and to create theologies and to express them in a dialectic which appealed to the mentality of the age. The mind of Peter worked more slowly. He wavered and shifted until he saw things plain; and then he was apt to see them in a vision, and act on them by impulse. In the long run, after hesitations and even mistakes, he was the rock which could not be shifted. When he was converted, the Lord had said, he would establish the brethren.

When he got to Jerusalem, he encountered criticism from a party which Luke describes as 'those of the circumcision'. These critics are not represented as objecting to the baptism of a Gentile, though the title given to them suggests that they were of the opinion that baptized Gentiles should be circumcised. What they objected to was Peter's going into a Gentile house, and eating and drinking with the uncircumcised and so making himself 'unclean'. He made his report, and the critics were silenced. They were silenced, but were they satisfied? Was his spiritual ascendancy weakened a little at this point?

It is no small merit of Luke's collection of narratives and 'speeches' that they enable us to follow, under the surface so to speak, the political trends and currents in the church. The Stephen stories showed us the emergence of a broad-minded left-wing group in the Jerusalem church, principally among the Hellenists, which may have advanced beyond the

5. (i) THE MOUNT OF OLIVES

5. (ii) THE VALLEY OF JEHOSHAPHAT

6. THE INSCRIPTION OF THEODOTUS

position of the church as a whole. The Cornelius story enables us to see the emergence of a narrow-minded right-wing group among the stricter brethren. There was by no means a unity of policy and practice in the mother-church; in fact it would seem that the seeds of most of the later dissensions were to be found there already.

Luke does not allow these painful differences to come into full view. He wrote at a later date, it is thought, when some of the great men he dealt with had become martyrs; he revives no memories of old unhappy controversies; and yet, since his sources are good and his historical instinct is sound, we are able to infer a great deal, some of which can be confirmed when we have other sources to draw upon, such as the Epistle to the Galatians. In this instance we have no such help; but judging by the cases in which we have, we must surely infer that the episode of the baptism of Cornelius and his household caused a violent and far-reaching controversy.

We are in a position now to make a conjecture about the original form and purpose of the narrative which Luke has preserved for us, and told for the most part twice over. We are told that Peter made a report when he got back to Jerusalem, and what would such a report consist of, if not the record which we have been following? This suggestion explains the whole form and content of the sequence; the miracles at Lydda and Joppa which proved that the divine agency was working in this apostolic mission; the emphasis on Jewish piety with its hours of prayer, its fasting, its alms-deeds and so forth, which proved its orthodoxy; the visions which announced the new principle of action, and led the apostle irresistibly to the house of the pious Gentile; and finally the outpouring of the Holy Spirit, which sealed the whole enterprise, and was actually compared by Peter with the outpouring of the Holy Spirit on the day of Pentecost in Jerusalem.

Such is the general pattern or outline of the kind of document which modern theology has labelled as a 'missionary journey'. There are others of the same sort in the Acts. But, whatever was its origin or purpose, such a document existed, and found its way into the hands of the author of Acts.

CHAPTER 4

ANTIOCH AND GALATIA

The Gospel in Antioch, *p.* 66. Prophets from Jerusalem, *p.* 67. King Herod Agrippa I, *p.* 70. Caligula's image, A.D. 39–40, *p.* 71. The Christian prophets, *p.* 72. King Agrippa's persecution, A.D. 44, *p.* 75. The rule of the procurators, *p.* 77. The famine in Jerusalem, A.D. 45–46, *p.* 78. The mission to Galatia, *p.* 80. The Pauline gospel, *p.* 82. The Galatian church, *p.* 84. The end of the mission, *p.* 85.

THE GOSPEL IN ANTIOCH

The power and purpose pent up in the apostolic church were so great that it was bound to break through its Jewish confines and pour out into the Gentile world; all the more because it had been unable to induce the Jewish people to accept Jesus as their promised Messiah. Paul distinctly states that the rejection of Jesus by the Jewish people provided the stimulus which brought in the Gentiles. Luke has strangely little to tell us about the way it happened; but he makes it clear that it was not the work of Paul; or of Paul alone.

The impetus was supplied by the persecution in which Stephen was put to death. There were enthusiasts in his party whose original home had been in Cyprus and Cyrene, a region of Africa to the west of Egypt, where Jews were numerous. These men fled for refuge to Phoenicia and Cyprus, and some of them found their way to Antioch on the Orontes, where they addressed themselves to the 'Greeks', that is to say non-Jews, speaking the Greek language and enjoying the Greco-Roman culture.

Antioch had been the capital of the old Seleucid empire, and was the third greatest city in the Roman world. It was the place of residence of the 'legate' of Syria, who was sent by the Roman senate to govern their oriental dominions, and to watch over the frontier defences on the River Euphrates. He exercised a general supervision over southern Syria and Judaea, as we have already seen. He had authority over the procurator at Caesarea.

Luke had little source-material about the foundation of this important church; no story of heavenly guidance or spectacular conversions; no miracles; no inspired kerugmata; and what he had not got, he could not give. Perhaps there was nothing very spectacular about the beginnings in Antioch? When the news reached Jerusalem, they sent Barnabas, who now apparently ranked as an apostle, to Antioch. He rejoiced at what he found there, and urged them to persevere; they may have needed the encouragement which he knew how to provide. He went on as far as Tarsus in Cilicia, where he found Saul, as he was still called; and he brought him to Antioch, where they worked together for a whole year. This allusion to a whole year illustrates the disconnected character of Luke's information; it hangs in vacancy without any indication of a beginning or ending; it does not help us to date the foundation of the Antiochene church. Some scholars would like to place it before Peter's visit to Caesarea. The plan of the Acts is really more geographical than chronological; it follows the outward expansion of the gospel from one Roman province to another until it reaches Rome itself.

One thing of interest he does mention. The believers in Antioch were given a nickname, which, it seems, was not liked. They were called *Christians*, a Latin formation meaning soldiers or dependants of the Christus. The word Christus or Messiah could not help suggesting the idea of a claimant to the throne of David, and it may be that these political associations of the word give us the clue to its use. It suggests that the faith had come to the attention of the Roman authorities, and this, in its turn, suggests that the course of evangelization was not running smoothly. The word Christian seems to crop up at first in connexion with legal trials and persecutions.

PROPHETS FROM JERUSALEM

Luke also mentions a visit from some Jerusalem prophets under the leadership of a certain Agabus. It is the first time that we hear of prophets in the church, though the church itself was thought of as a continuation of the prophetic succession. They seem to have made their appearance between 35 and 40. Their ministry in Antioch may be dated in this way. They prophesied a famine 'which came to pass in the days of Claudius Caesar', the inference being that the prophecy was uttered in the previous reign, which was that of Caligula, 37–41.

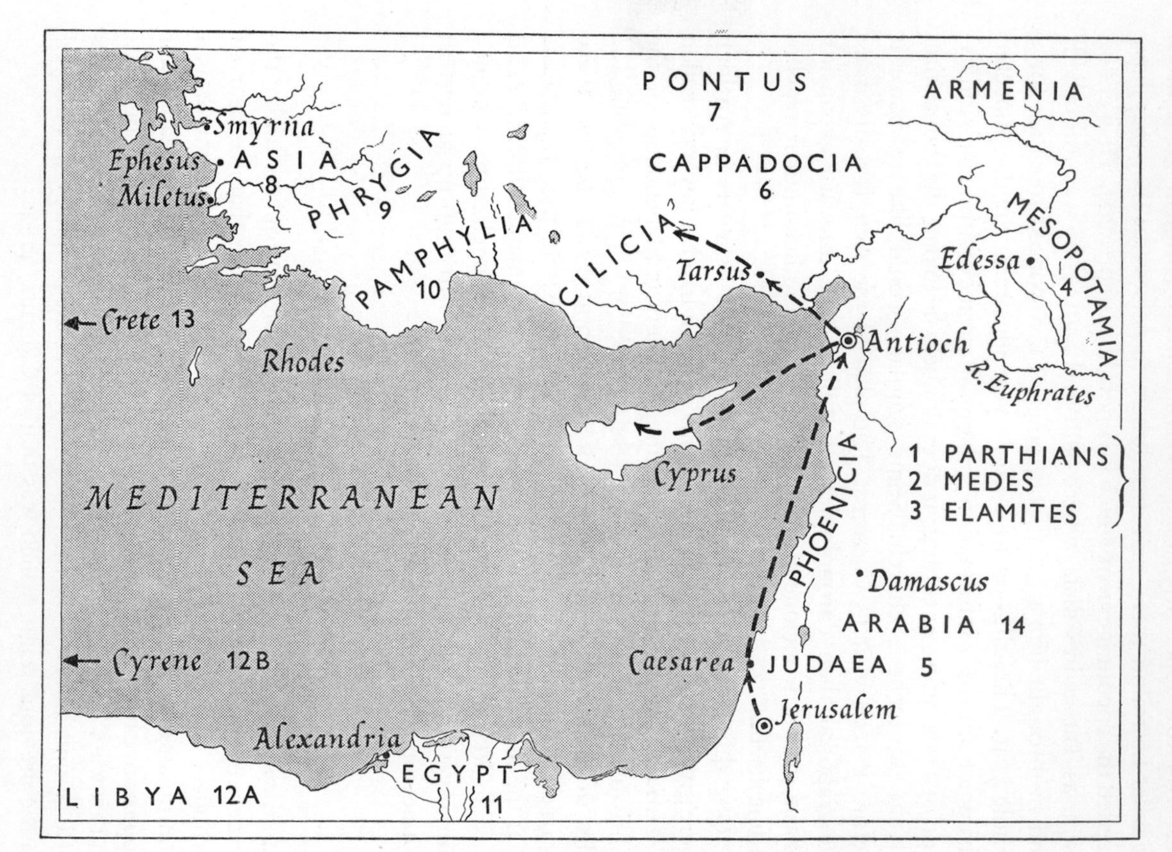

Map 2. The Christian Dispersion prior to A.D. 50.

The first centre of expansion is *Jerusalem*, which soon sets up a second centre in the nearby coast city of *Caesarea*, the centre of government for the country; this was the work of Hellenistic refugees from Jerusalem. Other refugees carried the gospel northward along the coast of Phoenicia to Cyprus and *Antioch*, which becomes a third centre. Saul, or Paul, who had been sent out from Jerusalem and Caesarea to his native city of Tarsus in Cilicia, joined the apostolic staff at Antioch. Paul and Barnabas are sent out from Antioch, and take the gospel into Pamphylia and Galatia (eastern Phrygia). This is the full extent of the expansion prior to A.D. 50, so far as Luke's narrative reveals it.

Egypt. Christians from Cyrene were among the first evangelists in Antioch, but no other Africans appear in the narrative except for the Ethiopian chancellor. Nothing is said about expansion into Egypt or into points east of Palestine or Antioch. There must have been such expansion.

The Pentecostal List. The expansion in and from Antioch was being conducted in Greek, but was cradled in an older expansion which was conducted in Aramaic for Jews and others who spoke this language. How far this expansion went, we cannot say, but perhaps there is a clue to it in the list of nations from which pilgrims came to Jerusalem according to the first chapter of Acts. This list is commonly regarded by scholars as a preview of the Jewish diaspora, into which the gospel radiated. The picture is oriental.

1, 2, and 3, are the *Parthians*, *Medes*, and *Elamites*, non-Semitic races in the mountainous country east of the Tigris; they are not included on the map. The Parthians, in common speech, meant the oriental empire which was the rival of Rome. *Mesopotamia* (4) is the land between the two rivers, where the capital of the Parthian king was situated; there were numbers of Jews there. 6 to 10 make up what we call *Asia Minor*; they are Cappadocia, Pontus, Asia, Phrygia, and Pamphylia; this was a field of missionary enterprise which may have been opened up from Antioch already. 11 is *Egypt* and 12 A and B are the parts of *Libya* around *Cyrene*, from which country the Antiochene evangelists had come. *Cretans* (13) and *Arabs* (14) seem to be added to round out the list. The Romans who are then mentioned are residents in Jerusalem, not visitors.

This picture recalls two others; one is the old oriental empire at its largest expansion, which became the dominions of the Seleucids and the Ptolemies; it is an oriental view of the world. The other is the list of Hellenistic synagogues in Jerusalem which is mentioned in Acts. It does not extend to Greece or Rome; it ignores the western world and the future work of Paul. It is a picture of the Christian dispersion as it existed in the year 50, when the Jerusalem council was held; it is a clue to the date of the sources which Luke uses in the first half of the Acts, and the geographical horizon of those who composed them. It is not really an introduction to Acts as a whole. It envisages an oriental expansion in which Peter is the most important figure.

KING HEROD AGRIPPA I

The Emperor Tiberius, in whose reign the crucifixion took place, was appointed co-emperor by Augustus in A.D. 13, succeeding him in 14. He did so with great caution and an elaborate deference to the old republican forms. When Caligula succeeded Tiberius in 37, it was quite another matter. The 'principate' was now an established institution. The 'princeps' was the master of the world, and was entitled to divine honours everywhere. His personal name was Gaius (or Caius), the name 'caligula' being a nickname which had been bestowed upon him by the soldiers; it means 'little boots'. He was a lunatic, and took his deity seriously. He set himself up in Rome as a divine ruler, and surrounded himself with a German bodyguard. Under this emperor a strong line was taken with the Jews.

We noted that during the last years of Tiberius, Herod Antipas, the 'tetrarch' of Galilee, had been engaged in a war with his ci-devant father-in-law Aretas, the king of Arabia.[1] He had been unsuccessful, and Vitellius had been obliged to come to his aid. Now his new wife Herodias, who was a daughter of old Herod, had a brother named Agrippa, an agreeable and clever adventurer, who was usually in debt or trouble of some kind. After living in Galilee for a while, he went off to Rome, attempted to influence Tiberius against Antipas, made some unguarded remarks about Tiberius, and found himself in prison. When Tiberius died, Caligula restored Agrippa to favour, and made him king of Trachonitis (or Decapolis), the 'tetrarchy' on the eastern side of the Sea of Galilee which was vacant by the death of the amiable Herod Philip.

His elevation to the rank of king did not please everybody. When he passed through Alexandria, late in 38 perhaps, there were serious riots in which synagogues were attacked and destroyed; and when he reached Palestine, he found his sister Herodias, and his brother-in-law (and uncle) Antipas very angry. Antipas had ruled Galilee for forty years without having the title of king, and Herodias insisted that the time had come for him to go to Rome and demand it. Agrippa sent a representative, who suggested to the emperor that he had troops at his

[1] Arabia, at this time, meant a strip of territory east of the River Jordan, containing the important cities of Bostra and Petra, and commanding the trade routes which ran north and south.

disposal on a war basis, and was inclined to make common cause with the Parthians against the Roman empire. The result was that Antipas was deposed and banished to Lyons in Gaul, where he ended his days. His tetrarchy of Galilee was added to the kingdom of Agrippa. These events occupied the years 39 and 40.

There were Christians in the immediate entourage of Antipas, whose names were known to Luke; Joanna, the wife of his 'steward' Chuza, had been a personal follower of Jesus; and Manaen his 'foster-brother' was a leader in the Antiochene church. It is possible that the faith reached Gaul in this strange manner. In any case the third of the sinister figures in the gospel narrative was gone.

CALIGULA'S IMAGE, A.D. 39–40

The friendship of Caligula for Agrippa did not imply that he was fond of the Jews. They were to feel the full weight of his tyranny.

The disturbances at Alexandria developed into an organized campaign of violence, destruction and massacre. Synagogues were torn down, and many Jews died for their faith and nation. They could not, of course, accept the deity of the emperor, or offer him the divine honours which they were now required to do. This had been recognized in times past, and it had been held to be sufficient if they prayed for the emperor and offered sacrifices for him in the Temple. Conformity to the law of the empire was now insisted upon, and in this respect the later persecution of the Christians was anticipated. But possibly Caligula had good reason for suspecting that the thought of an alliance with the Parthians, and a revolt against Rome, which Agrippa had suggested was the policy of Antipas, did exist in the minds of the more turbulent Jewish parties. Perhaps it had existed in the mind of Antipas? Such political ambitions must have been very tempting.

A reasonable emperor would have dealt with these disturbances by making wise concessions; but Caligula was not the man to be so easily mollified on a point of personal prestige and possibly of military danger. A deputation of Alexandrian Jews waited upon him in Italy, headed by the illustrious scholar and philosopher, Philo; but they were kept waiting at the imperial palace through the summer months, and finally went home without an answer. There was a counter-deputation under the leadership of a Greek scholar named Apion, who had written some anti-Jewish tracts, in which he made some extraordinary statements. He affirmed that the Jewish people had originated as a group of rebels of Egyptian origin, that they worshipped a god with an ass's head, and that they fattened up Greeks in their Temple to be sacrificed to this god. These extraordinary libels were believed by so intelligent a Roman as Tacitus.

Orders were sent to Petronius, the legate of Syria, to have an image of the emperor made, and to install it in the Temple at Jerusalem. Petronius knew the folly of this policy, but dared not disobey. In the summer of 40, he advanced into Galilee and quartered his army at the sea-port of Ptolemais, the modern Acre. Here he received a dignified protest from the leading Jews. He visited Tiberias on the Sea of Galilee, where further protests were made. He was met by thousands of Jewish peasants, who had neglected their farms in order to appear before him; they declared their willingness to die, rather than submit to the desecration of the Temple. Such is the story in Josephus. The proconsul made a brave decision. He agreed to delay proceedings and recommend the emperor to give up the project. He relied, no doubt, on the support of King Agrippa.

The end of the affair was most dramatic. Caligula was persuaded to give up the project, but Petronius must pay the price. Orders were sent to him to kill himself; but before these orders reached him, a faster messenger brought him the news that the emperor had been assassinated on 24 January 41. King Agrippa played an important part in bringing the new emperor, Claudius, to the throne. He was rewarded by having Judaea and Samaria added to his kingdom. The kingdom of Israel was thus restored to its fullest extent; but he was the last monarch to occupy the throne of David, and his reign was short. He enjoyed the kingdom for three years, A.D. 41-44.

THE CHRISTIAN PROPHETS

Luke does not refer to any of these events in the Acts, for he was not engaged in writing a history of his times, like Josephus; but they are of importance to us, since they supply the background which helps to explain the rise of the Christian prophets.

We know of a Jerusalem prophet of this period named Silas (or Silvanus) who co-operated with Paul, some ten years later, in the evangelization of Macedonia, and was a co-author with him of the Epistles to the Thessalonians, which contain some fragmentary apocalyptic texts. They speak darkly of 'a man of lawlessness, or son of perdition, who lifts himself up and exalts himself above every god or object of worship, to the extent of enthroning himself in the Temple of God, and displaying himself as God'. The reference to Caligula is unmistakable. The authors of the Epistles go on to state that the danger was not past; the 'mystery of lawlessness' was still at work; there was for the moment a restraining influence, but before long the evil thing would appear again in even greater force.

There is also a dated reference in II Corinthians to a man who was well known to Paul about the year 40 ('fourteen years ago' is the phrase used), who had marvellous visions and revelations, and was 'caught up into the third heaven, into the Paradise', whether in the body or out of the body Paul was not able to say. This man heard 'unutterable utterances' which it was not lawful for a man to speak. We do not know who he was; for the traditional theory that it was Paul himself is hard to reconcile with the wording of the epistle; but the reference sheds a little light on the nature of the prophetic movement as it existed among Christians in Syria in the reign of Caligula.

In the opinion of many scholars we may also take into consideration some of the older visions which were incorporated into the Revelation of St John. Some of these were the work of a Jerusalem prophet; for the first commission of the seer, after receiving his call from the hand of an angel, was to 'measure the Temple of God, and the altar, and those that worship at it'; and this was succeeded by the picture of the martyrdom of the witnesses of God in 'the great city which is spiritually called Sodom and Egypt, where their Lord was crucified too'; from which we can see that the Jerusalem prophets maintained their witness against the authorities in Jerusalem who were responsible for the policy of persecution. Now we find, in the thirteenth chapter of this book, a horrible 'wild beast' which rises up out of the sea (that is to say the west), and demands the homage of the whole world, and makes war on the saints; and there is a second wild beast, from the land, which makes an image of the first, and puts to death those who will not worship it. This prophecy has been rewritten to accord with the times of Nero, but it appears to retain features which were suggested by the episode of Caligula and Petronius.

We shall have to come to terms with the idiom of Judaeo-Christian prophecy, and to recognize it as a form of historical writing with its own idiom and conventions. It is far removed, however, from the kind of history in which men make plain factual statements, weighed and measured; it is a kind of poetry which may sometimes have been composed in a state of vision or ecstasy. It is not entirely fantasy, however. Stern facts appear, disguised in dream-like shapes, which embody the terrors and perils of the existent historical situation. It used a language which had been inherited from the old prophetic and apocalyptic tradition, but what it had to say was relevant to the 'last times', which simply meant the time in which men were actually living.

The apocalyptic tradition visualizes the universe as a scene of conflict between God Almighty and the powers of evil; a conflict which was concentrated for the moment in a trial of strength between the people of God and the empire of the world. It declares its unconquerable faith in the triumph of God's people, which will be consummated in the glorious appearance of the Messiah or Son of Man. The popular talk of the Christians in Antioch may have approximated more closely to the speech of Silas or of the Revelation, than to the spiritual wisdom of Paul or the well-measured prose of Luke; and if veiled references to the emperor as the abomination of desolation, spoken of by Daniel the prophet, were passing from mouth to mouth, or cryptic statements to the effect that the Lamb would overcome him because he was King of kings and Lord of lords, it is easy to understand how Christianity might come to be regarded as a revolutionary movement. Of course Christianity is in some sense a revolutionary movement.

Such visions and revelations were in line with the utterances of the Hebrew prophets which were read every Sabbath in the synagogues, and with later apocalypses, too, which were not in the canon; but their starting-point will have been those sayings of Jesus himself which were expressed in this idiom. It is considered likely that collections of his sayings of this sort, perhaps with explanatory notes, were being made and even reduced to writing about this time; such as the 'Little Apocalypse', for instance, in the thirteenth chapter of Mark.

When Agabus and his friends reached Antioch, we may feel confident that they had revelations and visions to offer of this sort, and the famine which they predicted for the future would be only one of the woes which were to come upon the earth. When a bad famine did actually come in the years 45–46, the church at Antioch decided to send relief to the church in Jerusalem 'by the hands of Barnabas and Saul'; but in saying this, Luke seems to have pursued one of his sources of information a little too far, and has to retrace his steps to take up another.

KING AGRIPPA'S PERSECUTION, A.D. 44

In Rome King Agrippa had wielded a good deal of influence with two successive emperors; in Palestine he had won considerable prestige by his handling of Caligula; and the way was open for the revival of the old Jewish kingdom in some of its ancient glory. He was an astute politician with dreams of grandeur. He adopted a highly orthodox policy on religious affairs, but this did not prevent him from showering favours on the numerous independent Greek cities which came under his rule. He made the best of both worlds.

The Nazareans at Jerusalem were in a difficult position. Strong passions had been aroused by the attempted desecration of the Temple by Caligula, and the anti-Gentile feeling in the hearts of many Jews must have been intensified; the feeling of loyalty to the Temple must have been deepened; and the church was already suspect on that point. It was now fraternizing with the Gentiles, and semi-Gentile congregations were coming into existence in Syria and Cilicia and even as near home as Caesarea.

Early in the year A.D. 44 the king gave his sanction to the persecution of Christians in Jerusalem, and this time members of the Twelve were singled out. James the son of Zebedee was killed, but there are no Acts of his martyrdom. It pleased the Jews, Luke tells us, and Agrippa proceeded to arrest Peter about the time of the Passover. A great change had taken place since the days of Peter's popularity, when it was said that people used to bring out their sick and lay them in the street, so that his shadow might fall upon them as he passed.

The document which Luke is using gives a remarkable narrative of his escape from prison, which was regarded as an intervention of providence; or, as they expressed it, an angel of the Lord. The element of the marvellous in the first half of the Acts cannot be passed over without any consideration, and a few observations are offered.

The first is that the element of the marvellous, apart from the question of the Resurrection itself, does not determine the course of history;

it blends into it. There were of course the 'pneumatic' gifts, such as tongues, prophecy, visions, healings, and so forth, which every one admits to have been features of primitive Christian religion; but above and beyond that, there was the sense of being controlled by great spiritual powers, a faith which was frequently expressed in the language of vision or apocalypse. It was the angel, or the Spirit, that directed and preserved the apostle or evangelist in all his ways; and the Syro-Hellenistic mind enjoyed a colourful sensuous presentation of this evangelical conviction. It liked to externalize it in concrete images. But, even so, the angel of Hebrew thought was not a Michelangelo angel with a superb physique and uplifted wings; it was a sudden inrush of invisible spiritual energy. The light that woke Peter in his prison cell was not, of necessity, a visible light; the voice that commanded him to rise up was not, of necessity, an audible voice; his condition at the time was not a normal one; he was in a dream or trance; he did not realize that it was true until he found himself in the street, and 'came to himself'. *Then* he believed. The Lord had indubitably sent his angel to deliver him. We have the talk of Peter to himself as he walked down the street.

It is plain that we have no idea what 'actually happened'; and it almost looks as if Peter had no idea either; but, in any case, there were excellent reasons for not revealing the mechanics of the escape, if there were mechanics. There were Christians in Herod's household perhaps, who might have to pay the penalty. The language of apocalyptic was the best language to use, and fully expressed the facts of the situation on the plane that really mattered to the Christian mind. It was a wonderful escape; it was an act of God; no need to say more.

It is characteristic of these stories that they are full of realistic and interesting detail. This one shows us the church met together in earnest prayer in the house of Mary the mother of Mark; we are even given the name of the maid who opened the door; it was Rose (Rhoda). Once again a Lucan source which many would describe as legendary enables us to follow new developments in the life of the church. The position of the Twelve has altered; they no longer dominate the scene in Jerusalem. Peter goes away 'to another place'; but before doing so he indicates the future leader of the Jerusalem church. It was, of course, James the brother of the Lord.

Even this Jerusalem story ends with a reference to Caesarea. The persecution is brought to an end by the sudden death of Herod Agrippa at Caesarea later in the same year; a death which was regarded as a judgement of God, both in the Acts and by Josephus. He was celebrating some imperial festival, and in the course of it he gave himself some of the airs of a divine king after the Gentile pattern. The angel of the Lord struck him, Luke says, because he gave not God the glory. Josephus gives unpleasant details with regard to the loathsome disease of which he died. The Jewish monarchy, on the grand scale, was extinguished. His son, who was also called Herod Agrippa, was a minor; and though he was given royal status some six years later, it was only as king of Chalcis, a small district in the Lebanon. We shall hear of him in connexion with St Paul. Indeed, he retained his position as king until his death in about A.D. 100.

THE RULE OF THE PROCURATORS

And now the Jews were placed once again under the rule of agents of the emperor called 'procurators', and the loss of their independence, nominal as it had been, provoked bitter resentment. We hear now of the Zealot or Cananean party, and hostility to Rome was further inflamed by the misgovernment and avarice and atrocities of the procurators. Rebellion now became endemic, as one modern historian says.

Cuspius Fadus became procurator in 44, and was succeeded by Tiberius Alexander, a renegade Jew from Alexandria and a nephew of the philosopher Philo. It was under Fadus that a 'magician' named Theudas led a company of his followers to the River Jordan which, he assured them, would divide at his command. He should not be confused with the earlier Theudas, who is mentioned by Gamaliel in his speech before the sanhedrin which is reported in the Acts; unless, indeed, Luke has introduced his name into Gamaliel's speech by error. Tiberius Alexander took strong action against the Zealots, and crucified two of their leaders, James and Simon, who were sons of that Judas of Galilee who had founded the party. Is it possible that the Zealot Simon, who was executed by Tiberius Alexander, was the disciple of Jesus who holds the eleventh place in the list of the Twelve, next to Judas Iscariot, and is always called Simon the Zealot, or Cananean?

THE FAMINE IN JERUSALEM, A.D. 45–46

The disorders of this time were made worse by an extensive famine which began in 45 and continued through 46. Josephus tells us how Helen, the dowager-queen of Adiabene, brought relief to the people of Jerusalem, on behalf of her son King Izates, who was a circumcised Jew. Adiabene was a small Syrian principality in the Parthian sphere of influence, beyond the Euphrates and Tigris Rivers. Judaism was extending its religious and political influence in those regions. It is our misfortune that we know nothing of the expansion of the gospel in this direction, for some expansion there must have been.

No doubt help came in from many parts of the world to the hungry city, including the help brought by Barnabas and Saul from the church at Antioch. It must have been a considerable task to make the collection from the brethren, 'from each according to his means', to convert it into goods, and to bring it to Jerusalem; for a gift of cash would not have given immediate relief, and is therefore unlikely. In making all these arrangements the two apostles had the help of a Gentile Christian named Titus, who came up with them to Jerusalem, as we learn from Galatians.[1] The visit may have coincided with one of the great festivals, when many pilgrims came up to Jerusalem. The gifts were received on behalf of the Jerusalem church by the elders. We have not met with elders before; but every Jewish community was traditionally governed by the elders of the people. In this atmosphere of benevolence and of gratitude, a conference on outstanding difficulties might have some chance of success; and we learn from Galatians that such a conference was held.

Peter and John were there as well as James. It is noticeable that Paul uses, and continues to use, the Aramaic name 'Kephas', of which the name Peter is a translation into Greek. He calls him Peter twice, but we infer that this name had not come into general use, and that he still moved for the most part in circles where Aramaic was spoken. This agrees with the information that he was regarded as the 'apostle of the circumcision', that is to say of the Jewish world; Paul (who is still called Saul in Acts) was now regarded as the 'apostle of the uncircum-

[1] In this reconstruction we identify the visit to Jerusalem described in Galatians ii with the visit described in Acts xii; not that in Acts xv. See the discussion in the next chapter.

cision', that is to say of the Gentile world; his stature had greatly increased. We get the impression that Peter exercised a travelling and supervising ministry among the predominantly Jewish congregations of Judaea, Samaria, and Galilee, while Paul did the same for the more largely Gentile congregations of Cilicia and Syria. We have no clear evidence, as yet, of entirely Gentile congregations.

Barnabas and Paul held a private conference with Peter and James and John, who were held in high honour in the Jerusalem church, Paul says; 'they were highly regarded as the pillars'; 'they appeared to be of importance'; though that, he adds, made no difference to him. An undoubted note of asperity creeps into his writings; for he was in a very uncomfortable position. He asserts emphatically that his apostolate had come to him from heaven, so that his position was every bit as good as theirs; and yet he was in desperate need of reassurance or support on some point or points, 'lest he was running in vain'. Their full recognition was essential to him, and he was relieved when they formally recognized his apostolate, and extended the right hand of fellowship. They would go to the Jews; he and Barnabas would go to the Gentiles. Only, it was stipulated, he must remember the poor; that is to say he must continue to bring further material help from time to time to the Jerusalem church, which had suffered from persecution and famine; the very thing, he says, that he was occupied with at the time.

Paul honoured this pledge in the most generous way. Never for one moment did he think of breaking away, or forming his own sect or party. The gospel, the apostolate, and the church, formed a unity in Christ, a point which he emphasizes increasingly as he grows older.

The understanding was not final. There were problems of practice and procedure which would have to be thought out; and there were strong groups in the Jerusalem church which were far from friendly. He had made many enemies there. False brethren, he says, were privily smuggled in to spy out 'our liberty which we have in Christ Jesus'; that is to say, the freedom of the Gentile mission from the yoke of the Jewish Law. These men were offended by the presence of Titus, a Gentile convert who had never been circumcised. Pressure was brought to bear; and though Paul says that he did not yield even for an hour, 'by way of subordination', this peculiar modifying clause rather suggests that he did yield by way of voluntary concession, or that

Titus agreed to be circumcised for the sake of peace. The true interpretation of this sentence will never be known.

We learn from the Acts that they took back with them to Antioch John Mark, who was a cousin of Barnabas, and a son of the Mary in whose house Peter had sought temporary refuge after his escape from prison. At a later date he became the 'interpreter' of Peter and the composer of the gospel which bears his name. The stage was set for new adventures.

THE MISSION TO GALATIA

Luke now introduces into the Acts the Antiochene document for which he has been preparing the way; or perhaps we have been dealing with it already. It may have begun with the account of the foundation of the Antiochene church which we suggested was composed by Luke out of his own personal knowledge. He has deviated from it to introduce the events of the Jerusalem persecution under Agrippa I, which may be derived from Caesarean sources. He comes back again to Antioch.

The church of Antioch is now furnished with prophets and teachers, like the church in Jerusalem we may suppose. This does not imply that they had no other ministry, as some scholars have assumed; it means that they were now well endowed with spiritual leaders of their own in addition to their apostles Paul and Barnabas. Among these leaders were Symeon the Black and Lucius of Cyrene, who would appear to have been two of the original evangelists of the city; both may have been of African origin. Another was Manaen (or Menahem), who is described as the foster-brother of Herod Antipas of Galilee; his connexion with the gospel might date back to the time of the ministry of Jesus himself, for Luke mentions in his Gospel a steward of Herod named Chuza, whose wife Joanna belonged to the immediate circle of Jesus.

There was a public act of worship or service of God, in which the Spirit made known his will, doubtless through the prophets; 'Separate me Barnabas and Saul', he said, 'for the work to which I have called them.' This powerful, largely Gentile church was fully 'pneumatic'; it knew the Spirit as a living force from which it received direction.

We may, if we please, in company with the scholars to whom we have referred, recognize here a characteristic feature of Syrian Christianity; the feeling for God as living Spirit infused into the hearts of the believers; into their bodies, Paul would say; for Paul, in his earlier

7. THE TYCHE OF ANTIOCH

8. CALIGULA

writings, is an exponent of this type of theology. In his Epistle to the Galatians, which we assign to Antioch at this period, his gospel of the Spirit is as strong and determinative as his gospel of the Son of God. It comes upon the believer in his baptism; it expresses itself in prayer to the Father; it overcomes the lusts of the flesh; it generates love and joy and peace and other Christian graces. In a church filled with such a consciousness of spiritual power, we would expect to find inspired teachers and prophets, earnest services of prayer and fasting, revelations of the will of heaven, and missionary enterprise. In Galatians, and in I Corinthians as well, the Spirit makes its presence felt by these powerful demonstrations; it is the real substitute in the ecclesia for the Jewish Law. Moses gave the Law; but Jesus Christ gives life and spiritual power.

It is a decisive moment in Luke's narrative. The course of the gospel is decided; it strikes westward. The two apostles who have given leadership in the Syrian capital have finished their work there, and, with Mark as their assistant, they are designated for a new field of labour.

This was done with fasting and prayer and the laying on of hands. It was not an 'ordination', for both men had been working as apostles for some years, and Paul quite defiantly asserts that his apostolate had not been given him by men or through a man, but came to him directly from Christ. It was a commission for new work, and an outward expression of the fact that the church at Antioch had reached its full stature, and had become a missionary centre in its own right, like Jerusalem. It was the sending body which now stood behind the apostles and supported them, financially no doubt as well as spiritually. It was to Paul and Barnabas what Jerusalem was to Peter and John.

It cannot be part of our plan to tell in detail the story of these 'missionary journeys', as they have been called in the modern literature on the subject. We can only pick out what appear to be the indications of important historical developments. The island of Cyprus was their immediate destination. It had already heard the gospel from evangelists of the school to which Stephen had belonged. It was the native land of Barnabas; but it is clear that Paul now took the leading part. It may be more than a coincidence that after his discomfiture of the 'magician' Elymas (a figure of the same type as Simon of Samaria), and the favourable impression which he made on the proconsul Sergius Paulus, his old name of Saul ceases to be used. Saul the Jew gives way to Paul the Roman citizen. The narrative reads 'Paul and his party left for Perga of Pamphylia', a country which was situated on the southern coast of Asia Minor.

Paul and Barnabas proceeded into the mountainous interior. Mark returned to Jerusalem for reasons unknown to us, which Paul considered inadequate. His arrival there would serve to inform the mother-church of the progress of the Pauline mission. Mark perhaps had never bargained on going farther than Cyprus, where of course he had relations.

The first stop was at Pisidian Antioch in the south-eastern part of the Roman province of Galatia. This city must not be confused with the Syrian Antioch, and it will be convenient to adopt the French expedient of calling it Little Antioch (Antiochette). It was one of the Hellenistic cities which had been founded more than two centuries before by the Seleucid monarchs from the greater Antioch, and there had been a strong Jewish element in these cities from the beginning. The story of the preaching of the gospel in Little Antioch is told with freshness and charm, and the detail is of great interest. It gives us the only authentic picture which we possess of a Sabbath service in a Jewish synagogue of our period, except for the companion picture (also given by Luke) of the preaching of Jesus in the synagogue at Nazareth. It vouches for the reading of the Law and the prophets, which seems to be a point of importance in the source which Luke is now using. It also mentions the 'word of exhortation' which followed the prophetic lection, thus indicating the point of the service at which the preaching of the gospel was in order.

THE PAULINE GOSPEL

We turn to the report of Paul's preaching with some interest, as we are about to see him in action for the first time; and frankly we are disappointed. There is no apparent power or magnetism or personality in it. It is a rather colourless proclamation of Jesus as the Jewish Messiah of David's line. Its content does not differ much from what Peter preached in Jerusalem, but it is devoid of his poetic diction. It ends on what seems to be a Pauline note, the doctrine of 'justification' (or right standing with God) through faith, and not through Law; but the evidence of Galatians shows that this too was common ground with Peter.

We naturally do not expect Paul to speak to Jews in a Jewish synagogue as he did later, in his Epistles, when writing to his own churches. We know that his policy was to come to the Jews as a Jew, and that he did preach Jesus as the 'seed of David according to the flesh'. But we feel that this 'speech' is not in his style. At the best it is a summary of his message, and the message itself was the conventional evangelistic material. On the other hand, the Jews who heard it would be more excited about it than we are when we read it after nineteen centuries of Christian history. It proclaimed a successor to the throne of David; it sharply criticized the Jewish authorities who had crucified him; it announced the Resurrection; it made the gospel superior to the Law; and it ended on a stern note of warning. It would have been disturbing.

Was this summary composed by Luke, or did he find it in his source? We shall give reasons for supposing that he found it in his source. It has every appearance of being put where it is to convince those who read it that the preaching of Paul was on sound Jerusalem lines, even if it was sharply expressed.

We are entering into the famous Galatian controversy which has exercised the minds of the leading critics and scholars for the past century. These are the churches of Galatia to which Paul wrote his most effective and warlike epistle, not sparing his colleagues in the apostolate Peter and Barnabas. It is true that the great scholar, Bishop Lightfoot, transported this controversy, and the destination of that Epistle, to a region farther north; but that famous theory was a paradox which the history of later criticism justifies us in rejecting. Nor can we find the time when Paul could have fared so far north, or any convincing evidence that he ever did so.

The narrative, apart from the kerugma itself, is alive with colour and detail. It conveys something of the feeling of exhilaration which was in the air. The gospel was the sensation of the town for those few days. There may of course have been some individual believers in Little Antioch already; but it had never yet received an official mission from apostles of the Messiah who claimed to have seen him after his resurrection. The prestige of the apostles rose to incredible heights; but deadly hostility was created in the hearts of the unbelieving Jews, who were able to influence certain socially elect ladies of 'Greek' descent, who in their turn brought influence to bear upon the magistrates. The authorities took action, and the apostles fled to Iconium.

Before they left Little Antioch, however, there had been a definite schism between the Gentile believers and the Jewish disbelievers. In accordance with the Galilean precedent, the apostles 'shook off the dust from under their feet'. A complete cleavage now existed between the old Jewish synagogue and the company of the disciples, which was filled with joy and the Holy Spirit.

THE GALATIAN CHURCH

St Paul himself gives some impressions of the new churches which he founded on this tour. He speaks of his bad health, his 'infirmity of the flesh' which humbled him and made him a trial to others; yet they received him as if he were an angel of God, as if he were Messiah Jesus himself. They believed, they were baptized, they became sons of God, they received the Holy Spirit. We have no difficulty in visualizing the baptismal scene, and the working of the Spirit in their hearts, and the spontaneous outpouring of prayer in which they sang or shouted the words 'Abba, Father'; an Aramaic word out of the prayer-life of the Palestinian church. There were no more worldly distinctions among them; neither Jew nor Greek, neither slave nor free, neither male nor female; they were 'in the Messiah'; they were seed of Abraham.

It is amazing. The religion of the Spirit, for all its breadth and freedom and humanity, was still the religion of the old Israel. The old religion had not been abandoned or cast aside or repudiated; on the contrary, the Gentile converts had been incorporated into it. But it was a Judaism without the Law, and without the feeling of racial exclusiveness. Faith in the Messiah gave these Gentile converts perfect standing with God as members of his ancient people. And that is what the 'speech' which Paul made at Antioch had finally said.

There is another question, however, which the narrative of Acts compels us to ask. Why were the Gentile authorities so easily persuaded to take action against the apostles if the gospel was simply a spiritual message? Why did the chief men of Little Antioch and the rulers of Iconium drive them out of town? What did the Jews say about the gospel which justified them in taking such strong action? Paul supplies no answer to this question, but perhaps Luke does. Perhaps it was the formal proclamation in the synagogue of a new king,

Jesus the son of David; an ineradicable semi-political element in the gospel tradition; the charge on which he had been crucified.

This point explains in a very precise way the nickname given to the disciples in Antioch; they were *Christians*: Messiah's men. It also explains Paul's theology; they were 'in Messiah'; and because they were in Messiah, they were in David and therefore in Abraham, and therefore in Israel. The sermon of Paul in Little Antioch seems to fit very well into its place. A year or two later, in the evangelization of Greece, the apostles are charged with acting contrary to the decrees of Caesar and saying that there is another king, one Jesus. It is the same accusation.

THE END OF THE MISSION

At Iconium the same course of events was repeated, and the apostles fled to the village of Lystra. Their success here was so great that they were thought to be pagan gods come down to earth. Barnabas was identified with Zeus, the bearded paternal 'father of gods and men'; Paul with Hermes, a smooth-faced young man with a trim athletic figure and the gift of speech. He was the chief speaker, they noticed. Barnabas was approaching old age; he was perhaps a little older than most of the apostles; Paul was a little younger. He was a 'young man' at the time of his conversion, and even now may not have been much more than forty. Fifteen years later he describes himself, perhaps in a half-comic vein, as 'such a one as Paul the aged'; hardship, ill-health and ceaseless work had taken their toll.

A hundred years later the legends which had grown up in Galatia about this mission were collected and worked into a novel called the *Acts of Paul*. It contains a description of the apostle which is hardly flattering, and may be based on personal tradition:

> a man of small stature, thin-haired upon the head, crooked in the legs, of good condition of body, with eyebrows joining, his nose somewhat hooked; full of grace; for sometimes he appeared like a man, and sometimes he had the face of an angel. (*Acts of Paul*, ii. 3.)

The apostles were stoned out of Lystra, Paul being seriously injured, and took refuge in Derbe. After recuperating, they turned back and re-entered each town in turn, gathering the disciples, urging them to stand firm, and imparting some degree of organization to their churches by appointing 'elders', whom they commended to God with prayer and fasting, warning the disciples at the same time that we can only enter into the Kingdom of God through many afflictions. There is a 'we' in the last sentence which adds immensely to the personal feeling with which this narrative is marked throughout, and comes no doubt from the original document used by Luke. It is a first-hand story, with some literary touches of its own.

When the apostles returned to Antioch, they lost no time in gathering the church together, and reporting what God had done through their means, and how he had 'opened a door' to the Gentiles. The narrative which Luke has been reproducing in his own style gives the substance of that report, and may depend upon some written form of it.

CHAPTER 5

CONFERENCE IN JERUSALEM

The counter-mission in Galatia, A.D. 48, *p.* 87. The Antioch controversy, *p.* 89. The Epistle to the Galatians, *p.* 91. The Jerusalem council, A.D. 49, *p.* 92. The 'speeches' in Acts, *p.* 93. James the brother of the Lord, *p.* 96. The speech of James, *p.* 98. The conciliar epistle, *p.* 99. The Judaeo-Christian tradition, *p.* 100. The neo-Levitical code, *p.* 102. The state of the church, *p.* 105. Christians in Rome, *p.* 106.

THE COUNTER-MISSION IN GALATIA, A.D. 48

We are not surprised to read in the Acts of the arrival of a counter-mission in Antioch from the more conservative Jewish Christians in Jerusalem, who insisted that 'you cannot be saved unless you are circumcised according to the Law of Moses'. It seemed to be the logical position to adopt, since the gospel movement regarded itself as the perfect form of the old Jewish revelation of God on earth. It had not dreamed of separating from it. What it had done was to draw into its fellowship of faith the 'God-fearing' Gentiles who were already adherents of the synagogue, and along with them other Gentiles who thus came into an analogous relationship.

It was maintained by Paul that these Gentiles, having been united with the Messiah, were Israelites now, and nothing further was necessary. What comes into view is an enlarged and transformed Judaism, whose essence consisted in recognition by faith of the Jewish Messiah; and this took the place in Paul's mind of the submission to the Law of Moses which had constituted the essence of Judaism for him prior to the Messiah's appearance. He therefore adopted the shocking policy that it would be wrong for the Gentile converts to be circumcised.

There was a political side to this argument, since Gentiles who submitted to circumcision after their baptism would have become Israelites in all respects; to use a modernism, they would have forfeited their old nationality. Paul held that in some sense they had done this by their baptism. They were seed of Abraham. He developed this idea in Ephesians.

There was no small argument, it says in Acts, with Paul and Barnabas; but we learn more about this controversy from the Epistle to the

Galatians which we place at this point. Many scholars place it about five years later; but if this is done, it is not possible to reconcile its evidence with that of Acts; and certain features in Galatians itself are more readily explained on the hypothesis of the earlier date.

We learn from this Epistle that an emissary of the circumcision party had arrived among the Galatian churches and had met with some success; which of course Paul may have over-estimated. He marvels that the 'foolish Galatians', as he calls them in all tenderness, have been 'bewitched' by this exponent of a more fully Jewish gospel, and have turned so soon from the gospel of pure faith by which they had received the spirit of liberty, to 'another gospel', which insisted on obedience to the Law of Moses which he regards now as a species of slavery. He weeps for their simplicity, and his love for them overflows as he writes. They are his own dear children in Christ, and once again he is in pain and labour in bringing them to birth in the gospel as he understands it.

There was scope, no doubt, for a mission of this kind in Galatia. It would serve to reassure the local Jews who had been shocked by Paul's radicalism. It was admitted, apparently, that he was an apostle, but not an apostle of Jesus Christ in the highest sense; he was an envoy sent out by church authorities, and he had exceeded his instructions by dispensing his Gentile converts from obedience to the Law of Moses. He was taking the easier way, and courting popularity. Nor was he consistent. There were cases, it was hinted, in which he had himself 'preached circumcision'; the case of Titus may have been in their minds, in which a concession of some sort may have been made. They were not entirely unsuccessful. They may have planted churches of their own sort in the Phrygian cities, where Jews were numerous; for Christians of this sort appear as far west as Philadelphia in the writings of John and Ignatius; and there was no stopping them presenting their case in the Jewish synagogues after the reading of the Law and the Prophets; or even in the new Christian communities which were probably organized along synagogue lines.

On the other hand, they had done wrong in invading the apostolate of another man; for it had been agreed that Paul had been entrusted with the apostolate of the Gentile world.

Paul does not hesitate to assert his authority. The Epistle was a powerful weapon. We make a great mistake if we think of it simply as a piece of personal correspondence, or even as a literary contribution to a theological controversy. It was a powerful intervention by the apostolic founder. It laid down a firm decision that it would be a denial of the gospel, and a repudiation of the Holy Spirit, and an act of apostasy to the faith, to yield to the new propaganda and receive circumcision. It even spoke of the 'anathema', the spiritual censure of the church, with its dreaded effects upon soul and body. Its words were officially read in the churches of Galatia by the ministers who carried the Epistle; who they were, we are not told; and it was preserved in the churches and continued to be read in them as an authoritative document; otherwise we would not have it today. Paul had acted with peremptory decisiveness.

THE ANTIOCH CONTROVERSY

A second point which we learn from the Epistle is that the controversy in Antioch itself was so severe that Peter came down and took part in a conference, or what developed into a conference. His attitude, Paul tells us, was favourable to the Gentiles; he joined in their sacred and sacramental meals; he lived like a Gentile rather than a Jew. He admitted that Christians were 'justified' by faith in the Messiah Jesus, and not by works of the Law. All this was common ground between the two great apostles.

The harmony was disturbed by the arrival of a new delegation from Jerusalem which claimed to have the authority of James the brother of the Lord. They were men whose strict adhesion to the Law made it impossible for them to join in table-fellowship with Gentiles of any sort, even if they were baptized; but it is not necessary to infer that James himself had dictated this policy. They were in a position to bring considerable pressure to bear upon Peter, who was obviously anxious to occupy a position of mediation, and to keep in touch with both sides. If he continued to mix with the Gentile believers, he would find himself debarred from intercourse with his old Jerusalem associates. He would have defiled himself by eating and drinking with 'sinners'; for this word was undoubtedly bandied about in the heat of the argument. The consequence was that he ceased to attend the Gentile gatherings. 'He began to draw back and separate himself', Paul says, adding with some bitterness that Barnabas was involved in the same hypocrisy.

These were hard words; but it was natural that Peter and Barnabas should act as they did in order to establish contact with the Jerusalem Christians. After all, Peter was the apostle of the circumcision; the situation was more complex for him than it was for Paul. But it was equally natural for Paul to feel as he did about their action, and entirely in accordance with his impulsive nature to tax Peter publicly with his inconsistency, and to say that Peter was not 'walking straight' in regard to the truth of the gospel.

It is necessary to go very thoroughly into this painful episode, in order to make it clear that the inconsistency of the older apostles, if it was an inconsistency, was a matter of accommodation to circumstances rather than a matter of principle; for Paul clears Peter on that account; he regards his actions as inconsistent with the principles on which both apostles agreed. There was nothing here which could not be mended on the assumption that Peter and Paul were Christian men; but Galatians does not tell the sequel of the argument; it breaks off into further argument without finishing the story; and the simplest explanation of the failure to finish the story is that it was written when the argument was still at its height.

The Epistle to the Galatians was composed in a remarkable flow of passionate eloquence. Paul may have written it right through with his own hand, which was an unusual thing for him; at any rate he added a personal message in his own handwriting; the large handwriting which is often characteristic of men and women with indomitable character and large ideas and considerable self-confidence.

> See with what large letters I write to you with my own hand.... Those who are forcing circumcision upon you, want to make a good show in the flesh. They are doing it to avoid persecution for the cross of Christ.... But henceforth let no man trouble me; for I bear in my body the scars of the Lord Jesus. (Galatians vi. 11ff.)

He had suffered much at the hands of his own nation, and would suffer more as the hostility to him grew more intense. His readers would remember the persecutions in Little Antioch and the stones at Lystra which nearly ended his life, as he did himself years later when he was facing martyrdom in Rome. It was the unanswerable argument which demonstrated his complete sincerity. The gospel was written in his flesh and blood.

THE EPISTLE TO THE GALATIANS

We have adopted the early date for Galatians, and have constructed our history on this basis. The question has been debated among scholars for two full generations, and agreement has not been registered; but it is a fact that, with the early date, every event falls naturally into place. Those who adopt the later date are obliged to identify Paul's visit to Jerusalem in Galatians ii with the Jerusalem council of Acts xv (which we now proceed to discuss) instead of the earlier visit of Acts xii (which Paul fails to mention on this hypothesis). It introduces confusions and difficulty at many points. The arguments which perplexed the older theologians and still go on in the schools were due in no small degree to the fact that they accepted the later date of Galatians, which was traditional in their time; yet the earlier date which we have adopted was suggested four centuries ago by John Calvin. It has many advocates today, and gives perfectly satisfactory results.

We must not leave the Epistle to the Galatians with the suggestion that its value was purely controversial. It is the first great exercise in the dialectic of the gospel as the supreme saving power, and the Spirit as a personal gift; and it is by far the greatest. Its logic is rapid and its style compressed; and yet it as clear as crystal. It may be compared with a great revolutionary manifesto. Its use of the Old Testament is not in accordance with modern critical principles; but that is a small matter; it used Rabbinic argumentation to convince Rabbinic men; and it probably drew on the treasury of 'testimonies' which was generally accepted in the church. It lays down, with the help of this allegorical exegesis, the principles of a free spiritual religion, lived by faith, and it abounds in great epigrams which have inspired heroic men and women in all ages.

I am crucified with Christ: I live no longer myself but Christ lives in me.

Neither Jew nor Greek, neither slave nor free, neither male nor female; but all one man in Christ Jesus.

Circumcision has no value and neither has uncircumcision, but only faith which operates through love.

And the fruit of the Spirit is love, joy, peace, patience, goodness, faith, humility, self-control: against these things there is no Law.

THE JERUSALEM COUNCIL, A.D. 49

We will not go far wrong in placing the mission to Galatia in 47 and the counter-mission in 48, and there is very general agreement in placing the council or conference at Jerusalem in 49, probably at the midsummer festival of Pentecost, so that the Antioch conference may have taken place at Passover in the same year. It thus took place under the new procurator Ventidius Cumanus who was appointed in 48; he seems to have been a bad man and a bad governor, so that disturbances among the Jews increased under his rule; there were also riots in the Jewish quarter in Rome. They had to do with a certain 'Chrestus'.

Herod Agrippa II, the son of Herod Agrippa I, succeeded his uncle about this time as king of Chalcis, an unimportant principality in the Lebanon; it was no doubt a concession to the Jewish national feeling, since he was given a protectorate over the Temple in Jerusalem. He deposed the high priest Joseph ben Cami, and appointed Ananias ben Nebediah, one of the most unprincipled men who ever held that position.

We turn now to the pages of the Acts for the story of the council. Luke is still using his Antiochene source, which he edits no doubt for his purpose. It tells how Paul and Barnabas passed along the Syrian sea-coast, traversing Phoenicia and Samaria, and giving their report of the foundation of the Galatian churches. When they reached Jerusalem, this report was presented to the 'apostles and elders'. The Pharisee party in the church responded to it by urging their contention that the Gentile converts should be circumcised and instructed to observe the Law of Moses; and there was an assembly of apostles and elders 'to see about the matter'. This body is sometimes regarded as a formal council of the Jerusalem church, which had been formed on the model of the Jewish sanhedrin, with James the brother of the Lord as its president; and such a development had no doubt taken place; but it is also possible that widely representative conferences were held at Pentecost or other festivals, when pilgrims came up to Jerusalem.

We are now told that Peter was present, an interesting point, as this is the last time that he is mentioned in Acts. He made a short speech in which he pointed out that he had initiated the extension of the gospel to the Gentiles by the baptism of Cornelius in Caesarea; he asserted the equal status of Gentiles and Jews under the gospel, guaranteed as it was by their equal reception of the Holy Spirit; 'Why, then, should we lay a yoke on the neck of the disciples which neither we nor our fathers were able to bear?'

It was a strong speech, and it seems to be entirely in accord with what we know of the position of Peter, both from Acts and from Galatians; but it does not appear to be very much more than a summary of his position. Luke has already related in some detail the events at Caesarea to which he referred, and does not need to repeat them now; but it is likely that Peter related the story in full; for Barnabas and Paul had related the story of the foundation of their churches in Galatia. We see now why Luke has given such a detailed account of both missionary journeys; they were required as an introduction to the story of the council; they were indeed the material on which the council was asked to make up its mind. The apostles rested their case, so far as we can see, not on general theological reasoning, but on the record of actual work which God had done through their labours; for their actions had been sealed by the approval of the Holy Spirit. Yet there was a 'theological' principle on which they both agreed, the complete sufficiency of faith in the Messiah as a saving power; but this was a pragmatic fact of the apostolic mission.

Conversely, the story of the council enables us to see why these reports of missionary journeys were composed, written down and preserved.

THE 'SPEECHES' IN ACTS

We are on controversial ground in a double sense at this point, for the radical wing in modern criticism is more than dubious about the historicity of Luke's reconstruction of the story of the council. They doubt whether Peter and Paul were so closely in accord; they doubt whether the council was so harmonious as appears; they even doubt whether there was a council at all; or they turn to Galatians ii for the true picture of it. These views are not unconnected with modern theological controversies; they require a drastic criticism of the evidence; and they have little respect for the historical ability of the author of Acts or the intelligence of his readers. It is regrettable, perhaps, that it is not possible to survey the literature on the subject in detail; all that seems possible is to adopt a moderate position which does justice to the evidence, the trustworthiness of which there is no real reason to doubt.

The story of the council appears in a source or series of sources, which begins as early as chapter xii, and is connected with Antioch; and this is natural, since Antioch was vitally concerned in its outcome. But it is quite possible that the author of Acts took a good deal of trouble in writing up the council and reconstructing it from various accounts which he had received. In particular he may have composed the 'speeches'.

It does not seem possible or necessary to accept the speeches in Acts as verbatim records of what was said by the speaker on the occasion, though this may come near to being the truth in some instances. On the other hand, no reason has appeared for regarding them as free compositions after the manner of Thucydides and other Greek historians: speeches, that is, which were never actually delivered. One can test this very simply by reading the numerous speeches in Josephus which were produced in this way, to be put into the mouth of some ancient person of Old Testament times or even some contemporary person of note such as the Emperor Titus or King Herod Agrippa II. They are all alike, all written in one style, all products of the workshop of Josephus. He makes no attempt to vary their style or to fit them to the character of the person speaking. This does not mean, of course, that they do not contain sentiments appropriate to the speaker, or even matter which he did include in a speech on the occasion under consideration; but this is not always so; the speeches are often quite unreal.

When we turn to the speeches in Acts, if we may so call them, it becomes clear at once that the precedent of Thucydides may be forgotten. Their style, their matter, and their personal character, vary from one to another. The kerugmata of Peter, for instance (if we may use this plural form), contain material of an Aramaic character, which shows some signs of poetic diction, and possibly of rhythm. The defence of Stephen consists for the most part of theological argument of a connected character. The word of exhortation given by Paul at Little Antioch consists of rather conventional kerugma, which reminds us sometimes of Peter and sometimes of Stephen; though it lacks the poetic diction of the former, and the forceful argumentation of the latter. His appeal at Lystra is of quite another type.

It seems natural to suppose that the author of Acts (or the composer of his sources) was making a sincere effort to give the matter or substance of what Peter or Paul or Stephen had to say on the occasion. He thought he had a good idea of what it was, but preferred to express it, as the ancients commonly did, in direct speech, that is to say in the form of an address delivered in the first person. If this impression is correct, there are two factors to be considered; one is the excellence of the sources or other information at the author's disposal, and the other is his skill and judgement in working them up so as to fall into line with the course of his narrative.

The question then arises, can they be used with confidence by the modern historian in constructing a historical record? And the answer will depend on the degree of confidence which he has in the dependability of Luke as a historian. This dependability may be checked in three ways. The first is by comparing his narrative, where this can be done, with the course of events as it may be inferred from the Epistles of Paul; a comparison which gives us the high degree of historical certainty which arises from the cross-fire of two independent witnesses who sometimes disagree with one another on matters of detail or judgement. We have already made use of this double witness to give stability to our reconstruction of the story in one or two instances, and have found that it coheres very well in spite of the minor divergences which always appear in the evidence of honest independent witnesses. We have indicated, however, that there is an alternative arrangement of the evidence which does not cohere so well.

The second is the testing of his accuracy with regard to local background in the light of the evidence which has been derived from other ancient authors, archaeology, and kindred researches; and the Acts has passed through this trial so triumphantly, especially in the light of modern discoveries due to excavation, that it stands high today as a historical work, even though it is not written in the manner of the incomparable Thucydides.

The author of Acts can make mistakes, no doubt, on small matters of fact. He may be at fault, for instance, in the chronology of events in Jewish history prior to his own generation. He can over-emphasize one element in a situation or under-emphasize another. There are gaps in his information which he does not know how to fill. But the fact remains that he took the trouble to find good sources of information, that he judged and arranged them well, and that his own personality appears in the telling as that of an observer with a balanced mind and a just appreciation of the human factor. Has any other book of the same size handled so successfully so many different scenes and characters?

There is a third way, actually, in which his fidelity may be tested, and that is his reproduction of passages from Mark in his Gospel. These stories are re-told; the Marcan style and manner has disappeared; but they are faithfully reproduced.

JAMES THE BROTHER OF THE LORD

This disquisition is necessary in passing from the speech attributed to Peter to the speech attributed to James; but the name of James raises further questions. Why is it that Acts has so little to say about this important man whose stature we must now recognize? We know from the writings of Paul that he was the brother of the Lord and had seen him after his resurrection; why does Luke fail to mention either of these points, either in his Gospel or in the Acts? or tell by what steps he became the bishop of the Jerusalem church? And why does he now bring him into sudden prominence without any adequate preparation? His position as a pillar of the church (we use the language of St Paul) seems to be taken for granted as if every one would know it; just as it seems to be in the epistle which goes out under his name but without any identifying title. The mere name of James is all that is given in either document. It is the other James (or Jameses) who require some identifying epithet.

The brother of Jesus was not one of the Twelve; he had not followed Jesus in the Galilean days; but he could not fail to have a commanding position in the church, once his standing in the evangelical tradition was secure. He left behind him in the Jewish church an effective memory which was quite equal to that of Paul or Peter or John. The Jewish Christians looked back to him as their patron saint, superior possibly to Peter himself. His figure assumed legendary proportions, and he was honoured as a paragon of the ascetic life after the style of John the Baptist. This tradition was preserved by Hegesippus, who received the Jewish-Christian traditions early in the second century. He said that James had been given the title of 'the Righteous' or 'the Just', from the times of the Lord.

Holy was he from the womb of his mother,
Wine and strong drink he drank not,
Nor ate animate food.[1]
The razor went not up upon his head;
With oil he anointed not nor used the bath-house.

For him alone it was lawful to enter the holy places:
Nor did he wear wool but linens;
And he entered alone into the sanctuary,
And was found kneeling upon his knees,
And asking forgiveness for the sins of his people,
Till his knees were hardened like the knees of a camel.
(Hegesippus, *Note-books*: in Eusebius, *E.H.* II. 23, 5–7.)

He was a Nazirite, therefore, and his title of the Just, or the Righteous, was not given him on account of any devotion to Pharisee legalism, but because he was a holy man and ascetic; and so he was known, says Hegesippus, even in the lifetime of Jesus. The tradition has acquired a legendary character; it cannot be taken literally, since no one but the high priest could go into the actual sanctuary; but it preserves a mode of thought about James and his position in the church in which he was compared to the high priest.

He had another claim, however, upon the devotion of the Jewish people, which was of a more substantial character; he was a successor with Jesus of the royal line of David. Jewish Christianity boasted two lines of succession from Jesus; one was the royal succession in the family of David, the other was the apostolic succession from Peter and the Twelve. There has been considerable discussion in modern times on the question of who 'presided' in the council of Jerusalem; but actually the text of Acts does not answer this question. Both successions were represented by their chiefs. Peter, for his tradition, laid down the principle that Gentile converts should not be obliged to keep the Law; James, for his tradition, assented to this principle, but added a 'judgement' or decision or suggestion as to the terms on which intercommunion would be possible between the divergent parties. The council as a whole accepted their views.

[1] 'Empsuchon': food with soul or life in it; flesh meat.

THE SPEECH OF JAMES

The speech which Luke puts into the mouth of James is exceedingly interesting, even if it only represents his own summary of what the position of James was. It is the point on which the whole structure of the Acts turns.

The descent of Jesus from David was an element in his claim to be the Messiah which was not emphasized at all in Galilee so far as we know; but it was the popular cry in Jerusalem. It was an important point in the kerugmata of Peter, in which he quotes verses from the Psalms of David which appear to have some reference to the death and resurrection of the Messiah or anointed king. It passed into the general tradition of the church, and was included in the sermon which Paul preached in the synagogue at Little Antioch; and a report of this mission had just been presented to the council. It is not surprising, therefore, that James takes it up. He quotes an oracle from the prophet Amos which declares that the rallying-point for the 'residue of mankind' will be the 'tabernacle of David', which had fallen down but was to be restored and rebuilt, so that the Gentiles might resort to it; and this suggests that the Gentiles ought to find their way to the God of Israel, not merely by turning to the Messiah Jesus, but by turning to the tradition of the royal line of David, which James also represented. Now Jerusalem was in some sense the mother-church;[1] it was the primary centre of the apostolic mission to all Christians everywhere; it had a claim upon the loyalty of the Gentile churches which Paul himself recognized by periodical pilgrimages with offerings. The speech was very apt to the character of the speaker and the circumstances under which he spoke.

The quotation from Amos is given according to the Septuagint version, and James may have used this well-known Greek translation at this mixed gathering, or else some Hebrew text on which it was based; but it is quite possible that Luke has substituted the accepted translation in writing up his Greek narrative. The Hebrew text in the surviving manuscripts says that the house of David will 'possess the remnant of Edom, and all the nations on whom the Lord's name is called'. If this is what James said, it is even more apposite, since the Jews commonly used the name of Edom to refer to Rome.

[1] It was surely not without significance that Paul had told the Galatians in a controversial moment that Jerusalem above was the 'mother of us all'.

The 'judgement' of James was not to lay unnecessary burdens upon the Gentiles who were turning to God, but to be content with directing them to abstain from the abomination of idols and from fornication and from blood; we shall discuss this recommendation later; at present we turn our attention to the interesting remark with which the speech closes, to the effect that Moses, 'from of old has his preachers in every city in the synagogues, being read every sabbath'.

This looks like another echo from the report of the preaching at Little Antioch, which speaks twice of the reading of the prophets on the Sabbath in the synagogue. James disclaims for Christian evangelists the duty of preaching the Law of Moses, since ample provision has been made for that throughout the world; but we can hardly avoid making the inference that, in his opinion, the Gentile believers would hear it preached by qualified persons. It may even have been his hope that they would accept it. Certainly the diehard Pharisee Christians, who wanted all the Gentile converts to be circumcised, would have derived very little comfort from his argument unless such an idea could be read into it.

It would seem that as James looked out upon the Jewish and Christian dispersion, he saw the Gentile converts listening to the Law of Moses on the Sabbath in the synagogue. Either they were attending the orthodox Jewish synagogue on the Sabbath, which hardly seems likely; or their own places of assembly were called synagogues, and the Law was read there; or he may make no clear distinction. The Gentile fringe of the synagogues of the dispersion (Christian or otherwise) may not have been thought of by him as a distinct group. They might approximate in his mind to the 'god-fearers' who formed a fringe to the old orthodox Judaism; though, indeed, separate Gentile churches had now been formed.

THE CONCILIAR EPISTLE

Modern controversy and discussion have been so much occupied with the true text and true interpretation of the clauses about idolatry, fornication, and blood, that it is hard for those who have followed them closely to realize that they were not the most important work of the council. The most important work of the council was the settlement of the circumcision question. The Epistle which it issued makes this quite clear, and here we have definite documentary evidence, unless indeed we are to suppose that it was composed by the author of Acts: a very arbitrary proceeding.

(1) It was sent out under the authority of the apostles and elders, and expressed their full confidence in the devoted work of Barnabas and Paul.

(2) It was addressed to the brethren in Antioch, Syria, and Cilicia, the churches of Cyprus and Galatia not being mentioned. We may suppose that it would be for the Antiochene church to communicate with them, as indeed it proceeded to do.

(3) It repudiated the Jewish-Christian counter-mission; and this was a victory of great magnitude for Paul and his party.

(4) It associated with Barnabas and Paul two leading men of the Jerusalem church, Judas and Silas, who were to carry the letter, and support it by their personal testimony. These men were prophets, a fact which shows that the prophetic movement in the Jerusalem church, as we would expect, supported the policy of a free Gentile Christianity.

(5) It left the Gentile believers free from any obligation to the Law of Moses, except for three necessary points: the abstinence from things offered to idols, from fornication, from things strangled and from blood; 'If you keep yourselves from these,' the Epistle concludes, 'you will do well. Farewell.'

This letter was read to the church at Antioch, and there were great rejoicings, in which we recognize the end of a controversy, and also the end of a source which Luke has been using, the Antiochene source which began with apostles and prophets going down from Jerusalem to Antioch, and ends with apostles and prophets going down from Jerusalem to Antioch.

However artificial we may consider Luke's reconstruction of the council to be, we must recognize two points about it. The first is that it is the climax of the first half of the Acts, and is presented as an event of great historical importance. The second is that it satisfactorily accounts for the form which historical Christianity actually took.

THE JUDAEO-CHRISTIAN TRADITION

The Christian churches in the Gentile world inherited from their founders a tradition which cannot be explained simply as the work of St Paul, though he was the pioneer apostle and herald of the gospel as it made its way westward. It may be described perhaps as a Petro-Pauline synthesis, and so it appears in the very earliest records, in Syria, in Asia Minor, and in Rome. But this Petro-Pauline synthesis is always found operating within a historical and liturgical tradition of a Jewish character with which the apostolic gospel is fully integrated. The Gentile churches resemble Jewish synagogues which have been transformed by the action of the gospel and the Spirit and the apostolate. Their structure and worship is a form of Hebrew structure and worship; their Bible is the Hebrew Bible; their theology is a Hebrew theology; their ancestors are the Hebrew patriarchs; they are the true descendants of the ancient Israel. There is no sign of any argument or difficulty or protest about this matter until we come to the heresiarchs of the second century.

The substance of Christian worship and piety and catechism and church order was Jewish. The old-fashioned Jewish piety flowed right on into Christianity without a break. It was the main current of the succession which carried along with it all the other successions, and formed the medium in which the gospel displayed its creative power. It was the historical basis of the existence of Christianity in the world. How astonishing, therefore, is the complementary fact that the Law of Moses was not binding in these Gentile churches.... There is no argument about this either. At some period early in the first century, in the height of the apostolic period itself, a universal agreement had been come to that the Law of Moses had ceased to be effective. It had receded into the past, so far as the Gentile Christian churches were concerned.

We have suggested two formulas which may help us to understand the genesis of what came to be called the catholic church. One is the Petro-Pauline synthesis,[1] the other is the Judaeo-Christian tradition; both hyphenated phrases implying solidarity, not co-existence. There is a third formula which helps to unify them; it is the Jewish diaspora, a word which includes all the synagogues of the Hellenistic world, with their fringe of devout Gentile adherents who were moving on in theory towards full acceptance of the Law. There was established in the Roman empire long before the arrival of the gospel, a Hellenistic Judaism in which a genuine Jewish piety was cultivated, in close

[1] It was not the only possible 'synthesis'; there is evidence in the second century of a Palestinian synthesis of Peter and James.

relation with the synagogue order but without the legalities of the Mosaic revelation; it accepted all that mass of liturgy, Bible, catechism, prophecy, apocalypse, and so forth, which passed on without a break into the Christian church; but it stopped short at circumcision, the Sabbath, laws of clean and unclean, and so forth. It was Jewish, but not nationally Jewish or legally Jewish. The apostolic gospel united itself with this kind of Judaism in the Gentile mission, and the apostolic Christianity of the Roman world naturally followed this form.

This is not to say that the Law of Moses left no mark or inheritance in the church. Far from it. It was a revelation of the will of God for the Israelites in the desert who received it, and for the Jewish nation itself; and many of the principles to which it gave symbolic form were regarded as being more perfectly exemplified in the Christian mysteries; a process which we can see at work five years after the council, in St Paul's Epistles to the Corinthians. Nevertheless, wherever Gentile and Jewish Christians came into social or sacramental contact, as they did in Antioch, it was necessary for the Gentile Christians to accept a certain quantity of the Levitical discipline in order to remove difficulties in the way of intercommunion, and so avoid a schism in the ranks of the believers.

James the Just had suggested that they should be asked to abstain from the sources of defilement connected with idolatry, from fornication, [from things strangled] and from blood. These conditions were incorporated into the conciliar epistle, and laid down as 'necessary'.

THE NEO-LEVITICAL CODE

The precise meaning of this formula will probably never be discovered, and may not have been clear at the time. The council may have grasped at it when it was proposed without pausing to define it clearly; local authorities would have to work out its implications in view of local conditions.

It is possible that similar requirements had already been laid down in the synagogues of the diaspora for the devout Gentile adherents; for they could hardly have been attached to the synagogue without accepting some minimum obligations of this sort; less stringent of course in the Gentile world than they would be in Palestine. Here, too, without serious doubt, the Christian mission could make use of a Jewish tradition which already existed, the tradition which is sometimes called catechism.

The general reader today is rather at a disadvantage in not knowing the extent to which the worship of pagan deities was mixed up with sexual licence of the most shocking kind. In the world-famed groves of Daphne, for instance, at Antioch, the rites of Apollo were celebrated as a matter of religion with every circumstance of beauty, luxury and licence. The festivals of the gods were occasions for banquets which were marked by drunkenness, obscenity and immorality. It was perfectly obvious that 'things offered to idols and fornication' had to be renounced, to use a word which found its way into the later baptismal rites; but the renunciation of 'blood' is a more difficult matter.

This renunciation seems to refer to certain rules which were imposed upon the Israelites in the seventeenth chapter of Leviticus, which is part of a section of that book which is known as the 'Law of Holiness'. This portion of the book deals with the prohibition of blood, the rite of immersion in water by which defilement is cleansed, and various forms of prohibited sexual intercourse. This rite of immersion ('tebilah') seems to be the Jewish antecedent of Christian baptism, and it is followed by a general exhortation on the subject of religious duties in the nineteenth chapter which has left a distinct mark on the Christian catechetical documents; it contains the famous command to love one's neighbour as oneself. It would seem very probable that James had this whole section of Leviticus in mind; and it is a curious fact that the passage from Amos which he quoted in his speech is set in the Hebrew lectionary as the appropriate 'haftarah' or prophetic lection to be read after it. Hebrew scholars do not think that the system of prophetic lections was fixed as early as this; but nobody knows how old such associations may be.

According to the 'Law of Holiness', the blood was to be drained from the carcass after the animal was killed, and poured out on the ground as an offering to the Lord; it was the life of the creature and belonged to the Lord. Meat killed in this way is called kosher, and it is the only kind that devout Jews will touch. If the Gentile believer would abstain from meat which had the blood in it, and from meat which had been killed for a pagan sacrifice, many of the difficulties which were felt by pious Jews in mixing with them would automatically disappear.

The addition of the words 'and from things strangled', which appear in some manuscripts, would seem to be intended to clarify the text of the decree by interpreting it in this way; but it is not likely that they are original.

An alternative explanation of the shorter text has been proposed by some modern scholars. It is suggested that the word 'blood' means murder, and if so we have a reference to the three major sins of idolatry, fornication, and murder. This cannot be said to be a natural interpretation, but it has its attractions, since Jewish moral theology did often speak of this triad of deadly sins which defile the land and cause the glory to depart. If we could accept this view, there would be no reference to Jewish ritual at all, but only to what could be regarded as the fundamental moral and spiritual law. It seems practically certain, however, that the formula belongs to the category of ecclesiastical order, and was designed to ease the situation at Antioch and elsewhere, where there was real difficulty over the question of relations between Jewish and Gentile Christians.

Understood in this way, the formula offered terms of intercommunion which would make it possible to grant the Gentile converts the freedom from the Law of Moses as a whole, which is what Paul was fighting for. It would hardly be possible for him to refuse so reasonable a condition. He could accept it for the sake of peace in mixed communities like that at Antioch, though not of course as an essential part of the gospel; nor are we surprised if it does not appear in the fully Gentile communities which grew up farther west. Syrian Christianity had a form and character of its own which was distinct from that of Asia Minor or Greece.

It is agreed that this formula was put forth from Jerusalem at some time, and did make its way into various parts of the church. It must have been so accepted, for instance, in the communities for which the Acts was written. It is alluded to in the Revelation, and it appears that there were Christians as far away as Gaul and Africa and Alexandria who were still abstaining from meat with the blood in it, late in the second century. The variations in the text of the Acts seem to show that it was not interpreted everywhere in the same way, however.

There was another way by which the difficulty could be evaded, and that was by not eating flesh meat at all; and this was already the practice among ascetic sects among the Jews. It was the practice of John the Baptist, and of James the Just according to the tradition quoted from Hegesippus. We learn from the Epistle to the Romans that there were Christians in Rome who adhered to this rule of abstinence, and Paul himself once swore that he would never eat flesh meat again if that would save a brother from taking offence. It was part of that strong vein of asceticism which appears in some of the Jewish and Jewish-Christian sects; but it receives no encouragement in the gospels. Jesus had differed from John the Baptist on the subject of asceticism. The whole subject is obviously much more complicated than we can gather from the notices in the existing documents.

The formula as a whole helped to fix the character of historic Christianity. The Gentile Christians were to repudiate their old way of life; they were to break with the cult of idols and with the sexual excesses which they had thought of as natural and normal; there come into sight those great denials of the world and the flesh which run through the epistolary literature, the catechisms, the baptismal rites, and even the martyr's witness: the whole conflict with a pagan society. Only the reference to kosher food seems strange and unreal to the modern Christian; it is an archaic touch. Paul did not carry it with him into the life of his new churches. He left it behind.

THE STATE OF THE CHURCH

We are unable to say how long these tempests continued to agitate the church, how soon they subsided, or to what extent they subsided, or in what localities they continued to rage. We may be sure that complete calm was not established all at once even by an apostolic concordat, which was capable apparently of more than one interpretation; a concordat which only concerned Antioch and Syria and Cilicia according to the terms of the epistle.

The author of Acts has placed all his Antiochene material in chapters xii–xv and he has nothing to tell us about Syrian Christianity except what he gives there. It contains two accounts of visits to Jerusalem by Barnabas and Paul, in both of which the name of James the Just appears. There is a great deal of coming and going. Numerous high-ranking visitors from Jerusalem descend upon the Antiochenes, and Antioch is obviously much indebted to Jerusalem. There is a sharp controversy which divides the church in both cities; but it is not a controversy *between* Jerusalem and Antioch; it reaches an acute stage in Antioch, and it is settled in Jerusalem.

In the Epistle to the Galatians we have a few vivid pictures of the same controversy taken from a particular point of view. We have the same phenomena; a visit by Paul and Barnabas to Jerusalem; the stream of visitors from Jerusalem to Antioch; the strong position of James; and the acute controversy. But it breaks off here. We are left with the two great apostles confronting one another; and if we accept the later date for Galatians, the controversy was *not* settled at the Jerusalem council, for the argument between Peter and Paul at Antioch broke out *after* it; and it was as much as five years later still that the circumcision party descended upon Galatia, and provoked Paul's great epistle. In this case the story in the Acts has been very highly idealized indeed; it has even been distorted, and it took much longer for the apostolic consolidation to be effected. Indeed, it is thought by a few that it never was effected.

The consolidation in question is a fact of history, however. Controversy of various kinds continued, but not the controversy about the circumcision of the Gentiles. It was possible for Jewish 'apostles', only five years later, to invade Paul's Corinthian church and attack his theology and belittle his standing as an apostle; it was possible for parties in that church to invoke the authority of Peter against the authority of Paul; but it is significant that they did not argue that Gentile Christians should be circumcised and keep the Law. Jewish Christian teachers continued to invade Paul's territory, and promote their peculiar views, but this kind of propaganda is not heard of again. The question had been settled, somehow or other.

CHRISTIANS IN ROME

We know no more about the movements of Peter except that he reached Rome at last and died there as a martyr. The so-called tradition that he visited the imperial city as early as the forties is exceedingly late and has no claims to serious consideration.

Vacant periods can be found, of course, when he could have done so. There are the years between his escape from prison in 44 and his appearance at the council in Jerusalem in 49, for instance; but if Peter preached the Gospel in Rome at this time, it seems impossible to explain why the story is omitted from the Acts, and why the Acts is constructed as it is.

It seems certain, however, that the gospel had reached Rome by this time in some shape or form. There were riots in the Jewish quarter which roused the anger of the Emperor Claudius, who banished the Jews from Rome, as Luke and Suetonius and Dion Cassius all report. Orosius, in the fifth century, gives the date of this edict as the ninth year of Claudius, which is 49, the year of the council. Suetonius, who is the earliest non-Christian writer to mention it, gives the name of the leader of these riots as Chrestus; and it looks very much as if he has made an error. The gospel may have reached the Jewish synagogues with its usual results. The Romans may have heard the name of Christus or Chrestus bandied about and taken it to be the name of the person who was stirring up the trouble. The two names were pronounced in much the same way.

There must, of course, have been individual Christians in Rome, but we shall be wise to accept the general picture which we receive from the Acts, which is that the official apostolic mission and the formation of recognized churches had not proceeded so far or so fast. At any rate the only line of expansion which the writer follows in the remaining ten years of his narrative is the Pauline progress through Asia and into Greece and back to Asia again, of which he had his own first-hand knowledge.

CHAPTER 6

MACEDONIA AND ACHAIA

The disagreement over Mark, *p.* 108. Silas and Timothy, *p.* 109. The new Pauline mission, A.D. 49, *p.* 112. The journals of Luke, *p.* 113. Paul in Macedonia, *p.* 113. The church in Thessalonica, *p.* 115. Questions from Thessalonica, *p.* 117. The catechism of holy love, *p.* 118. Athens, *p.* 119. Corinth, *p.* 121. The Corinthian church, *p.* 122. Gallio, A.D. 52, *p.* 123.

THE DISAGREEMENT OVER MARK

Immediately after the Jerusalem council, Paul and Barnabas resolved to visit their churches in Galatia and deliver the decisions of the council; but a serious difference of opinion ended in their parting company. It concerned Mark, the cousin of Barnabas, who had been their assistant when they left Antioch on their first mission, but had parted from them at Perga of Pamphylia and returned to Jerusalem. Paul felt that he could not accept his services, and so the two cousins went off to Cyprus where they had family connexions, leaving the Galatian field open to Paul. It was approached through Cilicia, where *he* had family connexions.

Luke is now approaching the point at which he has immediate personal knowledge; and when we consider how careful he has been to pass over disagreements among the Christian leaders, we find it hard to understand why he allows this one to come to the surface. He does not conceal the fact that Paul was not satisfied with Mark, and we know from our reading of Galatians that he had not been pleased with Barnabas either. The storms of controversy had not completely subsided. Something occurred which Luke felt could not be entirely omitted even if it did seem to cast a slur on Mark. Why did he feel obliged to mention it at all? Possibly to make it clear that the situation was no worse? There may have been impressions abroad which he thought should be corrected? It is one of the many indications that Acts was written not long after the events with which it deals in its second half.

Barnabas and Mark are not mentioned again in Acts; but Mark came back again into the Pauline orbit about ten years later. When

Acts was written, he was a well-known figure in the church. Some reference to him would be required, but fuller explanations were not necessary.

SILAS AND TIMOTHY

Paul now adopted Silas (or Silvanus, as he is also called) as his colleague in the ministry of the gospel. He was one of the Jerusalem prophets who had stood by him in the great controversy, and was mentioned in the conciliar letter. He was an influential man about whom we would like to know more. We find him later on collaborating with Peter.

They began by visiting Cilicia. Paul had been born in Tarsus of Cilicia, and had preached the gospel there before taking up work at Antioch. This is another point about which we would like to know more.

Cilicia was a base from which he could reach his Galatian churches. The great arterial highway ran west from Tarsus, through a narrow defile in the Taurus Mountains, and on into the highlands of Asia Minor. Persian armies had marched westward along this road earlier in history to attack the Greek city-states. Greek armies had marched eastward to humble the Persian power. Roman armies had followed in their train. It was the historic communication overland between East and West, by which oriental commerce and oriental religion made their way to Rome. It now became the life-line of the Christian gospel in its western expansion.

Paul and Silas took this road and made a visitation of the Galatian churches. In Lystra, where Paul and Barnabas had been taken for gods and Paul had nearly met his end, they found a young man who was willing to accompany them in the place of Mark. This was Timothy. He was a studious young man and the offspring of a mixed marriage. His father was a Greek, but his mother Lois and his grandmother Eunice were devout Jewesses who had embraced the gospel. He had studied the 'sacred letters' of the Jewish faith, that is to say the Old Testament literature, but he had not yet been circumcised. Paul agreed to his being circumcised, it says in Acts, 'because of the Jews who were in those parts; for they all knew that his father was a Greek'. Critics have detected an inconsistency here, and not without reason; for Paul and Silas were promulgating the decision of the apostles and elders,

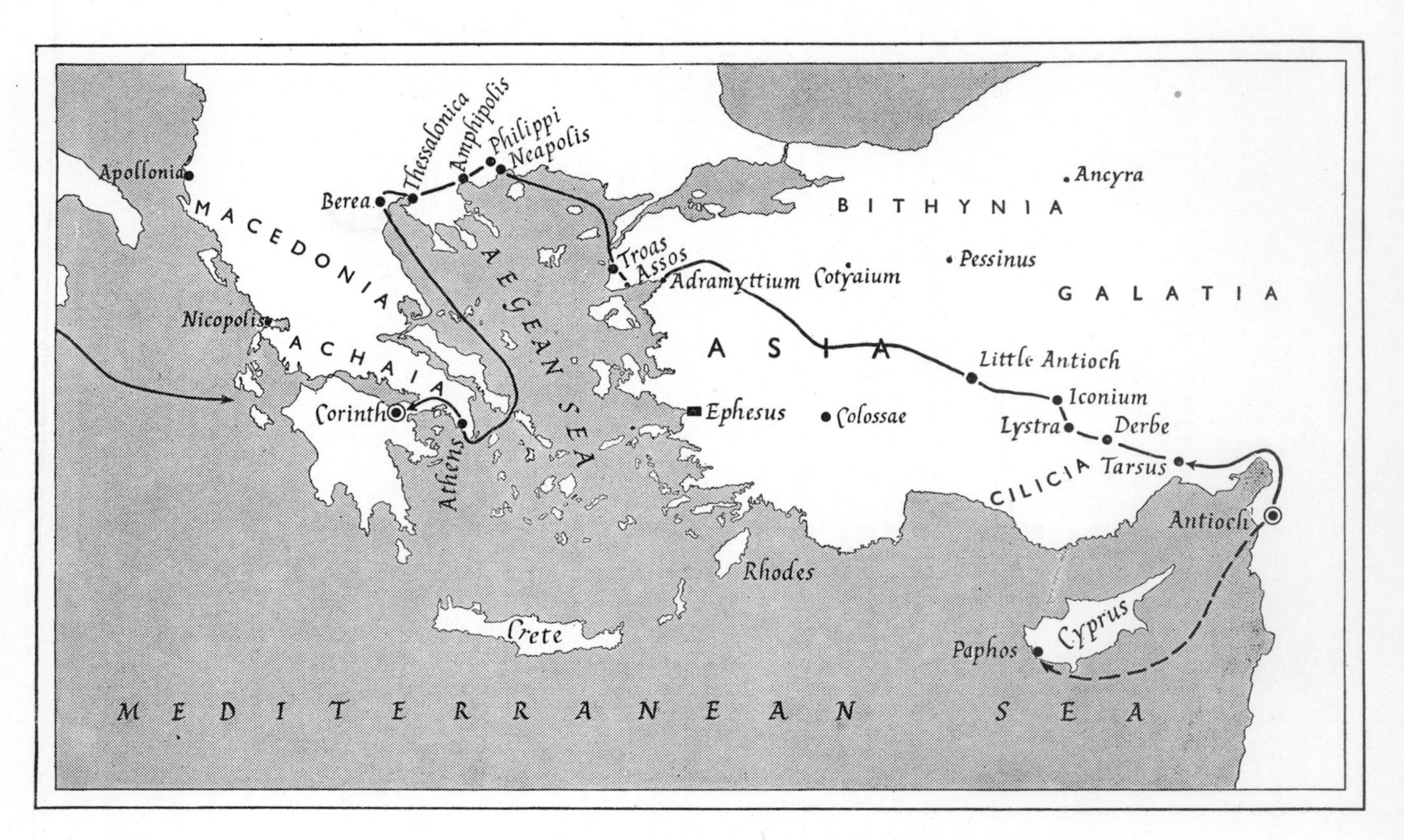

Map 3. The new Pauline missions, A.D. 49–50.

NOTES ON MAP 3

The right-hand bottom corner shows the base from which the new Pauline mission went out; it was *Antioch* with its expansion into Cyprus and Cilicia, and through either of these into the Galatian cities of Iconium, Lystra, and Derbe. Barnabas takes Mark and goes to Cyprus, which Paul thereby abandons. He takes Silas and goes overland to the Galatian cities, where he picks up Timothy.

He finds himself on the great highway from east to west. He is forbidden to go on to Ephesus, or to turn north into Bithynia, which is thus abandoned to other evangelists. He comes out at Troas to the north-west. He finds Luke. He breaks out of the oriental area into the true Hellenic world: Philippi, Thessalonica, Athens, Corinth. At *Corinth* he founded a new base for evangelization. He was joined by Christians from *Rome*, Priscilla and Aquila, who were fugitives like himself.

Relations between Rome and Corinth were very close; the coming of Aquila and Priscilla from Rome to Corinth; Paul writing his Epistle from Corinth to Rome; Hebrews in some way linking the two cities; Clement writing an Epistle from Rome to Corinth; Soter and Dionysius exchanging letters in the next century.

The western expansion is in sight now.

which dispensed Gentile Christians from such observances. But Timothy was more of a Jew than Gentile, and Paul was surprisingly ready to adapt his policy to circumstances, if it seemed necessary, in order to promote the gospel. He found it hard to defend this apparent inconsistency. 'To the Jews I became a Jew', he wrote later on to the Corinthians, 'in order to win the Jews.... I became all things to all men in order to save some'; and again 'Circumcision is of no force, and neither is uncircumcision, but a new creation.' It was probably necessary to him at this stage that his staff should be in good standing as Jews, but his action is surprising, and Luke feels that it requires an explanation.

THE NEW PAULINE MISSION, A.D. 49

From the East-Phrygian part of Galatia, Paul and his companions passed into western Phrygia. The main road led westward into the province of 'Asia', terminating at the great sea-coast city of Ephesus, which was the natural objective; but as they were passing south of Mysia, a mountainous region in western Phrygia, they were 'prevented by the Spirit' from continuing any further in that direction, or from turning northward into Bithynia. 'The Spirit of Jesus would not allow them.' These promptings of the Spirit were the most real thing in their lives, and they could not disregard them. They continued their journey in a north-westerly direction, and came out at Troas on the Aegean Sea near the Bosphorus. There a positive indication was given to them. Paul had the famous dream in which he saw a man of Macedonia, who said, 'Come over into Macedonia and help us.'

'Immediately', we read in Acts, 'we sought entrance into Macedonia.'

We are reading now the introductory material to the second part of Acts, which is very different in tone and texture from the first part. Its scene is laid in the cities of the Aegean Sea, and above all in Ephesus. Its hero is Paul, whom it ultimately takes to Rome. It bids farewell to Barnabas and Mark; it introduces Silas, or Silvanus as he was called in the west; it introduces Timothy and Luke. Three of these men appear together with Paul in Rome ten years later, and send affectionate messages to the churches of western Phrygia, the very region where Paul is now prevented from preaching. Two of them appear in Rome with Peter in the Epistle which he addressed to Christians in Asia Minor. It would seem that a local interest is being served in these introductory

9. THE CILICIAN GATES

10. (i) ATHENS: THE AREOPAGUS

10. (ii) CORINTH: THE 'BEMA'

passages, which answer such questions as these: Why did Paul pass by Phrygia? Why did he not strike northward into Bithynia? Above all, why did he not press onward into Asia, and set up his headquarters in Ephesus, thus saving valuable years, during which others were at work there?

The city of Ephesus plays the same part in the second half of Acts as that of Caesarea plays in the first half; and the author has it in mind from the beginning of his narrative; but it was not in the purpose of God, he intimates, that Paul should have gone there at once. He was led onward by the Spirit to Troas, and so into Macedonia and Achaia.

THE JOURNALS OF LUKE

The use of the word 'we' in the text of the Acts at this stage indicates that we are reading a portion of a journal or report, written by a travel-companion of Paul. This document was the work of Luke himself, who now appears for the first time. Luke and Timothy were destined to become Paul's closest friends and remained faithful to him to the end. Luke is the 'beloved physician' and Timothy is the 'true child', his own son, not only in the evangelistic ministry, but also in his love and affection. A new chapter in his life is opening up. Six or seven years of ceaseless labour were to follow, in which he would build up a circle of churches round the Aegean Sea and work out his mature philosophy of evangelism and church-building.

The word 'we' appears in the narrative as far as Philippi. It does not occur again until the journey to Jerusalem six years later.

PAUL IN MACEDONIA

We inferred from a close study of the documents that the apostles had run into persecution during their mission to Galatia, because the gospel had been construed by the authorities as a political movement. This impression is confirmed by the records of the evangelization of Macedonia; persecution, political conflict and apocalyptic vision appear in close connexion with one another. These topics are handled with considerable restraint by the author of the Acts; he is anxious to show that the gospel was not a political movement, and that the civil authorities did not accept this description of it.

The apostles found themselves on much more foreign soil when they landed in Philippi. The northern part of Greece, which was called Macedonia, was the birthplace of Alexander the Great, but it was regarded as 'barbarian' by some Athenian intellectuals. Philippi, which was named after Alexander's father, was now a 'colony', that is to say a Roman military settlement, governed by Roman magistrates on Roman lines. There were not many Jews there. The apostles found a 'house of prayer' by the side of the river, where a few Jewish ladies, or ladies interested in Judaism, welcomed them. Amongst these was a successful business-woman named Lydia, whose house became the headquarters of the church. Paul and Timothy wrote a letter to the Philippians ten years later which mentions some of the women who were prominent in these early days. These and other facts dispel the legend that Paul had some antipathy to women; he had friends among women, and knew how to make use of their gifts in church work.

There was a dispute with a local pagan priesthood over a prophesying girl, and Paul and Silas were dragged before the magistrates, beaten and imprisoned. The charge made against them was political. They were teaching customs which it was not lawful for Romans to accept. A curious point now emerges; both the apostles possessed the Roman citizenship, which should have made them immune from such summary treatment. The magistrates are said to have admitted their error, but the apostles left the town, taking Timothy with them. Luke, apparently, was left behind.

They preached in the synagogue at Thessalonica for three months, with the usual results. The Jews incited the mob to bring pressure on the authorities. The charge this time was that they were defying the laws of the emperor, and proclaiming a new king, whose name was Jesus: 'The men who are upsetting the world have come here', they said. Jerusalem, Antioch, Galatia, and Rome; and now Macedonia; it looked like a world-wide conspiracy.

The mob attacked the house of Jason, where the apostles had made their headquarters; but they were not to be found. They made good their escape to Berea, where the local Jews treated them with respect, and took their appeals to scripture seriously; but Thessalonian Jews followed them up, and it was thought wise to get Paul out of the way. He was shipped off to Athens by himself, where Timothy paid him a visit to keep him in touch with developments.[1] From Athens he went to Corinth, where Silas and Timothy rejoined him. It was from Corinth that they wrote the Epistles to the Thessalonians.

THE CHURCH IN THESSALONICA

These Epistles shed a bright light upon the inner life of the new-born church, which had gone through persecution after the departure of the apostles such as the Judaean churches had suffered from their compatriots. They had been warned that it would be so.

The conversion of the Thessalonians is described in a brief but pregnant phrase; they had turned from idols to serve a living and true God, and to wait for his Son from heaven, whom he had raised from the dead, even Jesus who saves us from the wrath to come. It is a fully apocalyptic credo, very different in tone from the spiritual fervour of the Epistle to the Galatians; but it was a theology for a time of persecution; and it must be remembered that Silas, the Jerusalem prophet, was a co-author of these Epistles, which contain pieces of apocalypse which seem to have originated in the first flush of the prophetic movement, some ten years earlier, in the time of Caligula. These prophetic utterances had been delivered to the Thessalonians during their period of evangelization.

The apocalyptic passages in the New Testament are such things as dreams are made on; they are great hymns sung or chanted in the heat of the moment; they are brilliant pictures painted in passionate words. The glowing faith in Jesus as God's Son projected itself into a future, when his glory would become manifest to all. The prophet used old literary material for his purposes; he introduced the trumpets and cloud and fire of Mount Sinai, because these were part of his native speech; he spoke of angels because he was familiar with angels; and he wove such concepts with absolute creative freedom into his vision of things to come. It would be stupid to take such a vision as a matter-of-fact prediction of future events. Prophets seldom predict. They imagine, they interpret, they bless, and they curse; they have hopes and dreams; and their visions of the future are their own heart's desire in the form of a dream.

When an artist designs a stained-glass window, he fills it with angelic

[1] There are minor discrepancies between Acts and the Thessalonian Epistles with regard to the movements of Silas and Timothy.

forms, and golden rays of light, and shining vestments and crowns and trumpets, because these are the language of his art; they have value for him because they express his ideas; ideas of such daring and beauty that ordinary words cannot do them justice. The hymn-writers do exactly the same. The congregation gazes at the window, and sings the hymns, and is lifted up into another world. Rather in this way the gospel brought with it an accompaniment of apocalyptic which was actually a kind of poetry or art. It expressed non-dogmatically a sublime hope about the future. It was not intellectually fixed, or nailed down to one interpretation or another. It was in a fluid state. Each prophet or singer could use it for his own purposes, and remould it nearer to his heart's desire.

These inspired poems of the first Christians expressed two deep convictions; their total faith in God Almighty through Christ, and their unconquerable hope of the immediate victory of the Christ and his saints. This indeed is what the words faith and hope meant to them. It is important to realize that these convictions were not eschatological in the sense in which the word is often used. They did not imply a violent 'end of the world', including a universal resurrection, a final judgement on all souls and eternal destinies in heaven or hell. These apocalypses were quite separate from all that. It is precisely because they were non-eschatological (in this sense) that intellectual difficulties arose. Everything in them was at close range; it was visualized as taking place within this present world-order, and within the life-time of the present generation.

The advent of the Son of God in the immediate future was the counterpart and balance of his appearance in the immediate past when he was crucified and raised from the dead. The display of glory in the advent balanced the display of glory in the Resurrection; each conception irradiated the other. Without the gospel of the Resurrection, there would have been no expectation of the advent.

Here, then, is the other side of the pagan view of Christianity as a political movement which was setting up a new king. It actually did so. The hope of the glorious advent had a local and political setting. Originally it had been the city of Jerusalem, and the Temple of God, and the rule of the high priests, which the Lord would supersede when he came 'on the clouds of heaven with the holy angels'. But the whole framework had been extended since then; it included the Roman empire, and the Roman emperor himself, who had aspired to be worshipped as a god in that same Temple, and so became the rival of the God of heaven and his Messiah.

There are two ways, of course, in which this kind of language could be taken. It could be a pageant or poem, symbolizing a spiritual victory of the gospel in history, which is how the author of the Revelation took it; or it could be a physical bodily appearance of the Lord in the sky for all to see. This is the way it seems to be taken in the Thessalonian Epistles. Doubtless the prophet who composed these visions felt free to clothe them in such symbols of glory as appealed to the imagination of the time, without expecting to have them taken literally; but the heart of it was the actual return of Jesus himself to his saints as their Saviour in the evil day.

QUESTIONS FROM THESSALONICA

The limited nature of this conception of the advent is proved by the questions which came in from Thessalonica. It was so far from being a form of eschatology that the question of the resurrection of the dead had not yet been related to it at all; and even now this question was only raised in a special form. Nor was it a theological question, it was a personal one. It had to do with the case of Christians who died before the advent. It was a serious question, and it was not settled all at once.

Silas, if it is he, answers in the idiom of apocalypse; those who died in Jesus had not lost their right to share in the advent glory; they would rise again. He boldly welds his answer into the apocalyptic vision. The trumpet is blown; the Lord descends; and they will rise from the dead. They are to rise first; then 'we who are alive' will be taken up in clouds to meet the Lord in the air; and so we will be for ever with the Lord. The advent of the Lord will solve all problems. There is a mixture of what we would regard as inconsistent values, the literal and the mystical, the fleshly and the spiritual, the advent vision and the resurrection hope. It is only the language of vision that holds together these contrasting elements in a unity which is fundamentally pictorial; it only satisfies the soul so long as it remains on the pedestal of vision; but it has proved an embarrassment to the more rationalistic mind which tries to operate the dream as if it were a dogma. Even as early as I Corinthians, we find an attempt to explain it or advance beyond it.

The second difficulty was also occasioned by the intensity of the expectation, which had created so much excitement that some of the brethren had been encouraged to abandon their daily occupation. Such men lived on the bounty of the *ecclesia*, and passed no doubt as spirituals. One answer is that if they will not work, they ought not to eat; but the apostles go on to say that the advent is not coming so soon as they suppose; nor has 'the day' broken upon them already, as some assert. Some warnings had already been given on this point. There was to be a general 'apostasy' or falling away from the faith, and this would come first; and then follows the passage about the 'man of lawlessness, the son of perdition', in whom we recognized the lineaments of Caligula. The language of vision, therefore, is capable of coming to terms with history, and perhaps it is not until it comes to terms with history that Christian apocalypse can be rightly understood; and conversely it is not until we understand Christian apocalypse that we will be able to understand the early Christian view of history.

It is apparent that the language of apocalypse is not really suitable for every purpose, except perhaps in the hands of such a master as the author of the Revelation, but we are on grounds now where it is clear and strong. The 'energy of Satan', that is to say the power of evil which had possessed the mad emperor Caligula, with his claim to be the god of this world, was at work. It was being restrained, it is true, under the providence of God; but a further outbreak must be looked for, 'with powers and signs and lying wonders', only to be destroyed by the Lord Jesus 'with the breath of his mouth'. In other words, the prophet correctly saw that the conflict with the empire was not over. It would be renewed in a more desperate form, and its next phase would be a contest between the divine claims of the emperor and the divine claims of the Messiah.

The apocalyptic vision is the reflexion in the Christian mind of the conflict between Christ and Caesar which appears in the Acts of the Apostles on the historical level.

THE CATECHISM OF HOLY LOVE

It is a relief to turn to the forms of exhortation or instruction which were delivered to the converts, apparently in connexion with their baptism. They open with the word 'consecration' or hallowing, an idea which was connected with the reception of the Holy Spirit at baptism.

The first point in the catechism is the consecration of the body by abstaining from 'fornication', an echo of the epistle of the Jerusalem council. The brethren must learn to live faithfully together in holy matrimony. The second is the love of the brethren; for the doctrine of Christian love was based on the idea of the one Spirit sanctifying the *ecclesia* and uniting the saints in one body: a divine presence as real as the advent itself.

The catechism is related to the Jerusalem decree, and therefore to the Levitical Law of Holiness on which the decree is based; and especially to the magnificent nineteenth chapter of Leviticus, with its continual refrain, 'Be ye holy, for I am holy, the Lord your God'; and its supreme sentence which Jesus himself had commended as fundamental, 'Thou shalt love thy neighbour as thyself'.

This 'neo-Levitical' catechism was the inner law and inspiration of a holy community which was separated from the world, and indwelt by God himself as Spirit; a temple of the Lord, consecrated and set apart; a circle of pure light in a dark and evil world; for God had taken his saints out of the 'evil aeon' and translated them into the kingdom of his son. This picture of an *ecclesia* of the saints is intimately related to the apocalyptic vision. It is the elect community which waits for the Lord.

ATHENS

The cities of the classical Greek culture were situated in southern Italy, southern Greece (Achaia), and the sea-coast of Asia Minor. The most famous of these was Athens, which had led the opposition to Persia in the fifth century before Christ, and had become the head of a great maritime empire. It had led the world in art, science, philosophy, poetry, and political theory, and our modern western civilization is built on these foundations, with an infusion of Christian faith or sentiment. Athens was still a centre of culture and learning, though we cannot be sure that this made any strong appeal to Paul. He was lonely, and grieved over his separation from his Thessalonian converts. Once Timothy came, and told him that they were standing firm under continued persecution; and this gave him comfort.

He walked about the streets, and was vexed by the sight of so many 'idols', by which he meant the masterpieces of Pheidias and Praxiteles and other famous sculptors. He passed by the famous altar of which no trace remains now,[1] on which were engraved the words *Agnosto Theo*, (to an) 'unknown god'. He disputed in the synagogue, and took his chance with other exponents of religion and philosophy in the market-place. It appeared to his hearers that he had a few scraps of learning and that he was introducing new deities, Jesus and Anastasis (the Resurrection). His apologia before the world-famed Areopagus was a masterpiece of Jewish apologetic. There is no sign that he was a 'university man', and his acquaintance with Greek philosophy was not very profound. The Stoic commonplaces which he used may all have been current in the Hellenistic synagogue; they represented the kind of monotheism which Seneca was trying to inculcate into Nero in Rome; the one God, the one world, the one purpose; 'we too are his children'; 'in him we live and move and have our being'. Paul opens his address with an ironical compliment on their devotion to many deities and their altar to their unknown God; but he is not satisfied with that vague universal concept of the philosophers, and he is outraged by their bronze and marble images; he resorts suddenly to the Living God of Hebrew revelation, who has appointed a day on which he will judge the world, and a Man by whom he will judge it, even Jesus whom he has raised from the dead. It is a mistake to suppose that Paul attempted to charm the Athenians by means of their own philosophy; he only dallies with it to enhance the high contrast of his own barbarian faith. He comes very close to pure eschatology. The passage seems to imply, though it does not state, that the judgement is imminent.

They laughed at his reference to a resurrection of a dead man; but some were induced to believe. There was a man called Dionysius, who was a member of the Areopagus, the time-honoured court before which Paul had spoken, and there was a woman of importance named Damaris. Once more Luke carefully records the local names. Such information would still be useful or interesting when he wrote.

We receive the impression that Christianity was no very strong plant in the centre of Hellenic culture; yet it would not be very long before the first reasoned statements about the new religion in the Gentile manner would come forth from Athens. Quadratus, Aristides, and Athenagoras promoted the cause of a Christian philosophy; and it was claimed that Dionysius, the convert of Paul, had been their first bishop.

[1] There is an actual altar with the inscription *Agnostois Theois*—'to unknown gods'. The expression 'unknown' or 'unknowable god' was in use, however.

CORINTH

No reason is given why Paul 'separated himself' from Athens (the word is rather a strong one) and chose Corinth as his next city of refuge. It had been destroyed by the Romans two hundred years before, and then refounded on the old site. It had become the largest and wealthiest city in Greece, and was the residence of the Roman proconsul and the seat of the government. It had two harbours, one facing west towards Rome, and the other east towards Ephesus; ships were transported overland from one to the other on rollers. It was strongly Roman in sentiment, and closely in touch with Rome. Business-men from Italy could here mix with traders and sailors from Syria, as well as from the Greek sea-coast and islands. Many deities were worshipped, and in particular the goddess of Love, who had one thousand sacred prostitutes in her service for the pleasure and convenience of the worshippers.

Paul was still lonely and in need; but he met with the greatest of good fortune. Many of the Jews banished by Claudius from Rome must have found refuge in Corinth. Among them was a Jew named Aquila, 'of Pontic race', which may mean[1] that his family came from Pontus by the Black Sea. With him was his wife Prisca, or Priscilla. They were tent-makers by trade and were willing to join forces with Paul, for he was a tent-maker too. No doubt they were already Christians, the first Roman Christians of whom we know. On this slender basis Paul established himself and began to 'reason in the synagogue every sabbath, and persuaded many, both Jews and Greeks'.

It is interesting that the ruins of a Corinthian synagogue of this period have actually been discovered; on the stone lintel of the door were engraved these words in weak and straggling characters: *sunagoge ebreon*, 'assembly of the Hebrews'. There were few wise, few important, few noble, Paul tells us, among the converts at Corinth. There was no Stoic philosophy either in Paul's preaching. He was resolved to preach the word of the cross in all its simplicity. 'Jesus only and him crucified' was the burden of his message.

[1] More likely perhaps that he was connected with the 'Pontian' family in Rome, like Pontius Pilate.

THE CORINTHIAN CHURCH

Early in his stay at Corinth, Silas and Timothy arrived, and he was able to devote himself more intensely to the Word. He also composed two Epistles to the Thessalonians, about whom he had received the most encouraging reports; or rather the three colleagues composed joint epistles, for we shall take quite literally the wording of the salutation which denominates all three as authors; in particular we shall look for the hand of Silas in the apocalyptic passages and perhaps, too, in the catechetical formulae. They shed brilliant light on the conflicts and exaltations of this hazardous year. Persecution from their Gentile compatriots has been the lot of these infant churches, and they were now suffering exactly as the churches in Judaea had suffered; but the apostles had warned them that it would be so.

According to the statement in the Acts, Paul had won converts in Corinth even before the arrival of Silas and Timothy and the dispatch of the Thessalonian letters. He says in I Corinthians that he personally baptized Crispus and Gaius, and as it was his usual custom to leave this work to others, it is possible that they were baptized in the period before his colleagues arrived. Crispus was the synagogue-ruler of the Jews, and his accession brought others in. The name of Gaius appears a few years later in the Epistle to the Romans: 'He is my host', Paul says, 'and the host of the whole city.' The saints at Corinth felt very much at home in his house.

Paul also baptized Stephanas and his household, and says that they were the 'first fruits of Achaia'; they had by that time undertaken the ministry to the saints. The appointment of 'elders' was mentioned in Acts in connexion with the foundation of the Galatian churches; and Paul mentions men in the Galatian churches who presided and gave instruction in the Word and were entitled to financial support. In writing to the Thessalonians he commends 'those who labour among you and are over you in the Lord, and admonish you'. Obviously all these descriptions refer to the same sort of officers, the 'rulers' or ministers in charge of the local *ecclesia;* but the word 'first-fruits' requires a special note.

Writing to the Corinthians about forty-five years later, Clement of Rome says that the apostles appointed their 'first-fruits' to be bishops and deacons for the future believers, referring particularly to what had happened at the evangelization of Corinth itself, and therefore, we may infer, to Stephanas among others. It seems a little unnatural to suppose that the first convert, whoever he was, would have a claim on the ministry, or be expected to take it up, as such. The word 'first-fruit' is a sacrificial term from the Hebrew tradition, and visualizes a special portion taken from the first of the harvest to be offered to the Lord. It may simply be that the person or family among the first crop of believers who did so offer himself was spoken of as the first-fruit, and that such a self-offering was looked for. There is Old Testament precedent for the idea; when the Levites were devoted to the Temple service, they were said to have been given to the Lord by Israel as a substitute for the offering of the 'first-born', which was the equivalent of the first-fruit of the harvest in the case of a human family.

It seems to be another example of the continuation in the new Israel of the sacred order of the old Israel, on the new spiritual evangelical level. Both Paul and Clement are conscious of this continuity in the ministerial and liturgical order. Paul defends the right of apostles to be maintained at the expense of the church by referring to the precedent of the priests in the Temple.

This organization occurred of course after the separation from the old synagogue. A church was formed in the house next door, which belonged to a certain Titius Justus. It has been suggested that Gaius and Titius Justus are the same man; for Gaius Titius Justus makes a complete Roman name. Eighteen months of steady work followed. The gospel had struck root. The series of escapes from one city to another now looked like a divine plan which led the apostles to Corinth. The gospel had penetrated deep into Greece, and had formed a new centre of evangelization there, comparable to Caesarea or Antioch.

GALLIO, A.D. 52

In the year 51 or 52, a new proconsul arrived in Achaia and took up residence in Corinth; he was Gallio, the charming and cultured brother of the philosopher Seneca. The Jews lost no time in bringing Paul before Gallio, and accused him of 'teaching men to worship God contrary to the Law'; a very different matter from the popular outcry at Thessalonica that he was promoting the claims of a rival emperor. It would appear that the facts of the case were now being seen in better proportion. When Gallio discovered that the law in question was the Law of Moses, and not the decrees of Caesar, he lost interest and drove them away from his tribunal. 'And the Greeks took Sosthenes the synagogue-ruler and beat him before the tribunal; but Gallio took no notice of any of these things.' The statement is a mystery, especially as some texts omit the word 'Greeks', and leave it uncertain who beat the unfortunate Sosthenes. The natural explanation is that some of Gallio's attendants administered a beating to him in the course of driving away the Jews; and this is possible, since the Romans looked with disfavour on ill-founded accusations. But there is a Sosthenes who appears with Paul three years later, when he is writing to the Corinthians; and if this is the same Sosthenes, the word 'synagogue-ruler' may perhaps have been applied to him as an official in the church; though indeed there is no other instance of this on record, churches are called synagogues here and there.

Gallio, it will be noticed, did not distinguish between Jews and Christians; they were all one to him. The Christians would agree with this attitude, and welcome it. It had been the claim of Paul all along that his Gentile converts were to be accepted as Jews. This legal decision from the highest court in the province gave protection of a sort to the Christians, and we hear no more for a while of the charge that they were a seditious organization.

CHAPTER 7

EPHESUS

The move to Ephesus, A.D. 52, *p.* 126. Paul visits Syria, *p.* 127. Apollos, *p.* 129. The Ephesian church, *p.* 130. The last year at Ephesus, A.D. 54, *p.* 132. The troubles in Corinth, *p.* 133. I Corinthians, *p.* 135. The Corinthian questions, *p.* 136. The resurrection of the body, *p.* 138. The crisis at Ephesus, *p.* 139. The severe letter, II Corinthians B, *p.* 140. The letter of thanksgiving, II Corinthians A, *p.* 142. The return to Corinth, *p.* 144. The Epistle to the Romans, A.D. 54–55, *p.* 145.

THE FIRST CHRISTIAN GENERATION, A.D. 30–70

(Chronological Synopsis)

A.D.

29/30 Crucifixion, Resurrection, founding of the Jerusalem church.

31/32 The martyrdom of Stephen; persecution of the church; expansion into Samaria.

33 Conversion of Paul.

34–38 The church spreads throughout Palestine, Syria, Cilicia among Greek-speaking Jews: church founded in Antioch, where the gospel is preached to the Greeks. Paul in Antioch. Prophets come down from Jerusalem.

39/40 *The Affair of Caligula's image*: II Thess. ii. 4; Rev. xiii. 14?

41 *Caligula dies; Claudius emperor; Agrippa I king.*

44 Martyrdom of James the Apostle; Peter leaves Jerusalem. *Death of Agrippa I*; Palestine governed by 'procurators'.

45 Famine year; Paul in Antioch.

46 Famine continues. Paul, Barnabas, Titus visit Jerusalem.

47/48 Mission of Paul and Barnabas to Galatia.

48 Return to Antioch; controversy over circumcision.

49 *Claudius expels Jews from Rome.* Galatians written. *Council in Jerusalem.* Paul in Macedonia, with Luke.

50 Paul in Corinth. Thessalonian Epistles.

51/52 *Gallio arrives in Corinth.*

52/53 Paul visits Ephesus; then Syria; then back to Ephesus.

53/54 Paul in Ephesus for three years.

54 *Death of Claudius; Nero emperor.*

54/55 Corinthians and Romans written. (Some would add Galatians.)

55/56 Pilgrimage to Jerusalem; Paul arrested and imprisoned.

A.D.	
56/57	Paul a prisoner at Caesarea; with Luke.
57/58	Paul appeals to Caesar; voyage to Rome; winter at Malta.
58/59	Paul arrives in Rome for two years; Luke, Timothy, Mark, etc.
59/60	Philemon, Colossians, Ephesians, Philippians written in Rome.
60/61	Paul in Rome. Work done on Acts by Luke? Release of Paul? Paul's voyage to Spain?
62	*Martyrdom of James the brother of the Lord*; Simeon succeeds him.
63	Paul in Asia Minor; see I Timothy and Titus.
64	*The Fire in Rome, July 19; Nero's persecution.*
65	Martyrdoms of Peter and Paul 64–67. II Timothy; I Peter.
66	*Outbreak of Jewish War.*
67	Suicide of Nero. The Gospel of Mark.
68	*Civil War in the Empire*; Galba, Otho, Vitellius.
69	*Vespasian becomes emperor*; Jerusalem Christians flee to Pella.
70	*Destruction of Jerusalem by Titus*; earlier sources of the Revelation composed.

Notes. Entries in italics are ascertained dates; the Jerusalem Council has been included with these since there is very general agreement about it. The remaining dates will be right within a very small margin of error.

(Some scholars regard Ephesians and I Peter as later pseudonymous writings; but even so their historical references relate to the period to which they ostensibly belong. It is assumed that the Pastoral Epistles contain authentic correspondence of Paul.)

THE MOVE TO EPHESUS, A.D. 52

We have already pointed out that in Roman times the word Asia was applied to the Roman province which was situated on the western coast of Asia Minor. Its principal city, Ephesus, had been a centre of trade and of Greek philosophy before Athens was much heard of. In fact the Greek scientific tradition may be said to have begun with the Ionian philosophers of the sixth and fifth centuries before Christ, of whom Thales was the first, and Heraclitus the best known. It was Heraclitus who introduced into this school of philosophy the doctrine of the 'Logos' or immanent reason, which the Stoics accepted as a basis for their 'theology'. The city was larger and more important than Corinth, and had communication overland with the Galatian cities. It was dedicated to the most ancient and august of all east Mediterranean deities, the Great Mother, known here as Artemis. Her image, which had fallen from heaven, doubtless a large meteorite, was treasured in one of the largest temples which had ever been built. She was 'great Artemis who is reverenced by the whole world'.

It was in the spring of 52 that Aquila and Prisca moved from Corinth to Ephesus, quite possibly to open a new branch of their business, combining business expansion with evangelization. Certainly the tent-making went on at Ephesus as it had at Corinth. Paul went with them and spent three months there, during which he preached acceptably in the synagogue, and was actually asked to stay; but he had made up his mind to visit Jerusalem again. According to an early reviser of the text of Acts, whose work will be discussed in chapter 15, he wanted to keep the feast of Pentecost there.

PAUL VISITS SYRIA

He arrived in Caesarea, from which city he 'went up and saluted the church', presumably the church in Jerusalem. No particulars are given of this visit, and we are left wondering who accompanied him, and why it was recorded. An answer may be suggested. We seem to see a systolic, as well as a diastolic motion in the apostolic mission; the evangelists go forth, but they also come back. The rhythm is observable even in the Gospels. The apostles are sent out two by two, but they are gathered together again unto the Lord; they report what they have done and taught; and the occasion seems to be connected with a festal convocation.

Paul makes four such journeys to Jerusalem in the forties and fifties.

(1) In 45 or 46 he went with Barnabas and Titus, taking offerings from Antioch; there was a conference or council in which Peter and John and James the Just took part.

(2) In 49 he went up again from Antioch with Barnabas; there was a conference of apostles and elders, in which Peter and James the Just took part.

(3) In 52 he went again; this is the present instance.

(4) In 55 or 56 he went a fourth time with a number of Gentile Christians taking offerings; there was a conference with James the Just and the elders.

In the case of (1), (2), and (4), Paul made a report on his work. In the case of (4) the visit occurred at Pentecost; in the case of (2) many modern scholars think it may have been Pentecost; in the case of (3) the reviser of Acts makes it Pentecost. This reviser, to whom we shall refer again, did his work shortly after Acts was written, frequently showing that he possessed some special knowledge or understanding of the material he was working on.

The evidence suggests that such gatherings were held at Jerusalem, at Pentecost every three years for report and conference; the request made in 46 that Paul and Barnabas would remember the poor in Jerusalem implies that they expected him to visit Jerusalem officially again; the council in 49 falls into place as one of a series; the visit in 52 becomes understandable without further explanation. Luke has prepared the way for this idea at the very beginning of Acts by describing the feast of Pentecost so fully, and emphasizing the great number of pilgrims who came up to it from all parts of the diaspora. Doubtless travelling conditions were better then, in May or June, than at Passover in the spring, or Tabernacles in the autumn.

When reports of this kind were made, and we have indubitable instances of this occurring, the question may be asked, to whom did the apostles report? Was it to Peter or James as superior? Or to the body of apostles and elder brethren? The latter would be the only answer that could possibly be justified by the evidence; for Peter himself was called upon to make such a report on one occasion. When the reports had been heard, the opportunity was there to come to an agreement on difficult controversial questions.

We have suggested that the composer of Acts made use of such reports, including some which he had penned himself. The stories in Acts about the Christian beginnings at Philippi, Thessalonica, Berea, Athens, and Corinth, may have been taken from the reports which were compiled for the conference of 52. When Paul had completed his business in Jerusalem, he paid a visit to Antioch, and returned to Ephesus by way of Galatia and Phrygia. The reviser did not take the view that Paul had actually reached Jerusalem, for he says at this point, 'And when Paul wanted, according to his own idea, to go to Jerusalem, the Spirit said to him to return to Asia'; thus making his work in Asia the result of a new revelation.

II. (i) CORINTH: RUINS OF THE TEMPLE

II. (ii) EPHESUS: THE TEMPLE OF DIANA

12. A ROMAN SHIP

APOLLOS

During the absence of Paul in the East, a new preacher of the gospel had arrived in Ephesus, the mysterious Apollos; mysterious to us, but not to the readers of Acts, who must have known more about him. It is as in the case of Mark; Luke gives a sufficient account for those who knew something of the man already, but not enough for us.

The reviser makes his name Apollonius, but Apollos is simply a short form of this name. The reviser is more ceremonious. Apollos was a learned or eloquent man. He was an Alexandrian by race, and was 'powerful in the scriptures', meaning of course the Hebrew scriptures. Possibly he had learned to allegorize them in the Alexandrian manner. The true text, or what we take to be the true text, says that he was instructed in the way of the Lord and was fervent in the spirit; he taught accurately the things about Jesus, but he only knew the baptism of John. The reviser says that he had been instructed in the word of the Lord in his native land. If this alteration in the text is correct, we have our only example of Alexandrian Christianity in the New Testament. It would appear to have been defective on some point; but it is not possible for us to say just how. Priscilla and Aquila took him and instructed him more accurately; but it is not said that they baptized him again, so that his case does not seem to be the same as that of the twelve adherents of the Baptist who are introduced shortly after.

The reviser says 'Aquila and Priscilla', putting the name of the husband first. This was more correct, no doubt, but it was not the usual order; for some reason the name of Priscilla came first. It is thought that she must have been a lady of some social standing in Rome. These points of divergence are very small, but they have their interest. The reviser had his own views about the impression that should be given. He is practically a second witness to the events. It is worth giving the next paragraph side by side.

ORIGINAL TEXT	REVISER'S TEXT
And when he wanted to cross over to Achaia, the brethren sent him on his way, and wrote to the brethren to receive him; and when he arrived, he spent some time with	And certain Corinthians who were dwelling in Ephesus, heard him, and urged him to cross over with them to their native land; and when he consented, the Ephesians

those who had believed through faith; for he refuted the Jews excellently, proving publicly through the scriptures that the Messiah was Jesus.
(From the Vatican MS. B.)

wrote to the disciples in Corinth, that they should receive the man; and he dwelt in Achaia, and spent some time in the churches; for he refuted the Jews excellently, arguing publicly and proving through the scriptures that Jesus was the Messiah.
(From the Cambridge MS. D.)

The fuller text which we have described as the Reviser's Text, may appear to many superior; and who can say that some points in it may not give the correct reading? But scholars generally are convinced, by studying all the evidence, that B represents what Luke wrote, and that D represents a rewriting.

Apollos made a profound impression on the Corinthian church, so much so that many were convinced that he was far superior intellectually to Paul.

THE EPHESIAN CHURCH

When Paul had finished his work in Galatia, he proceeded westward along the Asian highway until he reached Ephesus, passing once more by the cities of western Phrygia. It was not customary for apostles to travel alone, so he may have had Timothy with him. But there were changes in the missionary personnel at this time. The name of Silas disappears from the epistles of Paul, and the name of Titus is found there. Paul may have brought back Titus with him from Antioch. He may have left Silas there, perhaps with Peter; for he is associated with Peter when his name reappears some ten years later. It is a good conjecture that Peter and Silas visited the northern parts of Asia Minor from Antioch, including Cappadocia, Bithynia, and Pontus; for Peter's Epistle, which was written 'through Silvanus', was addressed to the Gentile Christians of these provinces, along with those of Asia and Galatia.

When Paul arrived in Ephesus he found a group of twelve men who were interested in the gospel, but the only baptism they had received was that of John, and they had heard nothing about the gift of the Holy Spirit. Paul persuaded them to accept Christian baptism and the laying on of hands. We cannot quite read the significance of the story, but it illustrates the mixed material out of which the Ephesian church was made. We must be careful, however, not to assume that the status of these men was the same as that of Apollos. He was said to be fervent in the Spirit, whereas they had never heard of such a thing; and they were given Christian baptism, which is not said in his case. They then received the Holy Spirit, like the Samaritan converts who were confirmed by Peter and John.

The preaching of Paul was not, of course, the first introduction of the gospel to Ephesus. It was the point at which an independent church was organized. He soon parted company with the synagogue, and organized his disciples in the school of a certain Tyrannus, where he gave lectures, according to the reviser of Acts, 'from the fifth hour to the tenth', that is to say, from 11.0 a.m. to 4.0 p.m. or thereabouts. It would be rather rash to infer that his association with Tyrannus imparted a share of Ionian philosophy to the Ephesian church. On the other hand, it may have supplied facilities for writing and book-production, and we shall see that Ephesus did become a centre of literary activity.

Another ingredient in the mixed background of the Ephesian church was magic. It was commonly believed at the time, though it was not necessarily thought to be respectable, that the course of life could be influenced by age-old ceremonies and charms and incantations in which an expert invoked the names of gods or daemons, the latter word simply meaning a disembodied spirit, who might be either good or evil. A degraded and contaminated form of Judaism produced its quota of these impostors, who knew the names of aeons and angels and dominions and powers. Some 'Jewish' exorcists with priestly pretensions, who called themselves the Sons of Scaeva (the left-handed), impressed by the healings and casting out of evil spirits which were a standing feature of the Christian mission, added the names of Jesus and Paul to their own repertoire; the response from the patient was not favourable. This incident led to confessions by many of Paul's converts that they were still using these curious arts, and there was a great burning of magical papyri.

We have passed rather lightly over Luke's rogues' gallery, that is to say his portraits of pseudo-religionists who opposed the progress of the gospel, often by assimilating themselves to it; but these portraits, even if they seem rather slight, make a valuable series for study. They are Ananias of Jerusalem, Simon of Samaria, Elymas of Cyprus, the soothsayers of Philippi, and the Sons of Scaeva. Brands plucked from the burning are Apollos of Alexandria and the 'Baptist' circle at Ephesus.

THE LAST YEAR AT EPHESUS, A.D. 54

Paul spent three years at Ephesus, which we may allot to 52–55 A.D. We can shift them a year or two later if we wish to, by allowing a longer time for the journey to Syria in 52; but the journey does not seem to require it. During this time he built up a considerable staff of assistants, whose names are scattered over the Acts and the Epistles. Among these Timothy acquired a position second only to Paul himself. By means of epistles and visits from these assistants, he continued to administer the affairs of the churches which he had founded, and those which had sprung up in their vicinity. It is in this period that he compares himself to the 'wise master-builder', and indeed a structure was going up all round the Aegean Sea which would provide a foundation for the church as a whole when the 'day' came with its storms and afflictions. At present, however, there was comparative peace. The Roman power was neutral and therefore, in a real sense, protective. Gallio had refused to take action against Paul in Corinth; the 'Asiarchs' who were men of influence in Ephesus were his friends.

Early in 54, according to our computation, he was meditating a new move. It was a pilgrimage to Jerusalem by representatives of all his churches, taking up a substantial offering for the 'poor saints'. It is interesting to note that in spite of the antagonism of the more narrow-minded Jewish Christians in Jerusalem there existed in the Pauline churches a genuine sentiment of loyalty and affection for the mother church, which was maintaining its own witness under great difficulties. The modern theological interest in the ecclesiastical controversies of the period tends to obscure the broader facts of the situation, and one of these was the solidarity of all Christians in the Messiah; one spirit and one body, as Paul expressed it.

These Gentile Christians had become members of a religious movement which was grounded in the Jewish tradition; and just as born Jews went up to Jerusalem from time to time to appear before the Lord and to offer their gifts, so the believers from among the Gentiles, who had the same status in Israel as the 'God-fearers' of the synagogue, could go up and offer theirs. Paul had taken part in a mission of this sort from Antioch in 45 or 46, and had pledged himself to bring further gifts from his distant churches, but it would be an error of judgement to suppose that the purpose of his visit was primarily financial. It must have been a spiritual enterprise. His Gentile converts would make personal contact with the old Jerusalem church; they would view the sacred sites; they would meet the original eye-witnesses and ministers of the word; they would hear the story of the early days for themselves.

Conversely, their presence might commend the Gentile mission to the hard hearts of the all-too-Jewish Jewish-Christian, a hope which Paul expresses in his Epistle to the Romans. It was a generous impulse, because he was no longer beholden to Jerusalem for recognition or encouragement. In these few years the Gentile mission had made great strides. The gospel was definitely passing to the Gentiles. Perhaps they were more numerous? Paul claims that he had laboured 'more abundantly than they all'.

THE TROUBLES IN CORINTH

These preparations were interrupted by serious troubles in the Corinthian ecclesia. Doubtless such troubles were part of the growing pains of all churches; but those in Corinth were especially severe, and we happen to have a good deal of the correspondence to which they gave rise. But not all. There was a letter which was written to the Corinthians previous to any which we now possess, in which Paul told them not to be 'unequally yoked with unbelievers', and to have no association with fornicators; a counsel which some in Corinth regarded as unpractical, human society being what it is. Paul had to explain that what he meant was that such persons should not be admitted to the fellowship meals and eucharists: 'with such a one not to eat in common'.

Early in 54, some persons representing a lady named Chloe gave him information about certain divisions and dissensions, which had become a danger to the peace of the church.

Every one says, I am of Paul, I am of Apollos, I am of Kephas; I am of the Messiah. Is the Messiah divided? Was Paul crucified for you? Or were you baptized into Paul's name? I am thankful that I baptized none of you, except

Crispus and Gaius, lest anyone should say that I baptized into my own name. I also baptized the household of Stephanas. I forget whether I baptized any other. (I Cor. i. 12–16.)

This typical piece of Pauline prose illuminates the situation, but does not enable us to analyse it. No success has attended the efforts to form a clear view of a Paul-party, an Apollos-party, or a Peter-party; let alone a Messiah-party. Yet parties there were, or at least violent opposition of different points of view, and debates in which the names of the leaders were recklessly used.

No doubt the controversies which had divided the church in 49 were not extinct; Jew and Gentile may still have found it hard to sit down at table together. But we can distinguish divisions of another kind now. We can detect a broad-minded or over-emancipated ultra-Gentile propaganda or trend, which, for all we know, may have appealed to a certain type of Jewish convert too; it would appear to have been favourable to Paul and favoured by him to some extent. There was also a narrow-minded, rather Judaistic propaganda which was critical of Paul, and may have been promoted by some Jewish 'apostles' of unknown origin, who had made their nests in the Corinthian ecclesia. There was much talk about wisdom and knowledge on the part of superior persons who thought that Paul was deficient in these respects. In the first part of his first Epistle he reads one side, or perhaps both sides, a lesson in which he commends the simple gospel of the cross, and attempts to put wisdom in a subordinate place; but in the very act of doing this he cannot help spinning a theory of esoteric knowledge or spiritual wisdom which was soon to prove too fascinating for weaker minds. There is a general air of intellectual ferment. It may be that both parties, or all parties, were rather inclined to what later would be called heresy.

This spiritual wisdom is thought by many to owe something to the language of what are called the 'mystery religions'. No doubt it is more in line with this kind of Hellenistic religious life than with the apocalypses and catechisms of the Thessalonian epistles, which it appears to desire to transcend; but we may not have to look farther than the Hellenistic synagogue for the origin of the idiom, allowing fully for the possibility of border-line tendencies in Judaism of a liberal, mystical, or ascetic character, and for the influence of a Syrian mysticism or gnosis in Palestine itself. Of course the converts from 'idolatry' brought in with them their own way of thinking and speaking on religious subjects, and we may allow for the possibility that Paul picked up a phrase or two from them, becoming 'all things to all men', as he says, 'that he might gain some at least'. He could certainly put on the manner of the Stoic or Cynic philosopher when he pleased, and why not of the master of the mysteries?

I CORINTHIANS

Paul had Timothy by him when he began to frame his great Epistle to the Corinthians, and the name of Sosthenes appears as a co-author. He was probably the Sosthenes who is mentioned in the Acts as a Corinthian synagogue-ruler. Stephanas had also arrived from Corinth, with two members of the ecclesia, Achaicus and Fortunatus. They carried a letter from the ecclesia which asked for guidance on a number of subjects; and they were able to supply him with further information on the condition of affairs. It was a staff-conference. Apollos was there.

Paul deals in succession with the various questions which were referred to him, beginning with a case of outrageous sexual immorality, which unfortunately had failed to disturb the serenity of the intellectuals. Stephanas and his colleagues had been unable to get the ecclesia to take action. The vigorous directive of Paul shows exactly what was meant by his picture of the church as a sanctuary of light in a dark world, and also the nature of his own authority as the Apostle who had founded the church. The offender must be cut off; he must be thrown back into the outer darkness; he must be 'delivered over to Satan for the destruction of his carnal nature' in the hope that his soul would be saved in the Day of the Lord. It is the Christian form of the anathema or solemn excommunication which was customary in Israel. We should bear it in mind in considering the cases of Ananias of Jerusalem and Elymas of Cyprus, Simon of Samaria even.

The apostle had made his decision so far as he was concerned; but his spiritual authority in such matters was normally exercised in the bosom of the ecclesia concerned. On this occasion he boldly anticipates the concurrence of the ecclesia; he acts as if he were present in the spirit, and calls upon the ecclesia to concur and to make the sentence effective. He was prepared to risk everything on this exercise of authority and this expectation of obedience. His appeal was supported by certain refrains of a liturgical character based on the Passover ritual of the searching for the leaven; it was the Passover season when he wrote

> Cleanse out the old leaven that you may have a new lump;
> For our Passover is slain, even the Messiah;
> Therefore let us keep the Festival.

THE CORINTHIAN QUESTIONS

There was a profusion of questions on the subject of marriage, divorce, and virginity; and also on social relations with pagan society. There was a group (or groups) which prided itself on its strength of purpose in Christ, and held to a course of virginity as the highest ideal. Apparently there were cases of men and women living together with nothing more than a spiritual bond. Even though Paul favoured virginity, he thought some were flying too high.

It was the same 'strong' group no doubt that frequented the pagan banquets, and ate the food which had been offered to idols; even it would seem in the temple-precincts, on the grounds that an idol was 'nothing in the world'. These were the views with which Paul most nearly sympathized, and it would seem that he had been known to partake of such food, though he strongly condemns any participation in the pagan rites themselves, or with the 'table of daemons' as he calls the banquets of the gods. It would appear that he had been attacked on this point, and we find him defending himself in a vigorous way, asserting his freedom on such matters, but also declaring that he would eat no flesh at all 'while the world endureth', if it offended the conscience of a weaker brother, that is to say a member of the party that attributed importance to such matters.

We are here, for one short moment, on the grounds of the decision which had been made for Gentile Christians in Syria by the Jerusalem council, five years before. Paul agrees to act in accordance with it, but only as a concession to the weaker brethren. It would be interesting to know how it had fared during five years of history. Paul does not refer to it at all.[1]

On the other hand, he quotes more than once from 'commandments' of the Lord. He has a commandment of the Lord on the subject of the

[1] Some scholars regard this silence as a proof that Luke's account of the Jerusalem council cannot be regarded as historical.

marriage bond, another on the support of apostles when preaching the gospel, and a third on the sacrament of the breaking of the bread; indeed, he tells the story of the Last Supper with the command to 'Do this in remembrance of me'. It is interesting to note that it is only in this Epistle, in connexion with these pastoral problems, that he introduces direct quotations from the teaching of Jesus, and direct references to the sacrament of the eucharist. But for the Corinthian scandals, they would never have been mentioned, and it would have been possible to argue that he knew nothing of them; which is a lesson on the limitations of documentary sources, and the fallibility of the argument from silence.

The Last Supper naturally suggests the Passover, and a Paschal background is provided by a mystical treatment of the Exodus story, based on Exodus and Numbers, or a 'Midrash' on Exodus and Numbers. Paul draws out the liturgical and sacramental implications of the sacred text, very much as we find it was done in the Jewish tradition; but he claims that its true significance is only revealed in the Christian mysteries. 'These things occurred as types', he says, meaning patterns which would be examples for us; 'and were written down for our admonition on whom the ends of the world have come.' The Hebrew scriptures only exist now to provide lessons for the Christian ecclesia.

After dealing with a number of liturgical and pastoral questions, such as the veiling of women during prayer and the scandals which marred the solemnity of the eucharist, he passes to the ministry of the 'spirituals', the men and women, moved by the Holy Spirit, who rose up and spoke with tongues or prophesied. It was no doubt in this very activity that the dissensions and debates arose. He presents his parable of the church as the body of the Messiah, and every member of it the recipient of a 'charisma' or special gift of grace, given to him for the service of the whole. He reviews some of these gifts of the Spirit, and insists that Christian love is a gift which outshines all the teaching and all the prophecy and all the wisdom. He does something to regulate the exercise of the ecstatic gifts, revealing as he does so how song and praise and thanksgiving were mingled together promiscuously and unintelligibly, to the perplexity of the average Christian, who knew not when to say Amen. He supplies rules of order. He insists that God is not a god of chaos.

THE RESURRECTION OF THE BODY

From this subject he passes to the question of the resurrection; for there were persons in Corinth who denied the resurrection of the dead. They probably believed that the soul passed away to some more heavenly sphere or was born again in another body; and, if this was the case, it may have been a piece of pagan mysticism such as could have been derived from the mystery religions or from the higher paganism of the East. No doubt men who had drifted in from these cults could make nothing of the apocalyptic vision in Thessalonians. Paul himself has advanced beyond the Thessalonian stage, and bases what he has to say about the resurrection of believers on the Resurrection of Jesus Christ himself, in which they all believed. He reminds them of the credal formula which he had taught them four or five years before and had received himself at an early stage in his Christian life.

He pointed out that the gospel of the resurrection rested on the concurrent testimony of Peter and James and all the apostles, including himself; and his insistence on this point suggests that the question about the resurrection of the dead was the very one which had divided the ecclesia into parties. The same question had occasioned doubts at Thessalonica.

He preaches them an Easter sermon on the resurrection of the body, in which his doctrine is neither all-too-bodily nor all-too-spiritual. He speaks of the transformation of bodily life by spiritual energy. The creative power of God, which raised the Lord Jesus from the dead, will also transform our earthly body from its present mortal condition, and make it a glorious incorruptible garment of the spirit. This new idea is boldly infused into the Thessalonian apocalypse. In a sudden access of inspiration, he re-fashions it to include the doctrine of transformation. The trumpet will sound, he asserts; but *we* will be changed. It is a 'mystery'; a kind of speech, that is, in which the heavenly truth is presented in a veiled form; but the veils have grown thinner and more transparent; the heavenly infuses the earthly and shines through it. And this new language of spirit-infused myth, or spirit-infused apocalypse, becomes Paul's natural mode of speech with regard to the eternal realities; it is not in words taught by man's wisdom, he explains, but in words taught by the Spirit, matching spiritual realities with spiritual realities. It is trans-apocalyptic, to coin a phrase.

The final chapter descends to earth again and deals with the method of organizing the collection for the saints in Jerusalem, which is to be effected by asking everybody to lay by such money as he can afford on the first day of each week, which is the earliest reference to the Christian Sunday after the event of Easter morning itself. He intends to stay on at Ephesus until Pentecost, but is sending Timothy to them, probably in connexion with the offering. Apollos prefers to remain in Ephesus.

THE CRISIS AT EPHESUS

In the chapter of I Corinthians which deals with the resurrection, there is a strange line which begins with these words: 'If, after the manner of men, I had fought with beasts at Ephesus'; and there are not wanting one or two scholars who suggest that it should be taken literally; but such an encounter could not have been passed over by Luke or omitted by Paul from his list of sufferings on behalf of Christ. It is, of course, one of his strong figures of speech, which is what he usually means by the phrase 'after the manner of men'. He has already pictured his life as an apostle as being like an appearance in the amphitheatre. The whole universe was a great arena for him, with all the hosts of heaven looking on.

A crisis occurred in Ephesus, however, which is the subject of one of Luke's most skilful pieces of writing. The trouble was due this time to the Christian (and Jewish) polemic against the 'idolatry' of the pagan world, about which very little is said in our sources. There was a guild of craftsmen who made and sold silver shrines of the great goddess Artemis, whom, they asserted, all the world adored. One of their number, named Demetrius, raised a great outcry against Paul, on the grounds that he was injuring their trade by preaching that gods which were 'made with hands' were not gods at all; which nobody knew better than he. There was a rowdy and disorderly gathering of the citizens in the enormous theatre, at which a Jew named Alexander was put up to speak, and howled down by the mob. Who he was, or what he was going to say, we have no idea; doubtless the readers of the Acts knew something about him, or the author would have given more information. Gaius and Aristarchus, two Christian leaders from Macedonia, were seized upon, but escaped with their lives. Paul was put under 'police protection'. Now though Paul received the personal protection of the Asiarchs, and though the city secretary succeeded in calming down the assembly, the hints in the Pauline correspondence rather suggest that the situation was uglier than it is allowed to appear in Acts.

The light and amusing style of Luke must not prevent us from recognizing the gravity of the crisis. The theatre at Ephesus held over twenty thousand people, and if it was filled by a riotous assembly of non-Jews it is a proof that there was an ugly anti-Christian feeling in the city; a growing hatred and fear of this new oriental movement which spread throughout the Roman world until it was sated in the martyrdoms in Rome ten years later. The first stages of this reaction appear quite clearly in Philippi and Thessalonica, and were perhaps set off by the disturbances in Rome of the year 49; it was being held in check now by the authorities, as was mysteriously adumbrated in the Thessalonian Epistles, but we can see what it was like when Nero turned it loose and hounded it on in 64.

There is a theory that Paul suffered an imprisonment in Ephesus, and that the Epistles written by him in prison should be assigned to this period; but it is not easy to fit an imprisonment of any length into the known course of events; and the silence of Acts is fatal to the theory. It is not possible to explain why Luke should omit a fact of such importance, and so give a false view of the course of events, which were in any case public property; the story as given in Acts impresses most readers as a particularly good piece of reporting. Nevertheless, the theory has the value of drawing attention to the gravity of the occasion, which is apt to be overlooked. Paul looks back to it in II Corinthians as a period of deadly peril, unless perhaps he is referring to some serious illness which he went through at the time.

THE SEVERE LETTER: II CORINTHIANS B

Meanwhile affairs at Corinth went from bad to worse. There was a good deal of coming and going at this time, and it is not easy to co-ordinate all the information we possess. It is certain, however, that Paul visited Corinth, as he had said in his first Epistle that he might do. This visit was not a success. He did not make a good showing, or that is what his enemies said. His bodily presence was weak, they remarked, and his speech beneath contempt. There was opposition and even defiance, in connexion with which one person was prominent, though we cannot give the one person a name, or form a very clear idea of him. He appears to have been the leader of a Jewish-Christian faction, and ranked as an apostle of some sort.

On his return to Ephesus Paul decided to take a strong line, and to send a severe epistle, even though it might give pain. He composed it, he says, in tears and great distress of mind. He sent it by Titus.

Titus was occupied in organizing the collection of the offering for the church in Jerusalem. It will be remembered that he had accompanied Paul to Jerusalem on a similar mission about eight years before. It would appear that he was a practical man with a talent for such work. He had gone through a conflict with difficult Jewish Christians on their home ground. He was the man for the occasion.

Part of this 'severe letter', or possibly the whole of it, has been appended to the second Epistle to the Corinthians, forming its last four chapters. It contains an onslaught on certain 'pseudo-apostles' who had egged on the opposition party; for Paul does not hesitate to call them by harsh names; 'false apostles, deceitful workmen, disguising themselves as apostles of Christ'. He also refers to them as the 'super-apostles' or the 'extra-super-apostles', if we may be allowed in this way to paraphrase his double superlatives. They were 'Israelites', and 'seed of Abraham' and 'servants of the Messiah'. Perhaps they had listened to Jesus. But they relied on letters of commendation, and collected them from the churches as they went round. They depended for their living on the bounty of the faithful, which Paul had not done. In return they performed miracles and supplied visions and revelations. They accused Paul of pride and arrogance and boasting and making money out of his churches; he was inconsistent, and his word was not to be trusted.

They were apostles of a sort, it seems; envoys or agents of some church, possibly the Jerusalem church. Paul makes mention of such envoys, men who had been chosen by his own churches to travel with him in the ministry of the gospel. He calls them 'apostles of the churches'. He designates one of them now, 'the brother whose praise is in the gospel', to accompany Titus when he makes the final appeal to the Corinthian church. They take the severe letter and present it. It used hard language in places, and Paul had felt compelled to give some account of what he had suffered on behalf of the gospel, and to remind them of all he had done for them. He descends to this level of 'boasting' with half-pitiful, half-comic apologies.

The mission was brilliantly successful. The opposition to Paul had probably discredited itself by now. The ecclesia as a whole had come to its senses. Titus and his unnamed colleague were received with 'fear and trembling'. An offender of importance, perhaps some doughty patron of the opposition, was censured by a majority vote. Titus returned in triumph.

THE LETTER OF THANKSGIVING, II CORINTHIANS A

It all took a little longer than Paul had expected. He arrived at Troas to preach the gospel of Christ, and a door was opened in the Lord; but his spirit found no rest. He went on into Macedonia with Timothy, where the churches had suffered some sort of persecution too. Everywhere there was trouble. Somewhere in Macedonia, in Philippi perhaps, he met Titus; and Titus brought him good news. His joy overflows in the opening chapters of his 'Second Epistle' to the Corinthians.

The liturgical background of this Epistle was the feast of Pentecost which was now past. It commemorated the giving of the Law by Almighty God in clouds of light upon Mount Sinai; how much more glorious, he says, is the ministry of love and grace with which the apostles are entrusted in the church; shining forth upon the world in the face of Jesus the Messiah, and written by the Spirit in the hearts of men through the proclamation of the gospel; not graven in rock to be a sentence of death. It is the Lord himself with the gift of liberty.[1] It is the promise and assurance of endless inexpressible life and glory, when these worn-out bodies in which we tabernacle now, are exchanged for those in which we hope to be 'clothed upon', when sorrow and conflict and persecution have been passed through.

In this passionate and realistic mysticism, we have travelled far from the thorough-going apocalyptic of the Thessalonian epistles. The Christian still stands between the Resurrection and the Advent, the two creative moments in which divine glory breaks through into this dark cosmos; but they are almost eclipsed by the glory of the

[1] Based apparently upon a rabbinic play upon words, substituting *hēruth* (liberty) for *hāruth* (graven).

present moment, when the unlimited Grace of God flows in upon the apostle and his people in their hour of need. It is most powerful of all in the pain and suffering and mortification by which he fills up in his own mortal body the sufferings and sorrows of the Messiah himself.

This is the Pauline doctrine of the 'perisseuma' or excess of grace which is translated in the famous phrase of 'grace abounding'. It is the main theme of the Epistle to the Romans, in which he develops the paradox that where sin increases, the grace of God is more abundant still. The sin of man provokes the wrath of God, and in surpassingly greater degree it provokes his grace.

Infusion of grace is the heart of the Pauline religion. Paul's Epistles and especially the Epistle to the Romans have provided raw material for a hundred schemes of salvation, doctrines of atonement, and theories of predestination; but the real Paul moved freely from one mode of thought to another, using all but selling himself to none. He penetrates into profound mysteries with uncanny analytic genius; he captures a mood of frustration or exaltation with a few magic words; he writes inspired passages which are like solemn music; but he has no consistent theology. When he argues he can be very fatiguing; when he theorizes he can be very obscure; but time after time he produces exactly the right phrase. He is a gold-mine for the preacher.

There is one consistent thought, however, which holds together everything he says and does. It is the inundation of the soul by power from heaven. It is a dynamic advent of deity here and now in this evil world; God in Christ; God in the man's soul and body, contending with sin and death and winning the victory; whether he calls it grace or justification or comfort or new creation or redemption or *charisma* or apocalypse, it is all one thing; God in action; Holy Spirit; grace abounding.

The greatness of Paul is his pure religious genius; the sense that he, so worthless and evil, was yet the chosen instrument which God filled with his supernatural power to do his will; too much power indeed for the weak body to sustain. His theology fails to embody or express it; it often obscures it and complicates it even as he labours to clarify it. It is in himself, not in his theology. He works it out in his flesh and blood. He is himself the theological factum; the sinner that God saved through Jesus Christ; the apostle that he equipped with so much power for building up but not for tearing down. God's power never fails. All around him the infinite glory and grace of it is poured out richly, and operates in all his churches, beyond all measure or hope or expectation; the excess, the overflowing, the generous superfluity, the completeness and fullness of the divine love that fills all in all.

It will be observed that we have here an advent or *parousia* taking place spiritually by grace in the church.

THE RETURN TO CORINTH

Paul finished his letter and sent it to Corinth. It is typical of his generous heart that he urged the Corinthians to restore to communion the offender who had been excommunicated. He sends him full forgiveness if the ecclesia will concur.

It was getting late in the year, but he pushed westward along the Egnatian Road, across the Balkan mountains, until he had crossed the boundary of the Adriatic province which was known as Illyricum. How much farther he went we do not know. He was on the main road to Rome; ships sailed from Nicopolis to Brundisium in Italy, but his hour had not yet come to see Rome. He retraced his steps and spent three months in Corinth.

A great change was taking place which would once more turn the current of the gospel. On October 12 the Emperor Claudius died, and his young stepson Nero came to the throne. The ban against the Jews was lifted and the Jewish exiles could go back to Rome. Aquila and Priscilla had already gone, and doubtless many others went with them. There was Phoebe, for instance, a lady from Cenchreae who is described as a patroness of the church there; it was seven miles out of Corinth. Paul could not go with them; there was his 'ministry' or 'act of grace' to be fulfilled in Jerusalem first; he decided to send a letter which Phoebe could take with her.

During this winter of 54–55 (or 55–56) Paul wrote his Epistle to the Romans, which gives us his mature thought on the deepest problems of religion, as they were illuminated by the gospel which he preached. He paused for a while and surveyed the scene. He was the apostle of the Gentiles. He saw himself as a priest ministering before the Messiah Jesus, as it were at an altar, that their offering might be acceptable to God, being consecrated by the Holy Spirit. Looking westward he felt his responsibility for Rome, and beyond that for Spain. Others had laid the foundations in Rome; and it was his principle not to build on foundations which were not his own; he had suffered sufficiently from other men building on his. But he could address an epistle to the Christians in Rome, and he could pay them a visit later on, and impart some spiritual gift, and then be sent forward by them on his way to Spain.

Looking eastward, he felt a responsibility for Jerusalem, where he had launched that first violent persecution. By now the Jews had been left behind. They had rejected the gospel, and it had passed to the Gentiles; perhaps its rejection by the Jews had stimulated the Gentiles to take it up. The purposes of God were strange; past tracing out. Perhaps the coming in of the Gentiles would stimulate the Jews? At any rate the appeal must be made. He must go up to Jerusalem once more, this time in all the spiritual strength that could be supplied by the prayers and gifts of his Gentile churches, which were themselves a thank-offering to God. It would be a costly and dangerous enterprise, but it must be taken in hand. If their rejection had been the occasion of the reconciliation of the Gentile world to God, what would their acceptance be but something very like life from the dead?

Such is the picture which is brought before us as we read the Epistle to the Romans; a steady picture of the whole Christian world, with Rome at one pole of it in the West, and Jerusalem at the other in the East; and the gospel encircling both.

THE EPISTLE TO THE ROMANS, A.D. 54–55

The task of producing this long Epistle was no light one, and we know that Paul had help. Indeed, it is unlikely that he ever produced any epistle entirely by himself, except possibly Galatians; for he wrote the last sentences at least in his own hand; perhaps the whole. It looks rather as if one copy was taken round and read in each church, the apostle's handwriting being the guarantee of its genuineness; and if so, this is another indication of the haste in which it was written. Copies must have been made in Galatia itself for the churches affected.

The Thessalonian Epistles were written at Corinth. It took three people to write them in the intervals of manual labour and evangelizing. They were certified by Paul's signature on each copy.

The Corinthian Epistles were written from Ephesus, and there, we have suggested, there may have been better facilities for book-production. The First Epistle was carefully composed and arranged, and two people worked on it, Paul and Sosthenes. The earlier Epistles had now proved their value, and had been retained in the churches which had received them, but I Corinthians was designed to be a permanent work of reference. It was certainly not intended to be read through at one session from start to finish, and then put away. On the contrary it was a well-organized manual for church rulers on the subject of church management. It was written for such use at the request of the household of Stephanas, who had assumed the ministerial authority in the church. Nor was it intended to be limited in use to one particular church, a point which is made clear in the address.

> Paul, called to be an apostle of Jesus Christ by the will of God, and Sosthenes the brother,
>
> To the church of God that is in Corinth...with all who call upon the name of the Lord Jesus Christ in every place.

Some scholars have suggested that an editor added this clause at a later date when the Pauline Epistles were prepared for 'publication'. It seems more probable that it was intended for wider circulation from the beginning. It is the epistle which left the clearest impression on the writers of the next generation, and in the old lists and manuscripts it often comes first.

II Corinthians is another matter. Its interest is largely local and personal, and it was connected with a crisis which the Corinthian church might well wish to forget. It may have been at a later date, when Pauline Epistles were in demand, that it was given to the church at large, the 'severe letter' being added as an appendix.

In Romans we recognize another letter which seems to have been intended for wider circulation. It has been thought that there was more than one version of it put out, since a shortened version, in fact, two shortened versions, were in use in the second century. It is not at all likely, however, that either of these existed in the first century. This difficult learned argumentative epistle went out now as the supreme expression of the mind of Paul on the gospel of free forgiveness and grace abounding for all sinners, whether Jew or Gentile. The succeeding generation did not understand it. It was too Jewish.

It may be that the winter of 54–55 saw I Corinthians and Romans sent out for wider distribution. It would seem that there was some sort of literary workshop or scriptorium in connexion with the Corinthian church where copies of such literature could be made. At any rate there was a scribe named Tertius, one of the many who had friends in Rome; he adds his salutations, and affirms that he 'wrote the Epistle in the Lord'. He seems to take some credit.

CHAPTER 8

PILGRIMAGE TO JERUSALEM

Origins of the Roman church, *p.* 148. Christianity in Rome, *p.* 150. The journal of the pilgrimage, A.D. 55 or 56, *p.* 151. Philippi and Troas, *p.* 152. The elders at Ephesus, *p.* 153. The voyage to Caesarea, *p.* 155. James and the elders, *p.* 156. The Epistle of James, *p.* 157. Paul in Jerusalem, A.D. 55–56, *p.* 158. Paul in Caesarea, *p.* 159. The Caesarean imprisonment, A.D. 55–57 or 56–58, *p.* 160. The written gospels, *p.* 161. Festus and Agrippa II, *p.* 163.

ORIGINS OF THE ROMAN CHURCH

It was twenty-four years after the Crucifixion when Paul wrote his Epistle to the Romans, and we are able to make a survey, of a sort, of a remarkable expansion which was still proceeding very vigorously. He could claim that he had brought the gospel in all its fullness from Jerusalem and its neighbourhood, as far as the coast of the Adriatic Sea. It was his *métier*, however, to introduce it where Christ was not named, and that is the reason which he gives for not planning to work in Rome. He has planned to visit the city time and time again, but he has always been prevented. He hopes to visit it now on his way to Spain, where there will be scope for his special type of work. He feels that his work in the regions where he now is has been done; and this was actually true; he had laid foundations which would bear up the weight of Gentile Christianity in those parts.

We do not know what man or men had laid the foundations in Rome. The English translation speaks of them as having been laid by 'another man'; but this is too precise. The word only means that they had been laid by others.

We see no sign of an organized church. The Epistle is directed to all those in Rome who are loved by God and called to be saints. It looks as if the saints in the imperial city were divided into small groups or households. Paul seems to know of about six groups, together with a number of individuals. The Epistle was carried by a 'deacon' of the church at Cenchreae, a lady of the name of Phoebe, who had been a patroness of many; she was one of those prominent women whose services he was an adept at enlisting. The word 'deacon' would not yet seem to have been confined to its technical usage.

She would take the Epistle first to the church in the house of Prisca and Aquila, who had risked their lives for his sake in time past. He mentions with them a certain Epaenetus, whom he calls the first-fruits of Asia. Here was a Roman household with Asian and Corinthian connexions. The next name, Mary, may belong to it, too. Some scholars are surprised to find this group in Rome since we last heard of it in Ephesus. They are also surprised that Paul should send salutations to so many Christians in Rome. A theory has been proposed, therefore, that the chapter was originally part of a lost letter to Ephesus, and has been mistakenly attached to the Epistle to the Romans. On the other hand, it has been pointed out that Aquila would naturally go back to Rome in the interests of his business as soon as the ban against the Jews was lifted; and so would many others.

Next on Paul's list come Andronicus and Junias; or Junia, for this name may be feminine. Paul describes them as his kinsmen, a word which may simply mean that they were Jews. He also calls them fellow-prisoners; and we wonder where this imprisonment may have taken place, for the only imprisonment of which we know so far was the night at Philippi. This reference can be fitted in with the theory that Paul suffered an imprisonment at Ephesus, especially if this salutation was part of an Ephesian letter. Ingenious as this kind of work is, there seems no reason why we should not accept the Epistle as it stands and the history as it comes to us.

Andronicus and Junias were veteran Christians, very likely of Palestinian origin, since their conversion had taken place before Paul's. He describes them as well known, or distinguished, among the apostles. Here was a second centre of active evangelization. The four names which follow may have been attached to this household; three of them, at least, were known to Paul: Ampliatus, Urbanus, and Stachys; he describes Apelles as a man approved in Christ. (Urban had been a fellow worker.)

Two more groups are then mentioned; 'those of Aristobulus', and 'those of Narcissus'. The Aristobulus group and the Narcissus group have been explained as follows. A prince of the house of Herod named Aristobulus had lived in Rome (and Herodion, a Jew, is associated with this group); and there had been a wealthy Roman freedman named Narcissus. Both of these men were dead, and their estates, which would have included many slaves and dependants, may have passed intact into the hands of the emperor, and kept the names of their deceased owners. The name of Narcissus is followed by the names of three women, who were 'workers in the Lord', like Phoebe herself; Tryphaena, Tryphosa, and Persis; and then comes Rufus, and his mother Mary, whom Paul describes as 'his mother, and mine'.

A fifth group now follows, Asyncritus, Phlegon, Hermes, Patrobas, and Hermas, 'and the brethren who are with them'. And these are followed by a sixth, Philologus and Julia, Nereus and his sister, and Olympas, 'and all the saints who are with them'. These are obviously Gentile groups. Paul does not claim any acquaintance with them. They may be examples of a non-Pauline Gentile evangelism.

CHRISTIANITY IN ROME

Is it possible to deduce anything from the Epistle about the special problems of the Roman church? It is a delicate task. We may assume, perhaps, that the responsibility had fallen rather heavily on the Gentile Christians during the five years in which Jews were excluded from the city. Now they were returning, and beginning to play their part again. The apostle sends them an epistle in which a theology of the gospel is worked out in its relation to the state of tension which existed between the Gentile and the Jew in the existing situation. It works out in great detail the doctrine of 'justification by faith' and supports it from the story of Abraham as well as from the gospel of Christ. It speaks of the non-Christian Jews with the greatest tenderness, but its gospel of grace abounding has no room at all for a religion based upon Law. It is a considerable advance upon the Epistle to the Galatians, in which the fighting principles were laid down.

The Christians in Rome seem to have been in danger of the same kind of dissensions as had occurred in Corinth; for there were unworthy evangelists about, who served their own base appetites and deceived the simple-hearted by fair and flattering words. There were differences of opinion and practice among the believers. Some of them observed special days, whereas others regarded all days as alike. Some observed food-rules and others did not. There were some who would not touch flesh-meat at all, which reminds us of the asceticism of John the Baptist and James the Just, who may have had some followers among them. Paul refers to such people as the weaker brethren, since they took seriously these Levitical ordinances; but he urges toleration; they should be 'received', but not to contentious arguments. The groups which Paul is addressing seem to be on the whole of his own way of thought.

There is a third point which may have some significance. He seems to go out of his way, in the catechetical material, to underline the customary Jewish teaching on submission to the civil power, and the payment of tolls and taxes. Any appearance of resistance to the government is to be avoided. Is he thinking perhaps of the riots of 49, when the emperor had taken strong action, and the Christians seem to have got a bad name?

He tells them about his visit to Jerusalem; he asks for their prayers; and he promises to visit them later on.

THE JOURNAL OF THE PILGRIMAGE, A.D. 55 or 56

We now turn to the Acts for Luke's narrative of the pilgrimage to Jerusalem. He comes back into the story himself, for the word 'we' now reappears in the text.

Luke has not told a great deal about Paul's work at Ephesus. He has only given the pictures which he requires to get his dramatic effect. The healings by Paul in Ephesus balance the healing by Peter in Jerusalem. The uproar in the theatre balances the uproar in the Temple at Jerusalem, which was instigated by the same people. (Perhaps Luke is endeavouring to make it clear how riots of this kind actually started.) Ephesus is assimilated to Jerusalem in every way. It even has the coming of the gospel prepared for by disciples of the Baptist. But he does not give much detail about the progress of the church.

Why then does he suddenly give us so much minor detail in his lengthy travel-document? The answer depends upon the character and purpose of the document in the first instance. Why did he write it? What purpose did it serve before it was incorporated into the Acts? The simple theory that he kept a diary is hardly adequate. It is more likely that the journal was intended to serve a definite purpose in the life of the church. Now there is evidence in the Acts that reports were made of what we call 'missionary journeys'; and this pilgrimage had a similar character; for Paul had it in mind that the faith of the Gentiles might stimulate the unbelieving Jews, and so all Israel might be saved. It was an act of ministry and grace.

The Christian public which would be interested in Luke's report would unquestionably be the churches of Greece and Asia from which the pilgrims set forth; for others might make this journey in due course. It demonstrates the establishment of a new life-line of the gospel, a route by sea from Ephesus to Caesarea, and so to Jerusalem, by which of course numbers of Jewish pilgrims (and Gentile God-fearers too, no doubt) were accustomed to travel every year. Gentile Christians could make the same pilgrimage, in association with these groups, or profiting from their experience. It is interesting that Josephus records a number of edicts put out by the authority of the Roman government which protected the rights of the Jews of Ephesus to travel to Jerusalem for the purpose of presenting their devotions and first-fruits (see *Antiquities*, XVI, 6, 7), and this is exactly what Paul claims to have been doing in Acts xxiv. 17.

Luke says nothing about the offering which was being taken up for the church in Jerusalem. His story is not on this level; and to tell the truth, trouble had arisen from time to time in Rome over Jews who collected money to take to Jerusalem. It was better perhaps not to say too much about the financial side of the enterprise; and yet we can deduce from the pages of the Acts that Paul had money at his disposal.

PHILIPPI AND TROAS

When Paul arrived at Philippi, he had seven members of his party with him; Sopater of Berea (perhaps identical with Sosipater); Aristarchus and Secundus of Thessalonica; Gaius of Doberium in Macedonia, who is coupled with Timothy; and Tychicus and Trophimus who represented Ephesus. The use of the word 'we' begins again in this town, where it was dropped five years before, showing that Luke had now joined them. Philippi had been the starting-point for the evangelization of Paul's whole province; it was the one that he remembered with special affection; it was the only one to send him gifts of money when he was in dire need. The seven went on to Troas, but Paul and Luke stayed on for the Passover festival and the seven days of 'unleavened bread' which followed it.

It is worth asking who was put in charge of the church at Philippi when Luke left it. Three or four years later Paul wrote the Philippians a letter, in which he sends greetings to a 'fellow-worker' of the name of

Clement, who would seem, therefore, to have been a member of his own staff. He also sends greetings to the 'bishops and deacons'. This terminology is new to us, and represents a clarification in the organization of the local ministry which seems to have taken place about this time. Some strengthening of the organization had been proved necessary, and all the more because Paul's own guiding hand was being withdrawn. The bishops would appear to have been the men on whom the apostle and his 'fellow-workers' could rely for pastoral oversight. It was a new name, of a non-Jewish character, for those rulers or leaders of the congregation who had been referred to in earlier epistles in more general terms. Clement of Rome, writing to the Corinthians forty years later, gives an account of the appointment of the bishops by the apostles.

They arrived in Troas after five days (which suggests that they had bad weather) and stayed there for a week. A grand farewell service was held for them in an upper room. It is the first description which we possess of a Sunday service. It began on the eve, that is to say the Saturday night, and lasted all through the night, the 'breaking of the bread' taking place before dawn. The inference is that it commemorated the resurrection of the Lord, of which the Passover at Philippi had been the twenty-fifth anniversary.

THE ELDERS AT EPHESUS

Paul took the twenty-mile journey to Assos overland, sending Luke and some of the others by boat, with orders to wait for him there. It is one of the signs that he had money at his disposal. He was in a position to give orders to the skipper.

A four-day sail from Assus brought them to Miletus, a seaport not far from Ephesus. Paul had decided not to visit Ephesus, for one reason or another. He had summoned the elders to meet him at Miletus, no doubt on the following Sunday. The word 'elder' or 'presbyter' is Luke's word for the rulers or leaders of the church. It denotes an honourable or aged man, especially one enrolled in a council or senate. It was a Jewish title of honour, and was used by Luke, of the Rabbis, or members of the Sanhedrin in Jerusalem. Luke's use of the word 'elder' in this instance emphasizes the fact that the church in Ephesus had a council of elders like the church in Jerusalem.

The speech of Paul to the Ephesian elders is a masterpiece of reporting, and in every sentence we can feel the personality of the apostle. He gives a strong charge to the elders. 'Take heed', he says, 'to yourselves, and to the whole flock, in which the Holy Spirit has placed you as bishops, to shepherd the church of God, which he purchased with his own blood.' The feeling of the new word is unmistakable; it indicates here the active pastoral responsibility which had been conferred upon these elders, either individually or as a corporation. The church is confided to their care. Perhaps similar scenes had taken place at other centres, or was this a council of superintendence for all the Pauline churches?

While the words 'elder' and 'bishop' have distinct meanings, it would seem that they are applied here to the same persons; but it does not follow that all elders were bishops. We have here an early stage in the development of a native ministry. A greater degree of personal responsibility was being conferred on the local leadership in the new missions.

The events of the past year had demonstrated the necessity for continual, firm, skilled, tactful supervision of the new converts. It appears that the condition of the Ephesian church had given cause for alarm. A vein of bitterness runs through this great speech. Paul does not altogether trust the men who stand before him. He knows full well that after his departure grievous wolves will enter in, not sparing the flock; but there is worse than that. Some of his own elders or bishops or pastors will teach perversions of the truth, so as to have schools or parties of their own among the disciples. It may be that some of these men had not supported him during the recent troubles. Someone had certainly accused him of making money out of his churches, a charge which had also been flung against him at Corinth. 'I coveted no man's silver or gold', he says suddenly. 'You yourselves know well that these hands have ministered to my needs!'

Obviously he thrust forth his hands or gestured with them; a habit of his in speaking to which Luke alludes more than once. We see him there, eager, and passionately sincere, and full of love for his people; seeing things so much clearer than any of them. It was an emotional scene, and there were tears and laments as they knelt on the shore to receive his blessing; for he had said that they would never see his face again.

There are a number of scholars who believe that they never did see his face again; but the Pastoral Epistles contain evidence which makes it highly probable that he came back, and found matters every bit as bad as he had feared.

THE VOYAGE TO CAESAREA

At Patara they found a boat which was taking on freight for Tyre on the Phoenician coast, and they succeeded in getting passages on her. There must have been a great deal of coastwise trade for them to trust to such casual connexions, but no doubt they were on the regular pilgrim route.

In his speech at Miletus Paul had said that the prophets in every city had advised him against going up to Jerusalem, where chains and imprisonment would be his lot. The prophets at Tyre were no exception to the rule. The ship touched at Ptolemais, the sea-port of Galilee, before going on to Caesarea. There they stayed with Philip, who was now styled the 'evangelist', still another new word which seems to have come in at this time. It was a title for those 'fellow-workers' or colleagues of the apostles who shared their missionary labours and some of their responsibilities, but could not rank as apostles themselves. Timothy is so described in the Pastorals; and in Ephesians the word is slipped in after the apostles and prophets, and before the pastors and teachers, who may be much the same as the elders and bishops. The word did not survive; but some word did seem to be needed at the time to distinguish these missionaries and evangelists from the local ministries in the missions.

Philip had been at Caesarea for twenty years now. He was married, and had four daughters who 'prophesied'. These daughters were called 'virgins'; and in the context the word seems to refer to the ascetic life. There were celibates at Corinth, and Paul had indicated his preference for this condition of life, which was not, however, a lifelong obligation. Philip himself, it may be inferred, had not shared this view. Agabus the prophet came down from Jerusalem to welcome them and added his word of warning to those who had been predicting imprisonment or possible death for Paul when he reached the city. He reinforced his message with solemn symbolic acts. All present implored Paul not to go; but nothing could shake his resolution. In narrating these scenes, Luke does not hesitate to indicate a certain likeness to the story of Jesus going up to Jerusalem for the Passion.

They cannot have expected Paul to come back alive; and that is what may have been understood at Miletus, when he said that they would see his face no more; but there lingered at the back of his own mind the thought that he was destined to see Rome before he died.

JAMES AND THE ELDERS

The party was conducted to Jerusalem by Christians from Caesarea, who brought them to the house of an 'original disciple' named Mnason, who was a Cypriot like Barnabas. Here they lodged. It was the Feast of Pentecost, fifty days after the Passover at Philippi, and twenty-five years after the historic day when the Holy Spirit had descended upon the mother-church; undoubtedly Luke heard the story at first hand now, and saw for himself what Pentecost was like in Jerusalem. We know that Luke, Aristarchus and Trophimus were in the party; and we assume that the other delegates who had gathered at Philippi were there too. It was certainly a bold stroke of genius which had brought these Gentile converts face to face with the oldest Christian church, in the city where the Lord himself had been crucified and risen from the dead. They were received gladly by the brethren, and here the word 'we' fades out of the narrative for a while. The tale of the pilgrimage was told.

On the following day James the Just summoned his sanhedrin of elders to hear the report of progress from the Gentile churches there represented. The offering for the needs of the poor saints must have been handed over, though Luke says nothing about this. James, on his part, did not disguise the great danger that Paul was in. There seems by now to have been an intense hatred for him personally, which had been methodically fostered by his enemies; and conditions in Palestine had steadily deteriorated under the rule of the procurators. Misgovernment on one side had been matched by lawlessness on the other, and Josephus speaks of impostors who deluded the multitude, and fanatics who advocated violence. He was a young man of nineteen at this time, and he tells us with a feeling of personal horror of the murder in the temple of the high priest Jonathan by bandits who were in the pay of Felix the new procurator, only a year or two after his visit. He also mentions the appearance about this time of an Egyptian 'prophet', who gathered his followers on the Mount of Olives to see the walls of

Jerusalem fall down at his command. Four hundred of these had been massacred by the cavalry and footmen of Felix; but the Egyptian had escaped.

THE EPISTLE OF JAMES

There are passages in the Epistle of St James which fit this period well:

> From whence come wars and fightings among you? Come they not even hence, even of your lusts that war in your members? Ye lust and have not; ye kill, and desire to have, and cannot obtain.... Go to now, ye rich men, weep and howl for your miseries that shall come upon you. Your riches are corrupt.... Behold the hire of the labourers who have reaped your fields, which is of you kept back by fraud, crieth out; and the cries of them which have reaped, are entered into the ears of the Lord of hosts.

The picture of the wealthy magnates which we gather from the pages of Josephus, with their bands of armed men and their oppression of the poor, is in line with this prophetic denunciation.

There is insufficient evidence to come to a firm conclusion about the date and destination of this Epistle, which is addressed to the Jewish or Christian 'dispersion' overseas; but many passages in it seem to have a Palestinian background. If the teaching of James was given by him in a fixed oral form according to the Rabbinic custom, and recited in a fixed order, and translated into Greek for the Hellenists, and written down in that language, and given conventional literary form for wider distribution, the result might be something very like the Epistle of St James. The theory of so early a date as this is supported by the fact that it deals with the same argument about faith and works which Paul handled in his Epistle to the Romans; though it comes to it from a very different point of view. This early date is certainly not impossible, though not many scholars would think it likely.

James explained to Paul that the extreme Judaizing party in the Jerusalem church was now very powerful, numbering tens of thousands, he says in a typical oriental exaggeration. He was satisfied himself with the decision of the council of six years before, but they had been infected with another spirit. They had been told that Paul was preaching apostasy from the Law of Moses, and teaching the Jews of the Dispersion not to circumcise their children or walk in the customs. They would need further assurance.

He therefore suggested that Paul should associate himself in a public way with a group of men who were under a Nazirite vow, and so demonstrate his adhesion to the Law. It would also be an act of piety, as he would pay the expenses of these men. Paul had no objection to this. He had taken a vow of this sort himself, Luke says, on the occasion of his visit to Jerusalem three years before. But it does not sound a very promising scheme; and it did not work. It was not the Jerusalem Christians, however, who caused the trouble; it was a gang of Jewish pilgrims from Ephesus, who set upon him when he appeared in the Temple to take part in these ceremonies. There was a scene of violence and confusion which rivalled the uproar in Ephesus the previous year. It was with great difficulty that the Roman commanding officer, Claudius Lysias, saved him from the hands of the mob.

PAUL IN JERUSALEM, A.D. 55–56

The first task of the officer was to find out the identity of his prisoner and the cause of the riot. The Ephesian Jews accused him of bringing the uncircumcised Gentile, Trophimus, into the Temple; and this was not an altogether ridiculous insinuation, if Paul had claimed that his Gentiles were fellow-citizens with the saints, and members of the house of God, Jesus the Messiah having destroyed the partition or fence which had divided them, as we read in the Epistle to the Ephesians.

The officer was under the impression that he was the Egyptian prophet mentioned by Josephus. It is odd that he permitted Paul to address the crowd, but perhaps he thought he might get some information that way, or at any rate gain time. The crowd was prepared to hear Paul speak in Greek, a fact which shows how general the knowledge of this language was; and they were delighted when he used Aramaic. The speech gives the best account we have of Paul's early life, and mentions his instruction by Gamaliel and the part he had played in the stoning of Stephen. It was twenty years ago now, but the memory disturbed him at this moment of crisis. Does it give the clue to the tremendous determination with which he had persisted in his visit to Jerusalem? Was it an act of oblation and atonement and satisfaction? Was there in his mind at all times the picture of the body of the martyr, broken and buried under its pile of huge stones, and then a blaze of light, and a voice which said, 'Saul, Saul, why are you persecuting me?'

The crowd listened in silence until he came to the vision in the Temple in which he had been sent 'far off to the Gentiles'; and then a roar of enmity and hatred went up, comparable to that which had greeted Jesus when he had stood in the same place on the morning of his crucifixion.

Paul was hurried into the safety of the fortress of Antonia, the military headquarters on the north side of the Temple enclosure, which contained the *praetorium* which had once been occupied by Pilate. The next expedient was examination by torture; but this was illegal in the case of a Roman citizen, and Paul successfully claimed this privilege for a second time. The next expedient was unsuccessful too; it was an inquiry before the high priest, Ananias the son of Nebediah, an unprincipled ruffian, who had amassed wealth by the use of violence. He ordered Paul to be struck on the mouth when he began to speak, and there was a hot exchange of words, for which Paul apologized. Then, looking round the sanhedrin, he played with success for the support of his old friends. For there would be Simon ben Gamaliel, the son of his old tutor, and the wise and broad-minded Johanan ben Zakkai, who would give spiritual leadership to Israel after the fall of Jerusalem; and others who were neither Zealots nor fanatics. Some moderation still existed in Israel, and we would look for it among the more judicious Pharisees. They had something in common with the Nazaraeans, for they believed in an angelic world and in a resurrection from the dead; some were even disposed to admit that an angel or spirit had appeared to Paul on the Damascus road. The solemn discussion turned into a loud and angry battle, and Lysias had to rescue his prisoner a second time.

PAUL IN CAESAREA

A second inquiry was planned, but information came in through a young nephew of Paul that there was a plan to assassinate him on the way to the hall in which the sanhedrin met; and Lysias thought it better to get him out of the city. He sent him to Caesarea, where an inquiry was held by that accomplished politician the procurator Felix. The Sadducee hierarchy knew that a theological approach was useless, so they hired an 'orator' or professional lawyer, named Tertullus, to do his best on their behalf; Luke summarizes his speech, preserving the Latin turn of his sentences. Paul heard himself described as a pestilential person, a promoter of revolution throughout the world, and a ringleader of the sect called the Nazaraeans. We have heard nothing since Gallio's judgement of this accusation of sedition against the Roman empire; but it comes out in an official form now, sponsored by the Jerusalem hierarchy.

Paul's reply is also summarized. It becomes clear that Luke is keeping a careful record of the riots and imprisonments and legal investigations in which Paul was concerned. He is building up a case for the defence, and this is an important motive in both his volumes, being prepared for in his account of the trial of Jesus.

Paul followed the example of Tertullus in paying a conventional compliment to Felix. He gave a picture of himself as an orthodox Jewish pilgrim, coming up to Jerusalem after many years 'to give alms to my nation'; for there had to be some reference to the financial side of his visit. He asked for evidence of his alleged desecration of the Temple; but the Ephesian Jews were no longer available, and the case was adjourned indefinitely.

THE CAESAREAN IMPRISONMENT, A.D. 55–57 or 56–58

Paul was kept a prisoner in Caesarea for two years under fairly easy conditions. His friends were allowed access to him. Sometimes Felix would send for him and listen to his preaching on righteousness and self-mastery and the coming judgement; but though he trembled at the words, he was not convicted of sin. In just the same way Herod Antipas, the late tetrarch of Galilee, had listened to the preaching of his formidable prisoner John the Baptist; and Drusilla, the wife of Felix, was a daughter of Herod Agrippa, and therefore a niece by marriage of Herod Antipas, and a cousin of the daughter of Herodias, whose dancing had cost John his head. She sat beside her husband when Paul preached.

Actually it was an understood thing that a Roman governor made a fortune out of the province that he administered, and Felix was holding out for a bribe; another sign that Paul had money at his command at this time. The economic factor has to be remembered, even in church history.

13. NERO

14. CHRISTIAN FUNERARY SYMBOLISM

The two years at Caesarea were spent by Luke in literary labours; an assumption which explains in the most natural way the appearance in his two volumes of excellent Palestinian material, and particularly of Caesarean material in the Acts. He states that he obtained his material from men who had been eyewitnesses of the 'Word' from the beginning; and this is the occasion when he had the time and opportunity to collect it. We note a few interesting references to the Herodian family; in his Gospel he speaks of Joanna the wife of Chuza who had been Herod's steward, and in the Acts he mentions Menahem whom he describes as a foster-brother of Herod himself. Both of these were Christians. We think of Drusilla in Caesarea, and are not surprised to discover this special knowledge.

It has been suggested that some of Paul's Epistles were written from Caesarea. Philippians, Colossians, Ephesians, and Philemon were written during an imprisonment, but they seem to fit better into the Roman imprisonment, to which they are generally assigned. The suggestion has its value, however. It reminds us that, during these years, there must have been a close connexion between the churches of Palestine and the churches of Asia. A line of communication had been established from Caesarea to Ephesus along which the current of the gospel would flow. It was a route which by-passed Antioch, Galatia, and Phrygia. The importance of Caesarea in the Acts fits into this new geographical pattern.

THE WRITTEN GOSPELS

It is very generally assumed by scholars that written gospel documents were now in circulation; and one of these was the document which is alluded to by the symbol 'Q'; a document which Luke made use of in the composition of his Gospel, which may have been taking some sort of shape at this time.

This statement is made as a result of the literary analysis of the Gospels which has been carried on by scholars of various nationalities and points of view for over a hundred years now. The first step of importance was the recognition of the fact that Matthew and Luke both made use of Mark in composing their own Gospels. When the material obtained from Mark has been eliminated from consideration, it is possible to see that there was another document or group of documents which Matthew and Luke both made use of. It may safely be regarded as a single document. It cannot be reconstructed in its entirety, but we have a fairly good view of its contents. This is the document known as 'Q', and it may have been available as early as the fifties.

The third step was the theory of 'Proto-Luke'. It was observed that the material which Luke obtained from Mark was incorporated into his Gospel at a late stage in its composition. If this Marcan material is eliminated from consideration, we are left with what appears to be an older form of Luke, or possibly an earlier draft of his Gospel, which he made before Mark came his way. This hypothetical first stage in the making of Luke is called Proto-Luke. It is one of those rare things, a satisfactory literary theory. It creates no difficulties of its own, and fits very happily into the ascertainable facts. On the other hand, the arguments in its favour have not convinced all scholars by any means; but, while it may not be safe to think of it in terms of a completed Lucan Gospel earlier than Mark, the evidence does seem to point to considerable literary work on good Palestinian material independently of Mark.

One component part of this Lucan groundwork was the document Q, whose existence has been independently demonstrated. The remainder (which may be called L) appears to consist of good Palestinian material which assumed its present form in surroundings of a Hellenistic character; that is to say in some church of the type of Caesarea which had access to the primary tradition. There must have been numbers of 'original disciples' like Mnason the Cypriot; and there were also the teachers and evangelists of the Palestinian church with their organized tradition of the sayings and doings of Jesus; and men like Philip himself, who was the principal representative of the old Hellenistic tradition of Jerusalem. Luke also obtained some stories about the birth of Jesus and John the Baptist, which would naturally have come to him from their families, whose place of residence he gives as the hill-country of Judaea. It has often been remarked that he tells these stories from the point of view of the women. There are other women mentioned in his Gospel; Mary and Martha for instance; and Joanna the wife of Chuza.

An interesting point now emerges. The collector and editor of the Proto-Luke material does not seem to have had direct access to the Galilean or Petrine tradition. His Resurrection narratives, for instance, are all connected with Jerusalem, and he tells them in a way which appears to leave no room for the appearance in Galilee which is promised in Mark, and actually related in Matthew. Each locality, and each apostolic school, may still, to some extent, have been working with its own special form of the tradition. Certainly the Galilean tradition of Peter as Mark knew it cannot have been personally available to Luke when he collected his earliest material or made the first draft of his Gospel; we must suppose that it was being carried on elsewhere, in Galilee perhaps, or even farther afield now.

This is simply an inference from the literary phenomena; but it is confirmed by the record of the Acts at this point. Peter was not present at Jerusalem or Caesarea for this visit of Paul and Luke; he is not mentioned in Luke's journal; and this evidence falls into line with the second-century legends which place him in Antioch, where indeed we heard of him prior to his appearance at the Jerusalem Council.

FESTUS AND AGRIPPA II

If we knew at what date Porcius Festus succeeded Felix in Caesarea, we would be able to regulate our dates with greater exactness. As it is we have to fall back upon our general chronological plan, and assign it to 57 or 58; a date which is obtained by working forward from the arrival of Gallio in Corinth in 51 or 52.

Felix was recalled to Rome to answer for his misdeeds, but he was shielded from their consequences, apparently by the wealth of his brother Pallas. When Festus arrived in Palestine, he found the country infested by dagger-men (*sicarii*); and the high-priestly families were using their organized gangs to attack one another. The new high priest Ishmael, who had succeeded the murdered Jonathan, suggested that Paul should be brought back to Jerusalem for trial, with the intention, Luke says, of arranging for his assassination en route; but Paul stood on his rights as a Roman citizen and refused to go. He was ready for martyrdom, but had no intention of disappearing from sight as part of the new procurator's policy of appeasement. The priests came down to Caesarea, but did no more than repeat their charges of political activity. Paul, weary with the long delay, played his last card. He appealed to Caesar.

He could do this as a Roman citizen. This citizenship had been artificially extended to include large numbers of people who were in no sense Roman. It could be bought at a price, like most things in the political world, but once it was obtained it was hereditary. Paul had inherited it from his father.

Festus was as much at a loss as Lysias had been to understand what offence Paul was charged with; and he took advantage of a courtesy visit from King Herod Agrippa II, and his sister Bernice, to hear a statement from Paul on the subject. Agrippa had now given up his Lebanese kingdom in exchange for territory east and west of the Sea of Galilee, and this was further added to from time to time. He was also given a certain oversight of the Temple and its services; for the sacred books required the presence of a king at certain rituals. He would be the right person for the procurator to consult on a point affecting the Jewish religion.

Paul made the best of this opportunity of placing his own story and the claims of the gospel before the young king who would reign over northern Israel for more than forty years. He stood before him in chains, and faithfully unfolded the story of his conversion, which Luke thus gives us for the third time. He attempted to argue the case for the Resurrection. He insisted on his loyalty to the old religion, which he asserted had not been impaired by his adherence to the gospel. It was all in line with the Law and the Prophets, and was the fulfilment of the hope which every Israelite cherished.

It is one of the commonplaces of criticism to contrast the Paul who walks through the pages of Acts with the Paul who talks through the pages of his Epistles. We may note one fundamental quality which they have in common. He is a fanatic; for all his infinite variety, his mind runs on one thing: the gospel. He presses forward to his goal; he evangelizes in season and out of season; he strikes recklessly but with the accuracy of genius. He scandalizes. He shocks.

In the Jewish synagogue he proclaims Jesus as the king; in the home of Greek philosophy he proclaims him as judge of the world; to the hostile mob of Jews in the Temple, he speaks of a mission to the Gentiles; when he stands before Felix, he terrifies him with the thought of a judgement to come (and it came): standing now before the descendant of the Herods and the Maccabees, he attempts to convert him.

The procurator sees a power in Paul's eyes which makes him uneasy. He takes it for insanity, and breaks in on his discourse. 'You're mad, Paul,' he says, 'Your great learning is driving you insane.'

The apostle attempts to tighten his hold on the situation. He turns to the young king.

'King Agrippa, believest thou the scriptures? I know that thou believest.'

Agrippa tries to laugh it off.

'You and your believing', he says. 'You are certainly losing no time in trying to make a *Christian* out of *me*', using the new name which was finding its way into use in Roman official circles. But he agreed with Festus that there was no serious charge against him; he could have been released if he had not appealed to Caesar.

CHAPTER 9

PAUL IN ROME

The emperor Nero, *p.* 166. Paul in Rome, A.D. 59–61, *p.* 170. Paul's staff and correspondence, *p.* 171. Philemon and Onesimus, *p.* 172. The Epistle to the Colossians, *p.* 173. The Colossian 'heresy', *p.* 173. Christianity as a world-religion, *p.* 175. The Epistle to the Ephesians, *p.* 177. The church in the world, *p.* 179. The Epistle to the Philippians, *p.* 180. Bishops and deacons, *p.* 181. The date of the Acts, *p.* 182. The release of Paul, *p.* 184.

THE EMPEROR NERO

The story of the Roman empire in the first half of the first century lends colour to the constant refrain of the Jewish apocalypses that everything was gradually getting worse. The excellent system of administration inaugurated by Augustus was preserved by his successor Tiberius; but the funds which had been accumulated by his frugality were wasted by the extravagance of Caligula. The reorganization of the imperial civil service under Claudius and the careful economy of his management left the administration in a good condition, but it suffered severely under Nero.

Claudius had married a widow named Agrippina with a boy of seven named Nero, who was soon married to his daughter Octavia. When Nero was seventeen, Agrippina arranged for Claudius to be poisoned, so that Nero could succeed him as emperor. Britannicus, the son of Claudius, did not long survive, and neither did Octavia.

During the first eight years of Nero's rule, from 54 to 62, the government was administered under the direction of Seneca and Burrhus. Seneca was the brother of the proconsul Gallio who had acquitted Paul at Corinth or at any rate dismissed the charge against him. He was a philosopher of the Stoic persuasion, and believed in a providence which overruled human affairs. He identified the highest promptings of the human heart with the voice of God. He even tried to teach these views to Nero. Burrhus was a soldier of high reputation, in charge of the praetorian cohort, that is to say the military guards attached to the emperor's person. As 'praetorian prefect', he had the supreme jurisdiction over criminal cases, including such as came from a distance.

He was also the head of the Greek secretariat, which meant that he handled the correspondence affecting the eastern part of the empire.

In the time of Augustus the civil service, as we would call it, had been housed in the emperor's palace; by now it overflowed these limits, but the expression 'Caesar's household' was still in use. Ambitious provincials from all over the world found their way into the departments of state; they included Jews, Syrians, Samaritans, and even Christians, since Paul speaks of the saints in Caesar's household. There was scope here for the 'freedmen' or ex-slaves, some of whom had made great fortunes and exercised considerable influence. One of these plutocrats was Pallas, the brother of the procurator Felix; and when Felix arrived back in Rome in disgrace it was the influence of his brother that saved him from punishment. So two at least of Paul's judges were in Rome when he arrived there, Felix and Gallio; and it is easy to understand why Luke points out, in the Acts, that they had not taken the case against him seriously.

Two deputations from Caesarea, one Greek and one Jewish, came to Rome in connexion with the case of Felix, and also with complaints against one another; and the Greeks are said to have won their case against the Jews by bribing Burrhus. Josephus, from whose history we glean this information, was in Rome himself a couple of years later, with a deputation of the higher priestly officials from Jerusalem. Affairs in Palestine, therefore, were by no means unfamiliar to official circles in Rome. Members of the Herodian royal family resided there permanently.

Nero was twenty-two years old, and was enjoying his unrivalled opportunities of cultivating pleasures of all kinds. He is quite a notable figure in the dreary annals of sex-perversion. His desire to excel in poetry and music and chariot-racing seems to have been genuine; and perhaps he was not without talent. An emperor who was a play-boy was a novelty and won the popular fancy. Shortly after the arrival of Paul in the city, he shocked society by the murder of his mother, who had committed every crime to place him on the throne. His fantastic figure passed into legend, and appears in myth and apocalypse and oracular verse.

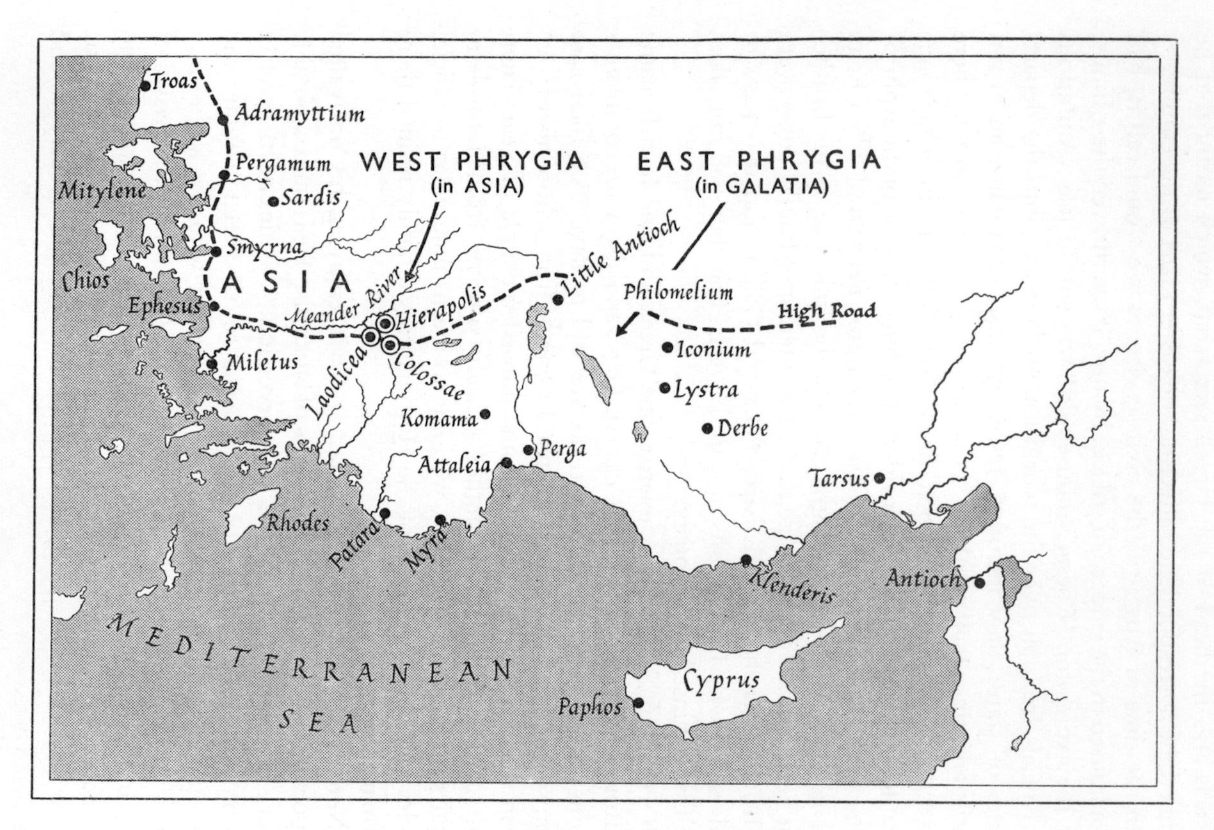

Map 4. Asia, showing St Paul's churches A.D. 60.

NOTES ON MAP 4

The main feature of this map is the high road from east to west, which we have described as the life-line of the gospel.

The first step in the evangelization of this area had been when Paul and Barnabas landed at Attaleia in 48, and made their way north to Little Antioch; it was at Perga that Mark had left them. Paul and Barnabas had evangelized the east-Phrygian cities of *Little Antioch*, *Iconium*, *Lystra*, and *Derbe*. They were situated in the Roman province of 'Galatia'; the west-Phrygian cities were situated in the Roman province of 'Asia'.

In 49 he visited them the second time, coming by road from his native city of Tarsus in Cilicia, striking north-west to Troas, and finally reaching Corinth.

In 52 he came along this road again from Antioch, his 'third missionary journey', and reached *Ephesus*, where he worked for three years. It became the next centre of evangelism. The gospel was heard throughout the province of Asia; but Paul never visited the west-Phrygian cities; nor did he evangelize Smyrna.

Over two hundred miles separated Ephesus from Little Antioch, and it was desirable to have bases of operation at some intermediate point. The evangelist of *Laodicea*, *Hierapolis*, and *Colossae* was an agent of Paul's named Epaphroditus, of whom we hear during Paul's imprisonment at Rome in 59–61. Paul sent an epistle to Laodicea which is lost; and one to Colossae which has been preserved; it has attached to it the Epistle to Philemon. Hierapolis is mentioned.

Mark, who had failed to accompany Paul in the task of evangelizing eastern Phrygia, has now come into contact with the new churches in western Phrygia. Some years later the apostle Philip settled at Hierapolis and made it his headquarters.

PAUL IN ROME, A.D. 59–61

When Paul arrived in Rome, early in 58 or 59 according to our computation (or possibly a year later), he was treated with indulgence, and allowed to take up his residence, with the soldier who guarded him, in a house or apartment, of which he paid the rent. This is the final piece of evidence, in the Acts, to show that he had funds at his disposal at this time.

He invited the leaders of the Jewish community to his lodgings and stated his case, making it clear that he had never attacked the old religion and that he had been betrayed into the hands of the Romans, who were prepared to release him, had he not been forced to appeal to Nero by the continued pressure of the Jerusalem authorities on the government at Caesarea. In reply they professed blandly that they had received no letters from Jerusalem, and that none of the brethren who had come from Judaea had brought an adverse report about him. It sounds rather smooth, but there may well have been some truth in it, so far as strictly official communications were concerned. The commotion in the Temple had taken place two and a half years before, the witnesses were dispersed, and there was no case against Paul worth mentioning. Silence and delay might be the best tactics for Paul's opponents.

As for the 'sect of the Nazareans', the Jewish leaders went on to say, all they knew was that it was everywhere spoken against. They professed their willingness to hear what Paul had to say in its favour, but naturally there was no agreement. Some believed and some disbelieved, a statement which shows that there were Christians in Rome among the synagogue-rulers themselves. Paul turned to the Gentiles once more.

This narrative rather confirms our impression that no Christian ecclesia had yet been formed in Rome. If various Christian groups or households were loosely attached to the synagogues, or were good members of them, we can understand the reluctance of the Jewish authorities to antagonize Paul. The hiving-off of the believers must have been a financial and social loss to the synagogue as well as a spiritual humiliation; and in view of the disturbances in the reign of Claudius and the consequent banishment of the Jews from Rome, they may have thought it best to keep the peace and let the matter settle itself.

PAUL'S STAFF AND CORRESPONDENCE

The Acts ends by telling us that Paul lived for two years at Rome in his own house, receiving visitors, preaching about Jesus and the kingdom of God, and meeting with no let and hindrance in his work. This house, or church, became a centre or headquarters for his evangelistic work, not only in Rome, but also in distant lands. He gathered about him some of his old colleagues, and added more. He wrote a number of letters, of which four are preserved. Philemon, Colossians, and Ephesians form a single group, and are linked together by obvious literary connexions; Philippians was written independently.

Timothy appears as a co-author in Philemon, Colossians, and Philippians; he had joined Paul in Rome, therefore, and was now his trusted colleague in his apostolic work. Other arrivals from Asia Minor were Tychicus of Ephesus, and an evangelist named Epaphras, who had been at work in Colossae and other Phrygian cities. Still another was Mark, who may have arrived with Epaphras. Luke and Aristarchus were still with him; and there were two new members of his staff, Demas, who was a Gentile like Luke, and Jesus Justus, who was a Jew like Aristarchus. As they all send greetings to Colossae, it would seem that they had some prior connexion with Asia Minor. It looks as if the Pauline household in Rome was an extension of his Aegean mission, though of course Demas and Justus may have been Romans.

The question has been asked whether these Epistles might not have been written in some other place, during some other imprisonment. It has been suggested that they were written during some imprisonment at Ephesus, where all these men might congregate more easily; but no evidence for such an imprisonment can be found. The suggestion that they were written from Caesarea creates no insuperable difficulty; but the picture which we derive from them of a large group of assistants and busy evangelistic activity seems to fit better into the two years at Rome, where there was no impediment to the preaching of the gospel, than into the two years at Caesarea, of which nothing of the sort is said.

PHILEMON AND ONESIMUS

In the Lycus valley of the Phrygian country, which Paul had passed by on his 'second missionary journey', there were three important cities, Colossae (or Colossi), Hierapolis, and Laodicea. Epaphras had been directing the work of evangelization in these three cities; and in one of them (probably Colossae) there was a church in the house of a man named Philemon, who was also one of Paul's colleagues. 'To Philemon our fellow-worker', he writes, 'and to Appia the sister, and Archippus our fellow-soldier, and the church that is in thy house.' We have before us here a little picture of the local unit in the church order; the 'bishop' or 'man in charge', and possibly his wife, since the word 'sister' obviously means a believer; and the house in which he lives, which is both a church and a guest-house. At the end of the Epistle, Paul bids him to prepare a room for him which he can occupy after his release, which he hopes for as the outcome of their prayers. He does not give Philemon the title of bishop, but he was the manager, or even the owner, of a house-church, where Paul claims the right (if he cared to exercise it) to give orders. Archippus, too, had a ministerial position, as we learn from Colossians.

Onesimus was a slave in this household. He was not yet a Christian; but he had taken advantage of his master's forbearance to go off to Rome, following Epaphras perhaps, to seek out Paul in his imprisonment. Paul had received him and given him baptism. It is clear that he was an attractive young man and must have had some education; for Paul would have preferred to keep him as a member of his staff. But this would not have been right, and he had persuaded him to return, giving him a letter to Philemon in which he urged him to take him back, no longer as a slave, but as a brother beloved. 'If you regard me as your partner,' he goes on to say, 'receive him as you would myself; if he has defrauded you, or if he owes you anything, charge it to my account; I will repay it; I Paul; I write it with my own hand.' We observe once more that he has money at his disposal.

This letter, with its personal touches, is unlike any other in the Pauline collection, but it is not altogether a personal letter. It is a letter to a church, like the others; the church in the house of Philemon. It was carried by Tychicus, an Ephesian Christian, who had been one of the seven who were chosen to accompany Paul to Jerusalem. He carried with it the Epistle to the Colossians and the so-called Epistle to the Ephesians. He also carried a letter to the church at Laodicea; but this has not been preserved. They went in the same mail-bag. They are all related, by various small touches, to the same group of persons. They appear as a group in later collections or catalogues of Pauline writings.

THE EPISTLE TO THE COLOSSIANS

Paul had never visited these Phrygian churches, but they had been constantly in his prayers. He was delighted to hear of their faith and their hope and their love; and so intensely real was his prayer-life that he felt that he was actually with them, watching their strong discipline and excellent church order.

As we read the Epistle to the Colossians, we are conscious of still another shift in the direction of Paul's thinking. It is one of the fascinating things about this man that we can see his mind grow and mature and put out new branches. He appears in a purely evangelical phase in Galatians; he passes very close to an adventist phase in Thessalonians; he was in a church-building and organizing phase in I Corinthians; he went through a crisis of mystical experience in II Corinthians; in Romans he attempted to work out a broad level theology and achieved it; in Colossians he has become a teacher of mysteries. He is still, of course, the servant of Almighty God, and the ambassador of Jesus Christ in the work of evangelization, but this work now includes the task of admonishing every man and teaching every man in all wisdom, and this he says because he does not want to see the new converts made the fools of false logic and persuasive speaking, or the prey of philosophy and vain deceit.

THE COLOSSIAN 'HERESY'

We have watched the growth in the Pauline churches of an attitude of mind and a type of teaching and practice which was apt to cause divisions. It has not been sufficiently organized to be called a heresy or a party, but it has produced a crop of talkers, some of them local elders or prophets, no doubt; but others seem to have been professionals passing from church to church and making their living thereby; false copies of the true evangelist or teacher. Such men have appeared in Colossae and

Laodicea, and that is why Epaphras has come to Rome for advice and instructions, Nymphas being left in charge at Laodicea, and Philemon with Archippus at Colossae (or Hierapolis?).

There had been previous correspondence with the Colossians in which the name of Mark had been mentioned; if he came to them, they were to receive him. We last heard of Mark ten years previously, when Paul had refused to accept his services and he had gone off to Cyprus with his cousin Barnabas. We do not know what had happened in the interval. Even now it looks as if his status in the Pauline mission was open to question. Paul may be trying to efface some unfavourable impression or to counteract criticism of some sort.

The false teachers who had come to Colossae were Jews,[1] as most evangelists and teachers must still have been, but the Judaism which they promoted was neither of the Law nor of the Gospel. It was a Judaism which had been assimilated to the prevailing oriental philosophy of religion. It was the precursor of what came to be known as 'gnosis' or knowledge; a bold claim to a mystical understanding about unseen worlds and a more holy life in this one. It gloried in 'myth' and was familiar with the names of spirits and daemons and angels—the 'authorities and powers' as Paul calls them. It cultivated the magical, the ascetic and the ritualistic. It was a case of 'touch not, taste not, handle not'. The old Hebrew tradition supplied them with names of angels, and even of the deity; it provided fast-days and rituals and forms of asceticism, Sabbaths and new moons and feasts, distinctions of food, and abstinences for certain occasions. Out of such material it was not difficult to build up a magico-philosophic system that seemed to confer superior wisdom and superior holiness. Circumcision was mentioned, apparently; sacrifice apparently not. It was from a ferment of this kind that the Jewish heresies in Palestine emerged.

What place these teachers assigned to Christ in their hierarchy of authorities and powers, we do not know; but Paul is careful in the first part of his Epistle to give him a position of divine sovereignty, superior to any angels or 'thrones or principalities or authorities or powers'; for he is the head and ruler over all things, and in him and through him and unto him were all things created; furthermore he 'cast off' the principalities and powers, and paraded them openly, by triumphing

[1] They may have been in occupation of the territory before the Pauline mission established itself.

over them in the cross. The passage which we have lamely represented here is conceived in a vein of high imaginative mysticism, which Paul had caught perhaps from the gnostic teachers themselves. When Paul faces a new situation, or enters into a new controversy, we see a new vocabulary emerge to suit the situation and, if we may suggest it, a new personality to suit the controversy. He outdoes the rival teachers themselves in asserting the divine sovereignty of the Christ, and the glory of his triumph on this earth.

But this is not a complete explanation of the new emphasis in his theology. Three years of imprisonment did not leave him unchanged.

He advises the new ecclesia to adhere firmly to the traditions which it had been taught 'in Christ'; and he supplies an interesting text of the baptismal catechism or exhortation. They have died with Christ and risen with Christ in the baptismal waters. They have shared in his exaltation and triumph. They must clothe themselves with the Christ, casting off the sinful self and putting on the new man. They must wear the Christian graces of mercy and kindness and lowliness and humility. They must practise mutual forbearance and love, following the example of Christ. The peace of Christ must reign in their hearts. The word of Christ must dwell in them richly in all knowledge; it must manifest itself in wisdom and sound teaching, in psalms and spiritual hymns, and in eucharistic worship addressed to God the Father in the name of the Lord Jesus. This is a notable catechetical and eucharistic text, another version of which is given in Ephesians. The word Christ runs through it—the divine king.

He subjoins the code of domestic and social relations, rather elaborating the section on slaves and their masters, perhaps with his eye on Philemon and Onesimus. He ends with the admonition to watch and pray.

CHRISTIANITY AS A WORLD-RELIGION

There had been times when Paul seemed to embrace a thorough-going apocalypticism and to be absorbed in the dream of the second advent; and there were other times when he seemed to incline dangerously near to the super-spiritual view that the spirit is all and the flesh is nothing. Actually, in spite of many unguarded utterances, he saved the church from falling into either of these extremes, though his too-fervid admirers deviated into the ultra-spiritual heresy. It was as a teacher of wisdom that he was remembered in the sub-apostolic church. The churches valued his admonitions, which touched so many points of real difficulty and perplexity.

What the Roman world saw in Paul, if we may trust Tertullus, was a ringleader of the sect of the Nazareans, a semi-political figure, promoting an international revolutionary form of Judaism which was gaining converts fast and was a menace to law and order. It had even been alleged that he spoke of another king or emperor, a man called Jesus or Christus. Paul did indeed speak of a 'Lord' whom he called Christus—the divine king; but how far is it true that Christianity was a revolutionary force?

There were two dominions or sovereignties in the Christian imagination, the sovereignty of this age or 'aeon', and the sovereignty of God in the higher realms. This sovereignty of God was focused somehow in the person of the Christ, who was exalted as Lord high above every imaginable authority or power which could have dominion over the world. In this evil aeon or cosmos men were enslaved to false gods and to unruly passions and desires. The whole creation was made subject to illusion or vanity, he had said in Romans; it was under the sway of the tyrants called Sin and Death. As Paul meditated in his imprisonment these ideas assumed a more mysterious form. He struggled to express his view of man's tragic situation by the use of other ancient mythological ideas which he freely transformed into a language of the spirit. He took the figure of Adam, who was the symbol of the human race in its evil state; he took the stars of heaven exercising their baneful influence upon the lives of men; the multitudes of unclean deities claiming the homage of mankind; the strain of evil infused into human existence; the world in bondage to evil powers.

He begins to use a new kind of poetry which dramatizes this pessimistic theology of the old pagan world. He does not mention in so many words the hierarchy of the gods, or the seven heavens, or the sinister astrological influences; but he talks in a general way about principalities in the skies which have usurped the dominion of the universe, and about a prince of the power of the air, and a world-ruler of this aeon. The odd thing is that he nowhere appears to touch upon the god-emperor in Rome who was the earthly embodiment of the world-power against which the gospel was now contending, the head of

15. THE 'CROSS' AT HERCULANEUM

16. WRITING MATERIALS: A PAPYRUS ROLL, INKWELLS, STYLI

the state and the patron of the false gods. Yet he cannot have omitted the emperor and his subordinate rulers in his meditations; all the more because his imaginative vision of an evil power enthroned in the heavens was a projection into the spirit world of the pagan empire.

Is it possible that he chose the words 'authorities and powers' for their political associations? and that they were intended to suggest more than one meaning? Such a double meaning seems to appear in I Corinthians, in which he speaks of the 'rulers of this aeon' who had crucified the lord of glory; and in Colossians he expands this phrase into more mysterious and more dramatic and more incomprehensible language. The Messiah had stripped bare the authorities and powers; he had shown them up in public; he had triumphed over them in the cross. The picture from which Paul is working is the 'triumph' of a Roman emperor, along the Sacred Way, through the heart of Rome, with captive kings and trains of slaves and prisoners and displays of looted treasure. Jesus was a conqueror and emperor in the spiritual world, and the cross was the sign of this triumph. Over what? Over every conceivable enemy. Over Death and Sin. And surely, too, over the human rulers of this sinful world who had actually crucified the Lord of glory: over Caiaphas and Pilate and Caesar. His was the triumph on Golgotha, not theirs. In the Epistles of the imprisonment there is not a word which actually makes this identification; but it is done in Thessalonians, and the Revelation and the *Ascension of Isaiah*; Caligula and Nero are daemonic figures—incarnations of evil. The revolutionary quality of the thinking can hardly be denied. The Christians were united in their loyalty to a heavenly lord or emperor who had been slain on Calvary, was their lord and king, and would come again to assert his sovereignty over the whole world. But they were not belligerent. They were not rebels. They claimed to be model citizens. They accepted the paradox that the civil power was ordained by God and must be obeyed.

THE EPISTLE TO THE EPHESIANS

Such were the thoughts which were worked up into the communication known as the Epistle to the Ephesians. The title is ancient, though it may not be original. It was in general use by the end of the second century and appears at the head of the Epistle in the Chester Beatty papyrus, which is thought to have been produced not much later than

A.D. 200. In Marcion's church it was known as Laodiceans. The original text did not specify the destination, the words 'in Ephesus' having been added later to bring the text into line with the title. It has been suggested that there was a blank in the original manuscript. It looks very much as if it was a general manifesto or encyclical, for use anywhere within the Pauline jurisdiction and particularly in churches which he had not visited himself. Ephesus was probably the centre of distribution.

It is, to some extent, an enlarged and elaborated form of Colossians, the general structure of which is repeated and many phrases used over again. The style is magnificent but rather formal. It contains majestic passages of a liturgical character. We miss Paul's conversational manner: its echoes of the Stoic philosopher and the Jewish Rabbi, and its sudden alternations of rhetoric, and exposition, and colloquial appeal. This is not to say that Paul did not write it, for no other mind but Paul's was responsible for the range of vision and height of genius which it achieved; but possibly it was produced for him by members of his staff or in some literary workshop attached to the Roman church. And what is meant by a Pauline Epistle in any case? Did the apostle always write, or personally dictate, every word of the documents which he sent out? A captive, suffering from chronic bad health and feeling himself to be an old man, may have been glad to accept assistance. We know too, from Corinthians that his style had not made a good impression on everyone; his 'logos' or diction had been criticized; he was said to be unpractised or amateurish in speech. He may have decided to issue an Epistle for general use which would be less open to such criticism.

This is as far as any reasonable criticism need take us in questioning the Pauline authorship. The view that Ephesians was a fictitious composition of a later date is supported principally by the argument from literary style, which is not very strong in this instance. It is also felt that the thought is more carefully worked out and more closely articulated than is usual with Paul; and that it shows a more advanced and reflective theology. This is a matter of opinion; it seems to others that we have here the mind of the apostle himself, still thinking creatively and expressing itself with vigour. It is a piece of original work, not a mere imitation.

THE CHURCH IN THE WORLD

The thought of the Epistle is firmly rooted in history. There is a world-wide church which is substantially identified with the old Israel. The Gentile converts are full members of the Israelite state. They are not to be content with the name of 'strangers and sojourners', which Peter does not hesitate to bestow upon them in his Epistle. This was a technical term in Judaism for the alien resident, or even the convert, the 'stranger within the gate', who was referred to in Greek Judaism as the 'proselyte', the one who had approached or come near.

He even goes so far as to say that they were 'no longer Gentiles'. They were fellow-citizens with the saints and native-born with God; the word 'native-born' being the technical term which contrasts with the word 'stranger', as in Leviticus xix. 33. They were citizens of Israel through their membership in the church, which was founded upon the apostles and prophets, the Messiah himself being the chief corner-stone. This phrase is thought by some to be non-Pauline, but it refers to specific historical functions of the apostles and prophets. Paul admits that in previous generations it had not been realized that the Gentiles were to be incorporated into Israel; this truth has now been revealed to the holy apostles and prophets by the Spirit; the Gentiles are to be joint-heirs, one body, and full partners in the promise.

These apostles and prophets are the gift of the ascended and enthroned Messiah to his church; and so are the evangelists, shepherds, and teachers, who are closely associated with them. They are Christian apostles and prophets, of course; Jewish-Christian apostles and prophets so far as we know, though there may have been Gentile prophets by now.

The idea of the expansion of the Israelite state into a world-church by the grace and favour of its divine king is entirely in line with the claims made by Paul for his Gentile converts in the earlier controversies; and it had a strong political and apologetic consequence; Christianity was the true form of Judaism, and as such it was a *religio licita*, a religion sanctioned by the Roman empire; all of which is easier to understand if the Epistle was composed prior to the persecution of A.D. 64 and the fall of Jerusalem in 70.

In the catechetical parts of this Epistle the new converts are solemnly urged to maintain the unity of christendom; 'there is one body and one

Spirit, one hope of your calling, one Lord, one faith, one baptism, one God and Father of us all.' They are to separate themselves completely from the social and religious life of the pagan world with its foolishness and ignorance, and licentiousness, and uncleanness. They are to walk as children of the light, and have no partnership in the unfruitful works of darkness. They are not 'Gentile' any more.

The Epistle ends with a magnificent picture in which the old apocalyptic imagery suffers yet another transformation in order to paint the picture of the Christian martyr or witness unto death. It is not the Messiah now who confronts the powers of evil in the evil day, as he did once on Calvary according to Colossians, and will do in the future according to Thessalonians; it is Paul himself, his apostle and ambassador in chains. He confronts the imperial power, but his warfare is not merely with flesh and blood; it is with authorities and powers and the evil that is enthroned in the high places of the pagan world. He must take up the spiritual weapons; the breastplate of righteousness; the shield of faith; and the sword of the Spirit, which is the Word of God. He must stand fast against all the wiles of the evil one.

The spiritualized apocalyptic of Paul is never at any time mere myth or gnosis. It is not impalpable or dematerialized. It is, to use a modern word, existential. The drama is conceived within the movement of history and the substance of bodily existence; it becomes actual and operative in the cross, and in the proclamation of the gospel in the world by apostles and prophets, and in the growth of the church which he describes as a body, and in the mortal conflict of Christian believers with a sinful world.

THE EPISTLE TO THE PHILIPPIANS

Philippi was a favourite congregation of Paul's, being the first of his Aegean churches to be founded. This church had sent him a substantial gift by the hand of one of its leading members, Epaphroditus, who was another old colleague. The means at his disposal were perhaps dwindling. He remarks, in acknowledging the gift, that he had had experience of both poverty and riches; he knew 'how to lack and how to abound'. Epaphroditus had fallen seriously ill, and the news of this had got back to Philippi. Paul writes to tell the Philippians about Epaphroditus and himself; it is a personal letter, written in his old familiar style.

The cause of the gospel is making progress. He sends greetings from the 'saints in Caesar's household', that is to say the Christians in the palace or in the civil service. He had become a well-known figure in Rome now, and was pointed out in his chains as one of the sights of the *praetorium* or military headquarters.[1] There was bitter opposition on the part of Christian Jews; but controversy had only served to spread the knowledge of the gospel.

He shows no signs of undue optimism about his case. He is fully prepared for whatever may befall him. He feels now that he is an old man; 'such a one as Paul the aged', as he wrote to Philemon. He has a desire to be dissolved and to be with Christ; and yet it may be necessary, for the good of his churches, that he should remain in the flesh. We detect here a note of weariness after so much labour and suffering and delay, but there is a change that is taking place in his mind. The simple naïve apocalyptic of the Jerusalem prophets no longer satisfied him; there had been a time when he naturally thought of remaining alive until the advent of the Lord, but what he wanted now was to depart from the body and make his home with the Lord. Yet he seems to think that he will be acquitted. He trusts that he will soon visit Philippi.

BISHOPS AND DEACONS

Not very many names are mentioned in this Epistle. There are two ladies, Euodia and Syntyche, who do not get on very well together; perhaps they were two 'deacons' or 'patronesses', like Phoebe at Cenchrea, who had preceded him to Rome. He reminds them how they were in the forefront of the battle with him when the gospel came to Philippi, using the Greek verb *athlein*, to play the part of an athlete, which was destined to become a technical term in the vocabulary of martyrdom. With them he associates a certain 'Synzygos' (or does the word simply mean a yoke-fellow or team-mate?), and of course his colleague or fellow-worker, Clement, whom some identify with the Clement who was the leader of the Roman church thirty years later.

The new departure is the inclusion of bishops and deacons in the form of address. The word 'bishop' (*episkopos*) had been used in the speech to the Ephesian elders three or four years previously; or so we

[1] His words are not inconsistent with the theory that the Epistle was written from Caesarea or Ephesus.

are told in Acts. It meant a watchman or superintendent or manager; but it is related in the apostolic texts to the idea of the shepherd. The word 'deacon' (*diakonos*) meant a servant or attendant, and was used by Paul in a very general way of assistant ministries in the church, even of the lady who carried his Epistle to the Romans three or four years previously. These words are now applied to definite ministries in the church, but we do not know how their offices were defined. Perhaps the author of the Acts would have alluded to the bishops as elders; Paul had referred to such officers in earlier letters simply as rulers. All we can say is that some clarification was taking place. Clement of Rome alludes to this period or earlier when he says that the apostles appointed the first-fruits of their mission to be bishops and deacons of the future believers.

THE DATE OF THE ACTS

What was the outcome of the imprisonment of St Paul? The last verses of Acts say that he remained at Rome for two years in his own hired house (or at his own expense) receiving guests, and evangelizing and preaching without impediment; an easy form of imprisonment. Does this imply that Paul was then released? Or that he was beheaded? Or that no decision had yet been made? The third is the most natural explanation; and if it is correct, Acts was written during the two-year period with the object of presenting the case for Paul and the case for Christianity. But this common-sense explanation has not passed unchallenged. Let us consider it first.

This theory of the writing of Acts accords well with its plan and style. It is deeply interested in the history up to the two-years' imprisonment. Christianity has an even chance of securing toleration from the authorities. The claim can be made out that it is a form of Judaism and therefore a *religio licita*. The attitude of the Roman officials is fair or at any rate neutral. This whole picture was changed in 64 by the sudden fierce persecution launched by the Emperor Nero. If Acts was composed later than 64, it is hard to believe that no sign of these altered circumstances would appear. And yet it *might* be that a Christian writer, under Vespasian, might wish to present for consideration and as an argument in favour of toleration the policy of the earlier period.

But if it was written at a later date, why should it not state clearly what happened to Paul at the end of the two years? Why should it devote so much labour to the task of working up to the crisis of his imprisonment and presenting the case in his favour in every detail, when the case had been decided years ago and it was no longer a crisis of great importance? And why does it not refer to later events? Why is it silent about Paul's martyrdom? And why is there nothing about the later labours and martyrdom of Peter? There is a perfect answer to these questions; Luke intended to write a third volume which would have dealt with these points. But this is a hypothetical answer. No evidence exists to prove that he had any such intention.

A third characteristic also points to an early date. There is a certain historical perspective about the book. The earlier narratives down to the Jerusalem council are lucidly told and are perfectly convincing; but they have not got the detail and sharp definition of the later ones. As we come down to the last chapters we are dealing with vivid and recent memories; the events are virtually contemporary and it is expected that the reader will understand the local references. The book stops short at this point. Peter has been allowed to drift out of sight; it has never been explained who James is; we know that he is the brother of the Lord, but it is not Acts that tells us this. The last reference to Mark is far from self-explanatory. Apollos remains something of a mystery. The Alexander of the Ephesian riot is never identified. The reader is supposed to know all these things. That is not how a book would have been written to satisfy the curiosity of the eighties or nineties; but it is exactly how it might have been written in the early sixties.

There is a partial answer to this. The features we have mentioned are features of the *sources* of the Acts, and these sources were left as they were in spite of the abrupt effect which they give. Or perhaps the sources were worked up into a first draft to serve a useful purpose in Rome in the early sixties to be used again later in a completed book.

The character of the Acts is best explained by the theory that it was composed at this early date, but there is a strong argument against it. It comes from the field of literary criticism. It is assumed that the Acts was written after the composition of the Gospel, which it refers to as the former treatise or first volume; but the Gospel was not written as we know it till after the author had come across Mark's Gospel, and most scholars do not date Mark's Gospel before 67–70. We have to allow time for Luke to study the work of Mark and to insert the greater part of it into the draft which he had already made; and for this reason few scholars at present would accept the early date of Acts.

We shall, therefore, without denying that Luke must have done a great deal of work on the Acts and on the Gospel during Paul's imprisonment, nevertheless defer our consideration of it as a finished work of literature to the period of the seventies.

THE RELEASE OF PAUL

No certain conclusion can be drawn from the abrupt ending of the Acts with regard to the fate of Paul; for while the case against him, as we see it in the Acts, would not warrant a condemnation, we must allow fully for the legal ability of any prosecutors who may have appeared against him, and also for political and financial influence. On the other hand, no prosecutors may have appeared, and if so the case would lapse after the expiry of a stated period. We do not happen to know what the length of that period was, but it is possible that it was the two years which are referred to in the Acts. There are, however, two other ways of approaching this problem.

There is a Roman document of the end of the second century, called the *Muratorian Fragment*, which definitely states that Paul visited Spain. The belief of the Roman church at so late a date could not be taken as conclusive evidence by itself, since it might have come into being as a deduction from the passage in Romans in which Paul expresses his intention of going on from Rome to Spain; but Clement of Rome, writing about 96, speaks of Paul as teaching the whole world righteousness, and coming 'even to the boundary of the west and bearing witness before rulers', before he departed from the world. It has been suggested that the boundary of the west is used here for Rome itself; but it is rather hard to believe that a Roman writer could have thought of Rome in this way. Perhaps Paul did visit Spain, and if so, the visit has to be placed after his Roman imprisonment.

We also have to find a place for the movements of Paul which are mentioned in the Pastoral Epistles, namely those which are addressed to Timothy and Titus. These events cannot plausibly be fitted into Paul's history prior to his Roman imprisonment. The attempt has been made, but it can only be done by cutting the passages in question into smaller fragments, and allotting each fragment to a separate context.

Whether these Epistles were written by Paul himself exactly as they stand, or whether they were worked up into their present form by another hand at a later date, does not concern us here. These movements and activities of Paul and his colleagues require a further period of missionary activity in Asia.

As a decision has to be made in the arrangement of a history, we shall follow the indications in the evidence, such as they are, and assume that Paul was released, as he, on the whole, seemed to expect when he was writing to the Philippians and to Philemon. We shall find that he feels very differently in the imprisonment from which he writes in certain passages in II Timothy.

Note. The theory that Ephesians, the Pastoral Epistles, and I Peter are 'pseudonymous' works, that is to say fictitious literature composed by a skilled writer who impersonates the apostle, will be discussed in chapters 14 and 15.

CHAPTER 10

THE MARTYRDOMS

The events of A.D. 62, *p.* 187. Annas the high priest, *p.* 188. Josephus and the Christ, *p.* 189. The Martyrdom of James, A.D. 62, *p.* 190. The persecution in Rome, A.D. 64, *p.* 191. The evidence of Tacitus, *p.* 193. The two apostles, the evidence of Clement, *p.* 195. The movements of Paul, the evidence of II Timothy, *p.* 196. Paul in Rome, *p.* 198. Peter in Rome, the evidence of his Epistle, *p.* 200. The martyrdom of Peter, *p.* 202. The Beliar Apocalypse, *p.* 203.

LIST OF HIGH PRIESTS IN JERUSALEM

after the death of Herod, 4 B.C.

Annas I (Ananus) appointed by the procurator Quirinus; deposed by the next procurator Gratus; but he and his dynasty continued to have great power.

Gratus appointed in quick succession

Ishmael, son of Fabi,

Eleazar, *son of Annas*,

Simon, son of Camithus,

Joseph called *Caiaphas*, *a son-in-law of Annas*.

Caiaphas was the high priest under Pontius Pilate, who condemned Jesus in 29 or 30. He was deposed by Vitellius in 37, who appointed in his place

Jonathan, *son of Annas*, who was deposed in favour of his brother,

Theophilus, *son of Annas*, who was deposed by King Agrippa I and succeeded by

Simon called Cantheras,

Matthias *son of Annas*,

Elionaeus son of Cantheras,

Joseph, son of Cainus, appointed by Herod Agrippa II,

Ananias, son of Nebedaeus, who presided at the trial of Paul about A.D. 55; he was killed by the Zealots A.D. 66. He was the father of Eleazar: see p. 226.

Jonathan (restored), who was killed at the instigation of the procurator Felix,

Ishmael son of Fabi, who was detained in Rome as a hostage, and beheaded after the fall of Jerusalem,

Joseph called Cabi, son of Simon.

Annas II (Ananus), *son of Annas I*, who condemned James the Just, the brother of Jesus in 62: deposed by the procurator Albinus and murdered in the insurrection A.D. 67.

Jesus son of Damnaeus,

Jesus son of Gamaliel (or Gamala), killed by the Zealots A.D. 67,

Matthias, *son of Theophilus, and grandson of Annas I*: was the last legitimate high priest, killed A.D. 70.

A rival high priest, Phanni or Phineas, had been set up by the insurgents.

THE EVENTS OF A.D. 62

According to our chronological plan, we have placed the end of St Paul's Roman imprisonment early in 61, or possibly in 62.

In the year 62 changes for the worse occurred in the political world. Nero, who was now twenty-five, took over the government of the empire. Burrhus, his praetorian prefect and Greek secretary, was replaced by Tigellinus, a man of bad character. Seneca had already retired into that melancholy seclusion in which he wrote his last philosophical works; and he committed suicide by Nero's orders in 65. Burrhus had died, not without suspicion of poison.

In the year 62 Nero divorced his wife Octavia, who was the daughter of the previous emperor, Claudius, and banished her to an island, where she was put to death. He lost no time in marrying Poppaea, the Jewish wife of M. Salvius Otho, a lady who is described by Josephus as devout. She is said to have used her influence in favour of her nation.

In Palestine King Agrippa II, who had the support of the procurator Festus, was not in harmony with his high priest, Ishmael ben Fabi, in whose pontificate Paul had appealed to Nero. A dispute had arisen about King Agrippa's palace, which overlooked the altar of the Temple. It was referred to Rome, and the high priest, accompanied by ten other Jews, came to Rome to plead their cause. They won their case through the good offices of Poppaea, Josephus says; but they were detained as hostages. Among the visitors in connexion with this case was Josephus the historian, who was shipwrecked on the way, as Paul had been three or four years before.

ANNAS THE HIGH PRIEST

Agrippa in the meantime acquiesced in the appointment of a new high priest, Joseph ben Simon, who was called Cabi; but on the death of Festus, which happened soon after, he deposed Joseph and appointed Annas (or Ananus), the fifth son of the Annas in whose palace Jesus had been examined. This older Annas had been the father-in-law of Caiaphas, and five of his own sons had held the high priesthood. Annas II was the last of them.

Josephus had a high opinion of this prelate, but the character of the man may be gauged from a rather frank account of him which he gives after relating the story of his deposition.

> The high priest Ananias [as the name now appears in the text] advanced every day in popularity, and won the favour and esteem of the citizens in a signal manner, and ingratiated himself with the (new) high priest and with Albinus [the new procurator] by making them gifts. But he had servants of bad character, who associated with overbearing men, and went to the threshing-floors, and took the tithes that were due to the priests by violence; and did not refrain from beating those who would not pay them. And the high priests behaved in the same way as their servants, since no one had the power to prevent it; and some of the [lesser] priests, who used to be supported from the tithes, died from lack of food. (Josephus, *Ant.* XX, 9, 2.)

What led to his deposition was this. He was a bold and overbearing man, Josephus says, and very insolent. He was a member of the sect of the Sadducees, who were very severe in judging offenders. Festus was dead and Albinus, the new procurator, had not arrived from Rome; 'so he assembled a sanhedrin of judges, and brought before them the brother of Jesus who was called the Messiah, whose name was James, with some others'; and when he had framed an accusation against them as breakers of the Law, he caused them to be stoned.

But those who seemed the most reasonable, and the most accurate in regard to the Law (and Josephus meant by this the Pharisees), complained to the new procurator, who deposed him on the grounds that he had exceeded his authority. Joshua (or Jesus) the son of Damnaeus succeeded him; but he increased in power, and was doubtless the real ruler, as his father Annas I had been before him.

We notice here the same chaotic social conditions as appear in the

Epistle of St James, and the same alignment of parties in the sanhedrin as appears in the pages of the Acts. Doubtless the real crime of James was his protest in favour of the poor and the oppressed, with which the more judicious Pharisees would sympathize. These sympathies appear in the Epistle which bears his name.

JOSEPHUS AND THE CHRIST

Josephus was now twenty-five years old and had attached himself to the Pharisees, so that he is narrating what came under his personal observation. There is no reason to question the authenticity of his report of the murder of St James; but unfortunately the passage in which he refers to Jesus himself has received some additions from the hand of a Christian scribe at a later date, so that it cannot be used with confidence for historical purposes. It is necessary, however, to quote it, since it appears possible to discern, at least partially, what Josephus wrote. It follows his account of Pontius Pilate. We eliminate three clauses which appear to be Christian additions, and print them below the remainder of the text.

About this time appeared Jesus, a wise man [1], a teacher of such men as received the truth with pleasure; and he influenced many of the Jews and of the Greek race [2]. And when he was condemned to the cross by Pilate, on the information of the leading men among us, those who had loved him at first, did not cease to do so; [3] and even now the tribe of *Christians*, who are named after him, is not extinct.

The Christian additions. [1] If indeed it is right to call him a man, for he was a doer of marvellous works. [2] This man was the Christ. [3] For he appeared to them again on the third day, living, the divine prophets having stated these and many other marvellous things about him.

(Josephus, *Ant.* XVIII, 3, 3.)

The clauses which have been separated from the text and printed below it are obviously unlikely to have been written by Josephus, though he may have made some allusion to the miracles and Resurrection of Jesus. They look much more like the comments of a Christian scribe, which were written first in the margin and then found their way into the text, as often happened in the production of ancient manuscripts. On the other hand, the remaining sentences are not written in the manner of a believing Christian, though their tone is not unsympathetic; and they probably represent what Josephus actually wrote. It is unfortunate, however, that no manuscript preserves the original text.

THE MARTYRDOM OF JAMES, A.D. 62

The Jewish-Christian church preserved its memories and traditions of these events, and some of them were collected early in the second century by the oriental teacher Hegesippus, and included in his *Hupomnemata* or 'Note-books'. Unfortunately this important book has not been preserved and we have to be content with the extracts and quotations which are given by church historians. We have already quoted his account of the sanctity of James the Just from the history of Eusebius, where it is followed by the story of his martyrdom. This story is also preserved by Epiphanius. We shall consider it more closely in a later chapter, since it sheds light on the development of tradition in the Jewish church.

Its form is legendary, but its substance is perfectly credible, and no doubt historical. After some debate and questioning with the leaders of the religious sects, James was thrown down from a high point in the Temple, and stoned to death; he was finished off by a blow from a wooden club. 'And immediately', Hegesippus adds, 'Vespasian besieged them.'

This is a homiletic addition; it is dramatic, but not strictly accurate. The evidence of Josephus shows that it was four or five years later before any Roman advance upon Jerusalem began. This homiletic touch has confused the chronology of Eusebius, or even Hegesippus, leaving no alternative but to place the appointment of a successor to James after the destruction of the city; and we should therefore disregard the italicized words in the following paragraph of Eusebius.

After the martyrdom of James, *and the taking of Jerusalem, which took place immediately afterwards*, it is recorded that those apostles and disciples of the Lord who still survived met together from all quarters and, together with the Lord's relatives according to the flesh (for the majority of these were still living), took counsel together as to whom they would judge worthy to be the successor of James; and furthermore they all unanimously approved Symeon the son of Clopas...who was a cousin of the Lord.

(Eusebius, *E.H.* III, 11.)

The words 'it is recorded' show that Eusebius here comes back to the text of the document which he is following, that is to say the *Notebooks* of Hegesippus; but we would suppose that Symeon must have been appointed some years before the war broke out.

We have here a narrative of the martyrdom of James which is completely independent of that of Josephus and therefore confirms it; so that we are more fortunate than in the cases of Peter and Paul, for no narrative of their martyrdoms seems ever to have been drawn up. The composition of 'Acts of Martyrs' for commemoration in church seems to have begun in Palestine; in Jerusalem even, since Stephen and James the Just are our oldest specimens. Like other old Christian traditions, it originated in the East and spread to the West in due course.

James had endeavoured to keep a steady balance between the Judaistic zeal of his own extreme party-men, and the pro-Gentile enthusiasm of Paul and his following. According to the record in the Acts, the statesmanship and moderation of the brother of Jesus had materially helped to bring the church safe through some of its early internal dissensions. He continued to extend recognition to Paul in spite of growing hostility in Jerusalem and of personal danger; and there was a moderate Jewish-Christian tradition in Palestine after his death in which a tolerant attitude towards Paul was maintained. The more extreme parties, who came to be known as the Ebionites, remained implacably hostile.

THE PERSECUTION IN ROME, A.D. 64

The deposition of the high priest for the persecution of Christians in Jerusalem must not be regarded as an intervention of the Roman power in favour of the church. It was done because he had arrogated to himself the right to act as the executive head of the state. The high priest was only a subordinate ruler and had no right to hold courts and to impose the penalty of death. On the other hand, his action was a more serious one for the Christians than a casual reading of Josephus might suggest; for James was not the only victim. He was put to death 'with others'.

This outbreak of persecution in Jerusalem was a symptom of the deterioration in the political situation. The Jews and the Romans were working up to a desperate war, and the Christians occupied an ambiguous intermediate position. They claimed to be a kind of Jew, but the Jews repudiated them; or at any rate they repudiated the Gentile Christians, whose claim to be regarded as true Israelites was championed in Ephesians and I Peter. It was not at all unnatural that the Jewish authorities should disown them, but we have evidence that they went further. They influenced the Romans against them. They suggested that they were hostile to the empire, a point which appears clearly in the trials of Paul; and, according to Justin Martyr, who wrote some seventy years later, they sent out picked men from Jerusalem into all countries to inform them that the irreligious sect of *Christians* which had recently sprung up, worshipped no God and was guilty of secret crimes. He may be too definite in his statement of the case, but the factor of Jewish pressure cannot be ignored in considering the causes of Roman persecution.

In the eyes of the Roman governing class Christianity had appeared as an obscure movement among poor and depressed and foreign groups, with wild and extravagant talk about a new kingdom and a new king, who was somehow identified with a man who had been executed in the time of Pontius Pilate for raising an insurrection in Judaea. He would appear again to claim his kingdom.

The flare-up in Jerusalem was not long in communicating itself to Rome, and doubtless to many other places. Any favourable impression which may ever have been made by Nero on judicious men had now been effaced by his cruelty, extravagance, vanity and self-indulgence. Unnatural murder and unnatural sexual vice fill the brief chronicles of his life. No doubt he had inherited a streak of lunacy along with his touch of genius. Nevertheless, he remained the idol of the multitude.

On July 18 of the year 64, a fire broke out in Rome and burned for nine days. It completely destroyed three out of the fourteen civic districts, and partially destroyed another seven. The theory that Nero engineered it himself is most unlikely. He threw himself with great energy into the organization of relief and opened his splendid gardens on the Vatican Hill to the thousands of homeless citizens; and in order to find victims to placate the people, and amusements to occupy their attention, he laid the blame for the fire on the Christians.

THE EVIDENCE OF TACITUS

The historian Tacitus, who was a child of eight or ten at the time, describes it in his *Annals*; it is our first picture of Christianity as it appeared to an external observer.

They were called *Christians*. The Christus from whom the name was derived had been put to death in the reign of Tiberius by the procurator Pontius Pilate, and the pestilent superstition was checked for a while; but it began to break out again, not only in Judaea, the birthplace of the evil thing, but also in Rome, where everything that is horrible and shameless flows together and becomes fashionable.

In the first place, then, some were arrested and confessed. Then, on their testimony, a vast multitude was convicted, not so much of responsibility for the fire as for hatred of the human race. They were put to death with mockery and insult. They were dressed in the skins of wild animals to be torn to death by dogs; they were fixed to crosses or condemned to the flames; and when the daylight failed, they were burned to give light by night.

Nero had granted the use of his gardens for that display, and gave a circus performance, mixing with the common people in the dress of a charioteer or seated in his chariot; and so a feeling of compassion arose (though it was for guilty persons who deserved severe punishment), since they were being done to death, not for the public good, but to satisfy the cruelty of a single individual. (Tacitus, *Annals*, xv, 44.)

This very important document deserves the most careful study. Let us grant that there may be some exaggeration about the 'immense multitude', the *ingens multitudo*, which was ready to die for Christ in Rome under the leadership of the apostles; even so we are impressed by the power and momentum of the spiritual forces which had been liberated in Jerusalem thirty-five years previously, when Jesus died on Calvary and of the people there were none with him. We are amazed at the progress which had been made in the interval. It is greater than we would have gathered from the apostolic writings.

We may draw attention to two points. The first is that Tacitus was aware of a second 'outbreak' of Christianity in Judaea, which seems to have occurred not long before the fire in Rome; and this would mean an outbreak of which the authorities took notice. It looks as if the persecution in Jerusalem two years earlier, in which James was put to death, was a larger thing than Josephus had cared to reveal, and that it started off a more general persecution which flared up before long in Rome. This is in line with the evidence of the Acts, which shows how a movement which could be more or less ignored at one time, as it was on the advice of men like Gamaliel and Gallio, could, not long afterwards, be regarded as a menace.

The second point is that he is uneasy about the situation. He is even on the defensive. If Christianity was the vicious and criminal movement which he says it is, why was there so much sympathy for it? He puts it down to the excessive cruelty of the punishments, in which Nero showed an obvious personal pleasure. There could be an alternative explanation, however; it could be due to the innocence of the Christians, and the impression made on some observers by their courage and sincerity; for during his own lifetime the sentiment in favour of the Christians had permeated all classes, even the highest. He admits that the Christians were innocent of the crime they were charged with, but their condemnation by the judges was justified by the fact that they were public enemies, a statement which he fails to support in any way. He admits, too, that the sentences were too severe and the scenes of violence inexcusable, but it was possible to blame Nero for this; and Nero was regarded as a monster of evil when Tacitus wrote. Under the new emperors Christians were sent to their deaths with the utmost decorum.

The explanations attempted by Tacitus were doubtless partially correct; but it is possible that the pro-Christian sentiment, the existence of which he admits, was greater than he would allow. We may mention a case of special interest which illustrates this point. There was a Roman of high rank, who was 'prefect of the city' at this time. His name was Flavius Sabinus. He died in 69, which was the year in which his brother Vespasian became emperor. His son Titus Flavius Clemens became a Christian, or was interested in Christianity. This is an instance of the kind of noble Roman family which was not impressed by the slanders which had been set going against the Christians. It would appear that the finest elements in Roman society, like the finest elements in Jewish society, were not always among the persecutors.

THE TWO APOSTLES, THE EVIDENCE OF CLEMENT

We have said that the martyrs met their deaths under the leadership of Peter and Paul, and we must justify this statement.

Only thirty years later Clement of Rome, writing to the Corinthians in the name of his church, refers in a rhetorical passage to the events of this time.

Let us finish with examples from ancient times [he writes] and come to the athletes *of our own time*. Let us take the glorious examples *of our own generation*.

It was through jealousy and envy that the greatest and most righteous 'pillars' [of the church] were persecuted, and contended as athletes, even unto death. Let us set before our eyes the noble apostles. Peter, through unrighteous jealousy, endured not one or two, but many labours, and so he bore his witness and went his way to the place of glory which was his due. Through jealousy and strife, Paul pointed out the prize of endurance; seven times in chains, living the life of a fugitive and pelted with stones, he became a herald both in the east and in the west, and won a glorious fame for his faith; he taught righteousness to the whole world, coming even to the boundaries of the west; he witnessed before the rulers, and passed away from the world, and went his way to the holy place, having become the greatest pattern of endurance. (Clement, *I Corinthians*, v.)

We would rather, from our point of view, have had a simple statement, with a few details, to the effect that Peter and Paul had suffered martyrdom under Nero; but such plain statements about things which everybody knew are seldom made in communications of this character. All we get is the occasional allusion or comment. But the evidence of Clement is strong enough, for he goes on to connect the witness of the two noble apostles with a 'great multitude' who are plainly to be identified with the 'great multitude' of Tacitus. The thing did not happen in this way twice.

Along with these great men of holy life and character, *there was associated a great multitude of the elect*, who endured many indignities and tortures because of jealousy, and became a splendid example *in our midst*. Because of jealousy, women were persecuted, Danaids and Dirces, who endured strange and impious outrages, and completed the strong course of faith, receiving the glorious prize, though weak in body. (*Ibid.* vi.)

The passage is far from clear, but it leaves no doubt that a mass-persecution such as Tacitus describes was the occasion of the martyrdom of the two apostles. The Danaids and Dirces have been much discussed. The daughters of Danaus were figures in an old Greek myth, who were punished in Hades by being obliged endlessly to fill with water barrels which were riddled with holes; Dirce was killed by being tied to the horns of a bull. It seems that the victims in the arena were sometimes forced to take part in the representation of myths of this sort and to undergo the actual torture or death; and perhaps something of the sort happened in this case. It fits in with the picture of a theatrical spectacle on a large scale which Tacitus describes. The word jealousy is not to be taken too seriously, as this is the general theme of which these martyrdoms are examples in the exhortation of Clement. Yet it may have played a part. We have evidence in other cases of anonymous and slanderous communications sent in to the magistrates; and, of course, of vindictive feeling on the part of neighbours; and the hostility of the Jewish authorities.

Despite the absence of detailed contemporary reporting, the martyrdoms of St Peter and St Paul in Rome must be accepted on the evidence as a fact of history. It was regarded as a fact of history in the second century, and their burial places were marked by monuments: St Peter's on the Vatican Hill, and St Paul's on the Ostian Way, both of them outside the city wall. The high altars of St Peter's on the Vatican Hill and St Paul's 'Outside the Walls' are erected over these second-century sites. The historicity of their martyrdoms is no longer seriously questioned by scholars.

THE MOVEMENTS OF PAUL, THE EVIDENCE OF II TIMOTHY

It is another matter to go further in reconstructing the course of events.

It will be well to take first the movements of Paul, so far as they can be traced in the Pastoral Epistles, leaving over for a time the literary problems which they present. On any reasonable theory of their date and authorship, they contain information which belongs to this period.

The journey to Spain, if it is accepted as historical, cannot be taken into account. If it ever actually occurred, the apostle must have landed in Gaul, and there is a possible reference to Gaul in II Timothy. A member of Paul's staff named Crescens had left him for 'Galatia'. Some good manuscripts read 'Gallia', and a number of the fathers were acquainted with this reading. The word Galatia could be used for Gallia, and it is perfectly possible that Crescens was sent to the south of France. It seems likely that evangelization had begun west of Rome. Clement's boast that Paul had taught the whole world is hardly justified if he had got no further than Rome.

There is no reference to persecution in I Timothy and Titus, and we may therefore place the events which they mention before the year 64, or no later than the first six months of it. Paul may have spent the winter in the island of Crete, where he had left Titus to establish elders and 'supply what was lacking'. He arrived in Ephesus, it would appear, in the spring, and a painful scene took place. He found the ecclesia under the control of unworthy teachers of the pseudo-Jewish type, and could only regard them as adventurers preying upon the faithful. With his customary courage he excommunicated two of them, Hymenaeus and Alexander, and left Timothy with a strong charge to reduce the elders and teachers to some sort of order and to resist their doctrines, which consisted of old wives' tales and endless genealogies. Timothy was specially commissioned for this work with the laying on of hands, after prophecy and prayer.

Paul went on to Troas, and we learn from II Timothy that he stayed there with a man named Carpus, and left in his house a cloak, a number of scrolls, and some parchments. He was then intending to return that way, but subsequently changed his plans. It must have been further along the road westward, possibly in Philippi, that he changed his mind; for in his letter to Titus, he says that he intends to winter at Nicopolis on the Dalmatian coast; he would follow the Egnatian Road to its terminal point on the Adriatic Sea. We may place the writing of I Timothy and Titus at this point, or at any rate some of the epistolary material that was worked into them. It is the Epistle to Titus that helps us now. He was bidden to join Paul at Nicopolis. He was to welcome Zenas the lawyer and Apollos, whom we would judge to have been the men who carried the letter. Paul promises to send Artemas or Tychicus to Crete for the winter.

Such is the picture which may be put together from the references in I Timothy and Titus; but when we come to II Timothy, the picture has changed. Paul is now a prisoner in Rome, and is asking for his scrolls, his parchments, and the cloak which he left at Troas. Timothy is to bring them when he comes; and he is urged to come before the winter. Titus has left Crete in accordance with Paul's instructions, and is actually in Dalmatia, the Adriatic province in which Nicopolis was situated. The various references do seem to tell a story when we combine them together, though our reconstruction is admittedly hypothetical.

PAUL IN ROME

Paul may have been arrested in Macedonia or Dalmatia; or of course he may have made his own way to Rome on hearing the news of the great persecution in July and August. In any case he is in prison. The tone of II Timothy is not at all what the Christian imagination would have fancied. No writer of pious fiction would have pictured him in this mood. He writes in deep dejection. There is no sign of the easy conditions of imprisonment which had been his lot before. There is no sign of optimism about the outcome. The time of his dissolution is at hand. He must hand on his charge to another.

He is very much alone. 'At my first hearing', he says, 'nobody stood by me; may it not be laid to their account.' (He almost seems to quote from Stephen.) 'But the Lord stood by me,' he says, 'and gave me power, that by my mouth the gospel might be fully preached, and all the Gentiles hear it; and I was delivered out of the lion's mouth.' He has the Book of Daniel in his mind here, the martyr's handbook. (Stephen quoted words from Daniel, too.)

Perhaps he overstated the case a little, for he also says, 'Only Luke is with me.' Demas had abandoned him, having loved this present world; but Crescens and Titus were absent on missionary work, one in Galatia (or Gaul) and one in Dalmatia. Even now this extraordinary man is spiritually in touch with churches of his making, or of his inspiration, all over the world; for Spain and Gaul can quite possibly be added to Italy, Dalmatia, Achaia, Macedonia, Asia, Cyprus, Syria, Arabia, and Palestine, as the scenes of his conflicts and labours. Egypt, Cyrene, and Africa were the only major provinces, so far as we know, where he had made no effort to preach the gospel; and Britain, of course, which had only been part of the empire for ten years; Cappadocia, Pontus, and Bithynia also seem to have been outside his range.

One hero of the faith, by name Onesiphorus, had found his way to Rome to bring him comfort and support. A late and perhaps worthless tradition connects him with Little Antioch. 'He often refreshed me, and was not ashamed of my chain', says Paul. He may have performed this service at the cost of his life; at any rate he had died before Paul wrote. 'The Lord grant mercy to the house of Onesiphorus', Paul prays; 'may the Lord grant him to find mercy from the Lord in that day.'

Onesiphorus had brought him no good news. 'Everyone in Asia has turned from me,' Paul writes, 'including Phygelus and Hermogenes'; he mentions also Hymenaeus and Philetus, who have erred concerning the truth by saying that the resurrection is past, and have disturbed the faith of many. This total victory of the false teaching in Asia may indeed be an exaggeration; but we must remember the mixed origin of the Ephesian church and the apprehensions which Paul had entertained about the character of its elders. The church order which he had built up had not been altogether equal to the strain; but, as in the case of Corinth, he may have been too pessimistic.

His mind turns affectionately to Timothy, his 'dear child' or 'genuine son' in the work of the gospel. He has sent Tychicus, who was an Ephesian himself, to take over his charge, and summons him now to his side. He is the only one who really understands his mind and purpose. He is the man to take over his tradition and hand it on to others. Paul's mind goes back to the early days when he first met him; what persecutions he had endured, what sufferings he went through, at Little Antioch, at Iconium, at Lystra. He thinks of Timothy as he then was and recalls the simple faith of his grandmother Lois and his mother Eunice.

A further thought comes into his mind. He asks Timothy to get hold of Mark and bring him with him, because he is a useful man for the ministry. Amends have been made for any past disapprovals or misunderstandings. It would appear that Timothy did get hold of Mark; for Mark came. Or was Mark already with Peter, and on his way? Whether any of them reached Rome in time to see Paul, we do not know; our evidence is beginning to fail us, and the picture which it creates is fading out. We may end with the words of faith which are worthy of his unconquerable spirit,

I have fought the good fight, I have finished the course, I have kept the faith. Henceforth there is laid up for me the crown of righteousness, which the Lord will give me in that day, the righteous judge; and not to me only, but to all who love his appearing.

Tradition must be right in saying that Paul was beheaded; for this was the form of execution which was legal in the case of a Roman citizen.

We find at the end of II Timothy the names of a family or group with which he was in close touch, friends of Aquila and Priscilla perhaps, who are back in Asia now, and receive salutations. 'Eubulus and Pudens and Linus and Claudia and all the brethren send thee greetings.' These are the only Roman Christians who are mentioned in the Epistle; and the name of Linus appears in the tradition of the Roman church as the name of their first bishop. Pudens appears in the late tradition as the name of a Roman senator who received Peter into his house; according to this tradition his mother's name was Priscilla.

PETER IN ROME, THE EVIDENCE OF HIS EPISTLE

We would give a good deal to possess a sequel to the Acts giving the story of the missionary journeys of Peter; but in the absence of such records, we must make the best of such traces and indications as remain. We will begin with the 'first Epistle'.

Our New Testament today contains two Epistles ascribed to St Peter. The second bears every mark of being a literary fiction composed in the second century; but the marks which prove it to be a work of the imagination are conspicuous by their absence in the case of the first. The 'first Epistle' is a first-century production which was used by Clement and Polycarp; and such arguments as have been advanced against its authenticity have certainly not been strengthened by recent study. There is a tendency now among the scholars who deny its authenticity to award it what might be called a deutero-historical character; it is suggested that it was issued under the name of Peter, not long after his death, to instruct and encourage Gentile converts; and of course it could not be effective, even as a work of pious affection and recollection, unless its references to the familiar historical background were correct. Since this conclusion appears to be inevitable, we may use this document for our purposes.

The Epistle is directed to the 'elect sojourners of the dispersion', which is a mystical description of the whole field of Gentile Christianity, recalling the opening words of the Epistle of St James. In Peter, however, the range of the address is limited to the provinces of Pontus, Galatia, Cappadocia, Asia, and Bithynia; some manuscripts omitting

Asia and Bithynia. The Pauline provinces of Asia and Galatia, which have lost their apostolic leader (if our historical reconstruction is correct), are grouped with others lying north and east, so covering virtually the whole of Asia Minor. It will be remembered that Paul and Silas had attempted to move into the northern provinces, but had been prevented by the Spirit from doing so; evangelization had now taken place in these regions, perhaps under the auspices of Peter (working from Antioch?), or of Silas, who appears in this Epistle as a co-author, under his Latin name of Silvanus.

Actually Silvanus was the writer of the Epistle. 'Through Silvanus, a faithful brother as I account him, I have briefly written', we read in the postscript, among the salutations. In the same way the church of Smyrna wrote its story of Polycarp's martyrdom 'through Marcianus'; and the Roman church wrote its epistle to Corinth 'through Clement', according to Dionysius of Corinth. Silvanus, Clement, and Marcianus were men of literary ability who composed epistles on behalf of higher authorities. It does not surprise us. Mediate authorship, or co-operative authorship, was not uncommon in the ancient world, especially in the east; and it is not unknown even today. If the apostle of the circumcision wished to address the Gentile churches, the natural thing for him to do would be to get the literary labour done for him by a competent Hellenist. Silvanus had co-operated with Paul in writing to the Thessalonians; and it is interesting that the catechetical portions of I Peter and I Thessalonians both echo the holiness catechism of Leviticus. The apocalyptic passages of I Peter are much more restrained than those in Thessalonians.

It is conceivable, too, that the literary staff which had helped Paul in the production of Ephesians and other Epistles was available to help Peter in his address to the Gentiles. There are phrases in I Peter which seem to be echoes of phrases in Romans and Ephesians; and there would be nothing surprising if they had been imitated from these Epistles. It has been shown to be quite likely, however, that they can be explained by the use of a common catechetical tradition, probably of an oral character.[1] The furthest we are entitled to go in framing a hypothesis of dependence of I Peter on the Pauline literature is to suppose that the idea of writing such an Epistle, and the general literary form which it took, were suggested to Peter by the fact that Paul had produced such

[1] See my book, *The Primitive Christian Catechism* (Cambridge, 1950).

Epistles and distributed them. The lines of theological thought which are characteristic of Paul himself are not to be found in it.

The reference among the salutations to 'her that is co-elect with you in Babylon' is taken to indicate that the Epistle was written in Rome; but the word Babylon is something more than a code-word for the word Rome. The phrase means: this church, which like yours is a stranger and an exile in an alien and persecuting society; for the churches which are addressed are also 'in Babylon'.

The same paragraph contains a greeting from 'my son Mark', an expression which recalls Paul's reference to his 'true son Timothy', and implies the idea of the recognized pupil and successor in the tradition of teaching. This reference supplies the only point of contact with the picture of the Roman background material which appears in II Timothy. In that Epistle Paul had sent for Mark to come to him. He was not at that time with Peter; or if he was, Paul did not know it. By now Mark had come to Rome and was working with Peter.

THE MARTYRDOM OF PETER

Considerable discussion has taken place about the legal grounds of the persecution to which I Peter is related, which seems to have extended to Asia Minor as well as to Rome. It has been argued that the terminology implies definite legislation or legal procedure which made the profession of the Christian name a capital offence. The words of the Epistle do not warrant this inference. Christians are reproached on account of the name of the Christus; and they suffer as Christians, which is exactly what Tacitus says they did. Peter simply advises his readers to accept the popular nickname and glory in it.

We may turn to the Epistle itself, and see what it says as the persecution becomes more intense.

> Beloved, think it not strange concerning the fiery trial which is come to test and prove you....
>
> If you are reproached for the name of the *Christ*, blessed are ye; for the Spirit of glory and of God rests upon you....
>
> But let none of you suffer as a murderer or as a thief or as an evil-doer or as a meddler in affairs that do not concern him; but if any one of you suffers as a *Christian*, do not let him be ashamed; let him glorify God in this name: for the time is come for judgement to begin at the house of God.

The name *Christian*, which was first given to the disciples in Antioch and was then used rather scornfully by King Agrippa II, appears here for the third and last time, so far as the New Testament goes. It was the name by which the new sect of Jews was generally known, as appears too in Josephus and Tacitus. It had been invented by an unsympathetic world; it was being made the basis of unfair accusations and cruel punishments; but the apostle advises the church to accept it and glory in it.

The legends of the end of the second century cannot be taken into account in considering the martyrdom of Peter. All we are certain of is the actual fact, which is vouched for by St Clement and St John and the general tradition of the church. At the end of St John's Gospel, Jesus says to Peter: 'When you were young, you girt yourself and walked where you wished; but when you are old, you shall stretch out your hands and another man will gird you and carry you where you do not wish to go'; and these enigmatic words are explained as indicating the death by which he would glorify God. Peter had died as a martyr, therefore, before this Gospel was written; and it may be possible to see in the wording of the text a reference to the crucifixion which was the mode of his death according to the legends; but on this point complete certainty seems to elude us.

THE BELIAR APOCALYPSE

The oldest surviving reference to the martyrdom of Peter may be that which is preserved in the *Ascension of Isaiah*. The third and fourth chapters of this imaginative writing contain a brief Christian apocalypse which seems to have been written in the first century. The Son of God, or Beloved, descends from the highest heavens without being recognized by the angels who guard their portals; he gathers twelve apostles; he dies, descends into hell, and rises again; he sends his apostles out into the world and then returns to the Father. Beliar, the spirit of evil and ruler of the world, then descends from his firmament, and takes the form of a king of lawlessness who was the murderer of his mother. He persecutes the 'planting' of the twelve apostles, and one of them is delivered into his hands. The reference to Nero and to Peter is perfectly clear.

It goes on to describe the divine pretensions of Nero and the apostasy of many Christians;[1] but after thirteen hundred and thirty-five days (a figure taken from Daniel), the Beloved will descend from heaven a second time and will cast Beliar and his armies into hell. Those Christians who have remained faithful will ascend into the highest heaven with the Beloved, their garments or bodies of flesh being exchanged for new. Some of those who had seen him when he was on earth the first time will still be living when he comes the second time; and this is what proves the early date of the apocalypse.

Here are some of the leading ideas of the Thessalonian apocalypses and of the Ephesian mysticism; or at any rate we have the same set of images; but the religious insight is on a much lower level. They are woven into a connected myth on the lines of the old oriental myths such as the descent of the goddess Ishtar into the underworld to deliver Tammuz from the powers of death and hell. The idea of the incarnation of the evil spirit in a Roman emperor is no longer concealed; it is made perfectly clear by factual references. The idea of Nero as the embodiment of evil was widely accepted in the first century and appears in the Revelation of St John.

The curious description of the church as the 'planting of the apostles' appears again in the Epistle of Dionysius of Corinth, about 160, in the passage in which he refers to the martyrdoms of Peter and Paul in Rome at the same time. ('I planted', Paul had said in writing to the Corinthians.)

[1] The reference to apostasies in *Beliar* should be compared with the statement in Tacitus that some who were arrested as Christians gave information against others, and this in turn with Clement's reference to jealousy.

CHAPTER 11

THE TRADITION OF PETER

On historical evidence, *p.* 205. Reorganization of the Roman church, *p.* 206. The Epistle of Peter, *p.* 207. The Marcan Gospel, *p.* 209. Oral and literary methods, *p.* 210. The earliest documents, *p.* 211. The making of a book, *p.* 212. The tradition of Peter, *p.* 213. Jesus and the scribes, *p.* 216. Other sources of Mark, *p.* 216. The Passion narrative, *p.* 218. Parables and hard sayings, *p.* 219. The Son of Man, *p.* 220.

ON HISTORICAL EVIDENCE

The stupendous spiritual missile of the gospel, which had been prepared and launched in Galilee in the years 27–30, had completed its trajectory and had exploded in Rome in the years 64–67. As Roman citizens walked about the blackened ruins of their city, they talked of a new people who were called Christians. The church, meanwhile, was reconstructing its corporate life and laying the foundations of its future strength.

It would be easier for us, no doubt, if numbers of contemporary records and biographies had been preserved, but we must do without these guides. Minute traces of evidence are often sufficient to establish great events; and the importance of events bears no proportion to the amount of evidence which happens to survive about them. The footprint of a dinosaur preserved in a rock in one's garden is not a big thing, but it is a sign that a big animal once passed that way. The absence of dinosaurs' footprints in neighbouring gardens does nothing to invalidate this conclusion; the significant thing is that a footprint has survived. This is a principle which is equally true in the consideration of early Christian history; there is no mystery about the meagreness of the evidence; the marvel is that so much has survived.

Two pieces of evidence of the dinosaur's footprint variety have recently come to light. One is a Christian sepulchre not far from Jerusalem, the date of which is necessarily prior to A.D. 70, when the city was destroyed and the country depopulated. The stone coffers which contain the bones are marked with the sign of the cross and the name of Jesus; in one case in Greek letters. The other is a chapel at Herculaneum, the date of which is necessarily prior to A.D. 79, when the city was covered with lava from the eruption of Mount Vesuvius. Above the little altar or *prie-dieu* is a stone slab with an incised cross. So soon, therefore, as the obnoxious word *Christian* becomes known in the Roman world, the sign of the cross appears as its emblem both in Palestine and in Italy. So old are the intimate Christian traditions.

REORGANIZATION OF THE ROMAN CHURCH

The reorganization after a savage persecution was naturally a difficult matter, calling for faith, firmness, and sympathy. There were always, at one end of the scale, the 'confessors' (to use a later technical term), who had stood firm and not denied the Name, and at the other those who had stumbled and fallen, the 'apostates' as they soon came to be called. Many of these would ask for restoration. The numerous problems would be intensified in this instance by the loss of the two masters and leaders, the two 'great pillars', Peter and Paul. As the survivors looked backward and forward, they would realize that they were passing into a new era.

Our documentary evidence shows us that the Roman church was not without leadership of apostolic quality. Silas, we may suppose, had gone off to Pontus with the Epistle of Peter; but Mark and Luke were available. Mark was a great man now. His first experience had been gained in the early days in Jerusalem, where his mother's house had been a centre of prayer for the brethren. He had personally attended upon his cousin Barnabas and upon Paul and Peter in their missionary work. He had been designated by the latter as his 'son' or successor in the faith. In his Gospel he ranks himself as a man of the younger generation; for he identifies the actors in the Passion narrative by the names of their children; the father of Alexander and Rufus, he says, or the mother of James and Joses. (There was a man named Rufus living in Rome whose mother was known to Paul; he had been very much at home in her house.)

Luke had been the close friend and medical adviser of Paul. He was the custodian of important documents, some of which were journals or reports of his own composition. It is likely that he had already begun work on his important history of Christian origins: the Acts may have existed in something very like its present form. Mark had oral traditions and written documents which came to him from Peter and others;

when these received their completed literary form, Luke was obliged to re-model his own work, and could then produce his full-length Gospel.

Timothy had been designated by Paul as his son or successor in the ministry of the gospel.

No doubt the principal activities of Luke and Timothy were in Greece and Asia Minor; but we must not forget that the intercourse which had been established between Rome and Asia by Paul himself continued to be an important factor in church history for a hundred and fifty years. We should think in terms of a curve of continuous interaction which passes through Corinth from Ephesus to Rome and back again.

To these names we must add that of Linus, who was mentioned in Paul's last communication with Timothy, and appears in the Roman tradition as the first bishop of Rome. The second name on the list of Roman bishops is that of Cletus or Anencletus, of whom nothing is known. The third is Clement, who was the leader of the church thirty years later, and wrote an Epistle to the Corinthians which we have already used. Apart from this by no means negligible information, our sense of history would tell us that excellent leadership was available in the Roman church, since in point of fact it was successfully reorganized on rather conservative lines which were based on the Judaeo-Christian liturgical order, the apostolic gospel-preaching, and the apostolic epistles.

THE EPISTLE OF PETER

The Epistle of Peter was a precious legacy, or, if we decide to follow the lead of more sceptical critics, an important production, of the Roman church in this period. It falls into three sections. The first is Paschal in character, and seems to presuppose a baptismal occasion at the Passover season; Christ is described as the lamb without blemish who was slain before the foundation of the world, and the sprinkling of the blood is given a mystical application to the sanctification of the converts. The Gentile Christians are addressed as a diaspora, an Israel of God dispersed among the nations; they are strangers and sojourners in the modern Babylon. The language which Peter uses is taken from Exodus texts which were in order at the Passover. He calls them a chosen race, a royal priesthood, a holy nation, a people for God's own possession, the very titles which the old Israel had received from God on Mount Sinai. They appear again in a liturgical context in the Revelation of St John as a doxology.

> Unto him that loved us,
> And loosed us from our sins by his own blood;
> And made us a kingdom, priests to his God and Father:
> To him be glory and might unto the ages of the ages. Amen.
> (Exodus xix. 5–6; I Peter ii. 5; Revelation i. 5–6 and v. 10.)

This is a Gentile Israel, redeemed from the earth, praising and glorifying God. It gives us a glimpse of the oldest Christian liturgy, which appears again in a more fixed form in Clement; but in I Peter and in the Revelation its Israelite character and inheritance are still dominant; contact with the Jewish antecedents has not been lost; it is Jewish liturgy transformed. In I Peter the worshipping church is described as a spiritual temple in which spiritual sacrifices are offered.

The peculiar destiny of the new Israel was to suffer. The word is repeated twelve times in I Peter, and is balanced by twelve repetitions of the word 'glory'.

The second part of the Epistle is catechetical, and follows naturally from the sacramental thinking of the first part. It is similar in substance and outline to the catechetical material in certain other New Testament Epistles; but each author develops it freely in accordance with his own special tradition. The key-note of the Petrine form is the compound word 'doing-good', which Clement so often echoes.

After some advice on the honour and submission due to the emperor, Peter introduces the topic of domestic and social relations, the 'code of submission' as Clement calls it; but this old Jewish material has been more successfully christianized than in Paul. He considers the case of the Christian wife who is married to a pagan husband, and the Christian slave who belongs to a pagan master and has to suffer violence unjustly, in silence, as Christ himself had done in his Passion; a passage which calls to mind the silence of Christ in Mark's story of the Passion, and the conception of the Messiah who came to be a servant. It is expressed in the time-honoured language of the Song of the Suffering Servant in Isaiah.

The third part has the fiery ordeal of persecution in view, and here the author writes, as an elder and a witness of the sufferings of the

17. A SCRIBE

18. THE APPIAN WAY

Messiah, to men of another race, who love him though they have never seen him. There is an emphasis here which is found in Mark, but is not characteristic of Paul; it is the adoption of the life and passion of Christ as a pattern to be imitated. He turns to his 'fellow-elders' in the church, and exhorts them to shepherd their flock; and when the chief shepherd shall appear, they will receive the crown of glory that passeth not away.

The Epistle is often compared, to its disadvantage, with the writings of Paul. It has none of his mystic dreams, or intellectual flights, or spiritual exaltations, or apocalyptic visions. Its message is to be sober and vigilant and watch unto prayer. Its beauty is always restrained. Its fundamentally Hebrew mode of thought is not in the least disguised by the formal excellence of the Greek it is written in. It is the work of a pastor. Its appeal is simply that of the firm, tender-hearted, rather sad personality of the man who speaks through it so earnestly and simply; with nothing original to say.

THE MARCAN GOSPEL

The traditional view that the Gospel of St Mark is Petrine and Roman has been found to harmonize with the literary evidence and the historical indications. Its use by the other three evangelists proves that it was early written, widely distributed, and everywhere received as authoritative; but not as scripture, of course, for that time had not come. The other evangelists do not hesitate to recast its rather unliterary Greek, and to omit or transpose some of the short sections of which it is mainly composed. It would appear that its order was not approved of by some of the brethren in Asia Minor, who must have had some other form of the gospel, which they preferred.

The disciple John, who flourished in Ephesus not long after it was written, came to its defence. He made a judgement upon it which was preserved by his pupil Papias.[1] Mark was the interpreter of Peter, he said; but Peter had never made any systematic arrangement of the gospel material; he composed his teachings as the need arose; and Mark had written them down accurately, though not in order. Not that he had made any errors; he had taken care to avoid errors or omissions. Now this John was a disciple of Jesus and a master in the Ephesian school; and such a statement, made by such a man, may be

[1] See chapter 17, *p.* 317.

taken to be authoritative. His guarantee of the accuracy of Mark implies that he was familiar himself with the tradition of Peter; and his picture of Mark interpreting for Peter confirms and amplifies the picture of Mark in Peter's Epistle as his 'son'.

Nevertheless it is possible that the opinion which he gave may have acquired a rather too precise form in the minds of his hearers; and perhaps we are not bound to restrict ourselves too closely to the words in which Papias reported it. A careful study of the text suggests that Mark was more than a translator and a scribe; he may have had access to other material; he may have had predecessors in the art of Gospel-writing; he may have spent some years in literary experimentation; but whatever may be thought of these possibilities, the fact remains that his Gospel, as a whole, has a Petrine quality, which supports the evidence which it preserves. Papias does not record that it was written in Rome, so far as our meagre knowledge of his writings takes us, but the connexion seems well enough vouched for.

ORAL AND LITERARY METHODS

The oral form of the oldest apostolic tradition is vouched for in this quotation from the lips of John, and it is fully recognized by modern scholars. It is implied in the title Rabbi, which was freely used in addressing Jesus. The rabbis taught their pupils to memorize, and, so far as their own teaching about the Law was concerned, they did not tolerate writing. One of their favourite maxims was to commit nothing to writing. Now oral teaching naturally assumes a set form for easier memorization; and these oral documents, as we may call them, became the stock in trade of the pupils when they set up as masters or teachers. This method of transmission explains the fixity of form which the gospel traditions assumed, and at the same time the variability in the telling. The method was necessarily conservative, one memory checking another at each repetition of the material. There was nothing vague or haphazard about it; it was the normal method of transmitting knowledge from one generation to another. The teaching of the first-century rabbis continued to be handed down in this way, through a succession of disciples, until it was written down in the Mishnah about the end of the second century.

It is fortunate that the oral tradition of the disciples of Jesus was reduced to writing while it was still fresh in their minds. This development was due to the fact that it had passed into the Greek world, where literary methods were the natural ones. There may have been Aramaic transcripts, but if there were, they led to no literary tradition in that language. Papias made a statement about an Aramaic transcript which was composed by Matthew.

THE EARLIEST DOCUMENTS

The only early gospel document, apart from Mark, about which we can feel any certainty is the document called 'Q', portions of which can be reconstructed by a comparison of Matthew and Luke when both writers make use of it; but the resultant reconstruction is far from satisfying.

It consisted of fairly short paragraphs which contained sayings of Jesus, dialogue, and even anecdote. Its order can be determined in part. It opened, as Mark does, with the preaching of John the Baptist, of which it gives a much fuller account. It went on from the baptism of Jesus to the three temptations, for which it is our only authority. It appears to have contained a short version of the Sermon on the Mount, which was followed by the healing of the centurion's servant or son. It included some account of the calling of the Twelve, and possibly a list of their names, and certainly the various instructions or exhortations which were addressed to them from time to time, including the mystical passage about the revelation of the Father in the Son, and the exaltation of the faculty of spiritual vision, and the counsels not to harbour fear or doubt, but to trust wholly in the Father. The gracious style of this author was well adapted to convey the poetic power of these passages. He retains their Old Testament colour. The Queen of Sheba appears before Solomon; Jonah confronts the Ninevites; the Gentiles are to sit down with Abraham and Isaac and Jacob in the kingdom: all of them pro-Gentile passages. It is rich in controversy with Scribes and Pharisees; and denunciations of an unspiritual generation, worse than Sodom and Gomorrha, which failed to appreciate either the Baptist or the Son of Man; and apocalyptic pictures of a day on which he would come again in glory. Its scene is laid in Galilee, though it ends in Jerusalem, or with Jerusalem in sight; Jerusalem that killed the prophets and stoned those who were sent to her.

It is thought to have been older than Mark, possibly a production of the fifties; and so was the Passion narrative in one form or another; and possibly other sequences of teaching or narrative. It has been suggested that Mark drew upon Q, but this is quite unlikely. It would appear that the form of the tradition which he followed sometimes included independent versions of the same events or forms of teaching. The recent school of criticism known as 'Form Criticism' believes that short units of oral teaching or narrative were current in the churches in more than one form; that they were combined into sequences for the use of teachers; and that these sequences were the sources from which the more ambitious literary efforts were constructed. A somewhat restricted theory.

THE MAKING OF A BOOK

It is desirable now to have some knowledge about book-production in the Roman world. Books were made of a material called papyrus, in the form of a roll. The most convenient width seems to have been about ten inches, the length running to as much as forty feet. Matthew, Luke, John, and Acts would all conform to this average or optimum size; and these are the longest books in the New Testament. In composing a book, the author would have to take into account the amount of footage at his disposal, and plan accordingly. The Gospel of Mark would not work out at more than about twenty feet, allowing the writing to take up the same amount of room as it does on the Vatican Codex.

The Greek word for such a roll was 'biblos' or 'biblion', and our word Bible (*Biblia Sacra*) is simply a continuation of the use of this word. The corresponding Latin word was 'volumen', a rolling or volume.

So far as we know the modern book-form was not yet in use; but within a hundred years the book-producers in Egypt began to fold sheets of parchment in quires, and sew them together along the folds, so producing the 'codex' or book-form that we know. It was a cheaper method, since both sides of the material could be used for writing. Christians were quick to adopt it, and the oldest surviving Gospel manuscripts, or fragments of Gospel manuscripts, are of this type. Nevertheless, it is still thought that the originals appeared in the form of rolls, and this type of Gospel was used at Rome as late as the end of the second century.

The roll was not so inconvenient to use as is sometimes suggested. It was held transversely in both hands, one end in one and one in the other; not up and down as is sometimes supposed. It was rolled up on a wooden roller which was not attached to the papyrus, a second roller being used to take up the part which had been read. The text began at the left-hand end of the roll, and was written in narrow vertical columns, so that a small amount could be exposed for reading at any point. If one wished to refer from one part of the book to another, all that was necessary was to lay it on a table, where a large amount of it could be rapidly unrolled at once. Three or four feet of ten-inch papyrus would reveal one-sixth of Mark, allowing the writing to be on the same scale as in the Vatican Codex. Figures in the margin made reference to chapters or paragraphs perfectly simple. First lines of chapters were sometimes written in red ink. The general plan of a book could be made out more rapidly and more easily than in a codex or modern book.

The text was written with a reed pen. Capital letters, called 'uncials', were used in formal texts, but running hands, called 'cursives', were also in use. In the case of uncials, there was no division between the words, and a word might break at the end of a line. This continuous succession of letters made the art of reading, and copying, rather more difficult. It would be better to have a lector, or reader-aloud, who knew his text; and there is a definite reference to this minister in Mark's Gospel, who was expected apparently to explain hard passages. Most books in the ancient world were planned to be read aloud to reading circles, and the Gospels are no exception; they were planned to be effective when operated as part of the church procedure.

THE TRADITION OF PETER

We know from Paul's Epistles that there were different parties or traditions in the Roman church or churches, some of which may never have coalesced into the resultant Roman church. There had been arguments about the lawfulness of certain foods and the observance of certain days. Jewish Christians had strongly opposed Paul himself during his first imprisonment. The great achievement of the thirty years which followed the martyrdoms was the fusion of the traditions of Peter and Paul, within the liberal Judaeo-Christian tradition, into a unified church which commanded the respect of the Christian world. Clement's Epistle is the literary monument of this achievement. Mark, who had been closely connected with both apostles, was admirably fitted to play a leading part in this development; and it is clear that he did so, not only for the Roman church, but through the Roman church for the church at large.

It is possible, by careful literary criticism of his Gospel, to make reliable inferences about the state of the church which it was designed to serve. The material of which it is composed, and even the phraseology in which it is expressed, must have come, of course, from the apostolic tradition; but the principles of selection, arrangement, and emphasis must often have been decided in view of local needs; and a certain amount of editing would be required; many sentences and paragraphs must have been written freely by the author.

The word 'gospel' did not at that time mean a book. It meant the apostolic message and mission, particularly among the Gentiles. Mark does not hesitate to use it, in his prologue, for the preaching of the Kingdom of God by Jesus in Galilee; implying that the message about Jesus which had been preached to the nations was continuous and identical with that original proclamation. Their baptism was the same baptism; the Spirit which they received was the same Spirit. The space allotted to the preaching of the Baptist is curtailed in order to give prominence to the baptism of Jesus, and the descent of the Spirit upon him; which precede the preaching in Galilee.

How, then, did a written book come to be called a gospel? Possibly because this one began with the words: 'Beginning of the Gospel of Jesus Christ, the Son of God.' Hebrew books were commonly called by their first words, and since the word 'beginning' had already been appropriated for the Book of Genesis, this one would be called 'The Gospel'; and when it had to compete with other similar books, it would be called The Gospel 'according to Mark'. But we do not know when this occurred.

The use of the word is no accident, however. The primary purpose of the book was evangelism. The figure of Jesus of Nazareth is cast on the screen in motion and in colour. He lives again as he lived in Galilee and Jerusalem, among the crowds and with his disciples. He calls, he heals, he forgives, he blesses; and as he does so, the power that was operative to heal and bless and forgive in Galilee becomes operative in

Rome. It is the person of Jesus, rather than his teaching, that is presented throughout.

This tradition of evangelism is not merely Galilean; it is Petrine. The 'mystery of the kingdom', it says, was entrusted to twelve disciples, whose call, training, and authorization form one of the leading themes of the book; the right tradition would therefore be that of the Twelve. But there was a special group of three (or four) disciples within the Twelve, whose position was closer to Jesus than the rest; and therefore it would be inferred that their tradition would be better still. Best of all would be the tradition of Peter, who was their spokesman.

Those who were outside the circle of the Twelve and their company did not properly understand; 'everything came to them in riddles (or parables)'; and among those who 'stood outside' was the family of Jesus. The suggestion would undoubtedly have been that their tradition was inferior to that of Peter and the Twelve. Roman Christians could not help noting these points; they might remember them if Jewish Christians who insisted on some particular provision of the Law of Moses chanced to invoke the authority of James. The Petrine tradition would thus come to the help of the Pauline.

Mark produced his written roll by piecing together various short stories or units of teaching, or sequences of such units which had already taken form in the apostolic tradition. Each unit could stand alone as a Sunday lesson, and quite probably did. They were written in a rough uncultured Greek with a strong Jewish flavour, occasionally retaining such Aramaic words as *epphathah* or *talitha cumi* or *gehenna*. We notice a number of touches which are marks of personal recollection or colloquial anecdote. He thus retained in his literary work something of the impression which was created when the old fisherman told his stories over the bread and wine. It is not the language of the Hellenistic schools, but it is surprisingly vivid and effective, especially when it is read aloud by one who knows how. It is awkwardly expressed now and then, but it is good, robust, well-knit prose. It is all sinew and bone and muscle; it has no superfluous fat. And it is remarkable how much material it comprises in its twenty feet.

It cannot be called an artless composition. Its repetitions and recurrences form an artistic pattern. Its short units are grouped into sequences, and advance from climax to climax. The Passion narrative is in view from the start, and everything moves towards it.

JESUS AND THE SCRIBES

The second Galilean sequence opens with the call of a fifth disciple, Levi the publican, elsewhere identified with Matthew; and its theme is the conflict between Jesus and the scribes who expounded and administered the Law. As the volume unrolls further, it becomes clear that the 'house' or school of Jesus was built up in opposition to the official Rabbinic schools, which were also called 'houses'. Jesus eats and drinks with sinners in the house of Levi, even on a fast day which the Pharisees are observing. The new teaching supersedes the scribal legalism on many points; even the Sabbath has to give way before the gospel. The Son of Man has power to forgive sins; the Son of Man is master of the Sabbath. Later on in the book there is a strong scene in which he opposes the oral tradition of the Pharisees and makes a formal pronouncement on the subject of clean and unclean, virtually abolishing the distinction. It was a subject of keen controversy in the apostolic church, wherever Jew met Greek; and so no doubt were the other subjects touched on in this series.

Jesus brings in a new spiritual authority. The old legalism cannot come to terms with him, for the great spiritualities override the small technicalities, and the needs of humanity can be more important than the demands of the ceremonial system. The supreme commandments, however, still occupy their fundamental position, especially those which proclaim the unity of the God of Israel and enjoin the love of God and the love of one's neighbour. This pronouncement won the approbation of an unnamed Pharisee scribe, thus confirming the evidence of the Acts that there were Pharisees who were not unfriendly. (It is not intended to suggest that the Rabbinic authority, as it developed in Judaism, did not temper the ceremonial law in view of human needs. It did. Human life came first.)

These passages support the picture of Peter in the Acts and in Galatians as the chief apostle of Jewish Christianity, and, in spite of that, the exponent of a liberal policy towards the Gentiles. Roman Christians would learn that a liberal form of Jewish Christianity was legitimately descended from the teaching and example of Jesus himself.

OTHER SOURCES OF MARK

The question has been asked whether Mark had other material to draw upon in addition to the tradition of Peter. Our common sense tells us that he must have, for we are still in the period when the facts about Jesus were common knowledge, and there were many disciples and eyewitnesses still available; and Mark himself had been immersed in this stream of talk and testimony from his youth. The detection of it in his narrative is a somewhat speculative enterprise, however.

It is considered likely by many scholars that the stories of the feeding of the five thousand and the feeding of the four thousand are only different versions of the same event; and if this is so, one of them, probably the four thousand, may reasonably be considered to be derived from a non-Petrine tradition; and if this is so, there may be other connected material of a non-Petrine character. It is also possible to detect in the Gospel, as it stands, certain sequences of teaching which look as if they had attained written form before they were included in it. The most convincing cases are the collection of parables in the fourth chapter and the 'Little Apocalypse' in the thirteenth; but it does not follow that these collections of teaching had not been put together in the school of Peter.

On the other hand, the evangelist did not use all the material which was known to him. Jesus is constantly represented as teaching; but not much of this teaching is actually given. The 'Sermon on the Mount' and the 'Our Father' are neither of them included. Such material must have been handled in the Roman ecclesia and in the school of Peter; but it did not serve the purposes for which this volume was designed. It probably continued to be handled on a purely oral basis.

The Gospel begins and ends abruptly. There are no stories of the birth, childhood, or early manhood of Jesus; and no Resurrection stories, though the fact of the Resurrection is declared beforehand and the tomb is found empty on the Sunday morning after the Passover. There has been much discussion about this sudden ending; the women depart from the tomb trembling and beside themselves; fear makes them speechless.

Some scholars have suggested that the end of the book has been lost by some mishap, but this view is not very easy to accept, since it reached Matthew and Luke in this form. After all, we do not know what happened when the lector came to the end of the roll. There may have been a benediction like the opening words of I Peter: 'Blessed be the God and Father of our Lord Jesus Christ, who has begotten us again to a living hope by the resurrection of Jesus Christ from the dead'; or psalms and hymns and spiritual songs; or the breaking of the bread.

THE PASSION NARRATIVE

The fact is that everything in the book is subordinated to the story of the crucifixion, and leads up to it. This narrative is a well organized literary whole, and had probably existed in written form for some time. It shows the marks of liturgical usage. It was built to fit into the twenty-four hours of the Jewish day, beginning at sunset with the Passover meal, and lasting till the sunset of the following day, when the Lord's body was laid in the tomb. Everything leads up to the cross: the conflict with the scribes, the choice and training of the Twelve, Peter's act of faith in Jesus, the great wonder of the transfiguration, and the three Passion predictions with their pendent sequences of teaching. The figure of Peter comes into prominence as he makes his act of faith in Jesus as the Messiah, and the story of the Passion makes much of his act of denial.

Interwoven with this progression of thought is the theme of martyrdom, of following Jesus and confessing Jesus, which had become a dire reality for Roman Christians in the Neronian persecution. Peter appears throughout as the man who had faith but failed to understand and failed to witness. There is no attempt whatever to glorify him; and in this sad picture we are bound to recognize the self-witness of the great apostle. No one else would have pictured him so. The humiliation of Peter in the Marcan Gospel is of one piece with the grave restraint of his own Epistle; the emphasis in both is on suffering here and glory hereafter. But, for the first hearers, this sombre self-portrait had been transfigured by the glory of his recent martyrdom, and the example of his earlier years may have been used to justify and inspire a sympathetic attitude towards brethren who had failed to take up the cross in Rome.

The pattern of martyrdom in this Gospel is not Peter; it is Jesus. He had been executed by the Romans as a pretender from the family of David who had tried to make himself king; and it was necessary to combat the impression which had been made by this fact and to place in their true light certain words and actions of his in Jerusalem. It is made clear that Pilate was never convinced that the charge against him was true, and that the sanhedrin had engineered his death for quite other reasons. The opinion of Pilate was reinforced by the comment of the Roman officer who had been put in charge of the crucifixion: 'Doubtless this man was a Son of God'; or, of course, 'a son of a god'. In these respects we see signs of a legitimate and necessary 'apologetic' in this Roman gospel.

PARABLES AND HARD SAYINGS

It was necessary, too, to explain certain hard sayings of Jesus which were not intended by him to be taken literally. It seems that the Gentile mind had some difficulty in understanding some of his 'parables' or 'riddles', and we learn from Mark that the Jews themselves had not found it easy. The speech of Jesus was full of gigantic figures of speech: stars fall from heaven, wheat sprouts from the earth in marvellous fertility, camels pass through the eyes of needles, and mountains are cast into the midst of the sea. This was no artifice; it was a natural way of talking about profound spiritual truth; it gave pleasure. It was the product of a peasant culture, and was obviously akin to folk-lore, folk-song, and folk-dance; it was the humble descendant of the old oriental culture which expressed its heavenly wisdom in a language which was drawn from myth and ritual and the rotation of the seasons and the revolution of the heavens. This idiom had been purified and glorified by the sages of Israel, both priests and prophets, and it lent itself superlatively well to the genius and purpose of Jesus. Only the household of personal disciples, however, could understand the mysticism of it, and even they had been slow to see and hear; to those outside it all came in riddles; or parables—for that is one meaning of the word. Such is the theory of parables which Mark emphasizes. The vision of the spiritual realities was a gift from heaven which was strangely missing in the wise men of Israel, an idea which is expressed equally strongly in Q.

The use of parables seems to have impressed the Roman ecclesia. A Marcan parable, with a correct mystical interpretation, is quoted by Clement; and the prophet Hermas composed a number of parables on the Marcan lines, though naturally very much inferior in power and far too complicated; these formed part of his regular teaching ministry, and he is careful to explain that the understanding of parables is a special gift which is received in answer to prayer.

The first considerable section of parabolic teaching in Mark is the fourth chapter which contains the three seed parables and the theory of mystical vision. The second is the thirteenth or 'Little Apocalypse'. This apocalyptic teaching in Mark is non-eschatological. Jesus alludes in earlier chapters to the resurrection of the dead and the destinies of eternal life and eternal destruction; but he does not suggest the approach of what is called in modern theology the 'end of the world'; he does not say that these things are to come soon.

The imagery of falling stars and eclipses and earthquakes falls very far short of this, and seems to be used to indicate a period of world-war and confusion. They are well-worn prophetic images which occur as a matter of course, in any apocalypse, to suggest the intervention of the deity in human affairs. The strong sense of expectation in this Gospel is focused entirely upon the coming of the Son of Man in his glory to this generation. The meaning of this mysterious promise is not revealed. It must have engaged the attention of the Roman church at this time.

THE SON OF MAN

The Son of Man, in Jewish thought, was a man from heaven, a being of heavenly origin, who was the image or likeness of the eternal deity; God's man comes to put everything right; but the idea of pre-existence is never so much as mentioned by Mark, though the use of the title may be thought to imply it. Within the glory of the Son of Man title, however, is enfolded the more august title of Son of God; for the Son of Man will be displayed 'in the glory of his Father'. During his earthly life, he has unlimited spiritual authority, but his true being is hidden and his teaching veiled in mystery. As the volume is unrolled, eyes are opened and ears unstopped and mysteries revealed, and in due course it becomes clear that its supreme theme is that of conflict with the powers of evil which comes to a climax on the cross when he says, 'My God, my God, why hast thou forsaken me?' Beyond that, it indicates, are the Resurrection and the coming in glory.

The Gospel thus falls into line with the Epistle. It is a study of the Passion of Jesus for a martyr church; it is a Gospel of suffering now and glory hereafter.

CHAPTER 12

THE FALL OF JERUSALEM

The apocalyptic view of history, *p.* 221. John the seer, *p.* 223. The Little Apocalypse of Mark, *p.* 224. The revolt in Judaea, A.D. 66, *p.* 226. Prophecies and oracles, *p.* 228. Vespasian in Palestine, A.D. 67, *p.* 229. The War of the Emperors, A.D. 68–69, *p.* 231. The dissension in Jerusalem, *p.* 233. The destruction of Jerusalem, A.D. 70, *p.* 234. The Revelation of St John, *p.* 236.

THE APOCALYPTIC VIEW OF HISTORY

We must now turn to the writings of the Christian prophets for help in our reading of history, and in the first place to the older stratum or strata in the Revelation of John. In these visions the persecuting world-power appears as a 'beast arising out of the sea', an expression which bears witness to the Palestinian origin of the vision, for in Hebrew the word 'sea' is used to mean the west; though of course the sea was a symbol which had important imaginative associations, derived ultimately from the chaos and darkness of the creation myth of the oriental world.

The beast is a horrible monster who wins the worship of the world. He is the devil's champion against the saints of God; he is the opponent of the Lamb of God, or Son of Man, who is the leader of the saints. His general likeness to a leopard, his claws like those of a bear, and his mouth like that of a lion, would remind the Christian reader of the aspects of Roman government which he met with in Nero's garden or in the amphitheatre. Those who follow and worship him are said to have 'his mark, the number of the beast or the number of his name upon their right hand or upon their forehead, just as a pious Jew wore the name of his God upon his left hand or upon his forehead. This mysterious number is six hundred and sixty and six. Those who resist the beast are the 'hundred and forty and four thousand' who stand with the Lamb on Mount Zion, and follow him wherever he goes.

These figures were symbols in their own right, and we can partially unravel their meaning. Twelve is the number of the signs of the zodiac and of the months of the year; of the sons of Jacob and the disciples of Jesus; of the true Israel and of the elect people of God. The twelve tribes or the twelve-times-twelve clans are the full and total number of all the faithful who encircle their sun Jesus Christ and are the heirs of his universal kingdom. Such explanations always seem to fall short of the glory of the poetry which the prophet wrote, but they point the way to its understanding. The figure six seems to stand for the 'ungodly', man as he exists apart from God and in defiance of him; it just falls short of the perfect number seven; it is only half of the heavenly number twelve. The half of seven appears in the symbolic time which is allotted to the tyranny of the 'beast'; it is 'a time and [two] times and half a time': one period plus two periods plus half a period, making three and a half periods. The ungodly kingdom cannot finish a perfect course; it crashes half-way through it.

Another image in the Revelation which belongs to this period is that of the Great Harlot, or Whore of Babylon, who is 'arrayed in purple and scarlet colour, and decked with gold and precious stones and pearls . . . and drunken with the blood of the martyrs of Jesus'. A majority of scholars still believe this repellent figure to be the city of Rome, but we commend the identification with Jerusalem,[1] the first great centre of persecution, where Jesus, Stephen, James the son of Zebedee, and James the Just, with many others, had been murdered at the instigation of a corrupt priesthood. The figure of the harlot throughout Hebrew prophecy has the meaning of the community of Israel or city of Jerusalem, which was meant to be the bride of God but had proved unfaithful to him. 'How is the faithful city become a harlot', says Isaiah; and when the city which is called Babylon in the Revelation is destroyed by fire, its place is taken by the descent from heaven of a new Jerusalem which is called the bride of the Lamb.

We have here a mode of writing history which is strange to us, though it has a modern parallel in the political cartoonist, with his bears and lions and eagles, or his bull-dogs and elephants and donkeys. The mind which thinks in images can sometimes portray the true character of a political movement or public personality more effectively and dramatically than the critic or commentator, and in half the time. But there is more than this in the Judaeo-Christian apocalyptic. There is a philosophy of history which is based on the conviction that Almighty God is all-active and all-powerful in the world of nature and in the world of men; he pulls down one and sets up another; he gives the

[1] There is a compromise suggestion: earlier prophecies dealing with Jerusalem have been fused with later prophecies dealing with Rome.

kingdom to whom he will. The real independence of nature in its sphere is not denied, nor the free will of men; they are asserted; but the supreme 'pantocratoric' power is of God. He rules over all things, for that is the meaning of the word *pantocrator*, which is translated 'Almighty'. The emperor (or the devil) is only *cosmocrator*; he rules the world. This sheer faith in Almighty God runs through the whole Hebrew scriptures and is expressed especially vividly in the symbolic tales of Daniel. It is the origin and root of the gospel of God's 'kingdom' which Jesus proclaimed in Galilee. Everyone who has this faith sees, at every point in history, the will of God working out his purposes with men and nations, despite their unruly wills and affections.

JOHN THE SEER

There are two possible views about the oldest visions of the Revelation. According to one view they were the work of an unknown prophet or school of prophets who witnessed in Palestine about this time; and they were incorporated into the Revelation when John composed it in Ephesus about thirty years later. Others think that the John who wrote in Ephesus was himself the author of the early prophecies. He certainly made the claim.

In his tenth chapter he describes his call to be a prophet. A mighty angel descends from heaven with an open scroll in his hand. His face is like the sun; the rainbow encircles his head; he plants one foot on the sea and the other on the land; he lifts up his right hand into heaven and declares with a voice like a lion roaring that there will be no more time; that is to say no more delay in executing the judgement of God. The angel represents the 'Word of God' which had come to all the prophets and now came to the author of the Revelation. The scroll is delivered to him, and likewise a 'reed' like a rod with which he is to measure the sanctuary of God, and the altar, and those who worship there. His ministry, that is to say, is in Jerusalem. In the continuation of this passage Jerusalem is described as the place where God's witnesses are opposed and persecuted; their dead bodies lie 'in the street of the Great City, which is spiritually called Sodom and Egypt, where also their Lord was crucified'. There is no doubt, therefore, where we are. We have the inspired utterances of a Christian prophet who maintained his witness in the 'Great City' during the bad years.

It is the eleventh chapter which contains this Jerusalem oracle. The twelfth tells of the mystical birth of the Saviour; the thirteenth contains the vision of the beast from the sea, originally perhaps Caligula, but now Nero; in the fourteenth we have the 'hundred and forty and four thousands' on the Mount Zion, that is to say the followers of Jesus who are destined to be martyrs; and this is followed by a brief vision of the gospel sweeping through the world. It is the only use of the word 'gospel' in all the Johannine writings.[1]

I saw another angel fly in the midst of heaven, having the everlasting gospel to announce to those that dwell upon the earth, and to every nation and kindred and people and tongue. (Rev. xiv. 6.)

This is precisely the same historical moment that is emphasized so strongly in Mark: 'This Gospel must first be announced to all the nations.' It is the point in history which we have now reached.

THE LITTLE APOCALYPSE OF MARK

The Revelation gives us a contemporary Christian voice from Jerusalem, and the 'Little Apocalypse' of Mark gives us a contemporary voice from Rome. They enable us to understand how Christians spoke and prayed when they attended their meetings under the shadow of persecution and impending world-chaos. Many scholars think that the thirteenth chapter of Mark had been reduced to writing before it was incorporated in his Gospel as an introduction to the Passion narrative. Like John's vision of the beast rising from the sea, it may be as old as the period of Caligula, 37–41; and it bears the names of the first four apostles, Peter and Andrew, and James, and John. No doubt it was widely circulated. It was designed to be read in the ecclesia with explanations by the lector; for at one point there is a note which says, 'Let the reader understand', that is to say exercise his intelligence; he was to give an explanation, or possibly substitute some plainer form of speech. We see in the Revelation of John and the *Pastor* of Hermas that prophetic material was written down and then read to the ecclesia; we gather from the note in Mark that comment or expansion or paraphrase was in order; for it was a living tradition which elucidated current history. This would explain a certain freedom of handling

[1] It is used only once in I Peter (in reference to persecution); twice in the Acts (once by Peter and once by Paul); commonly in Paul, Mark, and Matthew.

19. THE ARCH OF TITUS

20. THE ARCH OF TITUS: DETAIL

which can be observed when we study how Matthew and Luke reproduce this chapter.

It resembles the visions of John in another particular; its background is Palestinian, and yet it extends its view to cover the world-situation. It begins with a warning against false leaders who will arise in the nation and make misleading pretensions. It goes on to speak of a period of world-war and world-confusion. It gives warning of persecutions, so bringing the martyrdoms into its view of history. The apostles will be universally hated because of Christ's name; and yet the gospel will be proclaimed to all the nations; nothing can prevent that. And we are just at the point when Mark is making his transcript in Rome and John is bearing his witness in Jerusalem: and both are looking for a dénouement. It is the time when the world-harvest will be reaped. The Son of Man, who came sowing the seed when the generation opened, will come again to reap the harvest as the generation closes. The Jerusalem which rejected him forty years before will be judged now, and the whole system of priesthood and sacrifice will be swept away for ever. Not one stone will be left to stand upon another.

A third point in common thus comes to light. In both cases the scene of the oracles has the Temple as its background. In Mark the opening words are uttered in the Temple and predict its destruction, and the rest of the Little Apocalypse is an expansion of this utterance. In the Revelation the first work of the seer is succeeded by his commission to 'measure' the Temple. We can see therefore without difficulty the view of current history which unifies Christian apocalyptic. The city which crucified the Lord and killed his prophets is to be judged; the Temple and priestly system are to be destroyed; and the agent is to be the ungodly imperial power, evil though it is. Our minds go back to the 'blasphemous words' which Stephen was said to have uttered against this 'holy place'; and not only to Stephen, but to words which Jesus was alleged to have spoken when he was examined in the house of Annas, who was the father and evil genius of the Jerusalem priesthood. Time had been allowed for repentance; the old policy of violence and oppression had continued; judgement will now take place.

We turn to the pages of Josephus for the record of the actual events; and we shall find that he, too, thinks that the destruction of the holy city was due to the judgement of God.

THE REVOLT IN JUDAEA, A.D. 66

Law and order would appear to have broken down altogether in Judaea. The new procurator Gessius Florus, who succeeded Albinus in 64, seems to have been the worst of a bad series, and openly plundered the unfortunate country. According to Josephus, he goaded the Jews into rebellion in order to cover up his own tyranny and misgovernment. At the Passover of 66 he went up to Jerusalem with the idea of getting possession of the Temple treasure, and there was resistance and scenes of violence in the streets. He retired after an indiscriminate massacre, but had not been successful in his design.

The revolutionary parties among the people, known as Zealots or Cananeans or Sicarii (dagger-men), were eager for war. They had a fanatical faith which made them entirely confident that God would defend his city; but the wealthy and respectable were on the side of conciliation. King Agrippa II made a speech in favour of submission to Rome, or at any rate Josephus, who wrote under his patronage, put such a speech into his mouth. It was, of course, the policy which Agrippa advocated. It had no effect upon the people whatever, and he went off to his kingdom in Galilee and Trachonitis.

The first gesture of defiance was made by the governor of the Temple, a young man named Eleazar, whose father was the ex-high priest Ananias, before whom St Paul had been tried eight years previously. He refused to allow any gift to be accepted on behalf of a non-Jew; and this meant that the customary sacrifice for the emperor could not be offered. It was a breach of allegiance. The high priests and other magnates protested, but Eleazar had the support of the Zealots. Fighting broke out in the streets between the two factions. Eleazar and the Zealots took possession of the Temple and the eastern part of the city, where it stood; the high priests and their party, who were all for peace, held the higher part of the city which rose up toward the west of the Temple. Here the palace and fortresses of King Herod the Great were situated.

While this was going on, a picturesque figure arrived from Galilee. This was Menahem, a third son of the famous Judas of Galilee, the founder of the Zealot party. Menahem ensconced himself in the Transjordanian fortress of Masada, which had been seized by the insurgents. He seized the arms and supplies which he found there, and entered

Jerusalem, where he gave himself the airs of a king. He attacked the party of the high priests, murdering the ex-high priest Ananias. Eleazar the son of Ananias rallied some support, attacked Menahem, and killed him.

What remained of the Roman garrison was induced to surrender by a promise that their lives would be spared; but as soon as they laid down their arms they were massacred by order of Eleazar. The troops which had been sent by King Agrippa were permitted to leave. It is not to be wondered at that a wave of violence spread throughout the eastern world. There was a massacre of Jews in Caesarea and desperate fighting between Jews and Syrians in the Gentile cities of Galilee and Decapolis. It was at this time that Gadara, Pella, and other Peraean cities fell into the hands of the insurgent Jews.

It fell to Cestius, who was the legate in Antioch, to deal with the revolt. He lost no time in marching southward to Ptolemais with the twelfth legion. He left his assistant Gallus at Sepphoris, with the legion, to subdue Galilee, and went on to Caesarea to restore order there. Gallus soon rejoined him, though it would seem that he had not reduced Galilee to order, many of the Gentile cities in Galilee and Decapolis remaining in Jewish hands. He had decided to march immediately on Jerusalem, and Josephus thought that the war could have been brought to an end then by resolute action; but, for some unknown reason, Cestius retired after establishing himself in sight of the gates of the city. His retreat to Caesarea became a rout, for he was pursued by Zealot troops under Simon the son of Geiora. This occurred after the Feast of Tabernacles in 66, that is to say in September or October. Nothing more would be done in the way of hostilities till the following spring.

There was an interval, therefore, before hostilities began in real earnest; and, as Josephus quaintly says, 'many of the most eminent of the Jews swam away from the city as from a ship when it is going to sink'. By these he probably meant the wealthier citizens and some of the reputable Jewish Rabbis who settled in Jamnia (Jabneh) and became the founders of the new Judaism. Their leader was Johanan ben Zakkai, a pupil of Hillel, who, according to Mishnaic traditions, was carried out of the city in a coffin by his pupils Rabbi Eliezer ben Hyrcanus and Rabbi Joshua ben Hananya. A Jewish-Christian tradition which is preserved by Eusebius and Epiphanius tells how the Christians left Jerusalem before the siege and migrated to a Gentile city named Pella in Peraea, in obedience to 'a certain oracle which was vouchsafed by way of revelation to approved men'. They abandoned the witness to the gospel which they had maintained for forty years. They left the city to its doom.

According to Josephus, however, the city of Pella had been 'laid waste' (looted?) by insurgent Jews, and may still have been in their hands. The condition of Jamnia is uncertain. Perhaps Jerusalem Christians took refuge in the hill-country of Judaea during the winter of 66–67 and organized their flight to Pella in 67. Or perhaps they did not leave Jerusalem until a year or more later.

PROPHECIES AND ORACLES

The record of Josephus is full of prophecies and oracles. As early as 62, the year in which James the Just was murdered, a peasant named Jesus ben Ananus appeared at the Feast of Tabernacles, repeating in a melancholy sing-song,

> A voice from the east, a voice from the west,
> A voice from the four winds!
> A voice against Jerusalem and the holy house,
> A voice against the bridegrooms and the brides,
> A voice against the whole people!

He maintained his witness for a period of seven years, in spite of torture and punishment inflicted upon him by the authorities, and he died in the last year of the war. It may have been in the springtime of that same year, 62, a week before the Passover, that the priests whose duty it was to tend the altar fire, entering in the dark hour before dawn, found a light shining round the altar as bright as day; and a month later, also in the night-time, the great eastern gate, which could with difficulty be shut by twenty men, opened of its own accord. At the Feast of Pentecost, also in the night, the priests felt a quaking and heard a great noise, and after that the sound of a multitude saying, 'Let us remove hence.' The Mishnah, too, preserves such stories; for there was a night, it was said, when the eastern gate of the Temple flew open of its own accord, and Rabbi Johanan ben Zakkai quote the ominous prophecy, 'Open thy doors, O Lebanon, that the fire may devour thy cedars.' Such were the tales men told one another.

In comparison with such portents the Christian signs and oracles seem plain and straightforward. If we turn, for instance, to the Little Apocalypse in Mark, we find these words:

When ye shall see the abomination of desolation standing where it ought not—let the reader take note—then let those who are in Judaea fly to the mountains. (Mark xiii. 14.)

Fortunately the only enigma in this sentence presents no problem. The 'abomination of desolation', as Matthew points out, was 'spoken of by Daniel the prophet', who meant by it the capture of Jerusalem by the army of the world-emperor, and the desecration of the temple.[1] Christians were warned to flee when this desolating force appeared. The hill-country of Judaea would be the natural place of refuge in such an emergency; and we have suggested that a flight to the hills may have preceded the migration to Pella.

VESPASIAN IN PALESTINE, A.D. 67

Nero now sent to Palestine one of his most distinguished generals, Vespasian, an unemotional, fair-minded, practical man, who took his time and looked after every detail. He had had experience of similar work in Britain. He was in no hurry to begin operations; for the Jews in Jerusalem were not of one mind, though they were co-operating with one another for the moment. The fierce and ruthless Simon ben Geiora had taken to banditry in the country east and south of Jerusalem, which was at that time the preserve of the Idumaeans (Edomites). He finally joined forces with the Galilean Zealots who held the fortress of Masada and had lost their old leader Menahem.

In June of 67 Vespasian moved into Galilee, where he was welcomed by the important, mainly Gentile, city of Sepphoris. He methodically reduced the various towns and villages of Galilee, which held out against him under the command of the historian Josephus, who acted with admirable energy and courage. How Josephus managed to extricate himself from the attentions of his countrymen after the fall of Jotapata, and attach himself to Vespasian, must be read in his own words; we admire his nerve and ingenuity, but not so whole-heartedly

[1] Luke paraphrases the words of Daniel so as to make their meaning clear: 'When ye see Jerusalem encompassed by armies' (xxi. 20).

as he did himself. Arrived at the Roman headquarters, he posed as a prophet and delivered oracles which hinted that Vespasian would become the master of the world. This was confirmed by a response from the shrine of Elijah on Mount Carmel.

The last city in Galilee to be taken by Vespasian was the small town of Gischala, which was fiercely defended by a redoubtable rival of Josephus named John. John of Gischala slipped out and arrived safely in Jerusalem, where he inflamed the anti-Roman feeling. He was a stronger character than any one he found there. Eleazar was still in command of the Temple and its area. The priests and other magnates still held their own on the higher part of the city to the west, where Herod's palaces and fortresses were. Their leader was the ex-high priest Ananus (Annas II) who had directed the persecution in which James the Just had died as a martyr. Josephus now paints him as a wise, strong, public-spirited leader, by which he means that he was pro-Roman at heart. Ananus made the mistake of confiding fully in John who was a revolutionary at heart; for a social revolution was in progress. The chief supporters of the Zealot insurrection were the oppressed peasantry or young penniless hot-heads who had nothing to lose. They looted and burned the palaces of the wealthy, and destroyed the records of their indebtedness.

As the movement gathered force they decided to set up a high priest of their own, whom they chose by lot, which they claimed was the ancient tradition; the apostles had used the same method in filling a vacancy in the numbers of the Twelve.[1] This revolutionary high priest was an ignorant rustic named Phanni, Josephus says, and was probably named after Phineas the Zealot high priest in the book of Numbers. The legitimate high priest, Matthias the son of Theophilus, still held out in the upper city, but the Zealots with their new high priest had control of the Temple. At some point after this schism John of Gischala parted from the old high priests and went over to the Zealots and became their leader. Ananus still had a strong following, however, in the upper city and managed to establish control of the outer courts of the temple on the western side.

Since the Zealots were too weak to overcome Ananus without help,

[1] Casting lots was a sacred ceremony. In ancient times the high priest had charge of the sacred lots, Urim and Thummim, through which God made known his will.

they made an alliance with the Edomites, whose territory at this time extended as near to Jerusalem as Hebron. They were closely akin to the Jews, and had been incorporated into the Jewish national and religious life, but it seems that old feelings of enmity persisted. John succeeded in admitting them into the city by night, and there was a fearful slaughter which included two ex-high priests, Ananus himself and Jesus the son of Gamaliel, with many of their supporters. There was a revolutionary orgy. Mock tribunals were set up which convicted them of collaboration with the Romans; and among the victims was a certain Zachariah the son of Baruch (or Barachias) whose name has found its way, by a curious error, into St Matthew's Gospel (xxiii. 35).

The remains of the more conservative party continued to hold out in the upper city under the legitimate high priest Matthias.

Meanwhile Vespasian had occupied Gadara, and left his legate Placidus to complete the occupation of Peraea, which he was very successful in doing. By the spring of the following year the whole of Transjordania was in Roman hands.

In March of 68 Vespasian was in Caesarea, and began the subjugation of the villages and towns of Judaea, including Lydda and Jamnia, in preparation for an attack on Jerusalem later in the summer. Officers were assigned to the task of rebuilding devastated towns and villages. Unfortunately his whole plan of campaign was interrupted by the news of civil war in Europe and the suicide of Nero on 9 June. When the news reached him he was at Jericho, where he had joined forces with Placidus; he returned to Caesarea in order to have his army ready for any eventuality. It was in this way that a second suspension of hostilities occurred; and this may be the more likely point at which to place the Christian migration to Pella and the Rabbinic migration to Jamnia, since these towns were now in Roman hands.

THE WAR OF THE EMPERORS, A.D. 68–69

The revolt against Nero had begun in Gaul, and the legions in Spain proclaimed their commander Galba as emperor and marched on Rome. Public feeling in Rome had turned against Nero and he was declared a 'public enemy' by the senate. He committed suicide, with some assistance, in order to avoid arrest and execution. Galba arrived in Rome in October with Otho, who was the previous husband of Nero's late second wife Poppaea; but he was not popular, and it became clear that this would not be a final settlement. There was another year of confusion and conflict in the empire. Perhaps the author of the Revelation had this in mind when he made his 'fifth angel' pour out his vial of retribution upon the 'throne of the beast', so that the 'kingdom of the beast was darkened'.

In January of 69 another emperor, Vitellius by name, was proclaimed by the legions of Germany, which proceeded to invade Italy in order to establish him at Rome. At the same time Galba was assassinated by the praetorian guard, and replaced as emperor by his friend Otho. The forces of Otho met the forces of Vitellius in battle, and were defeated. Otho committed suicide.

Vitellius was now emperor, but the legions of the east had not spoken. Under the proconsul of Syria, Mucianus, they declared their allegiance to Vespasian and began the long march on Rome. The Danubian legions, one of which had recently come from Syria, made the same decision. They reached Italy, and defeated the forces of Vitellius at Cremona. In the westward march of these legions from the Danube and Euphrates we may perhaps see the historical events which suggested to the author of the Revelation that his sixth angel should pour out his vial 'on the great River Euphrates, to prepare the way for the kings from the east'; a march which would be a prelude to world-wide war, and the battle in 'the place called Armageddon'.

Vitellius was put to death on 20 December 69 and Vespasian, who had been declared emperor at Alexandria on July 1, was accepted in Rome, Mucianus with his Syrian legions taking command of the city on his behalf. In these wars the whole 'world' was set in confusion by the armed rising of three different groups of legions, each with its candidate for the position of emperor. Italy suffered the horrors of civil war, and Rome witnessed scenes of violence in which emperors and aristocrats were put to death and the old temple of Jupiter on the Capitoline Hill was burned to the ground. In these events Roman Christians could recognize the 'wars and rumours of wars' of the Little Apocalypse of Mark. 'Do not be disturbed,' it adds, 'the end is not yet.'

THE DISSENSION IN JERUSALEM

A long respite, therefore, was granted to the Jews, and they may well have thought that God had intervened for a second time to save Jerusalem from the ungodly. The various parties in the city made good use of their time to strengthen their positions and resources, but not to compose their differences.

The conflict between the Zealots in the Temple area under John and Eleazar and the priestly party in the upper city under Matthias was still going on. The withdrawal of the Roman armies had permitted Simon the son of Geiora, whom Josephus regards as the most ruthless of them all, to occupy the Edomite territory, including the ancient city of Hebron, about twenty-five miles south of Jerusalem. In the spring of 69 the fatal idea occurred to Matthias and his supporters (who were now allied with the intruding Edomites) of making an agreement with Simon, who was terrorizing the country outside the city. Simon established himself in the city, but failed to get control of the Temple; he shared the control of the upper city with the priestly party.

Early in 70 Eleazar, the original leader of the rebellion, parted company with John, who was now aiming at the leadership of the Zealot forces, and the city was divided into three zones. Between the upper city, where Simon was now established, and the 'mountain of the Lord's house', where Eleazar was established, there was at that time a depression which was called the Valley of the Cheese-makers; here John was in control. The three leaders indulged in mutual warfare, loot, and massacre.

We may illustrate this state of affairs from the oracle in the Revelation, in which the 'seventh angel' pours out his vial upon the air, and a voice comes out of the Temple, which says, 'It is done'; and there are lightnings and thunders and a great earthquake and 'the Great City was *divided into three parts*'; the Great City having been previously defined (Rev. xi. 8) as the city in which the Lord of the martyrs had been crucified.

Babylon the Great was remembered before God (the Revelation continues), and 'great hail *weighing as much as a talent* fell from heaven upon men'; this apocalyptic touch may also be illustrated from Josephus, to whom we now turn for the last phase in the tragic story.

THE DESTRUCTION OF JERUSALEM, A.D. 70

At the beginning of A.D. 70 Vespasian had left Alexandria for Rome and Titus, his eldest son, returned to Caesarea and marched against Jerusalem, not long before the Feast of the Passover. He occupied the heights of Mount Scopus and the Mount of Olives, to the north and east of the city. The need to unite in battle against the Romans did not modify in the least the ferocity with which the three parties in the city fought against one another, or the savagery with which they treated the unfortunate inhabitants of the city, especially if they were suspected of attempting to escape to the enemy. Great crowds came in as usual for the Passover, and John took advantage of this situation to attack and defeat his rival Eleazar, thus gaining control of the Temple area which was well stocked with provisions. Not long after this Simon got the high priest Matthias and his sons into his power, and after a mock trial put them to death. And so the Jewish high priesthood came to an end.

Meanwhile Titus had brought up his siege train, and had begun to batter the walls and towers with his catapults; and this bombardment may have suggested the oracle about the hail in the Revelation.

> *The stones that were cast were of the weight of a talent*, and carried two furlongs or more....The Jews at first used to watch the coming of the stone, for *it was of a white colour*, and therefore...it could be seen before it came, by its brightness. Accordingly the watchmen that sat upon the towers used to give them warning when the catapults were let go, and the stone came from them, by shouting in their own language, *The son is coming*.
>
> (Josephus, *Wars*, v, 6, 3.)

This odd scrap of Christian apocalyptic is sometimes emended by the translators into 'The stone is coming'; but the Greek text of Josephus reads *huios* (son); and the irreverent use of a Christian sacred text by Jewish soldiers is a lively and likely touch.[1] Josephus adds that the Romans soon made their stones invisible by painting them black.

The summer months came on, and the Roman soldiers penetrated into the northern part of the city, taking three successive fortifications by

[1] There may be a deliberate play on words here, the Hebrew word 'ben' (a son) being often equated with 'eben' a stone. 'The stone is coming' would have brought to mind Dan. ii. 35.

grim and bloody fighting. They took possession of the 'Tower of Antonia', the fortress or castle adjoining the Temple on the north, which had been the headquarters of successive Roman governors. All hope of any further deserters escaping from the city, or of food getting in, or of sorties breaking out, was effectively blocked by a wall or mound which was built by the orders of Titus so as completely to surround the city.

The days will come [we find written in St Luke's gospel as an oracle of Jesus] when thine enemies shall surround thee with a wall, and keep thee in on every side, and shall lay thee even with the ground, and thy children within thee, and shall not leave in thee one stone upon another, because thou knewest not the time of thy visitation. (Luke xix. 43–4.)

It has been held that this oracle, unlike the oracle quoted from Mark, has been so paraphrased by the evangelist as to reflect clearly the events of the siege; and if this view is correct, it gives us an additional reason for assigning this gospel to a date after A.D. 70. It is a quite conventional picture of a siege, however, and closely resembles Isaiah xxix. 3, on which it may be modelled.

The Tower of Antonia was in the hands of the Romans by the seventeenth day of the Jewish midsummer month Tammuz. This day was observed by the Jews as a solemn fast, for it was the anniversary of the day, more than six hundred years before, when the Babylonian armies had broken into the holy city and captured it. Josephus adds that the daily sacrifices ceased to be offered on this day. Just as he fortifies his narrative with prophetic utterances, so he marks the coincidences of place and time which have so powerfully affected the Jewish liturgical tradition; for these dates are found in the Mishnah as well as in Josephus, and the days are still observed.

Three weeks after Tammuz 17 came another dark day. It was the tenth day of the month Ab (July–August), on which Nebuchadnezzar, the king of Babylon, had burned the Temple of King Solomon in the year 586 B.C. This day, too, was observed as a solemn fast until the Temple was rebuilt in the days of Haggai and Zechariah, when the latter prophet ordained that it should henceforth be a joyful festival. On the first day of this month the Roman soldiers fought their way to the gates of the Temple, where great numbers had taken refuge, trusting in the assurances of Zealot prophets that the sanctuary of God could not fall into the hands of his enemies. On the eighth the battering rams were brought up, and there was fierce fighting. On the ninth fire was applied to the gates, which were still burning on the tenth. On the tenth the Roman soldiers broke into the inner courts, and, in spite of orders given by Titus to the contrary, a soldier set fire to 'the holy house' as Josephus calls it. It burned so fiercely that nothing could save it; but not before Titus was able to go into the Holy of Holies, as Pompey the Great had done a hundred and thirty-three years before, and save the gorgeous veils and other ornaments, which later on adorned the imperial palace in Rome.

The old Hebrew religious and national tradition had now come to an end, never more to be revived. The Romans brought their military ensigns, many of them bearing the effigy of the eagle, and set them up opposite the eastern gate. There they offered sacrifices to the ensigns and hailed Titus as emperor. Thus the 'abomination of desolation' was set up 'where it ought not'; or as it is paraphrased in Matthew, 'in the holy place'.

THE REVELATION OF ST JOHN

We have interwoven with our narrative, which is taken from Josephus and corroborated by Tacitus so far as Tacitus is extant, the Jewish and Christian interpretation of history which is called apocalypse. History and prophecy are identical in the Hebrew way of thinking. Both are dramatic presentations of God's dealings with men, whether in creative symbols or in poetic narrative. In the Old Testament the so-called historical books of Samuel and Kings are classified as 'the former prophets'. In the New Testament the Revelation is as much a book of history as Acts itself. It is a mistake, therefore, to say that we have no contemporary study of the fall of Jerusalem and the other great historical events of our period.[1] We have the Christian analysis of the history; our difficulty is to interpret it.

We have applied to the historical events of our present period three oracles from the Revelation which certainly agree with them very well; but it cannot be said that scholars generally would agree with our application. There is another oracle, however, which belongs to the series of Jerusalem visions without any reasonable doubt. It is the

[1] As in S. G. F. Brandon, *The Fall of Jerusalem.*

vision of the white cloud in chapter xiv, and one sitting upon it like the Son of Man, having a golden crown upon his head, and a sharp sickle in his hand. 'Send out the sickle and reap,' cries an angel who appears from the Temple, 'for the hour is come to reap and the harvest of the land is over-ripe.' So the sickle is cast into the earth and the earth is reaped.

Another sickle is then brought, and another angel calls for the cutting of the clusters of the vine of the land. The angel with the sickle casts it upon the land, and the vine is cut down and cast into the great wine-press of the wrath of God; 'and the wine-press was trodden outside the city, and blood came out of the wine-press up to the bridles of the horses, from one thousand six hundred furlongs'. We cannot altogether thread our way through this imagery, and perhaps the details are not meant to be interpreted with meticulous accuracy; but two great thoughts are entwined together which we can readily separate; one is the Crucifixion of the Son of Man in the year 30, when he trod the wine-press alone outside the City, and of the people there was none with him; the other is the day of judgement in the year 70, when he came again, and the vine of Israel was cut down and trodden in the wine-press of war. This vision is followed by that of the seven angels from which we have already quoted three oracles; the darkening of the kingdom of the beast, the coming of the kings from the east, the division of the great city into three parts, and the falling of the great hail. These lead up to the battle of Armageddon and the destruction of the Whore of Babylon. A majority of scholars identify Babylon with Rome and consider that the vision of its destruction anticipates a fearful vengeance upon that city; we advocate the identification with Jerusalem, whose fearful and dramatic end was the most terrifying event of the century.

On any interpretation of this evidence enough remains to inform us in what terms the Christian churches discussed the wars of the emperors and the fall of Jerusalem.

CHAPTER 13

JEWISH CHRISTIANITY

The passing of the old Judaism, *p.* 238. The Flavian emperors, *p.* 239. Josephus in Rome, *p.* 240. Rabbinic Judaism, *p.* 241. Rabbinic traditions about Jesus, *p.* 243. Samaria, *p.* 244. Simon of Gitta (Simon Magus), *p.* 245. Jewish gnosis, *p.* 247. The legend of James the Just, *p.* 248. The fate of the Jewish church, *p.* 249. The Matthew tradition, *p.* 251. Jewish-Christian missionaries, *p.* 253. The Epistles of James and Jude, *p.* 254.

THE PASSING OF THE OLD JUDAISM

The fall of Jerusalem was the greatest historical event of the century next to the crucifixion of Jesus Christ. Rome had once again annihilated a rival; in this case an oriental city of great wealth, high antiquity, and world-wide influence, for she was the metropolis of a vast dispersion. There were millions of Jews in Europe, Asia, and Africa; and all their synagogues paid tribute to Jerusalem. The Christian churches were part of this Dispersion, for they had not altogether emerged from the synagogue stage, or severed themselves from the old Judaism; but now the great city was gone, and only the Dispersion was left. The lamentations over Babylon express their grief in dramatic form:

> Woe, woe, the great city!
> *Babylon* the strong city!
> For in one hour thy judgement came.
>
> (Rev. xviii. 10.)

The city, the throne, the Temple, the priesthood, and the sacrifice, renowned through all the ages, had vanished. Cries of mourning are mixed with chants of triumph as her smoke goeth up for ever and ever.

The old Judaism left two principal sons or successors; one was the tradition of the Law in the Pharisee schools, which gave birth to modern Judaism; the other was the gospel of Jesus in the apostolic schools, which gave birth to catholic Christianity. There were other successors, of course, but they had no future. These are both with us.

The old Jerusalem church had been the mother-church of apostolic christendom. Judaea and Samaria owed their evangelization to Jerusalem, and Antioch received her missions of many sorts. The Pauline churches sent up their pilgrims with gifts for the saints, and in all probability received their envoys, as Antioch did. In some sense she had provided a centre of affection and loyalty, to which the Gentile churches responded; but it is not possible to define the extent of her leadership. In any case it was gone now. No other earthly metropolis ever took her place. The Christian church became a dispersion pure and simple.

It would seem that the Jewish Christians in Palestine had always regarded the Gentile mission rather in this light. Peter, the apostle of the circumcision, and James, the brother of the Lord, had both addressed the Christian world at large as the 'dispersion' in their Epistles, or were so represented by persons writing in their names, if we prefer that theory. This Christian dispersion provided the main body of the world-church which was now taking form; Jewish Christianity was sadly reduced in importance; but it still had a part to play in the development and formulation of a catholic Christianity. Its influence may have been greater than is usually suspected.

THE FLAVIAN EMPERORS

The old line of Roman emperors which had begun with Julius Caesar and Augustus came to an end with Nero, who left no possible claimants from this family alive. Vespasian, who became emperor in 69, came from a country family whose middle name was Flavius. He had two sons, Titus and Domitian, who succeeded him as emperors. We have mentioned his brother, Flavius Sabinus, who was prefect of the city in the sixties and lost his life in the civil wars; his children were brought up with the imperial family, and one of these, Titus Flavius Clemens, became a Christian, or was favourably interested in Christianity.

After the war Vespasian remained personally responsible for the administration of Judaea, and put in another procurator or imperial agent. Caesarea became an even more important city, for it was independent of the proconsul of Syria. No suggestion of an independent Jewish state was allowed to remain. The system of government by high priests disappears from history. Jerusalem was not rebuilt. Nothing was left of it, Josephus says, but a piece of the wall (the piece which is still standing) and three towers. This, no doubt, was something of an exaggeration; but modern excavation has not found any signs of rebuilding or resettlement before the reign of Hadrian. Nevertheless Epiphanius, copying some old manuscript in the fourth century, says that houses were left standing on the south-eastern hill which was known as Ophel. These included a Christian church and seven synagogues. We shall give this narrative, for what it is worth, when we come to the reign of Hadrian.

JOSEPHUS IN ROME

Vespasian and Titus celebrated a triumph in Rome. That is to say they rode through the streets of Rome on white horses, clothed in white robes and purple silk. There were troops of soldiers in the procession, and lines of captives, and displays of loot, which included such religious ornaments from the Temple as the seven-branched candlestick and the golden trumpets, which may still be seen in the sculptures on the Arch of Titus. The official scrolls of the Law, which were said to be written on skins in letters of gold, were deposited in the imperial palace, where the gorgeous veils or curtains of the holy place were also hung. Simon the son of Geiora was dragged along at the end of a rope, subjected to torture, and put to death in the Forum. John of Gischala was imprisoned for life. Josephus, his mortal enemy, who had been useful to Vespasian, was granted the Roman citizenship and an estate in Judaea, the revenues of which he was permitted to enjoy in Rome. He was a favourite at court and devoted himself to writing history, in which such characters as Ananus the high priest, Agrippa the king, Vespasian, Titus, and Josephus himself all appear in an extremely favourable light, the blame for the war being laid on the lunatic emperors, the bad procurators, and the Zealot parties.

His first literary effort was a history of the war written in Aramaic for the benefit of the barbarians in the upper regions, that is to say for non-Greeks in the Syrian principalities. This book has not been preserved, but it appeared in an enlarged form in the *Jewish Wars*, and was followed by other works, which occupied him until the end of the century. These books were written in Greek, with some help; and his mastery of the Greek language and literature does him great credit. They show, too, how a Jew from Palestine could put out literature in Greek, with some assistance, as it seems the apostolic writers did.

His friendship with the Flavian emperors suggests that they were by no means prejudiced against the Jews. Indeed, when Agrippa and Bernice visited Rome in 75, they were well entertained, and Titus showed considerable interest in Bernice; but the Roman people did not hesitate to show their displeasure at such a friendship.

RABBINIC JUDAISM

Meanwhile there had to be a restoration of the Jewish social and religious life in northern Palestine, where Jews were still to be found in some numbers. A conquering power is bound to establish or recognize some native authority through which it may work with the conquered people; and this recognition fell upon the group of Pharisee Rabbis who were settled at Jamnia, not far from Caesarea. 'Give me Jabneh', Johanan ben Zakkai had said to Vespasian, according to the tradition in the Talmud; and this academy was the centre from which the new Judaism was organized and the old precepts adapted to the new conditions. We hear of other schools in the vicinity, that of Eliezer ben Hyrcanus at Lydda, and that of Gamaliel II at Caesarea; and both of these were Christian centres too, as we learn from Acts. Johanan was the leading extant representative of the old school of Hillel and represented his broad-minded tradition. Eliezer had listened with pleasure to a *halakah* or opinion on the Law which was said to have been expressed by Jesus of Nazareth, and would by no means deny him a place in the life to come. Gamaliel held classes in Greek.

We see them through the traditions which were handed down in later generations. By the end of the century a sanhedrin or council of Rabbis had come into existence, for which a sacred pedigree was worked out. The early tractate called *Pirke Aboth*, or 'Sentences of the Fathers', is virtually an anthology of their sayings arranged in genealogical form. Ezra, it was said, had delivered the whole Law, both oral and written, to the men of the Great Synagogue, a shadowy institution of whose existence there is no direct evidence. Since that time each generation had boasted of its 'pair' of great teachers, who had handed on the sacred tradition intact. When Jesus went up to the Temple in Jerusalem as a boy about A.D. 7 or 8, the pair of teachers were Hillel and Shammai, and their schools were still strongly organized bodies.

Hillel was a learned broad-minded scholar from the Jewish academies of 'Babylon'. His religious insight and intellectual powers were of the highest order; he was the founder of the dominant Pharisee school which was called the house of Hillel. He was affectionately referred to as *Za-ken*, or 'The Elder', which was explained by a characteristic rabbinic etymology as *Zēh-sh-Kanah*—'he who has gotten' or 'acquired'—the word 'wisdom' being supplied to complete the phrase. The grandson of Hillel was Gamaliel I, the master of St Paul, who had advised caution in handling the Nazarenes. The son of this Gamaliel was Simeon II, who perished in the siege of Jerusalem; and Simeon's son was the Gamaliel II to whom we have referred. It was he who became the head or prince of the sanhedrin towards the end of the century; he lived in great state at Caesarea, the capital city; his manner was imperious; he taught in both languages. The hereditary patriarchate was established in this way at this time. The descendants of Hillel presided over the sanhedrin and were the rulers of Israel.

In the earlier stages, however, immediately after the war, the most influential leader was Johanan ben Zakkai at Jamnia. He is said to have had five disciples, Eliezer ben Hyrcanus, Joshua ben Hananya, José the priest, Simon ben Nathaniel, and Eleazar ben Arach. A didactic succession was thus established, which passed from master to pupil, or, as it was sometimes expressed, from father to son. The sages were often referred to as *aboth* (pronounced *āvōth*), which is a specialized plural of the word *ab* which means father. They could also be called *z'kenim*, the elders, or *hakamim*, the wise; but the characteristic title for the sages of this generation came to be *tannaim*, the repeaters. They originated nothing; they repeated and explained what they had received from the elders before them.

It was in this way, by constant repetition within the schools, where one memory could be checked by another, that the mass of oral documents was handed down from one generation to another; until they were finally written down in the Mishnah in the days of Rabbi Judah the Holy, the seventh from Hillel, between about 180 and 220. It was precisely in this way, of course, that the words of Jesus were handed down in the school of disciples which he established. The disciples of the sages were admitted into the teaching succession by the laying-on of hands of three accredited teachers, a procedure which was continued in the ordination of a bishop in the Christian church. The bishop, sitting in his chair, is the descendant, by one line of descent, of the Jewish rabbi.

Western readers of the present age have to rid themselves of the notion that there was something uncertain or casual about an 'oral tradition' of this kind. On the contrary, it was a rigidly organized system of transmitting knowledge, the sages or wise men being the reference libraries of their day. The mode of transmission had nothing odd or peculiar about it, but was the normal method before the time came when books could be easily produced, and the trained memory was superseded and impaired by the use of note-books. The history of the Maoris of New Zealand, during their eight centuries of residence there, has been reconstructed from their organized oral tradition, which even sheds light on the period before they came to the islands, and the way they got there.

RABBINIC TRADITIONS ABOUT JESUS

Joseph Klausner, in his book *Jesus of Nazareth*, has collected some of the statements about Jesus in the Mishnah which may safely be credited to the *tannaim* of the first century. Among them are the following: he was illegitimate; he went down into Egypt where he learned magic; he gave opinions on the Law and scoffed at the words of the wise; he practised magic and deceived the people; he was hanged on the eve of the Passover. The tone of these remarks is naturally critical; the detail is not always accurate, and in some cases may not have been intended to be taken literally; nevertheless, the picture which they convey corroborates the picture given in the Gospels. The Egyptian story has a special affinity with the first Gospel, and the date assigned to the crucifixion agrees with the fourth.

In these rabbinic traditions we have clear references to sayings of Jesus, which always resemble those found in Matthew, and sometimes those found only in Matthew. We are also told of a certain Jacob (the name which is reproduced in our Bible as James) of Kefar Sama or Kefar Sekanya, who taught the *halakoth* of Jesus (his pronouncements about the Law), and healed the sick in his name. We are also given a list of five disciples of Jesus: Mattai, Naqai, Netser, Buni, and Todah. It looks as if he was thought of as the head of a teaching school like Johanan ben Zakkai, who is also allotted five principal disciples; or

Ezra, who had five disciples to help him to rewrite the Law, according to the *Apocalypse of Ezra*;[1] and it is worth noting that the Gospels know of five disciples of Jesus who were selected prior to the remainder of the twelve: Simon, Andrew, James, John, and Matthew (or Levi). The only recognizable names in the rabbinic list are Mattai (Matthew) and Todah (Thaddaeus). The attempts to identify the three others are mere guess-work: Naqai perhaps Nicodemus (representing the Mishnaic name Naq-dimon?); Netser perhaps Andrew; and Buni perhaps John the son of Zebedee, the surviving member of the pair who were given the name of Boanerges.

The picture in the Mishnah is not based on written Gospels, though such Gospels are mentioned by second-century Rabbis. It is their corporate memory of Jesus and his teaching succession, as it continued to operate in the first century after the destruction of Jerusalem. Its value consists in the fact that it is completely independent evidence, and not always of a friendly character. It tells of a teaching succession in which Matthew was now the leading name, a point which receives some corroboration from the similar oral tradition among the Christians. In Jacob of Kefar Sama (or Sekanya) Klausner is prepared to see James the brother of the Lord, though there are serious chronological difficulties about this identification; in the mysterious Naqai he sees Luke. Luke would not be a familiar name in Palestine, one would think; but the Epistle ascribed to James is very closely related at some points to the teaching of Jesus, which it calls the royal law or law of liberty; and it advocates anointing with oil in the name of Jesus.

The regular name for the Christians in the Mishnah is *notzrim*, which appears in the New Testament as Nazareans or Nazoreans, or even Nazarenes; they are sometimes alluded to as *minim* or heretics; and we shall see that Jewish Christianity was invaded by the heretical sects.

SAMARIA

After the Jewish war Samaria was rewarded for its loyalty to Rome. Vespasian built the Samaritans a fine city near the site of Shechem, the ancient city where Abraham had erected his first altar and Israel chose its first king. It was not far from Mount Gerizim, where the Samaritan

[1] There is a rabbinic tradition that five scholars made the translation known as the Septuagint.

temple was situated, and it must soon have become one of the leading cities of Palestine. The orthodox Samaritans of this period, apart from their attachment to their own temple, did not differ very greatly from the Jews, except that they had not canonized the prophets and were more open to Gentile ideas. They resembled the Sadducees rather than the Pharisees, but the Sadducees very soon died out in Judaism itself.

The new city was called Flavia Neapolis, the new town of the Flavian emperors, and it was predominantly Gentile. It provided the Christian church with its first philosopher of any eminence, Justin Martyr, who was born there not later than about A.D. 100. His father's name was Priscus, he says, and his grandfather's was Bacchius. They were Gentiles, and Bacchius may have been one of the first settlers. Of course Justin may have had a native Samaritan mother; he speaks of the Samaritans as 'my own race'.

SIMON OF GITTA (SIMON MAGUS)

Neither the Nazarean nor the Pharisee seems to have flourished in Samaria, which cultivated romantic systems of myth, ritual and magic, coloured by the fashionable religiosity of the day. Justin says that nearly all the Samaritans in his time were adherents of Simon of Gitta, a village not far from Flavia Neapolis. He practised magical arts, and was identified by later Christian writers with the Simon Magus mentioned in the Acts. Justin does not say this himself, but the identification may be accepted.

What Justin says about Simon of Gitta, in his surviving works, is that he claimed to be a god (or to be God); and that most of the Samaritans worshipped him as 'the First God'. There was a Simonian cult in Rome, too, presumably in the Samaritan community. According to the accounts which he had received, this cultus had originated in the reign of Claudius (prior to 54, that is) when Simon paid a visit to Rome, and the Senate had honoured him with a statue which Justin had seen. Modern scholars discern legendary features in this story, and are sceptical about the Simonian origin of the statue; but the Simonians may have been responsible for the legendary features rather than Justin.

The claim to be a god is in line with the statement in Acts that he called himself the power of God which is called Great. Some emanation from the high God had incorporated itself into him. Justin adds that he went about with a woman named Helen, who had been a prostitute, and that she was the 'First Thought' or 'First Thinking' of the deity.

Justin wrote a further account of Simon in his lost book on heresies, which was called the *Syntagma*, and Irenaeus made use of it in composing his own book on the subject. According to Irenaeus the Primal God of Simon was the supreme being who existed far above the visible heavens; and the Primal Intelligence or Thinking was evolved out of his own essence to be his consort. From this divine pair proceeded the angels and powers who created the visible universe; the chief of these being the God of the Jews. The creator and his angels managed to imprison in their material universe the female spirit whom they called the Primal Thinking. She entered into one human body after another. She was the Helen of Troy for whom the Greeks contended in the Homeric poems. She passed from body to body until the Primal God himself came down to earth, in the person of Simon Magus, to deliver her. She was found by him living in a house of ill-fame at Tyre, and they were united. In this way the 'lost sheep' was found and saved.

This myth makes use of the commonplaces of the mixed oriental gnosis: the remote immaterial deity; the planets as maleficent gods who ruled events in the world; the descent of the female spirit or goddess from the higher realms; the imprisonment of spirit in matter.

It is doubtful, of course, whether every detail of this myth can be attributed to Simon Magus, but it illustrates the main features of the cult which he initiated: the hostility to Judaism and the Jewish God, and of course to the Law of Moses; the idea of the wholly immaterial high God, whose spiritual nature is nevertheless divided into male and female selves; and the mythological mode of expressing the high mysteries. The material universe is evil, and spirit is somehow imprisoned in matter against its will; but the Simonian cult was not ascetic. Its moral standards were severely criticized. It is said to have cultivated magic and sexual mysticism.

Later legend had much to add. Simon was a disciple of John the Baptist. He had a rival named Dositheus. Such points as these may preserve some dim memory of the truth; but at this point all we can do is to register the historical existence of the Samaritan gnosis in the first century as a rival to Christianity and to Judaism.

JEWISH GNOSIS

Simonianism is one example of the heretical cults which developed on the borderland between Judaism and Syrianism. There were many others, though they did not become so famous. Philo tells us of an ascetic communist sect of Jews in Alexandria, called the Therapeutai, which was substantially orthodox. Pliny and Josephus tell us of similar sects by the Dead Sea and in Transjordania which were called the Essenes; these were orthodox in the sense of accepting the God of the Jews as the supreme deity; but they abstained from the Temple sacrifices and practised numerous ablutions and other rituals to preserve their purity. They were celibates, they had secret books and initiations, they knew the names of angels, they reverenced the sun; yet they were strict sabbatarians and devoted to the detail of the Law of Moses. Their principal monastery, with a library of their literature, has recently been discovered at Qumran by the Dead Sea, or so it is believed.

Hegesippus gives a list of seven sects into which the Jews were divided; he enumerates the Essaeans, the Galileans, the Daily-baptists, and the Masbothaeans, in addition to the Samaritans, Pharisees, and Sadducees. The Galileans may be the Zealots; the Masbothaeans are not otherwise known. He adds that similar sects soon appeared among the Jewish Christians, under the influence of such men as Simon, Dositheus, Cleobius, Gorthaeus, and Masbothaeus. They are mere names to us; but there is no doubt that Jewish heresy and gnosis made headway in the church very fast: they had points of contact with the religions of Syria, Iran, and possibly India as well.

Jewish teachers of this type had invaded St Paul's churches, as we see in the pages of Colossians and the Pastorals. They cultivated asceticism and ritualism and magic; they forbade marriage and the use of certain foods; they revelled in myths and endless genealogies; they knew the names of angels and authorities and powers. These were Jewish Christians of the 'Essene' or syncretist kind.

In the second century we have widespread evidence which gives some idea of the older Jewish gnosis and its mythological or pre-mythological mode of thought. It was natural to think of the Holy Spirit as a female manifestation of the deity, since the word spirit is feminine in the Semitic languages; the Word or Angel was the corresponding male manifestation: virtually God himself. The name 'Son of

Man' is another title of this male power. The male power is sometimes the right hand, the female power is the left. Or the right-hand power is Michael and the left-hand Sammael or Satan.

Modes of thought of this kind must have been familiar in Jewish and Jewish-Christian thought in this period. Strange teachers and prophets talked in this language and practised mysterious rites: ablutions, incantations, sacraments, fastings, and vigils. Some were other-worldly and ascetic; others opposed the Law of Moses and even the common morality; they were the professors of *anomia* or lawlessness. The Jewish church was subject to the influence of both kinds. It eventually developed its own form of gnosis of an orthodox Jewish type, which denounced the Temple sacrifices like the Essenes and glorified baptisms in water; this eclectic Christian-Jewish gnosis was known as Ebionism, and had a Hellenistic wing.

THE LEGEND OF JAMES THE JUST

According to the narrative preserved by Hegesippus, the martyrdom of James had been brought about by the Jewish 'sects'. We have already made some use of his account of the martyrdom, which he had obtained from the Jewish-Christian church of his day. It shows the figure of their first ruler as it appeared to them when he had assumed the proportions of a patron saint, second only to the Lord himself. The story, as preserved by Eusebius, begins with the description of the character of the martyr as a holy man and ascetic; and we have quoted this in an earlier chapter. It then gives a dialogue with the leaders of the sects in the Temple. This is followed by the Acts of the martyrdom which occurred at the Passover, when there were great crowds assembled in the temple.

The preliminary dialogue is a mere summary. The leaders of the sects ask James, 'What is the door of Jesus?', and he replies by saying that Jesus is the Saviour, a word which has the meaning of a judge in Hebrew. This suggests the saying in the Epistle of James that the judge standeth before the door. The sects are unable to accept the doctrines of the resurrection and the advent in judgement, but some of the people do believe through James; and this includes many of the rulers. The scribes and Pharisees then fear that the whole people may come to expect Jesus as the Messiah.

At the Passover the scribes and Pharisees place James on the pinnacle of the temple, and demand that he retract his teaching about Jesus, which is leading the people into error. They ask him again, what is the door of Jesus; and he now quotes the sentence about the Son of Man being seated at the right hand of power and coming on the clouds of heaven. Many in the crowd sing the anthem, 'Hosanna to the son of David'; but the scribes and Pharisees go up and throw him down. Then they proceed to stone him, since the fall had not killed him; but he turned and kneeled down and said, 'I beseech thee, O Lord God, Father, forgive them; for they know not what they do.' This sentence appears to echo the Passion story of Luke and the stoning of Stephen in the Acts; and there are other phrases from the Gospels which appear in the narrative; but on the whole it has a character of its own, and these may be second-century embellishments of a first-century tradition.

One of the priests who was a descendant of Rechab, the great patron of asceticism in the Old Testament, protested against the stoning; but another man standing by, who had a fuller's club in his hand, struck the head of the martyr, and so ended his life. They buried him at a spot by the Temple, and his monument was still standing when these Acts were composed. Perhaps they were to be read there on the annual commemoration.

Epiphanius also quotes the narrative in full, but in his version of it it is Symeon the son of Clopas, a cousin of James and Jesus, who makes the protest. He omits the preliminary dialogue, and it is possible that this dialogue was not an integral part of the Acts of the martyrdom; for such a dialogue, at much greater length, is to be found as an independent story in the Ebionite legends which are included in the *Recognitions of Clement*; in these legends James is on the point of persuading the rulers and people to believe in Christ when he is thrown down from his high position by an 'enemy' who is easily identifiable as St Paul. It is the same story, but it has been given a different twist.

THE FATE OF THE JEWISH CHURCH

The traditions of the Jewish Christians, as they have come down to us, have assumed a somewhat imaginative form, but their main content is clear enough. We have the exalted position of James, as bishop, ascetic and martyr; as high priest and prophetic witness; and as next in dignity to Jesus himself. We have the continued prestige of the family of Jesus. We have the background of liturgy and apocalyptic.

The succession of Simeon may also be regarded as a fact of history.

When Jerusalem was destroyed, its church was scattered. The Jerusalem Christians abandoned the city and made their way to Pella. Eusebius does not say what his authority for this statement was, but he was making use of a written document which was probably still Hegesippus; Epiphanius uses the same source. We may regard it as certain, at any rate, that there were two churches in Palestine which claimed to be the successors of the old Jerusalem church; one was the church at Pella, and the other was the church at Jerusalem, when it was reconstituted there. Simeon is called the bishop of Jerusalem, but it seems likely that he was the bishop of the Jerusalem church-in-exile at Pella.

Hegesippus had some information about Simeon. He was the son of Clopas, who is mentioned in the Gospels. Clopas was an uncle of Jesus, and Simeon was therefore his first cousin, though obviously a great deal younger. His pre-eminence in the church was not undisputed. A certain Thebuthis was disappointed at not being made bishop, and began to give secret encouragement to the heretical sects which were now appearing in the church. Under Simeon these sects were successfully resisted, but when he was put to death as a martyr they were the ones who laid the information and accused him of being a descendant of David and a Christian. But these accusers were also found to be of the family of David, Hegesippus says; and this rather suggests that the mysterious Thebuthis himself, who was the defeated candidate for the bishopric, may also have belonged to this much-divided family. We gather from these interesting traditions, which are obviously in touch with the facts, that the unanimity which was displayed in the election of Simeon must have been rather overdrawn by Hegesippus, or possibly by Eusebius in reproducing Hegesippus, in order to emphasize the legitimacy of his position.

The Davidic claim was a serious matter among the Jews, and may be compared to Jacobitism in Scotland in the eighteenth century, or royalism in France in the nineteenth. Hegesippus says that Vespasian had investigations made into the question, so that the menace of persecution overhung the church. No doubt there were numbers of families, Christian and otherwise, which claimed Davidic descent; and parallels to this could be found in the hills of Wales or Ireland today.

The sentiment in favour of Davidic descent was so strong that the Rabbis, in due course, produced a Davidic pedigree for their own Hillel-Gamaliel succession. This may have been a counterblast to the Christian propaganda; but it may equally well have been a legitimate tradition. Davidic families are said to have lingered in Babylon, the home of Hillel, for many centuries; and illustrious Jewish houses today claim descent from them.

The city of Pella was situated in Transjordania, only a few miles from the Sea of Galilee, where the gospel had been first announced. It was in the territory of Herod Agrippa II. The Nazarean refugees could hardly have settled in his domains unless he had extended them some degree of recognition or protection, which he would be likely to do, as they had not been in favour of the war with Rome. Their situation was similar to that of the non-belligerent Jewish Rabbis who had been allowed by Vespasian to settle at Jamnia.

Perhaps there were Christians already at Pella, since the refugees would hardly have chosen a place where they had none of their own kind to welcome them. At any rate they established themselves there, and, if fortune had been kind, they might have developed a Jewish-Christian patriarchate similar to the rabbinic patriarchate at Jamnia. The reverence for the royal family of David and Jesus continued among them into the third century, when the *desposunoi*, as they were called, were interrogated by Julius Africanus on the subject of the pedigree of Jesus. There were two branches of the family, they told him, one with its ancestral residence at Nazareth in Galilee, the other at Cochabha in Transjordania, one of which may have been the family of Jude (see p. 335). He does not mention the church at Pella. By the time of Epiphanius there were no Christians in Nazareth, but he has some statements which he can make about Pella and Cochabha. Another important Jewish centre was at Beroea, near Antioch, the modern Aleppo.

The question of the reconstitution of the Jerusalem church will be dealt with in a later chapter.

THE MATTHEW TRADITION

There is a third approach which can be made to the Jewish Christianity of this period; it is by way of certain words of Jesus which are incorporated into the 'Gospel according to St Matthew'. The Jewish-

Christian character of this material is easily recognized. 'No jot or tittle will pass from the law, until all be fulfilled', it asserts. 'Whoever shall break one of these commandments, and teach men so, shall be called least in the kingdom of heaven.' 'The scribes and the Pharisees sit in the seat of Moses', and their teaching must be obeyed. The Christians who cherished these sayings as their spiritual law were living on the soil of the Holy Land under the established Jewish religion. They were even offering sacrifices at the Temple, which is visualized as still standing (Matthew v. 23).

We are not surprised to find in this special material of Matthew a particular interest in the royal family of David, to which Jesus and his brothers belonged. The Gospel opens with a pedigree which traces the descent of Joseph from Abraham and David. The earlier names were obtained from the Old Testament; the later names may have been handed down orally in the family; and, if so, it was no great feat. A Maori chief can repeat the names of his ancestors for seven or eight hundred years back. But written pedigrees were carefully preserved among the Jews, so that this hypothesis is not strictly necessary.

In spite of its use of the word 'beget', this pedigree is not a record of descent from father to son, like the similar genealogy in Luke. It is a record of descent from each king to his successor, which was, of course, in oriental thought a succession from father to son just as real and potent as that of natural descent. The number of names has been reduced by certain omissions so as to make a series of six sequences of seven generations each. Six is a bad number, as we have already seen; but the name of Jesus Christ opens the seventh period. Such a succession-list would have the greatest value and importance for the Jewish Christians. It would be a necessary piece of evidence in their claim that Jesus was the true king of David's line, and it would constitute the title-deeds of the Davidic episcopate or patriarchate in the Jewish church.

The same purpose would be served by the numerous testimonies or proof-texts from the prophets. The early chapters of Matthew contain exactly seven of these, including references to the Virgin Birth of Jesus, and to Bethlehem, the city of David, as his birthplace. An interesting case is the oracle attributed to 'the prophets', that 'he shall be called a Nazarene'. There is no such prophecy in the canonical books, and the vagueness of the reference shows that the composer of Matthew could not find it in his Septuagint, which he made use of in rendering the other testimonies from the same source. It has been a puzzle to scholars of succeeding generations too. It has been conjectured that it was a play on words such as we frequently find in the rabbis, and that the reference is to Old Testament passages in which the Messiah was called *netser*, the Branch, or even to the word *nātsīr*, which means an ascetic or nazirite. But its value to the historian is that it indicates a state of affairs in which the epithet *notsri*, or Nazarean, had become an embarrassment, and needed some justification from scripture. How could a Messiah, or indeed any good thing, come out of Nazareth (see John i. 46)? It looks as if the Jewish Christians did not like the name Nazarene any more than the Gentile Christians liked the name Christian.

The seventh testimony aims at proving that the gospel was intended to be preached in Galilee; and this testimony would also answer the same kind of criticism. 'Out of Galilee ariseth no prophet', the Pharisees say in St John's Gospel. The background of this material seems to be northern Palestine rather than Jerusalem. It is natural to think that it is the teaching of the school of Matthew himself, after whom the Gospel was named.

JEWISH-CHRISTIAN MISSIONARIES

It is unfortunate for the historian that Jewish Christianity did not propagate its faith by writing books. What it did was to send out apostles, prophets and teachers, whose repertoire of commandments, parables, narratives and prophecies was communicated orally. There were still in existence disciples of Jesus, or disciples of disciples; and we may assume that the flow from east to west continued in full force, along with the continual drift of other oriental preachers of religion, Samaritan, Syrian, and even Persian, who made their way along the roads which led to Rome. Indeed, the period A.D. 70–100 must have seen an influx into points east and west, which rivalled the records of the Book of Acts. A war sets in motion great numbers of people, including prisoners, refugees, and in ancient days slaves for sale. Thousands of Jews were sold as slaves and helped to swell the population of the great cities. The impact of the bearers of the Jewish-Christian gospel tradition on Greek-speaking Christianity may be measured by the extent to which it was incorporated into the Gospel of Matthew. We find its traces in the second century in Cappadocia, Commagene and Osrhoene. It passed along the highroads of Asia, through Phrygia, as far as the Pauline cities on the Aegean Sea. We know positively of apostles and elders and disciples of disciples who passed along these roads and settled down, Philip for instance in Hierapolis, and John in Ephesus; and we know of a tradition in the school of John that Matthew had composed a book of 'oracles' of the Lord in the Aramaic language.

The title 'apostles' was also used of a secondary class of evangelist, who, as we have seen, often carried letters of commendation. Perhaps we may venture to suggest that the Epistles of James and Jude may have been distributed by such men, since they claim to originate with the Jewish patriarchate. They are addressed to the 'dispersion' or Christian world at large, and are therefore written in good Greek. There would be no difficulty whatever in having that done.

The character of these Epistles is so general as to supply little evidence with regard to their date or the circumstances under which they were written. External evidence is also equally meagre. We know, of course, that Hermas made use of James early in the second century, and that the author of II Peter used Jude not much later; but they do not seem to have been received on quite the same level of authority as the letters which were written by apostles. A date in the fifties has been suggested for James, since it has some points of contact with Romans and Corinthians. James and Romans both deal with the faith and works controversy, and there may be some relation between them, indirect probably rather than direct; but it seems better to think of James as belonging to the same class and period as Colossians and Ephesians and I Peter, since all four draw upon a common catechetical tradition, and reproduce some of its phrases in the same order. Many scholars place it even later.

THE EPISTLES OF JAMES AND JUDE

The Epistle of St James reflects a social and economic life of a rural character, and describes the church officers as elders, like I Peter and Acts. One of their duties was to visit the sick, to pray for them, and to anoint them with oil in the name of the Lord; they also exercised a ministry of penitence. The picture which it presents agrees perfectly with the Palestinian origin which it claims. We remember, too, the James (or Jacob) of Kefar Sekanya (or Sama) in the Mishnah, who anointed the sick in the name of Jesus; and we think of a few touches in the Epistle which would be not unsuited to the Day of Atonement.[1] Its purpose might seem to be to sound a note of repentance, and to recall Christians to a disciplined moral life, lived in accordance with the precepts of Jesus which it refers to as the royal law of liberty. It opposes a religion of 'faith' which expends itself in talk.

The Jacob, or James, who writes this Epistle describes himself as 'the servant of God and of the Lord Jesus Christ', as if no further identification were required. Jude identifies himself quite simply as 'the brother of James', which suggests that the two Epistles travelled together. The Epistle of Jude contains severe warnings against heretical teachers who 'denied the glory', and spoke evil of 'dignities', that is to say the Creator and his angels. They lived an immoral life, and preyed upon the faithful. They walked in the pathway of Cain, and surrendered themselves to the wages of Balaam, and were corrupted by the rebellious talk of Korah. They remind us, therefore, of the Ophites or Serpent-gnostics, who detested Jehovah, and regarded Cain and Balaam and Korah as the great heroes of the Old Testament. Jude refers his hearers to the apostles who had predicted that such mockers would arise; their ministry lies in the past now, so that we can hardly place the composition of the Epistle before 75–85.

We must recollect that these Epistles were not published by business firms or sold in shops. They were operative documents, designed to fulfil some definite purpose within the church order of their day. They were addressed to the church at large and were presumably carried by men who had a mission to the church at large. They bear the names of great men in the Palestinian church, and therefore it looks as if the men who first carried them came from that quarter. The simplest and most satisfactory conclusion about their origin is that they were prepared on the order of the men whose names they bear; but there is no external evidence on the subject one way or another, and no chronological references in the Epistles themselves. If this conclusion is correct, James must have been written before A.D. 62, and Jude, as we have said, some ten or twenty years later. They have every appearance of being first-century productions, and the evidence of Hermas confirms such a date in the case of James.

[1] It has a dramatic call to repentance in iv. 8 ff. It mentions the harvest, prayers for rain, and the day of judgement. It refers to Job, a book which was read on the eve of the Atonement Day.

CHAPTER 14

THE PAULINE SUCCESSORS

Background of the Pastoral Epistles, *p.* 256. The style of the Epistles, *p.* 257. On pseudonymity, *p.* 259. Theories of authorship, *p.* 260. Timothy and Titus, *p.* 261. Combating the strange teachers, *p.* 263. The witness of the prophets, *p.* 264. The bishop and the deacons, *p.* 265. The elders and teachers, *p.* 267. The elders in the Pastoral Epistles, *p.* 268. The church order, *p.* 270. The Epistle to Titus, *p.* 270. II Timothy, *p.* 271.

BACKGROUND OF THE PASTORAL EPISTLES

We must now retrace our steps in order to consider the Epistles of Paul which were addressed to Timothy and Titus, and the picture which they give of the conditions in his churches during the period of transition, before they had passed out of their missionary phase into autonomy and independence. They depended, in this period of transition, upon the Pauline successors for guidance and supervision. The elders and bishops who were established in every city were subject to their direction and control; and the 'Pastoral Epistles', as they have been christened in fairly modern times, were the credentials of these apostolic men and the authority for their policies.

There is no suggestion in these Epistles that the churches will be guided into autonomy; and we have no contemporary evidence which tells us how this autonomy was achieved. All we can see is that it was completed and well established before the visit of Ignatius of Antioch to Asia Minor about 115, by which time every city had its single bishop with a council of elders or presbyters, as we may call them indifferently, using either the English or the Greek word. We can hardly suppose that this important change was first introduced any later than the nineties, when John and his companions were exercising paramount influence in Asia; and this conclusion provides us with a chronological point towards which we can work; for the Pastoral Epistles reflect a state of affairs previous to the introduction of this system of self-government. They are not likely, therefore, to have been composed later than about 80 or 85; they may have been earlier.

The earliest period to which they can be assigned is about 64, when the persecution of Nero broke out; for II Timothy contains passages which were written in the heat of this persecution. I Timothy and Titus have no references to it at all; their ostensible background is a little earlier. In all three, Paul is fighting a desperate battle against antagonists of the Jewish-gnostic type, who are endeavouring to control his churches and are coming very near to success. The battle was not over in the nineties, when the Revelation speaks of false Jews and false apostles who were still invading the churches; and its earliest phases can be seen in Corinthians and in Colossians. These Jewish-Christian teachers no longer demanded that all the Gentile Christians should be circumcised and keep the Law, as they did in the Galatian period. They posed as teachers of the Law, it is true, but they brought in 'Jewish myths and endless genealogies', which suggest gnostical dreams about the other world. They advocated asceticism, like the Essenes, forbidding marriage, and prohibiting certain foods, including wine and fleshmeats no doubt.

They made personal attacks on Paul and his claims to be an apostle, for he defends himself on both counts. He admits that he had been a blasphemer, a persecutor and a scorner, the chief of sinners he says, but he bears witness at the same time that he had become, for that very reason, the supreme example of God's mercy; and he affirms in the most solemn manner that he has been appointed by the Lord as the herald, apostle and teacher of the Gentiles. Thirty years had passed since the days when he had persecuted the church, and yet the hatred engendered in those days was still alive in somebody's mind.

The task of combating these enemy teachers fell upon his assistants and colleagues, who formed his missionary staff. It was vitally necessary for them to instal bishops and deacons of exemplary character in the churches, in order to reform abuses and to prevent the repetition of scandals, which had been taken advantage of by the enemy. Similar scandals had occurred a few years earlier at Corinth.

THE STYLE OF THE EPISTLES

Literary critics have found it hard to believe that these Epistles were written personally by Paul. There are many passages where we feel that it is not Paul who is writing. We miss his rapid fluent style or styles. They are fortified with rather pretentious words, some of which are characteristic of pagan authors. Their language is forcible enough, but seldom mystical or imaginative. They have a legislative manner; they appeal to precedent; their conception of faith is less dynamic; their insistence on good works is rather unexpected. On the other hand there are plenty of passages which, we feel, are indubitably Pauline, especially in II Timothy.

These impressions have been confirmed by patient literary analysis. The counting of words and phrases in a document is usually only a subsidiary consideration in the formation of literary judgements; but there are cases in which it is decisive; and in this case it is enough by itself to provide the proof. There are many passages in these Epistles which Paul did not write himself.

There are not wanting critics in the extreme school who solve the problem much too simply by saying that they are fictitious compositions of a much later date; and it has even been suggested that they belong to the middle of the second century and have the heresy of Marcion in view. It is true that they condemn asceticism, and Marcion was an ascetic; but Marcion was the arch-foe of the Jews; and the ascetics of the Pastoral Epistles were exponents of the Law of Moses. These Epistles fit much more readily into the actual historical situation to which they ostensibly refer. They do not fit a second-century situation.

There are many passages too, which a sound literary judgement is bound to recognize as Paul's own work. There are the personal expressions of faith in which the judicious reader recognizes at once the marks of his genius and personality; and there are the numerous references, *en passant*, to persons, movements, places, and events.

Erastus remained at Corinth. I left Trophimus sick at Miletus. Make haste to come before the winter. Eubulus salutes thee; and Pudens and Linus and Claudia and the brethren all.

These are pieces from authentic letters. They are occasional and incomplete and convey no significant information as they stand, or rather they have no clear meaning or significance except for the original recipients of the letter, who knew who the people were and were interested in their welfare. Pseudonymous writers did not compose their fictions in this way.

ON PSEUDONYMITY

It is assumed by a number of scholars, without adequate discussion, that the writing of an epistle of a fictitious character, in the name and person of an apostle, would be an innocent and customary practice which would be well understood at the time. The assumption is an extremely dubious one, and seems to be based on the fact that pseudonymous apocalypses were current in the synagogues and received in the church. A review of these apocalypses reveals a very different kind of literature.

Books like Ezra and Baruch give romantic pictures of a period in the remote past, when it was believed that holy men still saw visions.[1] There is always an elaborate supernatural setting, in which the ancient sage is introduced at some crisis in the history of Israel; he goes into the field and fasts and prays; angels descend with revelations from heaven in answer to his prayers; the course of world-history is unfolded in conventional apocalyptic forms; the end of all things is set forth in mysterious symbols.

This is a very different thing from the realism of the New Testament Epistles, with their plain straightforward messages from known persons to known churches, and especially the Pastoral Epistles with their practical unimaginative content. There seems to be no evidence at all that such missives were freely composed in the names of contemporary persons who had recently died. Fictitious letters do appear in the pseudonymous apocalypses and the romantic histories, but always within the framework of the legend, not from the fictitious situation to the actual: the *Letter of Aristeas*, the *Epistle of Jeremy*, and the first chapter of II Maccabees, for instance.

If the first-century Christians had been moved to follow this precedent, they would have put their message for the times into the mouth of some ancient prophet of Israel and written it up in an imaginative style, with supernatural machinery, which is precisely what one of them did in the second century, when he wrote the *Ascension of Isaiah*. At that time, too, they began to write an imaginative literature of this sort round the figure of St Peter, who was now sufficiently far in the past to have an aura of the marvellous about him. He was canonized, as we would say. The second Epistle of Peter is an example. It builds

[1] See chapter 18 for the character of these books.

up a romantic picture of the apostle; it gives its message for the times; it adds some apocalypse; and it refers to the first-century Epistles which were by now regarded as scripture.

The 'device' of pseudonymity, as it is actually known to exist, cannot be brought into relation with such realistic literature as Ephesians, I Peter, the Pastorals, James, or Jude, which belong to the first century and fail to build up the elaborate dramatic background which it was the whole purpose of pseudonymity to effect. The references to the contemporary situation are the natural or casual references which occur in actual letters.

THEORIES OF AUTHORSHIP

We are left with two common-sense views which may be taken with regard to the Pastoral Epistles. Either they were made for Paul in his lifetime, on his order, by members of his staff like Apollos or Zenas; or they were put together after his death, with the object of making available portions of his surviving correspondence, policies which had been sanctioned by him, material which had received his *imprimatur*, sayings current in his school, and precious personal memories. If so, we have an extension of the kind of mediate authorship which we found in I Peter, which claims to have been written by Silvanus on Peter's order. Modern literary executors would not animate their editorial work by casting it in continuous epistolary form; but it is possible that the ancient world would not think it so strange. They certainly preferred the form of direct speech to the form of indirect; they liked to have a man represented as speaking his thoughts in person, rather than a report or discussion or analysis by a third person. The speeches in the Acts may be examples of this 'animated' reporting of authentic material.

Perhaps we may provisionally adopt, for historical purposes, the latter of these theories; the publication in the Pauline school, with some degree of editing, of Pauline material and Pauline views, by men who knew his mind. It involves certain elements of dramatization in the preparation of the text, and there was a traditional literary form which it recalls at a few points, the 'testament' or last words of some distinguished and heroic figure; either of a great religious founder as in the case of Moses in the last chapters of Deuteronomy, or of the father of a family as in the case of Jacob at the end of Genesis. This form had been used for purely literary purposes in the fictitious *Testaments of the Twelve Patriarchs*, which Paul himself seems to have known. But the resemblance is only a fleeting one.

The Epistles show him face to face with martyrdom, without of course telling the story; but that would have been well known. He is almost overwhelmed by his enemies; he is almost deserted by his friends. There is a suggestion here of the betrayal and Passion of Jesus; 'they all forsook him and fled'. But it would look as if it was precisely his martyrdom that won the day. Paul the martyr was an even more potent force than Paul the evangelist. Every word and act and characteristic of the marvellous man would be of interest to his followers, even down to the books and the parchments and the cloak which he left at Troas. Perhaps they were still there.

The publication of the Epistles would minister to the same demand for information about Paul as the publication of the Acts, which worked up other old memories and documents into a continuous literary form. Without any literary dependence of the one on the other being apparent, it would seem that they must have appeared in the same circle about the same time. They are interested in the same persons and places.

TIMOTHY AND TITUS

The two principal successors of Paul were Timothy and Titus. Timothy is prominent in the Acts and Pauline Epistles; Titus is never mentioned in the Acts, and is not very prominent in the Epistles. He seems to have been a practical man. He appears in connexion with the two collections of money which were made on behalf of the church in Jerusalem; he settled Paul's troubles at Corinth. He appears in his own Epistle organizing new missions in Crete; but he is to leave when this work is done and join Paul in Dalmatia. Artemas or Tychicus will succeed him. He is described as Paul's true child according to the common faith; a genuine and legitimate successor in his evangelistic work.

Timothy is given a similar title of honour in the First Epistle, but appears in the Second as 'beloved child', a more affectionate and personal form of address, with a suggestion of unique status about it; for 'beloved son' in New Testament language is almost the same as 'only son'.

If Timothy was a young man in his twenties when Paul first adopted him to take the place of Mark on his staff, he would be about forty at the date which is presupposed in the Pastorals and forty was the age, Irenaeus tells us, when a man might begin work as a teacher, according to the Christian tradition in Asia Minor. This agrees with other signs, in the Pastoral Epistles themselves, that Timothy was rather a young man for a high administrative position; but this occasion demanded a teacher as much as an administrator and he had the qualifications for that. He was left at Ephesus for a time to combat certain strange doctrines. He was to assert a sound and healthy teaching, which was built on the Hebrew scriptures and the gospel preaching and the baptismal catechisms, in opposition to a false teaching, which was also based on the Hebrew scriptures, but gloried in fantastic myths and endless genealogies, and advocated asceticism and celibacy. Paul had no misgivings about Timothy's ability to cope with that part of the situation. He was an intellectual and had his special *charisma* or gift of grace. There had been prophecies which pointed forward in this direction. There had also been a laying on of hands by the 'presbytery'; which rather recalls the service at Antioch in Acts xiii, in which Barnabas and Paul had been sent out on a special mission some fifteen years before.

Who the 'presbytery' was we do not know. The word is used of the Jewish sanhedrin in Jerusalem and suggests a council of senior rank.

Timothy had the special qualification of being well-versed in the sacred literature, by which we may understand the Old Testament in the Greek version. He had known it from childhood and had studied it perhaps in some formal way, since he was prepared to meet antagonists who posed as experts, though Paul was very scornful about their competence. He was something of an ascetic. There is a quaint reference to 'bodily exercise' as being of some slight benefit, though it cannot be compared with 'exercise according to godliness'. It is most unlikely that Paul was referring to athletics; the word almost certainly meant some rule of fasting or other hardships voluntarily undertaken. He urges Timothy to keep himself 'pure', *hagnos*; a word which often has an ascetic connotation; and he goes on to say, 'Drink no longer water only, but use a little wine for your stomach and for your frequent sicknesses.' The word for water-drinking is a pretentious word which is used perhaps with a touch of impatience: 'Don't go on with your water-drinking craze!' Who seriously supposes that sentences like these were invented by an ecclesiastical writer to liven his admonitions?

We learn from this passage that Timothy was far from robust; in fact dyspeptic. We have now gone almost as far as we can in deriving a portrait of Timothy from the counsels which are showered upon him. Can we go further? Was he possibly rather fond of argument? Was he a little timid in making decisions? The various traits which emerge are certainly not those which would have been invented by a writer of ecclesiastical fiction. We are dealing with genuine Pauline counsels, even though they may be expressed in a style which is not always exactly that of the apostle.

COMBATING THE STRANGE TEACHERS

Paul does not encourage Timothy to enter into argument with the men who introduce the strange teachings. They like argument and thrive upon it; and the servant of God must not be argumentative. It hardly seems yet a question of heretical theologies or theories which have to be refuted. It was a question of how to deal with men and women with brilliant gifts, unbalanced temperament, fantastic imagination, personal ambition, and dubious morals; undisciplined men, Paul calls them; evil men and impostors. The word for 'impostor' is the word *goēs*, which can also mean magician; and it recalls men like Elymas and Simon Magus in Acts, who are given, no doubt, as specimens of their class. They are compared with the magicians who opposed Moses in Egypt.

The first line of defence was to hold fast to the patterns of 'sound (or healthy) teaching', which had been received by the faithful in the early days; a piece of advice which Paul had given as early as his Thessalonian period. These forms of oral teaching included sayings of Jesus; for the trouble-makers refused to come near to 'the sound words of our Lord Jesus Christ', or the 'teaching which is in line with godliness'. Godliness, *eusebeia*, is a favourite word, and seems to mean the whole established tradition of liturgy, worship, and catechism; it suggests a habit of worship and piety along the lines of the 'God-fearers' (the *eusebeis*) of the old synagogue. The Pastoral Epistles are full of little fixed forms and phrases which had become current in the tradition of teaching and worship. Occasionally we find what looks like a piece of a hymn or a benediction or a creed. Occasionally a sentence is introduced or rounded off with the words, 'This is a faithful and true saying', which suggests a technique of oral teaching; though not exactly a Pauline technique.

It is interesting to observe that there is no reference at all to a *written* Gospel. We are still in the stage when reliance was placed upon oral teaching and prophetic guidance.

THE WITNESS OF THE PROPHETS

Appeal is also made to prophecy, for Timothy had the support of the prophets. It had been foretold that these troubles would come in the last days.

> The Spirit expressly says that in the latter seasons some will apostasize from the faith, adhering to spirits of error and teachings of daemons.
>
> (I Timothy iv. 1.)

The connexion of false teachers with the world of evil spirits seems to be implied in Jude and I John and Polycarp, and has become practically an article of faith in Justin Martyr. It is often said that their coming had been prophesied; but where are we to look for the statement of the Spirit 'in so many words' that some will apostasize? We remember the 'apostasy' predicted as early as I Thessalonians; we remember the false prophets predicted in Mark's 'Little Apocalypse'. The Epistle of Jude refers to these predictions: 'Remember the words which were spoken beforehand by the apostles of our Lord Jesus Christ, how they told you that there would be mockers in the last time....'

The Pastoral Epistles have more contact with the prophetic tradition than their sedate manner would suggest. The deterioration of the church as the advent approached was part of the apocalyptic message. The *Ascension of Isaiah* had much to say about it. It appears again in the case of the Pauline churches, in the Revelation of St John. It runs through all the literature of the second generation. The writer of the Pastorals was working on a widespread church tradition which had apocalyptic connexions.

Paul saw clearly before he died that the power of these antagonists of his would grow; 'they will advance', he said, possibly echoing one of their favourite phrases; but they would advance for the worse. It is possible, however, that these predictive and forward-looking passages owe something of their character to the editors who were responsible for their final form.

THE BISHOP AND THE DEACONS

There also comes into partial view an outline of the local organization, which is of considerable historical interest; but we must not suppose that the object of the Pastorals was to provide what is called a church order; or even to assume that such a thing existed. The motive of the writer was to reform and correct the local ministry in certain phases of its operation, in view of criticisms which had been launched upon it, apparently with some justification. Why should it be necessary to insist that bishops and deacons must be content with one wife, or not addicted to drinking, or not quarrelsome, or not given to making money out of their office, if there were no good grounds for these accusations? Why should there be so strong an emphasis on marriage throughout these epistles? Why should it be necessary to insist on decency and good behaviour among Christian women, and especially among the widows?

The emotional preaching, the 'spiritual' excitement, the indiscriminate and immediate baptisms of the earliest days, had brought the church a mixed collection of converts, whose change of heart may not always have been very profound. Five, ten, or fifteen years, would be enough to show them up in their true colours. Three years were long enough in the case of Corinth. The first flush of spiritual exaltation would decline; the moral deficiencies would appear; it would become necessary to insist upon the virtues which this epistle sums up under the term 'godliness'.

There is a long section at the beginning of I Timothy, the background of which is the service of prayer and worship with its sacrament or holy meal. The cautions about the bishop and his deacons are inserted into this context. The bishop has the responsibility for the house or household of God, 'which is the church of the living God, the pillar and ground of the truth'—a phrase which rather sounds as if it were derived from the story of Jacob at Bethel (the house of God). It would seem that an actual house or church-building was in the mind of the writer; for the bishop has to provide hospitality for strangers, among his other duties. In such a church-house, especially if eucharists and common meals were held there, social and financial irregularities would be likely to appear as the number of the converts outgrew the rather rudimentary organization. It was a question therefore of the moral character of the 'caretaker' or bishop. Men must be found for this work who were above suspicion, and not open to cavil from the outside world.

The word *episkopos* or bishop was in common use in the pagan world to mean a supervisor or manager; but such a translation would be quite inadequate and misleading in its New Testament connotation; and the word 'overseer', with its suggestion of the slave-gang would be even worse. It would appear that it was deliberately chosen, in the fifties, by the apostles as the title of a specific office in the local church, to which liturgical, pastoral, and administrative duties were attached. It was closely associated with the idea of the shepherd or pastor.

In I Timothy the bishop is mentioned in the singular, and the deacons in the plural. If we are not prepared for the idea of one bishop in each city, we may, if we please, think of several church-houses or households, each under its bishop and deacons. This would satisfy the terms of the Epistle and fall into line with the plural bishops of Acts and Philippians; and also, of course, with the various references to a church in the house of some individual, such as Aquila, or Philemon, or even Onesiphorus.

The bishop or curator, who is left in charge of the house of God, as his house-steward (*oikonomos*), is the counterpart in the Pauline mission of the faithful and wise servant in the parables of Jesus who is left by the master in control of all his property. The master may return at any time, and therefore the steward must be sober and watchful; he is not to eat and drink with the drunken or beat the slaves. This is echoed very precisely in the Pastorals; 'no drinker', 'no striker'.

The Pastorals refer explicitly to the health-giving words of our Lord Jesus Christ, and it is not surprising to find them echoed. The *charisma* which Timothy is to stir up, and the 'deposit' which he is to guard, recall the parables in which the master of the house entrusts to his servants a number of 'talents' or 'pounds' which they are to trade with until his return. The adventist touch is not missing from the Pastorals either; 'I charge thee', it says, 'to preserve the commandment unspotted and blameless until the appearing of our Lord Jesus Christ.'

Throughout these Epistles the ecclesiastical language, with its infusion of secular words and its stresses on godliness and sound morals, is in closer touch with the oldest evangelical traditions than might at first be supposed.

The section which contains the paragraphs on the bishop and the deacons also contains interesting references to the worship of the congregation, with its prayers and supplications and intercessions and thanksgiving for all men. The men stand for prayer with uplifted hands. The women stand in silence, in sober array, doubtless apart from the men. There are snatches of liturgical material, and even perhaps a piece of a eucharistic anaphora: 'One God and one mediator between God and man, the man Christ Jesus, who gave himself as a ransom for all'; cf. Mark x. 45. The arguments about unlawful foods are mentioned in this connexion, because it would be at the Lord's table that they would cause dissension. 'All the creations of God are good', Paul asserts, 'and nothing is to be rejected; it is to be received with thanksgiving (or eucharist): for it is hallowed by a Word of God and by prayer'. The thanksgiving here seems to be connected with a fellowship meal rather than a purely sacramental occasion, unless indeed the two were combined, as they seem to be in I Corinthians.

THE ELDERS AND TEACHERS

We now come to the main body of the Epistle, which deals mainly with elders and teachers, though a long section on widows has been incorporated into it. It is at this point that Timothy will need all his resolution: 'Let no man despise thy youth', Paul says. Timothy might well be daunted; for he was to take over the full responsibility for the 'admonition' and discipline of the congregation, including the older men and women.

> Rebuke not an older man but exhort him as a father,
> The younger men as brothers;
> The older women as mothers,
> The younger women as sisters. (I Tim. v. 2.)

This general introduction to the subject of the elders (or olders) is in striking contrast with the more precise directions about the bishop and the deacons. The elders in this case seem to be the veteran Christians who were the fathers of the community; the younger may be the more recent converts. After some lengthy directions about the widows, the writer returns to the subject of the elders, and says,

> Let the elders who preside well be counted worthy of double honour, particularly those who labour in the word and the teaching. (I Tim. v. 17.)

It looks as if he was now considering a select council of elders who formed a governing body, some of them being preachers or teachers as well. The word 'honour' has the meaning of financial recognition, like our word honorarium. All the elders, therefore, were on pension; but those who were members of the *praesidium* could receive twice as much, especially if they preached or taught.

It is at this point, in connexion with the teachers and elders, that the most difficult part of Timothy's work of admonition lay. He must carry out his work of inquiry and reform with the utmost impartiality. He must be exceedingly careful how he receives an accusation against an elder, and yet he must be prepared to admonish him in public if he is in error. The text is in confusion, and possibly we have only the relics of the counsels which were originally given with regard to a rather unpleasant situation; there are a number of cautions and admonitions on too rapid ordinations, on getting involved in the sins or errors of others, on purity, on the good effects of a little wine, on the detection of sins, and on the position of slaves. It comes back, however, to the topic of the false teachers, with their passion for argument and their love of money, which it calls the root of all evils. Paul has in view, of course, the scandals which have appeared in the church, and one doubts not that he was right; money is at the bottom of most scandals.

The false teachers were not satisfied with the food and shelter which is all they got, we may suppose, within the provisions which were made by the church and, indeed, the counsels of Christ himself. This touch completes our picture of the complex financial organization which had come into existence within the rapidly growing church. There were bishops and deacons as executive and pastoral officers; elders or older men receiving a pension, which was doubled if they were on the governing body; older women and widows to be supported; strangers who required hospitality; and wandering teachers to be suitably entertained and sent on their way.

THE ELDERS IN THE PASTORAL EPISTLES

The picture of the bishop and deacons, separate from the elders and teachers, which we find in I Timothy, is not identical with the impression which we receive from the Epistle to Titus. Titus was left in Crete to establish the local organization; 'to appoint elders in every city;

if a man is blameless, the husband of one wife', and so forth; 'for', it continues, 'the bishop must be above reproach as the house-manager of God'. Here the natural interpretation must be that the house-bishop is the same person as the elder whose appointment was mentioned in the previous clause; or possibly that he would be selected from among them. These appointed elders, however, are clearly distinguished from the wider class of senior men in the church, since a different Greek word is used for them.

If the organization is identical with the organization in Ephesus, we are obliged to admit that no clear picture of it emerges; but perhaps there was no strict uniformity. The Ephesian church had existed for some years, and had its veteran Christians, and its well organized house-churches. The Cretan church was at the beginning of its development; at the same stage in fact as those Galatian churches for which Paul and Barnabas had appointed elders not long after they were evangelized. We see how far these Epistles are from providing what was called a 'church order' in later ecclesiastical history. The organization was still in a rudimentary stage. Its outline is not made clear.

We are not told how the local ministers had been appointed in Ephesus, but we see that they were appointed in Crete by apostolic men. There is no sign that congregations could elect their ministers or that bishops or elders had acquired the powers of ordination. The new churches, and probably the old ones too, were still dependent on the apostolic order for ministerial appointments and discipline. Yet when Timothy himself had received the *charisma* or gift of grace for the work he was doing, there had been a laying on of hands by a 'presbytery', which means a sanhedrin or council of elders. Were they the local elders of Ephesus? or were they the apostolic men? or did the teachers and prophets intervene, as they did at Antioch when Paul and Barnabas were sent out on their first mission? Was it an ordination at all? or a service of commission for a special piece of work, as we have assumed in our narrative?[1]

The apostolic church was rich in ministries and spiritual ordinances and works of charity and traditions of teaching and sacraments and

[1] The text reads '*through* prophecy *with* the laying on of hands of the presbytery': I Tim. iv. 14. In II Timothy Paul says, '*through* the laying on of my hands'. The two statements are not at all incompatible.

modes of liturgical action, but did it have a church order? Was it not the mission and authority of the apostolate that held it together? The indigenous ministry was only in process of formation.

THE CHURCH ORDER

Another picture comes into our mind as we read these Epistles. It is that which is revealed in the early chapters of the Acts, which describes the struggles and problems of the Jerusalem church, which had become or soon would become a memory and a tradition. We think of the apostolic kerugmata, the breaking of the bread in the house-churches, the common fund and the common meals, the murmuring of the Hellenist widows, the ordination of the seven Hellenists to administer this part of the work, the council of elders who acted with the apostles, the house-churches established in Joppa and Caesarea, the prophesyings at Antioch, the mission of Barnabas and Saul with the laying on of hands, and the appointment of elders by the apostles in the Galatian churches. The only considerable deviation from these Palestinian precedents is that where we find the seven so-called deacons in the pages of the Acts we find a bishop and deacons in the Pastoral Epistles; the administrative staff has divided into two orders.

We are looking here at an historical and literary succession. The church order with which the Pastoral Epistles have to do is a Palestinian church order which had reached Asia Minor by way of Antioch and Caesarea; and Acts presented pictures of this Palestinian church order so as to provide models for the churches of Asia Minor.

At the conclusion of the first Epistle Timothy is urged in the most solemn terms, drawn from the gospel kerugma itself, to preserve the commandment unspotted and unblemished until the Epiphany of our Lord Jesus Christ. He is to guard the 'deposit'; he is to reject the contradictions of a 'knowledge' (or *gnosis*) which is falsely so called. The word *gnosis* here makes its appearance as a technical term.

THE EPISTLE TO TITUS

The Epistle to Titus is by no means a pale shadow of I Timothy, though it resembles it closely. It opens with the reference to the establishment of elders in every city, which passes into a sketch of the character and work of the bishop; but more stress is laid upon the position of the bishop as a teacher and a guardian of the true doctrine. He is to be familiar with the traditional oral forms, so as to be able to refute the talkers of vanity, especially those 'of the circumcision', whose mouths it is necessary to stop. The Epistle goes on to give an unfavourable remark about the Cretans, which is taken from one of their own poets. This passage suggests very strongly that the Epistle was not intended to be read aloud in their churches.

Then comes a simple catechism dealing with social relations, and a beautiful exposition of the gospel message. The grace of God has been revealed and offers salvation to all men; but its more glorious revelation is to be the 'Epiphany' of our great God and Saviour Jesus Christ, for which we are now waiting. The words Epiphany and Saviour[1] (or 'God and Saviour') are examples of the developed vocabulary of these Epistles, which clothes the old Pauline gospel in more stately language. These thoughts come to a climax in the reference to the sacrament of baptism, which is described as the bath of regeneration and renewing by the Holy Spirit, which is poured out upon us richly, by Jesus Christ our Saviour. The language of new birth scarcely appears before except in I Peter.

The Epistle to Titus is as well adapted to the circumstances of a new church as I Timothy is to the circumstances of an older church.

II TIMOTHY

In II Timothy the Pauline manner and spirit is far more evident, and comes out clearly in certain passages which are undoubtedly his own writing. It is only a very insensitive criticism which can attribute these deeply personal sentences to the work of the literary editor, whose own style is formal and impersonal.

II Timothy picks up the idea of the 'deposit', which was mentioned in the last chapter of I Timothy. The 'deposit' is a metaphor taken from banking, and means a sum of money or property left in trust for safe-keeping. In this case the deposit is the ministration of the gospel, which the Saviour had entrusted to his servant Paul, as a herald, apostle, and teacher of the Gentiles. This sacred trust is now handed on to Timothy, his 'beloved child', his son and heir in the tradition, just as Mark, who had been Timothy's predecessor on Paul's staff, was designated as the

[1] But the word Saviour is found in the *Martyrdom* of James and the preachings of Peter in the Acts. The word Epiphany seems to replace the word *Apokalupsis* (Revelation).

spiritual heir of Peter. Timothy, in his turn, was to hand it on to 'faithful men who would be qualified in their turn to teach others'. He provides, in short, for an apostolic succession.

Timothy is not called an apostle, however. He is called an evangelist, like Philip of Caesarea, another man of the second rank, who was not an apostle himself and yet preached and supervised churches. 'Be sober in all things', says Paul, 'endure hardships, do the work of an evangelist, fulfil your ministry'; and it is in connexion with this charge that he urges him to 'stir up the *charisma* that is in you through the laying-on of my hands'; the personal reference was necessary here, where the continuation of his own ministry was in his mind.

An interesting critical point now follows. If the Pastoral Epistles were composed in Paul's lifetime and issued by him, we are bound to accept it as an historical fact that he did so designate and authorize Timothy to be his successor in the Gentile churches of his own creation; but we have little evidence in this case as to Timothy's success in this capacity. If, on the other hand, we decide that they were composed in the Pauline school in the seventies or eighties on the basis of Pauline documents and personal memories, we miss the direct statement by the apostle which we would like to have; but in this case it becomes certain that the Pauline churches in the seventies and eighties did accept Timothy in this capacity, and believed that Paul had so designated him. The Pastoral Epistles also formed the credentials of Titus, Zenas, Artemas and others who are mentioned in them in an indirect way.

These letters are a massive literary and ecclesiastical monument, though their bulk is not great. We have allowed ample room for legitimate difference of opinion with regard to the date and circumstances of their production; but when the utmost allowance has been made in deference to the most sceptical schools, they remain firmly established as working documents in the Pauline churches between the years 65 and 85. They give us a valuable picture of a period of transition, when the churches were not yet autonomous, and were still subject to the visits of wandering teachers of Jewish origin. They do not provide a church order or constitution. The directions which they give are related to the emergent problems of a situation which was still plastic; it was for the successors and old colleagues of St Paul to uphold his good name, to administer his churches in their hour of need, and to reform the abuses whose existence was frankly admitted.

CHAPTER 15

CHRISTIAN LITERATURE UNDER VESPASIAN

Apostles, prophets, and teachers, *p.* 273. The Epistle as a literary form, *p.* 275. The Gospel as a literary form, *p.* 277. The excellent Theophilus, *p.* 278. The writing of Luke-Acts, *p.* 279. Luke as an author, *p.* 280. The Pauline controversy, *p.* 283. Collections of Epistles, *p.* 285. Textual variation, *p.* 287. The appendix to Mark, *p.* 289.

It is a fact of considerable significance that when the gospel made its first impact upon the world, it created a literature of the highest genius, which became a classic. It is still a best-seller. The great literary lights of the day were men like Seneca and Pliny the Elder; but the creative immortal literature was produced among the despised and persecuted Christians. Jesus lives for all time in this literature, as Socrates lives in the pages of Plato and Xenophon, so far as the reading public is concerned. Indeed, Plato and Xenophon are left far behind.

APOSTLES, PROPHETS, AND TEACHERS

The first stages in the presentation of the gospel were oral; that is to say it was popular and dramatic. It was in immediate personal contact with the interested public. The first masters of this evangelical mode of communication were the apostles, prophets and teachers, who are mentioned in that order in I Corinthians, in a catalogue of 'graces' or special gifts which were bestowed by the Holy Spirit. Paul is not thinking here of ministerial orders in the ecclesiastical organization; he is thinking of inspired utterance.

The apostles were the primary gospel-bearers and spirit-bearers. The first on the list were the Twelve who had been named and authorized in Galilee; but their ranks were extended from time to time, and if we may judge from the cases of Matthias and Paul it was done on the authority of a sign from heaven, coupled with recognition by the existing apostles; for the solemn casting of lots in the case of Matthias seems to have been a request for the intervention of heaven. Barnabas and Silas may also have been called apostles in this sense of the word; and some would add

Andronicus and Junias. These apostles were envoys of the Messiah personally; it would seem that they had 'seen the Lord'.

The word was used on a lower level of envoys sent out by church authority, the apostles from men or through a man, mentioned by Paul in Galatians; like the Jewish 'apostles' who invaded his Corinthian church or the representatives appointed by his Greek and Asian churches. The former carried with them letters of commendation, and collected more as they went their rounds. Apollos was given one by the Ephesian brethren when he went to visit Corinth. A model of such a letter is preserved in the epistle of the Jerusalem Council of Acts xv: 'We send unto you Judas and Silas, and them to tell you[1] the same things orally.' The letters were the credentials of the men; the men were the official exponents of the contents of the letters.

We may place in a different class the accredited colleagues of the primary apostles, such men as Mark or Timothy, who may be called for convenience 'apostolic men' (a phrase coined by Tertullian), to whom the apostles delegated some of their own authority in the missionary field; a picture which is necessarily derived from a view of the situation in which the Pauline churches are in the foreground.

The prophets appear fairly clearly in the documents. They were men and women who possessed unusual gifts of vision and poetic utterance; they spoke as God moved them. Sometimes, like Hermas, they resided principally in one centre; sometimes, like Agabus, they made extensive journeys; sometimes, it would appear, especially in Syria and Palestine, they travelled from church to church living on the bounty of the faithful. Asia Minor may have received its share of these. A study of the *Didache* and of Matthew suggests that there was a prophetic quality about the original apostolate, so that the prophets could be thought of as conforming in some degree to the apostolic character; the attention in both documents seems to shift very readily from the apostle to the prophet; commandments which were designed for apostles were also binding upon prophets; whoever received a prophet in the name of a prophet would receive a suitable reward.

About the teachers we know less. They were no doubt the equivalent of the Jewish rabbi, the *tanna*, who repeated and expounded the words of the wise; and we may conjecture that they used their special gifts in transmitting the sayings of Jesus, or the catechisms which have left

[1] An interesting 'semitism': *kai autous apaggellontas*.

their traces in the epistles, or the 'testimonies' which were gathered from the Old Testament; or apparently more speculative matter from less reliable sources. Some of them were undoubtedly local elders. If their work was mainly personal and oral it would help to explain why it has left few obvious traces in the New Testament literature. No doubt the prophets expressed themselves orally, too, and even more freely; but they were sometimes commanded to write down their visions. Hermas wrote down his catechism material as well, but it was at the express command of his angel.

The didactic and prophetic gifts might be found in any one, and were not confined to the male sex. In the Epistle of Titus the elder women were told to instruct the younger. In the Acts we read of Priscilla instructing Apollos, and the daughters of Philip prophesying. Paul himself does not object to women praying or prophesying in the Spirit. In fact he contemplates all Christians prophesying.

Such, then, were the sources from which a Christian literature might be expected to appear; and when it comes it has the character of a substitute for the living voice.

THE EPISTLE AS A LITERARY FORM

It is probable that various oral forms were committed to writing in the first generation, words of Jesus, sequences of stories, prophecies, and so forth; but only one literary form emerges into prominence, and that is the Epistle. It was Paul apparently who first realized its possibilities. To hear a Pauline Epistle read aloud in the ecclesia by one of his young men must have been like hearing him talking; the presence of Timothy or Titus with an Epistle in his hand was a substitute for his own presence, and word-of-mouth utterance. Indeed, he visualizes the congregation so vividly as he writes, and puts so much personality into the words, that he feels that he is genuinely present with them. 'I am absent in body, but I am present in spirit, and I give my judgement as being present.'

The Pauline Epistles bear little resemblance to ordinary secular correspondence, or even to formal theology. They have a 'pneumatic' or sacramental quality. They are the effective spiritual means by which he intervenes with power, as an apostle of the Messiah, in a church crisis which requires action to be taken. His relation to his converts is one of spiritual paternity; he writes to them as his little children whom he has brought to birth in the gospel;[1] he sends them brothers in the gospel who bring them his message personally; he brims over with love and pride, or mourns over their folly. He writes exactly as if he was there speaking, and that is what gives his epistles their literary power.

Once it was established in the church the Epistle became a literary model; the personal touch weakens as more ambitious efforts are produced. I Corinthians overruns the natural limitations of an Epistle and becomes in part a manual of church order. Romans is a theological manifesto, and so is Ephesians. Ephesians is written in a more formal manner. I Peter, the Pastorals (in part), James, and Jude, are other examples of the more formal, less personal type. For this reason a certain school of critics calls them 'deutero-pauline'. The form which Paul brought into prominence is imitated and used as a mode of communicating ideas and policies to an extended group of churches; or even to the church as a whole. Some scholars hold that these documents were the work of skilled writers who did not hesitate to commend their own views to the church by giving them what appeared to be an apostolic form.

We have not adopted this theory. The production of operative Epistles of an apostolic character went on into the period of Clement and Ignatius and Polycarp. It was a traditional element in the apostolic mission which brought the living voice to the ears of the distant community: 'I Paul the prisoner of the Lord'; 'Peter an apostle of Jesus Christ...and a witness of the sufferings of the Messiah'; 'I John your brother and companion'; 'Ignatius who is also Theophorus'; 'Polycarp and the elders who are with him.' They form a continuous series. A number of persons were involved in the work. There were co-authors like Silas and Sosthenes and Timothy; literary assistants like Tertius and Burrhus; members of the staff who read them in church and expounded their meaning, like Titus and Phoebe and Crescens and Claudius Ephebus; copyists, secretaries, and doubtless translators.

The production of some of these epistles in a more formal style is amply accounted for by the co-operation of these auxiliary workers and the variety of needs which they were designed to serve. This view

[1] A good rabbinic phrase: 'He who teaches Torah to the son of a fellow-man, has it ascribed to him as if he had begotten him.'

of the matter is in line with the evidence as a whole and has the merit of accounting for the personal references which they contain, which otherwise can only be regarded as insincere touches, designed to convey an impression which was not true, and to suggest an authenticity which they did not possess: 'Marcus my boy salutes you'; 'I left Trophimus at Miletus sick'; 'Take a little wine for the sake of your digestion.' The theory that they are fictitious falls foul of such personal touches; it is gratuitous and unnecessary.

They went on being read in the churches. They were passed from church to church. They were collected into volumes. They were widely known at the end of the century. They were the models which were sedulously studied by Clement and Polycarp. They were the ordinances of the apostles, Ignatius said.

THE GOSPEL AS A LITERARY FORM

The second literary form which emerged from the spiritual ferment of the apostolic church was the gospel; and here too the literary form was at first the next-best substitute for the living voice. St Mark's Gospel, which we have assigned to a date prior to A.D. 70, retains the grammatical informalities and characteristics of conversational speech, and requires the tone of voice or gesture to animate it. The question may be asked whether it is literature in its own right, or whether it should be regarded simply as a script to be used by a lector who knew his business. To some extent, at any rate, it is oral material still.

The strong feature artistically of this Gospel is that it preserves the voice of a story-teller of genius; but the work of the story-teller is brought to us by the craft of a writer. He lacks the arts and graces of the Greek schools; his manner is Semitic; his vocabulary and style are rough and plebeian. Nevertheless his work is not a mere collection of anecdotes. It is a unified work of art, similar in construction to a modern film, with its succession of shots and sequences, and its devices which ensure 'continuity'. Indeed, the making of Mark's twenty-foot roll of papyrus involved techniques very like the techniques used in making a film. His motion-picture of the life of Jesus is a new literary form, which has been the basis of all subsequent lives of Jesus.

The Gospel of Mark was not the only attempt to provide a script of the familiar material. We have the definite statement of Luke that many had taken this in hand, so much so that the excellent Theophilus, to whom he dedicated his own volumes, was perplexed, and even had a sense of insecurity which needed to be allayed. Luke includes Mark among the many efforts of which he speaks, and he incorporates the greater part of it into his own Gospel.

THE EXCELLENT THEOPHILUS

Many a learned eighteenth-century book bears on its first page a dedication to some noble or royal personage, which was composed on the classical model. The dedication which Luke wrote for his own Gospel can be set out in the same form.

DEDICATION

To the Most Excellent THEOPHILUS

Since so many Authors have assay'd to set in order a Narrative of the Events which have been Fulfilled in our midst, as they were delivered unto us by such as were Eye-witnesses and ministers of the Word from the Beginning; I did determine, Your Excellency, to write it down for you myself, in due Order, seeing that I have follow'd all things with the utmost care from the first; so that you might be well Assured with regard to the matters in which you have already been instructed.

The eighteenth-century writer would have concluded with some such phrase as 'Your Excellency's Humble and Obdt Servant the Author', and then subscribed his name; but this was not the ancient custom. Luke does not append his name.

While he does not name himself, his dedication makes it clear that he was known personally in the circle for which he wrote, and that the reliability of his work was guaranteed by his own researches and by his personal association with apostolic persons. His famous 'we passages' would show exactly where he had enjoyed this personal association. There are many scholars who hold that this judgement is incorrect; they think that the author of Luke and Acts was a later writer, who made use of Luke's journals and reports and left in the word 'we' out of carelessness or indifference, or to retain the realistic feeling it conveys. To many others, it would seem that this procedure is out of harmony with the unified and competent character of the books, and with the personal claims in the dedication. The man who writes the word 'I' in the dedication also writes the word 'we' in the passages in question: it is a relation which cannot be ignored.

The production of these volumes was not an ecclesiastical enterprise. We have the regular relations between the author and the patron which governed the production of books in the ancient world. The patron found the funds, and the author rewarded him by inserting his name in the dedication. If our reconstruction is not seriously astray, the author had a large amount of material on which he had been working for some years; but other writers had reached the stage of publication before him. He needed time and leisure to put his own work into satisfactory literary form. It was no small service to posterity to make possible the production of Luke and Acts.

Theophilus was a Roman official of similar rank to Felix, since Luke makes use of the title 'Most Excellent' in both cases. He represents a new class of Christian, which may be described as a reading public. He was anxious to have a written narrative which would give solid support to the form of the tradition which he had received in the normal way in the church.

THE WRITING OF LUKE-ACTS

We have already seen that the whole character of the Acts makes it difficult to place the date of writing too long after the Roman imprisonment of Paul with which it ends. It adheres closely to the situation of the Pauline churches in the sixties. It seems to have been known to the author of John,[1] who composed his Gospel in Asia probably at the end of the century. It is certain that it was not known to the author of Matthew, who composed his Gospel in Syria no later than John. Its place, therefore, must be in Asia Minor or westward, not in the east; and it must have come into circulation well before the end of the century. This terminal date is confirmed by another weighty consideration. The author of the Acts makes no use of the Epistles of Paul, which seems to show that they had not yet gone into circulation in their collected form as literature. Nothing encourages us to place his work so late as the nineties, as some scholars do. A date in the seventies seems to satisfy all the indications.

[1] Unless both are making independent use of some unknown source such as the hypothetical 'Proto-Luke'. Even so they are related with one another, and not with Matthew.

There is a church tradition which makes Luke a native of Antioch, but the internal evidence of the Acts does not suggest any close association with that city during the period of history which he covers, though he regards Antioch as the mother-city of the Gentile mission, and uses an Antiochene source.

Some manuscripts of the New Testament provide little prologues to the various books, and some scholars regard these prologues as second-century work. What is called the anti-Marcionite prologue to Luke's Gospel describes him as a Syrian of Antioch, a physician by profession, a disciple of apostles, and later on a companion of Paul. He had no wife or children, and died in Boeotia at the age of eighty-four. He wrote his Gospel in Achaia, to which province Boeotia belongs. There is nothing in the least improbable about any of this, and some scholars take it seriously.

A further consideration supports Greece (or Asia) as the place of writing. The immediate background in Acts is very similar to what we find in the Pastorals. It closes about 61 or 62, with bright fresh narratives which concern the same persons and the same places and the same sort of activities as the personal allusions in the Pastorals. It is to this historical situation that both of these literary productions adhere; they minister to the same demand for information in literary form about the labours of Paul and his colleagues, in the churches of Greece and Asia, prior to about 60 and 65. The preservation of numerous local names and other details seems to be a sign of a close connexion with those communities at that time.

LUKE AS AN AUTHOR

The work of Luke is very different from the other books which have been accepted for inclusion in the New Testament. It is fortunate that this Greek physician, with his literary training and his gift for easy narrative prose, should have intervened at this point. He was a keen observer of men and manners, and provides us with a survey of the origins of Christianity which also gives us our best picture of the old Roman empire, its political life, social conditions, modes of travel, and so forth. He is a forerunner of the modern journalist or reporter. He likes a story with a human interest. Even today the average reader finds his Gospel the easiest of the four to read; and the Acts is a good travel-book, apart from the 'speeches', which require special study for their appreciation.

Luke models his style on the Septuagint and on previous Hellenistic works in the Jewish tradition. He shows a marked tenderness for the old-fashioned piety and devotion of the people among whom Jesus was born, though he strongly emphasizes the guilt of the Jerusalem authorities and regards the destruction of the city as a judgement upon them. He is on the side of the poor against a wealthy and tyrannical aristocracy, of which he had seen something in Judaea. He has an eye for the human values. There is an element in his writing which may almost be described as sentiment and humour. He gives us a picture of Jesus in his normal social life. He takes us to the dinner-parties of the Pharisees, and into the home of Martha and Mary. He gives us the story of the woman who was a sinner, and was forgiven because she loved much. It is not at all what the conventional rabbi would approve. He preserves the less formal parables of the prodigal son, the good Samaritan, the unjust steward, and the Pharisee and the publican, which depend for their effect on sympathetic delineation of character. His historical figures are equally clearly visualized; and there is a host of them.

It is natural that such a writer does not care to resurrect the painful scenes which necessarily occurred in the course of violent controversy. Paul is his hero undoubtedly; but the place of priority is given to Peter, whom he does not appear to have known so well personally. He depends upon his Jerusalem and Caesarean sources for Peter. Throughout the Gospel, and well into Acts, Peter, with the Twelve, occupies the central position. It is Peter who first breaks through the Jewish restrictions and advises the council at Jerusalem to liberate the Gentiles from the yoke of the Law. Paul hardly appears as a controversialist or as a master of speculative thought. It is said that he argued; but he is never delineated in argument. He is guided by visions and premonitions as we would expect; but he is not depicted as a thinker and mystic. He is always the man of action. His speeches seldom remind us of the kind of prose he wrote in his epistles. At Little Antioch he proclaims the Jerusalem kerugma, though he ends on a 'Pauline' note. At Athens he makes use of Stoic commonplaces, but ends on an 'eschatological' note. At Miletus he grieves over the strange doctrines which he sees arising in the Ephesian church, but no account of the strange doctrines is given. He defends the sect of the Nazareans before governors and kings. He is always the pioneer evangelist and, on occasion, the Roman citizen; on the other hand, he is the pupil of Gamaliel, and still invokes the Pharisee name. Something of the many-sided quality of the man comes to light.

Luke loved the wonder-stories which abounded in the Palestinian church and were highly appreciated in the Gentile mission. He took them over, and re-told them in his Hellenistic style. The supernatural, as he saw it, was not a foreign or alien thing; it permeated human life and expressed itself through the devoted personalities who were his heroes. The angel or Spirit was a friendly and familiar influence from heaven which guided the apostle or evangelist in all his work. He tells the tales in all simplicity as objective occurrences.

He gives the stories of the wonderful birth of John the Baptist, the Virgin Birth of Jesus, the Resurrection appearances in Jerusalem, and the Ascension on the Mount of Olives. Different minds will evaluate them in different ways. Matthew has a narrative of the Virgin Birth which also comes from a Jewish-Christian source, but it is of independent origin; even the genealogies of Joseph are not the same. Here is one conclusive reason, among others, for believing that neither evangelist had seen the work of the other. It has often been pointed out that Matthew tells everything from the point of view of Joseph, whereas Luke tells it from the point of view of the Virgin Mary and the women. His narrative contains the beautiful pictures of the Annunciation at Nazareth and the shepherds at Bethlehem. He preserves certain hymns or psalms which have passed into Christian liturgy, such as the *Hail Mary*,[1] the *Magnificat*, the *Benedictus*, and the *Nunc Dimittis*; for he is at his best as an artist and poet.

What a contrast there is with the last chapters of Acts, which refer to so many familiar names and places; the house of Lydia at Philippi; the house of Jason at Thessalonica; Dionysius the Areopagite at Athens and Stephanas at Corinth; and so forth. Then the reading circle which met in the house of Theophilus would hear the word 'we' which intimated to them that the author was giving his own experiences by sea and land, which had been shared by others who were still living and

[1] Luke i, 28: 'Hail thou that art highly favoured [*or* full of grace]: the Lord be with thee'; and i. 42: 'Blessed art thou among women and blessed is the fruit of thy womb.' The additional sentence is medieval.

possibly present. His sea voyages are specially characteristic: 'Loosing from Troas, we came with a straight course to Samothrace, and the next day to Neapolis, and from thence to Philippi',...'And we sailed away from Philippi after the days of unleavened bread, and came unto Troas in five days',...'And we being exceedingly tossed with the tempest, the next day they lightened the ship, and the third day we cast out with our own hands the tackling of the ship.'

The narrative thus came to its close among scenes and personalities of which everybody had some knowledge.

THE PAULINE CONTROVERSY

Rather more than a hundred years ago, this broad inclusive harmonious picture of the apostolic church was called in question by the leading radical scholars of the day, and it was dismissed as a romantic invention of the second century. It was asserted that no such harmony existed. There was a Gentile party led by Paul, and a Jewish party led by Peter, and these two never made peace. The passage of time has antiquated this theory; the Acts of the Apostles has passed successfully through the fires of criticism, and very few scholars would assign it to the second century today. It is admitted on all hands that the gospel of Paul was rooted in Jewish religious life and thought, and that the policy of Peter towards the Gentiles was a liberal one; they were never the leaders of irreconcilable factions. Nevertheless, the old controversy has left its marks on the theological speculations of today, and appears in a modified form in the reconstructions of history which are attempted in the radical schools.

One reason for this is that the old radical criticism was not devoid of foundation. The state of the church was not so calm and happy as the narrative of the Acts might lead us to suppose. The epistles of Paul suggest otherwise and Acts itself shows knowledge of more than one crisis. We are told of many 'ten-thousands' of Jewish Christians who were violently opposed to Paul. Were there also narrow-minded Gentile Christians who claimed to be followers of Paul, and were strongly opposed to Peter and to everything Jewish? Such schools of thought do appear in the second century, and it is possible that they had their predecessors in the first; and if this suggestion is correct, their appearance would constitute an additional reason why Luke would lay so much stress on the solidarity of the apostolate and the Jewish origins of the apostolic mission.

The turning point of the Acts is the Jerusalem conference of A.D. 49 or 50 and its Epistle to the Gentile brethren of Syria and Cilicia which dispensed them from obedience to the Law of Moses, but laid upon them the obligation of refraining from eating food which had been offered to idols, and from 'fornication' and from 'blood'. The importance attached to it in the Acts shows that it must have been regarded as a basic historical document of the apostolic tradition in the circles for which the Acts was written. This is all the more important because Paul himself, in his Epistles, never refers to it; indeed, the bold statement in the Pastorals that Christians may eat of any food provided that a 'thanksgiving' has been said over it seems to contradict the requirements of the Jerusalem formula. In I Corinthians he sees no harm in eating food which has been offered to an idol, though he will abstain if the point is raised; to that extent, and for the sake of the 'weaker brethren', he will come into line.

It looks as if the Jerusalem Epistle had spread more widely, and become a rather more important document in the twenty-five years, more or less, which have passed since the council was held. This council had taken place in the bosom of the old Jerusalem church, which was now a thing of the past; its leading figures had become martyrs and saints in glory; but Luke is able, on the basis of information which was still available, to construct an acceptable account of what was done there, subjoining the text of the Epistle, which commended 'Barnabas and Saul' in glowing terms. He can bring in the weighty authority of James himself as well as Peter. But the fully historical character of his narrative is still assailed by the radical school, who think that the pious imagination has been at work upon it. If there was really a formal council which laid down such a decree for the Gentiles (in Syria and Cilicia at any rate), why is it that no sign of such a thing appears in the Epistles of Paul? There seems to be a difference of emphasis here which calls for some explanation.

There is a second place in Acts where the Pauline controversy comes to the surface. It is the noble charge which Paul delivers to the Ephesian elders at Miletus; and it is part of the report of an eye-witness. It is decidedly in the grand Pauline manner. It envisages the danger to the church from 'great wolves' who will bring in strange doctrines; and it predicts that some of his own elders will become the founders of perverse schools of thought. This forecast that Paul's own elders or bishops would develop into heresy may have had a distinct bearing upon the situation when Luke wrote. The Acts may be in part an antidote to novel theologies which had appeared among the followers of Paul and had given Theophilus and others a feeling of insecurity; and this may be one good reason why it preserves speeches of an apostolic character which are rooted and grounded in such old-fashioned Jewish material as the Law, the Prophets and the Psalms; and why Palestinian models of church order and procedure are so fully supplied.

In other words, it is possible to find points at which Acts seems to reflect conditions as they may have existed after the death of Paul. Some scholars have thought that it has an air of retrospect which suits a period after the fall of Jerusalem, better than the years 59–62 when its action closes. It looks back, with some regret perhaps, to the pre-war period when Jerusalem, in spite of the malign forces which it harboured, still existed as a centre and rallying-point for all Christians; and the great triumvirate of Peter, James and Paul could give guidance and direction to the thought and practice of the church as a whole. Now, however, the church of God, dispersed throughout the earth and deprived of its three canonized leaders, must direct its course in its several jurisdictions as best it can. An apostolic literature will assist it in this task.

It has been suggested, too, that it looks in much the same way on a period when Christianity had not yet been outlawed by the state, and depicts it as a form of Judaism in order to win reconsideration of the case from the Roman government, since Judaism was a *religio licita*. For the same reason it gives detailed information about Paul's various encounters with the civil power; but the later the date of Acts is placed, the less convincing this line of reconstruction becomes; for the Pauline instances can have had very little relevance to the legal situation after the middle sixties. It would be necessary to refer to later and more important cases.

COLLECTIONS OF EPISTLES

This analysis of the possible orientation of the Acts suggests that there was a literary movement in the second generation in the west which aimed at strengthening the authority of the church tradition by an appeal to the primary apostolic mission of the first generation, and especially to the names of the martyr apostles. This hypothesis enables the scholar to relate the Acts as well as the Pastorals to the needs of the church in this period of transition, and thus explain why the book was written and preserved. Indeed, he can go further. He can relate Ephesians and I Peter to the same needs at the same period, by a bold use of the hypothesis of pseudonymity.

The theory of a literary movement or a literary interest of this sort in the church of the west at this time is not just a piece of guess-work. We are obliged to place the collection and circulation of the Pauline Epistles at this point too. Doubtless the work of copying and distribution began soon after they were composed; in the case of I Corinthians, Romans and Ephesians it may have begun at once. Each church would have its collection of Epistles before long. New churches like Smyrna would demand copies; and we happen to know that Smyrna possessed a very full collection. Other churches no doubt were equally well provided.

There is no need to suppose that some one centre undertook the work of copying, collecting and distributing. There may have been more than one collection; for the evidence of the second century is by no means uniform on the matter. All we can say is that considerable progress had been made by the end of the first century; and that such Epistles had an authoritative position in the church before the time of Clement, Ignatius and Polycarp. On the other hand, the author of the Acts made no use of them, so that a relative chronology can be made out; Acts was written before the period when these epistolary collections were current in the churches.

The *Muratorian Fragment*, at the end of the second century, remarks that the Revelation of John was addressed to seven churches, and that the Epistles of Paul which were accepted in the catholic church were also addressed to seven churches; and some scholars have suggested that there was an early sevenfold Pauline corpus which established a literary form which was followed by John and Ignatius. This attractive theory is rather fragile, however. No one can prove that a corpus of Pauline Epistles to seven churches was established so early; it seems that his Epistle to Philemon usually accompanied his Epistles to the churches; the messages to the seven churches in the Revelation are not Epistles; and finally Ignatius addressed six churches and one individual bishop.

It seems more likely that collections of Epistles came into existence in various churches in accordance with their needs. Furthermore, there may have been mixed collections which included I Peter, and Hebrews too when it came along; possibly Clement had a mixed collection of this sort. The inclusion of Hebrews in a mixed collection would explain how it came to be attributed to Paul in Alexandria and the east. On the other hand, James and Jude may have had a rather different history.

This is the background against which the more radical school places the composition of a 'pseudonymous' apostolic literature. The successors of Peter composed an Epistle in his name on the regular Pauline model, to supply an apostolic message to the churches of Asia Minor in time of persecution. The successors of Paul composed the manifesto which is now known as Ephesians in order to supply a theology for the apostolic world-church. Both of them regard the church as an extension of the old Israel, and thus reflect the special interest of the period. The Pastorals, in the opinion of this school, also belong to the same class of literature.

In this way the successors of the apostles managed to provide themselves with an authoritative apostolic literature which helped to tide them over the period of transition.

TEXTUAL VARIATION

So soon as a book was launched on its way in the ancient world, the factor of textual variation would come into play. Each new copy was written out by hand, and it is impossible to make such a copy without errors and omissions, usually of a trifling character. No two manuscripts, therefore, ever agree. Every manuscript contains its 'variant readings', and these are transmitted to succeeding copies, so that 'families' of manuscripts come into existence. As there was no central authority in the church which could control this process of free variation, there was nothing to prevent the development of various types of text, each of which had its peculiar character. On the other hand, local church authorities could maintain some sort of control over the type of texts used in a given area, and so tend to standardize 'families' of manuscripts. The science which studies the existing variations with a view to establishing the pedigree of the different 'families' and so recovering the original text, is called textual criticism.

Luke-Acts was subjected to more variation than the other books of the New Testament, perhaps because it was not a church text in the first place. It could be altered with greater freedom. It is not merely a question of accidental variation, or of occasional correction by a well-meaning scribe, or of a little addition or alteration; it is a question of a process of revision and re-writing not very long after its composition; and in the case of Acts it has been done very thoroughly. The reviser recast many sentences, made the motivation clearer, and introduced new details. His work is secondary, and in most cases, inferior, but sometimes he makes interesting additions. He gives the Ethiopian a short creed to repeat at his baptism: 'I believe that Jesus Christ is the Son of God.' When Peter is delivered from prison, he goes out through the gates and 'down the seven steps'. When Paul preaches in the schoolroom of Tyrannus, he does so 'from the fifth hour to the tenth'. In the Epistle of the Jerusalem council, the reviser retains what appears to be the true text, 'to abstain from things offered to idols, and from fornication and from blood'; but he adds a few words: 'And what you do not wish to be done to you, not to do to another... the Holy Spirit supporting you.'

It is impossible to resist the impression that this reviser knew what he was doing. He wished to clarify certain passages where the sequence of events was not perfectly clear or where he was not satisfied that the facts were adequately presented. It looks occasionally as if he had good local information. He may have known the sources that Luke used, or it may be that he had heard or read the stories in some other form. His work bears witness to a lively interest in the history and suggests that the facts were still fresh in some minds, quite apart from the literary form which Luke had given them. We think of the other literary efforts to which Luke alluded in his dedication, and also of the sources which he employed.

The revised texts of Acts is found in a family of manuscripts and other authorities which are called collectively the 'Western Text', or Western Family. The Western Text of the New Testament was current in the Roman church in the middle of the second century, but scholars do not think it originated there. It is probable that it has a different origin, and the name 'Western' is probably misleading.

THE APPENDIX TO MARK

No addition could possibly find its way into all the manuscripts, once the process of distribution had begun. They could not be called back for correction or alteration. This may be illustrated from the textual history of Mark. This Gospel was a church book and was not subjected to the same kind of textual rewriting as Luke-Acts. The 'Western Text' of Mark is entirely free from the large-scale revision and rewriting which we have found in the 'Western Text' of Luke. There are a number of peculiar readings but many of them seem to preserve the original text. The Western Text of Mark is deserving of respect.

The only large change which occurred in the text of this Gospel was the provision of a supplementary lection at the end, for the Resurrection and Ascension of Jesus. The true text breaks off abruptly with the message of the angel to the women at the sepulchre in xvi. 1–8. The remaining verses, 9–20, are not found in the oldest surviving manuscripts, though they were in copies of Mark, of the Western family, which were known to Irenaeus in the second century. They gradually passed into the various official bibles, including the English Authorized Version, which was translated from late Greek manuscripts.

The additional verses appear to formulate the common oral tradition as to the resurrection appearances, the commission given by Jesus to the apostles, and his ascension into heaven, thus closing the narrative of the gospel. It incorporates features from Luke, but there is no proof of dependence upon Matthew or John. It may be assigned, therefore, quite possibly, to the point which we have now reached in our history: to a place in Greece or Asia Minor and to a time rather later than the publication of Luke-Acts; and this suggestion may be supported by a note in an Armenian manuscript, which attributes it to 'Ariston the Elder'; which looks very like the mysterious 'Aristion' who flourished in Asia Minor as a companion of John before the end of the century.

It must have been added by high ecclesiastical authority but it did not find its way into all manuscripts. The earliest and best evidence establishes in the most decisive way that it was not part of the original text. It is interesting that in Rome the gospel for Easter Day should be taken from Mark, and that it should still stop one verse short of the original ending.

CHAPTER 16

THE ELDERS IN ASIA MINOR

Philip the apostle, *p.* 291. Papias and the elders, *p.* 291. The traditions of the elders, *p.* 296. Polycarp of Smyrna, *p.* 297. The author of the Apocalypse, *p.* 298. The seven churches, *p.* 298. The prophet and the pastor, *p.* 300. John and the episcopate, *p.* 302. The prophet and the liturgy, *p.* 303. The writer of the Epistles, *p.* 304. The Fourth Gospel, *p.* 306. The docetic teachers, *p.* 308. Cerinthus, *p.* 309. The Johannine school, *p.* 310.

Before the end of the first century a condition of affairs had established itself in the churches of Phrygia and Asia which was quite different from the immediate post-Pauline situation, as we see it in the Acts and the Pastoral Epistles. The Pauline successors had obviously not been in a very strong position when confronted with Jewish evangelists and teachers who brought in peculiar doctrines which were not in accordance with the tradition; their churches now received reinforcements in the shape of apostolic missions of Jewish character; and it was this development that gave Ephesus and Smyrna the leading position in Christian thinking for a long time to come and produced schools of prophecy and evangelism and theology, the influence of which was not exhausted even at the end of the second century.

The leaders of these schools were Jews from Palestine and some of them were disciples of the Lord. They were called by the honorific title of 'the elders' like the masters in the rabbinic teaching tradition. Hillel, for instance, was called 'the elder', meaning the man who had gotten wisdom, and the same title was given to John by the Christians in Asia. Irenaeus speaks of John and the other 'elders' who had seen the Lord, that is to say disciples of Jesus. We have a good deal of evidence about them and their work, but the task of interpreting it is a complex one and scholars are by no means agreed on the subject. There is no question, however, about the importance and enduring influence of the schools which they established in Asia in the reign of Domitian.

PHILIP THE APOSTLE

It is convenient to begin with Philip the apostle, who settled in the city of Hierapolis in western Phrygia. It was an important city in the neighbourhood of Colossae and Laodicea, both of which had received evangelists and Epistles from Paul. This country became the home of the Montanist movement some fifty or sixty years later; and forty years or so later still the Montanist leader Proclus, who lived in Rome, is said by his opponent Gaius to have identified this Philip with the evangelist of the same name who had lived in Caesarea and had four daughters who prophesied. It was a natural error since this Philip had daughters too, and the Montanists seem to have claimed them as the forerunners of their own movement. Many scholars think that Proclus was right, but no evidence for this identification appears before his time (A.D. *c.* 200).

Papias, who was acquainted with the daughters and became bishop of Hierapolis, identified him with the apostle (or is so understood by Eusebius); and so did Irenaeus of Smyrna and Polycrates of Ephesus, who were scions of the Johannine school in the generation next after Papias. Polycrates and Proclus both state that Philip was buried at Hierapolis; and Polycrates adds the statement that two of his daughters, who lived to an advanced age in a state of virginity, were buried there too, a third daughter being buried at Ephesus.[1] Their tombs were probably still pointed out.

The daughters of Philip told Papias some extraordinary tales about Judas Iscariot, and Judas called Barsabbas, who drank a cup of deadly poison and took no harm from it; and he included these stories in his book. It does not seem at all certain that he knew Philip personally.

Stories about Philip are included in the Gospel of John, which was written at the close of this period.

PAPIAS AND THE ELDERS

In the introduction or dedication to his book, which was called *Expositions of the Oracles of the Lord*, Papias tells how, when he was a young man, men were still passing through the churches who could repeat the

[1] Proclus says that all 'four' daughters were buried at Hierapolis.

Map 5. The Seven Churches of Asia.

NOTES TO MAP 5

The seven churches addressed in the Revelation of John are numbered on the map in the order in which he mentions them, showing how the messenger who carried the Revelation could make a round trip, delivering it to each church as he went.

The first and the last are Pauline churches, Ephesus and Laodicea. The loop which he follows, as far north as Pergamum and down to Philadelphia, marks the notable expansion during the thirty years since the death of Paul. This must be attributed in part to the second wave of missionary expansion from Palestine, which occurred after the destruction of Jerusalem in 70. Hierapolis became the headquarters of Philip, Ephesus of John.

In this period Papias and Polycarp received their training. These churches remained open to strong influences from farther east, from Jewish or Syrian Christianity. Bishops, prophets and teachers passed and re-passed along this line of communication, which linked Syria with Rome.

This helps to explain why Alexandria had a rather different development.

words of the 'elders', by which he meant the disciples of Jesus. This book has not survived, but Eusebius gives an interesting extract from it.

> And if any one happened to arrive who had been a follower of the elders, I would make enquiries about the words of the elders, what Andrew or Peter had said, or Philip, or Thomas, or James, or John, or Matthew, or any other of the disciples of the Lord.
>
> (Papias, *Expositions*, in Eusebius, *E.H.* III, 39, 4.)

We note with interest that Papias claims to have listened to pupils or auditors of seven out of the twelve disciples (if the James he mentions is one of the Twelve, and not the brother of the Lord); and this disposes of the strange theory which we sometimes hear that the Twelve vanished from the scene of history at an early date leaving no trace. The order of the names is interesting; for Andrew and Peter and Philip appear in that order in the first chapter of John's Gospel. The fact that Thomas was given a second name Didymus, the 'twin', which is a translation into Greek of his Jewish name Thomas, suggests that he had found his way into the Greek-speaking churches; and a Roman tradition at the end of the second century says that it was Andrew who encouraged John to write his Gospel. All four have Greek names now.

The extract from Papias, as Eusebius gives it, continues as follows,

> And what Aristion and the elder John, the disciples of the Lord are saying.
>
> (*Ibid.*)

The addition of this clause confuses the effect, since it suggests that there were two Johns; but on a second examination of the text one is not so sure that this impression is correct; for John is described in both cases as an elder and a disciple of the Lord. Aristion does not rank as an elder, and we know nothing more about him except that Papias derived sayings of the Lord from his tradition. The distinction between the two clauses lies in the tense of the verb. In the first clause it is what the seven disciples *had said*, and in the second clause it is what the two disciples *were saying*. The distinction would seem to be between utterances which had been made in the past and utterances which were contemporary.

Here is a written document which does not give us all the help which we might hope for, and many ingenious explanations have been offered to account for this confusion. On the one side it has been suggested by some scholars that the word 'elder' in the first clause refers to pupils of the disciples, not to the disciples themselves, though the title 'elder' is indubitably given to a disciple in the second clause; they would then interpret the first clause as if it read, 'I would make enquiries about the words of the elders *who reported* what Andrew, etc.' On the other side it has been suggested that Eusebius has combined two distinct quotations from two separate sentences of Papias; Eusebius does do such things, and when he comments on the second clause, he modifies it with a peculiar phrase which may be translated 'after a break in the text'.[1]

This passage provides the whole of the historical evidence for the theory, which many modern scholars accept, that there were two Johns who were both of them elders and disciples of the Lord; but whatever conclusion we may come to on that question, it does not in any way affect the evidence of Justin, Irenaeus, Polycrates, and the church of the second century generally (both orthodox and heretical), which supports in the most substantial manner the fact of the residence of the apostle John at Ephesus in the reign of Domitian. If a lesser John revolved in his orbit, he was quite lost to sight so far as the church was concerned. He left no trace in subsequent history, except for the possible reference in Papias, and the amusing statement by Dionysius of Alexandria that two tombs of John were on exhibition at Ephesus in his time.

The theory of two Johns was first suggested by this Dionysius, in the third century, to account for the extraordinary difference in literary style between the Revelation and the fourth gospel, both of which are assigned in the tradition to the apostle John. It was taken up by Eusebius, who thought that the evidence of Papias supported it, and has been revived in modern times and widely accepted. We shall, for the most part, continue to speak of 'John' in accordance with the evidence as we find it, leaving on one side the problem of the Papian duplication and the Ephesian tombs. It is really the pressure of literary and theological considerations which will decide the problem one way or another.

[1] *Diasteilas ton logon:* This is the translation of F. J. A. Hort in the margin of his copy of Eusebius, which is in my possession. See also Lawlor and Oulton's translation of the *E.H.*, vol. II, pp. 22 and 113.

THE TRADITIONS OF THE ELDERS

Papias and Irenaeus record a few opinions of John and the other Elders who had seen the Lord. Sometimes Irenaeus says that he is quoting from Papias; at other times the information may have reached him by some other channel. These opinions seem to have been handed down orally in his school, as the opinions of the rabbis were handed down orally in their schools. They concerned the interpretation of parables or prophecy, the age of the Lord when he began teaching, the length of his ministry, the proper day for Christians to observe as the Pascha, and other points. The most important of these was his opinion on the merits of Mark's Gospel, and his reference to an Aramaic Gospel written by Matthew, which we will quote in the next chapter.

Papias was an enthusiast for the apocalyptic tradition, which he interpreted in a rather literal fashion, and he quoted in his fourth volume a 'saying of Jesus', which the elders of his period had received from John. It does not appear that he claims to have received it from John himself.

> The days will come when the vines will grow,
> Each vine with ten thousand shoots,
> Each shoot with ten thousand branches,
> Each branch with ten thousand clusters,
> Each cluster with ten thousand grapes,
> Each grape yielding twenty-five measures of wine.
> And when one of the saints would take hold of a bunch, another bunch would cry out, Take me: Bless the Lord through me.
> (Papias, *Expositions* IV, in Irenaeus, *Ad. Haer*. V, 33, 34.)

This interesting piece of oral tradition is not theology at all. It is a cumulative folk-song, and Irenaeus goes on to indicate the content of the other verses, about the wheat, the fruits, the seed and the grasses; and all the animals, he says, will eat food which grows out of the ground, and live together in peace and harmony and subjection to mankind. It was a harvest-song, such as might have been sung at the harvest-festivals in Israel, at Pentecost and Tabernacles, for instance. It is in line with the old prophets and the contemporary apocalypses and was widely known, since the verse about the vines is quoted in Baruch (xxix.3), and an allusion to it is found in Enoch (x. 17–19), where it is said that every one will beget ten thousand children. It is a fantasy about the redeemed earth in the millennial age.

Papias goes on to say that Judas asked the Lord how such things could be, and the Lord answered, 'They shall see it who come to it.'

It is natural to reject at once the idea that there could be any connexion between the thought of our Lord and material of this kind; but possibly there is no real incongruity in the idea of his joining in songs of this sort with the people of the land at their village festivals. It is not even inconceivable that some literal-minded person might have made the protest that Judas is said to have made, and that a mild remonstrance with a touch of irony in it might be the best reply. But however that may be, it is clear that Papias remembered a time when such songs were regarded in the Johannine circle as having the benediction of the Lord himself. He found no difficulty himself in taking this one literally; it is credible to the faithful, he said.

The tradition is valuable background material. It leads us directly into the old extravagant semi-apocalyptic, semi-liturgical lyrics, which must have been part of the religion of the soil in Palestine, and it helps us to understand the pre-theological phases of Christianity. It shows us the kind of material which flowed in on the popular level in the days when Judaism and Christianity were not yet severed from one another. A great deal of what turned into theology may at first have been poetry. Later on, in the second century, Papias and his friends hammered it into shape, and used it as material for the rather literal-minded apocalyptic of their day. We can see it as it passes through the medium of their tradition; from the elders to Papias and his generation; and from Papias and his generation to Justin Martyr and Irenaeus and their generation.

POLYCARP OF SMYRNA

The best-known disciple of the Elder John was Polycarp of Smyrna, who was born in 69 or 70. There is a new theory which places him twenty years later, but it runs into great difficulties; he would have been made bishop of Smyrna, for instance, before he was twenty-five. On the basis of the accepted chronology, he would have attended the school of John as early perhaps as the eighties, since such instruction began at an early age, when the memory could be trained. He was made bishop of Smyrna before about 110–115, when Ignatius addressed an Epistle to him; and Irenaeus, who was his pupil, states that he was so appointed by apostles. He loved to relate his memories of John and the others who had seen the Lord, and Irenaeus himself had vivid memories of these occasions; 'I am able to describe the very place', he said, 'in which the blessed Polycarp sat as he discoursed...and the accounts which he gave of his intercourse with John and with the others who had seen the Lord.' Polycarp wrote nothing himself which has survived, except one short epistle; but Irenaeus preserves his witness, and says that the John of whom he spoke was the apostle. Irenaeus knows nothing of a second John.

He also informs us that Papias was a contemporary[1] of Polycarp, and a hearer of John; but according to his own account he depended on reports by John's pupils. He lived a hundred miles from Ephesus, and his contact with John himself may only have been occasional.

THE AUTHOR OF THE APOCALYPSE

We can now turn to quite another field of evidence and examine the local and personal references in the Revelation. The author of this book gives his name as John, but does not add any title. He was well enough known not to need it. He had a commanding position in the churches which he addressed, and describes himself to his hearers as their brother and companion in persecution. This persecution occurred in the last years of Domitian, who died in 96; but the relation of the prophet to the churches which he addresses must have been established well before that date; no later than 85 to 90, one would suppose.

Justin Martyr, who was teaching in Ephesus about forty years later, states that he was John the apostle. Other church writers after his time make the same statement. The Revelation itself does not say so. It says 'John your brother' without further identification.

THE SEVEN CHURCHES

The Revelation is addressed to seven churches in Asia and Phrygia, and contains a message for each, from which we can obtain information about the evangelistic and prophetic expansion since the Pauline period.

The envoy who carried this important book would begin with the

[1] *Hetairos:* literally 'companion'. It recalls the rabbinic term *habēr* which means an associate in the oral tradition of the schools.

old Pauline centre of Ephesus. This church had suffered a further influx of false teachers, and had survived the impact well. It had tested those who said they were apostles but were not. It had learned the lesson of faithfulness to the tradition, which Timothy had been commissioned to impress upon it; and it had lost the mystic love which had once been its glory. Yet it was in its favour that it hated the deeds of the Nicolaitans. Who the Nicolaitans were we frankly do not know. Irenaeus connects them with Nicolas of Antioch, who is mentioned in the Acts, and says that his error lay in self-indulgence. Clement of Alexandria credits him with the saying that we ought to abuse the flesh, whatever that may mean; he also refers to an odd story about his treatment of his wife, which, however, he does not believe. He claims to have some knowledge about him.

From Ephesus the envoy proceeded to the younger churches. The first of these was Smyrna, a busy seaport which lay a few miles to the north. This church was founded in the post-Pauline period, as Polycarp states in his Epistle to the Philippians. It was about to undergo a serious persecution. It had enemies who said they were Jews but were not; they were a synagogue of Satan, John says.

North of Smyrna was Pergamum, and east of Pergamum Thyatira. Pergamum was an old royal city, and the principal centre of the emperor-worship in Asia Minor; Satan's throne was there, John said. A Christian with the Herodian name of Antipas had died there recently as a martyr. These new churches were not lacking in faith and courage, but they were wide open to strange doctrines. Pergamum had some who held the teaching of Balaam, who taught the children of Israel to 'eat things offered to idols and to commit fornication'. Thyatira harboured similar teachers, and had accepted the ministrations of a woman-prophet, who encouraged her children to explore the deep things of Satan. This woman, who is referred to as Jezebel, will come to no good end.

The references to the false teachers are not so cryptic that we cannot make out their anti-Jewish character; for Balaam and Jezebel were opponents of the Mosaic or prophetic religion. We can also make out definite references to the Jerusalem formula, which imposed upon the Gentile churches of Syria and Cilicia a modicum of respect for the Levitical Law.[1] It would be unwise, however, to infer that we have

[1] But it only mentions two points: idolatry and fornication.

here a reference to the Acts. The Jerusalem Epistle must have been well known apart from the Acts. The echoes of the words of Jesus which are found in the Revelation seem to be rather more in line with Matthew than Luke, but may be drawn from some independent version of the Matthew tradition. John knew of various attempts to render it in Greek, Papias says.

The envoy who carried the book struck south-east now in the direction of Phrygia, but made a halt at Sardis in Lydia, where the church had a reputation for being very much alive, though it was spiritually dead according to the message which John sent it. He then passed over the border into Phrygia, and came to Philadelphia, where a small congregation had remained faithful under persecution in spite of the opposition of those who said they were Jews and were not. The Jewish question was still a live one in Philadelphia when Ignatius visited it about twenty years after John wrote.

The envoy now came out on the main highway near the important cities of Hierapolis, Colossæ, and Laodicea. The daughters of Philip, who attained to a great age, must still have been living; Papias was a young man storing up reminiscences in his retentive memory. The Revelation had no special message for Hierapolis. Colossæ and Laodicea had received letters from Paul some thirty years before, though the Laodicean letter no longer survives. The seventh message in the Revelation is addressed to this city. It has little good to say about it; it was neither hot nor cold; self-satisfaction reigned supreme.

THE PROPHET AND THE PASTOR

The acquaintance of this John with these churches was far from superficial; his analysis of their strong and weak points is profound. He speaks with full prophetic inspiration. It is rather misleading to refer to his messages as Epistles, as is done in the *Muratorian Fragment*; they are the messages of the risen and glorified Christ who stands in the midst of his churches; they are given to John in a state of spiritual vision; they are what the Holy Spirit is saying to the churches.

The frontier of the gospel has been pushed forward in the last thirty years, and new churches established. Prophets and evangelists and even apostles, of all sorts, have continued to stream westward and ramify northward. The newer churches are bold and aggressive, though they are too inexperienced to discriminate between false and true teachers. The gospel is making progress in Phrygia, and Philadelphia has an open door before it. The prophetic form of the faith struck deep roots in Phrygia; in fifty years the Revelation would bear strange fruit there.

The strange style of the Revelation must have been familiar in all these churches. It is without parallel in Jewish Hellenism. John wrote in a barbaric Greek which moved according to the dictates of Hebrew grammar; but its success as a poetic medium is extraordinary, and survives well in the English translation. The Revelation is a work of genius. Its author was a Hebrew scholar, apparently, and knew the old prophets in the original language; his Hebrew thinking, based upon this classic literature, passed into the Greek language and took possession of it. It is open to question whether his linguistic style was his own creation, or whether it was the language of some semi-Hellenized circle of Jews in Palestine or elsewhere.

His older or earlier visions were composed in Jerusalem. Some of them are packed with unresolved and unexplained symbols drawn from a Hebrew mysticism which expressed itself in terms of ancient oriental myth and ritual. They are not like the realistic or representational art of the Greeks; the symbols do not cohere in such a way as to produce an illusion of reality; you cannot think in realistic terms of the figure of a man with a sharp two-edged sword going out of his mouth. The unity of each vision is spiritual, not three-dimensional. Yet they draw a sense of reality and vitality from the world of nature. We are conscious of the Palestinian landscape, the high mountain, the desert, the hot winds, the burned-up harvests, the cloud of locusts, the scorpion striking with its tail, the vulture in mid-heaven, and the voice like a lion roaring. In the later visions, the barbaric style has been modified a little by the grace and lucidity of Hellenism, and is said to have incorporated local symbolism, such as was familiar in Asia or Phrygia. A Jewish syncretism in Asia and Phrygia had doubtless prepared the way for this.

Scholars have debated whether these old Jerusalem visions were the work of John himself, or whether they were the work of previous prophets which he has incorporated into his book; if this is the case, he has impressed his own style and personality upon the book as a whole.

This prophet stood in a pastoral relation to the churches which he addressed. He was familiar with their spiritual conditions. He rebuked, he admonished, he commended; and all in the name of the Lord Jesus. Ezekiel, who was his literary master, had a similar sense of pastoral responsibility; and in the *Didache*, a generation later, we read of prophets who went from church to church exercising pastoral supervision.

JOHN AND THE EPISCOPATE

We may here record a statement of Clement of Alexandria, which was drawn from the oral tradition of his time, that John, on being invited, visited the neighbouring districts of the Gentiles, 'in one place appointing bishops, in another setting in order whole churches, in another ordaining a ministry or individuals from among those who were indicated by the Spirit'. There is nothing impossible, or even unlikely, about this, as the organization of the autonomous episcopate must have occurred during this period; after the situation which appears in the Pastoral Epistles, and previous to the situation which appears in the Epistles of Ignatius.

In this connexion Clement relates the story of how John confided to one of his bishops the care of a promising young convert, who subsequently abandoned the church and joined a band of robbers. The bishop took no steps to reclaim him, but John, on his next visit, rebuked the bishop, mounted his horse, pursued the young man, and brought him triumphantly back.

Clement tells the story at length, and is very confident about it. He found it current in more than one locality, some even giving the name of the city where it happened. It lacks confirmation from other sources, but it is interesting for more than one reason. It is the only story which shows a Christian evangelist riding a horse (like the heavenly Christ in the Revelation); and it gives a lively picture of an old man of extraordinary vigour hunting down his lost convert, and shouting after him as he goes. This was the impression which St John left in the mind of the church, not that of a mild unworldly dreamer, such as pious meditation has distilled from certain passages in the Gospel and Epistles.

It shows him at work building up the episcopal order, which was taking form at this time. Tertullian attributes this work to John, and Irenaeus states that Polycarp was made Bishop of Smyrna by apostles.

THE PROPHET AND THE LITURGY

The ministry of prophecy has some relation to the liturgy of prayer and worship in I Corinthians as well as in the *Didache* in which it has rather taken command of the situation. The movement of the Revelation is sustained throughout by organized liturgical action. Its literary structure is built up on the daily and yearly order of the Temple services, with their sacrificial worship and festal occasions and choral music. The incense-offering, the trumpets, the bowls of blood, and other liturgical features, provide the framework of the poem. It is preceded, however, by a heavenly vision, in which a Christian form of worship is set forth in symbolic form.

The worship of heaven is offered by a circle of twenty-four elders, who are described as kings and priests. They are seated in a circle and there is a throne in their midst. It consists of the four winds or spirits of life, with their six wings and their many eyes, which represent in Hebrew art and poetry the whole circle of created being. He who presides there has no form or likeness, but is compared to the glowing concentrated light of precious stones. Those who worship him sing the traditional chant in a new form,

> HOLY! HOLY! HOLY! LORD GOD THE ALMIGHTY!
> Who was and who is and who is to come.

This pattern is based on the order of the Jewish synagogue or Christian ecclesia. It recurs in Christian writings; in the Epistles of Ignatius, for instance, where the elders preside like the council of the apostles, and the bishop is in the place of God or of Christ. In heaven the Creator and Master of the Universe presides in his synagogue of watchers and holy ones; on earth the pattern is repeated in the Temple or synagogue or ecclesia.

This is the first phase in the heavenly worship and corresponds to the act of praise and thanksgiving in the sabbath service of the synagogue, in which God is visualized as enthroned in his creation on the seventh day; the refrain, 'Holy holy, holy', belongs to this act of thanksgiving. It appears in the synagogue ritual as the *Kedūshah* and is reproduced by Clement in his Epistle.

In the second phase John sees the sealed book in the right hand of God, but no lector appears who is worthy to open its seals or read its content; until the 'Lamb of God as it had been slain' takes the book and opens its seven seals. This vision combines the ideas of the crucified and risen Messiah with the idea of the mysterious Son of Man whose place is at the right hand of the deity. The sound of the harp is now heard, incense is offered, and all creation joins in the worship of the Lamb. The Christian 'Lord's day' worship is thus drawn into, and incorporated with, the Jewish sabbath-day worship.

This subject of the liturgy is one of the major interests of the prophet; and we may hazard the guess that his peculiar Greek, with its Hebrew colouring and structure, may preserve for us the language of some liturgical tradition of a Jewish or Jewish-Christian type. This side of his work was not forgotten. Polycrates, who was born in an episcopal family in Ephesus about 130, grew up in the Johannine tradition, and became Bishop of Ephesus himself about 190. He says that John was a witness and a teacher; he was also a priest, and wore the 'petalon'. The petalon was a golden plate which was suspended from the mitre of the Jewish high priest so as to cover his forehead. It was engraved with the words 'Holiness unto the Lord'. We have, here, the memory, as it was preserved in the Ephesian ecclesia, in words which must have been purely symbolic, of the prophet and seer of apostolic character, who led their worship at one time and left his mark upon the liturgy of the universal church. It recalls the picture of James the Just in the Jerusalem tradition.

THE WRITER OF THE EPISTLES

We turn from this half-legendary picture to another set of contemporary, documents, the three 'Epistles' which are attributed to St John. Only two of these are in true epistolary form, the Second and the Third. The author does not name himself. He calls himself 'The Elder' which recalls the nomenclature of Papias and Irenaeus. The title seems to have been sufficient identification.

The 'Second Epistle' is written to a church which is also not named; he calls it 'the elect Lady', a quaint piece of symbolism which may be matched in I Peter and Hermas. He sends greetings from his own church, or the church where he happens to be: 'The children of thy elect sister greet thee.' There is no sign of the harsh Hebraism of the Revelation. Instead we have the simple and correct Greek of the Johannine Gospel with its characteristic use of key-words like love and truth and commandment. The word truth replaces the word faith, which he does not use; the word commandment is connected with the word love. This is the kind of 'walking' which had been received from the beginning. On the other side are the deceivers, who do not confess that Jesus Christ has come 'in the flesh'. They are 'the Antichrist', and are not to be received into the house (by which he means the church) or given any greeting.

The 'Third Epistle' is a personal letter written to the well-beloved Gaius, who is the head of a local church, perhaps a bishop. The Elder commends him for his loving care in entertaining certain strangers who had come to him in the name of God, taking nothing from the Gentiles. He condemns another church official, named Diotrephes, who loves his position of importance, behaves roughly to strangers, and makes malicious remarks about the Elder himself. He commends Demetrius.

The writer is a pastor. He addresses the churches and their leaders with authority. He proposes to visit them soon, and these very slight and short Epistles are no more than preludes to his visit. As he does not give his name, it is possible to attribute them to the secondary John as was done at least as early as the fourth century, or to Aristion, or to some unknown elder. On the other hand, their style connects them with the First Epistle and with the Gospel. It has been suggested, however, that the style might have been imitated by a pupil, or that it might be a conventional style adopted in the Johannine school.

The 'First Epistle' is very closely connected with the Gospel. It is not an actual letter like the others. It is a manifesto of a personal character which may have formed an appendix to the Gospel. One passes from the last words of the Gospel to the first words of the 'Epistle' with a perfect sense of continuity. In the *Muratorian Fragment*, the Epistle is quoted from immediately after the paragraph which deals with the Gospel, and Clement of Alexandria speaks of it as 'following the Gospel'. It is written in the same distinctive style and develops many of the same ideas. Critics generally are agreed that it is by the same hand, though the question has been raised again recently by Dr C. H. Dodd. All think of it as emanating from the same circle, and this circle is associated with himself by the author.

THE FOURTH GOSPEL

The First Epistle begins by speaking in the name of a band of witnesses. They bear witness to 'that which was from the beginning; what we have heard, what we have seen with our eyes, what we have looked upon, and our hands have handled; of the Word of Life'. It begins with the plural form; but it soon passes into the singular, 'I write unto you, my children.' The single author, who now speaks, has a position of authority as a pastor and father in God and a witness to the evangelical truth. He speaks with deep affection and concern; but he does so with the support of a band of witnesses.

The Gospel gives us exactly the same picture of compound authority and witness. 'The Word was made flesh', we read in its first verses, 'and dwelt among us, and *we beheld* his glory.' A more precise affirmation occurs in the last chapter. There is an unnamed disciple in this Gospel, who appears first in the Passion narrative; he reclined next to the Lord at the Last Supper, he followed him into the judgement hall of Annas, he stood by the cross, he received the Lord's mother into his home, and he was a witness of the empty tomb on Easter Sunday morning. 'This is the Disciple who bears witness of these things, and wrote these things', we read 'and *we know* that his witness is true'.

The reader who was familiar with the earlier Gospels, or with the gospel material in any comparable tradition, could not fail to identify this disciple with John the son of Zebedee, who never appears in this Gospel under his own name.[1] Other suggestions have been made, of course. He is the shadowy second John who has been discerned by many scholars in the names recorded by Papias; or he is a purely allegorical figure emblematic of the true believer, though it would be hard indeed to make out the terms of the allegory. A bold few resolve the whole Gospel into allegory; but theories of this kind fail to come to terms with the definite statements which are made in the Gospel and Epistle; or, for that matter, with the theology of the Gospel itself.

The impression of compound authorship is reinforced by evidence from the church tradition. Clement of Alexandria, at the end of the second century, said that John wrote the Gospel at the request of his

[1] The 'sons of Zebedee' are mentioned, but not individually named, in John xxi. 2.

friends. The *Muratorian Fragment*, which was written in the Roman church about the same time, gives a similar picture:

Of the fourth of the Gospels: John, [one] of the disciples, when his disciples and fellow-bishops were urging him, said, 'Fast with me to-day for three days, and whatever may be revealed, let us narrate to one another'; the same night it was revealed to Andrew [one] of the apostles, that John should narrate all things in his own name, as they called them to mind [or: and they were all to certify].

This story may have assumed a slightly legendary form, and surprises us by its mention of Andrew; but it is completely in harmony with the evidence, and shows how long the tradition of compound authorship endured. Andrew is prominent in the Gospel where he is made the companion of Philip.

Another view appears in the so-called Anti-Marcionite prologues, which we referred to in our discussion of Luke as being quite probably second-century work. Their evidence on the fourth gospel is definitely anti-Marcionite, and not very helpful; but we include it for the sake of completeness.

The gospel of John was manifested and given to the churches by John, while still living in the body, as [one] Papias by name, a Hieropolitan, a dear disciple of John, has handed down in his 'Exoterica', that is in the last five books; indeed he wrote down the gospel as John dictated; but Marcion the heretic was cast out by John, because his opinions were contrary; he indeed had brought him writings or Epistles from the brethren who were in Pontus.

This statement is incoherent in itself, and does not agree with more reputable evidence.[1] The only question can be whether it contains some morsel of good tradition; and, since it is controversial in tone, whether it is possible to reconstruct the views which it is refuting. Was there a belief, for instance, that it was given to the churches when John was no longer living in the body?

[1] Possibly it meant in its original (Greek) form that Polycarp repelled Marcion on the authority of John?

THE DOCETIC TEACHERS

We may now return to the Epistles and examine the contemporary evidence which they supply with regard to a type of heresy which now appears clearly for the first time. The Second Epistle spoke of deceivers who refused to recognize that Jesus Christ had come in the flesh. The First Epistle has more to say about them.

The Pastoral Epistles and the Revelation have told us something about false teachers of the Jewish type who practised asceticism and revelled in mythology; and the Revelation spoke of false teachers who persuaded the brethren to eat things offered to idols and commit fornication, and were probably of the anti-Jewish type; but nobody has shown much concern about false teaching on the subject of the person of Christ.[1] The First Epistle of John refers to it very clearly. These 'false prophets' once belonged to the church, but are now in schism. They have gone out from us, the writer says; but this proves that they were never really 'of us', or else they would have stayed with us. Their appearance is a sign of the last times. They are manifestations of the Antichrist, about whom the hearers of the epistle have heard something. They claim to possess a *chrisma* or anointing, and a Spirit of truth; but what they really possess is a spirit of error. 'This is how you know the Spirit of God', the writer says. 'Every spirit which confesses that Jesus Christ has come in the flesh, is of God; and every spirit which does not confess that Jesus Christ has come in the flesh is not of God.'

The denial that Jesus Christ had come in the flesh was a bold thing, carrying with it, as it seems to do, a hostile attitude to the historical gospel tradition, that is to say the tradition which was vouched for by Peter and the Twelve. It is the form of belief about Christ which appears in the heresies of Marcion and the Syrian gnostics; and this may be one of the schools of thought from which those heresies were derived. Marcion based his theology on Paul, and it is considered possible that these heretics did the same. Paul had preached Jesus as the glorious Son of God who had entered into his life on the Damascus road. He had called him the Lord from heaven and a life-giving Spirit. He even went so far, on one occasion, as to deprecate a knowledge of Jesus 'according to the flesh', had he possessed it. The Jesus of Paul was a true man,

[1] Paul may have had such teaching in view when writing to the Colossians.

however; he had been born of a woman, and came of the seed of David according to the flesh; he had been brought up under the Jewish Law, and had been a 'minister of the circumcision'; he had had twelve apostles; he had died on the cross, and been buried, and risen again on the third day. The spirituals had an answer for that. He had only *appeared* or *seemed* to do these things. The life-giving Spirit could not actually have been born, or lived in the flesh, or suffered, or died. This form of faith is referred to as an organized heresy or sect in the Epistles of Ignatius a few years later; and heretics of this kind came to be called docetics, from the Greek word *dokei* it seems.

Looking again into John's Epistle, we infer that their faith in Jesus as pure Spirit was balanced by their confidence in the Spirit which they claimed to possess themselves. This Spirit had come to them 'by water'; that is to say they had received it at their baptism; it was their link with the spiritual Christ; it conferred on them unerring knowledge of the truth. The schism was prophetic or visionary in character: they were inspired persons.

The writer of the Epistle recalls his flock to the Word of Life and the message which they had received from the beginning, which he confirms by his own witness and the witness of his companions. 'What was from the beginning, what we have seen, and our hands have handled... that is what we declare unto you.' He reminds them of their baptism; 'The Spirit that is in you is greater than the Spirit that is in them; *you* have a *chrisma* from the holy one.'

The theology of this passage, no less than the mysterious rhythmical style, tells us that the author himself is a 'spiritual'. He writes in a condition of high spiritual tension.

CERINTHUS

A clarification of this confused situation was proposed by a certain Cerinthus who appeared in Ephesus about this time. Polycarp of Smyrna, who was now a young man in his twenties, used to tell a story of John going one day into the public bath-house and finding Cerinthus there; he rushed out again saying, 'Let us fly before the building collapses; Cerinthus the enemy of the truth is inside.' It is the sort of anecdote that goes on being told about men of strong personality; they are seldom false to the character of their hero, even when their authenticity is dubious, and this one gives the same picture of a determined and active old man that we found in the story of the robber band.

Irenaeus the pupil of Polycarp, who vouches for this story, informs us that Cerinthus had been trained in the Egyptian system of education. He taught that Christ was a Spirit from the high God and therefore incapable of suffering; and so far he was at one with pure docetism; but he had an arrangement by which he could accept the Jesus of history too. Jesus was a man like other men, the son of Joseph and Mary though not by a virgin birth. He was juster and wiser than the rest of mankind and after his baptism by John in the Jordan, the Christus (as it is convenient to call the heavenly Spirit in this kind of christology) came down upon him in the form of a dove; and from that time he began to work miracles and to proclaim the heavenly Father. At the end it departed from Jesus, and it was Jesus by himself who suffered on the cross and rose again from the dead, the Christus remaining impassible, incapable of suffering.

This clever idea of a separation of the Christus from the Jesus seemed to retain the values of both schools of thought; the angel or spirit from heaven on the one hand; and the man Jesus on the other who was a teacher and wonder-worker.

THE JOHANNINE SCHOOL

Against this background of myth and apocalypse and millenialism and other-worldly spirituality, the Johannine school continued to stress the idea of God in human history as the basis of gospel and apocalyptic. 'What we have seen', they kept on saying, 'What we have heard and our hands have handled'; or alternatively, 'What must swiftly come to pass.' Perhaps we may attempt some summary of the evidence which has been reviewed here.

They brought with them authentic traditions from Jerusalem, since Jerusalem visions are included in the Revelation and Jerusalem narratives in the Gospel. It is natural to identify the Elder of Papias, who communicated apocalyptic hymns to his pupils, with the John who wrote the Revelation; on the other hand, it is the writer of II John and III John who actually calls himself the Elder. We are bound to equate the Elder of Papias with the tutor of Polycarp, as Irenaeus actually does. On the other hand, many scholars feel that the author of the Gospel (with which I John is closely associated) cannot be the same man as the author of Revelation; the style and emotional feeling of the two books are so different, they think. Here is the beginning of the perplexities which are felt by modern scholars in approaching the subject; they are led to question the evidence of the second-century fathers, since they regard the whole Johannine tradition as one and indivisible, and identify the master of it with John the apostle. They fall back on the theory of the existence of two Johns, which the evidence of Papias permits and the mind of a third-century father originated; but some are reluctant to identify either of them with John the apostle. This question is taken up again on page 362 below.

CHAPTER 17

THE SYRIAN GOSPEL

The oriental Gospel, *p.* 312. Alexandria, *p.* 313. The church in Antioch, *p.* 314. Menander and his sect, *p.* 315. 'According to Matthew', *p.* 316. The oracles of the Lord, *p.* 318. The five books of teaching, *p.* 319. The kingdom of the heavens, *p.* 320. The Scribes and Pharisees, *p.* 322. The author of the Gospel, *p.* 324. Matthew and Peter, *p.* 325. Peter the stone, *p.* 327. The Matthaean narratives, *p.* 328. The false Prophets, *p.* 329. Apocalypse and eschatology, *p.* 330.

Vespasian died in 79 and was succeeded by his elder son Titus, the conqueror of Judaea. Titus died in 81, and was succeeded by his brother Domitian, who reigned until 96. In Gentile history Titus comes down as the good honest brother and Domitian as the mean crafty brother. In the Jewish tradition, the estimate of Titus is naturally not so favourable; or indeed of the Flavian emperors as a whole.

THE ORIENTAL GOSPEL

It was during the reign of Domitian, 81–96, that the schools of John and the other elders were flourishing in Asia Minor, and doubtless there were similar schools in Palestine and Syria; for these were the lands of the older and better-equipped churches, from which the Gentile west had received the faith; they were the sources from which the apostles and elders and prophets and teachers came. Unfortunately we know next to nothing about them, because they had no literary tradition; or at any rate no literature has survived, except for the Gospel 'according to Matthew', which was made in some centre of Syrian Hellenistic Christianity where the pressure of Jewish Christianity was strong. It made use of a number of sources, including Mark and Q; but the author had no knowledge of Luke or John. It follows that it must have been produced about the same time as Luke or not very much later, and in a distant region; in Alexandria, or Caesarea, or Antioch, for instance. It cannot be placed earlier than Luke, since time has to be allowed for the Gospel of Mark to arrive from Rome and make its impression. And the Matthaean gospel was not written in a hurry;

it may have gone through several stages. We may place its composition in the reign of Domitian without fear of serious error one way or another.

ALEXANDRIA

There is little if any reason for thinking of Alexandria as the place where Matthew was composed; but the deficiency of evidence about Alexandrian Christianity leaves us in the dark. It produced no literature at all, so far as we know.

There is no strong reason for connecting any New Testament book with Alexandria. Scholars have found some evidence for the influence of Alexandrian thought in the Epistle to the Hebrews or the Gospel of John, but the influence, such as it is, looks very remote. Only the mysterious Apollos, who preceded Paul at Ephesus and intervened in his mission at Corinth, can be claimed for Alexandria. The early reviser whose work appears in the Western Text of Acts says that he learned his Christianity in his native land; and he may be writing out of his personal knowledge. If this additional information is correct, then we can say that there was a form of Christianity in Alexandria which had a close connexion with John the Baptist, and was defective in some way when judged by the Pauline standards. We are not much farther advanced.

There is of course the legend, not to be dignified by the name of a tradition, which Eusebius was the first to place on record, that Mark was the founder of the Alexandrian church:

> Now it is said that this Mark journeyed to Egypt, and was the first to preach there the gospel which he had also written; and that he was the first to form churches in Alexandria itself. (Eusebius, *E.H.* II, 16, 1.)

Eusebius may have received this legend from the tradition of the great Alexandrian scholar Origen, with which he was familiar; but he does not say so; and he is not supported by the oldest Alexandrian writers such as Dionysius, who fails to mention Mark in his discussion of the travels of apostles and evangelists. On the other hand, if we take the reference to Mark's Gospel to be the main point of the tradition which Eusebius had received, it does fit in with certain indications which suggest that this Gospel had a strong position in the early Alexandrian church. The first clear statements about Alexandrian Christianity which are of any historical value have to do with the activities of important heretical teachers and the first of these is Cerinthus, whose peculiar views about the descent of the Christus into the man Jesus would seem to require a Gospel like that of Mark, which began with the baptism of Jesus by John. The school of elders or teachers in Egypt where Cerinthus received his training, may therefore have used Mark.

THE CHURCH IN ANTIOCH

We must pass by the churches of Caesarea and southern Syria for the moment, so far as Gentile Christianity is concerned; for no contemporary evidence about them is to be found. Later Palestinian legend, in the romances attributed to Clement, fills up this void by giving Caesarea a bishop named Zacchaeus, appointed by Peter, accommodating other cities of the sea-coast in a similar way. Peter goes on, and fixes his own headquarters at Antioch. This may be taken to represent the second-century tradition.

About the year 115 we have the Epistles of the martyr-bishop, Ignatius, which enable us to make some inferences about the kind of development which had taken place in his lifetime. It is not likely that Ignatius was born any later than the sixties, and a study of his thinking suggests that he was a convert from paganism rather than a born Christian. In any case his Christian education and spiritual development must have taken place in the reign of Domitian, when the Gospel of Matthew was in the making. During this period, and later, he saw the church in Antioch achieve a high degree of unity which was focused in the 'assemblies' and the acts of worship; the one altar, as he calls it; the one bishop with his council of apostolic elders; and the one gospel, which was that according to Matthew. Tradition gives him a single predecessor as bishop: his name was Euodius.

We are not free to say that the episcopal order or the Matthaean gospel originated in Antioch. They probably have a longer history. They seem to be based on Jewish-Christian precedents or antecedents, and may have been received from Palestine or South Syria. In Acts and in Galatians the church in Antioch receives one mission after another from Jerusalem, and there is no reason at all to suppose that this pressure from Jewish Christianity ceased. Indeed, the adoption or production of the Matthaean gospel, with its strongly Jewish-Christian content, is a proof that it was welcomed; and it is interesting that it appears in Matthew as a tradition of Peter.

The church in Antioch was the oldest of the great Gentile churches, and the mother-city of Gentile Christianity. It had been the scene of many conflicts. Its elders and teachers could tell Ignatius the whole truth about the historic occasion on which Paul had resisted Peter face to face; and it would seem that extreme men still carried on the argument. Ignatius had to deal with irreconcilable champions of what he called Judaism, and with equally irreconcilable 'docetics', who believed in a Jesus who was an angel or spirit. They may have been ardent followers of Paul.

MENANDER AND HIS SECT

Samaria, too, was sending out its evangelists and teachers, and among these was a certain Menander. Justin Martyr, who was a native of Samaria, is our oldest authority on his teaching, and Irenaeus, who made use of lost works of Justin, is our second. Menander belonged to the school of Simon Magus, the opponent of Peter. Justin can name the birthplace of both men; Simon came from Gitta, and Menander from Cappareteia. He is said to have announced himself as the Saviour, who had come down to earth from invisible realms to overcome the angels who hold this world in bondage. He had a magical knowledge by which they could be vanquished, which probably means that he was an exorcist. Those who received his baptism became recipients of the resurrection and were incapable of death. They grew not old but became immortal, Irenaeus said. He made Antioch his headquarters, and founded a school there. His date cannot be precisely determined; he followed Simon Magus and preceded Satornilus. Justin had met adherents of his who still cherished their faith in him in their old age.

It is possible that Justin and Irenaeus took the words of Menander too literally. He may have taught a mystical and spiritual doctrine along the lines of the Pauline sacramentalism; for Paul spoke constantly of baptism as a new creation or moral resurrection. A resurrection in the sense of a spiritual regeneration may have been all he cared for, like Hymenaeus and Philetus in Asia, who held that the resurrection was already past. Similar language is used by Ignatius about the eucharist;

he calls it the elixir of immortality, and the antidote against death, which is the language of poetry, not of theology.

The story of the Menandrian sect in Antioch, with its Samaritan background, reminds us of an important fact. The medium in which the gospel spread was the omnipresent Jewish diaspora, which radiated from Jerusalem and filled the world; 'Every land is full of thee, and every sea', as the Sibyl had said; but there was an eastern dispersion as well as a western; for Judaism was an oriental religion, which had affinities with other oriental religions. Jewish ideas had been combined in certain circles with the monotheisms or near-monotheisms of the Syrian kingdoms and the Parthian empire; the high 'dualistic' monotheism of Iran for instance, and the astrological monotheism of the Chaldeans, and the polymorphous spirituality of the Syrians, which had already blended into various mixed forms, which could express themselves either as myth or philosophy. Simon and Menander were mystics and philosophers who took the gospel of Jesus into union with such 'syncretized' versions of the higher paganism of their time.

'ACCORDING TO MATTHEW'

The Syrian Gospel appeared in the church at large and won its way to the premier position among the four, under the name of Matthew; but it does not lay claim to apostolic authorship in the actual text. Ignatius refers to it simply as 'The Gospel', and that may have been its original name; and if it was intended to provide the whole available evangelical material, for church use, in one volume, no further words would be required; but they would become necessary so soon as Luke and John appeared as competitors, or when it became apparent that it would not supersede Mark. Perhaps the words 'according to Matthew' were added to the title as it moved westward into Asia Minor.

These words do not imply that the book was written by Matthew himself; they would be sufficiently accounted for if it was believed that it faithfully preserved the tradition of Matthew as it was carried on by him or by his school. The existence of a Matthaean tradition of teaching can hardly be disputed. It is mentioned in the Mishnah and in the church tradition, and is suggested by the name of the Gospel itself. The oldest extant authority to refer to it is probably the Elder John, according to a statement of Papias which is preserved by Eusebius.

(Eusebius) And Papias delivers in his book accounts of the words of the Lord by the aforesaid Aristion, and *traditions of John the Elder*, to which we refer the student; but we are bound to add to the words of his which we have already quoted, *a tradition which he set forth concerning Mark who wrote the gospel*, in these words:

(Papias) *And this is what the Elder said:* Mark, who had been an interpreter of Peter, wrote down accurately what he related [*or* remembered?], though not in order, of things which were said or done by the Lord; for he had not heard the Lord or followed him, but afterwards, as I said, he followed Peter; and Peter composed his teachings to meet the needs [*or* requirements], but not with the idea of making an orderly arrangement of the oracles of the Lord; so that Mark made no error when he wrote certain things down as he remembered [*or* related] them; for there was one point to which he paid attention, not to omit anything that he had heard, and not to make any error about it.

(Eusebius) *So this is what is recorded by Papias with regard to Mark; but with regard to Matthew, this is what is said:*

(Papias) 'Matthew, however, made a written arrangement of the oracles of the Lord in the Hebrew [i.e. Aramaic] language, and everybody interpreted them as best they could.' (Eusebius, *E.H.* III, 39, 14–16.)

Naturally there has been considerable discussion among the learned about these important extracts. How much of the first paragraph comes from the Elder, for instance, and how much is explanatory matter by Papias? And is the statement about Matthew intended to be a quotation from the Elder or not? Since no agreement exists on these points, it will be best to take the whole of it as the fruit of the researches of Papias made at this period.

Papias knew of a collection of the 'oracles' of Jesus which Matthew had written in Aramaic; he remembered about the difficulty that there was in getting it translated in the Gentile churches. The memory of it was not lost in the church, some confusing it with the 'Hebrew' gospel which was written early in the second century, and some even with the canonical Matthew;[1] but it is not necessary to pursue the various references to it here.

[1] Some scholars think that Papias was guilty of this confusion, or that he invented the idea of the Aramaic *logia* to account for the canonical Matthew. His statement seems to be innocent of any such ideas.

THE ORACLES OF THE LORD

There has also been a great deal of discussion about the meaning of the word *logia*, which has been translated 'oracles'. It used to be rather widely held that it meant sayings of Jesus, and therefore, it was argued, the Aramaic Matthew could not have included his acts; and this led to the rather unscientific habit of referring to an isolated saying of Jesus as a *logion*. Another theory which has been advanced from time to time is that it referred to a collection of extracts from the Old Testament.

The meaning of the word *logion* which is given in the dictionary is 'brief utterances or oracles'. The word was in regular use in Christian writers in connexion with the Law of Moses, which Stephen called the living *logia*, and Paul the *logia* of God. Now the Law of Moses contains the whole story of the patriarchs, as well as the narrative of the Exodus and the wanderings of Israel in the wilderness, so that there can be no justification for the exclusion of acts of Jesus from the *logia* of Matthew. Indeed, the word suggests that it was a Christian counterpart of Genesis and Exodus. Furthermore, the Aramaic Matthew and the Marcan Gospel, in the Papias quotation, are referred to and compared as books of the same type. The difference lay in the fact that Peter had a translator who produced a report of his teachings in Greek, whereas Matthew produced his arrangement of the *logia* in Aramaic, which everybody had to translate for himself. Mark's book had a less satisfactory order than Matthew's, but Matthew's was less accessible to the Gentile churches for language reasons. And this is the state of affairs which Papias knew about through his personal researches.

A number of scholars take the very natural view that the Aramaic Matthew was one of the sources which was used by the author of the canonical Matthew, and that the title 'according to Matthew' was given to it because it preserved in an acceptable Greek form the contents of the older book. It was customary at one time to identify it with Q; but this is not satisfactory, since Q was written in Greek and is even better preserved in Luke than it is in Matthew. The element in the canonical Matthew which gave it its name should be looked for in the material which is peculiar to it, or the special character which it possesses.

THE FIVE BOOKS OF TEACHING

The most striking feature of Matthew is the fact that it collects into five distinct masses or blocks of teaching the sayings of Jesus which were given to Israel, or through the apostles to the church. In each case the material is woven into a continuous dramatic discourse and given an appropriate narrative setting. The author takes in material out of Mark or Q, when it is relevant, and blends it freely with material from his own special tradition or from other sources.

The first of these is the Sermon on the Mount, in which Jesus is presented as the supreme teacher in Israel. His function was to fulfil the Law and the Prophets, not to destroy them as was apparently supposed by some. The Law of Moses was eternally valid, but not in the sense in which the scribes and the Pharisees expounded it. The righteousness of God's kingdom was implanted in the heart; a pure heart; a heart devoid of anger or malice or lust or fear or even anxiety; a heart full of faith and love; a childlike heart trusting implicitly in the Father in the heavens, and showing forth its relation to the Father by gentleness and goodness and love even towards one's enemies; for he makes his sun to shine on the unjust as well as the just, and sheds his rain on the evil as well as the good. A sublime spiritual monotheism is here revealed which is concentrated in the word 'Father'. It teaches a simple childlike heaven-and-earth mysticism in which the sons of God are the middle term; and a conflict with evil in which those who suffer for righteousness' sake inherit the kingdom of heaven.

The second discourse concerns the founding of the apostolate, which is a Marcan theme; but it gathers the various stages into one; the choice of the Twelve, their names, their sending, the counsels for the journey, the warnings of persecution, and the command to confess the Messiah even at the cost of martyrdom. It stands well within the historical framework; their mission is limited to the lost sheep of the house of Israel; but the material is so arranged as to serve the needs of the church at a later time.

The third discourse is an enlargement of the Marcan parable chapter. It contains several new parables, including the tares and the fish-net, which introduce important new themes, such as the thought of the church on earth as an intermediate form of the kingdom, and the more elaborate eschatology to which this thought is related, and the 'consummation of the age' to which everything moves.

The fourth discourse concerns the household of the church, and is broken by narrative. The figure of Peter is prominent in it, and it follows Peter's confession of faith, which is left in its Marcan position, but has appended to it the famous word, 'Thou art Peter, and on this rock I will build my church.' The setting of the discourse is the Marcan conclave at Capernaum, with its teaching on mutual service, and humility, and concern for the little ones, to which it adds the duty of unlimited forgiveness. It affirms the divine character of the church in a new form of the heaven-and-earth mysticism, in which the church on earth is the middle term which links the two.

The fifth discourse is a double one. First come the lamentations over the Pharisees, which balance the beatitudes in the Sermon on the Mount; for here is the unspiritual externalized religion, which masquerades as the Law and the prophets in action. This long prophetic diatribe ends with the lamentation over Jerusalem and the Temple, which was taken from Q; and this provides a background for the Marcan 'Little Apocalypse' which immediately follows in an extended form. Three parables of judgement are added, the Talents, the Ten Virgins, and the Sheep and the Goats; and this ends the ministry of Jesus to Israel. The Passion narrative follows.

THE KINGDOM OF THE HEAVENS

These five long discourses are fitted into the framework supplied by the Marcan narrative, and so successfully was this done that the same system of lection-division could be used for both Gospels in the ancient manuscripts, with a surprisingly small degree of variation.[1] One Gospel could be substituted for the other in a continuous reading course with very little difficulty. They were both built according to the same pattern. But it would be an error to consider Matthew as nothing but an ingenious arrangement of traditional sources for liturgical or didactic purposes in the ecclesia. Our author has his own vision of what he is doing, which appears in his peculiar source-material, his explanatory handling of the text, and his general structure.

Matthew repudiates the Judaism of his day in order to present a new Judaism of superior authority. He does not begin, like Mark, with John the Baptist; he begins with Abraham, who appears in the litera-

[1] See my *Primitive Christian Calendar*, Cambridge.

ture of Jewish Hellenism as the first instructor of the old civilizations of Babylon, Syria and Egypt. He produces a genealogical scroll which introduces Jesus as the son of Abraham and the son of 'David the king'; and this ancient and royal genealogy[1] is divided into six periods of time, thus indicating that a seventh and last era of history had opened with the Messianic kingdom. John the Baptist announces the 'kingdom of the heavens', which he does not do in Mark. Jesus begins his ministry in Galilee with the 'gospel of the kingdom', an interesting new phrase.

We turn to the end of the book. The eleven apostles are sent out from a mountain in Galilee to make disciples of all the nations, and the risen Messiah will be with them to the consummation of the age. The oriental mind would have no difficulty about this; the new seventh age had begun; the final age of Sibylline song.

After the genealogy and the birth of the Messiah, Matthew brings in the Magian pilgrims, who are the representatives of the old oriental civilization, to offer their homage at his cradle. They are led by a star and the suggestion is that the heavens belong to God; the stars are good —not evil as the prevailing astral religion declared.

It is a remarkable fact that Matthew uses the phrase 'kingdom of the heavens', not 'kingdom of God'. It recalls the words of Daniel to the king of Babylon, 'that thou mightest know, O king, that the heavens do rule'. The Rabbis often spoke of God by the title of 'the heavens', and no doubt it was done out of motives of reverence to avoid profaning the word 'God'; but it also offset the current suggestion in astral or gnostic religion that there were evil powers in the heavens; a form of thought which is used in the Epistle to the Ephesians for a special purpose. Such gnostic teachers as Simon of Samaria took it seriously. Jesus used the word 'God' with great freedom, as his Pharisee opponents sarcastically observed: 'Rabbi, we know that thou art true, and regardest not the person of man, but teachest the way of God *in truth*' (they are mocking at his solemn asseveration, 'Amen I say unto you'). Nevertheless Matthew prefers the word 'heavens' when speaking of the divine kingdom; it makes it perfectly clear which God was meant; it was the Hebrew God.

The Magian pilgrims to Jerusalem and Bethlehem hail Jesus as the one who was born to be king. Egypt affords him a refuge from the evil

[1] In the period of the monarchy it gives successive kings rather than an actual family tree.

designs of the tyrant who had usurped the throne which rightly belonged to him. The Gentile world to which Matthew relates his Gospel is that of the old orient, with Egypt on the one hand and Babylonia on the other. When we read of a mission to the Gentiles, or rather to the nations, at the end of it, we should think of it in terms of this oriental world. The Hellenism of this evangelist is that of a Judaism which was expanding into a Syrian world. He says that people came from the whole of Syria to hear the Sermon on the Mount.

THE SCRIBES AND PHARISEES

We have already given some account of the strongly Jewish-Christian traditions which were incorporated into this Gospel. When we examine this material we find that the Christians among whom it was formulated were commanded to submit to the scribes and Pharisees who occupied the seat of Moses, though they were not to imitate their conduct. These Christians were still offering sacrifices at the Temple, which shows that it took form before the destruction of the city in A.D. 70; Jerusalem is the holy city, or the city of the great king, in this Gospel; and the Great King was the title of the Persian or Parthian monarch, and was equivalent to 'king of kings'.

A note of irony often creeps into these Jewish contexts. The personal ministry of Jesus was confined to the 'lost sheep of the house of Israel'; but this way of putting it was no compliment to Israel. The missions on which he sent his disciples were limited in the same way; they were not to go along the road to Samaria, or enter the Gentile cities; it would take them till doomsday to convert Israel; 'You will not have finished with the cities of Israel before the Son of Man comes.' The word 'Gentile' is often used in an ironical context. 'Do not even the Gentiles do the same?' we read; or 'After all these things do the Gentiles seek'; as if no Jew ever gave a thought to the material goods of this world. A powerful intellectual ferment was at work wherever this teaching went. It was no wonder that the rabbis in the Mishnah said that he mocked at the words of the wise.

The controversy with the scribes and the Pharisees is given more space in Matthew than Mark, and is treated in a more dramatic style. They are the principal opponents of Jesus, a point of view which is in marked contrast with that of the Acts, in which we are told that a measure of toleration was secured for the Christians at one time by the intercession of the influential Pharisee, Gamaliel I. But this was before the destruction of Jerusalem, and after that date the policy changed. So soon as the rabbis at Jamnia had consolidated their power, they proceeded to enforce their own interpretation of the Law on all Jews; henceforward there would be only one interpretation of the Law. This unifying policy must have taken some time to formulate and enforce, and the turning-point must have come at some point in the second Christian generation, when the leadership in Israel passed from the broad-minded and scholarly Johanan ben Zakkai to the princely and dictatorial rabbi Gamaliel II. One sign of the accomplishment of the change was the definition of the canon of scripture about the year 95; henceforward there would be no additional creative or interpretative literature which might compete with the oral tradition of the sages. Another was the so-called Blessing of the Minim.

The word 'blessing' was sometimes used euphemistically in the Hebrew language to mean 'cursing', and that is what it means in this phrase. It was actually an anathema, and contained such words as these: 'May the Notzrim and the Minim be suddenly laid low and not inscribed with the righteous'; the Notzrim or Nazareans being the Christians, and the Minim being heretics in general. Wherever this 'benediction' was adopted, the 'Nazareans' would be forced out of the orthodox synagogue; and when we turn to Matthew, we find that they were in serious danger of persecution and punishment. This fact is to be found in Mark and Q of course, and is confirmed by the evidence of Thessalonians; but it is much more strongly emphasized in Matthew.

This historical background helps us to understand why this Gospel sets out in such a dramatic style the lamentations over the scribes and Pharisees, and sets up the gospel tradition as the true interpretation of the Law. Just as we can dimly see a Matthew tradition in the pages of the Mishnah, so we can discern the earliest Mishnaic tradition behind the special tradition of our canonical Matthew. It looks as if they were in touch with one another. We now think of the new conditions in northern Israel; of the rabbinic schools at Jamnia and Lydda and Caesarea; and particularly the patriarchal establishment of Gamaliel II in the capital city. Caesarea and Lydda had Christian churches, as we know from the Acts, and conflict would be bound to occur there.

The production of the canonical Matthew has been assigned by some scholars to this region of southern Syria or northern Israel; it certainly looks as if its special tradition took form there.

THE AUTHOR OF THE GOSPEL

The author of the canonical Matthew gave the place of honour in his record to the Jewish-Christian tradition. Whether he mastered it himself in Aramaic or depended upon translations we cannot say. He was a Hellenist and wrote an excellent synagogue Greek. He knew the Law and the Prophets in the Septuagint version and generally adjusted his quotations to agree with it. The combination of his different sources was done with extraordinary literary felicity, so as to form an all-inclusive gospel for actual use in church. It was a sacred text.

His style is powerful, direct and clear. He rounds off, supplements and fills out whatever in Mark was meagre or uncertain or enigmatic. Mark, for instance, speaks of Pilate without saying who he was; and he speaks of the high priest without giving his name. Matthew corrects these omissions. On the other hand, he dispenses with a great deal of Mark's vivid detail, holding simply to what was essential to tell the story. He rolls out a magnificent liturgical prose which is always moving and impressive. His Gospel has become the most important book in the world. When we consider what the influence of his version of the Sermon on the Mount has been, and how often his version of the Lord's Prayer is used throughout the world every day, we can see no exaggeration in this statement.

The world-wide scope of its influence was anticipated in the book itself, in the commission given to the eleven apostles after the Resurrection. They are to go out and make disciples of all the nations, baptizing them and teaching them to observe all the things which had been commanded by the Lord, meaning of course the teaching contained in the book. The gospel teaching thus breaks out of its original Jewish limitations, and a world-wide expansion begins from the mountains of Galilee. The Jewish-Christian tradition of the teaching of Jesus, in which the Law and the Prophets have been spiritually interpreted, is promulgated as a spiritual law for all nations. The apostolate is the power-line through which this gospel was transmitted.

It would be a very crude interpretation of our documentary studies to suppose that this presentation of the gospel was effected by making a few additions to Mark and Q from some later stratum of documents or from the inner consciousness of the author himself. He is drawing upon an oriental form of the gospel tradition which was independent of Mark and Q and had its own pedigree and history; he does not hesitate to interpret Mark and Q in the light of it.

It would also be a mistake to suppose that the presentation of the Messiah as the supreme exponent of the Law involved some lower view of his person or function; in oriental thought the teacher of heavenly truth was a being with divine authority. Matthew retains and strengthens the evangelical theology of Mark, if we may call it a theology; but he has a theology of his own, or rather of the school which he represents. His Messiah is the Son of God; a middle term in a heaven-and-earth mysticism; and also a middle term between the past and the future, between the first beginnings of the historical revelation in Abraham and Moses and its final consummation when the Son of Man appears again to sit on the throne of his glory and judge the nations.

In the meantime he is present in his church through the ministry of his apostles, who are to be received as himself. He is with them to the end of time.

MATTHEW AND PETER

There is one point, however, where the author seems to reveal a personal interest; it is a little change which he introduces into the text of Mark. In that gospel there is a story of a 'publican' named Levi the son of Alphaeus, who is called to follow Jesus; and his house becomes a centre of evangelism and teaching for the 'publicans and sinners'; but there is no Levi in Mark's list of the twelve. In Matthew there is no Levi at all; his name has been altered to Matthew, and the Matthew in the list of the Twelve is distinguished as the 'publican'.[1] This change clarifies the Marcan text. Many Jews had two names, and it is recorded that Jesus conferred new names on his disciples. It would be perfectly natural if Levi, the exactor of taxes, preferred to use a new name when he went about as an apostle of the Lord. Simon had denied his Lord, Saul had persecuted, Levi had exercised an offensive profession; under the new names of Peter and Paul and Matthew they redeemed their past

[1] In some texts we find the name 'Lebbaeus' among the twelve. It may be an attempt to get Levi in.

and won praise in the church. This identification connects the master of the special tradition of this Gospel with the ministry of Jesus to the non-religious or non-respectable classes; and the extension of the gospel to these classes was regarded as a first stage in its extension to the nations of the world.

Our author does not name Matthew as the master of his special tradition. It is Peter who occupies this place. The Matthew tradition, therefore, was not simply the Matthew tradition; it was the Matthaean form of the tradition of Peter and the Twelve. This, in turn, clarifies the statement of Papias. Matthew and Mark both made arrangements of the oracles of the Lord, and these oracles turn out, in both cases, to be the tradition of Peter. And what else could they be?

In Mark and Q, the word 'house' or 'family' is in very frequent use for the circle of disciples who accepted Jesus as their Lord and master. Jesus is the 'master of the house', and the Twelve are his trusted servants who are given authority in it. In Matthew, however, we twice find the word *ecclesia* or 'church'. It may be that Jesus used the Hebrew or Aramaic equivalent, *kahal*, which was in common use for the whole assembly of Israel in the desert or in the Temple; but it is thought that Matthew may have introduced the word in order to clarify the situation, just as Mark may have introduced the word *euangelion* or *gospel*. The word 'ecclesia' is used once of the local group of disciples, and once of the whole household or new Israel, which Jesus was bringing into being.

In the fourth discourse, this household or church is the principal theme, and it is stated that what they bind on earth is bound in heaven, and what they loose on earth is loosed in heaven. Jesus himself is with them when they meet in his name, and what they agree together to ask of the Father the Father will do for them. There is nothing ambiguous about these sayings. Binding and loosing were terms of the Rabbinic tradition, and referred to the interpretation of the Law. The 'house' of Hillel might bind; the 'house' of Shammai might loose; the one permitted, the other forbade. The authority to make these binding interpretations no longer belonged to the scribes; it had been committed to the disciples of Jesus meeting in his name, that is to say with him in their midst. In particular it had passed to the Twelve, who formed a sanhedrin of judgement, 'sitting upon twelve thrones'; and among them a high position of responsibility was conferred upon Simon Peter, with the new name of the Stone.

PETER THE STONE

The stone symbolism is connected with the ideas of building a house or raising a family; for the Hebrew word *bānāh* had both meanings; and there was a well-known play on words as between *bānīm* which means 'children', and *ăbānīm* which means 'stones'. 'Out of these *stones* God can raise up *children* to Abraham', John the Baptist says; and raising up children means building a house.

Peter had been, at times, a man of little faith. He had been swift to speak and slow to understand, though never harsh or ambitious like the sons of Zebedee. He had opposed the doctrine of the cross, and would deny his Lord. He was a *skandalon*, the Lord says in Matthew, a stone on which a man might stumble and fall; he impeded progress; and yet, when he confessed Christ as Messiah and Son of God, he could be described as a 'petra', a stone on which a house might be built.

> Thou art Petros, and on this petra I will build my church, and the gates of death [*hades*] shall not conquer it. I will give unto thee the keys of the kingdom of heaven, and whatever thou shalt bind on earth shall be bound in heaven, and whatever thou shalt loose on earth shall be loosed in heaven.
>
> (Matthew xvi. 18–19.)

It is true that the powers of binding and loosing had been conferred by Jesus on the Twelve as a whole already, or possibly on the whole household of disciples acting in his name; but they are now conferred personally upon Peter as the leader of the Twelve and the first exponent of their faith. He is the chief steward in God's kingdom, for the keys were the symbol of the authority of the chief steward in the house. They also symbolized the office of the scribe.

We are bound to infer that in the tradition from which these words were received, and in any church where they were accepted or taught or recorded, the brethren looked back to a time when, as they believed, Peter had occupied such a position, and had presided, with the college of the Twelve, in the Jewish-Christian church and pronounced such decisions. Certain other evidence from Palestine falls into line with this. Paul calls him the apostle of the circumcision, that is to say of the original Jewish churches; and in the first half of the Acts, he is the leader of the Jerusalem church, and forms the first Gentile church at Caesarea, under its wing so to speak. He enunciates the policy of freedom for the Gentiles in the council of the apostles and elders at Jerusalem. Among the Hellenistic Jewish-Christians of the second century, and in eastern Christianity generally his position of leadership among the Twelve was increasingly emphasized; and the Gospel of Matthew must have contributed to this view of the gospel tradition.

On the other hand, it says nothing to support the claims of James the Just or of the family of Jesus. We can see where it stands in relation to the Palestinian tradition. It is not a tradition of the old Jerusalem church. It is not promoting the claims of the Lord's family.

THE MATTHAEAN NARRATIVES

There does not seem to be any considerable body of new narrative in Matthew. Apart from the stories of the nativity, which must have been derived from the tradition of the brethren of the Lord, it appears mostly in the form of additions and appendages to the narrative of Mark. It is distinctly secondary. This leads us to wonder what this church in Syria had before Mark's Gospel reached it from Rome; and the most reasonable hypothesis is that they had something not unlike Mark's Gospel. They could not have possessed the story of Pilate's wife's dream, or the remorse of Judas, without any Passion narrative to attach them to. They must have had a Passion narrative very like that of Mark, that is to say a Petrine Passion narrative. Many scholars think that the Passion narrative was one of the first things to be written down, and that it circulated separately before any of the surviving Gospels were written. There was other material available, of course; Luke had access to non-Petrine Passion sources, but Matthew shows no sign of them apart from what is plainly additional and secondary material; that is to say there is no sign that the Passion narrative which he was familiar with before the Marcan Gospel arrived differed from it much in order or substance.

How far these arguments could be applied to the rest of the Marcan material is a matter of speculation.

Some of the additional material in Matthew is thought to be of a symbolic or apocalyptic character, reinforcing the spiritual significance of the original tale; Peter's walking on the water may be an example; or the sentence in the transfiguration story, 'His face shone like the sun'; or the earthquake at the Crucifixion and the opening of the graves. They may be poetry rather than factual reporting, many scholars think.

Some are local tales. The Jerusalem stories seem to be of this type; the story of the death of Judas is connected with a site that was pointed out; in another case a story was told among the Jews 'unto this day'. Perhaps he gives these stories for what they were worth. There must have been many of them about in his time; disciples, and disciples of disciples, were still telling their memories, and he seems to have gathered up the fragments that nothing might be lost. Perhaps he gives a miniature portrait of himself in one of his minor parables: 'Every scribe who becomes a disciple of the kingdom of the heavens is like the master of a house who can bring out of his storeroom things new and old.'

It would appear that the special tradition which he followed was mainly Galilean, and that its contact with Jerusalem was slight. In Luke the risen Lord appears to his disciples in Jerusalem, and Matthew must have known that such appearances had occurred; nevertheless he concentrates upon a single resurrection appearance in Galilee, and leaves the impression that the presence of the risen Lord was in the church continually everywhere. It looks as if the glory has departed from Jerusalem.

THE FALSE PROPHETS

The effect of this Gospel was to establish the doctrine of an omnipresent spiritual deity who worked continually through human agents in history, and supremely in a flesh-and-blood Jesus who was a descendant of Abraham and David. He came in succession to the Law and the prophets; he fulfilled his mission to Israel; he died on the cross at a place called Golgotha and rose again on the third day; he was the builder of the apostolic church. It would be the answer to the spiritualizing gnostic or mystic who rejected Judaism and thought of the Saviour as an angel or spirit. Such an answer could only be given with the help of the Jewish tradition. Jesus was not only a real human being; he was a Jew, the greatest Jew of them all.

The composer of this Gospel was aware of certain dangers in the church, and draws attention to them by his treatment of the prophetic passages in the Little Apocalypse. The wars and persecutions and martyrdoms are to be succeeded by the appearance of false prophets as in Mark. 'Many shall be offended', he adds, a word which implies a falling away from the faith; 'many false prophets will appear, and will lead many astray, lawlessness will increase, and the love of many will grow cold.' We hear this from every source. 'You have left your first love...you are neither hot nor cold', the author of the Revelation writes. 'Love shall be turned into hate', we read in the *Didache* and the *Ascension of Isaiah*. Strife and envy have broken out among the elders and pastors, Hermas and the *Ascension* complain. And there are always the false prophets.

The enemy as Matthew sees it is lawlessness, the spirit which rejects the kingdom of God and his righteousness. It assumes a Christian exterior and it wears sheep's clothing; but actually it is a beast of prey. It is a noxious weed, and it is not possible to root it out. Everything must grow together till the harvest. This is an 'eschatological' situation; for the harvest is the end of the 'aeon', the climax of the present historical time-process. He presents his picture in high apocalyptic style in his explanation of the parable of the tares. God will send his angels; he will gather out of his earthly kingdom everything that offends; the evil will go into the furnace of fire; the righteous will shine like the stars in the firmament. He explains his parable with new figures of speech more astonishing still. They are taken from the prophet Daniel.

APOCALYPSE AND ESCHATOLOGY

Matthew underlines apocalypse, for apocalypse is one of the answers to 'lawlessness'. Law and righteousness are great historical principles in Matthew. The book is dominated by the ideas of retribution and maturation. Everybody will get his reward or wages. They will all be paid in full. It is in the grain of God's creation; it is not something to be added to it. Even the 'end of the aeon' is simply a universal harvest or maturation, not an act of violence done to the natural processes. It will be the fulfilment of all divine and natural processes; the *sunteleia* or maturity.

All the imagery, including the payment of wages, belongs to the harvest-fields and the harvest-festivals. Out of these harvest-festivals of Judaism comes the liturgical and apocalyptic imagery, including the harvest parables,[1] the vineyard parables, the pay-day parables, the judgement parables, and the nuptial parables, in all of which he rejoices. The final scene of this panorama passes into sheer allegory. A king sits upon a throne, but he is not a king; he is a shepherd. All the nations

[1] Compare the harvest-songs in Papias (chapter 16) and the harvest rituals in the *Didache* (chapter 26).

pass before him, but they are not nations; they are individuals. There is no need for any act of judgement; it took place long ago when the poor beggar was turned away from the gate, or the prisoner left to pine, or the sick man to die. It was the king himself who was rejected in that humble form. The eschatology of Matthew takes a strange form; it is incorporated into the time-process. It is going on now. It is God in action.

There is terror in Matthew as well as irony; but it is more than balanced by an amazing tenderness of heart, which is all the more effective because of the contrast. There is a perpetual concern for little children and the little ones, and the 'least of these my brethren', and even for those of little faith. The lastcomer to the vineyard gets as good as the rest; and there is more joy in heaven over one sinner who repents than over ninety and nine righteous persons who need no repentance. These passages are sometimes forgotten when critics come to assess the eschatology of Matthew, though they are of the essence of it. What is safeguarded in it is the teaching of Jesus, along time-honoured Jewish lines, about the dealings of God with men, and about his mercy as well as his justice.

The style of Matthew tends to give further definition to the teaching of Jesus, and to strengthen the visual imagery. It is a didactic style at some points, and an apocalyptic style at others; but it is always a dramatic style. We have suggested that the apocalyptic style sometimes breaks into the narrative, or lends more glory and terror to the apocalyptic utterances. The Angel is actually seen descending from heaven and rolling away the stone from the tomb. The coming of the Son of Man, the sound of the trumpet, the sending out of the angels to gather in the elect, the happiness of the blessed and the despair of the lost, are presented in strong and realistic colours. An over-spiritual mysticism, which thought itself superior to common morality, would not be allowed to escape from the full impact and effect of these traditional Jewish concepts, which were taken into Christianity as images of the eternal realities which condition life in this world; representing in dramatic and moving forms the doctrine of an inevitable judgement upon all the works of man, and of a final separation between good and evil, in accordance with a divine law which is operative in history at all times and works continually towards its perfect fulfilment and consummation: the kingship or kingdom of God.

CHAPTER 18

THE TYRANNY OF DOMITIAN

The philosophers, *p.* 333. Domitian and the Jews, *p.* 333. The grandsons of Jude, *p.* 334. The last works of Josephus, *p.* 335. Baruch and Esdras, *p.* 336. Some apocalyptic conventions, *p.* 339. The Sibyl, *p.* 340. The Apocalypse of John, *p.* 341. The date of the Revelation, *p.* 343. The return of Nero, *p.* 344. The victorious word of God, *p.* 346. The thousand years, *p.* 347. The new Jerusalem, *p.* 348.

The Emperor Domitian appears in Christian history and tradition as a tyrant and a persecutor, and he has left an equally sinister impression in the works of Roman writers. Tacitus and Suetonius, who lived as young men under his 'tyranny', may have been tempted to blacken his memory in order to please the subsequent emperors, but their writings leave no doubt in our minds that the unpleasant impression was justified. He was secretive and suspicious. He loved the exercise of power and he took seriously his claim to divine honours. He adopted the designation of 'Our Lord God Domitian': *deus et dominus noster Domitianus*. Such a title might accord well with the adoration offered to an eastern king, but it would not be taken seriously in Rome.

Vespasian had restored the authority of the senate, and had respected the constitution as it had been settled by Augustus; but under Domitian the relations between emperor and senate progressively deteriorated. A rebellion on the German frontier in the year 88 or 89, headed by a general named Saturninus, was put down with difficulty, and a number of senators who were implicated in it were executed. The emperor was now on the defensive. He surrounded himself with guards, and organized a secret police. The reign of terror began.

From this time the senate was forced to comply with his will; and there were others who felt the force of his tyranny. In 89 the philosophers were expelled from Rome, and in 93 there was a second edict under which a number of the Stoics were put to death.

THE PHILOSOPHERS

Stoic philosophy, with its sombre outlook and its feeling for self-discipline, made a strong appeal to the Roman mind. There was something about it which harmonized well with the rather puritanical traditions which were handed down in the patrician families. Often a Stoic philosopher was attached to a great household as a tutor and spiritual adviser; for conduct was now the main concern of philosophy. There was less interest in the classical systems of physics and metaphysics. The philosophers of the day were what was known as eclectics; they selected from the philosophies of the past. Many of them believed that the world was animated and controlled by a universal mind or spirit which ordered all things in accordance with reason. In morals they tended towards the Platonic view of a conflict between reason and the passions. Seneca, the tutor of Nero, is our main authority for this rather severe form of monotheism, and it was his unhappy lot to have to reconcile his idealistic views with his duties as a high dignitary at Nero's court.

The Stoic philosopher, feeling as he did that the divine reason was speaking in his breast, was bound to regard himself as the envoy of the deity to mankind. There was a tradition that he must oppose the rule of the one man over the many, whom he was prepared to regard as the kinsmen of God. He could hardly help becoming interested in politics. Seneca had been accused of complicity in the Pisonian conspiracy against Nero and was commanded to commit suicide. Other Stoics were put to death under Nero, including Musonius Rufus, who said that all men were made in the likeness of God. Even under Vespasian the philosophers suffered. Under Domitian more of them were put to death.

There grew up in this way a legend or tradition of resistance to tyranny which was not unlike the Christian tradition about the martyr; the Christian teacher Justin, fifty years later, paid homage to this tradition, and mentioned Musonius by name.

DOMITIAN AND THE JEWS

There is no reason to suppose that Domitian put out any special edict of a general nature against the Christians; but there is plenty of evidence that martyrdoms occurred in his reign. The Revelation is sufficient evidence by itself. It mentions the name of Antipas, who died as a martyr at Pergamum, and it sees persecution coming in Smyrna.

It is also known that Domitian acted unfavourably towards the Jews. He exacted with some severity the half-shekel tax which the Jews used to pay towards the maintenance of the Jerusalem Temple but which was diverted now to the new temple of Jupiter on the Capitoline Hill at Rome, which was dedicated in 81. Nerva, his successor, took some credit for abolishing this levy, which was an aftermath of the war of 66–70. It was an excellent conjecture of the historian Gibbon that the exaction of this tax served to make clear the distinction between Christians and Jews, since Gentile Christians would not be liable to pay it and would be quick to prove that they were not Jews; on the other hand, their position in the eyes of the Law might then become very ambiguous and uncomfortable.

THE GRANDSONS OF JUDE

Hegesippus, the collector of Jewish-Christian traditions, who lived in Rome sixty or seventy years later, states that Vespasian and Domitian both made investigations in Palestine about the descendants of David; and nothing is more likely, since it was known that many Jews were interested in the idea of a king from the old royal family. He says that there were some sons or grandsons of Jude the brother of the Lord, against whom information was laid. Eusebius quotes his words, and a later writer, who may be Philip of Side,[1] gives their names as Zoker (Zacharias?) and Jacob (that is, James). They were brought into the presence of Domitian by a Roman official called the 'evocatus', and Domitian asked them how much property they owned. They said that they only had property to the value of nine thousand denarii between them. It was in the form of land, which they worked themselves, paying the taxes out of the proceeds; and they showed him their tough bodies and horny hands as a proof of their statement. The area of this farm would not be more than nine or ten acres; thirty-nine 'plethra' they said.

The emperor then asked them about the Messiah and his kingdom, and they explained that it was not a worldly or earthly kingdom; it was

[1] The de Boor fragment: see note at end of chapter 19.

heavenly or angelic, and would appear at the 'end of the aeon', when the Messiah would come in glory to judge both the quick and the dead. He dismissed the case with contempt, Hegesippus says, and ordered the two men to be sent home, issuing a directive that the persecution should cease. They returned home and ruled over the churches, not only as 'martyrs', but as members of the Lord's family. Peace was established, and they remained alive into the reign of Trajan.

There seems little reason for doubting this story, which is full of good detail and is devoid of legendary features. It shows Domitian in an amiable mood, which is not how the Christian imagination would have pictured him. The payment of taxes was an acknowledgement of the worldly sovereignty of the emperor; the sovereignty of the Messiah was of another order altogether. The conversation between Jesus and Pilate in the fourth Gospel brings out the same points.

THE LAST WORKS OF JOSEPHUS

The Jewish general and historian, Josephus, was still living in Rome at this time under the patronage of the emperor, and in the enjoyment of considerable wealth. His enormous work, the *Archaeologia*, or *Antiquities of the Jews*, was finished not long before the year 96. It surveyed the whole field of Hebrew history from the earliest times down to 66, when the rebellion against the Romans had broken out. The events from 66 to 70 had been covered in his previous book, the *Jewish War*. The *Antiquities* draws on other sources besides the Bible, and its preservation of older Hellenistic Jewish material is of great value today. One of its purposes was to answer the many accusations and slanders which had been levelled against the Jews. It makes out as good a case as it can to show that the wars in Palestine were due to the extreme policies of small misguided minorities among the people. Josephus himself belonged to the aristocratic class which cultivated good relations with the Romans. His royal patron, King Agrippa II, held similar views, and was still reigning as king in northern Palestine under the Roman patronage. There was a rival Jewish historian in Galilee, Justus of Tiberias, who criticized Josephus severely both as a general and as an author; Josephus defended himself in a short autobiography which is attached to the *Antiquities*.

The *Antiquities* was also an 'apology' in the religious and philosophical sense of the word; that is to say, a reasoned presentation of the case in favour of the Hebrew religion; but he also wrote a book *Against Apion*, the anti-Jewish writer in Alexandria, which meets his unfair history and false accusations.

In the *Antiquities* he is at great pains to exhibit the sublime character of Hebrew monotheism, the role played by Abraham as an instructor of the old oriental civilizations, the unfailing wisdom of Moses, the priority of the Hebrew prophets to the Greek philosophers, and many other points of Jewish propaganda which were soon taken over by Christian 'apologists' for their purposes. The picture which he gives of the national religion was so coloured as to appeal to the educated classes among the Greeks and Romans. He sometimes talks about God rather in the style of the philosopher of his day. He even goes so far as to compare the Pharisees with the Stoics and the Sadducees with the Epicureans.

Josephus was a sincere believer himself. His conviction that the destruction of Jerusalem was a judgement of God, which was brought upon the people because of their sins, was perfectly genuine. His references to Christianity are brief and formal; he practically ignores it; but it was Christian scholarship that preserved his writings, and men like Clement of Alexandria and Origen and Eusebius made use of them. There are medieval versions of Josephus, with additional material, which have given rise to interesting discussions among scholars; but it scarcely seems likely that they have any authentic information to add to what we have already.

BARUCH AND ESDRAS

Creative literature was still being produced among the Jews for use in connexion with their religious life, but the new books were written in the name and person of some ancient worthy who had lived in the days of Ezra, or earlier, when it was believed that visions were still seen and revelations received from heaven.

This convention of pseudonymity is worthy of closer inquiry than it has yet received; it seems to be something more than the insertion of a false name and a few false facts into an otherwise realistic document. The element of make-believe or fantasy runs right through them. They are in the nature of popular drama or fiction. They seem for the most part to have been written in Hebrew or Aramaic, or to depend on

21. DOMITIAN

22. A GALLERY IN THE CEMETERY OF DOMITILLA

Hebrew or Aramaic originals. They belong to the category of oriental religious romance, and have affinities with such works of fiction as Tobit and Esther, or even such imaginative histories as 2, 3, or 4 Maccabees. It has been shown that some of them, at any rate, were designed for use at the minor commemorations of the Jewish calendar, which were supplementary to the great fasts and festivals of the Law of Moses: for instance,

Tammuz 17 (midsummer). The golden calf worshipped in the desert: Jerusalem entered by the armies of Nebuchadnezzar or Titus. *The Apocalypses of Esdras and Baruch; The Epistle of Jeremy.*

Ab 9 and 15 (midsummer). The 'rebellion' at Kadesh in the desert; the burning of the Temple by Nebuchadnezzar or Titus. *The Apocalypses of Esdras and Baruch; The Lamentations of Jeremiah; Solomon's Song.*

Kislev 25 (midwinter). The re-dedication of the Temple by Judas Maccabaeus; commemoration of the Maccabaean martyrs. *3 and 4 Maccabees.* (Hanukkah.)

Adar 13–15 (spring). Maccabaean victory over Nicanor; Mordecai and Esther in Persia. *Book of Esther; 2 Maccabees.* (Purim.)

Could it be that on these popular commemorations, which were not regulated by the Law and coincided in three cases at least with the old pagan festivals of nature, there was a less solemn presentation of a less sacred literature on a more popular level? With some miming perhaps, or folk dances, or ritual dramas? In the case of Ab 15 (and the Day of Atonement), Rabbi Simeon ben Gamaliel, who died in the siege of Jerusalem by Titus, mentions dancing in the vineyards by the young people in white garments, the choosing of wives, and a song about King Solomon wearing the crown with which his mother crowned him on his wedding day, which is a quotation from Canticles. The popular demonstrations at Adar have continued into modern times, and other evidence of the sort could doubtless be found in the Rabbinic records. Were these apocalyptic books compilations of traditional material on traditional lines, but with new references to current history added or substituted from time to time?

The religious troubles of the time were presented in the form of drama or dialogue. The seer lies on his couch, like Daniel, and an angel descends to converse with him. He remonstrates with God in long rhetorical prayers; he laments; he is prostrated with grief or terror. The angel replies with mysterious words of rebuke or comfort, but condescends in due course to answer his questions. He unveils the future. It is the time-honoured device of the play within the play, which induces the audience to identify itself emotionally with the seer, which is not the case with the authentic Old Testament prophets.

In his vision or revelation we encounter the favourite characters of myth and apocalypse; the remote timeless deity who is far above man's feeble intelligence; the spirit who descends from the higher realms, or sometimes the seer himself ascending to the throne; the dying hero or king; the weeping mother or bride; the mysterious symbols of the woman with child, or the growing seed, or the spreading tree; the beast or dragon who comes up out of the waters; the hero or king who slays the beast; and so forth. Running through it is the question of the destiny of the soul in a tragic universe; the destiny of Israel as God's favoured nation, and yet trampled down by the kings of the earth; the inexplicable fate of Jerusalem; the loss of the Temple. The answers come in eschatological symbols; the future is not really disclosed as a rule.

Such is the character of the pseudonymous books which were composed under Vespasian and Domitian: the Apocalypse of Esdras (Ezra) and the Apocalypse of Baruch. Both contain older material; both received later additions.

These books look back upon the recent destruction of Jerusalem by Titus with grief and horror. They question the goodness of God in bringing this calamity upon this generation and in creating so many human beings for misery and destruction. The dramatic form makes possible the frank expression of these sceptical views. No clear answer is returned; but faith is maintained. This world is for the many, but the world to come is for the few. It is not for the seer to inquire too closely into the purposes of God. We are reminded of the dialectic of predestination in Paul's Epistle to the Romans; for these authors fall back, as he did once, and as all pious Jews tend to do, on the doctrine of inscrutability. It was impiety, as well as folly, to question the purposes of Almighty God, whose love for his creation must excel all human love and compassion.

It is strange that these books, with their profoundly Jewish outlook, should have passed into use in the Christian church. The Apocalypse of Baruch, with the Epistle of Jeremy, is included in the Christian Apocrypha. The Apocalypse of Esdras, in a Latin translation, is appended to the Apocrypha of the western church; the Greek does not survive.

SOME APOCALYPTIC CONVENTIONS

There are several conventions in this type of literature which are of interest. One is the picture of the ancient oriental sage, who lived so many centuries ago, peering into the future, writing down his vision of the things which are to come in the last days (a conventional phrase for the times men were living in), and sealing them up, or storing them away, to be revealed when their time comes. Another is the relation between the gift of vision and the practice of asceticism. These ostensible authors are represented as going apart into deserts or mountains to pray and fast. They eat herbs or flowers of the field; they abstain from domestic life. We cannot help thinking of a succession of instances from John the Baptist to Hermas and later, in which asceticism and prophecy are connected. Even in the Mishnah we read of Jews who fasted in order to obtain dreams. It was a common practice in certain Greek temples. The Montanists did it in Phrygia.

The idea can be traced back as far as Daniel, but hardly to the older books of the Hebrew canon. The worthies of the Old Testament fasted and afflicted themselves in order to express their penitence or show their humility or submission to God. Now we have a new kind of mysticism, probably of Syrian or oriental origin, which links fasting and virginity with the vision of heavenly beings or the revelation of divine mysteries. Such, no doubt, was the practice of the erratic Jewish teachers who are referred to in Colossians and the Pastorals. It harmonizes with the little we know about the ascetic Jewish sects.

The content of the vision had also been conventionalized. Esdras gives an affecting picture of an aged woman who laments over the death of her son who died on his wedding night; a picture which is in line with the myth and ritual of Adonis or Tammuz; but this woman is the holy city of Jerusalem, and the death of her son is the destruction of the city. The piece was made up out of ancient mythological features, and was set for the midsummer fast, when the Syrians mourned for Adonis and the Jews for Jerusalem.

> And it came to pass, while I was talking to her, behold her face shone exceeding bright, and her countenance was like lightning, and I feared greatly ... and I saw, and behold, the woman was no longer visible to me, but a city that was builded, and a place of great foundations.
>
> (II Esdras, x. 25–7.)

A similar vision of a woman who is also a city is found in the Revelation; and Hermas of Rome, after his period of prayer and fasting, was permitted to see a vision of an aged woman whom he believed at first to be the Sibyl; but it was explained to him later that she was the church, and that she was to be identified with a tower which was being built. The two images are also found in Ephesians, but are not combined into a myth.

THE SIBYL

The grief over the loss of Jerusalem, and the certitude about divine vengeance in the future, are expressed for the most part in cryptic forms which conceal the strong anti-Roman feeling which was present in the heart; but this feeling was expressed openly in the *Sibylline Oracles*, which purported to be pagan productions.

The Sibyl did not see visions. She was a wild incoherent creature who uttered dooms; a god spoke through her. Doubtless there had been real Sibyls in ancient Greece and Asia Minor, who prophesied at the temples; but we are concerned with the Sibyls of literature and legend, and particularly the 'Babylonian Sibyl', who was the imaginary author of some of the oldest oracles. Her verses dealt with myth and current history and things to come. In the days of the Maccabees, Jewish authors had taken up these pagan prophecies, and added more of the same style, in which they proclaimed a pure Jewish monotheism, and foretold the destruction of the godless kingdom, and the way the world would end. After the destruction of Jerusalem by Titus, these verses were taken up again by Jewish poets and brought up to date. They were bitterly hostile to the Flavian emperors, and reserved a rather special position for Nero, who is said to have favoured the Jews.

The idea existed that Nero still lived. A false Nero had appeared as early as 69, in the reign of Otho, but had been captured and put to death. Rather later, an Asiatic actor and musician of the name of Terentius Maximus, who resembled Nero, appeared in Asia Minor. He collected quite a following and took refuge in Mesopotamia. His claims were recognized by the Parthian King, Artabanus, who found him a convenient political tool; but neither empire was actually prepared for war. The new *Sibylline Oracles* espoused the cause of the false Nero and of the Parthian empire. They proclaimed the destruction of Rome.

Sibylline verses were collected together, and some centuries after our period a mixed assortment of them was collected into a single corpus. Book III seems to be a second-century production, and is based on the old Babylonian Sibyl with successive Jewish additions. Book IV contains some oracles from the time of the Flavian emperors; it refers to the earthquake at Laodicea in 76, and the eruption of Vesuvius in 79. Doom is predicted for all the nations, and especially for Rome, which is given the mystic name of Babylon in one passage.

And a great star shall fall from heaven upon the dread ocean, and burn up the deep sea, with Babylon itself; by reason of which many Hebrews perished; holy and faithful were they, the people of the truth. (*Or. Sib.* IV, 11.)

In some of these oracles, the instrument of vengeance will be the Emperor Nero, returning from the east at the head of Parthian armies.

To the men of Jerusalem shall come an evil storm-blast of war from Italy, and shall lay waste the great temple of God...then shall a great king from Italy [Nero] flee away like a deserter, unseen, unheard, beyond the ford of the Euphrates....

But when a flame of fire from a cleft in the earth [Vesuvius] in the land of Italy shoots out its light to the broad heaven, to burn up many cities, and to slay men...then the strife of war shall be stirred up, and shall come to the west, and the exiled man [Nero], lifting up a mighty sword, and crossing the Euphrates with tens of thousands. (*Or. Sib.* IV, 11.)

This kind of literature, therefore, was political as well as eschatological, and we are not surprised when Justin Martyr informs us that the reading of the Sibyllines in his time was punished by death. The apocalyptic literature may have served the purpose of inflaming an anti-Roman feeling among the oppressed classes and nations.

THE APOCALYPSE OF JOHN

The study of this literature shows us that the Revelation of St John was written in an idiom that would not be altogether strange in Jewish and Christian circles, and that it dealt with contemporary historical problems. In every respect, however, it forms a striking contrast with the Jewish apocalypses, and especially in the fact that it was not put forward under a borrowed name. No ancient seer wrote these visions, and ordered them to be sealed up and stowed away until the last times.

Their author was the great prophet of Asia who was well known in the churches; 'I am John your brother', he says, and insists that he is writing about what is happening now, or must shortly come to pass. 'Seal *not* the sayings of the prophecy of this book; for the time is at hand.'

The angel of his vision is no Gabriel or Raphael; he is the Lord himself, descended from heaven; we have here an advent or *parousia* taking place in the church. The book opens with the messages to the seven churches of Asia. It is the Lord's Day, and the prophet is in the Spirit. He sees the angel of the risen and glorified Christ standing in the midst of seven golden lamps, which are also seven angels. The seven angels are said to be the seven churches, and so are the seven stars in his right hand; the alternative symbols are combined in a single pattern. The glorious central angel, who is like a Son of Man, has messages for the churches, and the prophet is commanded to write down his words. He is the interpreter of the divine voice which should be audible to all; he ends each message with the same refrain: 'He that hath an ear, let him hear what the Spirit is saying to the churches.'

The literal meaning of the word angel is 'a messenger'. In the higher religious thought of our period, it meant a spiritual power or impulse which made itself known or felt; thus Hermas speaks of an angel from the Holy Spirit coming to the prophet; it is a charge of divine energy which is personal in character; God making his impact upon man.[1] It may be said that an angel represents its original and in some sense is its original. The seven angels represent the churches; for purposes of this poetry they are the churches; and so are the stars and lamps.

The vision was seen on an island called Patmos, not far from the shore of Asia Minor. John was on the island 'for the Word of God and the witness of Jesus'. Irenaeus and other writers in the second century believed that John had been condemned to banishment on the island as a Christian under Domitian. This second-century belief that John's confinement on the island took place in the reign of Domitian is confirmed by the internal evidence of the Revelation itself, which was certainly composed at this time, though it incorporates so much older material.

[1] But the angel or impulse which comes to the prophet may not be absolutely identified with God; Rev. xix. 10; xxii. 9.

THE DATE OF THE REVELATION

Three stages can be distinguished in the composition of the Revelation, or three strata of material which have been worked into it. The first is the old Jerusalem material, which was directed against the 'great city' where God's witnesses were killed and their Lord crucified; some of this may be as old as the time of Caligula, when the 'wild beast' which represented the world power wore the features of that monarch. Then comes the intermediate period, when the wild beast wears the features of Nero, and the action of the apocalyptic drama is determined by the tragic events of the sixties; it is probable that a continuous text of some sort came into existence in the reign of Nero's successor Vespasian; but it was completed, in the form in which we now have it, in the reign of Domitian. This is the third stage.

In the earliest stratum the prophet receives his call from an angel to prophesy again upon many peoples and nations and tongues, and many kings; and it is the many kings who give us the clue to the chronology. As the book is now, it contains three rather extended and elaborate visions, which belong in their present form to the last stages of composition, in each of which the prophet is again instructed by an angel. The first is the vision on the island in chapter i, with which we have already dealt; this vision sanctions the book in its final form. The second is the vision in the desert in chapter xvii; this vision explains the historical setting. The third is the vision on the mountain, in the last chapters, in which he sees the New Jerusalem which is coming down from heaven.

In the vision in the desert, the prophet is shown the figure of the 'great harlot' who is also a city; a parody of the mother or virgin who is also a city. Her mystic name is 'Babylon'. She is seated upon a scarlet wild beast, which is allotted seven heads, which the angel says represent seven kings; 'five are fallen, one is, and one is yet to come'. The wild beast is easy to interpret; it is the imperial world-power, and the heads fall into line with history fairly easily, too. The five who have fallen are Augustus, Tiberius, Caligula, Claudius and Nero; Galba, Otho and Vitellius are ignored; the one who now is, is Vespasian; the one who is yet to come is Titus. A great number of commentators accept this explanation.

The allotment is confirmed by the statement that the seventh Caesar will endure only for a short time; and this is Titus, who only reigned for two years, 79 to 81; but our author, or his angel, goes on to speak of an eighth Caesar, who is Domitian, saving his symbolism by saying that 'he is one of the seven and goeth unto destruction'. He could not alter the number of heads, which was fixed as far back as the prophet Daniel.

It is perfectly clear that these notes must have been added to the text after Domitian came to the throne, when the vision on the island was composed as a prologue to the book as a whole. The substance of the book was not altered, however; it continues to speak as if from the reign of Vespasian; Nero is in the immediate past, and Titus in the immediate future. The historical standpoint of the book is still the standpoint of the sixties.

THE RETURN OF NERO

In order to bridge over the historical gap between the sixties and the nineties, our author makes use of the myth of the return of Nero, which could no longer be expected in the normal course of history. It now takes the form of a return from the realms of the dead. Domitian, the eighth Caesar, is Nero over again; for Nero was the typical form of the bestial idea. 'The wild beast which thou sawest, was and is not, and shall ascend out of the abyss...even he is the eighth, and goeth unto destruction.'

Many scholars make use of the Nero expectation to explain the reference to the River Euphrates in chapter xvi, and the march of the kings from the east which we suggested might refer to the march of the Syrian legions from the Euphrates to Rome in the civil wars of 67 to 69. They suggest that this means the return of the living Nero with the aid of Parthian armies, which is what the Sibyl hoped for. The words of John himself which we have quoted above envisage a very different idea; the return of Nero from hell in the person of the eighth Caesar; that is to say Domitian is Nero over again. But there is an ingenious suggestion by which these views can be reconciled. Perhaps in the sixties the seer did look forward to the return of the living Nero, and later on in the nineties, when this had not occurred, he transformed this expectation and adapted it to the new circumstances.

We suggested very strongly that the 'great harlot', whose mystical name was Babylon, should be identified with Jerusalem, as the centre of the Jewish diaspora and the persecutor of the saints; but most scholars hold that she is to be identified with the Rome of the Neronian persecutions, since the Sibyl uses this name for Rome, and so apparently does I Peter. They can point to the fact that she is said to be drunk with the blood of the saints and martyrs, that she is the 'great city' who reigns over the kings of the earth; that she is enriched with a great luxury trade; and finally that the seven heads of the beast on which she is seated are seven mountains; but these heads or mountains belong to the beast, not to the woman.[1] The destruction of the city of Rome by the beast, who undoubtedly represents the Roman empire or imperial power, can be explained by the Sibylline form of the Nero myth; it is the Emperor Nero with his Parthian armies who destroys Rome, though this idea must of course have been abandoned when the Revelation received its final form.

The great majority of commentators accept the traditional view that Babylon in the Revelation means Rome; but the same compromise has been suggested in this case; perhaps the prophecies about Jerusalem as a persecuting city, and the prophecies about Rome as a persecuting city, have been transferred from one to the other, or fused together in the processes of editing through which the book as a whole has passed. Scholars differ on many points in interpreting this difficult book, but there is no difference of opinion on two great principles. The first is that the author of the Revelation plunges deeply into contemporary history, and so provides a commentary on the events of his own time; the second is that this commentary is expressed in images which are drawn from the old oriental tradition of mythological thinking, which was the parent of gnosis and apocalypse and liturgy, all of which contribute their quota to the Revelation, and are indeed inseparable.

Many scholars think that the John who gave the book its final form need not be the author of what we have called the earlier strata. The old Jerusalem visions may have been the work of an earlier prophet or prophets; and the apparent confusions might be explained in this way. But it is very generally agreed that it is an artistic unity as it stands. One mind gave it its present form and breathed his genius into it.

[1] In the Mishnah Jerusalem is said to be built on seven hills.

THE VICTORIOUS WORD OF GOD

It would not be possible to attempt an 'explanation' of this amazing book, but we must take it into account in constructing the history, and in this respect it has often received less than justice. Its intellectual power and towering imagination must be obvious to all, and so must its immense influence upon Christian liturgy, art, hymnology and inspirational life. It is possibly the best expression we have of the faith and hope which burned so ardently in the breasts of the first Christians. It cannot be relegated to a minor position as a by-product of the Christian genius.

Its principal concepts are timeless. Contemporary movements were recognized as examples of recurrent types which had been observed and depicted by previous masters of the art, particularly Ezekiel and Daniel. The 'wild beast', for instance, is not a study of any particular Roman Caesar; it is the Roman world-power, which was, so to speak, incarnate in each of them; but even the Roman world-power was only one in a series. It was the contemporary form of a phenomenon in history which had been observed many times before; like so many of the imaginative concepts in the apostolic writings, it had been 'spoken of by the prophet Daniel'.

It is a study of the animal type of human polity, which knows no divine law superior to itself and seems to be devoid of justice and mercy, expressing its essential nature in the figure of an autocrat or conqueror who gives himself the airs of a god. In course of time it works its own ruin and 'goeth unto destruction'; but in due course it reconstitutes itself; it 'rises from the abyss', revealing itself in a new autocratic figure exactly like the last. It had appeared even in the streets of Jerusalem itself.

Against the kingdom of the beast John places the kingdom of the man. The heavens are opened and a king rides out on a white horse, accompanied by many of his own kind. His eyes are like a flame of fire and on his head are many crowns. His clothing is dipped in blood; his own blood that is, for this is he who trod the wine-press outside the city,[1] and of the people there was none with him. He and his legions are clad in white linen, pure and clean. Out of his mouth goeth a sharp

[1] A relic of the harvest symbolism; see Revelation xiv. 20 (=Isaiah lxiii. 3), where the identification is first made; a passage which definitely refers to Jerusalem.

two-edged sword. On his thigh, where the conqueror's sword should rightly be, there is nothing at all but a name written: 'King of kings and lord of lords' (the title of the Persian or Parthian monarch). But this conqueror is no soldier-king, after the manner of Cyrus or Alexander; we are looking at the victory of the bare unarmed truth. He has no weapon but the word that goes out of his mouth; and his own name is called the 'Word of God'.

It is the same name that is given to Jesus in the Fourth Gospel, but with what a difference of effect. The prophet sees Jesus as the supreme force in human history; but his victorious advance proceeds along the evangelical level, in the expansion of the gospel, in the ministry of the prophets, and in the faith of the martyrs; in witness to the Word. He thus records his conviction that the heavenly king will triumph over the earthly tyranny, and that the man-power of the church will not fail in the day of judgement and crisis. Our survey of the second apostolic generation would have been seriously defective without this kind of evidence. We would have noted the rise of curious heresies, the consolidation of the ministerial order, the development of a literary tradition, and the increasing emphasis on a glorious worship; but we might have missed the central fact that the proclamation of the gospel in faith and power, and the consequent defiance of the world, went on in the witness of men who loved not their lives even unto death.

It is this writer who first speaks with inspired confidence about the dead in Christ. 'I heard a voice from heaven which said, Blessed are the dead which die in the Lord: Yea, saith the Spirit, may they rest from their labours.'

THE THOUSAND YEARS

John has no doubt that the Word of God will be victorious over the kingdom of the beast. He has a sublime faith, like that of the Matthaean gospel, in the justice of Almighty God working itself out continuously in history. He uses the concepts which became traditional in Christian eschatology, but he does not hold out any prospect of a grand climax all at once.

He sees the outcome of the great war between the forces of Christ and the forces of the world-power. Christ will be victorious, and the wild beast and his prophet will go into the lake of fire; the old pagan empire will pass into oblivion; 'it goeth unto destruction'. But he interposes a long period before the final judgement of all souls; a period of a thousand years. The figures in the Revelation are never to be taken literally, and this one would seem to mean a long age in human history. He deals with it in obscure symbols, as is natural. Satan is bound but not disposed of; he is laid in the abyss, but at the end of the thousand years he will rise again and there will be further conflict.

Furthermore, during this thousand-year period the souls of the martyrs will receive their just reward; they will be given 'judgement'; they will reign with Christ; and this is the 'first resurrection'. On this slight foundation are built up all the grandiose expectations in later apocalyptic of a 'millennial kingdom' of Christ upon this earth; but that is not what is said; it is the *souls* of the martyrs which receive their reward as priests of God and of Christ; a very different assurance from the bodily resurrection which was promised to the Thessalonians by Silvanus and Paul.

As for the church on this earth during this period, nothing is said. He only speaks of the camp of the saints and the beloved city which will be assailed, at the end of the thousand years, by the nations which are in the four quarters of the earth. Let who will interpret this discreet symbolism.

THE NEW JERUSALEM

We are in the highest realms of poetic mysticism when we come to the vision on the mountain, of the bride of the Lamb, or new Jerusalem, which balances the ugly figure of the harlot city which we believe to represent the old Jerusalem; for the city of God is seen at one time on earth suffering, and at another descending from heaven, and finally in its glory. Like the other great concepts in his gallery of visions, it will not fit into the limitations of time and space; it transcends them. It is at once the martyr-church on earth, and the company of saints in heaven; the author never seems to draw any distinction between the two; and yet it has proved a satisfying concept in all ages for the martyr, the mystic, or the simple believer. It is Israel, it is Jerusalem, it is Paradise, it is the apostolic company, it is perhaps the pagan city of the gods. The genius of the poet infuses every word and every sentence with pure spirituality. It is not of this world; for it needs no sun nor moon to shine upon it, and he sees no temple in it; the Lord God Almighty and the Lamb are temple and glory and illumination enough. It is in this world, however; for the kings of the earth bring their honour and glory into it.

The shining symbols which go to make up this splendid vision are parted out among the seven churches of Asia in the messages with which the whole book begins; and there are other symbols which adhere closely to it; the new name, the key of David, the hidden manna, and the bright and morning star. It would be supposed that it would be obvious to all that this is poetry and not prose, and that whoever materialized it would do so at their peril; but the Christian mind in Asia and Phrygia could not quite rise to it. They brought it down to earth; they cramped it into the thousand years; they localized it. It had to wait for Augustine of Hippo, and Bernard of Morlaix, and Christina Rossetti and spirits of that sort to enter into its mysteries. Indeed, it may be that its day has not come yet.

CHAPTER 19

THE EPHESIAN GOSPEL

The question of philosophy, *p.* 350. Epictetus, Plutarch, Apollonius, *p.* 351. The higher paganism, *p.* 352. Jewish unbelief, *p.* 354. The literary relations, *p.* 355. The theological task, *p.* 356. The historical interest, *p.* 358. The liturgical structure, *p.* 359. The sayings of Jesus, *p.* 360. The Paraclete, *p.* 361. The advent in John, *p.* 362. The Gospel and the Revelation, *p.* 362. The Gospel Epilogue, *p.* 364. The Johannine school, *p.* 366. The production of the book, *p.* 367. The death of the master, *p.* 367. Note on the supposed martyrdom of John, p. 369.

THE QUESTION OF PHILOSOPHY

The study of the Revelation of St John is a difficult one, and different minds come to different conclusions on debatable points, but it has the great advantage to the student of being in touch with external history at many points; with the churches of Asia, with the prophets and martyrs, with the old Jerusalem, with the imperial power of Rome, and with the tyranny of Domitian. It gives us an excellent idea of the kind of ferment out of which it arose, and by doing this, it forms an introduction to the second great document which issued from the same ferment at the same period: the Fourth Gospel.

But this document surprises us by its completely different character. It does not seem to have any points of contact with the history which is reflected in such lurid colours in the Revelation. It has abandoned the apocalyptic modes of thought which appear so massively there. It speaks in a new language; a language of the spirit. It speaks of word and life and light and truth; of the bread of life and the water of life; and of the spirit of truth which leads the disciples into all truth. These concepts are all to be found in the Revelation, it is true; but they do not provide the drama of the Revelation. On the whole the poetry of the Revelation brings the mind into contact with all kinds of external historical forces; the poetry of the Gospel brings us into contact with the inner life of the church and the inner life of the believer.

All great literature is in contact with life, and the Fourth Gospel is no exception. It is in touch, as we have said, with the inner life of the church, which it illuminates with deep spiritual insight. It develops a special understanding of this inner life in a special terminology; and this special terminology must have a significance. This significance, according to many modern scholars, is derived from its relevance to the Hellenistic thought of the age; to philosophy, in short; but to what philosophy?

EPICTETUS, PLUTARCH, APOLLONIUS

Among the philosophers who left Rome in 93 or 94 was the famous Epictetus. He had come to Rome from Hierapolis in Phrygia as a slave. He had learned in the house of Epaphroditus, a notorious favourite of Nero, to endure pain and hardship with serenity. On gaining his freedom, he attended the lectures of Musonius Rufus and then began to give lectures himself. His style was direct and to the point; it reminds us at times of passages in St Paul, and both of them, no doubt, were familiar with the popular philosophic idiom. But it was his sincerity and deep religious conviction that gave him his hold over his pupils. It was said that he had looked a tyrant in the face. He lived for the rest of his life at Nicopolis in Epirus, and won the favour of the Emperor Hadrian. We know about him through his pupil Arrian, who wrote down his teaching. He must have died in the hundred-and-twenties.

Another philosopher who thought it prudent to leave Rome at this time was Plutarch of Chaeronea, who was at the beginning of his career, and died about 120. Unlike Epictetus, he was a writer, and composed 'Lives' of eminent Greeks and Romans, who were chosen as examples of the philosophic virtues. Biography was a fashionable literary form at this time; for we have the Gospels, Josephus and Plutarch in Greek, and Tacitus and Suetonius in Latin. The success of Plutarch as a writer was enormous; not only in his biographies, but in his mystical writings. He marks an important stage in the revival of Platonism, in which he had been anticipated by Philo the Alexandrian Jew. He had fallen victim to the spell of Egypt and to the cult of Isis, which was establishing itself in Rome at this time.

A very different type was Apollonius of Tyana, who compares with the austere Stoic much as the gnostic practitioner compares with the apostle. It is a pity that we have no contemporary account of this extraordinary man. Some very curious stories were handed down among circles of admirers, and were collected about the year 200 by Philostratus, who wove them, in a highly romanticized form, into his famous *Life of Apollonius*. He was born at Tyana in Cappadocia, a border-province in which an Iranian syncretism had been attempted. He had been to India, we are told, and had learned the spirituality of the Brahmins. He had also been to Ethiopia. He practised a life of such heroic asceticism and mystical discipline that he was able to work wonders by reason of his great holiness and his contact with the spirit world. Without doubt he was a historical character; but we are not required to accept the statement that when he stood before the judgement-seat of Domitian he vanished into thin air, a thing no Christian ever learned the secret of. He left Rome for Asia Minor, and fascinated great crowds in Ephesus by his eloquence and by his supernatural arts. He was a common type in his time, and we have seen another example of it in Simon of Samaria, whose legend developed in a very similar way. We may suppose that both of them were men of culture and possibly of character.

It is against this background that we must place the composition of the Acts, and the rivalries between John and Cerinthus, and the publication of the Fourth Gospel. It enables us to see, for instance, the special effectiveness of the dialogue in which Jesus confronts Pilate, the representative of the emperor of his day—

> Thou couldest have no power at all over me unless it were given thee from above.
>
> My kingdom is not of this world, else would my servants fight....
>
> For this cause was I born and came into the world, that I might witness to the truth. (John xix. 11; xviii. 36, 37.)

—the very principles, incidentally, which are enunciated in the Revelation in a more flamboyant idiom. The figure of Jesus as the divine unarmed defender of the truth was such as to have a special appeal to thoughtful readers in this period of moral earnestness, mystical piety and resistance to tyrants. There was a kinship, strange as it may sound to say it, between the Christian martyr, the Greek philosopher, and sometimes even the Roman aristocrat.

THE HIGHER PAGANISM

The new kind of Cynic like Epictetus, the new type of Platonist like Plutarch, and the new type of Pythagorean like Apollonius, are interesting figures; but it cannot be said that they help us to explain the language of the Fourth Gospel. Nor do we really get much farther by

23. THE SYNAGOGUE AT CAPERNAUM

24. TRAJAN

comparing John's doctrine of the Word of God with the Stoic doctrine of the Logos or universal reason, or by looking for the origin of his spiritual concepts in some Platonic other-world. The Fourth Gospel is made of different stuff from the metaphysical systems of the Hellenic schools. If it is Hellenic at all, it is a Hellenism which has learned much from the oriental world, and has been transformed or fertilized by a mystical faith in a universal deity who reveals himself spiritually to pure souls.

Where are we to look for this kind of philosophy, if we may call it a philosophy? Epictetus and Plutarch both had a touch of it; they recognized an intellectual deity who communicated something to the human mind. For all we know Apollonius had more than a touch of it. It was in the air.

Philo, the Jewish philosopher of Alexandria, knew and practised it; for 'knowing' was practising in this way of thought. To 'know' God was to be in touch with him. Philo fused together the deities of Moses and Plato; he spoke of a Logos or Word of God, who acted for God in relation to this world, and set it in order and illuminated the thinking mind. He used the old Hebrew modes of speech, but he also used the accepted language of the philosophers. He believed himself to be guided by this intellectual power of God, which came from God and was God. But it has never been shown that the Fourth Gospel owes anything to Philo. They seem to belong to different streams of thought.

We pass to the Hermetic writings, and there we find something more akin to the language of John. But there is a difficulty. The date of some of the Hermetic writings can be pushed back into the second century, but not with certainty into the first; the best that can be said is that a very small proportion of this Egyptian literature *may* belong to the first. On the whole it seems reasonable to suppose that a good deal of the Hermetic writings have been influenced by John, or by Johannine thought, but we may conjecture that some of the streams of thought which passed into them had passed at an earlier date into the Johannine writings. John may have been influenced by pre-Hermetic thought, or something akin to it.

These writings speak of the spiritual and intellectual deity, and the spiritual and intellectual powers which radiated from him into the pure soul. Such thought and language must have existed in the first century. It is the ancestor of other religious developments, the chief of which is gnosticism. In such circles the Johannine language about the Father and the Son, or about the Spirit of truth, may have been readily intelligible. At any rate it is to such a world of thought that this kind of language seems to relate itself. But it must have been a Jewish world of thought; or a world of thought into which Jewish ideas had entered, so becoming more intelligible to the Hellenistic mind. It was a pre-gnostic form of Judaism.

It is an important fact that the actual thought of the Johannine Gospel, though it may be expressed in the idiom of a Hellenistic spirituality, is nevertheless attached to Judaism at every point. It appropriates the authority of Moses and the prophets as definitely as Matthew does: it refers to Moses even more often. Its doctrine of the Word of God can be amply explained from rabbinic sources, and its other leading concepts are also taken from the Jewish tradition. Its sentence-construction is Semitic in character, and is readily retranslatable into Aramaic. It is fundamentally a Semitic book, not a Greco-Roman book.

Furthermore, while it can be maintained that certain hypothetical pre-Hermetic and pre-gnostic initiates might have understood very readily what was meant by the word of God as an intellectual and spiritual power consubstantial with the deity, they would have been shocked to hear that the Word had become flesh and dwelt among us. It would have been a rude blow to their over-spiritualized, over-intellectualized mode of thought. The impact of the divine being upon the ordinary world of flesh-and-blood in the evangelical history would have been just as difficult for them to accept as the impact of the divine being upon the world of flesh-and-blood in the apocalyptic vision of history.

JEWISH UNBELIEF

A further study of this Gospel reveals another form of contact with history. Its story of the ministry of Jesus, from the first chapter to the twelfth, is told so as to emphasize the unbelief and hostility of the Jews; and by the Jews the people of Jerusalem and their rulers are intended. Even the believers in Jerusalem are not very highly thought of. Jesus would not trust to them. Those who opposed Jesus were the children of the devil, not seed of Abraham at all; *he* was seed of Abraham; in fact he existed before Abraham.

They throw off their superficial objections to the Christhood of Jesus; but John does not take the trouble to answer them. 'Out of Galilee ariseth no prophet', they say; or 'Messiah cometh of the seed of David and of the town of Bethlehem': the kind of objections which Matthew answers with proof-texts. John says their failure to recognize him was due to their spiritual blindness; they did not recognize who he was; they thought they knew whence he came and whither he went; but actually they knew it not; they could not see his light or hear his word. They did not understand his speech.

It looks as if we are in touch with the historical situation here. We remember the hostility of the Ephesian Jews to Paul and their connexion with the Jews of Jerusalem. It looks as if the conflict with the Jews had not lessened since those days, and the Revelation seems to support this conclusion. The Johannine Gospel did on the plane of literature what Paul had done on the plane of evangelism; it turned to the Gentiles. It does not state this in such positive terms as Matthew does, but it intimates it dramatically in the twelfth chapter which concludes the story of the ministry of Jesus to Israel. The Gentiles come and ask to see Jesus, and Jesus gives the Jews their final warning.

THE LITERARY RELATIONS

We must take into account, too, the various circumstances which we learn of through the evidence of the Johannine Epistles, the remaining fragments of Papias, the witness of Polycarp and the statements of second-century writers. We must relate the Gospel somehow to the company of elders and disciples, among whom the prominent name (or names) was that of John; and also to the Docetic and Cerinthian schools, which we may now recognize perhaps as sharing in the 'philosophical' or pre-gnostic approach to religion which appears to have been coming into fashion at the time. For the Docetics of John's First Epistle laid considerable stress upon the idea of *gnosis* or knowledge, which was coming to mean a saving knowledge of divine mysteries; indeed, something of the sort may be traced in the various erratic schools to which Paul refers in his Epistles. It became one of the watchwords of the over-spiritual and over-intellectual heresies of the second century. It was not at all incompatible with a myth such as we find attributed to Cerinthus, in which a 'power' or 'spirit' from the sovereignty which is above the universe descends into the man Jesus, who is juster and wiser than others; a descent which occurs at a sacramental moment.

The Gospel of John shows no knowledge of Matthew; the very occasional coincidences of expression appear to be fortuitous; but it has a close relation to Mark, sometimes taking his narrative for granted, sometimes retelling it, and often making bold changes in its order. Some modern scholars would prefer to think in terms of a gospel-tradition which resembled Mark; but Mark had been in the world for some time now and had even reached Syria; it had come to the attention of the Asian schools and been criticized there, and John (or one of the Johns) had defended its accuracy though he did not accept its order. Other arguments in the Johannine school may be explained as attempts to correct views which were based on Mark; the question of the right day for the Christian *Pascha*, for instance, and the difference of opinion on the length of the Lord's ministry. The heresy of Cerinthus may have been based on a peculiar understanding of Mark; Mark was the favourite Gospel of those who separated the Jesus from the Christus, Irenaeus says.

John's Gospel has a number of interesting points of contact with Luke and Acts, though all scholars would not accept them as proofs that John was familiar with Luke's work. Nevertheless the fact is that the contacts are with Luke and not with Matthew. The background from which he works can be studied in Mark, Luke and even the Acts; some scholars would add Paul.

THE THEOLOGICAL TASK

We are now able to see the magnitude of the task which John attempted. There were various mental images of the Saviour, which were being made the basis of distinct theologies, if this word is appropriate yet. There was the eternal Son of God, older than creation, to borrow a phrase from Hermas; there was the historical Jesus of Nazareth, whether as legislator and prophet, or as the crucified and risen Messiah; there was the spiritual Lord who was at the right hand of God, or reigning in the church among the believers; there was the conquering king who was to come in glory. The task which John undertook was to unify these images, and present them as one picture and person, which he could do because he had passed through the various phases of experience and vision and saw them as one person.

He avoided the confusions which came from regarding the Holy Spirit of the baptism story as the person in whom Christians put their trust. It was Jesus himself who was the object of Christian faith; and therefore Jesus personally was the Son of God, or Word of God as John called him, using a title which we have already noticed in the Revelation. The Word of God was an established name in Hebrew thought for the revelation of the divine personality which broke into the soul of the prophet as light and truth. It created the fundamental evangelical or prophetic experience, whether in the old Hebrew religion or in the new. And it was personal; it was nothing less than God himself in creative action; it was life as well as light. All things were made by it; nothing was made apart from it. It became flesh in Jesus of Nazareth and dwelt among us. We beheld its glory.

The divine glory that men saw in Jesus of Nazareth was not something added to the man; it was the man himself; it was He. A unified picture thus becomes possible.

The words we have been using are taken from a psalm or hymn which John used as an overture to his prologue. The name of John the Baptist is woven into it. He was the spokesman of all that was best in the old Israel, and he had recognized Jesus. It is not said that he saw the glory as the disciples did; but he saw the Spirit which descended upon him, and he bore witness to the light. There had been disciples of the Baptist in Ephesus in Paul's time who were not at one with the church, and it may be that some of them still maintained their special form of faith. It is probable that the relation of John to the Christian faith needed to be defined. Perhaps there were some who claimed him as the Messiah, a claim which he abjures in this Gospel. Perhaps he was regarded as a witness to the Cerinthian or docetic type of faith. Later Ebionite legend regarded the Samaritan heretics, Simon and Dositheus, as disciples of the Baptist; and this Gospel says that John did preach and baptize in Samaria.

The story of the baptism of Jesus is so handled as to rule out the docetic and Cerinthian views, and to allot John his proper place; and yet the story is not actually told. It is taken for granted, and the effect built up by a supplementary dialogue. Mark's Gospel has not been replaced, therefore; it would have to be read before John's could be understood. John's is in the nature of supplement or commentary.

THE HISTORICAL INTEREST

As we read through the Gospel, we find that the glory of the divine nature of Jesus in no way obliterates or overrides his humanity, though it enters fully into his actions and experiences. He is tired; he weeps tears over the death of his friend; he suffers pain and thirst; he dies; 'And he that saw it bore witness, and *we know* that he saith true, that ye might believe.' No one can question the earnest emphasis on historic fact in this sentence. The historic quality is of the essence of the Gospel, and a necessary element in its high evangelical theology. It was written to persuade men that Jesus was the Messiah, and the Son of God, against the Jews; but just as much to prove that he was truly man against the Docetists. 'Then came Jesus forth, wearing the crown of thorns and the purple robe; and Pilate saith, Behold the Man'; not an angel or spirit, but a creature of flesh and blood. It is the dual emphasis that gives this Gospel its dramatic appeal. It also constitutes its problem.

In consequence of its special historical interest, we find it more loaded with minor detail than the other Gospels. There are a number of notes of time, and names of persons and places, and references to local customs. The background and atmosphere is fully Jewish. The style and diction is such that it has been seriously suggested that it is translated from Aramaic. It has been proved right in more than one instance on a historical detail. Has it ever been proved wrong? The case of the day of the crucifixion is an interesting example. The verdict of scholarship is not unanimous but it is given on the whole in favour of John. We note that he does not hesitate to correct the older Gospel.

John says that Pilate brought Jesus out wearing the crown of thorns and displayed him to the people at a place called the 'Pavement'. The site was pointed out in the Middle Ages, and the Ecce Homo Arch was said to mark the spot. Recent research has unearthed a stone pavement of twenty-five hundred square feet on this site, on the north of the old Temple area and just outside the site of the Roman *praetorium* or military headquarters. It was covered by rubble and debris by the destruction of the city in A.D. 70, so that the knowledge of the site in medieval times must have been a good tradition coming down unbroken through the centuries, and confirming now the statement of John. It is the one solidly authenticated Gospel site in Jerusalem, apart from the Temple enclosure itself.

The author of this Gospel, or the disciple whose 'witness' he used, seems to have had a photographic memory for places and circumstances which fully warrants his repeated claims to have his evidence taken seriously as history; and critical scholarship today is receding from the view that everything he wrote was allegory and imagination. It is being recognized that he worked from authentic memories and traditions.

Why, then, is there any objection to taking his Gospel seriously as what it professes to be? The difficulty arises from literary and theological features, which will appear more clearly as we continue.

THE LITURGICAL STRUCTURE

We said that John does not hesitate to change the order of Mark; but in reality he uses a different outline of history. In Mark the scene is laid in Galilee and the north, until Jesus goes up to Jerusalem to be crucified; in John much of the action takes place during visits to Jerusalem, and a great deal of it in the Temple courts. It is connected with the great festivals of the Hebrew calendar. The writer or his informant is well acquainted with Jerusalem and the Temple and the customary rites and ceremonies, just as we found the author of the Revelation to be.

In Mark there is only one Passover mentioned; and it was seriously contended in the second century that all the events of the ministry, from the baptism to the Passion, took place within twelve months. John has three Passovers, and his Gospel occupies parts of three years. This difference is not very serious, since the events in Mark cannot easily be compressed into twelve months, and a second Passover is indicated, though it is not named. More difficult for the old-fashioned harmonizer are the changes in the order of the events; the placing of the 'cleansing of the Temple', for instance, at the beginning of the ministry rather than at the end. But perhaps the order in both Gospels is sometimes liturgical rather than 'historical'? John groups his 'Marcan' material round his three Passovers. The first of them is followed by teaching about baptism; the second by teaching on the eucharist; and the third by the Last Supper. Now when we find a Christian sacramental mysticism developed in connexion with the festivals of the Judaeo-Christian calendar (for John uses other Jewish festivals in a similar way), we are bound to ask whether this teaching was not placed where it is for liturgical reasons. We may even ask whether these passages in his Gospel were not composed in the first place for delivery in church on these festal occasions, to which they are so well fitted.

THE SAYINGS OF JESUS

The greatest divergence from the other Gospels, however, is not in the historical order, in which we may venture to say that John can hold his own against Mark; it is in the character and style of the sayings of Jesus. In the other Gospels, we have as a rule rather brief utterances, full of amazing visual images; the camel passes through the needle's eye; the mountain is cast into the sea; the stars fall from the skies. In John we have a smooth connected style of deceptive simplicity. It makes use of figures of speech, but seldom figures of speech which are calculated to startle the hearers. The manna in the wilderness, the serpent lifted up by Moses and the Paraclete coming from God are certainly not self-explanatory; but these are exceptions. The shepherd of the sheep, the bread from heaven and the living waters are not difficult ideas. The keywords of the Johannine discourses are Hebrew in origin, and are derived from prophecy and liturgy, but they are taken one by one and their inner significance drawn out. The apocalyptic element, which is so strongly fortified in Matthew, has been largely abandoned. The parable form hardly exists; it is merged into continuous discourse.

This simplification of style is not all. It has been compensated for by a different kind of dramatic effect. In the synoptists Jesus does not commonly speak at length about himself in the first person.

In John there are a number of cases in which he makes solemn utterances in the first person. 'I am the good shepherd'; 'I am the light of the world'; 'I am the true vine'; and so forth; and such sayings often introduce a connected monologue or dialogue, dealing with the relations of Jesus as Son of God with the Father, or with the disciples, or with the world. We receive the impression that these discourses or dialogues owe a good deal to the art and genius of the evangelist himself, who has perhaps given free expression to his own personal understanding of the Master's mission and message. It is still the Jesus of history who is speaking, but he has moved forward into the church, and is speaking there in a new idiom through his disciple, thus interpreting himself to his own, and to the Hellenistic world in which the church lives.

The Gospel itself announces such an idea. Jesus departs from the world, it says, and goes to the Father, but he will not leave his disciples as 'orphans'; he will come to them.

THE PARACLETE

In the discourses which follow the Last Supper, Jesus tells them of another Paraclete,[1] a champion or defender, who will come to them from the Father. He is the Spirit of Truth, who will develop further the revelation which has been given them in and through himself. 'He will lead you into all the truth.' It is a bold statement. The revelation which was given by the Son of God in Jerusalem was not final or complete. There comes from the Father a second divine teacher who continues the revelation which he has begun. 'He will take of mine and show it unto you.' The coming of the Holy Spirit in the church is the mode by which the Son of God continues to make himself known, or be made known, to his friends whom he has chosen. The Son of God is still the object of their faith and the medium of God's revelation; but the revelation goes on among them in the Spirit.

This theology illuminates one or two verses in the Gospel which say that the disciples did not understand at the time something that Jesus was saying or doing; the understanding of it came to them later.

Of course this can be turned round and expressed in another way, if desired. There has been progress and development in the understanding of the words and acts of Jesus, as they were originally delivered by the disciples and eyewitnesses; and this development, it might be argued, was expressed by a literary convention, as his continued revelation of himself through the action of the Spirit in the church; but this would not fairly represent the thinking of John and his associates. For the Christian heart and mind, the power which was present in the church was the historic Jesus himself, who was the Word of the eternal Father.

[1] Paraclete in Greek means a lawyer or advocate for the defence, one who stands by an accused man: see Mark xiii. 11. But in rabbinic thought it has the further meaning of a champion or vindicator. It seems to contrast with the Satan, or adversary, or accuser.

THE ADVENT IN JOHN

This thought of a progressive clarification of the gospel in the church by the Lord through the Spirit is the most original feature of the Fourth Gospel. It is the form which the old doctrine of the advent or *parousia* now takes. In Mark the Lord had promised that he would come 'in glory' and his disciples would 'see' him. When we turn to the Revelation we find the conviction that this promise had been fulfilled in more ways than one. He had come in judgement when Jerusalem was destroyed; and he came in conquering power wherever his gospel was preached in the world or his martyrs bore their witness to him; but according to this Gospel, he came to his friends and servants, as they prayed in his name, an idea which is found in Matthew, too. The coming of the Holy Spirit was a veritable advent, through which he was once more in their midst though, indeed, he was not identical with the Holy Spirit; but where the Spirit came, he came. The same idea is expressed in a different idiom in the prologue to the Revelation. He stands in the midst of the golden lamps which represent the churches; he speaks to the prophet, who is in the Spirit, words of admonition and comfort which he is to convey to the churches. He convicts them of sin and of righteousness and of judgement.

It may be added that, while the hope of the advent of Jesus is quite fully realized in the internal coming within the church, the genuinely eschatological features are not altered. The resurrection of the dead and the general judgement remain for the future; but, as in Mark, there is no suggestion whatever of an immediate expectation of these great events. In the Revelation they are deferred to a distant future.

THE GOSPEL AND THE REVELATION

We have been obliged to illustrate the Gospel from the Revelation, and the Revelation from the Gospel, since they emanate from the same literary circle, and the leading thoughts of one are so often found to be the leading thoughts of the other; but dare we identify the prophetic witness who interpreted apocalypse in one, with the apostolic witness who interpreted gospel in the other? The diction of the Revelation is almost another language when compared with that of the Gospel; the one so cryptic and Hebraic and barbarous, the other so much more successfully Hellenized, so lucid and musical. Could one man write in both styles, seeing, as the French critic said, that 'Le style est l'homme même'? Great scholars from Dionysius of Alexandria down to the present day have found it hard to believe; but perhaps it is easier to believe in one man of supreme creative genius and intellectual daring who could write in the two styles, than in two such men who lived in the same place at the same time. When we are further asked to believe that both of them were named John, both were called the Elder, and both were disciples of Jesus, the coincidence becomes very difficult to accept.

The Revelation picks up the old apocalyptic forms and makes a new thing of them. It works with stiff oriental imagery of an almost Babylonian rigidity; but it transforms it into a thing of vision and spiritual beauty. It creates a world of pure imagination. The living waters flow all through the city of God. It is amazing that it can be done in Greek at all; but it may have been the tension between the Hebrew and the Greek that made the miracle possible. The author was totally unsuccessful in what he attempted. He was not understood. He fell into the hands of the literalists and the millenarians, who could not understand his poetry. He had to wait for the Christian mystics and poets to interpret him.

It is the same with the Gospel. It picks up the old stories or parables. It takes the images one by one and meditates upon them. It writes clear and lucid sentences. It leaves no doubt that it is dealing with spiritual realities which need these images in order to make themselves actual and so become available to the human heart. It is obvious who the good shepherd is and what he does; it is obvious what is meant by the vine and its branches, or the wind that bloweth where it listeth, or the bread of life which cometh down from heaven. The words are spirit and truth; it is said so, in order that there may be no mistake.

The Gospel-writer also failed in his attempt. He fell into the hands of the philosophers and the gnostics, and they used him as a source-book for their systems of myth or dogma; and yet the ordinary preacher knows what to do with the story of Jesus seated weary by the well of Jacob or calling Lazarus from his four days' sleep.

The contrast between the two works of art is so striking as to suggest that it is not absolutely fortuitous. They occupy their different grounds so exclusively, and yet echo each other's deepest notes so constantly, that we are challenged at once with the problem of explaining their relations. They have so many things in common; and one of them is genius. Neither Paul nor Luke nor Matthew could have written the Revelation; it would have been beyond their compass; but can we feel so sure about the author of the Fourth Gospel?

Those who think it impossible (and they comprise a number of Protestant scholars) have the task of explaining the spiritual relations which belong to the inner life and thought of the two books. Did the great poet who put the Revelation into its final shape also provide dialogue for the Gospel? Can the work of the same mind be discerned, at least at certain levels? Most easily perhaps in the realm of a mystical and sacramental devotion.

The Spirit and the Bride say, Come: and let him that is athirst come.
Whosoever will; let him take of the water of life freely.
Whosoever drinketh of the water that I shall give him: shall never thirst.
Lord, give me this water, that I thirst not: neither come hither to draw.
Our father did eat manna in the desert: as it is written, he gave them bread from heaven to eat.
Then said they unto him: Lord, evermore give us this bread.
If any man hear my voice and open the door, I will come in to him; and will sup with him and he with me.
He that hath an ear: let him hear what the Spirit saith to the churches.
To him that overcometh will I give to eat of the hidden manna: and will give him a white stone.
And in the stone a new name written: which no man knoweth saving he that receiveth it.
Thou shalt be called Cephas: which is by interpretation a stone.

This jumble of texts out of both books serves to illustrate this point.

THE GOSPEL EPILOGUE

We recommended earlier in this chapter the identification of the 'beloved disciple' of the Fourth Gospel 'who wrote these things' with John the son of Zebedee, and rejected the theory that he was an allegorical figure. We must return to that subject.

The last chapter of the Gospel contains a dialogue between Peter and the risen Lord, in which Peter's pastoral authority and his martyrdom at an advanced age are both established as historical. They were in the past when the Gospel was written. The 'beloved disciple' is allotted a different destiny: 'If I will that he tarry till I come, what is that to thee? follow thou me.' And so the saying went abroad among the brethren, the Gospel continues, that the disciple in question would not die. But Jesus had not said this, the Gospel explains; he had said, '*If* he tarry till I come...'.

We learn from this passage that the 'beloved disciple' was a historical personality on the same level as Peter; that he lived to a great age; that he was well known among the brethren; and that there was a belief about him that he would survive until the coming of the Lord. A note was added to the Gospel to correct this mistaken idea. But nobody corrects ideas which do not exist, about persons who do not exist. The 'beloved disciple' was a person everybody knew, not merely a character in a book.

Those who wish to escape from this conclusion suggest that the final chapter was written by another hand and added at a later date; but even if this were true, the chapter would still prove the existence of the 'beloved disciple' among the brethren at the date when it was written or not long before it. It is quite true, as they point out, that the chapter is in the nature of an epilogue, which comes after the main action of the book seems to come to a natural close at xx. 31; but this literary form is a very common one and in this case it adds strength and beauty and significance to the book as a whole. The same literary convention is used by the author of the Revelation, who adds an epilogue of serene beauty after the close of the apocalyptic action at xxi. 8. 'Sleep after toil, port after stormy seas, ease after war, death after life does greatly please'; and 'Good plays prove the better by the help of good epilogues'; to quote two great English masters of the art.

There is nothing in the style or in the thought of either Johannine epilogue to suggest that it was written by another hand. The high standard of creative writing is maintained in both; indeed, the author surpasses himself. The tension is relaxed, but new beauty is introduced to compensate for that. This new element picks up thoughts which were introduced in the prologue; in the seven messages to the seven churches in the case of the Revelation, in the first seven days of the narrative in the case of the Gospel. There is no indication in any manuscript or other textual authority that either book ever circulated without its epilogue; and we have shown why such evidence was bound to survive.

Once a document was handed over to the copyists, and new copies began to circulate, there would be no way of recalling them in order to have the addition made. The history of the epilogue which was added to Mark illustrates this point. The conclusion is bound to be that the epilogue to John is an integral part of the Gospel, and that the 'beloved disciple' was a familiar and venerated figure among those who first read it or heard it read.

THE JOHANNINE SCHOOL

We are no longer looking at a book or books which can be treated as if they came to us with no pedigree, but at a massive historical fact which is vouched for by copious external evidence in the succeeding period of church history. It is the great Johannine school which dominated the Ephesian landscape in the nineties. It was so well grounded in history, and its spiritual authority was so secure, that it was able to stand firm against the Docetics, the Cerinthians, the non-believing Jews, and quite possibly some of the more extreme Jewish Christians. It was not entirely the tradition of one man; and yet its power and influence and appeal was due to the genius and originality of one man who won the homage of the whole church and inspired the most interesting developments of the following century in Syria, Asia, Phrygia, Alexandria and Rome. He appears as a faithful witness and teacher, a venerable elder, a disciple of Jesus, a master of liturgy, and a maker and visitor of bishops. We hear from all quarters that he was John the son of Zebedee.

A highly sceptical literary and theological criticism has doubted the truth of this identification, or has endeavoured to divide him into two or more personalities; and these doubts have confused the issue and clouded the view of the landscape. We have done our best to make fair allowance for them; but we have to record our conviction that the historical evidence is so strong, however harshly it may be criticized, as to leave John the son of Zebedee firmly enthroned as the master of his school, however his relation to the literature may be explained. The literature cannot be considered apart from the school and its history, nor the school apart from the literature. Its immense influence was not confined to the production of books. It produced scholars and evangelists who themselves became venerable 'elders' in due course; for the rabbinic notion of a teaching succession was one of its features. Its literature was accepted as part of the apostolic tradition. It is not until the end of the second century that a voice was raised against the Johannine literature, and this eccentric protest was caused by the excesses of the Montanist movement which made an eccentric use of the Johannine writings.

It is one of the ironies of history that the barbarous and fanatical prophet Montanus should have entered so deeply into the literature of this apostolic school, and wedded together in a fantastic union the exciting doctrines of the Paraclete and the New Jerusalem, thereby forcing their consideration upon the church as a whole; just as the 'eschatological' school of criticism today, for all its extravagances, forces the ecumenical church to take a new look at the apostolic literature.

THE PRODUCTION OF THE BOOK

The 'disciple who wrote these things' may not have written the whole Gospel, as we have it now, in connected form. The phrase may only mean that he left written documents. Others intervene with their attestation; and in this circle, if we please, we may place the second John. It is possible that the aged disciple had passed to his rest before the complete Gospel came into existence; for when it was published, as his work, the notion that he would never die needed to be corrected and explained; and this rather suggests that he had died. These others may have worked on it, and arranged it, and added some of the explanatory notes which we find here and there.

We have seen that books, in this period, sometimes took long to write. They were often the fruit of old age. The co-operation of others was not despised. The Johannine Gospel may have gone through many processes before it matured and came to perfection. It went out to all the churches as the last word of the old disciple, and the supreme expression of a great apostolic tradition which was widely venerated.

THE DEATH OF THE MASTER

The tradition states that John survived into the times of Trajan, the emperor who came to the throne in 98. There is no record of his death, any more than there is of Peter's or Paul's. It was fifty or sixty years later that a Valentinian Gnostic, whose name may have been Leucius Charinus, ventured to tell the story in a romantic piece of fiction called the *Acts of John*. It is a work of the pious imagination; but fiction has to accommodate itself to the main facts of history, and the main facts must have been well known at that time. In this book John died peacefully in Ephesus at a great age. After a long prayer he sealed himself in every part, saying, 'Thou art with me, O Lord Jesus'; then he lay down in the grave where he had strewn his garments; and when he had said 'Peace be with you, my brethren', he gave up his spirit with joy. There are elaborations in some manuscripts to this simple ending, as for instance that the body was found to have disappeared, or that the earth over it could be seen to move as if the buried apostle were still breathing; for was it not thought that this disciple could never die?

The story in the *Acts of John* has no historical value, of course, except so far as it shows what the general belief of the church was at the time when it was written. There is no good reason to question this belief, which is that of the first Christian centuries; but there are some scholars who have taken seriously a statement which may be traced back to a fifth-century historian named Philip of Side, who had a reputation for unreliability; it is to the effect that after John had written his Gospel he was slain by the Jews, and it is said to have been derived from the second volume of Papias. If Papias really said this, it must be taken seriously; but it is obvious that he did not. Irenaeus and Eusebius and others had studied Papias for themselves, and if the statement had stood in his book they would have known about it, and so would the church at large.

Nobody claims John as a martyr before the fifth century, that is to say a martyr who sealed his witness by death. He was a martyr in the primitive sense of the word, a man who bore witness to the truth. The grandsons of Jude were martyrs, Hegesippus said, and John was a martyr in that sense, too. It was the sense in which he used it himself.

> For this cause was I born and came into the world, that I should witness to the truth: (John xviii. 37.)[1]
>
> The spirit of prophecy is the witness of Jesus. (Rev. xix. 10.)

[1] The text of the quotation is that of the recently discovered papyrus fragment of the early second century, now in the John Rylands Library, Manchester. The word translated 'witness' is *marturia*.

NOTE ON THE SUPPOSED MARTYRDOM OF JOHN

George the Monk, who called himself *Hamartolos* or the Sinner, compiled a *Chronicle* in the ninth century, into which he copied extracts from previous compilations. There are twenty-six manuscripts of his work, and one of them (Codex Coislinianus at Paris) contains a statement which is said to have been made by Papias in his second volume, that 'John the Divine' and his brother James were slain by the Jews. It is embedded in argumentative material, and quotes the verse in Matthew which says that both brothers would drink of his cup. The other side of this argument seems to appear in an equally dubious quotation from Polycarp (which we owe to the fifth-century Victor of Capua), in which it is argued that actual martyrdom is not implied: it is printed by Feuardentius and Lightfoot.

The argument may safely be traced back to the fifth century. There is a manuscript at Oxford called the Codex Baroccianus, from which certain extracts were quoted and discussed by C. de Boor in *Texte und Untersuchungen* (Berlin, 1888). This manuscript is also of the chronicle type, and de Boor considered it to be an epitome or selection of extracts made by some unknown person in the seventh or eighth century from the fifth-century writer Philip of Side. Philip was a historian with a reputation for extreme inaccuracy. His works have not survived except for this dubious fragment and a few other quotations.

The 'de Boor' document contains the alleged quotation from Papias about the death of John; and also a few minor details which are not found in corresponding passages elsewhere. In the extract from Papias the name of a person miraculously raised from the dead is given. It looks as if Philip, or some source that he worked from, may have had independent access to these ancient authors, and it is just possible that some authentic information may have filtered down through these obscure channels. It is difficult to see, however, how any one could prefer this evidence to the solid tradition of the early church.

It has also been pointed out that a fourth-century Syrian martyrology commemorated James and John on the same day (December 27) and this implies the belief at this time, or even earlier, that both brothers were martyrs; but it is not at all clear in what sense the word martyr would have been used originally, or indeed which James and John were originally commemorated. An African calendar of the same century substitutes John the Baptist. These mid-winter commemorations are an obscure study, and shed no light on the history of the apostolic period.

See *Neue Fragmente* by C. de Boor, 1888; and discussions from different points of view by R. H. Charles, *Commentary on the Revelation* in I.C.C., and J. H. Bernard in *Commentary on St John's Gospel* in I.C.C.

CHAPTER 20

CORINTH AND ROME

The Epistle to the Hebrews, *p.* 370. Liturgical thinking, *p.* 372. Authorship and reception of Hebrews, *p.* 373. The Church in Corinth, *p.* 373. The Church in Rome, *p.* 376. Titus Flavius Clemens, A.D. 95, *p.* 377. The schism in Corinth, *p.* 379. The Epistle of Clement, *p.* 381. The character of the Epistle, *p.* 382. Hermas the prophet, *p.* 384. The new repentance, *p.* 385. The Judaeo-Christian tradition, *p.* 386. Nature and liturgy, *p.* 388. The Living God, *p.* 390.

We return now to Rome and to the reign of Domitian, and even to the earlier part of his reign, not long after the Neronian persecution. We come back to the western churches of Greece and Italy, which were unaffected as yet by the great spiritual movements from Syria and Asia Minor. These churches looked back to St Peter and St Paul; they cherished the literature which they had received from them or from their pupils; they maintained the church order which they had established. They begin to have an old-fashioned look.

THE EPISTLE TO THE HEBREWS

Somewhere on the line which passes from Ephesus, through Corinth, to Rome, the so-called Epistle to the Hebrews was produced in the seventies or eighties, by a writer of high authority whose name has not been preserved. It was not addressed to the Hebrews; that title was given to it in the second century, perhaps in Alexandria. The salutation 'They of Italy salute you' suggests to some minds that it was written from Italy; but it looks more like a salutation from an Italian group, and if so the destination might be Italy; most probably the Roman church. It conveys the information that Timothy has been released or acquitted, presumably from some imprisonment or legal process; though some scholars think that the word means that he was sent off on a journey. This is the last notice we possess of the movements of Timothy, who was last heard of at Ephesus.

A period of persecution lies in the past; it was doubtless the Neronian persecution. The church which it addresses had behaved with exemplary courage. The people had watched the 'departure' or 'exit' of their leaders or rulers, a word by which the author means their tragic deaths. They had endured with joy the insults and robberies to which they had been exposed; but there had been time since then for a change. Slackness had set in, and resistance unto blood was no longer the order of the day. Little progress had been made in the deeper understanding of the faith. So far from producing teachers, they were in need of elementary instruction themselves in the '*Logia* of the beginning', those fundamental traditions to which so much of the literature of this period refers. These traditions included the word of salvation which was originally spoken by the Lord, and had been preached locally by men who had heard him. It looks as if actual hearers and pupils of the Lord were no longer available in this branch of the church.

The writer was a theologian, and his 'Epistle' is the only theological treatise which has secured a place in the New Testament, unless indeed we are prepared to regard Romans or Ephesians in this light. St Paul had shown in I Corinthians, which was known to this author, how easily and naturally the gospel was expressing itself in terms of Jewish liturgy, and especially in the traditional commemorations from Exodus which were attached to Passover and Pentecost. I Peter makes use of the same tradition. The author of Hebrews continued this study by considering the work of the Levitical priesthood and especially the ritual of the great Day of Atonement. He was much concerned with the ideas of sin and forgiveness, and of discipline and suffering. He took a dark view of the ecclesiastical scene. The problem of apostasy loomed large. The rule of chastity was in danger; and he seems to deny that there could be any restoration for such lapses. How could offenders of this kind repeat the experience which he calls illumination, and pass again through the rites of baptism and confirmation, so as to receive for a second time the heavenly gifts and powers?

The old Jewish Law had a machinery of reconciliation in its various sin-offerings, and especially in the great Day of Atonement, when the high priest entered the Holy of Holies, with incense and with blood, to avert the divine indignation. This ancient ritual had come to an end with the destruction of the Temple; but 'The Day' continued to be observed as a solemn fast among the Israelites, and they were assured that if they turned to the Lord with all their heart, they would be forgiven. The author of this Epistle can find no further place for it. The whole paraphernalia of the Temple ceremonial, with its blood of bulls and goats, had been transitory and ineffective. It was rendered irrelevant now, not by the destruction of the Temple (to which he does not allude), but by the death of the Messiah on the cross, which was the true sacrifice offered once and for ever by the eternal high priest.

LITURGICAL THINKING

The most important thing, perhaps, about Hebrews is that it calls for a final break with the Jewish religious system. Historic Judaism, with its priesthood and rituals, had become a thing of the past. Christians must come out of it and leave it behind. They have an altar of their own, from which those who served the 'tabernacle' could not partake.

Was there a hankering after Jewish rituals in the Gentile churches? Was there a demand for ceremonies of absolution, or even for the Day of Atonement itself? Were such things practised? We recollect that the stock-in-trade of Paul's Jewish antagonists had been some form of Jewish myth or ceremony or asceticism. It is sometimes assumed that Gentile Christians were naturally hostile to Jewish teachers and Jewish rituals; it looks very much as if they were sometimes too much attracted by them. And could it have been easy, in any case, to decide which Jewish teachings and ceremonies should be retained? The Passover was retained in its christianized form, so why not the Atonement? Hebrews is an anti-Jewish document, at least in this respect. It antiquates and explodes the Levitical system, considered as an effective and final means of grace and righteousness.

On the other hand, it was impossible for the author to regard it as wrong or meaningless. It was the work of God and had served a certain purpose for a certain time. It had set forth publicly in ritual forms the redemptive religion which was to become real and effective in the life and death of Jesus. It was, so to speak, a shadow of the real revelation which was to be given in due time in the gospel; and when the gospel came, the idea of sacrifice was lifted from the old level of ritual action to that of moral and spiritual devotion. The consecrated will was to be offered to God in service and obedience, and suffering was willingly accepted as a discipline. These sublime thoughts had all been anticipated in the prophets and the psalms.

The old system of worship and sacrifice provided this author with the substance and material of his thinking. He had no theology in the sense of systematic dogma. His thinking about the incarnation and atonement was done in terms of liturgy. The Son of God was bound to share our flesh and blood, in order to become our high priest and offer himself on our behalf, and so bring many sons to glory. No doubt our author's actual knowledge of the Levitical rituals was not always accurate; no doubt, too, he was influenced by current Alexandrian theology; nevertheless his mind moved in the realm of the old liturgical action, which he now desired to transcend and leave behind. The theory which he worked out seems to have been of great assistance to the church in defining its relation to the Hebrew Bible and the Hebrew historic tradition.

AUTHORSHIP AND RECEPTION OF HEBREWS

There is no New Testament document in which the Petrine and Pauline elements are more perfectly fused than Hebrews. The author seems to know the Marcan story of the Passion, for he visualizes Jesus in Gethsemane and on the cross, and again when God brings up from the dead the great shepherd of the sheep with the blood of the eternal covenant (Mark xiv. 27 and 24). He makes use of Pauline Epistles, including Romans and Corinthians at any rate. His use of the Old Testament is in line with that of the Christian schools which produced the so-called *Books of Testimonies*. Clusters of prophetic quotations are a marked feature of his book. He chooses them with a sympathetic feeling for their poetic effect and for their spiritual power. He writes with great skill and ability. He has a profound feeling for the human appeal of the gospel.

Who he was is quite unknown. If we had to choose from among the church leaders known to us, we would pick the learned and literary Apollos. A possible place of writing might be Corinth. We judge from I Clement that it was well known both in Rome and Corinth.

THE CHURCH IN CORINTH

A great deal of light is shed on the Corinthian church as it was in the eighties by the Epistle of Clement, which reviews its history, rather idealizing it perhaps. It was a well-ordered community with a dignified worship which was offered by bishops and deacons. Due respect was paid to the elders. The younger generation, which may mean the more recent converts, did not take too much upon themselves. The women were taught to love their own husbands. The 'law of subordination' was observed by all. It is a state of affairs which is fully in accordance with the Pastoral Epistles, which were probably in Clement's mind when he wrote.

The Epistle contains a survey of the history of the local ministry which goes back to the period of apostolic evangelization in the fifties and sixties, when the first bishops and deacons were appointed.

> Jesus Christ was sent out from God: so the Christ was from God and the apostles from Christ; both coming in due order from God... they went out in the full conviction of the Holy Spirit, bringing the gospel that God's kingdom was about to come; so as they made the proclamation in country and town they appointed their first-fruits, after proving them by the Spirit, to be bishops and deacons for those who should believe.
>
> (I Clement xlii. 1–4.)

And after some argumentation based on the Old Testament he continues as follows:

> Our apostles knew through our Lord Jesus Christ that there would be contention over the name of the episcopate, so for that reason, since they had received perfect foreknowledge, they appointed the aforesaid, and for the meantime gave a direction by which, if they were to fall asleep, other approved men should succeed to their ministry.[1]
>
> So we do not think it right that those who were appointed by them, or in the meantime by other men of rank, with the consent of the whole church, ...should be cast out of their ministry. Blessed are the elders (or older men) who have trod the road before us, who had a fruitful and perfect release; for none of them are in fear that someone will remove them from their established place. (*Ibid.* xliv. 1–5.)

Certain historic facts stand out perfectly clearly in this survey. The first is the belief in the divine mission and authority of the original apostolate. The second is that the appointment of bishops and deacons came as part of this mission from Christ and from God. The third is

[1] This could mean 'to succeed to the apostolic ministry'; but this interpretation does not commend itself. If it is adopted the 'men of rank' in the next sentence will of course be these successors of the apostles.

that the ministry of bishops and deacons in the local church was for life. Clement calls it a 'liturgy'; he speaks of the 'offering of the gifts'; he compares it to the Jewish priesthood. This may be 'theology' of course, but it reveals the facts of the situation to which he was addressing himself. There was a permanent liturgical ministry in the church which had been instituted by the apostles themselves as part of their own God-given ministry in the gospel, and subordinate to it.

The second quotation bears this out. The apostles foresaw that there would be contention over the question of the episcopate (when there was a vacancy, that is), so they made provision for a succession (the word is an interesting one). The vacancy created by the death of a bishop was filled up by the apostles themselves, or else by other men of rank with the concurrence of the whole church. And this had actually taken place before Clement wrote.

What is meant by other men of rank? The word *ellogimos* means enrolled or registered; and then notable or famous. It appears that there were other men available whose standing was comparable with that of the apostles. We naturally think of apostolic men like Timothy and Titus, Mark and Luke, or possibly Clement himself; but some scholars believe that it is a way of referring to the surviving bishops (or bishops of surrounding cities), and the student must decide for himself whether this is the natural interpretation of the words.

A second controversial point is the question of the elders. There is a theory that bishop and elder were alternative names for the same official in the church. But is such a use of language natural?

It is a fact that Clement refers to the deceased bishops as elders in one of the passages which we have quoted: 'Blessed are the older men or elders who have trod the path before us.' But what does he mean by the word? Grand old stalwarts of the former generation? Venerable clergy? Veterans of the faith? The word is capable of many meanings.

May we infer that the word 'elder' was only used of bishops? Or has Clement a larger body of men in mind? He talks in a general way of the elders or rulers of the church, of respect due to them from the younger, and of responsibility resting upon them. He mentions established or appointed elders. But his way of speaking of the elders is rather different from the precise way in which he delineates the position of the bishop and deacons. It is always so in literature of this kind. Bishops and deacons are executive officers with definite duties; elders are the church authorities in general, or older men, or members of a council, or venerable teachers. The word appears to be used as a blanket designation for the senior ministries of the church. Peter can say that he writes to the elders as a fellow-elder. John was called 'the elder' in Asia Minor. Papias alludes to the disciples of Jesus as elders.

The word 'elder' is an old word inherited from the Jewish synagogue and requires no explanation. The word 'bishop' was the new word taken out of the Gentile world to be used for a new office instituted by the apostles and dependent upon them or other ranking men for its continuance in the church. These bishops are associated with deacons. Bishops and deacons is the expression in Paul, Clement, Ignatius and the Didache; the only exception is the Epistle of Polycarp which speaks of elders and deacons, and special reasons have been suggested for this. These bishops were the apostles' men in their newly formed churches; they could be called elders, but it would be rash indeed to assume that there were no others who could be given this ancient and honourable title.

In considering the function of the elders the simple factor of seniority should not be forgotten. In these western churches we can find no trace of any further influx of apostles, or disciples, or disciples of disciples, such as occurred in Asia, and presumably in points farther east. There was no enrichment or development of the apostolic gospel in reinforced apostolic schools. The responsibility seems to have fallen very heavily on the senior converts, especially upon those who had been appointed to be bishops or elders.

THE CHURCH IN ROME

It is reasonable to suppose that a similar church order prevailed in Rome; but the Roman church in the second century preserved a succession-list of single bishops, the first three of which were allotted to this period—Linus, Cletus and Clement. As each of these is allotted an episcopate of twelve years it looks as if no exact record had been preserved; it seems to be an artificial or even a symbolic number. The names must be accepted as those of famous men who exercised leadership in the church at this time; but, in order to harmonize the tradition with the picture which is given by Clement, it has been suggested that they exercised authority concurrently rather than successively; they may have been members of a presbytery, or heads of different 'houses', or indeed apostolic men of the same type as Timothy and Titus. The system of plural bishops required something of the sort. It always seems to depend on some higher or external authority for advice or supervision or direction, or even appointment.

Irenaeus, who wrote about 180, out of a very full knowledge of the Roman tradition, remarks that Clement had seen the blessed apostles, had accompanied them, and had their teaching sounding in his ears, 'and not only he, for there were many still surviving then who had been taught by the apostles'. This perhaps is no more than we would have surmised for ourselves.

TITUS FLAVIUS CLEMENS, A.D. 95

The Roman church in the second century looked back to the tyranny of Domitian as the occasion on which John the apostle was banished to the island of Patmos and wrote the Revelation; but there is no good reason for believing that he actually appeared in Rome before the emperor. No confidence can be placed in the legend, first related by Tertullian, that he was condemned to death there by immersion in boiling oil, and 'suffered nothing'. We do not know that John was ever in Rome.

On the other hand the appearance of the grandsons of Jude before the emperor must have made a profound impression upon the church; the kind of impression which we can study later in the similar case of Ignatius. It may be that it was in some such way as this that the Epistles of James and Jude came to the knowledge of the Roman church; for Hermas undoubtedly made use of James. The story rests, however, on the single authority of Hegesippus, and it is dismissed as a fiction by some critics, though its realistic and circumstantial character entitles it to respect.

Our most interesting evidence about the persecution comes from pagan authors. In 95 Domitian struck down certain leading members of the patrician and imperial families. One of these was his own first cousin, Titus Flavius Clemens, who held the high office of consul. Another was Manius Acilius Glabrio, who had been consul in 91. This particular Clemens or Clement must be distinguished from the Clement who wrote the Epistle. He was a first cousin of Domitian himself, and his two sons had been designated as next in succession to the throne. The charge on which the consul Clement was condemned, says Dio Cassius, a third-century historian, was 'atheism, under which charge many others were condemned as having been followers of Jewish customs'. Suetonius says that he was guilty of 'contemptible inactivity' which sounds a little like the modern phrase 'refusal to co-operate'. (Or does it mean that he was a person of no importance?)

The charge of atheism was a stock charge against the Jews and the Christians, and meant that they refused to worship the gods of the state or take part in their rituals. Inactivity (*inertia*) might cover non-appearance at various official functions or ceremonies or games, in which a Christian could not take part. The Jews have naturally claimed that the consul Clement was a convert to their religion, and he appears as such in the pages of the Talmud; but the blood-purge may not have distinguished very clearly between the allied sects of Judaism and Christianity, and there is another line of evidence which makes it practically certain that he was a Christian.

Clement was married to his cousin Domitilla, who was a niece of the emperor. She was banished to an island, but returned safely when Domitian died. She had an estate called the Villa Amaranthiana, which was situated on the Ardeatine Road to the south-east of the city; and here the visitor may still wander along the galleries of the subterranean 'Cemetery of Domitilla' which is one of the oldest Christian burying-places in Rome; so that the archaeological evidence points to Christianity, rather than Judaism, as the ostensible reason for the liquidation of the suspiciously inactive consul.

Another first-century place of burial which was used by Christians was the 'Cemetery of Priscilla', on the Salarian Road to the north-east; and among the burials in this cemetery are several which belonged to the Acilian family, including quite possibly the resting-place of Domitian's other illustrious victim, Acilius Glabrio. The names of Prisca or Priscilla, and Acilius or Aquilius, occur frequently as family names in these inscriptions; and it is not unnatural to connect this group of families with the Aquila and Priscilla (or Prisca) who appear in the New Testament as patrons and friends of St Paul. According to the catacomb tradition, the senator Pudens (who was said to be the son of Priscilla) was also buried here: and Paul mentions a Pudens along with Linus, who was remembered as the first bishop.

It must be realized, however, that while these cemeteries were indubitably established in the first century, there are no recognizably Christian inscriptions belonging to the first century or first half of the second century. It is the family connexions that are continuous. The oldest Roman churches of the third or fourth century claimed to have been founded by the Pudens–Priscilla family.

These connexions lead us to revise any romantic notions that we may have had of Christianity as a 'proletarian' movement, spreading solely among slaves and depressed foreign groups. Our survey of its literature has shown that its intellectual and literary standards were of the highest, even if they were not those of the classical schools. The evidence of the cemeteries shows that it was in touch with the noble families, and Hermas has much to say about the influence of the rich in the Roman church. Christianity had made great strides, and it had brought together persons and families of unlike types. If we underestimate the evidence for its phenomenal expansion at this point, we are unable to explain the fear which it created, or the fact that it did eventually overcome the pagan world.

We should like to know a great deal more than we do about the Christian expansion in the city of Rome, and the period of 'tyranny' which came at the end of Domitian's reign. What we have, however, is sufficient to give us some idea of its range; and we may add that it was still talked about sixty or seventy years later. It ended on September 18 of 95, when the 'tyrant' was assassinated by one Stephanas, a servant of the exiled Domitilla, with some help from his own servants and friends. The senate, who profited by his death, appointed one of its own members, an elderly lawyer named Nerva, a man of the highest integrity, to take his place. Jews, Christians, patricians and philosophers could begin to breathe again.

THE SCHISM IN CORINTH

It was during this time of crisis and persecution that a 'foul and unholy revolution' broke out in the peaceable Corinthian church. Clement describes it as a rebellion by the newer or younger against the older and more honourable. He even calls it a revolt of the ecclesia against the elders. It was a mutiny. He describes the leaders of the revolt as wilful and headstrong and precipitate and ambitious and arrogant. There were women among them as well as men; and certain exhortations suggest that they were not without their gifts of intellect and character and possibly of wealth and position.

He does not make the original cause of the dissension clear. If we may make an inference from the doctrinal character of the Epistle, the younger party may have been sceptical about the apocalyptic elements in the faith, the bodily resurrection, the day of the Lord, and the advent in judgement. On the other hand, they did not reject the Old Testament, since Clement appeals to it with great confidence. It is not possible to feel sure that doctrinal differences were at the root of the trouble.

Clement treats the problem as if it were largely personal or possibly constitutional; a clash between two parties, both of which were determined to control the church. In the course of this rivalry the younger group had met with some success. In particular they had succeeded in deposing or retiring from office some of the bishops who had been appointed by the apostles (or other eminent men), and had offered the gifts without criticism for many years; and this was the scandal as Clement saw it. They had no right to do that.

He urges them to submit themselves to the judgement of the whole church with the constituted elders. The bishops had been appointed in the first place with the concurrence of the whole church, and the present unfortunate position must be rectified in the forum of the whole church, in which Clement appears to have the greatest confidence; but the whole church had been guilty of rivalry and party strife; it had need of repentance and humility and Christian charity. The whole blame is not placed on the group of rebels.

The Corinthian dissension was of more than local importance. It had communicated itself to Rome, where it was the talk of the dissentient groups in that city. It had become a danger to the church in whose name Clement wrote. It is unfortunate from our point of view that his very discreet Epistle does not make it possible for us to discover more exactly what had actually occurred.

Naturally the support of the powerful and wealthy Roman church with its strong apostolic tradition would be of great importance to whichever side could obtain it. In all probability it was asked to intervene. Both sides may have sent emissaries to Rome with letters and explanations; and doubtless to other churches too.

The Roman church took a little time to consider the matter, for they had troubles of their own. They resolved finally to send two of their members with a well reasoned letter supporting the Corinthian elders. These envoys were Claudius Ephebus and Valerius Bito. They were no neophytes, but lifelong Christians, who had behaved themselves blamelessly from youth to old age; that is to say, they were veterans who could remember the Neronian persecutions and had seen and heard the apostles. With them went a man named Fortunatus, who is not described as an envoy of the Roman church. He may be the man who had come from Corinth to express the views of the older generation; he may even have been the man who had gone to see Paul at Ephesus on similar business a generation earlier; a contemporary of Clement.

The letter is described as an entreaty on behalf of peace; it was written through the Holy Spirit and should not be disregarded. It had, therefore, we would suppose, the support of a church council or conference in which it was believed that the Spirit had given guidance. Perhaps the prophets had spoken.

THE EPISTLE OF CLEMENT

The Epistle was written on behalf of the Roman church by Clement. His name does not appear in the text, which is addressed from the church of God sojourning at Rome to the church of God sojourning at Corinth. It is only from 'tradition' that we know that Clement was its actual author; but the word 'tradition' in this case, as so often, is a name which is used to cover explicit statements made by responsible men who could not help knowing all the facts; Hegesippus, for instance, who passed through Corinth about 150 or 160; and Dionysius who was bishop there a few years later and says that the Epistle was still being read on Sundays in his time. It ranked therefore with the apostolic Epistles. It was widely received on this level throughout the Christian church, and almost always as the 'Epistle of Clement'.

The Corinthians had been waiting for a message from Rome; for Clement begins by apologizing for the delay in sending it, which was due, he explains, to the series of accidents and misfortunes which had come so unexpectedly, one on top of another; he is referring, of course, to the events of the last years of Domitian. He takes a strong line, but argues his case with earnestness and moderation. He advises the younger men and women who have promoted rebellion to submit to the elders and to the judgement of the ecclesia. He urges the elders to be prepared to exercise unlimited forgiveness, which is rather at variance perhaps with the doctrine of the Epistle to the Hebrews, a book from which he often quotes. He supports his plea by numerous arguments from the holy scriptures of the Old Testament and from the apostolic traditions as they had been received in both churches.

But he goes further than this. He invites the whole church to make a corporate act of repentance for all its folly and strife and discord. 'Let us fall down before our Lord', he says, 'and implore him with lamentations to be merciful to us and be reconciled, and restore us to the holy and sacred paths of brotherly affection. Blessed are we, beloved, if we act according to the commandments of God, and in the unity of love, so that our sins may be forgiven us through love.'

Such a call from a church to a church was the strongest spiritual appeal which could be made under the circumstances, and doubtless the two Roman elders who presented the Epistle to the Corinthian church were prepared to back up this appeal with personal admonitions and advice; they were sent as 'witnesses' between the two churches. In the atmosphere of emotional and spiritual release which would be liberated in such a movement of mass-repentance, it would be possible for individuals to win respect by an outstanding act of apology or submission to the general will; or even, as the Epistle says, for a party-leader to cover himself with glory by making a great act of renunciation and offering to withdraw altogether. 'Is any among you noble?' Clement asks; 'Is any among you touched to the heart? Is any filled with love? Let him say: "If I am the cause of faction and strife and divisions, I depart; I go wherever you will; I do whatever the majority may decide; only let the flock of Christ be in peace with the established elders". Whoever does this will purchase for himself great renown in Christ; and any place will receive him.'

It was a fair offer. Clement backs it up with examples of heroic renunciation and self-sacrifice from Roman history and Jewish apocryphal literature.

THE CHARACTER OF THE EPISTLE

This Epistle is a monument of Christian synagogue Hellenism, the last of its kind. Clement knew the Old Testament in its Greek form, including some books of the Apocrypha. He knew the apostolic catechisms and household rules. He knew the liturgy. He refers to the two great columns or pillars of the church, Peter and Paul, and their departure to the place of glory which was their due. He seems to make use of Mark (e.g. I Clement xxiv. 5); but his quotations from the teaching of Jesus look as if they were drawn from an oral tradition.

Remember the words of the Lord Jesus [he says] which he spoke when teaching gentleness and patience:

> Show mercy that you may obtain mercy,
> Forgive that you may be forgiven,
> As you do, so will it be done to you,
> As you give, so will it be given to you,
> As you show kindness, so will kindness be shown to you;
> The measure that you measure with
> Is the measure with which it will be measured out to you.

(I Clement xiii. 2.)

He refers by name to I Corinthians, the letter in which Paul had spoken about the party divisions of forty years before. He often quotes from Hebrews. He has echoes of Romans and Ephesians; he writes in the style and vocabulary of I Peter and the Pastorals, with which we judge he was familiar. He does not quote them formally, but his Epistle is in the same tradition. It is remarkable that there should be so many traces of the apostolic writings in so short a document, and we would judge that he knew most of the Petro-Pauline epistolary literature; but the evidence for Luke and Acts is quite slight. The Johannine and Matthaean books had not reached him.

The medium in which Clement worked was still the Judaeo-Christian community tradition of the early apostolic period. He handled his material in a masterly manner; but his mind was not that of a theologian or philosopher, or even of an evangelist; it was that of a pastor or shepherd of souls; a statesman and administrator and man of wisdom after the old Hebrew pattern of wisdom; a teacher with a firm hand and a tender heart, but judging and making decisions without respect of persons. It was the supreme sign of his wisdom that he sank his own name and personality and wrote in the name of his church, which he had been able to carry with him. Had he been less self-effacing, we would know more about him. We infer that the spiritual unity and strength of the Roman church must have been due in no small measure to his leadership.

His name suggests that his family had some connexion with the family of the consul Clemens and his wife Domitilla, and consequently with the imperial family. This does not necessarily imply blood-relationship. It could mean for instance that he belonged to a family of Jewish origin which was associated with the family of Flavius Clemens in the dependent position of clients. His attitude to the new imperial government is friendly and respectful, and he follows the traditional Jewish and apostolic teaching in requiring submission to the emperors on the grounds that their authority comes from God. This is the main line of Judaeo-Christian theology, notwithstanding the apocalyptic pictures in which the imperial power is the incarnation of evil when it persecutes. At such times it is possessed by an evil spirit.

HERMAS THE PROPHET

As the ministry of Clement ends, the ministry of Hermas begins. Clement belonged to the apostolic period, when the church was still conscious of its family connexions with the synagogue and was under the influence of the synagogue tradition. Hermas belonged to a new generation. He was a well-known type; a slave of parts and character who had won his freedom, and we shall consider his autobiography in the next chapter. The Old Testament, which colours every page of Clement, left few marks on his. His New Testament allusions, such as they are, are accounted for by a knowledge of Mark and the sayings of Jesus, of Hebrews, James, I Corinthians, Ephesians and possibly I Peter. His style and manner is more in line with that of the recent apocalypses, Ezra, and Baruch, and the oracles of the Sibyl. He was familiar with many current Jewish ideas, but they reached him in an acutely Hellenized form which was akin to apocalypse and gnosis. When he first stood up in the ecclesia before the elders and claimed to have received a revelation from heaven, he said that it came to him through an aged woman whom he took to be the Sibyl. He did not correct this opinion for twelve months.

This lady of vision had given him the revelation in the form of a written scroll which he copied out faithfully letter by letter, not even pausing to distinguish the words or meaning as he did this manual

25. THE COLOSSEUM

26. (i) THE CHAIR OF MOSES

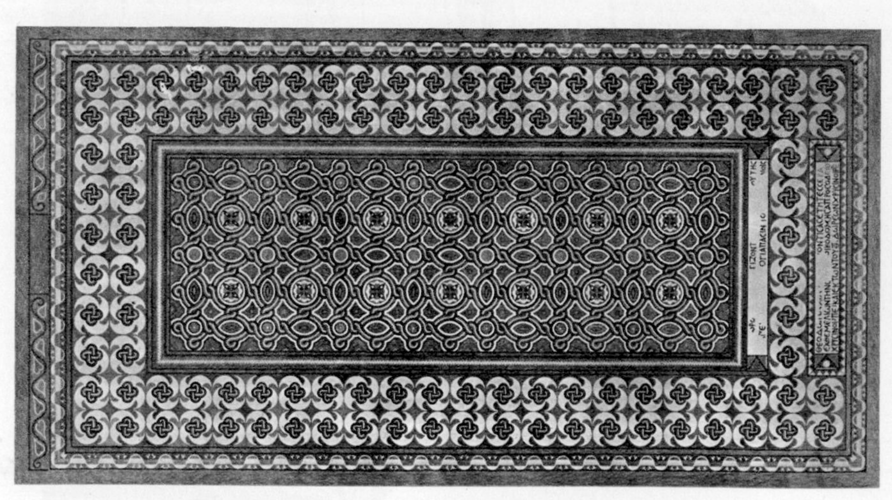

26. (ii) MOSAIC ON A SYNAGOGUE FLOOR

work; for in ancient writing there were no spaces between the words. When he had finished, the heavenly original vanished from his hands. It was a case of automatic writing; his conscious mind knew nothing as yet of what he was writing. He read this document in the ecclesia 'with the elders', who were very severely criticized in an appendix to it for their lives of luxury, their unconcern for the poor, their divisions and their personal ambitions. It was not meant only for Rome; it was for 'all the elect'. He was commanded to make two more copies of it, one for Clement, who was to send it to the 'outside cities', since that was his business, and one for a church official named Grapte, whose duty it was to admonish the widows and orphans. We find ourselves on the same ground as in the Epistle of Clement. The church authorizes publication, since the concurrence of the elders seems to be necessary; but it is Clement who has further copies made and sent to other churches.

THE NEW REPENTANCE

The document produced by Hermas in this dramatic manner was nothing less than a new revelation for the Christian church as a whole, on a question of policy which had become acute as a result of persecution. What was to be done with the apostates who had denied their Lord and now wished to be restored to communion? The author of Hebrews had stated that there was no way back into the fellowship for those who had departed from it; and he seems to have been thinking of those who relapsed into paganism, either by denial in persecution or by a return to pagan social life. He compares them with Esau, who sold his birthright and found no place of repentance though he sought for it with tears. It would appear that the church of the second generation was threatened by something very like a moral collapse, a state of affairs which had begun to show itself as early as the Pastoral Epistles. The strange teachers were feared more for their lax morals than their peculiar doctrines. Hence the emphasis on church order and Christian ethics which we find in the Pastorals and Clement. Equally necessary now was the provision of a 'place of repentance' or mode of absolution for erring church members who were clamouring for restoration.

Now Clement had urged the rebels in Corinth to repent, and had assured them of forgiveness if they did so. He had affirmed with a solemn oath, invoking the name of the Trinity, that penitents could be enrolled among the number of the saved; and similar affirmations are to be found in Hermas. But Hermas provided a procedure. His heavenly document was to be read aloud, and the penitents were to accept it in faith. It was in effect a prophetic supplement to the gospel. It is important to make no mistake about it. It did not announce that everybody was entitled to one repentance, though Hermas came very near to saying this at a later date. It said that there was repentance for the saints who had sinned *before the 'appointed day'*; the day perhaps on which this revelation had been received, or the day on which it was read in the Roman ecclesia, or the day on which the sinner happened to hear it. Those who had denied their Lord are specially mentioned in it; but those who deny in future will not be eligible for pardon. The indulgence did not apply to future sins of future believers; it was only for former sins committed before the 'appointed day'—a phrase which was borrowed from Hebrews itself. (See the fourth 'Commandment' of Hermas in addition to the second Vision.)

The effect of the Hermadic revelation, therefore, was to support the doctrine of no repentance after baptism which was maintained by a number of Roman teachers. Once the existing apostates and backsliders had been restored, the perfectionist ideal of the author of Hebrews could become the directing principle of church administration. Such therefore was the policy adopted by the Roman church, and communicated by it to the rest of the Christian world for their consideration. The two Roman books were received along with the New Testament literature without any great sense of difference; they were read in churches; they were often included in the New Testament when the New Testament began to be formed.

THE JUDAEO-CHRISTIAN TRADITION

Out of sheer necessity the literature of this kind was bound to emphasize the importance of ethics, repentance, the good life and church order. It could not help bringing to the front the 'Jewish' element which was taken for granted in the old apostolic tradition. In comparison with this the gospel of grace and power, as we see it in the Pauline literature, seems to be very much reduced. But this is an optical illusion, due to the fact that these books are supplementary treatises, handling the emergent problems of their time. They come as postscripts or appendices to the gospel and the epistolary literature, a knowledge of which is taken for granted; they confine themselves to their proper subjects. 'We have written to you', Clement says, 'concerning those matters which pertain to religious worship, and are most profitable for a virtuous life'; he lists faith, repentance, unfeigned love, self-control, soberness of mind and patience or endurance among these topics. It is a treatise on moral theology in its relation to church order or liturgy.

Under the conditions of the time, when the first enthusiasm had passed and ordinary human defects had appeared in the fabric of the church, attention to these grave problems was required. It was necessary to maintain some sort of spiritual discipline in order to preserve the unity of the church and also to deal with lapsed members who desired to return to the fold. On the one hand was the high perfectionist doctrine—that the church was a communion of saints and there was no room in it for the ex-Christian who had sinned against Christ; on the other was the spirit of the gospel itself with its message of mercy and forgiveness. It is interesting to see that it was the Roman church which found a way of building up church order and discipline, and yet leaving a place of forgiveness for the penitent. Hermas found the appropriate mystical language for this kind of work in the imagery of town-building.

Actually the beauty of the gospel is well expressed by Clement in his own style and manner; not only by his emphasis on love, patience, mercy and forgiveness, but also by the way in which he places the figure of Christ, as Son of God and high priest of our oblations, against the background of the supreme majesty and glory of God Almighty as it is given in Hebrew liturgy. He has no theological theory about the person of Christ; he expresses his faith, like the author of Hebrews, in terms of liturgical vision and in words borrowed from the Old Testament prophets and psalmists. The charm of the Roman church at this period may almost be said to be its immaturity. It was still waiting to receive the fullness of the apostolic gospel as it had been more fully interpreted in Antioch and Ephesus. It had made no attempt to explain itself as a new religion distinct from that of the Jews. The gospel had been received from the apostles as the central glory of the old Hebrew religion, and no change had been made in this historical situation. The concept of Law had receded into the background, of course, and the legal system was now no more than a type or shadow of the gospel truth. Faith in God through Christ had taken the place of works, as Clement knew; but the continuity of feeling with Judaism was perfect. Clement draws on the treasures of the Hebrew tradition without reserve. The patriarchs, prophets and priests of Israelite history are the saints, heroes and progenitors of the Christian church. The church has taken possession of them through Christ.

Neither Clement nor Hermas mentions the Jews. They are neither pro-Jewish nor anti-Jewish. This silence of theirs is in marked contrast to the anti-Jewish feeling which we can find in the contemporary traditions of Antioch and Ephesus. It could be explained if relations in Rome were a little more friendly,[1] if the synagogue had not yet accepted the new Rabbinic standards, if the ecclesia had not yet parted company with the synagogue in all respects, and if they had recently shared a persecution together in virtue of a common inheritance. At any rate the Christianity of Clement appears without any apology whatever as a form of the Jewish religion, and there is no evidence of hostility to Judaism proper. He does not refer to it.

NATURE AND LITURGY

There is a special theological note which is found in Clement, to which attention should be drawn, since it is also found in Hermas. It is the vision or sentiment about God which comes from the contemplation of nature; 'I was walking towards Cumae', Hermas says, 'and glorifying the creations of God, how honourable and powerful they are, and as I walked, I passed into a trance.' It is found in the Psalms and in the Gospels; it permeates the Hebrew liturgy; it is magnificently expressed in the Song of the Three Children, from the longer version of Daniel which Clement refers to in his forty-fifth chapter. But there are touches of it in the Greek poets and philosophers, in Plutarch for instance, and in an anonymous treatise mistakenly attributed to Aristotle. Its apologetic possibilities had been cultivated by those Jewish intellectuals who ventured to philosophize. It is voiced by the Sibyl. A train of argument along these lines is to be found in the Acts, in the speeches of St Paul at Lystra and at Athens. It is the opening phase in Christian apologetics, the presentation of Hebrew monotheism to the pagan world.

[1] The neutrality of Josephus deserves to be considered in this connexion.

Clement does not by any means equate the God of Hebrew revelation with the God of Greek philosophy. What he does do is to make us aware of a form of worship of the Hebrew God according to the rites of the Hellenistic synagogue, but adapted in some degree to the Greek intellectual climate. He invites his hearers to contemplate the Father and creator of the universe and to cleave to his excellent and magnificent gifts in peace.

Let us consider how free he is from anger with regard to his whole creation.
The heavens, which are set in motion by his government, are subordinate to him in peace.
Day and night pursue the course that is appointed by him, in no way hindering one another.
Sun and moon and the dances of the stars roll along their appointed courses....
Earth that brings multitudes to birth according to his will, in their proper seasons, makes food to spring up both for beasts and for men.
The trackless regions of the abyss... the mass of the unmeasurable sea... the ocean uncrossed by man, and the worlds that lie beyond it... the seasons of spring and summer and autumn and winter... the stations of the winds... the ever-flowing fountains... the smallest of living creatures, making their conventions in peace and unity of mind.
All these things the great Demiurge and Master of the universe commanded to live in peace and unity of mind; doing good in every way, and especially to us, who have fled for refuge to his mercies, through our Lord Jesus Christ, to whom be glory and majesty for ever and ever. Amen.

(I Clement xix, xx.)

The Greek word demiurge was an established word in the Judaeo-Christian tradition; it means workman or craftsman or technician; the gnostic sects who rejected Jewish liturgy and apocalypse would treat it with scorn. It belongs to the poetic or mythopoeic tradition, which is older than Christianity. In another place Clement reproduces very exactly a feature of the Sabbath service called the *Kedūshah* which is reproduced more freely in the Revelation.

Let us be subordinate to his will. Let us consider the whole multitude of his angels, how they stand by to minister to his will; for the Scripture saith,

Ten thousand times ten thousand stood by him,
And thousands of thousands ministered unto him: (Daniel vii. 10.)
And they cried Holy, Holy, Holy, Lord of Sabaoth:
Full is all creation of thy glory: (Isaiah vi. 3.)

And let us too, in unity of mind, gather in one place, and cry out earnestly to him as from one mouth.... (I Clement xxxiv.)

Clement continues his Epistle along liturgical lines of thought and concludes with a series of formal prayers which we may assume to represent the custom of the Roman church. Many of their phrases are still to be found in the synagogue liturgy.

THE LIVING GOD

It would appear, therefore, that the Roman church, like the Antiochene, had achieved a measure of order and harmony in its liturgical traditions and in the ministerial and fraternal relations of its members; Clement called it the canon of subordination.

The church in this generation found that it had a new task which had not seriously confronted the apostles. It was the indoctrination of the Gentile converts into the Hebrew faith in a living God, who was not only the ground of all being (as the philosophers say), but also the supreme factor in human history, and the salvation of the believing soul. It was useless and confusing to impose the Pauline gospel of the Saviour upon a substratum of polytheism which had not been purified, educated and disciplined in Jewish monotheism; indeed, this was the combination which produced the gnostic heresies. The church was actually forced to provide courses in elementary Judaism, and so lay the foundation of faith in the living God.

One way of doing this was to present him to the imagination in the thunders of apocalypse, but Clement does not advise this method; he defends it, but he does not fall back upon it. He has recourse to the method by which Christian people do actually form their idea of God as Lord of creation and Saviour of the lost; it is the way of worship.

'This is the way', he says, 'by which we found the saving power of Jesus Christ, the high priest of our oblations and the patron and support of our weakness; it is through him that we gaze into the height of the heavens.' Clement thinks of prayer and worship and devotion as a kind of vision; and it is to this vision of God and of his Son and of his saints and angels that he so confidently appeals. This literary formulation of the fundamental liturgical tradition explains the widespread appeal of this weighty Epistle and the universal respect in which it was held.

CHAPTER 21

HERMAS AND HIS ANGEL

The literary traditions, *p.* 391. The date of Hermas, *p.* 392. Inspiration and vision, *p.* 393. Hermas and Rhoda, *p.* 394. The elder lady, *p.* 396. The Italian Sibyl, *p.* 396. Hermas the prophet, *p.* 397. The family of Hermas, *p.* 398. The vision of the tower, *p.* 399. The gnosis of Hermas, *p.* 401. The appearance of the Shepherd, *p.* 403. The commandments (*Mandata*), *p.* 404. The moral theology of Hermas, *p.* 405. The parables (*Similitudines*), *p.* 406. The dedication of the tower, *p.* 407. Hermas as literature, *p.* 408.

THE LITERARY TRADITIONS

As we come to the close of the second apostolic generation we cannot help being impressed by its vigorous and creative character and by the variety in the types of Christianity which it develops. The task of the third generation will be to blend these various apostolic types into the harmony which is known as catholicism. We know of four Gospels, for instance, each of which represents a local apostolic tradition; what we do not know is how they came to be combined in one book, and received by the catholic church as *The Gospel*; but the creative phase of apostolic Christianity is not complete until this is done. And this, in its turn, is part of the larger process in which the various apostolic traditions were combined into a catholic or universal pattern.

Among these traditions were the liturgy, the creeds, the sacraments, the ministries, and so forth; but none was more important than the making of the New Testament.

When the outline and shape of the New Testament become visible in the second century, it is in some respects larger than we would expect; for it carries Clement and Hermas with it. It was not a question of including them in it; it was a question of detaching them from it. They circulated from the first with the rest of the church literature, to which Syria contributed Matthew, Asia the Johannine writings, and Greece (quite likely) the writings of Luke.

There was no New Testament at first. There was a church literature of an apostolic or ecclesiastical or prophetic character, made by inspired men to serve the needs of the time. It survived because it did serve the needs of the time, and therefore continued to be read in the churches. It included Clement and Hermas, and they lingered for a very long time on its confines. The fourth-century Bible known as Sinaiticus or Aleph (or S) contains Hermas; the fifth-century Bible known as Alexandrinus or A contains Clement.

THE DATE OF HERMAS

Strange to say, these books were excluded from the New Testament earlier in Rome than elsewhere, if we may judge by the *Muratorian Fragment*, which gives a list of New Testament books which were accepted for public reading about A.D. 180 to 200. It excludes Hermas by name, and gives a reason for doing so. Hermas composed *The Pastor* in our own times, it says, when his brother Pius was occupying the bishop's chair in the city of Rome. Now Pius did not become bishop until thirty-five or forty years after the death of Clement, and since the Visions of Hermas refer to Clement as living, the Muratorian author must be wrong;[1] or, more likely, the ministry of Hermas extended from about 100 to about 140, when a final edition of his writings may have been prepared by him for use in the Roman church.

Some scholars are inclined to date the whole book in the episcopate of Pius, but careful reading confirms the early date which is demanded by the reference to Clement. Its thought is simple and unreflective; its theology is untutored or non-existent; the church order which it reflects is undeveloped. The catholic form of the episcopate has not apparently been received. The writer appears to know nothing of Matthew or Luke or John. All his Gospel references can be explained as due to the influence of Mark, with a little help from the oral tradition. 'Ask and it shall be given you', and 'By their fruits ye shall know them', pretty well exhausts it.

Its reception with the books of the New Testament cannot be explained if it originated in the hundred-and-forties; Irenaeus and Clement of Alexandria would never have accepted it as Scripture if it had been so recent. It is easily explained if it first appeared in the same period as Matthew and John and the Revelation, when inspired creative literature was still being received; and if it went out as a prophetic message to the

[1] The suggestion that there was another Clement in Rome who also corresponded officially with other churches is not a happy one.

whole church under the sponsorship of Clement and with the sanction of the Roman elders. These data had to be given if the revelation which it contained was to be taken seriously; and that is why they were given. The *Visions*, therefore, went out to the Christian world in the nineties or early hundreds. The rest followed later.

A survey of the whole evidence suggests a ministry of Hermas during the first forty years of the second century, but whether the whole of this ministry was spent in Rome is another matter. He saw his first vision on the road to Cumae, in the part of Italy in which Naples is situated. He saw his second vision as he was walking along the Campanian Way, a name which is given to a road in this neighbourhood; but the commentators, for some reason, approve the idea that Hermas meant the road leading out of Rome along the right bank of the Tiber. The scene in his last 'parable', a most ambitious effort, is laid in Arcadia. Does this mean that Hermas visited Greece and received new inspiration there? His mission was addressed to the whole Christian world, and it is perfectly possible that he made extended journeys like other Christian prophets and teachers. We ought not to pin any early Christian teacher down to one locality; but the centre from which he worked was Rome, and it was Rome that received his first revelations and issued them to the world at large.

Hermas has no parables or imagery borrowed from sea-travel. His mental horizon is limited by his life on a farm or great estate and by his relations with the Roman church.

INSPIRATION AND VISION

The theologians and critics are baffled by the fact that the writers of the first Christian century expressed themselves in poetry and imaginative symbols. There is not one formal theologian among them. The parables, the epigrams of Jesus, the apocalypses, the mythology or gnosis of Paul, the visions of the Revelation, the mysticism of the Fourth Gospel, the eschatology of Matthew, the liturgy of Clement, wherever you look, it is all expressed in a succession of visual images and poetic diction which defy logical analysis. This is the language in which the first Christians talked about the great spiritual realities. Those who take it over-literally betray themselves into fearful absurdities. It is the language of inspiration.

Hermas 'saw' his visions in a condition of high emotional tension, which was created by a grievous personal humiliation. He wrote them as he saw them; but as he wrote them, he expanded them and conventionalized them. Somewhere on the borderland between conscious and unconscious cerebration, and in the realm where the divine and the human meet, we may place the thinking of Hermas. The visions which he saw were perfectly real to him; the heavenly scroll was present to the eyes of his mind; he copied it in a state of intense exaltation; and we are not astonished that when he had finished, it vanished from under his hand. The experiences which he communicated to the ecclesia were perfectly genuine; but we may assume that they had passed through the normal conscious literary processes before they reached their present form. The work of reflexion is to be seen in them, as well as the work of inspiration. Even so, the heavenly guidance was thought of as continuing through all the stages of composition. When Hermas had pen in hand, his 'angel' was never very far away.

HERMAS AND RHODA

Hermas is the first pagan convert who comes clearly into view, and his autobiography is valuable as a case-history. He had been a slave, born of slave parents or sold as a slave in infancy. He does not say that he was a foundling; the fact that his brother was known seems to prove the contrary. He had received a good education. Promising slave-boys were trained in medicine, literature, art, science, business or other vocations. His older contemporary, the philosopher Epictetus, was a slave from Phrygia; Phaedrus, the collector of Aesop's Fables, was a slave from Macedonia. Men of his class often obtained their freedom and rose to positions of wealth and influence, much to the disgust of Romans of the old school, such as Tacitus. Hermas rose to be the principal literary figure in the Christian world, and his brother Pius became the ninth bishop of Rome.

Hermas was sold by the man who brought him up to a lady named Rhoda, and his various interests and special knowledge suggest that he managed her estate. Many of his illustrations are taken from masonry, farming and technical processes. He gained his freedom and made money for himself in business. He married and had children. He met Rhoda again, he says, when she was bathing in the Tiber; or was he assisting at her baptism? He gave her his hand to help her out of the water, and a thought ascended in his heart, 'Happy were I, if I had such a wife, both for her beauty and her character!' This, and nothing more, he assures us, was his thought. He loved her as a sister, and revered her as an aunt; or perhaps the word should be translated goddess; but when she died, his sensitive imagination magnified the passing thought into a deadly sin. It preyed upon him.

How Rhoda died, we are not told, but possibly as a martyr in the persecution of Domitian; and Hermas saw her once again in a dream.

It was thus that Hermas saw her. A spirit took him and led him away through pathless country, where no man could travel. It is an opening like that of the first canto of Dante's *Inferno*.[1] The place was precipitous and broken off by the waters. He passed through the river and came to a level plain, where he went down on his knees and began to pray to the Lord and confess his sins. Then the heaven was opened, and he saw the woman whom he had desired, who greeted him by saying, 'Hermas, rejoice', or 'Hail, Hermas', as this common Greek salutation is generally translated.

'What are you doing here, my lady?' Hermas asked.

'I was taken up', she said, 'to convict you of your sin before the Lord.'

'Are you my accuser?' he asked in consternation.

She smiled as she answered him. 'The desire of evil ascended upon your heart. Surely you agree that it is a bad thing if an evil desire ascends upon the heart of a righteous man?'

Moral collapse followed this painful speech. 'I was overcome with terror and grief', he says. 'If this sin is entered against my account, I said to myself, how can I be saved?'

The moral theology of Hermas was worked out in fear and trembling in his own unduly sensitive conscience before it came to be worked out further in his domestic life and in the forum of the church.

[1] It has echoes from the first lection in the Gospel of Mark: the river, the desert, the opened skies, the spirit coming upon him. For Hermas, however, the desert is trackless; 'anodia'; like Dante, he cannot find the way.

THE ELDER LADY

The figure of Rhoda now fades out of his dream, and he sees a 'presbyteress' or venerable lady, in shining garments, seated on a great white throne, with a book in her hand.

'Why so downcast, Hermas', she asks, 'the patient and serene and ever-smiling?'

He tells her his story, and she agrees that such a thought must bring sin for the man who is holy and proven, and especially for Hermas the austere, who abstained from every evil desire and was full of all simplicity and great innocence. But this was not the real cause of God's anger; it was on account of his softness of heart in failing to discipline his children and so leaving them to spiritual ruin. God was full of tenderness and mercy, however, and would establish him in his former glory; but he was not to be so easy-going in the future; he must be fearless and strong, and admonish his family with the daily word of righteousness. From which we learn that there had been a family crisis.

THE ITALIAN SIBYL

The *presbutera* or 'elderess' was the Sibyl, or so Hermas thought. There was an Italian Sibyl, and in such a place Aeneas, the hero of Virgil's great poem, had found her in her cave among dense woods and broken rocks. She was his guide to the underworld and the abode of the dead. It was she who gave him the famous warning: *Facilis descensus Averno.*

> Easy is the going down to hell;
> The gates are ever open night and day;
> But to retrace the steps and gain the upper air,
> This is labour, this is toil. (Virgil, Aeneid VI.)

Virgil makes use of Sibylline literature and Orphic lore, not only in his Sixth Aeneid, but in his famous Fourth Eclogue.

> The last era of Cumaean song has come;
> The great order of the ages begins once more.
> Now the Virgin returns, and Saturn's kingdoms come:
> A new-born child descends from highest heaven.
> (Virgil, Eclogue IV.)

He draws on a Jewish Sibyl here, or even on the prophet Isaiah; and his Sibylline song is connected with Cumae, like the vision of Hermas.

Cumae, near Naples, was the legendary abode of the Italian Sibyl, and a temple existed there, where prophecies were given out. Cumae and Naples were ancient Greek colonies, so that the Sibyl of Cumaean legend was of Greek origin. She wrote her prophecies on leaves, which the wind soon dispersed. Rome itself had once possessed three 'Sibylline Books', which foretold its history and were consulted when disaster threatened the city; they had been purchased by the fifth king, Tarquinius Priscus, from a mysterious old woman. The Sibyl of Hermas resembles this old woman, since she appears with a mysterious scroll, from which she reads to him. Since her first words were terrible and unbearable, it is possible that they foretold the doom of the city, but Hermas professes that he could not even remember them. Her last words were agreeable and gentle.

Behold the God of hosts,
Who by his invisible power and great understanding created the world,
And by his glorious counsel adorned his creation with beauty...
Behold he moveth the heavens and the mountains and the hills and the seas;
And all shall be made level for the elect of God. (Isaiah xl. 4.)
(Hermas, Visions, I, III, IV.)

This Sibylline opening would serve to commend the *Visions* of Hermas to a Roman audience; but it was borne in upon him later that he had made a mistake.

We are given an exquisitely clear picture of this kindly and conscientious young man, who had so much charm but was rather too suggestible and imaginative and lacked the quality of decision. The elder lady read to him from her scroll, which terrified him with its vision of the judgement to come, and then comforted him with its promise of glory and joy for the righteous. When she had finished, four angelic beings appeared and carried her away towards the east. As she went she said, 'Hermas, be strong.'

HERMAS THE PROPHET

It was a year later, and at the same season of the year, that he had another vision, or rather a protracted series of visions lasting for three weeks. He had made but little progress in his domestic life. His seed had blasphemed against the Lord and had betrayed their parents; that is to say, his children had utterly failed him under the stress of persecution. Hermas himself had not denied the living God, and that had been his salvation, along with his simplicity and great continence. It would seem that his property had been confiscated or plundered; for, whereas he had been wealthy, he was now a poor man. Others had suffered more severely than he; they had endured whips, prisons, great afflictions, crosses, and wild beasts, for the sake of the Name; a passage which is forgotten by those scholars who think there was no noticeable persecution under Domitian.

It was a time of trial for the church as well as for Hermas, and the crisis was not over, for there was the usual aftermath of spiritual and moral problems. And it was at this point that he saw the elder lady again, and she handed him the scroll which assured all the saints who had sinned up to this day of forgiveness and restoration. He was to read it in the ecclesia with the elders and to tell the rulers of the church that they must direct their paths in righteousness. Hermas, the weak brother, had made good his glory by standing firm in persecution, and had been chosen to declare the will of God to the Saints. He was entrusted with a special message for one who had denied during the persecution, a rival prophet perhaps.

'Say unto Maximus, Behold affliction cometh if it seem good to thee to deny again; the Lord is near unto them that turn, as it is written in *Eldad and Modat* who prophesied in the wilderness.'

We know nothing of the apostate Maximus, or of the book of *Eldad and Modat*, which is the only Scripture that Hermas ever quotes by name; but these passages in his writings help us to visualize him in his important work as a prophetic teacher in the Roman church. The ex-slave had won his way to a place of honour in the counsels of the church and sat among the elders, some of whom, we do not doubt, belonged to noble Roman families.

THE FAMILY OF HERMAS

It seems incongruous to some scholars to find that the family affairs of the prophet should occupy so large a place in the document from heaven; but this is a social fact of great importance. Hermas did not find his way to heaven, apart from his wife and family, by some path of pure philosophy or pure mysticism. His emotional tension at this time was due to his mortification over the behaviour of his children, and his fear that they could not be forgiven or restored; it was for them in the first place that the message of forgiveness was required. It was incumbent, too, upon an elder or ruler in the church to have his family under control, which had not been the case with Hermas, as the ecclesia very well knew. The lapse from grace of his children reflected on his own standing in spiritual things. The social order of the day did not very readily consider individuals apart from the domestic or tribal group to which they belonged; the family was the legal, social and sacred unit with which it dealt.

Primitive Christianity constantly dedicated whole families to God in baptism. In the old Hebrew tradition the Law constantly addressed itself to a man and his family; 'thou and thy house' we read, or 'I and my house'. Hermas imitates this language when he gives directions about fast-days.

The families of the old prophets had been regarded as signs and patterns exemplifying God's dealings with Israel.[1] Hermas was in good company, therefore, in bringing his own family rather prominently into the scope of his prophetic activity. His sense of domestic solidarity was so strong in fact that he was prepared to suffer on account of their sins. When a sudden and severe affliction came upon him, an illness of some sort perhaps, his angel convinced him that he must accept it as a punishment for the sins of his children. How could they be afflicted unless he was afflicted?

It is the converse of the teaching of the Second Commandment; the sins of the children are visited upon the father.

THE VISION OF THE TOWER

Fifteen days after he had received his second revelation, he saw his famous vision of the building of the tower. He had been informed now that the elder lady of his visions was the church, 'which was created first of all things...for this reason she is very old, and for her sake the world was created'. In more modern language, the appearance of the Christian religion was the goal towards which creation and history had been moving; it had always existed in the eternal purposes of God. This was the regular Christian teaching, and was based on Hebrew thinking about Israel; and Israel appears as a venerable woman in

[1] See Isaiah viii. 18 and Hosea i. 2.

Jewish apocalypses which Hermas probably knew. In the vision of Hermas the familiar apocalyptic figure represents the church considered as a divine predestined factor in history and revelation and the final phase of all creation; the tower represents the church as it is actually being built on the earth, so realizing the divine purpose. There were four layers of stones in its foundations, and these represented four stages through which it had passed, or four classes of Christians who had emerged into notice: first, the apostles, bishops, teachers and deacons; secondly, the martyrs who had suffered for the Name of the Lord; thirdly, the upright men who observed the commandments of the Lord; and fourthly, the young, by which he means the new converts or hearers. So short has been the history of the church so far that this comprises it all; in his later rewriting of this vision he extends its past history back to Adam.

The building of the tower was very nearly complete, and there was little time left in which to take advantage of the preaching of repentance; those lapsed Christians who did repent would be built into an inferior part of it; and only then, after they had been tormented and had fulfilled the days of their sins. They are represented by stones which have been taken out of the tower, or are lying near the tower, or are rolling away from the tower.

This period of visionary experience continued until the twentieth day. In his fourth vision, he is again walking along the Campanian Way when he sees a fearful monster, with a body like a whale and a head like an urn, which is capable of destroying whole cities. It was the 'aeon', the age in which men were then living, in its aspect as persecuting world-power. He walked on in perfect faith, and the creature lay down and protruded his tongue. It reminds us of the story of the virgin martyr Thecla and the lion which licked her feet.

And now he sees advancing towards him a figure in white, dressed like a bride, who says 'Hermas, rejoice!' like the sainted Rhoda of his first vision; but this charming figure is not Rhoda, who has been forgotten now; she is the church, who has been renewed and rejuvenated during the twenty days of prayer, fasting, abstinence and revelation.[1] She explains certain symbolic features about the beast; but at this point the vision fades out; its nuptial or festal climax is not given.

[1] In Ezra and Baruch we have a three-week period of fasting in midsummer, in response to which visions and revelations are given: see chapter 18.

27. A ROMAN HOUSE

28. CATACOMB PAINTINGS

THE GNOSIS OF HERMAS

The theology of Hermas is based on a Hellenized Hebrew monotheism, but it has parted somewhat from its Old Testament moorings, and has taken aboard a certain amount of material from the dreamland of gnosis or apocalypse. It is not gnosticism, but it shows how a Syro-Italian gnosticism might have developed. The symbols or images which appear in the Judaeo-Christian imaginative writings of the period were quite limited in number. Many of the images used by Hermas were also used in the Revelation of St John, and yet careful investigation has not succeeded in establishing any direct literary connexion. The woman adorned like a bride, the tower or city which is being built and the beast which embodies the persecuting 'aeon', were not invented by either writer. They were familiar concepts in the poetic tradition quite apart from the gospel. Hermas affiliates the Marcan Gospel to a Judaism of this kind.

In these circles Jewish monotheism was interpreted by a number of symbolic elaborations, which had a respectable ancestry and sometimes expressed quite profound thoughts. The supreme deity was not thought of apart from the 'angels' or 'spirits' which emanated from his being or were created to serve him day and night without ceasing. Hermas has no exact definition of a spirit or angel; almost any impulse which comes to him was personified in this way.

Jewish mysticism of this sort knew of two principal Spirits of God which were prior in existence to all creation, one of them being personified as a male and the other as a female. In Egypt they were the Word of God and the Wisdom of God. Hermas calls them the Son of God and the Holy Spirit. He even calls the Holy Spirit a Son of God, for his nomenclature is disturbingly fluid. The Son of God is also called the Glorious Angel; for angels are normally male, and spirits female.

Hermas is enchanted with female spirits, and especially with the lady of his vision, who is said to be the Holy Spirit as well as the church. She guides the work of church-building, which is the final stage in the work of creation. She directs the six male angels who bring the stones and place them in the tower with the assistance of seven virgins; but these angels have a leader of their own who will appear in due course, making up the number seven (and finishing the seven days of creation?). His name is Michael; but he is generally called the Glorious

Angel. This is one of the two forms in which Christ appears in this book; but the name of Jesus and the title of Christ are never used.

This is similar to the pattern that we found in the myth of Simon Magus, to which Hermas may be providing an antidote; the divine spirit who guides the seven creator angels in their work. The nuptial element is suppressed, but the female spirit appears in the last vision adorned as a bride, and doubtless the implication is that the bridegroom will appear and be united with her. The Jewish and Christian literature of our period is full of this symbolism in which the spirit is a bride, and the bride is a city or a temple or a tower or the church. The Sibylline oracles, the Jewish apocalypses, and the Christian chiliasts like Papias, were concerned with the literal rebuilding of Jerusalem and its Temple; Ephesians, Revelation, Hermas and Barnabas refer these ideas mystically to the church as the bride of Christ. This idea underlies Hermas, though it is not expressed in so many words. As the lady of his vision waits for her lord to come and visit her tower, with which she identifies herself, the nuptial symbolism is not far off; she is waiting for a husband.

Setting on one side the possibility that the visions have been expurgated, it has to be remarked that Hermas does not combine his more difficult symbols very well; they coalesce like the symbols in dreams, one of them following another without logical sequence. His seven virgins are the elder lady over again; they are the Christian graces or gifts of the Holy Spirit, with which the Christian must clothe himself as he enters the tower. Their names are Faith, Temperance, Simplicity, Understanding, Innocence, Holiness, and Love. The meaning is clear enough when he explains it; the difficulty is that he crowds too many lessons into his more complicated efforts.

It is useless therefore to look for any gnostic or pseudo-theological scheme, which combined these concepts into a Christian pantheon. The day had not come for theology. They are such stuff as dreams are made on, and each vision or parable must stand on its own feet if it can. The figures fade into one another and re-form ranks. Hermas ought to be compared to Spenser or John Bunyan rather than to Cerinthus or Valentine; but we can see how it was that when the Gnostics arrived in Rome, and Valentine established his school there, his fantasies about the heavenly Wisdom cannot have looked too strange to the Roman Christians, whose minds had been formed on the scriptures of Hermas. The idea of a queen of heaven was not unfamiliar to them.

THE APPEARANCE OF THE SHEPHERD

As the fourth vision fades out, we find ourselves at the beginning of a totally new book, the *Pastor* or *Shepherd*, which consists of 'Commandments' and 'Parables' which were written down under the guidance of a male spirit. Hermas is no longer a mere recipient of heavenly messages or allegorical visions; his mind becomes more active, and he is the partner of the shepherd-spirit in the rebuilding and renewing of the church.

When this new book of Hermas was combined with the earlier collection of 'Visions', it lost its first paragraph or paragraphs, and what was left of its introduction was numbered as the fifth vision. We gather, however, that the 'Glorious Angel' had appeared, and had handed Hermas over to the care of a lesser angel, who was glorious of face, shepherd-like in appearance, clad in a white skin, with a wallet over his shoulder and a staff in his hand. This angel is with him in his house; he is about his bed and spies out all his ways. He is the 'Pastor' from whom this new book receives its name; but the word was soon extended to cover all his works, the *Visions*, the *Commandments*, and the *Parables*. The complete text exists only in the Latin translation, and consequently is often quoted by its Latin name, the *Pastor*, the three subdivisions appearing as *Visiones*, *Mandata*, and *Similitudines*.

This pastor and teacher is the inward monitor who teaches and illuminates the Christian mind; he is indeed, in some sense, the Christus himself; but Hermas never says that. He is a spiritual influence from the Christus; the Christus so far as he speaks in the heart of Hermas; but not as it were the Christus as he is in himself.

Relatively to the Pastor, Hermas occupies the position of a penitent. He is put back to the beginning of his Christian life. He must learn the commandments over again. He must even write them out, so that he can have them by him in a handy form, and be able to read and keep them. Does some dissatisfaction with oral methods appear here? It is perhaps the technique which Hermas began to use with his pupils, for every now and then he turns from his inner colloquy with the Pastor and addresses a class. At any rate we have here our only picture of an important stage in the evolution of the teaching technique, the making of a teacher's transcript of the oral tradition, a development which had to be defended on the authority of a revelation from heaven. At the end of the century Clement of Alexandria was still obliged to defend the writing down of the oral tradition, and did so by quoting this passage from Hermas (*Stromateis*, I, 1).

THE COMMANDMENTS (*MANDATA*)

The first commandment of Hermas was to believe in God, and to fear him, and to practise abstinence or self-control (*enkrateia*), a word which would acquire undertones of rigorism and asceticism and renunciation. His second was to be simple-hearted and innocent, like little children. His third was to love truth, an ideal which he finds strangely difficult. His fourth was to guard purity or consecration, a word which was already being associated with celibacy. These words came out of the Judaeo-Christian catechisms; they were words of authority in the church and part of the fabric of the tradition. They had been taken over from the synagogue and christianized in the first apostolic generation. We find material of this sort in the Epistles, especially in the Epistle of St James, which Hermas makes use of at this point. Some of it had been worked up into a document called *The Two Ways* which is used in the *Didache* and *Barnabas*.

Hermas expatiates on these commandments. He adds explanations and appendices. He answers questions. His chapters came very slowly into their present form, and we can trace certain developments in his teaching as he goes on. These must be reserved for a later chapter.

There is nothing legalistic about his presentation of these commandments. He sees his Christian virtues as dispositions of the soul, and calls them *pneumata* or spirits, like the author of the old Jewish treatise called the *Testaments of the Twelve Patriarchs*, which was well known in the church. Simplicity or sincerity, for instance, is a motion or disposition in the heart. It is the soul itself, or a spirit in the soul, trusting happily in God. Over such the world, the flesh and the evil spirits have no power; but the evil spirits are also dispositions in the soul, sad, angry, gloomy, destructive forces. The most dangerous condition of all is called *di-psychia*, the wavering or divided soul, the fluctuating or uncertain frame of mind which is the victim of doubt or anxiety or fear and so cannot pray in happy confidence, but gives way eventually to melancholia or even mania. This condition resembles the concept of schizophrenia in modern psychology, while the 'single' or simple-hearted individual is the properly integrated happy personality.

It is a little fanciful for our taste, but the fundamental thought is perfectly clear; it is the indwelling of the Holy Spirit. If the heart is pure, the indwelling Spirit will be happy and gay and childlike; but if it is forced to dwell with dark and gloomy spirits, it will depart and intercede against that man.

Needless to say Hermas personifies these spirits. They are virgins who tend and preserve the Christian soul. The evil dispositions are dark women in black raiment, who lead the soul to madness and destruction. His moral theology is sharply dualistic; there are two ways to walk in; two desires or inclinations in the soul; and two loyalties, God and the devil.

THE MORAL THEOLOGY OF HERMAS

Hermas gives twelve commandments in all, and later on he increased the number of his virgins to correspond.

The spirituality of Hermas is strangely difficult to classify because it is concealed under highly elusive symbolic forms. He adopts the traditional Jewish forms of apocalypse and commandments and parables, all of which are used in the Gospels; but the external features of traditional Judaism have disappeared. What is left is a de-Judaized Judaism for Gentile enquirers. Like the *Didache*, and certain other Christian literature, it was written out of a refined Hellenistic Judaism which was attempting to capture the pagan world. A theism of this kind had taken form prior to the gospel among the pious Gentiles who had attached themselves to the synagogue. It was carried on into the second century, and appears in the apologists. Aristides sums it up under three heads; first, the pure worship of the One God; secondly, the commandments which were engraved in the heart; and thirdly, the hope and expectation of the resurrection of the dead and the life of the coming 'aeon'.

This spiritual and moral Judaism, as it appears in Hermas, has been infused with the Christian spirit and related to the Christian mysteries, but it is expressed in a language of allegory which tends to conceal its Jewish and Christian origins. It speaks of commandments, but not of Moses; of the church, but not of Jesus Christ; of apostles and teachers and bishops and deacons, but not of the gospel. It uses its language of allegory as a disguise; the elder woman and the shepherd and the virgins and the towerbuilding are intended to *conceal* the Christian mysteries; Christians would understand what was being referred to; others would not. But he speaks perfectly openly and without disguise about the need of repentance in the church, which was a new thought altogether; and the importance of the moral life of its members, which was sadly in need of renewal. This was his mission from the church to the church, to rebuild its moral life by repentance and righteousness. The supernatural visions provided the authority for this mission.

THE PARABLES (*SIMILITUDINES*)

In the *Parables* we see quite another side of Hermas. We see him as he moves about his country estate, or the country estate of some wealthy Christian who has received him into his household. We see him among his elms and vines; he watches the trees dropping their leaves as winter approaches; he wears a linen apron, and sets out willow slips to see if they will grow; he stores his wine and honey in earthen jars. He knows the country techniques. He understands the mysteries of tending vineyards and building towers. He has a mystical feeling about his work which has been quickened by his study of the gospel parables. He has his angel with him, his touch of insight or inspiration which reveals unexpected lessons. The change of the seasons is like the course of the world; men have their winter and summer like the trees, and time will show whether they are fruitful or barren. The willow-slips remind him of his pupils; some have promise of life and some have not, but all are worth trying a second time. The rows of earthen jars teach another lesson; some are full and some are empty; but empty you put them away, and empty you find them when you come again. Your honey is good honey, but a little gall mixed with it spoils the whole pot. The rabbis used similes exactly like this.

Hermas has the observant eye and the uncanny inspiration of the poet. His little sketches are full of life. His picture of the old man, a prey to many infirmities, who sits in a chair and thinks of nothing but death, and is completely rejuvenated when he gets an unexpected legacy, was surely drawn from life and made people smile when they heard it. Such is the effect of the heavenly message, Hermas says.

A character in whom Hermas delighted was that of the young slave who was left to fence the vineyard, and occupied his spare time in weeding it, though he had not been told to do that. This exercise of initiative and intelligence won him his liberty. Hermas could identify himself in his imagination with that slave, since he had been a slave, too, and had somehow won his liberty. In the parable he stands for the Son of God, who took the form of a servant, and cleansed our sins by much toil and the endurance of many labours; it is his only picture of the Jesus of the gospel message. He uses this parable to enforce other lessons too; too many of them.

The use of parables, which Hermas learned from the gospel itself, is a method which brings the majesty and glory of God into the most intimate contact with the smallest things of everyday life. The everyday quality of the writing of Hermas may at times seem a little flat and homely, but it brought the magic of the gospel into the lives of the simple people to whom he ministered, and enables us to see something of their problems.

THE DEDICATION OF THE TOWER

Towards the end Hermas allows his parables to grow too complex. The parable of the willow tree is an example. It overshadows plains and mountains, and Michael the Glorious Angel slashes off slips which he distributes; the character and destiny of each recipient is indicated by the condition of the slip when he returns it. It suggests some spring or autumn ritual like the 'Gardens of Adonis' in Syria, or the Feast of Tabernacles of the Jews. There are no less than twelve classes of recipients, and this number corresponds to the twelve patriarchs of *Testaments*, the twelve tribes of the 'dispersion' in James, the twelve commandments of Hermas himself, and so forth; it is the conventional number of the Israelite or Christian dispensation. It is weary reading, but we are enabled to see the various classes of persons with whom Hermas had to deal.

Last of all he rewrites his vision of the tower, which has now expanded out of all recognition. It is in the middle of the earth, a locality which he places in Arcadia. Its building has occupied the whole of recorded history. It has been visited by its Lord and very strictly tested. This is the persecution of Domitian, which now lies in the past. It is interesting to see that a persecution may be regarded as an advent of the Christ.

Hermas and the shepherd are hard at work reconditioning the

rejected stones, and building as many as possible back into the tower. The new stones are more carefully selected and dealt with than the old. They are carried in by twelve virgins who represent the Christian graces, and no stone can be accepted unless it is clothed in these. Among the new stones are several beautiful white ones which will be very suitable when their curves are cut off; these are wealthy converts who will be splendid acquisitions to the church when they have been parted from some of their wealth.

The twelve virgins are the joy of Hermas' heart. There is a species of dedication of the tower, which is now cleansed and renewed. He walks round it with the shepherd and the virgins; everything is swept and cleaned up. The shepherd leaves him and he keeps vigil with the virgins, who constrain him to stay with him and sleep in their midst. We have to go back to the Song of Songs which is Solomon's, to find a background for this delightful scene.[1] Nothing unseemly occurred, Hermas assures us. They supped all night on the words of the Lord. It is the same sentimental Hermas who assured us at the beginning of his book that his feelings for Rhoda were of the most innocent character.

In the tenth and last chapter of the *Parables* the Glorious Angel in person appears, and authorizes him to continue his ministry of teaching and reconciliation. 'And when he had spoken, he rose from the bed, took the shepherd and the virgins with him, and went his way; but he said that he would send back the shepherd and the virgins to my house.' These are the last words of the book.

HERMAS AS LITERATURE

We have it on the highest theological authority that Hermas is dull, pious, and stupid; but those who take the trouble to go along with him will be rewarded by the discovery of an innocent charm spiced with a little innocent vanity. His sense of humour sometimes fails, but he has the social gift and we see him at his work of personal counselling, as it is called today. He is a shrewd judge of persons and things. He weaves something of his own everyday life and business into the prophetic and didactic tradition of the church, and in consequence it comes to life.

[1] See Song of Songs i. 2–4, iii. 4 and v. 1–6; also Proverbs vii. 4 and viii. 17; and Wisdom viii. 2. References to virgins or 'daughters of Jerusalem' are common in the festal lyrics of the Hebrew prophets.

His simple moralizing narratives appealed to the church public of his day, and so no doubt did his earnest and kind and conscientious character. They provided pleasant and profitable Sunday reading for the churches for some centuries, and that is more than can be said for most pious literature. He was in touch with ordinary Christian life, as it was lived by the average church members. He gives a first-hand picture of the work of a prophet or teacher among all classes in the Roman church in the first quarter, or longer, of the first century.

It is the first piece of imaginative Christian literature in the European tradition. He is the harbinger of Dante and Milton.

CHAPTER 22

ORIENTAL CHRISTIANITY

Roman expansion eastward, *p.* 410. Elkhasai the prophet, A.D. 100, *p.* 411. The Ebionite heresy, *p.* 412. The legend of Clement, *p.* 414. The descent of the Christus, *p.* 415. The martyrdom of St Symeon, A.D. 105–7, *p.* 417. The episcopate in Jerusalem, *p.* 418. The episcopate in Alexandria, *p.* 420. The Gospel of the Hebrews, *p.* 422. The 'Gospel of the Truth', *p.* 423. The break with the Synagogue, *p.* 424. Rabbi Akiba, *p.* 426.

ROMAN EXPANSION EASTWARD

The year 100 saw the death of King Herod Agrippa II, the same who had heard St Paul preach in Caesarea forty years before, and had said, 'Do you expect to make a Christian of me so easily?' He ruled on both sides of the Lake of Galilee, where a few very aged people must still have remembered the preaching of Jesus of Nazareth. After his death his kingdom was absorbed into the Roman province of Syria, which included Damascus now, and was being extended eastward towards Palmyra. A Romano-Syrian Hellenism was coming into existence in these regions, based on the increasing trade between east and west.

The years 105 to 108 saw the annexation of the old kingdom of the Nabatean Arabs with its strong cities of Bostra (Bozrah) east of Jordan, and Petra south of the Dead Sea, which were important trading centres on the caravan route which led further south to the Gulf of Akabah, and so by sea to India. The other route to India and farther east passed through Palmyra, which was situated to the north of the great desert which separated the Roman and the Parthian dominions. The Parthian empire, whose capital was at Seleuceia in southern Mesopotamia, was Persian in character, and professed a form of Zoroastrianism which had absorbed some features of the old Babylonian religion; this mixed form of 'monotheism' was accepted in turn by the Syrian cities and principalities, and combined with their own cults to create a tolerant solar monotheism which assumed a Hellenistic form in the second century.

The suppression of the Jewish kingdom completed the severance with the past. The bulk of the Jewish population was now in northern Palestine. The religious authority was vested in the rabbinic sanhedrin under its patriarch Gamaliel II, whose headquarters were at Caesarea, the old residence of the Roman procurator. This sanhedrin had the power to make religious enactments which were binding in the synagogue. This circumstance was adverse to the cause of Jewish Christianity.

It was the fate of Jewish Christianity to be submerged in the deluge of sects which were especially prolific on the eastern side of the Jordan. The researches of Hegesippus, Africanus and Epiphanius give us a picture of small Nazarean communities which acknowledged the leadership of descendants of the Lord's family, but were unduly influenced by erratic teachers, such as the mythical Ebion and the legendary Elkhasai. There were several branches of the family of the Lord, these writers report. Symeon the successor of James the Just was still presiding over the church at Pella when the century opened; but grandsons of Jude were also presiding over churches, Hegesippus says.

ELKHASAI THE PROPHET, A.D. 100

We know little or nothing about the sects which are mentioned by Hegesippus, the Simonians, Cleobians, Dositheans, Goratheni and Masbothaeans; but it so happens that we have documentary evidence about Elkhasai, whose name means 'the hidden power': *hēl khāsai.* He was an oriental counterpart of the Roman Hermas; for he promulgated a doctrine of a new repentance, on the authority of a revelation from heaven which came to him in the third year of the Emperor Trajan, that is to say A.D. 100; a date which is given in the scriptures of the sect, which were brought to Rome about the year 220 and quoted by Hippolytus. Elkhasai, or perhaps some earlier visionary named Sobiai, had seen the Christus or Son of God, together with the Holy Spirit, descend from heaven, in male and female form respectively, both of them being about ninety-six miles high; an estimate which was confirmed by measuring a foot-print, which proved to be about fourteen miles long.

Elkhasai was thus able to announce that there would be another opportunity for repentance and a new baptism for lapsed Christians, which would wash away sins of even the grossest description. The sinner immersed himself in water, in the name of the Great God the Most High, and of his Son the Great King. He was to be wearing his clothes, and he was to invoke the seven witnesses; the heaven, the water, the holy spirits (or winds?), the angels of intercession, the oil, the salt and the earth. The same procedure would prove effective in the case of sickness or the bite of a mad dog. The ethical element was not absent, however, for there was a promise of good behaviour; 'I call the seven witnesses to witness that I will sin no more; I will not commit adultery, I will not steal, I will not defraud, I will not covet, I will not hate, I will not forswear myself; I will not take pleasure in any evil thing.' Seven commandments in all. The recitation of commandments at baptism was a good Hebrew custom, and is vouched for in the case of the church by Ignatius.

Holy immersions were practised by pious Jews as a means of release from sin or defilement. Evidence for frequent or daily ablutions of a holy character comes in from the Gospels, the Mishnah, the Sibyllines and various quarters. Hegesippus mentions a sect of 'daily-baptists', and it may be that his sect of 'Masbothaeans' practised similar rites; their name might be connected with a verb which means to wash, which is said to appear in the name of a later sect called the Sebuai, the baptizers;[1] and again in the case of the Mesopotamian Sabians who were recognized by Mohammed; and these sects are possibly represented by the modern Mandaeans.

The religious ferment in the parts of Syria east of the Jordan is a factor of great importance in the history of religion, and Elkhasai played an important role there. Origen knew something about him in the third century, and Epiphanius found that his books were treasured among the various Ebionite sects in the fourth century. The family of Elkhasai was still held in great reverence (like the families of Jesus and Mohammed), and two female descendants, Marthous and Marthana, were venerated as goddesses.[2]

THE EBIONITE HERESY

Elkhasai must be accepted as a serious theologian or prophet or religious founder, in spite of the fantastic character of his apocalyptic and liturgical style. He was coeval with John and Hermas, and his book was offered equally with theirs as an inspired contribution to the life of the church. It was a period when it was still natural to express one's

[1] So W. Brandt; but J. Morgenstern suggests a derivation from a word meaning 'seven', which he connects with the calendar; but it could be connected with the word for oath, and the oath mentions seven witnesses.

[2] The syllable 'marth' (Martha) is the feminine form of the word 'mara' which means lord: as in the Christian prayer 'maranatha'.

religious convictions in this imaginative or mythological style, and there was an accepted language of symbolism which was widely understood. There is more than one connecting link between Elkhasai and Hermas, for instance.

The type of Jewish-Christian heresy known as Ebionism, which began to take form at this time, inherited imaginative concepts of this kind. Indeed, Elkhasai is simply a rather fantastic example of Ebionism. He shares its peculiar christology. The Christus of Ebionism was a divine teacher who had appeared on earth many times, beginning with Adam the first man. He had also come as Moses and as Jesus; and perhaps his last appearance was in Elkhasai himself, who may not have been called the 'hidden power' for nothing. The idea of the recurring world-teacher is widespread in oriental religions, including some varieties of Mohammedanism.

The attitude of the Ebionites to the Law of Moses was also in line with the teaching of Elkhasai. They adhered to circumcision and the Sabbath, with some added superstitions, in the case of Elkhasai, about the moon and certain stars. They turned towards Jerusalem when they prayed, but they rejected the system of sacrifices, a point which had no practical consequences after the destruction of Jerusalem, since they had ceased to be offered. They regarded the fire of the altar as evil and the water of baptism as good. Their emphasis on water as a purifying element was developed in order to replace the sacrifices as a means of absolution and forgiveness. It may be that fire represented the evil power in the cosmos.

They were also ascetics. They refrained from 'animate food', flesh with the soul in it; and in this respect they followed the example of James the Just and John the Baptist; but they differed from the ascetic Essenes in requiring all their membership to marry. The Elkhasaites are said to have practised astrology and magic and the invocation of angelic powers. They predicted the future.

Here is the classical picture of the gnostic or heretical streak in Jewish Christianity. It was an ascetic Judaism, divorced from the Temple cultus though it reverenced Jerusalem, infused with ideas from further east, profoundly conscious of the power of evil in the cosmos, and prone to magic and superstition. It was not the only form of Ebionism. Later writers distinguish a more conservative Ebionism which was orthodox from the Jewish point of view, but regarded Christ as a 'mere man' who received the Holy Spirit at his baptism and so became the Messiah; this type appears to be mentioned in the writings of Justin Martyr and he treats it with sympathy.

At the end of the second century the word was applied indiscriminately, at least in the west, to all the surviving Jewish Christians, with the implication that they were less than orthodox. It is thought that it was once an honourable name. The word *ebion* is a Hebrew word meaning poor, and it is constantly used in the Psalms and other literature for the religious and devout. It occurs in this sense in the first benediction of the Sermon on the Mount. It is thought that it may be one of the names by which the primitive Jewish Christians called themselves or were called. If so, its origin and meaning were soon forgotten. By the time of Tertullian we find references to a heresiarch named 'Ebion' or 'Hebion', who was regarded as the founder of the heresy. Epiphanius is confident of his historical character, but it is most unlikely that he ever existed.

As time went on the word 'Nazarean' seems to have been appropriated by the formally orthodox Jewish Christians, who believed in the Virgin Birth and accepted the apostle Paul.

THE LEGEND OF CLEMENT

One of the sources for our knowledge of gnostic Ebionism is the legends which were incorporated into the *Books of Clement*, so called from their ostensible author, Clement of Rome, who was regarded as the secretary of St Peter. Their theme is the contest between Simon Peter and Simon Magus, which may originally have been a dramatization of a rivalry between a Jewish gnosis and a Samaritan gnosis; but the figure of Simon Magus has been so treated in successive revisions as to become a mask for St Paul and even for later Gentile heresy.

The association of Clement with Peter is part of the legend which makes Peter the founder of the episcopate everywhere; a Jewish or Syrian view. It suggests that Clement's Epistle made a profound impression in the east at a very early date; its influence may be discerned in the writings of Bishop Theophilus of Antioch about 170–80, and it was accepted in Syria as part of the New Testament for four or five centuries. It is interesting to note that the visions of Hermas did not make a similar impression; the east had more exciting prophets of its own.

In their present form the stories in the *Books of Clement* represent the view-point of a sophisticated Hellenistic Ebionism of the end of the second and beginning of the third century which was at home in the sea-coast cities from Caesarea to Tripolis. They were further edited in the fourth century, and their value as historical evidence is most uncertain. No doubt they made use of old traditions of some sort, or were obliged to harmonize with the old traditions, such as they were.

THE DESCENT OF THE CHRISTUS

The imaginative christologies of Simon or Cerinthus or Elkhasai were based on a simple dramatic or mythological idea, the descent into this dark world of a spirit from the High God; and this was patterned in its turn on a well-known Syrian myth. The idea was very widely accepted and it entered into the gnostic theologies when the time for theologies came; but the poet had his innings first. He had near at hand, in the astral religion of the east, the magnificent picture of the seven spheres or heavens which separated this 'sub-lunary' world from the most high deity, whoever he was; and he pictured the Christus as descending through one heaven after another without being recognized by the angels who guarded their portals. He put off his glory by degrees, and assumed the form of the angels in each successive heaven; just as Ishtar surrendered one veil at each of the seven portals of hell. The lowest of these heavens was the firmament which we see, where Jehovah sat enthroned as the ruler of this 'aeon'; or Satan, in some versions of the myth.

Once arrived on earth, the Christus assumed human form, so as not to be recognized by the hostile powers who control the world. He was born of a virgin; or simulated such a birth; or made himself look like a man; or entered into the mortal man Jesus at his baptism. He selected and trained his twelve apostles. He died or seemed to die. He descended into Sheol, the underworld of the dead; 'but to Hagual, the place of destruction, he did not go down'. He despoiled the angel of death; he brought out the righteous dead; he ascended with them into heaven.

There was consternation in heaven after heaven as they passed upward. How was it that the Lord of Glory had descended and they had not known it? We are reminded of a sentence written by St Paul,

'Whom none of the rulers of this world knew, for if they had known, they would not have crucified the Lord of Glory.' It has been suggested, indeed, that the ignorance of the heavenly watchers might seem to have been anticipated in certain passages in Ephesians; for this disguised descent and triumphal return could plausibly be described as the mystery which was hidden from the aeons, a word which may mean either ages or worlds. In any case the poet who originated this Christian myth would seem to have been a student of St Paul.

This part of the myth has music to it, taken from the twenty-fourth psalm; it is oratorio. 'Lift up your heads, O ye gates, and be ye lift up, ye everlasting doors: and the King of Glory shall come in. Who is the King of Glory? even the Lord of hosts, he is the King of Glory.'

The ruler of the aeon is overcome with astonishment and fear as a loud voice breaks upon his ears. He had thought that he was God, and that there was none above him. He adores the Christus as he ascends to his proper place.

A version of this myth was included in the early Christian book called the *Ascension of Isaiah*. Other versions were woven into the Ophite and gnostic mythologies. Its origin can hardly have been 'theological'; it is psalmody or hymnology or exuberant fantasy. Ignatius of Antioch knew it. The Saviour came into the world unobserved by the devil, he says; the virginity and motherhood of Jesus deceived him. Justin knew this application of the twenty-fourth Psalm and probably knew the *Ascension of Isaiah*, too. The book had connexions with Samaria, and so had he; it is hostile to Samaritan prophetism, and he is hostile to Samaritan gnosis.[1]

The picture we have given is a composite one, based in the main on the *Ascension*, but enriched from the gnostic myths. It is fundamentally a descent into Hades like the descent of Ishtar. The idea of the seven heavens was not an authentic part of the Christian tradition; but the descent into Hades after the crucifixion is found in I Peter.

[1] Some scholars think that a similar hostility appears in the *Sibylline Oracles*, Book III, in which the evil spirit Beliar comes from 'Sebaste', which was the Gentile name of Samaria. The *Ascension* also uses the name Beliar for the spirit of evil. The hostility to Samaria flows on into the *Books of Clement*.

29. CATACOMB PAINTINGS

30. THE SABAZIAN PARADISE

THE MARTYRDOM OF ST SYMEON, A.D. 105–7

Such were the dreams and visions and songs of this imaginative eastern world; what we lack is plain contemporary information about events; but we can place the martyrdom of St Symeon between the years 105 and 107 with some confidence. Hegesippus, who preserves the story, gives the name of the 'consular' official who presided at the trial as 'Atticus', and this may be the Sextus Attius Suburanus whose years as a proconsul would fall due at this time. Symeon was accused by the 'sects' of being a member of the family of David and also of being a Christian. He was tortured for several days, till everyone marvelled at the fortitude of an old man of a hundred and twenty years of age. After that he was crucified. Let no one wonder at the hundred and twenty years, for this is simply a Jewish way of stating that he was a venerable elder and patriarch. Moses was a hundred and twenty years old when he died, and so were Hillel and Johanan ben Zakkai and Rabbi Akiba, according to the Talmud. One Jew still says to another, 'May you live to be a hundred and twenty.'

Narcissus, who had become bishop of Jerusalem by 190, claimed to have reached the age of one hundred and seventeen not long before he died; and if so, he was born as early as 100; but centenarians tend to exaggerate their ages, and Narcissus was a fantastic character.

Hegesippus adds that the accusers of Symeon were also members of the family of David, and were arrested themselves in the search which was being made by the Roman authorities. This admission that there were members of the Davidic family among the heretics who informed against Symeon is an indication of the divided state of the Jewish church, and illustrates the realistic character of the sources on which Hegesippus depends. He adds a comment of his own. Up to this time, he says, the heresies in the Jewish church had existed in a subterranean fashion, but now they lifted up their heads and publicly preached an opposition gospel; that is to say, there was an open schism. No doubt there were rival bishops. He adds that the church had formerly been like a pure virgin; now she was corrupted with heresy. He has no further bishops from the family of the Lord. His record ceases.

THE EPISCOPATE IN JERUSALEM

The church historian Eusebius preserved two statements from a written record (which was doubtless Hegesippus); one was the appointment of Symeon as Bishop of Jerusalem in succession to James the Just; the other was the flight of the Jerusalem church to Pella. They are also found in Epiphanius, who seems to have taken them from the same source. We took the step of placing the former event before the latter and assuming that Symeon accompanied the Jerusalem Christians to Pella. We now have two more pieces of information to consider.

Epiphanius gives a circumstantial account (which we will consider in our next chapter) of a return of disciples from Pella to Jerusalem which he places before the year 117; he took it from an ancient source, though he does not specify what it was. Eusebius has a list of Jerusalem bishops which he says was in the records of the Jerusalem church.

Nothing was more important among the Jews than the question of corporate continuity, and the Jewish-Christian tradition knew of two lines of succession, one in the family of Jesus, and the other through bishops. So far as Hegesippus is concerned, on whom we have depended so far for our information, the succession in the family of the Lord ends with the grandsons of Jude and the martyrdom of Symeon; after Symeon comes the deluge of heresy. But Eusebius tacks on, after James the Just and Symeon, his list of thirteen 'bishops of the circumcision' who officiated in Jerusalem prior to the disastrous war of 131–5. The document from which he copied it went on to give the names of fifteen Gentile bishops who held office after 135. The last on the list is that of the long-lived Narcissus whom we know to have become bishop of Jerusalem by 190. The list is quite obviously the pedigree of Narcissus himself. Eusebius states that he found it in the archives of Jerusalem.

There are two problems with regard to this episcopal list, the first of which is the problem of Jerusalem itself. It seems certain that the old Jerusalem church cannot have survived there, or been reconstituted there, after the destruction in 70; archaeologists support the statement of Josephus and the Mishnah that the city was not inhabited. But some settlement or rebuilding must have preceded the war of 131. Many historians think that nothing was done until 130; but, according to Epiphanius, the Emperor Hadrian sanctioned the rebuilding in 117, and though this narrative is not reliable it is possible that unofficial resettlement was tolerated before 130 and even that official action of some sort preceded that date; and the list of the thirteen bishops is evidence that the Gentile church after the war believed that they were the successors of a Jewish church prior to the war; and they would hardly have claimed descent from a church which had not existed.

Eusebius gives us no information about the re-establishment of the episcopate in Jerusalem. He covers it in the following words, which are quite formal:

And when Symeon had been perfected in the manner described, a certain Jew of the name of Justus, who was one of the ten-thousands of the circumcision who had then believed in Christ, succeeded to the throne of the episcopate in Jerusalem. (Eusebius, *E.H.* III, 35.)

The reference to the 'ten-thousands' seems to be lifted from the speech of James the Just in Acts xxi. 20; the sentence is the composition of Eusebius himself. He gives the complete list of bishops in a later chapter of his history (IV, 5, 3). It begins with James and Symeon, who are followed by Justus I, Zacchaeus, Tobias, Benjamin, John, Matthias, Philip, Sennekas, Justus II, Levi, Ephres, Joseph and Judas; such, he says, was the number of the bishops in the city of Jerusalem to the time of which we are speaking.

The second problem about this list is that it has too many bishops for so short a time, and this is an indication that it was not invented for the purpose of filling it up. The difficulty had been felt before the time of Eusebius, and the document from which he took the list had an explanation to the effect that these bishops were very short-lived. Perhaps a more plausible explanation can be advanced. Perhaps the thirteen names are the names of a bishop, Justus, together with twelve elders from whom a successor would be chosen when the necessity arose. And of course the list of fifteen Gentile bishops after 135 would allow room for the Gentile succession to have been started off in this way.

Two examples of this pattern are to be found in oriental legend. Eutychius, who was the patriarch of Alexandria in the tenth century, wrote a book of *Annals*, in which he said that St Mark had provided the first 'patriarch' of the city, whose name was Hananiah, with twelve elders from whom a successor was to be chosen and ordained by the remaining elders. The Ebionite legends which are preserved in the

Books of Clement provide Peter with twelve attendants, whose names are given; the first of these happens to have the name of Zacchaeus, like the successor of Justus in the Jerusalem list. Peter appoints Zacchaeus to be the first bishop of Caesarea, and provides him with twelve elders. He follows the same course in other cities.

At the end of the second century the churches of Alexandria, Caesarea and Jerusalem (then called Aelia) were closely connected, and it looks as if they had a common tradition about the primitive form of the episcopate. Each legend is weak by itself, but they combine to form what looks like a respectable tradition. Now if we look at Antioch, as we see it in the writings of Ignatius, we find that a similar pattern existed there at this time; for he compares the elders who sit with the bishop to the 'council of the apostles'. He does not specify the number twelve, but this was strongly emphasized in the Antiochene Gospel of Matthew. Ignatius is comparing the Syrian ministry of a bishop-and-elders with the pattern created by the Matthaean picture of Jesus and the Twelve, which was thus re-created in every church.

THE EPISCOPATE IN ALEXANDRIA

It may have occasioned some surprise to produce a tenth-century legend in favour of our suggestion; but the tradition that there was something unusual about the Alexandrian episcopate is older than that and has been treated with respect by numerous scholars. It was stated by St Jerome in the fourth century, and by Severus of Antioch in the sixth, that the bishop of Alexandria was originally appointed by the presbyters; but neither of them supports the statement of Eutychius that they ordained him. Jerome says that this system of presbyteral election continued into the time of Demetrius and Heraclas; and Demetrius was a contemporary of Narcissus at Jerusalem; he became bishop about 190. Eutychius says that it continued into the time of Bishop Alexander, who died in 328; and it is quite noteworthy that Alexander was succeeded by Athanasius, who was his deacon. Under the system of presbyteral election this would not have been possible. Perhaps the appointment of Athanasius did create a new precedent of some sort; and there is a legend that his enemies reproached him with having been ordained bishop by presbyters. Once more a number of weak legends do add up to something.

Other indications and analogies are to be found which support or explain this evidence; the independent position of presbyters in Alexandria as heads of distinct churches; the statement of Eutychius that down to the time of Demetrius and Heraclas there was only one bishop in the land of Egypt; the fact that the Patriarch of Alexandria had the right to consecrate the other bishops; the civil organization of Egypt, which was highly centralized; and the subjection of the Alexandrian synagogues to the rule of a 'Patriarch'.

We may look on the Alexandrian legend as the continuation, with some degree of tendentiousness, of a memory which existed at the end of the second century of an ecclesiastical pattern which had been dominant at the beginning of it and was not in all respects obsolete. The actual system may not have been so simple or so uniform as the legend made it appear; but it distinctly suggests that the bishop was the head of a closed corporation of presbyters who were jealous of their rights; and this is just what appears in the life-story of Origen under Demetrius. It looks too as if there was no popular election; no deacon could become bishop, as happened more than once at Rome.

This aristocratic form of organization, if it existed, was balanced by the variety and audacity of the intellectual life in the various academies. The church was shot through with heresy, just as the Jewish church was; and doubtless it came from that quarter. We may assign to this period the 'Petrine' school of Glaucias, who was claimed by the Basilidians as their master's predecessor; and the 'Pauline' school of Theodas, who was claimed as the predecessor of Valentinus. Somebody, it is said, was handing down esoteric gospel traditions in the name of Matthias. A peculiar interpretation of the parables of Jesus and of the mysticism of Paul was also coming into existence. The visions of Hermas and the Epistle of Clement were being accepted along with other New Testament material. The church was represented abroad by Cerinthus, with his ingenious theology and his enthusiasm for apocalypse. These at any rate are the names which were invoked in the various traditions.

Eusebius had received a list of Alexandrian bishops, with the length of each episcopate, which works out approximately as follows: A.D. 62 Annianus (Hananiah), 98 Cerdon, 109 Primus, 119 Justus, 130 Eumenes, 143 Marcus, 153 Celadion, 167 Agrippinus, 179 Julian, 190 Demetrius; but Demetrius is the only one of whom anything is known.

THE GOSPEL OF THE HEBREWS

A literary work which was produced in the Jewish-Christian church in Palestine, or perhaps in Alexandria, fairly early in the second century, was the Gospel of the Hebrews which was used by Hegesippus. Jerome found a copy of it in the library at Caesarea and was able to compare it with another, which was still being used by the Nazareans at Beroea, the modern Aleppo. It was not a free composition like the mass of apocryphal Gospels and Acts which we shall encounter later in the second century. It should be regarded as a fifth attempt at serious Gospel-making for church purposes. It was written in Aramaic for Aramaic-speaking Christians. It was not the Aramaic document written by the apostle Matthew, if that is conceded to have had a substantial and permanent existence; but it might have used such a document as a source. Nor does it seem that it appeared under the name of Matthew, though the time came when it acquired it.

The Hebrew Gospel has not survived, but there are enough quotations from it in Jerome and others to enable us to form some opinions about it. It was written subsequently to the synoptic Gospels and was dependent upon them; but it had its own characteristic versions of certain Gospel passages, some of which have an interesting mythological colour.

Jerome quotes part of the story of the baptism of Jesus, which describes the descent of the Holy Spirit in the character of divine mother.

> And it came to pass when the Lord was come out of the water, that the whole fountain of the Holy Spirit descended and rested upon him, and said unto him: My Son, in all the prophets I was waiting for thee, that thou shouldest come, and I might rest in thee: for thou art my rest, and thou art my first-begotten Son that reignest for ever.
>
> (*Hebrew Gospel*: in Jerome, *Epistle to Hedibia*.)

Here is a fanciful elaboration in mythological terms of an older story which we know from earlier sources. Origen gives a sentence from the story of the Temptation, which continues the theme; Jesus is the speaker, 'Even now did my mother the Holy Spirit take me by one of mine hairs, and carried me away even to the great mountain Tabor.'

Another passage describes the resurrection appearance to James the Just, which Paul mentioned in his first preaching to the Corinthians.

It appears to be regarded as the first of the resurrection appearances, and this would be natural in the Jewish church, whose patron he was. The story also supplies authority for the paschal fast, from the evening of the Last Supper (at which it is implied that James was present) to the morning of the Resurrection. It may also include the ministry of Jesus to the souls of the departed, which is mentioned in I Peter and the *Ascension of Isaiah*. The quotation has two gaps in it.

Now when he had given the linen cloth to the servant of the high priest, the Lord went unto James and appeared to him. For James had sworn that he would not eat bread from that hour wherein he had drunk the Lord's cup, until he had seen him risen from among the dead.... Bring ye, saith the Lord, a table and bread.... He took the bread and blessed and broke, and gave it to James the Just, and said unto him, My brother, eat thy bread, for the Son of Man is risen from among them that sleep.

(*Hebrew Gospel*: in Jerome, *De Viris Illustribus.*)

This piece of Jewish-Christian tradition about James may have belonged to the same cycle as his answers to the Jewish authorities in the Temple, and the glorification of his ascetic life, and the Acts of his martyrdom.

THE 'GOSPEL OF THE TRUTH'

Another experiment in Gospel-making was the Gospel which was used by the great anti-Jewish heretic, Marcion. His catholic opponents accused him of fabricating this Gospel himself, and modern scholars seem to accept their word for it. But he strenuously asserted that he found it in existence, and that it was the original 'Gospel of Truth' which was used by Paul. We consider this Gospel at this point in order to do him justice.

Marcion had his predecessors, some of whom appear fairly clearly in the correspondence of Ignatius and Polycarp; they were the Docetists, who believed in Christ as an angel or spirit without a body; and Polycarp accused them of dealing craftily with the '*Logia* of the Lord', a phrase which his contemporary Papias used in connexion with the writing of Gospels. They did not accept the birth from a virgin, or the human nature of Jesus, or the reality of his Passion. There was no ancient Gospel which embodied this point of view; so they took the Gospel of Luke, the companion of Paul, who was in all probability the apostle on whom they relied, and cut off its opening chapters. The birth from a virgin and the baptism by John were both rejected. It now began with the preaching of Jesus in Galilee; 'In the fifteenth year of Tiberius he descended into a city of Galilee named Capernaum...and they were all astonished at his teaching.' He descended 'as a saving Spirit', Marcion says. It is one of the strange paradoxes of Marcionism that the Passion story is retained.

The Gospel of Luke was further cut down until it bore some resemblance to Mark in outline and proportion. A church which had been accustomed to using Mark could easily substitute it, just as the more orthodox churches could substitute Matthew. It omitted a great deal of material which seemed to be of a pro-Jewish character or to be connected with the doctrine of the fulfilment of Jewish prophecy; and it made alterations in the text that it retained; but the work of omission and emendation is not entirely explained by these dogmatic prepossessions. It is hard to see why the good Samaritan or the prodigal son would be omitted on these grounds. It is known to us through the hostile commentary of Tertullian and some detailed notes which were made by Epiphanius, and minor notices in other catholic writers.

It seems to be a sixth attempt at serious Gospel-writing, on anti-Ebionite, and anti-Cerinthian, and anti-catholic lines. We would not venture to speculate as to where it was produced, but we think that it should be considered in the period before Marcion, who may have been born earlier than A.D. 100, and taught in Rome before 140.

THE BREAK WITH THE SYNAGOGUE

So early as the last twenty years of the first century, when the Matthaean gospel was in process of formation, the Jewish Christians were already being squeezed out of the national life, which was expressed locally in the synagogue. This process was in its last stages by now. Synagogue and ecclesia must part, and go their several ways.

The standard synagogue service already contained some of the fixed forms of prayer which are in use today, though their text was still in a plastic condition. It began with the Psalms and with the *Kedushah* or *Sanctus* and variations are found. After the prayers called *Yotzer* and *Ahabah*, came the *Shema*: 'Hear O Israel, the Lord is thy God, the Lord is One' and so forth. This text is at once the primary commandment and traditional creed-form of Judaism, proclaiming as it does the unity of the God of Israel and the duty of personal devotion to him. It was followed by the Ten Commandments, which were afterwards omitted from the service, 'because of the heretics'; an obscure phrase which suggests that their presence there was taken advantage of somehow by Christians or heretical propagandists; for Judaism was dealing with the same problem of competing sects which was the bane of the Christian church.

Then came the *Emeth-weyazzib*, and the important prayer known as the Eighteen Benedictions or *Amidah*, which preceded the solemn reading of the Law and the prophets. The Law was taken out of the ark with appropriate benedictions and responses and read with great ceremony. This was the central act of the service.

The synagogue service had already taken a Greek form in the Hellenistic synagogues, and its influence on the Christian liturgy can be observed in Clement of Rome and later authors. As late as the fourth century the synagogue prayers, in a Greek form, including the *Kedushah* and *Amidah*, are included in a Christian book of Syrian origin, called the *Apostolic Constitutions*. Christian liturgy develops out of Jewish liturgy under the transforming influence of the gospel and the Spirit.

The following extracts from the *Amidah* give some idea of the increasingly hostile tone of Palestinian Judaism early in the second century.

XII. Let the apostates have no hope, and may the wicked kingdom [Rome] be soon rooted out, and the Notzrim [Christians] and the Minim [heretics] perish in a moment, and be blotted out from the book of life.

XIII. Have pity, O Lord our God, on Israel thy people, on Jerusalem thy city, and on Zion the dwelling-place of thy glory, and on thine altar, and on thy Temple, and on the kingdom of the house of David the Messiah, thy Righteousness.

XIV. Be pleased, O Lord our God, to dwell in Zion, and may thy servants worship thee in Jerusalem; have pity and restore thy presence unto Zion thy city, and the order of worship to Jerusalem.

The thirteenth and fourteenth Benedictions express the profoundest aspirations of the Judaism of the day, and even, with a difference, of some Christians. The restoration of Jerusalem in all its glory was the ardent hope of the leaders of the nation; but there was no room in these devotions for the Nazareans, with their evangelical faith in Jesus as the Davidic Messiah, and their apocalyptic or gnostic speculations, and their prayers and rituals in the Name of Jesus.

RABBI AKIBA

What we have called the second apostolic generation, down to 110, is the equivalent of the first rabbinic generation subsequent to the destruction. The end of the first rabbinic generation saw a great change. Johanan ben Zakkai, the successor in the teaching order of St Paul's Gamaliel, had been a broad-minded man with a statesmanlike policy of friendly living. Eliezer ben Hyrcanus, his favourite pupil, had been a man of the same type. It would appear that he became involved in controversy and lost the day. He retired to the seclusion of his academy at Lydda. 'Warm thy hands at the fire of the wise,' he is reported to have said, 'but beware of their glowing coals lest thou be burned.' One of the points which had been brought against him had been his partiality for Jesus of Nazareth, which was by no means tolerable in the eyes of new men like Rabbi Ishmael ben Elishah, who taunted his wife, Imma Shalom, the daughter of the old Gamaliel, with the sin of seeking healing from a disciple of Jesus.

In the new generation, which flourished from about 90 to the war of 131, the greatest name was that of Akiba. He was a proselyte of Arabian origin, a convert to the faith. He set himself to master the precepts of the oral law, and to bring them into order. He spoke at Jamnia in favour of the inclusion of the Song of Solomon among the synagogue scriptures; but he was not one to resort to allegorical interpretations in order to bring such difficult books into line with the teaching of the sages. No doubt there were too many of these imaginative efforts. He resorted instead to artificial deductions (as they seem to be to the Gentile mind) of single words and even single letters in the sacred writings. It all came from the hand of God, and there must be a meaning in the minutest feature of it. Rabbi Ishmael, on the other hand, is said to have preferred a broad literary interpretation. It did not die out in Israel.

Akiba was responsible for the first energetic attempts to arrange and codify the mass of oral traditions which were handed down in the schools, and to impart order and system to the jungle of rulings and precedents and customs. We find references in old rabbinic sources to a First Mishnah, and a Mishnah of Rabbi Akiba, which may have been a written document; but many scholars think that it referred simply to the enterprise of arranging the various legal opinions in accordance with the topics they dealt with. It does not seem credible, however, that this could be done without making any notes or transcripts.

Jerome tells us that Akiba was the tutor of Aquila, another proselyte, who was a native of Sinope in Pontus, like Marcion. Aquila made a new Greek translation of the Hebrew scriptures. The translation known as the Septuagint often followed a different text from that which was favoured by the rabbis; it sometimes translates inexactly or even wrongly; and, worst of all, it had been appropriated by the Christians, who used it to prove the truth of their gospel. The new version of Aquila was painfully literal, representing every word and particle of the Hebrew text, so far as this could be done in Greek. It was intended for use in connexion with the theological methods of Aquila, which depended upon the study of every detail. It must also have involved the formulation of an authoritative Hebrew text from among the various texts which were available.

During the period from 90 to 130 the Christians had no leader who could compare with Akiba; but then, of course, they had no central organization in which such a man could exercise his powers of leadership. He was the St Paul of the New Judaism, the convert who excelled the home-born in energy and zeal and learning; always travelling, organizing, teaching, and even writing; and yet a man of fervent simple faith. He was destined to ruin Israel by his military and political adventures; and yet, by his genius, he laid the foundations of the New Judaism which would survive the disaster for which he was largely responsible.

CHAPTER 23

THE WARS OF TRAJAN

The Roman historians, *p.* 428. Pontus and Bithynia, *p.* 429. The church and the empire, *p.* 430. Pliny and the Christians, A.D. 111–12, *p.* 432. Trajan's rescript, *p.* 434. The Wars of Trajan, A.D. 114–17, *p.* 435. A story from Epiphanius; Aquila in Jerusalem, A.D. 117, *p.* 437. Anti-Jewish theologies, *p.* 439. Satornil and the Ophites, *p.* 441. Ignatius the bishop, *p.* 443.

THE ROMAN HISTORIANS

The reign of Trajan was the period of the last classical Latin literature. He belonged to the same circle in Rome as Tacitus and Pliny, who perpetuated the memory of the great aristocratic tradition in literature and government. Tacitus had gone through the offices of state under Domitian and had suffered spiritually as a result of his tyranny. In his numerous historical works the moralizing turn which was natural to the conservative Roman mind had been infected with pessimism and bitterness. The pictures which he drew of Rome under the bad Caesars are partly history and partly satire. He seems to have seen clearly the insecurity of the empire, and may have been doubtful about its future. We have made use of his *Annals* in describing the persecution under Nero in 64. He was about ten years old when those events took place, and would remember the burning of the city and the hunting down of the Christians in those hot summer months. He never troubled to correct the impression of the Christians which he had received from his elders at that time; nevertheless the account which he gives of the Christians is better informed than the account which he gives of the Jews.

Gaius Plinius Secundus is called Pliny the Younger, to distinguish him from his uncle the admiral, by whom he was brought up. Pliny the Elder wrote copiously on scientific subjects. It is possible that Clement of Rome drew from his writings the particulars about the bird called the phoenix, which he uses as an argument in favour of the resurrection; and if so, he erred, as theologians may, by following the accepted text-books of the day. Pliny the Elder had a genuine scientific interest in natural phenomena, and lost his life by investigating too closely the eruption of Mount Vesuvius in 79. His nephew, the younger Pliny, was a man of literary tastes and varied interests, whose letters shed light on many aspects of the social life of his time.

Suetonius was what we would call a civil servant. He was encouraged by the younger Pliny to devote himself to literature, and about 120 he published his *Lives of the Caesars*. He has been described in modern times as a gossip-writer; but his intimate stories, as they sometimes are, were often obtained from good sources and are of great value to the historian. He dismisses the persecution of the Christians by Nero in a single sentence.

PONTUS AND BITHYNIA

In September 111, the younger Pliny arrived in the province of Pontus and Bithynia to govern it as a special representative of the emperor. This province was situated in the northern part of Asia Minor along the shore of the Black Sea, where there were a number of flourishing sea-ports. Among these was Sinopē, which was the birthplace of Aquila, the convert to Judaism who made the new translation of the Hebrew scriptures for the Rabbi Akiba. It was also the birthplace of the heretic Marcion, who came to hate the Jewish religion and attempted to eradicate every trace of it from the Christian faith. He is said to have been the son of the Christian bishop, and must have been in his boyhood or youth when Pliny arrived.

The origin of Christianity in Pontus and Bithynia is not known. It was not Pauline territory. Some sign from heaven deterred Paul and his companions from visiting it in their missionary journey of A.D. 50. It would appear that it became Petrine territory. In the sixties it received an Epistle from Peter, written through Silvanus, from Rome, in which Mark also sent his salutations. It would seem likely, therefore, that the bishop of Sinopē was an adherent of the tradition of Peter, and probably too of Matthew. His celebrated son had a poor opinion of Peter, and rejected Matthew; he was intoxicated by the strong wine of the gospel of Paul, as he found it expressed in his Epistles, and expounded in the Docetic schools. He believed in liberty and the Spirit of the Lord.

The Epistle of Peter had been written under the shadow of a great persecution, the danger of which overhung the churches to which it was addressed; and it is possible that they were touched by further persecutions beginning in the nineties under Domitian; for Pliny speaks of apostasies from Christianity, the first of which occurred more than twenty years before the time at which he wrote. Some of those scholars who regard I Peter as a pious fiction assign it to the period of these hypothetical persecutions, or even to the period of Pliny himself; but here scepticism overreaches itself. It belongs to an earlier generation. It shows no awareness of the danger of Docetic heresy or indeed of any heresy. That is why it had to be supplemented by the writing of II Peter.

THE CHURCH AND THE EMPIRE

Pliny the Younger followed the example of Cicero, who had also been a governor in Asia Minor, by preparing his numerous letters for publication. It is fortunate for the historian of Christianity that he addressed one of them to the emperor on the difficult question of how to deal with the Christians. We do not, of course, expect to find in the case of Trajan and his successors instances of imperial savagery and mob-violence on a large scale, or the liquidation of obnoxious persons by police action. The lives and properties of Christians were no longer in danger from such causes; but they were far from secure.

There was no law or imperial decree, so far as we know, condemning Christianity by name; but there was no need for such a law. The church was an international organization of a semi-secret character which was universally regarded as a danger to the state. Its founder had been condemned in a Roman court, and executed as a criminal, but this had not checked its advance; his followers gloried in the fact of his crucifixion and took his cross as their emblem. It had spread with alarming rapidity to Rome, where its ringleaders had been seized and executed with numbers of their followers. The affair had not been very creditable to the emperor of the time, but, after all, these people had been justly hated for their secret crimes. Such is the account of them that Pliny would have received from his friend Tacitus; but fortunately he was broad-minded enough to make further inquiries.

There was another aspect of the case. The Roman administration was nervous about clubs and societies and associations of a voluntary character, since they could be used by disaffected persons for political purposes. Such free associations were not to be tolerated. It was part of that process by which a cultured and enlightened bureaucracy was slowly eliminating such human liberties as there were. Pliny had been ordered by the emperor to enforce this policy firmly, and he had done so, even to the extent of suppressing the fire brigade at Nicomedia. The church organization, therefore, would be liable to dissolution without any special law being passed. Furthermore, Christianity was not one of the religions which the state recognized, protected and supported; on the contrary, the new faith carried on an unremitting propaganda against all the old religions. Worst of all, when Christians were brought to trial, they refused to offer the accustomed religious homage to the emperor. This confirmed the view of Tacitus that they were enemies of the state.

The worship of the emperor was not taken very seriously from a theological point of view. It is difficult to suppose that anybody in Rome thought of Trajan as a god. It was an act of loyalty on which the security of the world-state reposed; but the idea of civic loyalty was so closely connected with the old rituals as to have taken the form of religion in some respects. It was capable, too, of explanation by the philosophers; for Seneca had taught Nero that he was the instrument of the deity, by whose providence he had been brought to the throne of the world. It was possible also to make a distinction between the emperor personally, and his 'genius' or guardian spirit.

In the east matters were otherwise. In ages past the oriental empires and kingdoms had been ruled by monarchs who were honoured as gods. Alexander the Great had conquered that empire and had been invested with divine honours, which his Greek subjects seem to have accorded him with some enthusiasm. His successors, the Seleucids and Ptolemies, had been gods too. When the Roman emperors acquired these kingdoms, they became gods in their turn. Many temples had been erected to the Roman emperors in Asia Minor. It would be a serious affair, therefore, in these regions. The conflict between Christ and Caesar would be acute. Each was called Lord and God and Saviour. To confess one was to deny the other. Some feeling for the dignity and freedom of man underlay this refusal to submit to the divinity of the ruler; for it was an inheritance from the old intolerant Hebrew monotheism that would bow the head to none but God Almighty; a conviction which is the only final bulwark of freedom.

PLINY AND THE CHRISTIANS, A.D. 111–12

Pliny soon found himself obliged to make investigations into the activities of the Christians. An anonymous letter came in which accused a number of people by name. He found to his alarm that Christians were numerous. It was not only a question of the cities, but of villages and farms. The temples were deserted, he was told, the sacred rites had ceased in some instances and animals put up for sale found few buyers. No doubt these pictures were rather highly coloured, and the situation, such as it was, may not have been entirely due to the spread of the gospel. Fifty years later Lucian remarked that Pontus was full of atheists and Christians; and by atheists he meant the philosophers of the school of Epicurus, who were devotees of a scientific rationalism. But it was natural to blame the mysterious sect of the Christians for the decline in the fortunes of the indigenous cults, whose follies, of course, they must have been pointing out. The church had made considerable progress; for Christianity appears to have begun its work in the cities; it would take time for it to establish itself there and then expand into the country districts in such force.

Pliny was not quite certain of the correct legal procedure, as he had not taken part in such trials before; either they were not very frequent in Rome now,[1] or else he had not happened to preside at a court where they had come up. He asked each accused person whether he was a Christian. If he confessed, he was asked the fatal question a second time with threats of punishment. If he still confessed after a third inquiry, he was condemned to death; for Pliny did not doubt that, quite apart from the confession of Christ, such inflexible obstinacy deserved to be punished. Some of the accused, however, had the Roman citizenship, and these were sent to the emperor himself for trial.

Some denied that they had ever been Christians, and these were asked to prove their sincerity by invoking the gods and offering incense and libations of wine before the emperor's statue, and cursing Christ; none of which things, he was advised, a real Christian could be compelled to do. There were others who began by confessing, but then denied, and proved their loyalty by complying with these ceremonies.

[1] There may have been no strong anti-Christian feeling in Rome now: the Roman church thought it could save Ignatius from the wild beasts.

31. A SABAZIAN HAND

Others said that they had once been Christians, but had ceased to be so, in some cases three years before, but many of them much earlier, and one of them more than twenty years ago. These apostasies may have been due to earlier persecutions.

The procedure sounds so satisfactory from the point of view of administrative routine that it is rather remarkable that he carried his investigations any farther; but he seems to have inherited some of his uncle's interest in finding out the actual facts of a situation. He made further inquiries of the apostates, in order to discover what the substance of their guilt or error amounted to. The impression which he received was rather confused, and perhaps they did not tell him everything. What he learned was that it was their custom to assemble together before sunrise on a fixed day and sing an antiphonal chant to Christ as to a god; they then bound themselves with a solemn oath (*sacramentum*) 'not to steal, not to rob, not to commit adultery, not to break their faith, and not to deny the deposit if called upon'; a catechetical or baptismal formula like that which Elkhasai demanded of his penitents at their immersion; and Ignatius speaks of commandments which were given when making disciples, that is to say at baptism; see Matthew xxviii. 19–20.

The deposit which must not be denied may be the confession of Christ which was first made at baptism.

When they had finished their worship, and bound themselves with their oath, they dispersed, but came together again later on for the purpose of taking food, which was of a harmless and ordinary sort; and even this had been given up after he had published his edict against the formation of clubs and associations, at the command of the emperor.

In order to confirm the evidence of the apostates, he examined with torture two slave-girls, who were called deaconesses (*ministrae*), and found out nothing at all but an evil and extravagant superstition. What he had expected to find, of course, was some particulars about the secret crimes of which Tacitus had spoken. It was fully believed, for a hundred years or more, that Christians met together to feed on the body of a murdered child, after which they indulged in promiscuous sexual intercourse. His resolution was obviously a little weakened by his discovery of the innocence of Christian religious life, and he decided to delay further action until he had found out from the emperor whether Christians were put to death solely on account of 'the name', or for the crimes which were supposed to be connected with it. No doubt his letter was carried by the officer who was in charge of the party of Christians who happened to be Roman citizens.

A second, and perhaps a more powerful motive for consulting the emperor, was that he found himself running into serious difficulties owing to the number of suspects involved, who were of all ages and social classes. Important persons might turn out to be Christians. The fear of touching such persons may have moderated more than one persecution.

TRAJAN'S RESCRIPT

The short reply, or 'rescript', of the emperor, is one of the important documents of the period, since it had the force of law. He admitted that it was difficult to lay down a definite procedure which could be adhered to in all cases, and commended Pliny for the policy which he had adopted. Christians were not to be inquired after; but if it happened that they were accused and found guilty, they must be punished; but any one who denied that he was a Christian, and proved it by offering worship to 'our gods', should be pardoned on account of his repentance, however suspicious his past behaviour might have been. On the other hand, papers that came in without any name signed to them ought not to be taken into account in any inquiry; 'that kind of thing is a bad precedent, and unworthy of the times in which we are living'.

The good emperor looked back with contempt on Domitian's policy of espionage and heresy-hunting, under which noble Romans and leading philosophers had been made to suffer. He wished to protect well-affected citizens from baseless and malicious accusations. Even in the case of Christians, he saw no point in persecutions and inquisitions; he extended to them a slight degree of protection in his '*conquirendi non sunt*'—'they are not to be sought out'. Nevertheless the position of the Christian remained insecure. He was at the mercy of a badly disposed neighbour who wanted revenge, or the violence of the mob which wanted blood and loot; and once he stood before the judge, his position was hopeless unless he was prepared to deny his faith, in which case his chance of restoration to his place in the church was small indeed.

A curious dualism of language had grown up in this horrible business, and martyrdom had its ritual and its terminology, half legal and half evangelical; we shall see more of it in the Epistles of Ignatius. The use of the word 'name' was common to the Christian Gospel and the Roman law-court; and so too were the words 'confess' and 'deny'. It was anticipated as long ago as the time when Peter wrote his Epistle. 'Let none of you suffer as a murderer or a thief or a busybody', the apostle had said, 'but if he suffer as a *Christian*, let him not be ashamed, but glorify God in this name.' In this short sentence, the words 'suffer' 'ashamed', 'glorify', and 'name', are taken out of the Gospel vocabulary, and set like jewels round the word *Christian*, which was new then, and apparently not liked by those who had it thrown at them. By Pliny's time, fifty years later, the usage was well established, and it was a point of honour for the martyrs to glory in it, as the apostle had urged.

THE WARS OF TRAJAN, A.D. 114–17

We must now turn our attention to the city of Antioch where the name *Christian* had been coined; but before taking up the story of persecution there, we must supply a sketch of the historical background.

In the year 113, in which Pliny returned to Rome and died, Trajan arrived in his eastern capital, and spent the winter there in preparation for his great eastern adventure. Antioch now saw its king (for this word was freely used of the Roman emperors in the Greek and Syrian tongues) for the first time since the Seleucid empire had petered out under the blows of the Parthian power and the Roman armies. He was a soldier of distinction, and his soul was fired with the ambition of reviving in his own person the military glories of Alexander and conquering on behalf of Rome the age-old empire of the far east. Progress had been made in the subjection of Britain, and protracted wars against the Germans had strengthened the frontier-line on the Rhine and the Danube. If these defences could be held, he could safely turn eastward and revenge certain ancient defeats which Rome had suffered from the Parthians, extend her boundaries as far as the Persian Gulf, and control the trade-routes to India and China.

In 114 Trajan occupied the buffer-state of Armenia, which was regarded as a Roman satellite, and then advanced into northern Mesopotamia, which he conquered without difficulty and proceeded to organize as a Roman province. Meanwhile his second-in-command, Lusius Quietus, who was a Moorish chieftain, marched down the

Euphrates River as far as Singara. In the following year, 115, Trajan joined forces with him, and proceeded to invade the south-eastern part of Mesopotamia. But during this campaign news came to him of Jewish rebellions in Egypt and in the adjoining province of Cyrene, under a 'king' named Lukuas or Andrew. Horrible massacres and barbarities are said to have occurred, and two hundred and twenty thousand people are said to have been killed by the insurgents. Soon the revolt spread to the island of Cyprus, where twenty-four thousand are said to have been murdered in a rising of the Jews. Unfortunately we have to depend on the evidence of third-century historians for this information, and our picture of the events lacks precision, or possibly has too much; but archaeological evidence shows that many cities in Cyrene were badly damaged. The Jews had obviously taken advantage of the eastern advance of Trajan to raise a rebellion in those countries. No doubt they had an understanding with the Parthians and other oriental nations; and it is natural to believe that they joined forces with other subject nations or oppressed classes. It is possible, too, that the massacres and barbarities were not all on one side. It was a serious crisis, and Trajan had to send one of his best generals, Martius Turbo, to Egypt, with forces that he must have been in need of himself, to quell the risings. They were put down with great severity, and it is probable that the decline of Judaism in Alexandria dates from this unhappy rebellion of which so little is known.

Trajan was not deterred by these events. Later in 115 he marched farther down the Euphrates to the site of the ancient Babylon, and captured Ctesiphon, the capital city of the Parthian monarch. He then continued his march to the shores of the Persian Gulf. The way to India was now open, and he exercised control of more territory than any other conqueror in human history; but he had moved too fast, and it would not be his destiny to outshine Alexander.

When he had reached his farthest point of conquest, Parthia renewed hostilities, and his new province of Mesopotamia rose against him. Quietus put down the Mesopotamian revolt, and is said to have slaughtered great numbers of Jews in doing so. There were many Jewish colonies in these parts, and we infer that they had joined in the rising. Palestine remained quiet; but trouble seems to have been expected there, since Quietus was put in charge. By the year 117 order is said to have been restored at terrible cost, but Trajan died on August 8 at

Selenus in Cilicia. The situation was uncertain, and all the eastern conquests of Trajan, with the exception of Arabia, were wisely abandoned by his successor Hadrian, though kings of his own choosing appear to have been left in command of the various principalities.

According to Epiphanius, Hadrian authorized reconstruction work in Jerusalem at this time, which is likely enough, since the frontier had to be strongly held.

A STORY FROM EPIPHANIUS; AQUILA IN JERUSALEM, A.D. 117

We have been making use from time to time of the evidence of Hegesippus, who may have been born about this time, probably in Palestine itself. We now turn to the pages of Epiphanius, who used the work of Hegesippus and other old documentary material, the origin of which is not known.

Epiphanius was a native of Cyprus who lived in the fourth century. After visiting Egypt, where he had some contact with the Gnostic sects, he settled for a time in Palestine. While he was there, he became head of a monastery at Eleutheropolis in Galilee, where he made researches into the history of Jewish and Jewish-Christian sects. He returned to Cyprus, and became bishop of Salamis. He was an important ecclesiastical figure in his day, and about the year 375 he composed his *Panarion*, in which he catalogued, described, derided and refuted every known kind of heresy which had ever existed. He has no historical ability, but he sometimes makes use of older sources without acknowledging the fact. He mentions in a general way his indebtedness to Irenaeus, Clement of Alexandria, Hippolytus and 'many others'; and among the many others was Hegesippus, from whom he took the stories of the asceticism and martyrdom of James, and doubtless too the story of the flight of the Jerusalem disciples to Pella, previous to A.D. 70.

He has some more passages of the same kind, dealing with events in the second century, and we find among them some acceptable dates, which commends them to us. In his book *Concerning Weights and Measures* he copies from some source a chronology of the Roman emperors, and remarks that sixty-five years elapsed between the crucifixion of Jesus and the 'desolation', by which he means the capture of Jerusalem by Titus in 70. Actually this is the period between the 'desolation' in 70 and the formal restoration in 135. He has garbled an accurate statement through sheer carelessness; but he is using a good source, which counts its dates from the 'desolation', not from the crucifixion, as he thought.

He goes on to give an account of Aquila the translator, and says that he achieved fame in the twelfth year of Hadrian, which was 129, a quite possible date which scholars have found acceptable. It then tells a curious tale about a sickness of Hadrian, and a journey of his through Antioch, Syria and Palestine, which sounds as if it ought to be the famous journey through Syria to Egypt in 129; but he dates it, very surprisingly, in the forty-seventh year after the 'desolation', that is to say in 117. Now this is the year in which Hadrian succeeded Trajan; and a journey from Antioch to Palestine is not impossible; but it looks more likely that two stories, each with a good date, have got hooked together.

The narrative goes on to give an account of the condition of Jerusalem. It says that Titus had torn down the whole city and levelled it to the ground, with the exception of a few dwelling-houses which were situated in the quarter known as Zion, that is to say the hill called Ophel which runs southward from the Temple-site on the eastern side of the city; not the western hill which is called Zion to-day. In addition to these houses, there were seven synagogues and a small Christian church. One of these synagogues was still standing in the reign of Constantine, Epiphanius says. He does not say whether the small Christian church remained standing so long; but Eusebius, in his *Demonstration of the Gospel*, speaks of a large Christian church which remained standing in Jerusalem up to the war of 131–35. This would seem to be a fourth-century form of the old story in Epiphanius.

This story in Epiphanius does not sound like a fourth-century invention, and the seven synagogues recall the theory of Hegesippus that the Jews were divided into seven sects. There were seven synagogues left over, but only one church. Is it possible that Epiphanius is making use of the *Note-books* of Hegesippus at this point?

The Christian church was the same building to which the apostles returned on the day of the Ascension, his document goes on to say. It had a congregation once more; for the disciples of the apostles, who had removed to Pella in obedience to an oracle given by an angel, had returned to Jerusalem and were flourishing in the faith and performing great signs. This statement suggests that the story of the flight to Pella must have stood in the document which Epiphanius was using, which numbered the years from the date of the 'desolation' when the flight occurred.

This is all introductory to the story of Aquila, who was now entrusted by Hadrian with the responsibility for the reconstruction of the city. He was still a Gentile, but he was deeply impressed by the Christian teachers whom he found in Jerusalem and asked for baptism, which was granted. Unfortunately he failed to renounce his interest in astrology and calculated horoscopes every day. He was warned by the Christian teachers, but persisted in his error. Finally he was excommunicated. Mortified by this treatment, he had himself enrolled as a Jewish proselyte and was circumcised. He devoted himself to the study of the Hebrew language, and produced his new translation of the Old Testament with the object of giving a new rendering of those passages on which the Christians principally relied in their arguments against the Jews.

The story of the relations between Aquila and the Christian teachers in Jerusalem has points of contact with the story of Marcion's relations with the Roman elders which Epiphanius uses in his *Panarion*.

ANTI-JEWISH THEOLOGIES

The story of Hadrian and Aquila has only a shadowy claim to consideration as history and certainly seems to have some legendary features. On the other hand, it is placed in a historical setting which seems to be well informed. It is not really known, however, when Hadrian authorized the rebuilding of Jerusalem, except that it was between 117 and 130; (which by the by would allow room for thirteen bishops of the circumcision if they presided for one year each); and it is not known whether Aquila became a Christian before his conversion to Judaism. As for the re-establishment of the Jewish church in Jerusalem, the evidence which we have reviewed seems to make it highly probable. It is unfortunate that the facts of this period of transition are so imperfectly known, since it was a period of crisis in the relations between the Christians and the Jews; and these relations must have been affected by the unrest on the Syrian border and the widespread wars and rebellions of the time.

A western power, the Roman empire, confronted an eastern power, the Parthian empire, with its Persian inheritance, which was situated in the territory of the old Babylon. The various satellites, protectorates and buffer-states which were situated in the border-zones were deeply involved in their rivalries, and were alternatively under the control of one power or the other. The Jews of Syria, Mesopotamia, Palestine and Egypt were on the Parthian side, and many of them took an active part in the wars of 114 to 117. They were determined to regain their independence and rebuild their city and Temple. Some progress may have been made.

The line taken by Christians in these areas cannot be determined; but we cannot exclude the possibility that there were Jewish and Syrian Christians who sympathized with these rebellions. Fragments of apocalypse or scraps of oracular verse may turn out to refer to such conflicts. The prophet Elkhasai, for instance, has a reference to Trajan and the Parthians, though it is far from clear. The additions made about this time to the *Apocalypse of Ezra* are anti-Roman; and this book commended itself to some Christian churches.

It is not surprising, therefore, that there are signs of an anti-Jewish trend in the thinking of the Gentile churches. It appears, for instance, in the so-called Epistle of Barnabas and in the nascent gnostic heresies. It would be natural, under war conditions, for Gentile Christians within the Roman empire to repudiate very strongly their connexion with the rebellious and nationalistic Jews; and we do find the distinction very clearly enunciated in the writings of the bishop of Antioch of this period, the martyr Ignatius; 'Judaism' was one thing, 'Christianism' was quite another. And it is not anticipating things too much to point out that the objection of Marcion to the Jewish God was that he was fierce and severe and delighted in war. The school of Basilides in Alexandria went farther; the God of the Jews was tyrannical and belligerent and tried to subdue all the other nations to his nation; so it was natural that the other heavenly rulers would combine against him, and their nations fight against his.

Just so Elkhasai traced the disturbances in the kingdoms of godlessness to certain stars of godlessness. The idea of patron gods or angels for nations was quite at home in Judaism, and seems to have passed into these Christian schools of thought. Enlightened Gentiles would not put up with a mere national deity such as Jehovah appeared to be. They looked for a 'strange' deity, from beyond time and space, who had never had any connexion with this unfortunate planet. He was of course the high God of Syrian Hellenism or Iranian faith, whose prophet had been the Persian Zoroaster; or a fusion of the two.

SATORNIL AND THE OPHITES

Marcion was not yet propagating his views, nor Basilides either in all probability, though precursors of theirs were at work who were forming their minds; but Satornil may have been at the beginning of his career. We have no means of dating him beyond the fact that Justin regarded him as the successor of Menander in Antioch. He appears to have come at an early stage in the development of gnosticism; and the Syrian gnosis appears to have preceded the Alexandrian. It was in his hands apparently that the gospel of Jesus Christ was first blended with oriental monotheism in a mythical form which commanded the attention of serious thinkers.

His God was the nameless and timeless deity who exists in infinite space; but he differed from Simon Magus in admitting no sexual element into his myth. He accepted the idea of the seven angels or planetary deities who made the world, the chief of them being the God of the Jews; but they had no female spirit to guide them, or give order and beauty to their work, such as we find in Simon and Hermas.

The nameless God emitted, from his own immaterial being, a luminous image in the form of a man, an idea which seems to be borrowed from the Iranian cosmology, though it lies hidden in the first chapter of Genesis; for God made man in his own image and likeness. The idea of a heavenly man, or something man-like in the being of God, was by now a widespread concept of oriental religious thought; we think of the Son of Man of Daniel and the Gospels, the heavenly man of Paul, the glorious angel of Hermas, and the Christus of Elkhasai who was also Adam. The seven creator angels had some vision of this man of light, and said one to another, 'Let us make a man according to the image and the likeness'. They did their best, but the thing which they made lay helpless on the earth, unable to stand erect. Then the power which is above took pity on it, because it was made in its image, and sent down a spark of light or life, which raised it up and made it live.

This beautiful myth may come from the repertoire of some pre-

Christian oriental sect which had already developed an ascetic gnosis based on a mythological handling of the Genesis story. Another version of it is to be found in the tangled mythology of the 'Ophite' gnostics who regarded the serpent as the highest symbol of the divine nature. Jehovah was the jealous god in the bad sense of the word; his law was evil and tyrannical; but the wise serpent persuaded Eve to take the forbidden fruit of the tree of knowledge (or 'gnosis') which was the food of eternal life.

Satornil may have thought rather less severely of the Hebrew God, since he admitted that he carried on a perpetual warfare against the devil and his daemons; and therefore he may have been wrongly quoted in saying that the Saviour came into the world to destroy him. He may have allowed him a middle position between the high God and the devil, which is what he had in some of the gnostic schools. On the other hand, his system of ethics was strictly dualistic. There were only two kinds of men, those who had the spark of heavenly light in their souls, and those who had not. The former would be saved and ascend to the heavenly realms where their souls belonged. The others were non-spiritual, and could not be saved; there was nothing in them to save.

The Saviour was pure spirit. He could not have had a body, because everything which had to do with the body was evil. Marrying and giving in marriage are works of the devil; wine and flesh-meat must be renounced. No moral charges seem to have been brought against the school of Satornil; on the contrary, he can be accused of imposing too severe a regime of self-denial; but the strict holy ascetic life was highly regarded in the east, and was adopted by Marcion and others as an essential part of the gospel. It invaded the church under the name of Encratism.

It was not so with the Ophites. Their complex myth was given a romantic turn by the incorporation into it of a lovely female being who was called the First Woman or Holy Spirit, or in the Egyptian versions of the myth, Sophia or heavenly Wisdom. Another name for her was Zoë, the Greek word for life, which is used in the Septuagint to represent the name Eve. She is the bride of the Primal Man (or highest deity) and the mother of the Second Man (the heavenly Adam), and the Mother of all living. Indeed, her names are endless, and she looks at times like the east Mediterranean earth-mother, or some heavenly lady from the Syrian pantheon. She may even be the formless matter from which the world was made. The sons of this mother were no enthusiasts for asceticism, or even for ordinary sexual morals. They appear in Egypt rather than Syria.

IGNATIUS THE BISHOP

If we had a first-hand record of the views and character of Satornil, we might not find him so easy to classify as we do when working from the miniature portrait which Irenaeus gives us, working no doubt from the lost works of Justin. We might find that certain unusual or fantastic features had been selected in such a way as to produce something of a caricature. We might find a poet or mystic of considerable genius, who had studied Paul and was interpreting the new gospel in the terms of the contemporary religious idealism. Nor should we allow ourselves to feel impatient about the myths. They were a serious mode of thought and have a facility of their own for the expression of spiritual truths. They appear in our history at this point, and are entitled to serious consideration.

When we come to Satornil's bishop, the great Ignatius, we have the man's own letters to judge by and the task is more complex. He, too, might be called a gnostic, since he has a touch of the myth-maker and the poet in his make-up; but if so, he was a flesh-and-blood gnostic of the school of John, whose theology he knew. He was no Hebraist, though he extols the divine prophets as pupils of Jesus before his time. His true interest was in the gospel itself, just as Satornil's probably was; but he asserts the flesh-and-blood character of the Saviour's life on earth, and in particular the reality of his death and resurrection.

Ignatius, or Egnatius, is a Latin name. He was also known by the Greek name of Theophorus or God-bearer; but he was neither a Greek nor a Roman by temperament; he was an oriental. He had the ardent Syrian spirit. He was without formal education of the classical Greek kind. He shows some knowledge of Greek literary models but his style must be classified as barbarous. Nevertheless, he dictated a vigorous poetic prose, which was highly dramatic and effective. A self-conscious modern taste finds itself embarrassed by the passionate feeling which embodies itself in his stream of paradoxes and epigrams and other figures of speech. He is always dramatizing himself, alternating as he does so between an excited exaltation and a profound abasement; but he is not unsteady. His rhetoric is brave and true and firm; for it is the rhetoric of a brave and true and firm man. And what it was on paper, that it was in the ecclesia; and what it was in the ecclesia, that it was as he stood in chains between the soldiers who guarded him.

Ignatius had a message to give to the Christian world which arose out of his own personal experience in this age of conflict and confusion. It was the importance, before everything else, of unity. He believed ardently in one God and one Lord Jesus Christ, not in a host of heavenly beings. He knew how the one Gospel of Matthew had been composed and adopted for use in his ecclesia. He knew how the worship of the one altar had given his congregation a sense of the divine harmony. He knew how the rule of one bishop presiding among his apostolic elders had made for peace and stability. He does not tell us about the origin of these things; for he was as little interested in the past as he was in the future. What interested him was the power of the living God which had taken possession of his spirit and flesh through the Lord and Master for whom he was glad to lay down his life.

CHAPTER 24

IGNATIUS THE MARTYR

The journey of Ignatius, A.D. 110–15, *p.* 445. Ignatius in Phrygia, *p.* 447. Ignatius at Smyrna, *p.* 449. The Epistles from Smyrna, *p.* 450. Syrian catholicism, *p.* 451. The gnosis of Ignatius, *p.* 453. The Epistle to the Romans, *p.* 453. Ignatius at Troas, *p.* 455. Ignatius at Philippi, *p.* 457. The Epistle to Polycarp, *p.* 458. The Epistle of Polycarp to the Philippians, *p.* 459. The case of Valens, *p.* 461. The conclusion of Polycarp's Epistle, *p.* 462.

THE JOURNEY OF IGNATIUS, A.D. 110–15

The account of the trial of St Ignatius before the Emperor Trajan in Antioch, and the Acts of his martyrdom in Rome, were composed at the end of the fourth century and are classified as pious fiction. We can infer from his own Epistles that he was the last of a number of martyrs; for he calls himself the last of all, and refers to other Syrians who have gone to Rome before him, who may have been martyrs too. Polycarp mentions two other martyrs, Zosimus and Rufus; but they were not travelling with him, and must have passed through a little earlier. It would seem that he caught up with them at Philippi.

Forty years later there was a severe persecution at Smyrna, in which Polycarp evaded capture for some time, so that his death came as the last of a number. Ignatius seems to have done something of this sort.

The sentence was to be carried out in Rome. A special example was to be made of this notable Christian, and in consequence the whole catholic church was stirred by his dramatic progress from east to west. It was incumbent upon him to preserve his spiritual morale; for the eyes of the world were upon him. He knew exactly what would be done with him. We have his own word for it; 'I am beginning to be a disciple; come fire, come cross; grapplings with wild beasts, cuttings and manglings, wrenching of bones, hacking of limbs, crushing of the whole body; let cruel torments of the devil come upon me; if only I may attain unto Jesus Christ.'

He travelled in the custody of ten soldiers; ten leopards, he called them; and remarked that the more kindly they were treated the worse

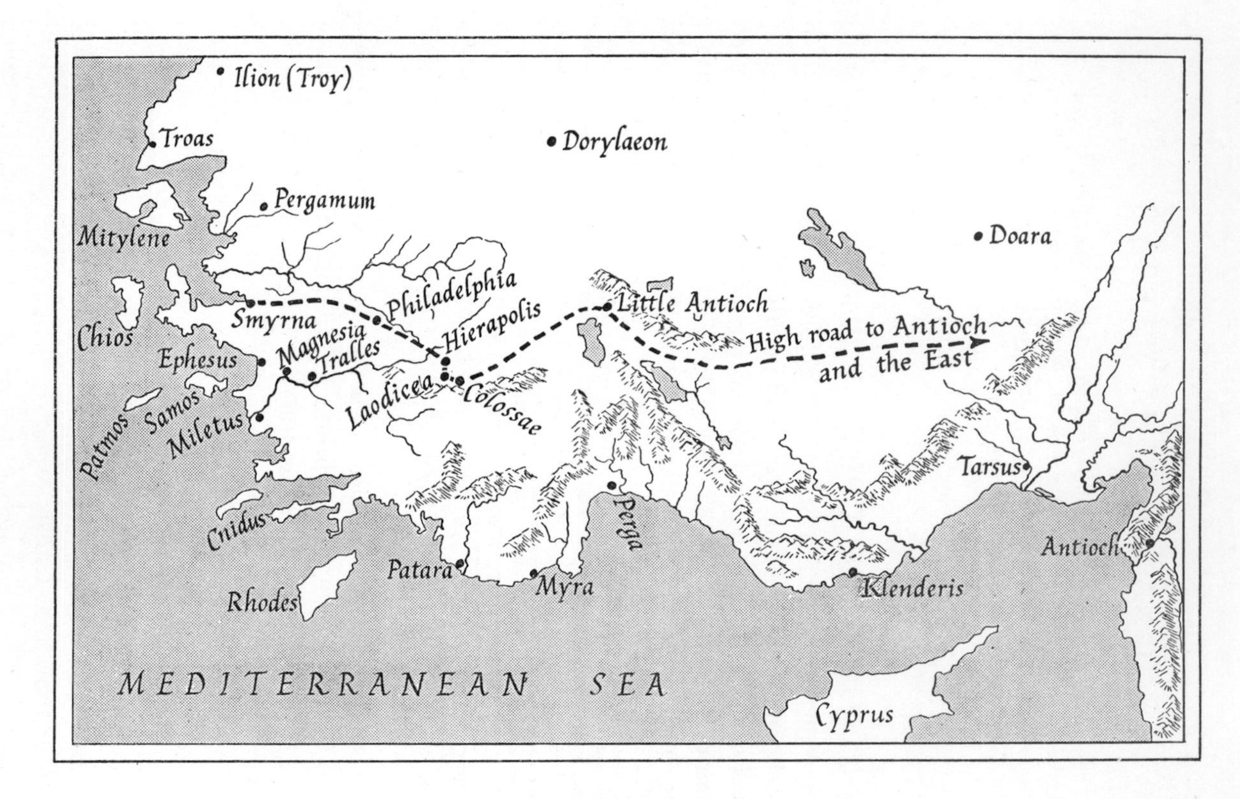

Map 6. The journey of Ignatius.

they behaved. No doubt the effects of a bribe soon wore off. There may have been other prisoners, though not apparently Christian ones. On his way Ignatius wrote seven Epistles; or seven have come down to us; he may have written more. Towards the end of the fourth century more were written in his name, and combined with the fictitious story of his trial and martyrdom to create a problem which baffled the learned world for some centuries. The seven genuine letters are now established beyond question. They are the most important Christian documents of the period.

One of our first surprises is to find that a prisoner of this sort, who had good friends to help him, was able to command a number of privileges. The soldiers were not inaccessible to bribes, and were willing to show off their prisoner locally if it was made worth their while; for we cannot suppose that they did it for nothing. Bishops and deacons could have access to him, and bring him comforts and facilities for correspondence. In later documents we even read of services conducted in the prison. Money must have been paid out for these privileges, and the church seems to have been able to find the money. It was a well-organized body with influential connexions.

IGNATIUS IN PHRYGIA

While it was possible to take the first part of the journey from Antioch by sea, it seems more likely that the party followed the Pauline trail overland, by taking the road which ran northward through Cilicia; for a Cilician deacon, named Philo, was moved to make an offer to accompany Ignatius to Rome and minister to him in the word. Even so early as this the bishop appears with a deacon by his side. Philo could not come immediately, but he followed later, bringing with him another deacon, from Antioch, whose name was Rhaius Agathopous. It is possible that Ignatius had sent Agathopous back to Antioch on business; perhaps with letters, though they do not actually survive. In Antioch the persecution had come to an end. A council had been held to which the neighbouring towns had sent bishops, and some of them elders and deacons as well.

Ignatius went on, without his deacon, along the road which Paul had first taken about sixty-five years before; unfortunately we have no information about his experiences in Galatia, where a few old men and women could still retail their memories of those early days. He gives no information, either, about the west Phrygian cities of Colossae, or Laodicea, or Hierapolis, where Papias may have heard him speak; but a halt was made at Philadelphia, and he was allowed to address the local church. It must have been a strange sight. We know that he was loaded with chains, his spiritual pearls, as he called them; and probably he was coupled to one of his 'leopards'. Twenty years earlier, as we learn from the Revelation, this church had been vexed by a 'synagogue of Satan', who claimed to be Jews but were not so in truth. The Jewish question was not yet settled. Christians of Jewish race or sympathies advocated the observance of the Sabbath, and championed the claims of the priesthood. More than that, they objected strongly to their bishop, whose name Ignatius does not give; they even made unpleasant charges about the way in which he had obtained his office.

The welcome which was extended to Ignatius was of a mixed character therefore. The minority was vocal, and the argument was heated. 'It is written,' Ignatius had asserted, as if settling a point. 'That is the very question', they retorted. The divine prophets were being discussed and the archives, whatever they were, and the written gospel; but there was some organized party at the back of it all, and he recognized the signs; some schism-maker, a would-be bishop perhaps. His prophetic soul was stirred, and he spoke in a loud voice, a voice of God. He commanded the situation.

> Adhere to the bishop and the council of elders!...
> Guard your flesh as the temple of God!
> Love the unity: flee from divisions.
> Be imitators of Jesus Christ even as he imitates the Father.
>
> (Ignatius, *Philad.* VII, I.)

It was the old catechetical material in the Ignatian idiom; or the Antiochene idiom possibly. It somehow hit the mark. The words were so apt to the situation that the malcontents thought that some hint had been given to Ignatius beforehand, and he had been told what to say; but he swears that this was not so; he knew nothing 'according to the flesh'; it was the Spirit that proclaimed. This utterance appears to be quoted in the so-called *Second Epistle of Clement*, ix. 3.

The scene is vividly impressed upon us, but we do not see clearly what gave rise to the altercation. Throughout the stormy assembly the local bishop sat still and said nothing; Ignatius praises his immovable unwrathful demeanour.

IGNATIUS AT SMYRNA

Ignatius never reached the apostolic city of Ephesus. After leaving Philadelphia the road forked, and his party took the northern highway, which led to Smyrna, where Polycarp was bishop. Ignatius spent several days there, and enjoyed the society of Polycarp, who had been a pupil of John; it is disappointing that he does not mention the name of John in his Epistles, though he shows knowledge of the Johannine teaching. He does not mention the name of Matthew either. His mind was set on the idea of martyrdom, and on the two martyr-apostles, Peter and Paul, who had taken the road from Antioch to Rome before him.

His intercourse with Polycarp during these few days was a most important point in church history, for the two men dominate the story of the church in the first half of the new century. He made other friends in Smyrna as well, among whom he mentions the family of Gaouia, and Alke, 'beloved name', and Daphnus the sincere, and Eutecnus. Alke was still living when Polycarp was martyred in 155 or 156.

The churches along the southern road, which could not receive the martyr in person, sent representatives to pay their homage to him at Smyrna. The old Pauline church of Ephesus sent its bishop, Onesimus, who assigned his deacon Burrhus to Ignatius as his secretary, in place of the absent Agathopous, thus making possible the production of the letters which we are now using; for Burrhus wrote at the dictation of the martyr. Other members of the Ephesian delegation were Crocus, Euplous, and Fronto. Crocus appears to have had some connexion with the Roman church and he was sufficiently influential to obtain considerable improvements in the treatment of Ignatius.

It is possible that the family of Alke had some influence in the official world, too, for her nephew Herod appears as the chief of police at a later date. He did not, unfortunately, turn out to be friendly to the Christians, for it was he who arrested Polycarp forty years later. His name suggests that this divided family was Jewish.

The first letter which Ignatius wrote was one of gratitude to the

Ephesian church, in which he recalls their connexion with St Paul and desires their prayers; he warns them against the Docetic heresy. There were two churches on the southern road whose names are new to us, Magnesia and Tralles. Magnesia sent its young bishop, Damas, with two elders, Bassus and Apollonius, and the deacon Zotion; Ignatius gave them a letter in which he warned them against what he calls Judaism, contrasting it with 'Christianism', or as we would say, Christianity. Polybius, the bishop of Tralles, came without an escort and took back with him a letter in which the views of the Docetics were attacked; the sect which could not bring itself to believe that the Christ had really taken a human body.

THE EPISTLES FROM SMYRNA

The thought of Ignatius can be traced back at one time to Paul (whom he names), at another to Matthew (whom he quotes without naming), and yet again to John (whom he also quotes without naming); 'the Spirit is not deceived, since it is from God; it knows whence it cometh and whither it goeth' (Ignatius, *Philad.* VII. 1, and John iii. 8). But the tradition which he represents is an independent one with a character of its own.

His presentation of Christianity is coloured by his own spiritual experience of God, which was developed in the intimate fellowship of the apostolic Syrian church. It was fixed unalterably on the figure of Jesus Christ as God and Saviour, whose true birth and sufferings and death and resurrection formed the sum total of his faith. Jesus was his God who had died for him, and his Master who was now teaching him how to die. This evangelical faith was expressed in credal formulas.

God was also made known to him as Spirit; the wind that blows about as it will; the breath that is infused into human hearts through faith and love; God himself coming as power and life, and taking possession of his 'flesh', and enabling him to overcome the ruler of this aeon. He had found him in the message of the gospel and in the worship of the Church; he would encounter him finally in martyrdom, when he would 'arrive at God'.

The language of Ignatius is not only the language of evangelism; it is the language of hymn and song and eucharistic worship. He has much to say about the church assembled in unity with its bishop and presbytery and deacons; for he is now a prisoner, and his memory dwells upon the familiar scene, and draws strength from it; but he does not write like a canonist or the author of a church order. He speaks of the one altar and the one sanctuary, but they are mystical names for the church at prayer. He speaks of it as a spiritual symphony with every instrument in harmony, like an orchestra; the elders tuned to the bishop, like the strings to the harp; the congregation like the chorus; every man taking his note; every man playing his part; all breaking one bread in the one eucharist in union with the one bishop who represents the one God. He must be thinking of the actual church music, which played its part in creating the unity and grounding it in the heart through the senses.

Ignatius does describe himself as the minstrel of the churches; and there must have been a Christian tradition of hymns and spiritual songs, which contributed something to the language in which he wrote. But of course he had other resources. There was the reading of the Law and the Prophets; there was the written Gospel according to Matthew; there were the 'ordinances' of the apostles, by which he seems to mean their epistles; there were the creed-forms to which he resorts for homiletic summaries of the faith.

Like any good preacher, he loved the parable from common life, in which the spiritual realities are made available to the imagination. He talks of the light, the bread, the cup, the leaven, the water, the salt and the herbs, which are the components of the daily meal. The members of the church are stones for the temple, swung up into their high place by the mechanism of the cross, the Holy Spirit being the rope; they are 'God-bearers, temple-bearers, Christ-bearers, Holy-Spirit-bearers'. The teachers of evil doctrines come sowing devil's weeds; they mix deadly poison with their honey-wine. He speaks of living water, living and speaking water. He does not say much about the sacrament of baptism, though he often mentions the eucharist, calling it the elixir of immortality and the antidote against death.

SYRIAN CATHOLICISM

We have here some of the elements of a Syrian catholicism, based on the Judaeo-Christian tradition, but singularly free from purely Judaistic language. The traditions of Peter and Paul have passed into it, but the spirituality of Ignatius is really closer to that of John. The Spirit fills the ecclesia; it infuses itself into the corporate and sacramental life; it imparts itself to the faithful, uniting itself with their 'flesh'. The Spirit is life, and to have life is to have Christ; for Christ is our true life; but this union with Christ in the Spirit can only be realized in the unity of the ecclesia. A native Syrianism appears in this flesh-and-spirit theology.

Antioch was a Semitic or oriental city despite its use of the Greek language. It had much to bestow upon the church as a whole, and there is no sign that its influence was at an end. It had sent forth the first apostolic missions. The word *Christian* (*christianos*) had been first used there; and the epistles of Ignatius contain more new words of profound spiritual importance; *Christianity* (*christianismos*); *the Gospel* (*to euangelion*), used now of a written book; and the *Catholic Church*, meaning the universal church. The episcopate in its autonomous and apostolic form appears very clearly, and so do the eucharistic worship as the fullest expression of the Christian unity and fellowship; the creed-forms as characteristic declarations of the faith; the apostolic literature as a holy library; and particularly the Matthaean Gospel which the western churches soon accepted as the premier Gospel of the four. Sunday is mentioned as the resurrection day, taking the place of the Jewish Sabbath.

Antioch had been a starting-point for the apostolic missions; Ephesus had been a port of call on the road; 'You have been a haven for those who have been slain for the sake of God', Ignatius says. Rome had been their final goal. This picture was in his mind as he made his own progress from the church in Syria to the church in Rome; from the land of sunrise to the land of sunset. He protests, of course, that he cannot be compared with Peter or Paul; he is not issuing 'ordinances' to the churches as they had done; he is only writing as a disciple to his fellow-disciples. Nevertheless the comparison does underlie these statements, which are an eloquent witness to the prestige of the Antiochene bishop; and the claims which he repudiates may have been made for him by others. He addresses the churches *en apostoliko charakteri* —after the apostolic pattern. Relatively to Rome, Antioch was an originating centre of the Christian faith; the land of sunrise.

The word 'apostolic' is another new word.

THE GNOSIS OF IGNATIUS

In theology, if we may use that word of his flights of imagination, it was his aim to oppose a human historical gospel 'in flesh' to the fantastic myths and dreams which the gnostic mind was evolving out of the apostolic tradition; such dreams as we have studied in the myth of the 'Descent of the Christus'; but Ignatius had his own dreams about the unseen world and his own poetic fancies. In his Epistle to the Trallians he speaks of his meditations on the heavenly realms, which included the places allotted to the angels and the stations of the rulers; and these phrases undoubtedly suggest the background of the gnostic myth. It would not be fair to credit Ignatius with a mythological system of the gnostic sort, but he loves its language, as Paul himself had done.

In writing to the Ephesians he says that our God was Jesus Christ. He was brought to birth of the Virgin Mary by a dispensation of God, from the seed of David and from the Holy Spirit; and the virginity of Mary deceived the ruler of this world. How was it made manifest to the aeons? He turns from creed-form to poetry at this point, and gives us what is virtually the first Christmas carol

A star in the heavens
  Shone brighter than any star;
Its light was beyond description
  Its newness created wonder.

And all the other stars
  Along with the sun and moon,
Became a chorus to this star,
  Whose light excelled them all.

So every charm and chain was broken,
  The ignorance born of evil vanished away;
The ancient throne was cast down,
  When God appeared as Man
  Unto newness of life eternal.

THE EPISTLE TO THE ROMANS

While Ignatius was in Smyrna a communication arrived from Rome which mentioned the arrival there of an earlier party of Syrian Christians and also informed him of some plan which was proposed by the

Roman church to save him from martyrdom, though we have no idea how this could have been done. Someone was leaving for Rome by a faster route than he was taking, and this made it possible for him to send an appeal to the Roman church.

It was written in a different tone altogether from the other Epistles, since it was not a message of spiritual counsel and advice, composed in answer to a request. It was an entreaty with regard to his own case. His heart was set on martyrdom, and he prayed his Roman friends not to do him so unreasonable a favour as to save him from it. He was beginning to be a disciple now, and longed to complete his course and to give his life for God.

> You have taught others [he says], and all I ask is that you should implement the commands which you give [them] when you make [them] disciples.
> (Ignatius, *Romans*, III, I.)

This is the famous passage which is so often twisted out of all recognition in the service of controversy, and is sometimes misquoted by scholars who ought to know better, in the form 'You taught other churches'. Ignatius has many complimentary things to say about the Roman church; but he does not say that it taught other churches. He is referring to the regular baptismal instruction.[1]

'Do not torment me', he goes on; 'and even if I implore you when I arrive among you, do not believe what I say then, but believe what I am writing now.' Just for a moment he seems to doubt his own resolution, and fears any possible efforts to weaken it. Hermas had said that the Christian who inwardly questioned his ability to stand firm was already lost. He must be sublimely certain of himself in the spirit. Ignatius was destined to become a pattern of such resolution and this Epistle of his to the Romans, which was circulated separately from the others, was destined to become an inspiration to others who were in his position.

He recovers himself, and in his exaltation of spirit, his words take lyrical form.

> Him do I seek, the one who died for me:
> Him do I seek, the one who rose for me:
> Birth lies before me!

[1] The words are based on Matthew xxviii. 19–20: 'Make disciples...baptizing ...teaching...whatsoever I have commanded.'

Hinder me not to live! Refuse me not to die!
Suffer me now to take pure Light,
And, there arriving, I shall be a Man—
  Suffer me now
To imitate the passion of my God.
(Ignatius, *Romans*, VII, 2.)

Living I write: falling in love with dying.
My Love is crucified in me, and now
There is no fire in me that loves dead matter,
But water, living and talking in my soul,
Saying, Come hither: To the Father: Come! (*Ibid.*)

This is the language of the mystic, of the Syrian mystery cults perhaps; but entirely sublimated, and devoted to the person of the crucified.

The letter is dated August 24, a week before the Greco-Syrian New Year. It is the first Christian document to be dated by the Roman calendar; the second such date is found in another Smyrnaean document, the martyrdom of Polycarp. Unfortunately Ignatius does not mention the year.

IGNATIUS AT TROAS

The party now went on to Troas, where Paul had received his original call to evangelize Macedonia. Five years later he had waited there impatiently to hear from Titus the outcome of the Corinthian conflict. In his last year of evangelizing, he had left his cloak and his books and his parchments there with Carpus; and the house of Carpus may still have been the centre of church life when Ignatius arrived there. Burrhus went with him and he was joined at last by his Cilician deacon Philo and his Antiochene deacon Agathopous, 'an elect man who had said good-bye to life'. The bishop must have been an elect man, too, to inspire such service. They brought him the news that the persecution in Antioch had ceased, and a great council was being organized.

The two deacons had passed through Philadelphia, where Ignatius had run into controversy, and they had encountered a similar heckling; but the church as a whole had given them a warm welcome. Ignatius now wrote his Epistle to the Philadelphians, and another to the Smyrnaeans. We note a new emphasis in these Epistles, which dealt with the problem of schism.

We would judge that the Jewish party in Philadelphia was not actually separated from the church; for men who professed Christianity were urging the claims of Judaism in the church assembly. The Docetics, on the other hand, appear to have separated themselves, or been separated, and this leads Ignatius to make a new point. Schismatics may be restored to the unity of the church provided they repent (a point in which he agreed with Clement); but those who follow a schism-maker have no inheritance in the kingdom of God.

The situation was serious. It was necessary to warn the Smyrnaeans against certain wild animals in human form, who were not to be received or even encountered, if this was possible. They were to be prayed for in the hope that they would repent, though this was a hard thing. Ignatius had encountered them personally, presumably at Troas, or on the way there, and they were now on the road to Smyrna. They had flattered him, but he had resisted their flatteries. They were not convinced by the Law or the Prophets, or even by the gospel as yet. They refused to confess the Lord as a human being 'in the flesh'. They had no faith in the blood of the Messiah. They had no fear of judgement to come. They were persons of influence and importance; 'Let no one be inflated by his *position*', Ignatius says.

He goes on to discuss their indifference to the common Christianity and its social order; they cared nothing for love or charity; for the widow or the orphan or the afflicted, or the prisoner or the hungry or the thirsty; they absented themselves from eucharist and prayer, because they did not confess the eucharist to be the flesh of our Saviour Christ. He could give their names, but he refuses to mention them unless they repent.

It is a crisis in the church, with which Polycarp would have to deal as bishop of Smyrna; and Ignatius writes him a personal letter urging him to be firm. Polycarp mentions these men in his own letter to the Philippians, and gives the same picture as Ignatius. These teachers of an over-spiritualized gospel, which had parted company with the human element in the gospel record, were the predecessors of the Marcionite heresy; and it is important to note that they were officially condemned at this early date in Antioch and Smyrna. It is not said, however, that they rejected the God of the Jews, or preached Jesus as the Son of some higher deity, as Satornil did in Antioch and Marcion afterwards in Rome.

Ignatius goes on, in his Epistle to the Smyrnaeans and in the companion Epistle to Polycarp, to dwell on the social order of the church, and all its complex ministrations and personal relations, domestic, educational and charitable. His farewell sounds a sadder and more personal note; he has to break the ties with a number of new friends, including the charming Alke and the faithful Burrhus, whom he commends as a pattern of God's diaconate.

IGNATIUS AT PHILIPPI

Ignatius tells us nothing about the church at Troas and the people he met there. One gets the impression that his party was waiting for a fair wind, an experience which serves as an illustration in his Epistle to Polycarp. The fair weather seems to have come suddenly, as such changes do, and it left him no time to complete his epistolary programme. He had to ask Polycarp to do this for him. He was sailing at once for Neapolis.

Or was the Epistle to Polycarp written from Neapolis? or even from Philippi? for a mail reached Polycarp from Philippi, by the hand of a certain Crescens, a Smyrnaean Christian who was planning to make his home there with his sister. It informed Polycarp of the welcome which had been given to Ignatius, and it must have mentioned Zosimus and Rufus too, since they are associated with Ignatius in Polycarp's reply. Ignatius had urged the Philippians to send delegates to the council at Antioch; but they contented themselves with sending letters which they entrusted to the Smyrnaeans to deliver. They asked Polycarp to send them copies of the Epistles which Ignatius had written to the churches in Asia.

There was other news of a less pleasant sort. A certain elder, named Valens, had misunderstood the position which was given him and had been guilty of various irregularities. The church at Philippi requested Polycarp to write them an 'Epistle concerning Righteousness' to help them over this crisis.

The epistle which the Philippians wrote to Polycarp has not survived, but it can be reconstructed to this extent out of Polycarp's reply. After that there is no further information about Ignatius. His party must have continued their journey overland to the Adriatic coast, with Zosimus and Rufus who seem to have been picked up at Philippi.

There they would take to sea again, and so reach Italy. The accounts of the martyrdom are late and worthless; but the day of the saint in the Syrian martyrology is October 17, and this agrees so well with the date August 24 in his Epistle to the Romans as to suggest that it may be a true tradition. If so, it is the earliest instance of the remembrance of the 'birthday' of a martyr; and we noted that Ignatius did allude to his death as a mystical birth, a birth into life eternal.

THE EPISTLE TO POLYCARP

We must now return to the Epistle which he wrote to Polycarp himself. It was addressed to him as bishop, but was intended to be read to him in church; it was semi-private, semi-public, like the epistle to Philemon, and possibly I Timothy. It salutes him not merely as bishop of Smyrna, but as the leader who was destined to bear the principal burden during the next generation. 'The times call for you', he says, 'as the shipmasters wait for winds, and the storm-driven mariners look for the harbour.'

Stand firm as an anvil under the blows of the hammer. It is the part of a great athlete to be beaten and to win the victory; how much more must we endure everything for the sake of God, that he may endure us.

(Ignatius, *To Polycarp*, III, I.)

The last clause seems to be an example of the lack of literary precision which is complained of in the writings of Ignatius; or did he mean to write 'who endured for us'?

Ignatius was more than a bishop, more even than a martyr. He was the athlete of the Christian church, the strong man of his time, whose life was given on behalf of all the churches, as he himself says in his rhetorical style. 'I am your off-scourings, your scapegoat, your soul-substitute.' My life is given for you, is what he means. Force of circumstances had made him the champion of the church and the defender of the faith. Polycarp would succeed him, and be for forty more years the central pillar of Christendom, until the day when he would give his life like Ignatius, as a bishop and a martyr and a prophetic teacher. Ignatius urged Polycarp to pray for more understanding, and to 'be more eager than thou art'. To his rapid mentality there was something slow and perhaps a little sluggish about the younger man, who is often dismissed by modern writers as conservative and lacking in originality; but in this respect he was a good representative of his period. The creative times were over and Ignatius, the ardent mystic and rhetorician, had no successors of his type; he was like Clement's phoenix, a rare and solitary bird.

Polycarp was no theologian, but an admirable teacher and pastor. He repeated the formulas of the apostolic kerugma and the apostolic tradition. He had a complete library of apostolic literature, including Clement; and he did not travel far from it. He stood firm just where he was like the anvil of the Ignatian metaphor. He was an iron man.

THE EPISTLE OF POLYCARP TO THE PHILIPPIANS

His Epistle is addressed from Polycarp and the elders who are with him, to the church of God which sojourns at Philippi. It mentions their reception of the martyrs in flowery language, which is almost worthy of Ignatius himself; but from that point it declines into a sober moralistic style which shows the influence of Clement.

He begins by recalling to the memory of the Philippians the faith which they had received in the earliest times, expressing it in words drawn from the apostolic writings, and notably from I Peter. He is emphasizing the true death and resurrection in opposition to the Docetics. He goes on to quote some words of the Lord which resemble Luke rather than Matthew, but are most likely drawn from the oral teaching:

> Judge not that ye be not judged,
> Forgive, and ye shall be forgiven,
> Show mercy that ye may receive mercy:
> With what measure ye measure,
> It shall be measured unto you.

and

> Blessed are the poor,
> And those who are persecuted for righteousness' sake:
> For theirs is the Kingdom of God.
>
> (Polycarp, *Philippians*, II.)

The first of these passages closely resembles the similar quotation in Clement.

He thus approaches the subject of 'righteousness', but pauses to apologize for his lack of qualification for dealing with it. He is totally unable to follow the wisdom of the blessed and glorious Paul, who had lived among them himself and written them Epistles; and this modesty is shown to be sincere by the way in which he continually falls back on the language of the apostolic writings, including Acts, I Peter, and I John. He confesses that he has no learning in the Old Testament scriptures. He mentions the three traditional virtues of faith, hope and charity. He goes on to the two commandments of love. Love, he maintains, is the fulfilment of righteousness, but the love of money is the beginning of all troubles, thus glancing at the case of Valens, we may suppose.

This echo of I Timothy introduces an exhortation in the style of that Epistle:

Let us arm ourselves with the armour of righteousness,
Let us begin by training ourselves to walk in the Lord's commandments,
And our women-folk to practise the domestic virtues.

(Polycarp, *Philippians*, IV, 1–2.)

He considers in turn the widows, the deacons, the young people, and finally the elders. The passage is also reminiscent of the Epistle of Clement, which was very much in Polycarp's mind.

He goes on to the question of forgiveness, and so to the false teachers who lead astray empty-headed men. He issues a strong warning against the Docetic heresy, in the course of which he quotes from the Epistle of John.

Whoever confesses not Jesus Christ as having come in the flesh is Antichrist.

(I John iv. 3.)

And whoever does not confess the witness of the cross, he is of the devil.
And whoever falsifies the Oracles of the Lord for his own lusts, and says there is neither resurrection nor judgement, he is the firstborn of Satan.

(Polycarp, *Philippians*, VII, 1.)

He urges the Philippians to follow the examples of Ignatius, Zosimus and Rufus, not to mention their own martyrs, and Paul himself and the rest of the apostles. He grieves over the erring elder and his wife, and prays that they may be granted true repentance and be restored as members of the church. The notion that Christians who have sinned cannot be restored is seldom found in the literature which appears at the top level in the early period.

THE CASE OF VALENS

The last Epistles of Ignatius had dealt with the same situation as the Epistle of Polycarp, the danger, locally, of the Docetic heresy. Ignatius knew the names of the leaders, but would not demean himself to give them. Perhaps Polycarp does mention one of them. 'I was deeply grieved about Valens', he says, 'who was at one time appointed a presbyter among you, that he should so *misunderstand the position* which was given to him'; and Ignatius had said, 'Let no one be *inflated by his position.*' It may be inferred from what Polycarp says that Valens and his wife were fond of money and not particularly chaste or truthful; but what he actually says about him is that he had a false view of his position in the church.

He prays that he may be granted true repentance, which is what Ignatius had said should be done. He advises the Philippians not to regard *such persons* as enemies, but to win them back as frail and erring members to the body, which shows that there were others of his type in Philippi who constituted a problem; a schismatic group in fact. It looks as if Valens were something more than an individual presbyter who had been found out in financial and social scandals. The terms of Polycarp's letter are consistent with the view that he had intellectual pretensions, had left Philippi under a cloud, had crossed swords with Ignatius at Troas, and then come on to Smyrna with his wife and possibly with a colleague or two. This reconstruction draws together the various references in the three closely related epistles, and so provides a more solid and realistic basis for the Epistle of Polycarp, which seems to require something more than the defalcations of one elder to explain. It has even been suggested that Valens had been the bishop of Philippi, and that Crescens was now designated as his successor.

A close examination of these possibilities seems to be called for, since there is a theory which explains the serious tone of the Epistle by dividing it in two and assigning the major part of it to a later date, so that Polycarp's anathema against Docetism can be regarded as a polemic against Marcion. He uses the provocative expression 'the first-born of Satan', which he applied to Marcion at a later date, according to a well attested story. But the heretics in the Epistle of Polycarp are not said to have repudiated the God of the Jewish revelation in favour of a higher deity, as Marcion did; and they are described in exactly the same terms as the Docetics mentioned by Ignatius. Furthermore Polycarp might use the same language about heresy more than once in his long life. His Epistle fits exactly into the background supplied by Ignatius.

THE CONCLUSION OF POLYCARP'S EPISTLE

The theory of a later date for the bulk of his Epistle, somewhere in the hundred-and-twenties possibly, or even in the hundred-and-thirties, requires that the two last paragraphs, 13 and 14, should be detached from the rest and regarded as a separate letter of an early date, since their reference to Ignatius is obviously contemporary; it would consist of the brief notes which follow the benediction and prayer. Polycarp promises the Philippians to send their letters to Antioch; he may even take them himself, as he hopes to attend the council there. He had also, at their request, had copies made of the Ignatian Epistles, which he sends with the letter. He asks for further news about Ignatius and his companions as soon as reliable information becomes available. Like Clement, he undertakes the management of the correspondence with distant churches. We see how collections of such Epistles were made and distributed.

The theory is that these short notes, after the benediction and prayer, were a 'covering letter', which Polycarp sent to Philippi with the Ignatian Epistles; the bulk of the Epistle, ending with the benediction and prayer, could then be regarded as a later composition which was designed to deal with two problems, the heresy of Marcion and the dishonesty of Valens; though indeed it mentions the patient endurance of Ignatius, Zosimus and Rufus, and speaks of prisoners wreathed in honourable chains who had recently received a welcome in Philippi.

Actually the position of these brief notes after the benediction is sufficiently accounted for by the fact that they would be out of place in the body of a solemn charge which was to be read, as such, to the congregation. There are few apostolic Epistles which end on the solemn benediction; and I Peter, which Polycarp takes as a model, has short notes after the benediction.

The letter was written for Polycarp by Crescens, who was returning to Philippi. His sister is to follow him in a few days. And so the story ends, so far as the historical evidence is concerned; but the scenes which we have been privileged to witness give us a lively view of church life as it was lived in the third apostolic generation, when men who could remember the apostles were still to be found, and their memory was yet green in the land.

We note that wherever the preservation of contemporary documents allows us a clear view of apostolic Christianity we are given a picture of busy activity and energetic administration. It is a scene of continual conflict and motion; conflict with the outside world and with the alien philosophy which was filtering its way into the church; motion of men and documents from one church to another. There was nothing aimless or left to chance. The churches were always interacting upon one another and giving one another assistance in the spiritual warfare. They were not afraid of strong leadership. Strong characters appear upon the scene who have an organic relation to the apostolic tradition and to the churches which they address. They stand firm and enable the whole church to gain strength and so pass through the crisis of the hour.

Clement, Hermas, Ignatius and Polycarp were men of this type. We are not at liberty to think of them simply as literary and theological figures whose works chanced to survive. They were proved and tested 'Elders' of apostolic and prophetic quality, whose labours crowned the apostolic tradition itself; and it is only by studying the whole mass of human and personal data, woven so far as is possible into a continuous story, that we are able to get the feel of the church life, and so relate our other studies to the realities of the situation. However we may reconstruct the story in this or that detail, this general picture remains the same.

CHAPTER 25

APOSTOLIC TRADITION

The gospel in the church, *p.* 464. The local unit, *p.* 465. The Jewish inheritance, *p.* 465. Lord's Day and *Pascha*, *p.* 466. The Hebrew Bible, *p.* 467. The apostolic literature, *p.* 467. The written Gospel, *p.* 469. The unified episcopate, *p.* 470. The two types of episcopacy, *p.* 472. The Roman bishops, *p.* 474. From Clement to Xystus, *p.* 475. The bishop's house, *p.* 476. The Jewish antecedents, *p.* 477. The life-line of the gospel, *p.* 478.

THE GOSPEL IN THE CHURCH

Perhaps an external observer would have seen little likelihood now of the emergence of a uniform Christian tradition out of the great variety of forms which were coming into existence; but the variety was of the very essence of the gospel tradition. The types of apostolic Christianity which were created in the second generation were derived from differences which had existed from the beginning of the first generation. They were continued into the third generation, but each area of Christian tradition, as it emerges into clearer light, is found to exhibit the same pattern, which is given the convenient name of catholicism. It appears as a whole for the first time in the pages of Ignatius.

There were two forces which constituted and maintained the unity of the church; and these two were one. They were the gospel and the apostolate; the message and the mission. The gospel was never a message or theory existing in a vacuum; it was always embodied in men and propagated through men; and it boasted of a divine power called the Holy Spirit which flowed through it into the church and worked wonders. It was 'in flesh' as Ignatius says.

Paul insists that whatever differences there may have been between Peter and James and himself, as heads of traditions, they had but one gospel. The core of this gospel was the death and resurrection of Jesus Christ. It follows that when the Docetic teachers denied the actual death and resurrection, the church could recognize that these teachers were not in line with the gospel; it made Ignatius look to his written Gospel and his theology and his creed-forms; it made Polycarp look to his apostolic records. The formation of schismatic groups made them look to the problem of church order and church unity.

THE LOCAL UNIT

The church had grown up on a territorial basis, a principle which was expressed in the conviction that there could only be one church in each city. Paul wrote to the church of God in Corinth. There were lesser units there, grouped in or round influential families or households, and one of these had a special ministerial position in relation to the whole; but the church to which he wrote was the church of Corinth. 'When your whole church meets together', he writes, in speaking of spiritual graces. This whole church, and every member of the body of it, was filled with the Holy Spirit.

When Clement wrote to the Corinthians, he also addressed them as a whole church, and expected action to be taken by the whole church with the constituted elders. He wrote on behalf of the whole church at Rome, which could therefore act as a unity despite its multiple origin. There were dissident groups, he says, but plainly such action had taken place as marked them off from the recognized unity. The Clementine church in Rome was as deeply concerned with the problem of unity as the Ignatian church in Antioch, and had found it in the same way, through the Spirit-filled worship of the whole ecclesia.

The maintenance of the local unity was the fundamental problem of the period of transition. It was solved on this level by the adoption of the form of the episcopate in which one bishop presided over the local ecclesia with a council of elders.

THE JEWISH INHERITANCE

The problem may now be approached from another angle. The evidence of the apostolic and sub-apostolic literature discloses a substantial identity of tradition everywhere, which was derived from the apostolic gospel as it expressed itself in the medium of Jewish synagogue order; or we may prefer to say, from the Jewish synagogue order as it was transformed by the gospel and the Spirit. The Law of Moses was not binding in the Gentile churches, but no objection was raised to its continuance in the Jewish churches; though there must have been serious problems where Jewish and Gentile churches co-existed in one community.

The historical tradition of Judaism provided the pattern for the

Christian liturgy and the substance out of which it was formed. It provided the faith in the one God, who was encountered in history and revelation and apocalypse as a living God. He and no other was the 'Father' of our Lord Jesus Christ. We have not yet found any evidence in Christian literature of Docetic theologians dispensing with the Jewish scriptures or the Jewish revelation of God; but as the views of Satornil and others like him spread more widely, various anti-Jewish schools of thought came into existence which were at once recognized as foreign to the apostolic tradition.

The liturgical tradition of the Christian churches exhibits everywhere a number of institutional features which were solidly based on Jewish antecedents. The most instructive of these is the observance of Sunday as the Lord's Day.

LORD'S DAY AND *PASCHA*

The observance of holy days is a good example to begin with, since it has not been clouded by modern inter-church dispute. All Christians keep Sunday, even where the Christian year generally speaking has been abandoned. It is not the Jewish Sabbath, but its observance was due to the existence of the Jewish Sabbath; for it depends upon the institution of the seven-day week. How did this remarkable shift in religious observance occur? It is obvious that the resurrection of Jesus Christ on the first Easter Sunday had this very powerful effect; but this is strictly speaking only an inference from the known facts. It cannot be directly documented. The occasional writings of the apostles and their successors do not happen to say this.

Paul refers once to the first day of the week; offerings of money were to be laid aside on this day. Luke refers to it once; he describes an all-night vigil, with the 'breaking of the bread' taking place at dawn. John refers to it once; his vision on the island took place on the Lord's Day. Ignatius connects it with the Resurrection. The *Didache* says that the eucharist should be celebrated every Lord's Day. 'Barnabas' discusses it. It is always a casual or accidental reference until we come to the *Didache*. Everybody is keeping Sunday; everybody knows what it is; and there is no need to explain it. It has never become a subject of argument. It is a 'catholic' custom which originated in apostolic times: it was part of the gospel tradition.

A similar custom was the keeping of the annual *Pascha* or Passover in its Christian form. In the second century we have evidence that a solemn fast was kept on or near this day, which was the anniversary of the Crucifixion. A very early documentary reference to it mentions a dispute at Rome in the hundred-and-twenties about the proper day on which to observe it, so that the custom must have been well established by that time. The New Testament evidence is entirely indirect; yet the paschal references in I Corinthians and other authorities are so numerous and appropriate as to compel the belief that serious attention was paid to it. The Gospels, and I Peter, and I Clement, in various ways support this belief.

THE HEBREW BIBLE

Another legacy from Judaism was the reading of the Law and the Prophets which had been canonized for some two centuries in the Jewish tradition. Along with these went Daniel and Job and the Psalms, and the Song of Songs and other books which were in actual use in the Temple and the synagogue. The limits of this third division of the scriptures were authoritatively defined for the synagogue by the rabbis at Jamnia, and their decision was accepted in due course in the church; a striking indication of the close affiliation of second generation Christianity with the Jewish liturgical practice.

The churches had followed the lead of the Hellenistic synagogue, however, in reading a much wider assortment of holy books, though it did not necessarily quote them as scripture. Quite recent books like the *Wisdom of Solomon* and the Apocalypses of Baruch and Ezra passed from the synagogue into the ecclesia, and were associated with the canonical scriptures. Older books like *Enoch* or *Testaments* were also read. There is no means of assessing their exact status, or discovering the steps by which they were ultimately classified or de-classified. Suffice it to say that a considerable library was inherited from Judaism along with the canonical scriptures.

THE APOSTOLIC LITERATURE

Next to these were the books which were written by the apostles or by their pupils preserving their teaching. When we reflect on the uncertainties of the period, we may safely conclude that nothing can have given the church leaders greater confidence than the possession of these documents.

It was a transition period in two different ways. It was a period of transition from the 'synagogue' condition in which the church was not completely separated from Judaism; and it was also a period of transition from the missionary phase in which it depended on an apostolic or missionary order which was almost entirely Jewish, for direction, supervision and even the appointment of an indigenous ministry. The churches of Asia, as we saw them in the Pastorals, and the churches of Corinth and Rome, as we saw them in I Clement, had not passed beyond this stage. The churches of Syria and Asia, as we see them in Ignatius, have completed the transition; and the leaders of the Syrian and Asian churches are armed with an apostolic literature which seems to be more complete than the Roman.

The modern text-books rightly insist that this literature was not grouped with the Old Testament *as scripture*. Its position was not defined; but it was highly authoritative. The supreme authority in the church was the Lord Jesus Christ himself, who was represented by his apostles and apostolic ministries; it was a living voice that resounded in the church through the lips of living men. As the authentic living voice receded into the past and strange teachers brought in new theologies, the surviving literature became supremely important. The written Gospels superseded the living voice of the actual disciples and disciples of disciples; the written Epistles took the place of the living voice of the apostolic founders. These books had been designed as substitutes for the living voice in the first place, and that continued to be their value. The third generation men used them with confidence to fortify their own messages.

There is a great advance in Ignatius and Polycarp in the use of apostolic literature. Clement, in the nineties, was still in the 'synagogue' stage. He writes in the succession of the apostolic Epistles, some of which he knows very well; but he works directly from the Old Testament, in the light of an education and training which was fundamentally that of the Hellenistic synagogue. Neither Ignatius nor Polycarp does this. They work directly from an apostolic literature. There is often room for doubt whether a certain book has been quoted or not; but there is no room for doubt or debate about the impressive fact that these writers were steeped in the apostolic literature, modelled their own writings on it, and made numerous references to it when addressing the churches, which must therefore have been familiar with it too.

The following summary will serve to illustrate these statements.

Mark is best attested by its use in the three later evangelists and by the statement of the elder John; it was probably used by Clement, and certainly by Hermas. Luke appears to have been known to John. Matthew is the authority to which Ignatius alludes as the gospel, but he has read Luke and John as well. Acts was used by Polycarp. The Pauline Epistles were used by Clement, Hermas, Ignatius, and Polycarp, though they are naturally not all attested by indubitable quotations. Ignatius speaks of 'ordinances' given by Peter as well as Paul. The Pastoral Epistles and I Peter were used by Clement and Polycarp. Hebrews was used by Clement and Hermas. I Peter and I John were used by Polycarp and Papias. James was used by Hermas. Clement was used by Polycarp. Papias used the Revelation. Clement and Hermas interlock, and so do Ignatius and Polycarp. There is no trace of the smaller epistles, Jude, and II or III John. II Peter was definitely not written till after this period.

It is amazing that so many traces of the apostolic literature can be found in so few pages. No writer can be expected to reveal the full range of his reading in indubitable quotations, or even in passing allusions, in the course of brief messages or exhortations designed to suit some special situation. The evidence that emerges justifies us in concluding that our New Testament books were, for the most part, in general use as part of the church order. One or two statements in the above notes might be questioned by this or that scholar or differently expressed; but the picture of a familiar, operative, interrelated literature is soundly established.

THE WRITTEN GOSPEL

We may not assume, however, that the tradition in every church, at the dawn of the second century, was uniform; far from it. The use of the Gospels is a case in point. Clement and Polycarp seem to quote the words of Jesus as from an oral tradition. It seems that they were repeating them as they had heard them from disciples of Jesus. Written Gospels were in general use, but it would seem that they had not superseded the oral tradition in Rome or Asia or Phrygia.

Now Ignatius brought with him a different conception. He had a written Gospel to which he appealed as a final authority; it was, of course, Matthew, and the position he claimed for it was virtually that of scripture. It is fair to say that this opinion is not accepted by every scholar, but it seems to be required by the evidence; he speaks of the Law, the Prophets, the Gospel, and the ordinances of the apostles, in close conjunction with one another, and makes use of them all.

His reference to a written Gospel had not passed without protest. There had been an argument at Philadelphia with the Judaizers, in which 'the Gospel' had been discussed (*Philad.* VIII, 2); he had said 'It is written', and they had said, 'That is the point under discussion'. They argued that what was in the Gospel should be supported by what they called the archives; very likely the Old Testament. It is impossible to unravel the argument, but it is clear that the written authority referred to by Ignatius was not accepted in Philadelphia as he would have liked it to be.

Our four Gospels were known to the church in Asia as they were in Antioch; but no four-Gospel canon for use in the church had yet come into existence. Even a one-Gospel canon was advancing against difficulties. The fourfold Gospel still existed in a dispersed form. It had not been gathered together, unified and corporately accepted. The condition of the episcopal ministry was rather similar.

THE UNIFIED EPISCOPATE

We come now to difficult ground, which has been traversed by hosts of theologians with different theories to maintain. The unified episcopate appears fully developed in the letters of Ignatius, and he speaks about it with his customary ardour.

The position of the bishop in the church is that of the representative of God or of Jesus Christ. He is in the place of God or is a 'type' of God. God is the universal bishop or shepherd or teacher, as we find in I Peter, where he is called the 'shepherd and bishop of your souls'. We have no adequate translation of the word in English; for we mentally interpose associations drawn from church experience or controversy. Even in the Greek world from which the word was taken, it had a wide range of meaning. The gods in pagan Greece were called the 'bishops' of solemn oaths or covenants; they were guardians or watchmen over men. In I Peter and Ignatius God is the supreme guardian or watchman over mankind. The pastoral care originates in God.

The idea of the ministry presented by Ignatius was not a new one. In Hebrew thought the divinely appointed authority speaks and acts for the deity, a principle which included the honour due to parents; he who honours his father and mother has it ascribed to him as if he honoured God. It was extended to the apostles through the divine mission of Jesus; he who receives you, Jesus says to his apostles, receives me; and he who receives me, receives him that sent me. He leaves them as stewards of his household. It is frequent in the *Didache*; the teacher, the apostle, or the prophet, is to be received 'as the Lord'. Ignatius gives no history of the episcopate, as Clement did, but he has this gospel tradition in mind.

Everyone whom the master of the house sends as his steward, we should receive as we would the one who sent him; it is obvious therefore that we should reverence the bishop as the Lord himself.

(Ignatius, *Ephesians*, VI.)

There is no sign in Ignatius that the bishop had any large powers apart from his council of elders, or indeed apart from the ecclesia, though he was of necessity the key-man and chief executive. He was responsible for the teaching; he had the care of the widow and orphan; he had some regulative power in connexion with marriage and the celibate life; he celebrated the eucharist or designated others to do so; and it is as master of the liturgy that his divine commission most clearly appears.

Ignatius is entirely in favour of having more frequent assemblies; 'let assemblies be more frequent', he writes to Polycarp. Now these assemblies, or 'synagogues', could be turbulent and stormy; and it would seem that the bishop could do nothing about it. The bishop of Philadelphia remained silent, and was highly commended for it. The bishop of Ephesus had also learned the value of silence. At the best, it would seem, the bishop could assert his spiritual leadership by a prophetic utterance. The promoters of Judaism, or even of Docetism, do not seem to have been ruled out of order. It would appear that they had the right to state their views. However strongly the bishop felt on the subject, his method had to be that of persuasion. Ignatius himself relied on persuasion; he did not issue ordinances like the apostles.

The position of the bishop was not strong, and Ignatius is urging the churches to support him. The word he uses means to submit or be subordinate; it is the standard word in all the apostolic catechisms; and it is the least a chairman can expect. In the last resort, it would seem, the bishop could stop his ears and leave the assembly, and Polycarp was known to do this. The assembly could do the same if it heard doctrine that it objected to. The procedure was actually adopted at the Council of Nicaea.

THE TWO TYPES OF EPISCOPACY

Much ingenuity has been expended in attempting to show how the plural bishops of the Pastoral Epistles and of I Clement 'developed' into the single bishop and presbytery of the eastern pattern; but there is no reason to suppose that any such 'development' occurred. The current of Christianity did not normally flow from west to east. It is better to say that we can distinguish two principal forms of the apostolic order: a system of plural bishops in the Pauline churches of the far west, lacking powers of ordination and dependent upon apostolic persons, or churches with apostolic leaders, for certain purposes or services; and an autonomous episcopate in the eastern churches, in which plenary authority was vested in a single bishop with a council of presbyters. It is obvious from the Epistles of Ignatius that the latter system was the dominant one in his time throughout Syria and Asia Minor; and he speaks of bishops established to the end of the earth; but it does not follow that these bishops were in every case single bishops. He knows and advocates the single-bishop system, but it does not follow that he would not have recognized plural bishops where they existed.

As a matter of fact we do not know what form of the episcopate was in use in the west when Ignatius wrote. The view of the situation which appears in his letters does not extend any further west than the churches of Asia, though of course he cannot have been without information about more distant churches. In Philippi, however, we have an old Pauline church which was not provided apparently with a bishop, since Polycarp only mentions presbyters and deacons in his salutation; but even so we must be on our guard; the expression 'presbyters' may include venerable clergy and teachers of all kinds, perhaps even a bishop or bishops.

Or there may have been a vacancy in the see when he wrote. It has even been suggested that the erring 'presbyter' Valens may have been the bishop; for bishops continued to be described by the honorific title of 'elder' for centuries. Valens may have been the old bishop, and Crescens the new one; his so-called sister may have been his wife, as we suggested in the case of Philemon. But let us assume that Philippi had no bishop. It is the assumption which is generally made.

It was not a large church with great resources, or it would have been able to send a delegate to the council at Antioch. It was in agreement with the general outlook of Ignatius, for it received him worthily and asked for copies of his letters. It had geared itself, perhaps, to the single-bishop system, by speaking of its clergy as elders and deacons, not bishops and deacons, which is what Paul had called them when he instituted the ministry there. It showed need of additional moral and spiritual oversight by asking for directions from Polycarp, possibly on the advice of Ignatius. Like the Corinth of twenty years before, it had an incomplete church order, which could not stand alone; it had not quite passed out of its missionary phase, when it had depended upon a superior ministry of apostles and apostolic men. It can be no accident that it was in Corinth and Philippi, where the single episcopate was not in operation, that it was found necessary to have recourse to a neighbouring church, with a stronger establishment, and a leading man of apostolic character, when trouble arose which affected the clergy themselves.

It was perfectly natural, therefore, that the Epistles of such apostolic men as Clement and Polycarp, written under such circumstances (with the concurrence of their churches), should be enrolled with the apostolic Epistles, since their production was a continuation of the old apostolic procedure. The distinction or gap which we mentally interpose is an unhistorical one, based on the subsequent fact that some of them have been canonized, whereas others have not. There was a difference of degree of course. Polycarp modestly disclaims any comparison between the advice he gives the Philippians and the advice which Paul gave them; but the disclaimer itself is an indication that he was doing for them very much what Paul used to do for them; otherwise it had no point.

THE ROMAN BISHOPS

We must now complete our survey by considering the case of Rome. The impression which we receive, from Clement and other sources, of the stability of the Roman church is strengthened by various references in Ignatius; for he uses an even greater number than usual of his compound polysyllabic adjectives in addressing her: she is God-worthy, honour-worthy, blessing-worthy, praise-worthy, good-fortune-worthy, and sanctification-worthy; she presides in love; she keeps the law of Christ and the name of the Father. He adds also that she 'presides in the place of the region of the Romans'; a phrase which suggests a position of leadership among the nearby churches. There is nothing in the form of address which would have been found extraordinary had it been written from Rome to the church of Antioch, which of course presided in the place of the region of the Syrians; and Ignatius does call himself bishop of Syria more than once. Antioch and Rome both enjoyed leading positions in their respective 'regions'.

On the other hand, Ignatius makes no reference to any bishop at Rome, as he does in his five other letters to churches; and it has been argued that he fails to do so because there was no bishop there of the type to which he was accustomed. The controversy has been long drawn out, but there is surely only one fair statement which can be made; he makes no reference and we are not entitled to draw conclusions.

We turn to the 'Visions' of Hermas and we find him referring to the elders as the authority which authorizes him to deliver his message in the church; the elders or rulers occupied the principal seats, and he sat with them. He refers to Clement as the person who communicated with the church at large; but he fails to give him a title. In his allegory of the tower, he mentions bishops, teachers, and deacons in close association with the apostles; but some years later, in his second version of it, he treats of bishops and deacons separately from the apostles and teachers who are now relegated to a past period. The use of the plural does not quite prove that there were several bishops in Rome. The tower signified the universal church, and the bishops who appear in the explanation of the allegory must be the bishops of the universal church. Pius the brother of Hermas was unquestionably a single bishop; but this was rather later than the period with which we are dealing.

FROM CLEMENT TO XYSTUS

The traditional date for the death of Clement is 100, but it rests on uncertain evidence. He may have survived a year or two longer. According to the episcopal list which was supplied to Hegesippus some fifty years later he was succeeded by Euarestus, and Euarestus by Hyginus. The later Roman list gives the years of their episcopates:

A.D. 64 Linus: 12 years.
Cletus (Anencletus): 12 years.
Clement: 12 years.
Euarestus: 8 or 9 years.
Alexander: 10 years.
Xystus or Sixtus: 10 years.

These are the names of historic leaders who were remembered in the Roman church as the legitimate bishops of their day; but nothing in the way of detailed information appears until we come to Xystus. The period between Clement and Xystus is a historical blank except for the martyrdom of Ignatius, of which no record remains.

Xystus had to deal with the problem of the day on which the *Pascha* should be observed, and allowed the Asians in Rome to keep the fast according to the Johannine custom. He sent them the eucharist from his own service. In later centuries the Popes still sent a portion of the eucharist to the parish churches as a symbol of unity; and it was called the *fermentum* or leaven, which suggests that the custom originated in connexion with the *Pascha*. This fact about Xystus, which is vouched for by Irenaeus, enables us to see that he was regarded in his day as the centre of liturgical unity for Christians in the city. His action was in line with the view of Ignatius that the eucharist should be under the bishop's control; and it illuminates the statement that he could give permission for others to celebrate it. It provided a method of recognizing minority groups. It suggests that the position in Antioch and in Smyrna may have been more complex than appears on the surface.

The martyrdom of Ignatius may have taken place as early as 110, and it can be placed as late as 117. The Syrian Chronicle allots it to 115. The accession date of Xystus is uncertain, but it was probably the later of the two events; and it has been suggested that the arrival of Ignatius in Rome, and the great influence which he exercised as a martyr and a prophetic man, may have helped to clarify the position of the single bishop in the city; but even so it must have been anticipated to some extent in the persons of Clement and Euarestus and Alexander, who exercised a degree of leadership which led to their being remembered by their younger contemporaries as the Roman bishops of their day.

THE BISHOP'S HOUSE

It is a reasonable conjecture that the wealthier Christian families in Rome allowed the halls in their great houses to be used for 'synagogues' or church assemblies. In his earlier *Visions* Hermas condemns the wealthy for their lack of consideration for the poor, but in his later *Parables* his tone is less severe. He speaks of bishops 'and hospitable men' *(episkopoi kai philoxenoi)*, 'who gladly receive the servants of God into their houses'.

This rather suggests that the bishops may have been, in the first case, those wealthy or prominent converts whose families or households became the first centres of church life; or in due course the managers of such buildings. At Corinth it was the household of Stephanas that undertook the ministry to the saints, and other cases of house-churches have appeared from time to time. If this conjecture is sound, it would follow that where there were several of these house-churches, as there were at Corinth and Rome, there would be several bishops, but where Christian life was sufficiently consolidated to have a central building, there would naturally be only one bishop, or one principal bishop if lesser house-churches continued to function. It was the business of the bishop, according to the Pastorals, to look after the house of God. He was a caretaker or warden, which is what the word 'bishop' means.

A process of unification certainly took place in the west in one way or another. The schism at Corinth had demonstrated the weakness of a plural episcopate. As the church in each city developed its spiritual autonomy it expressed it by subordinating the Sunday worship and the social life to the presidency of one bishop. Where there had been plural bishops, we may suppose that they came to terms with the lesser episcopal groups, as Xystus did with the Asian community and possibly with other communities too. Possibly they were enrolled among the elders and magnified their office. In Rome the elders wielded considerable power. They dealt firmly with Marcion, Epiphanius says; and Irenaeus describes the Roman Passover tradition as a tradition of the elders. The elders were the guardians of the tradition of preaching and teaching which had been committed to the church by the apostles, he says, but he links the successions of elders with the succession of bishops who traced their descent from a bishop who had been appointed by the apostles. The appointment of the first bishops by apostles appears very clearly in Clement, and Hermas associates them with the apostles.

It appears in the evidence of Hegesippus that in the hundred-and-fifties those bishops whom he found in every city presiding over the churches which he visited could establish their descent, to his satisfaction, from some predecessor who had been appointed by an apostle. The appearance of this pattern everywhere, without controversy or objection, is certainly a striking historical fact; but the internal situation, even under the presidency of the single bishop, may not have been so simple or uniform as some have supposed. He may have had to cope with national or social or domestic groups with well-rooted traditions of their own; or even with different 'apostolic' foundations. Alexandria, if the legend can be trusted, had a strong episcopal corporation, but it had to deal with a variety of academic schools. In Rome the record of schisms and disputed elections may be related to an original multiple ecclesiastical origin; and this may be reflected in the fourth-century legends which place the 'title-churches' of Pudentiana and Praxedis and Prisca in the first century.

These legends preserve a recollection, which may be true, that the first churches in Rome were formed in private houses and named after their owners. Attempts have been made to support this tradition on architectural grounds, and there is a theory that the oldest form of Christian church architecture is based on the architecture of the Roman house of the period.

THE JEWISH ANTECEDENTS

Another approach to the subject is by the study of the Jewish antecedents of the Christian institutions. The general outline of the church order in Ignatius repeats the synagogue pattern with its synagogue-ruler and council of elders and minor officials; and it is a fact that in some synagogues there were several such rulers, just as in some churches there were several bishops; but the system of one synagogue-ruler became the general one in Judaism, just as the system of one bishop became the general one in Christianity.

The problem of succession was common to both. Palestinian Judaism had two lines of succession, a teaching succession of Rabbis perpetuated by means of the ceremony of the laying on of hands, and a ruling succession which was vested in the family of Hillel and Gamaliel. Palestinian Christianity also had two lines of succession: an episcopal or teaching succession from Peter and the twelve, and a hereditary succession vested in the family of Jesus. In both cases it was claimed that the hereditary succession was Davidic.

A great divergence now appears. The Jews succeeded in establishing a central authority with a prince or president of the sanhedrin who was taken from the hereditary succession. James the Just, the brother of the Lord, had hinted at something of the same sort for Christianity, according to the sources which are preserved in the fifteenth chapter of the Acts; but the Gentiles had failed to respond; and no basis of any sort could be found for a central authority after the destruction of Jerusalem. The church was content with a dispersed authority, the original apostolic commission being vested in the various episcopal corporations throughout the world, the unity of the whole church being secured by the unity of the episcopate locally. It was both a teaching and a ruling succession, since the apostles had received plenary authority as trusted servants in the household of the Lord. This quality in the succession is emphasized by Ignatius in the passage already quoted; the more Rabbinic quality, with its emphasis on teaching, is emphasized by Papias; Clement emphasizes the preaching of the gospel and the offering of the gifts.

THE LIFE-LINE OF THE GOSPEL

The historical development of the unified episcopal system is not recorded, any more than the institution of the Lord's Day is recorded, or the canonization of the four Gospels. Nor is it recorded how they were disseminated. It is a fact, however, that they were received throughout the whole church as apostolic institutions. They were all present in the stream of apostolic and evangelical tradition which flowed like a river from east to west; from Judaea to Antioch; from Antioch to Ephesus or Smyrna; from Ephesus to Corinth or Rome.

It was not entirely a one-way traffic. The churches of the west had made their own contribution to the completed evangelical and catholic order by the dissemination of the Marcan Gospel and the Epistle of Clement and the *Visions* of Hermas; but they were naturally the last to receive everything in its fullness. Clement and Hermas, for instance, seem quite innocent of any knowledge of Matthew and John. The Roman church was far from the originating centres of Christianity; it had an admirable independence and a sturdy conservatism which would be its strength in the next generation; and it had a legitimate apostolic tradition of its own; but it developed slowly.

Some scholars have seen a certain native Roman character in this strength and conservatism; yet it was largely a foreign community, despite its conquests among the noble Roman families. Christianity was an oriental religion still; and the Roman church continued to absorb apostolic and quasi-apostolic missions from Palestine, Syria, Asia, and even Alexandria. This influx, which continued into the third century, was part of a general flow of orientals to the west, a process which would be speeded up with each successive oriental war. The Romanization of Syria was being compensated for by the Syrianization of Rome. The old Latin culture was being inundated by a tide of multi-coloured Hellenistic immigration.

The Roman poet Juvenal was writing his first satires in the episcopate of Xystus. He noted the familiar figure of the Jew, and bemoaned the undue influence in society of Greeks and orientals; and it was to Antioch on the Orontes River that he traced its origin: in *Tiberim defluxit Orontes*:

> What race is best received among our wealthy friends today,
> Though I'd avoid their company, I'm not ashamed to say.
> Ye doughty sons of Romulus, I boldly do declare
> Our sacred city Hellenized is more than I can bear.
> The sewage of the Greeks today infects our moral fibre,
> And the Syrian Orontes drains its filth into our Tiber.
>
> (Juvenal, *Satires*, III, 58.)

Tacitus, who wrote his story of Christianity about this time, made use of the same unsavoury metaphor; for Christianity, he remarked, soon found its way to Rome, 'where everything that is horrible and shameful flows together and becomes fashionable'.

Among these streams of unwelcome visitors came the bishops, prophets, teachers, evangelists and martyrs of Jesus Christ; Andronicus, Junia, Aquila, Priscilla, Epaenetus, Phoebe, Paul, Luke, Aristarchus, Mark, Timothy, Peter, Silvanus, the grandsons of Jude, Ignatius, Philo, Agathopous, Zosimus, Rufus and many more of whom these were the outstanding examples. Later on came Cerdo, Marcion, Valentine, Justin, Tatian, Irenaeus, Polycarp, Hegesippus, Marcellina, Avircius, Rhoda, Philumene, Praxeas, Epigonus, and Theodotus. This powerful westward-flowing current of evangelism from Jerusalem, Pella, Caesarea, Antioch, Hierapolis, Ephesus, Smyrna and Corinth, was the unifying and creative factor in the making of a homogeneous evangelical catholic Christianity, uniting east and west. The same gospel everywhere carried the same hereditary factors and assumed the same form. Its unity was a unity of momentum; its quality was cosmopolitan; and all its origins were Jewish. All apostolic types of Christianity flowed into it, and contributed to it. It assumed the catholic form in this period when the venerable 'elders' who had been trained in the apostolic tradition were giving leadership to the church as bishops, teachers, and pastors.

CHAPTER 26

CATECHISM AND SACRAMENT

Jewish proselyte catechisms, *p.* 481. The *Two Ways*, *p.* 483. The *Books of Testimonies*, *p.* 485. The Epistle of Barnabas, *p.* 486. The Jewish background, *p.* 487. Manifestation in flesh, *p.* 488. The new covenant, *p.* 488. The mystical exegesis, *p.* 490. The *Didache*, p. 491. Origin of the *Didache*, *p.* 494. The prophets in the *Didache*, *p.* 496. The primitive eucharist, *p.* 498. The evangelical context, *p.* 499.

JEWISH PROSELYTE CATECHISMS

We can now proceed to supplement our study of the early second century by the consideration of certain documents which are thought to belong to this period, though they come down to us without any author's name attached. They seem to contain the work of the teachers. We are not surprised to find that they concern the instruction of converts, catechism and baptism, continuation courses for the baptized, and participation in the prayers and eucharist.

Among the documents which originated in the apostolic period, and yet failed to get into the New Testament, except so far as they have been incorporated into some of the Epistles, were the catechisms. The Jews of the dispersion had been obliged to provide instruction in elementary piety for their converts and God-fearers; and when the church came to deal with its converts, who were often taken from this very class, it seems to have turned to the existing Jewish catechisms, which had already proved their usefulness. What these converts needed was a course in elementary Jewish piety, that is to say 'my duty towards God and my duty towards my neighbour'.

The proselyte catechisms were based on older forms of religious instruction, which were derived in their turn from the Hebrew scriptures. There was the fundamental commandment, for instance, called the *Shema*, which was to be repeated twice every day.

Hear, O Israel, the Lord is our God; the Lord is One; and thou shalt love the Lord thy God with all thy heart and with all thy soul and with all thy strength. (Deuteronomy vi. 4–5.)

And next in importance to this came the Ten Words or Ten Commandments, which were then a normal part of the synagogue service. There was also the nineteenth chapter of Leviticus,[1] the eighteenth verse of which was regarded by St Paul, and by Rabbi Akiba too, as the crown or summary of the whole Law.

Thou shalt not hate thy brother in thy heart;
    But thou shalt rebuke thy neighbour and not suffer sin on his account.
Thou shalt not avenge or bear any grudge against the children of thy people;
    But thou shalt love thy neighbour as thyself.

(Leviticus xix. 17–18.)

The founder of Christianity had commended these texts to his disciples, and Christians accepted them as the fundamental documents of religious faith and practice.

Catechetical material was also derived from such non-canonical books as the *Wisdom of Jesus ben Sirach*, commonly called *Ecclesiasticus*. This book was rejected by the rabbinic canon-makers, but it remained firmly fixed in the affections of the Christian church, and lingered on in the archives of some of the Jewish synagogues. Its seventh chapter provides a catechism of social relations which contains many excellent counsels: among them were these:

With all thy strength love him who made thee: and forsake not his ministers.
Fear the Lord and glorify his priest: and give him his portion as it is commanded thee.
The first-fruits and the trespass-offering: and the gift of the shoulder.

(Ecclesiasticus vii. 29–31.)

The Christian book called the *Didache* made a very powerful use of this text, as we shall see.

These and similar pieces of ancient wisdom were built into the Jewish proselyte catechisms, and into one in particular which was called the *Path of Life*. In the course of time a little appendix was added to it which was called the *Path of Death*; and so the whole document received the title of the *Two Paths* or *Two Ways*. The Two-Way symbolism is as old as Jeremiah and the Book of Proverbs. It was taken into the gospel, and there was a time and place early in the first

[1] Leviticus xix is the basis of the catechetical portion of the 'Zadokite Fragment', which is closely related to the community which produced the 'Dead Sea Scrolls'. It was also drawn on by the Jewish author of the gnomic poem which is ascribed to Phocylides.

century when Christianity itself was called by this name—'The Way'. The catechism called the *Two Ways* was adapted for use in the church, perhaps by the end of the first century, since Hermas may have made use of some form of it. It has been incorporated in slightly different forms into the *Didache* and the *Epistle of Barnabas*.

THE *TWO WAYS*

It began with the two great commandments in an expanded form which differs slightly in each of the Greek texts which have come down to us. There is a Latin version which runs as follows:

First, thou shalt love the eternal God who made thee. (Ecclus. vii. 29.)
Secondly, thy neighbour as thyself. (Lev. xix. 18.)
Everything, therefore, which thou wishest not to be done to thee;
Do not do to another.

They are well-worn maxims from the old Jewish piety, which was called the fear of the Lord and was more ancient than any Pharisaism. The combination of the love of God with the love of one's neighbour is first found in the Gospels, it is true; but according to Luke it was a Jewish lawyer who gave this answer. The golden rule in its negative form is found in the apocryphal book of Tobit and was one of the sayings of Rabbi Hillel the Elder. The reviser of the Acts added it to the decree of the Jerusalem council.

After this come a number of prohibitions in the style of the Ten Commandments and including most of them. It is interesting to note that in this kind of literature they are never quoted completely or entirely or even without additions; and the fourth commandment, which sanctifies the Sabbath, is never quoted at all. This document begins with 'Thou shalt not commit adultery' and 'Thou shalt do no murder' and 'Thou shalt not bear false witness'; but continues with 'Thou shalt not corrupt boys, commit fornication, curse, practise sorcery', and so forth. The text in the *Didache* enlarges this list to include augury, magic, witchcraft, the exposure of new-born infants, and so forth, thus giving us a picture of the actual cases with which the Christian teacher had to do and the kind of renunciations which were required of incipient Christians.

Another type of commandment is that which inculcates the virtues which were expected of hearers and learners; lowliness and humility and receptiveness.

> Thou shalt not exalt thyself but shall be humble-minded in all things:
> Thou shalt not take glory upon thyself;
> Thou shalt be meek: thou shalt be quiet:
> And tremble always at the words thou hearest: (from Isaiah lxvi. 2.)

The teacher is to be held in reverence as the spokesman of the Lord: 'Thou shalt love as the apple of thine eye every one who speaketh unto thee the word of the Lord.' Classes were held daily: 'Day by day shalt thou seek out the presence of the saints.' The learners must contribute to the support of their teacher from the work of their hands, a provision which we find as early as Galatians (vi. 6). Free-will offerings, not fees, were the rule.

There are counsels about family and social life, such as are found in several epistles: Colossians, Ephesians, James, I Peter, Clement, Polycarp, for instance.

> Thou shalt love thy neighbour more than thine own soul: (Leviticus xix. 18.)
> Thou shalt not lift thine hand from thy son or daughter, but shalt teach them the fear of the Lord: (compare Psalm xxxiv. 11.)
> Thou shalt not rebuke thy slave or bondmaid in thine anger, seeing that they set their hope upon the same God, lest they fear not the God who is above both: (compare Ephesians vi. 9.)

These counsels, in their various forms, illuminate the important position of the household as a subsidiary unit in the local church.

Few indeed of the finer points of character are overlooked. The *Two Ways* sets a high value on such virtues as modesty, sincerity and consideration for others. Its central ideal is integrity of character or 'simplicity'. The divided or hypocritical soul is the enemy; and its natural sequels are the double mind and the double tongue, which is a snare of death; the very points in moral theology with which Hermas dealt so fully. The second part, or *Way of Death* is a catalogue of sins and offences. It begins with idolatry, which is the source and origin of all other sins in Jewish moral theology; it closes with partiality towards the rich and censoriousness towards the poor.

As traces of this document appear in Syria and Alexandria and Rome, we are justified in regarding it as being in something very like general use, in one form or another, at the beginning of the century. It got the name, in due course, of being an apostolic document; it was doubtless a legacy from the apostolic period; but it seems that it was not of sufficiently high calibre or authority to find its way into the New Testament.

THE *BOOKS OF TESTIMONIES*

Another cycle of teaching which originated in apostolic times and yet never found its way into the New Testament except in substantial quotations was that which handled the Hebrew scriptures, and produced the *Book* or *Books of Testimonies*.

According to the classic theory on the subject, the *Book* was an anthology of Old Testament texts or passages transcribed under various heads, so as to prove or illustrate the gospel preaching. It has never been proved, however, that this hypothetical book ever actually existed; but doubtless there were numerous written transcripts or notes of 'testimony' material, that is to say Old Testament prophecies which were believed to refer to the person and mission of Christ, or the interpretation and validity of the Law of Moses, or the status and destiny of the Jewish people, or the claim of the Christian church to be the true heir of the promises which had been made to the patriarchs of Israel. These prophecies were, in a certain sense, the title-deeds of the Christian church as the people of God and played an important part in theology and apologetics. They are the proper area of study in which to approach the development of Christian theology.

We have here an enormous and complicated body of learned thought, which came into existence in the first place in the frontier country, or no-man's-land, between Judaism proper and the apostolic church, in the days when the separation was not complete. It continued to grow in bulk as the relation between the two became increasingly hostile. Its leading idea may be expressed in testimony language as the doctrine of the two nations. When Rachel, the mother of all Israelites (and therefore of all Christians), was about to become the mother of Jacob and Esau, it was said, 'Two nations are in thy womb; and the elder shall serve the younger.' It was not in the purposes of God that the birthright should pass to the older son without reference to spiritual values; and God repeated himself in history. In Christian thought the church was the true son or successor of the old Israel 'according to the spirit'. It was the younger son; but the younger form of Judaism would supersede the older.

This particular example of testimony interpretation appears as early as Galatians. The primary documents for this study, after the New Testament, are the so-called *Epistle of Barnabas* and the *Dialogue with Trypho* of Justin Martyr.

THE EPISTLE OF BARNABAS

The Epistle of Barnabas sheds light on the controversy with Judaism which burned so fiercely in the days of Trajan and Hadrian. The Jews believed that the Hebrew scriptures, which both sides accepted, commanded everybody to be circumcised and observe the Sabbath and obey the various Levitical ordinances; but the Gentile Christians maintained that they were free. The yoke of the Law had been placed on the Jews for their discipline and as a preparation for the gospel; but now the old Law had come to an end; there was a new Law 'without the yoke of compulsion'.

The author of 'Barnabas' felt that the Jewish propaganda was making headway, and that there was a danger of some Christians making a shipwreck of themselves upon it. His epistle is generally assigned to the early years of Hadrian. The references to current history are vague enough, but it seems clear that the fatal war of 131–5 had not been fought, and that it reflects the conditions of the hundred-and-twenties. Its author is unknown, but it is not a pseudonymous book. The author does not impersonate anyone. He makes no claim to be an apostle or apostolic man. He is a church teacher who has spent some time with the congregation which he is addressing. He is moving on now, but has consented to leave a written record of some of his teachings which have been much admired. We do not know how his epistle came by its name. Perhaps the author's name was Barnabas?

The burden of the introductory remarks is the importance of 'gnosis' or knowledge, as an addition to faith, hope and charity; that is to say as a continuation course after the elements of Christianity have been learned. But this gift of 'gnosis' was a very special thing. It was the gift of extracting a spiritual meaning from the Hebrew scriptures by means of allegorization. This kind of interpretation was a well-established literary and critical tradition at Alexandria, and it is considered probable that the author of this epistle was an Alexandrian. His point of view is Alexandrian, and he pleased Clement of Alexandria, who said, 'There are few who comprehend these things.' If this conjecture is correct, we have our first piece of documentary evidence from this centre of Jewish and Greek learning.

THE JEWISH BACKGROUND

To enter into the thinking of 'Barnabas' and his tradition requires great patience and a touch of imagination. It is very easy to be repelled by his hostility to the Jews, and by his artificial handling of the Jewish scriptures, which he claims exclusively for the Christians. The scriptures are *ours*, he says, and not *theirs*; the covenant is ours and not theirs; *they* had an opportunity of receiving the covenant, but they lost it by turning to the worship of idols, and so the covenant of the Beloved Jesus was sealed in *our* hearts.

It was a serious principle of Christian theology or controversy that the Jewish people fell from grace when they made the golden calf at the foot of Mount Sinai and Moses broke the tables of the Law. Something of the same sort is found in the contemporary rabbinic tradition, in *Mekilta* for instance. The whole subject is discussed in the Talmud treatise *Abodah Zarah*, where perhaps we have the Jewish answer to the Christian polemic.[1] There was a Jewish fast-day at midsummer, we read in *Taanit*, on Tammuz 17, which commemorated the golden calf incident and other dark days in Israelite history.

In other words the line of thought which we find in Barnabas goes back to an area of religious tradition which Jew and Christian both occupied, the area in which the Jewish scriptures were interpreted by both sides in their ancient liturgical setting. Barnabas continues along these lines. He goes on to consider other calendar days and other rituals of various kinds.

Barnabas was the heir of the author of Hebrews in his affiliation to the Jewish (and Christian) liturgy; he was the heir of Ignatius in his conviction of a complete separation from Judaism, and also, as it happens, in his theology of a manifestation of the Son of God 'in the flesh'; a theme which had been announced in Hebrews too.

[1] A suggestion which came to me from Rabbi Abraham Brachman of Fort Worth, Texas.

MANIFESTATION IN FLESH

The manifestation of the divine nature 'in flesh' is a principle which should not be too exclusively limited to the doctrine of the incarnation. The word 'flesh' was used to include the whole life and nature of man. Even in the Old Testament God is revealed through human lives. The emphasis on flesh and blood in Hebrews, John, Ignatius, and Barnabas, was an emphasis on the existential character of the gospel; the Son of God had entered personally into the tragedy of human existence; he had suffered; he had shed blood; he had died.

Barnabas inherited this tradition, which was affirmed more and more defiantly, in opposition to the Docetics who resolved everything into myth. In their system spirit expressed itself in the realm of ideas and aspirations; it remained immaterial. In the catholic authors it expressed itself in material and historic terms; in a human life which is lived 'in the flesh'; in a martyr's death; and in a bodily resurrection. There is nothing impalpable about it at any point.

The expression 'in flesh' does not stop here; for the terminology is sacramental as well as evangelical; the one category passes imperceptibly into the other. The references to flesh and blood in these four authors are all connected, explicitly or implicitly, with the sacrament of the Lord's Supper, and the new covenant which Jesus made there with his disciples in his body and his blood. That word covenant, which he chose, supplied the connecting link with the Jewish paschal tradition of the exodus of Israel from Egypt and the making of the old covenant at Mount Sinai, which was also sealed with blood These events were commemorated every year at Passover and Pentecost, and so the principle of manifestation 'in flesh' was extended into the corporate life of the church, along the line of the sacramental liturgy, in its Paschal setting, and with its old Jewish associations.

Barnabas came to his understanding of the work of Christ through this Judaeo-Christian medium.

THE NEW COVENANT

Barnabas believed, of course, that the actual rites and ceremonies of the old religion were no longer binding. They had been given to the Jews because of the 'hardness of their hearts', and were superseded now by the advent of the Messiah Jesus, who was the true Law and the true covenant, to which the greater prophets, like Jeremiah and Ezekiel, had looked forward. The 'New Covenant of the Beloved Jesus' had been sealed in our hearts, Barnabas says, and the phrase has more in it than barren controversy. The thoughts of the love of God in Jesus, and the religion implanted in the heart, are favourite ideas with him. They rose out of his own devotional and spiritual experience.

The Beloved Jesus was the eternal Son of God who had shared in the creation of the world. He had been manifested to the world in the flesh. He had been rejected by hard-hearted men. He had associated with the sinful, choosing twelve apostles from that class, and revealing his glory to them through the flesh. He had offered his flesh, his whole human self, for his new people on the cross; he had set his flesh like a stone; he had endured the blows and the nails and the death. He was the true sacrifice which the men of old had spoken of in figures of speech, and prefigured in the poor beasts who were buffeted and slain in the Temple ceremonies.

The thought of Barnabas runs on immediately into Christian baptism. The great paschal commemorations of the creation, and the exodus, and the entry into the promised land, are inextricably confused in his treatment of it. We are created over again; we are new-born children; we taste the milk and honey of the promised land, which is made to signify the 'flesh' of Jesus; and the milk and honey are the new life which he bestows upon us. We are within the circle of sacramental ideas which were touched on in Hebrews, and provided the material of the Christian baptismal ritual, as we see it in Hippolytus and Tertullian and later writers; a ritual which was closely associated with the paschal season.

Barnabas goes on to find some mystical meaning in all the Jewish rites and ceremonies and legal enactments. The rite of circumcision is interpreted mystically of the circumcision of the ears and heart to which the greater prophets had looked forward. The unclean birds and beasts and fishes are regarded as symbols of evil and predatory human beings. Texts are found which prefigure the association of the cross with the waters of baptism. The relations between the 'two peoples' and the meaning of the covenant are more fully expounded. The Sabbath is interpreted as a perpetual Sabbath, or as a seventh age of a thousand years at the end of the world; and authority is found for keeping the 'eighth day' instead of the seventh. The last section deals with the Temple itself, for which he substitutes the spiritual temple which is now being built upon the name of the Lord; it is the Christian church; 'he himself dwelling in us who were once enslaved to death, and opening to us the door of the temple which is not made with hands'.

The exposition thus ends on the note of a real presence of Jesus in the Christian heart and in the universal church. It goes on to give a version of the 'Two Ways', and a few counsels for the elders of the community.

THE MYSTICAL EXEGESIS

The modern reader finds this exegesis artificial and unreal. It seems to make it possible for the Christian teacher to make the Old Testament mean whatever he wants. This criticism is not entirely just; for if it was, the different teachers would each have gone his own way, and the result would have been chaos and confusion, whereas they reproduce the same ideas rather monotonously. There were principles of interpretation which were widely accepted among them. There was a body of allegorical or mythological interpretation which had a common origin and was promoted by teachers who had graduated in it. It was an organic part of the massive Judaeo-Christian tradition, and had relations with apocalyptic on one side and gnosis on the other which would be interesting to study.

One interesting example is the saga of Moses and Joshua. Moses prays on the hill-top with his hands extended in the form of a cross; and Joshua defeats Amalek while bearing the divine name of Jesus; for Joshua and Jesus are the same name. Moses makes a brazen serpent, and hangs it on a 'sign' or standard, which is thought of as having the form of a cross; and all Israel looks to it for healing. Joshua brings the old people through the River Jordan into the promised land, and divides the inheritance; Jesus brings the new people through the waters of baptism into the land of eternal life.

This sequence of testimonies is found again and again in the repertoire of the Christian teacher, and a rather similar exegesis is found in the contemporary Mishnaic tractate *Taanit*. It is explained that it was not the holding up of Moses' hands, or the lifting up of the serpent, that saved Israel; but the people looked at these things and were moved to direct their hearts towards their heavenly Father. This seems to be the rival 'spiritual' interpretation of these Old Testament pictures. Both sides used them to promote the religion of the heart. The Old Testament provided pictures and stories whose inward meaning was eternally relevant, and that is 'gnosis'.

Of course Barnabas can be artificial, irritating, and censorious; but it would not be fair to judge him by his less fortunate expositions. His interpretation of the unclean beasts and fishes was in line with the thought of his time, being found in the *Letter of Aristeas*, for instance. His numerology was also a fashionable mode of thought, though the modern scholar is often impatient with it. In reading the story of Abraham circumcising his household, his eye fell on the figure 318 which appeared in the scroll as T I H. Now I H was a familiar contraction of the sacred name of Jesus, and is so written in the Alexandrian papyri of the period; and the letter T looked like the cross. 'Barnabas' is inordinately proud of this discovery.

THE *DIDACHE*

Barnabas concludes his treatise by appending a version of the *Two Ways*, which he calls another kind of teaching or 'gnosis'. Another full-length version of it is to be found in the *Teaching of the Lord through the Twelve Apostles to the Gentiles* which is usually called the *Didache* for short. This elaborate title is only an indication of the subject-matter which it contains, and hardly ranks the book as a pseudonymous work. The apostles are not represented as speaking in it.

Archbishop Bryennios of Nicomedia discovered a copy of the text in a manuscript of the eleventh century, and published it in 1883 with learned notes and illustrative material. Its documentation previous to the fourth century is meagre. Some form of it left its traces apparently in a third-century Syrian church order; and Clement of Alexandria was familiar with its catechetical material, and quotes a sentence from it as 'scripture'. It is referred to by Eusebius and Athanasius as an extra-canonical book. The compiler of the *Apostolic Constitutions* incorporated it into his seventh book and, in spite of many editorial changes, we can recognize fairly clearly the document published by Bryennios.

The romantic enthusiasm which greeted it when it first appeared has somewhat faded, and few scholars now would assign it to the first century. It can hardly be older than the hundred-and-twenties or thirties, since it relies so heavily on Matthew as a written authority. Some of its source-material was undoubtedly older; some of its special features may be later; for it has been much edited. Some scholars place it far down the second century.

There is a ministry of teachers who pass from church to church, but no teacher is to be accepted who does not conform to the *Two Ways*. Their authority stands very high. They are to be honoured as the Lord; for wherever the Lordship is spoken of, there the Lord is; a sentiment which is almost exactly reproduced in the rabbinic document *Pirke Aboth*. Ignatius said much the same about the bishop.

The *Two Ways* was to be read or recited as a preliminary to baptism, which recalls the reference in Ignatius to the 'commandments which you enjoin when you are making disciples', and the Jewish custom of reciting commandments at proselyte-baptism, and the baptismal formula of Elkhasai. There are also some relics of directions about food-laws, which are reminiscent of the 'decree' of the Jerusalem council in Acts xv.

And concerning food, bear what thou canst, but be very careful to avoid meat sacrificed to an idol; for it is a worship of dead gods. (*Didache*, VI.)

This is the Bryennios text, but *Apostolic Constitutions* reads: 'Thou shalt pour out the blood.' Evidence for the continuation of this Jewish custom is also to be found in Irenaeus, the Acts of the Gallican martyrs, Tertullian and Clement of Alexandria.

With the allusion to baptism, another source seems to be welded on to the *Two Ways* which gives an outline of the sacramental order, and in this source the teachers fade out of the picture, their place being taken by prophets. Their authority stands even higher than that of the teachers; too high in fact. The sacramental order begins with baptism, which is to be preceded by prayer and fasting. Baptism is normally administered in 'living water' in the name of the Father and of the Son and of the Holy Spirit, in accordance with Matthew's Gospel. Living water means running water, which was also preferred by the Jews for their proselyte-baptisms. The Jewish custom of immersion is advised as the regular procedure; but pouring three times on the head is sufficient.

The references to prayer and fasting follow. The fasting-days are to be Wednesday and Friday, not Monday and Thursday according to the custom of the hypocrites, as the compiler unkindly describes the Jews or Judaizing Christians. The Lord's Prayer is given in its Matthaean form, with the addition of a doxology: 'For thine is the power and the glory unto the ages', very like the one which became traditional in the east.[1] Blessings and prayers are then supplied for the eucharistic service which succeeded the baptism. They resemble the benedictions or doxologies of the synagogue service and the Jewish domestic rituals. The cup comes first.

First concerning the cup: We give thanks to thee, our Father, for the holy vine of thy servant David, which thou hast made known to us through thy servant Jesus: Thine is the glory unto the ages.

Then concerning the fraction (the broken loaf): We give thanks to thee, our Father, for the Life and Knowledge which thou hast made known to us through thy servant Jesus: Thine is the glory unto the ages.

For as this fraction was once scattered upon the mountains, and was gathered together and became one, so may thy church be gathered together from the ends of the earth into thy Kingdom: For thine is the glory and the power through Jesus Christ unto the ages. (*Didache*, IX.)

None are to partake except those who have been baptized into the Name of the Lord.

A thanksgiving is added, after the reception of the communion, for the holy Name which the holy Father has caused to dwell in us, and for the knowledge and the faith and the immortality. Further prayers follow, and here the text is in some confusion, since the prayer for the unity of the church is repeated in a different form, and the final refrains seem to be intended to precede the communion.

May Grace come!
May this world pass away!
Hosanna to the God of David! (or 'son of David' in *The Apostolic Constitutions*).
If any man is holy, let him come: if any is not, let him repent.
Maranatha: Amen. (Come, O Lord: Amen.)

We seem to have a Hellenized version of some old Jewish-Christian devotions which are highly valued, but imperfectly understood.

[1] It was adopted by the Protestant churches from late Greek manuscripts.

They are followed by directions for the reception of apostles, prophets, and teachers, and other visitors, which have been much elaborated in the interest of the prophets, who are not bound to adhere to the set prayers which have been given. Directions are given for the regular Sunday eucharist, which is preceded by a confession of sins, and in this connexion we have a free quotation from Malachi, which is the only contact of *Didache* with the Testimony tradition. It was widely used as the charter of the universal worship of the Gentile churches.

In every place and time to offer me a pure sacrifice; for I am a great King, saith the Lord, and my name is great among the Gentiles.

(*Didache*, XIV. Malachi i. 11 and 14.)

Bishops and deacons are to be appointed by the congregations and to receive due honour, since they perform the functions of the prophets and teachers. References are made to admonishing offenders, disputes among the worshippers, prayer, and almsgiving, but without much detail, since information on these points is to be found in 'the Gospel'. All must keep watch and vigil. There must be frequent assemblies. There will be false prophets; love will be turned to hate; lawlessness will increase. It is the conventional apocalyptic material of this tradition. The 'world-deceiver' will appear as son of God; the whole creation will go through the ordeal of burning fire; and not till then will come the three signs of the truth, the sign of a spreading out in the heavens, the sign of the voice of the trumpet, and the sign of the resurrection of the dead.

Then shall the world see the Lord coming upon the clouds of heaven.

ORIGIN OF THE *DIDACHE*

The interesting point about the *Didache* is the preservation of what were originally Jewish-Christian forms in a Gentile document which is fully catholic in the sense of visualizing Christianity as a world religion. The tradition which it preserves had had a long history, and the document itself has passed through various stages. As it stands it is designed to meet the requirements of certain Gentile Christians who lived as farmers in a mountainous region where they were in contact with Jews or Judaizing Christians, from whom it was vitally necessary to distinguish themselves. They possessed copies of Matthew, which they called 'the Gospel', and referred to it as a sacred authority, the same situation that we found in the case of Ignatius; and for this reason it must be placed in a Matthew area, that is to say an area where Matthew was accepted as a one-gospel canon in line with the Hebrew scriptures. This is likely to be Syria, though Palestine or eastern Asia Minor should not be excluded. The land of Egypt seems to be ruled out by the reference to mountains in the prayer for the church; nobody scattered seed on the mountains in Egypt.

It was put out as a manual of guidance in church procedure and as a supplement to Matthew. From the same centre, wherever it was, it would appear that apostles, prophets and teachers were also sent out, since it lays down authoritative rules for their behaviour and reception. The arrival of an apostle is not seriously considered, but prophets are well-known visitors to the churches. Their association with the apostles may be explained as a memory inherited from earlier times, and a means of bringing them under the directions for apostles in the tenth chapter of Matthew, where prophets are mentioned with apostles as if partaking of their missionary office; and this suggests that there was some sort of commissioning or sending out in the case of the *Didache* prophets, like the service in Acts xiii which took place at Antioch.

The local churches had a ministry of bishops and deacons which they were directed to appoint for themselves, the first and indeed the only case in which appointments are said to be made by the congregation. In the Acts, the seven 'deacons' were nominated by the congregation for ordination by the apostles, and possibly the *Didache* visualized a similar procedure, but it says nothing about the manner of ordination. It is usually assumed that these were plural bishops such as we find mentioned in Clement; but this assumption is not free from doubt. In addressing a number of churches with single bishops, it would be perfectly natural to say, 'Appoint your bishops' as the *Didache* does. On the other hand, no elders are mentioned. If the Pauline system of plural bishops still lingered in the *Didache* country, it would explain why they were dependent upon a superior order which had a quasi-apostolic character. The system of plural bishops never appears without some higher authority on which it depends.

The *Didache* may be regarded, therefore, as a supplement to Matthew, taking its title and inspiration from the last verses of that Gospel, in which the apostles are commissioned to go out and 'make disciples' of the Gentiles, baptizing them and teaching them to observe what the Lord had commanded; that is to say, what he had commanded in that Gospel.

THE PROPHETS IN THE *DIDACHE*

The devotions for the baptismal eucharist in the *Didache* are followed by a comparatively detailed passage which explains what persons may be admitted to the eucharist, and what persons may offer it; and it is here that we find directions about the prophets which cause us to raise our eyebrows. The liberty to criticize the prophets, which Paul had freely permitted to the Corinthians, is withheld. There is no sign of the spirit-endowed ecclesia in which every one had his gift of grace, and all might prophesy. It is a sin against the Holy Spirit, the irremediable sin, to criticize a prophet; and yet it is granted that there are undesirable prophets who prey on the churches, and are Christ-mongers rather than Christians. They ask for money in the Spirit, or 'order a table'. Even an approved and true prophet may 'perform a cosmical mystery of the ecclesia', whatever that may be; but as the great 'mystery' of the ecclesia in St Paul is that she is the bride of Christ, it is to be feared that the prophet was accompanied by a virgin of some sort. The sentence also informs us that there were unidentified prophets travelling about, who were not approved or true. It is a sad fact that the deterioration of the prophetic order is attested on all hands; by Matthew and Jude and Hermas, for instance, as well as by this document.

A very practical object of this little pamphlet was to provide the prophets with more regular financial support. These prophets, unlike some others, travelled from village to village, though they may have had a permanent home in some centre from which they were sent out, if we are right in assuming that this was the system. They depended, during their travels, on free hospitality and free-will offerings, like the teachers; and they were inclined to outstay their welcome. A man who stayed more than three days was stigmatized as a false prophet; and even if we visualize a large area with a large number of villages, the system would still provide very meagre and uncertain support.

The suggestion of the *Didache* is that they should settle down as village priests. 'They are your high priests', it says, the first instance of any Christian minister being given this title. It refers back to the verse out of *Ecclesiasticus*, a part of which was quoted at the beginning of the document and may have been more fully quoted in the original text; for this passage (which we have given in full earlier in this chapter) provides for the support of the priests out of the first-fruits, and orders the people to give according to the commandment. The *Didache* now makes use of these phrases. The prophets, in their capacity of high priests, are entitled to the first-fruits of the winepress and the threshing-floor, and of oxen and sheep (the gift of the shoulder?); of bread and wine and oil; and even of money and clothes. The people are to give according to the commandment. The Jewish Levitical order is the pattern for the Christian ministry, as it is in Clement.

Although he could no longer offer animal sacrifices in Jerusalem, the Jewish village priest still performed many functions under the Law of Moses, and Jesus had recognized his position in the case of the cleansing of the leper. The priest was not to be done out of his offering. Many priests had become Christians, we are told in Acts, and there may have been Jewish-Christian communities in which they still functioned. It would appear, too, from the Epistles of Ignatius, that the Judaizing Christians at Philadelphia wanted to have, or possibly did have, priests in connexion with that church. The *Didache* suggests a way by which that demand might be met. The prophet, who was a liturgical expert and knew how to offer the appropriate benedictions, could take the place of the village priest in Judaism and officiate at the offering of the first-fruits of the harvest and the vintage, presumably at the appointed seasons of Passover, Pentecost and Tabernacles. The bishops and deacons performed the same functions as the prophets and teachers, the *Didache* says. We remember that the bishops and deacons at Corinth performed the duty of 'offering the gifts', and that Clement says that they should be offered at the correct Levitical seasons. Hippolytus preserves a first-fruits ritual which was still in use at the end of the second century.

We have a background now against which we can place the eucharistic benedictions and the permission to the prophets to offer them as they thought fit. That background was the old Jewish village life, the round of agricultural festivals, the offering of the first-fruits, the ministry of the priests and the old Hebrew rituals. The prayer after the fraction in the *Didache* looks like a harvest prayer. Traces of this rural background lingered in the liturgy for a long time.[1] Fifty or sixty

[1] Papias seems to have derived his 'eschatology' from sources of this kind.

years later, when Irenaeus was narrating the institution of the eucharist at the Last Supper by Jesus, he says that the Lord was counselling his disciples how to offer the first-fruits to God from his creatures; and the eucharist is associated by the second-century writers with the offering of all kinds of food. The development of Christian liturgy is in part the gradual loss of rural and agricultural features, as the worship of the church became more civilized and urbanized.

THE PRIMITIVE EUCHARIST

No doubt the sacramental order of the *Didache* contains some first-century traditions with regard to the baptismal and eucharistic ritual. Jewish liturgical forms have been christianized and then Hellenized in churches which were situated on the spiritual frontier between the Jew and the Gentile. They are in such a condition that they could easily be adapted for gnostic use. The stress on knowledge or gnosis is reminiscent of Barnabas; the emphasis on the name could pass into magic; the use of the word immortality, instead of life eternal, recalls Menander and Ignatius; the invocation of grace was taken over by gnostic heresy in Ephesus. There is obviously something rather peculiar about this document as it now stands, but it still remains a version of a widespread tradition of considerable antiquity. It is, at the same time, primitive and sophisticated, Hebraic and Hellenistic; but its primitive features have an authentic pedigree.

In considering the primitive eucharist, it should be noted first that the typical Jewish benediction does not bless the food in so many words. It blesses God *for* the food or for whatever gift is being considered; in Barnabas, for instance, we have benedictions in this form for the gift of wisdom or gnosis. The mind is directed upward to God, not downward to the gifts. An ancient second-century form of the eucharistic prayer, preserved by Hippolytus, begins with the admonition, 'Lift up your minds.' (Compare Colossians iii. 2: 'Set your minds on things above.')

Yet there is a real presence and an effective benediction; for the solemn naming of God, or 'invocation of the Name', is rewarded by a special presence where it is uttered. That is why the three names are invoked over the candidate at his baptism; and there is a special thanksgiving in the baptismal eucharist for the Name which God has caused to tabernacle in our hearts; and the great Malachi testimony assures the catholic church that in every place where the Gentiles offer the pure sacrifice of the eucharist, the presence of the Great King is vouchsafed through the Name.[1] The presence of God which was once localized in the Temple worship is transferred now to the Christian liturgical order. The covenanted presence which once existed in Jerusalem, 'the city which God chose to put his Name there', is granted to his new people universally; his Name is great among the Gentiles.

The forms of benediction in the *Didache* are similar to those used by the Jews, but there is a striking difference; the name of Jesus is associated with the name of the Father, as it is in the various apostolic and sub-apostolic precedents; for numerous examples could be given of blessings, praisings, glorifyings and thanksgivings, addressed through Jesus, or in the name of Jesus, to the God and Father. It will be sufficient to quote the rule on the subject which St Paul included in the catechism which he sent to the Colossians.

Let the Word of Christ dwell in you richly in all wisdom; teaching and admonishing one another in psalms and hymns and spiritual songs; singing with grace in your hearts unto the Lord; and whatever you do, in word or in deed, do it all in the name of the Lord Jesus, giving thanks to God and the Father through him. (Colossians iii. 16–17.)

The Christian benedictions, then, were to be on Hebrew lines, with the name of Jesus added.

THE EVANGELICAL CONTEXT

The *Didache* is quite silent about the Christian mysteries, thus falling into line with other didactic literature, like James and Hermas. The name of Jesus is not mentioned except in the doxologies, and even there nothing is said about his crucifixion and resurrection, or his body and blood. The narrative of the Last Supper is never referred to. Jesus is called the Messiah, but more often the child or servant of the Father, never the son, except of course in the baptismal formula. The word translated 'servant' is the greek word *pais*, which can mean boy or child. It is used about Jesus by Peter in the Acts of the Apostles; he also uses it of David, as the *Didache* does. It continued for a long time

[1] The Great King is a title of Christ in Hermas and Elkhasai; but see Matt. v. 35.

in the liturgical tradition of the church. It was connected, apparently, with old prophetic texts by means of which Jesus the Messiah was linked with David the king, or with Israel his people, or perhaps with the Song of the Suffering Servant in Isaiah. The word has special sacred associations, the nature of which is not known now. The paradox of the situation is that these associations are certainly Jewish, whereas there is said to be no Hebrew or Aramaic word which has the double meaning of child and servant.

Could the tradition have originated in the testimony from Isaiah: 'Unto us a *child* is born: Unto us a *son* is given', which is Davidic in character?

It must not be forgotten, however, that our document is an appendix to Matthew, to which the readers of the *Didache* are explicitly referred no less than four times. Any provision which it makes in the way of church order is supplementary to that Gospel. Turning to Matthew, then, we read that as they were eating, Jesus took bread, and uttered a benediction, and broke it and gave it to his disciples, and said, 'Take, eat; this is my body.' The words of the benediction which were uttered by Jesus are not given, and this is the deficiency which the *Didache* seems to supply. We read next that he took the cup, and uttered another benediction before he gave it to them, saying, 'Drink ye all of this; for this is my blood of the new covenant.' Again the words of the benediction are not given, and the *Didache* appears to supply the deficiency.

Why the *Didache* supplies the eucharistia over the cup before the eucharistia over the fraction, we are unable to say, though guesses can be made. If the narrative of the Last Supper was read without any break, the last point mentioned would be the cup, so that the eucharistia for the cup might naturally follow. If the bread was broken then, the eucharistia over the fraction would be in order at that point. And this is the shape of the liturgy as it appeared later. No ritual actions were interpolated into the narrative of the Last Supper.

The same order is followed by St Paul in writing to Corinth:

The cup of blessing which we bless, is it not the communion of the blood of the Messiah?
The loaf which we break, is it not the communion of the body of the Messiah?
For we, being many, are one loaf, one body; for we are all communicants in the one loaf. (I Corinthians x. 16–17.)

It will be noted that the third clause in Paul, like the third prayer in the *Didache*, regards the loaf as a symbol of the unity of those who share in it as communicants or partners. We are not suggesting that the *Didache* prayers were *derived* from I Corinthians; but it appears highly probable that they are reproducing the same pattern.

The fact is that we do not know how the benedictions and prayers of the *Didache* were combined with the Matthaean text; but of course they must have been, since the authority of Matthew was paramount. It is possible that a perfect unification did not take place all at once. Paul does not quote the Last Supper narrative until his succeeding chapter; Justin quotes it separately from his account of the eucharistic action; the disjunction is found as late as Cyril of Jerusalem in the fourth century.

The reader will not be surprised to hear that there is a theory that there were two 'types' of eucharist in the apostolic church, one of which was purely 'Jewish', and had no memorial of the death and resurrection of Jesus the Messiah; it was not inspired by the Last Supper narrative, it is claimed. The *Didache* is the main support, indeed the only reputable support, of this theory; and even so it has to be divorced from Matthew if the argument is to be taken seriously. Indeed, it has to be made as early as Matthew; or earlier.

On the other hand, there may by now have been two types of holy meal in the church order, the 'agape' or love-feast, and the 'eucharistia' or sacramental rite; for Ignatius says that it is wrong to celebrate either the eucharist or the agape without the presence or consent of the bishop; and II Peter, which may be about contemporary with the *Didache* (though the date of both is uncertain), speaks of 'the false teachers who are blots upon your love-feasts' (*agapai*). We have no evidence for this distinction earlier than the second century; in fact it would appear that the difficulties which are dealt with in I Corinthians arose from the fact that the distinction had not been made, and the eucharist took place in connexion with a community supper.

It has been suggested, therefore, that the eucharistic benedictions in the *Didache* were intended for use at the agape; but in view of their connexion with the baptismal rite, and their high mystical quality, this is not generally accepted.

The matter may now be left to the liturgiologists.

SELECT BIBLIOGRAPHY

The Bibliography to volume II may also be consulted. Further bibliographies will be found in a number of the books which are listed. Except for editions of original sources, the books listed are, for the most part, in English.

A. GENERAL INTRODUCTION

The Cambridge Ancient History, vols. XI and XII (Cambridge, 1939). (Contains very full bibliography.)

A History of the Jewish People in the time of Jesus Christ, Emil Schürer (English trans. Edinburgh, 1885 f. and New York, 1897f.).

Jerusalem under the High Priests, E. Bevan (London, 1904).

History of Israel, W. O. E. Oesterley and T. H. Robinson (Oxford, 1932).

Judaism in the First Centuries of the Christian Era, G. F. Moore (Cambridge, Mass., 1927).

Die Religion des Judenthums, W. Bousset (3rd ed. Tübingen, 1926).

Le Judaïsme avant Jésus-Christ, M. J. Lagrange (Paris, 1931).

Le Judaïsme palestinien au temps de Notre Seigneur, J. Bonsirven (Paris, 1950).

Religion and Worship of the Synagogue, W. O. E. Oesterley and C. H. Box (London, 1907).

Jewish Background of the Christian Liturgy, W. O. E. Oesterley (Oxford, 1925).

The Samaritans, J. A. Montgomery (Philadelphia, 1907).

Archaeology of Palestine, W. Albright (London (Pelican), 1951).

History of the Ancient World, M. I. Rostovtzeff (Oxford, 1926).

Hellenistic Civilization, W. W. Tarn and G. T. Griffiths (London, 1952).

Le Monde gréco-romain au temps de Notre Seigneur, A. J. Festugière (Paris, 1935).

Conflict of Religions in the Early Roman Empire, T. R. Glover (London, 1932).

Les Religions Orientales dans le Paganisme Romain, F. Cumont, ed. 4, Paris, 1929 (English trans. Chicago, 1911).

Environment of Early Christianity, S. Angus (London, 1914).

The Mystery Religions, S. Angus (London, 1925).

Roman Society from Nero to Marcus Aurelius, S. Dill (London, 1905).

Roman Life and Manners, L. Friedländer (English trans. London, 1908).

The Dead Sea Scrolls, Millar Burrows (New York, 1955).

Discoveries in the Judaean Desert, Qumran Cave I (Oxford, 1955).

B. CHURCH HISTORIES, ETC.

Duchesne, L. *Early History of the Church*, English trans. (London, 1909f.).

Kidd, B. J. *History of the Christian Church* (Oxford, 1922).

Gwatkin, H. M. *Early Church History* (London, 1909).

Hamilton, H. F. *The People of God* (Oxford, 1912).

Harnack, A. von. *Mission and Expansion of Christianity*, English trans. J. Moffatt, 2nd edn. (London, 1908).
Harnack, A. von. *History of Dogma*, English trans. N. Buchanan (London, 1894f.).
Le Breton, J. and Zeiller, J. *The History of the Primitive Church*, English trans. E. C. Messenger (New York, 1949).
Lietzmann, H. *Beginnings of the Christian Church*, English trans. L. B. Woolf (London and New York, 1937).
McGiffert, A. C. *A History of the Apostolic Age* (New York, 1912).
Ramsey, W. M. *The Church in the Roman Empire to 170 A.D.* (London, 1893).

C. ENCYCLOPAEDIAS, ETC.

Encyclopaedia of Religion and Ethics, J. Hastings (Edinburgh, 1908ff.).
New Schaff-Herzog Encyclopaedia of Religious Knowledge (New York, 1908).
Jewish Encyclopaedia (New York, 1906).
Encyclopaedia Judaica (Berlin, 1928).
Dictionary of the Bible, J. Hastings (Edinburgh, 1903ff.).
Dictionary of Christ and the Gospels, J. Hastings (Edinburgh, 1915ff.).
Dictionary of the Apostolic Church, J. Hastings (Edinburgh, 1915ff.).
Encyclopaedia Biblica, T. K. Cheyne and J. S. Black (London, 1899ff.).
Dictionary of Christian Biography, W. Smith (London, 1877ff.).
Dictionnaire d'archéologie chrétienne et de liturgie, F. Cabrol (Paris, 1907–53).
Catholic Encyclopaedia (New York, 1907).

D. LITERATURE OF THE PERIOD: TEXT AND INTRODUCTION

The Old Testament in Greek (according to the Septuagint), ed. with introduction by H. B. Swete (Cambridge, 1930) or A. Rahlfs (Göttingen, 1935).
Apocrypha and Pseudepigrapha of the Old Testament (translations with introductions and notes by various scholars), R. H. Charles (Oxford, 1913).
Translations of Early Documents (S.P.C.K. series), ed. W. O. E. Oesterley and C. H. Box (London, 1916–).
History of New Testament Times with an Introduction to the Books of the Apocrypha, R. H. Pfeiffer (New York, 1949).
The Books of the Apocrypha (introduction), W. O. Oesterley (London, 1914).
The New Testament in Greek, ed. L. F. Tischendorf (8th edn. Leipzig, 1878); Westcott and Hort (Cambridge, 1881); A. F. Souter (Oxford, 1910f.); H. von Soden (Göttingen, 1913); A. Merx (7th ed. Rome, 1951); E. Nestlé (Basel, 1945); and others.
Text and Canon of the Greek Bible, F. G. Kenyon (London, 1949).
Canon and Text of the New Testament, C. R. Gregory (English trans. Edinburgh, 1907).
Text and Canon of the New Testament, A. Souter (London, 1913).
Commentaries on the New Testament in various standard series: the International Critical Commentary, the Westminster Commentary, the Cambridge Bible,

the Cambridge Greek Testament for Schools and Colleges, the Clarendon Bible, etc.; see also the 'Handbuch' series, ed. H. Lietzmann (Tübingen).

One-volume commentaries with articles by various scholars, ed. A. S. Peake (London, 1920); C. Gore (London, 1928).

The Concise Bible Commentary, W. K. Lowther Clarke (London, 1952).

Introductions to the New Testament: A. Jülicher, trans. J. P. Ward (London, 1904); T. H. Zahn, trans. J. M. Trout (Edinburgh, 1909); J. Moffatt (Edinburgh, 1911); A. H. McNeile (Oxford, 1953); E. F. Scott (Literature of the New Testament) (New York, 1932).

See also for special points of view:

Case, S. J. *The Evolution of Early Christianity* (Chicago, 1927).

Dibelius, M. *A Fresh Approach to the New Testament* (English trans. New York, 1936).

Enslin, H. M. *Christian Beginnings* (New York, 1938).

Foakes-Jackson, F. J. and Lake, K. *The Beginnings of Christianity* (including introduction, text and commentary on the Acts). 5 vols. (London, 1920–33).

Grant, F. C. *An Introduction to New Testament Thought* (New York, 1950).

Goguel, M. *The Birth of Christianity*, trans. H. C. Snape (London, 1935).

Hoskyns, E. C. and Davey, F. N. *The Riddle of the New Testament* (London, 1931).

Weiss, J. *The History of Primitive Christianity*. 2 vols., trans. F. C. Grant (London, 1937).

The (Soncino) Talmud, 35 vols. (English trans. London, 1935–52).

The (Soncino) Midrash Rabba, 10 vols. (English trans. London, 1939).

The Mishnah, English trans. H. Danby (Oxford, 1933).

Introduction to Talmud and Midrash, H. L. Strack (English trans. Philadelphia, 1931).

Kommentar zum Neuen Testament aus Talmud und Midrasch, H. L. Strack and P. Billerbeck (München, 1922–8).

Prayer Book of the Jewish Synagogue.

The Letter of Aristeas, ed. H. St J. Thackeray (Manchester, 1935).

The Works of Josephus, text and trans. by H. St J. Thackeray and R. Marcus (Loeb Library, London and New York, 1926–43).

The Apostolic Fathers (introductions, text, trans. and notes), J. B. Lightfoot (2nd ed., 5 vols. London, 1889–90). (Texts and trans. in one volume, ed. J. Harmer, London, 1893.)

The Apostolic Fathers. (Text and trans. by K. Lake in the Loeb Library, London and New York, 1912–13.)

The Apostolic Fathers (translated) in the Translations of Christian Literature series (S.P.C.K.) in the Ante-Nicene Library, and in the Library of the Christian Classics series (S.C.M.), ed. C. C. Richardson, with others (London, 1953).

The New Testament in the Apostolic Fathers (Oxford, 1905).

The Ezra Apocalypse, ed. G. H. Box and W. Sanday (London, 1912).

L'Ascension d'Isaïe, ed. E. Tisserant (Paris, 1909).

The Sibylline Oracles, Books III–V (S.P.C.K. Translations), ed. H. N. Bate (London, 1918). Greek text ed. J. Geffcken in the Berlin corpus, 1902.

Sayings of the Jewish Fathers (Pirke Aboth), introduction, text, trans., notes and appendices by C. Taylor (Cambridge, 1897).

Early Greek Religion, and *Later Greek Religion*, E. Bevan. (Selected texts with trans. and introduction, London, 1927.)

Hellenistic Religions, F. C. Grant. (Selected texts with trans. and introductions, New York, 1953.)

Corpus Hermeticum, text ed. A. D. Nock. (French trans. A. J. Festugière, Paris, 1945–.)

Hermetica, ed. W. Scott (Oxford, 1924–).

The *Ecclesiastical History* of Eusebius, trans., introduction and notes by H. J. Lawlor and J. E. L. Oulton (London, 1928).

The *Ecclesiastical History* of Eusebius, text and trans. by K. Lake and J. E. L. Oulton, Loeb Library (London and New York, 1928).

The Apocryphal New Testament, trans. and introductions by M. R. James (Oxford, 1924.)

E. NEW TESTAMENT PERIOD: SPECIAL STUDIES

The Relevance of Apocalyptic, H. H. Rowley, 2nd ed. (New York, 1946).

Jewish and Christian Apocalypses, F. C. Burkitt (London, 1914).

Ancient Synagogues in Palestine and Greece, E. L. Sukenik (London, 1934).

The Dead Sea Scriptures (translation and notes), T. H. Gaster (New York, 1956).

The Greek Papyri and the New Testament, G. Milligan (Cambridge, 1910).

Jesus of Nazareth, J. Klausner, trans. H. Danby (London, 1925).

The Four Gospels, B. H. Streeter (London, 1924).

The Growth of the Gospels, F. C. Grant (New York, 1934).

Form Criticism, R. Bultmann, trans. F. C. Grant (New York, 1934).

From Tradition to Gospel, M. Dibelius, trans. B. L. Woolf (London, 1934).

The Formation of the Gospel Tradition, V. Taylor (London, 1952).

Form Criticism, E. B. Redlich (London, 1939).

The Making of the New Testament, B. W. Bacon (London, 1912).

The Bible and the Greeks, C. H. Dodd (London, 1935).

The Apostolic Preaching, C. H. Dodd (London, 1936).

Gospel and Law, C. H. Dodd (New York, 1951).

According to the Scriptures, C. H. Dodd (New York, 1953).

Jew and Greek, G. Dix (London, 1953).

The earlier Epistles of St. Paul, K. Lake, 2nd edn. (London, 1927).

St Paul and the Church of the Gentiles, W. L. Knox (Cambridge, 1939).

The Making of Luke-Acts, H. J. Cadbury (London, 1927).

The Gospel of St Mark, introduction, text, commentary, V. Taylor (London, 1952).

The Primitive Christian Calendar, P. Carrington (Cambridge, 1952).

Peter: disciple, apostle, and martyr, O. Cullmann, trans. F. V. Filson (Philadelphia, 1953).

Petrus und Paulus in Rom, H. Lietzmann (Berlin-Leipzig, 1927).
The Epistle to the Ephesians, C. L. Mitton (Oxford, 1951).
St Paul's Ephesian Ministry, G. S. Duncan (London, 1929).
The Problem of the Pastoral Epistles, P. N. Harrison (Cambridge, 1936).
The Pastoral Epistles, B. S. Easton (New York, 1947).
The First Epistle of St Peter, E. G. Selwyn (London, 1946).
The First Epistle of Peter, F. W. Beare (Oxford, 1947).
The Primitive Christian Catechism, P. Carrington (Cambridge, 1942).
Studies in Matthew, B. W. Bacon (London, 1930).
The Origins of the Gospel according to St Matthew, G. D. Kilpatrick (Oxford, 1946).
The School of Matthew, W. Stendhal (Uppsala, 1954).
The Fourth Gospel, E. C. Hoskyns and F. N. Davey, 2nd ed. (London, 1947).
The Fourth Gospel in Recent Criticism, W. F. Howard (London, 1931).
The Interpretation of the Fourth Gospel, C. H. Dodd (Cambridge, 1953).
The Revelation of St John, R. H. Charles, in International Critical Commentary (Edinburgh, 1920).
The Meaning of the Revelation, P. Carrington (London, 1931).
The Fall of Jerusalem, S. G. F. Brandon (London, 1951).
The Parousia, anonymous [J. S. Russel] (London, 1878).
The First Epistle of Clement, W. K. Lowther Clarke (London, 1937).
The Christianity of Ignatius of Antioch, C. C. Richardson (New York, 1935).
Polycarp's two Epistles to the Philippians, P. N. Harrison (Cambridge, 1936).
The Primitive Church, B. H. Streeter (London, 1929).
The Founding of the Church, B. W. Bacon (New York, 1909).
Three Measures of Meal, F. G. Vial (Oxford, 1923).
'Foreign groups in Rome during the first centuries of the empire', G. La Piana in *Harvard Theological Review*, 1927.
Testimonies, ed. J. R. Harris, vol. I (Cambridge, 1916); vol. II with G. V. Burch (Cambridge, 1920).
Die jüdischen Baptismen, W. Brandt (Giessen, 1910).
Barnabas, Hermas, and the Didache, J. A. Robinson (London, 1920).
Das Hirt des Hermas, M. Dibelius (Tübingen, 1923).
Elchasai, W. Brandt (Leipzig, 1912).
The Riddle of the Didache, F. E. Vokes (London, 1938).
Essays on the Early History of the Church and the Ministry, H. B. Swete and others (London, 1918).

INDEX

Ab (fifth month), fast of, 235, 337, 339
ab (father), pl. *aboth*, 242
ab-beth-din, 14
Abodah Zarah, 487
abomination of desolation, 22, 229, 236
Abraham, 18, 87 ff., 320 ff.
Achaia, 110 ff., 119
Acts of the Apostles, or Luke-Acts, *see* ch. 15; authorship, date, etc., 95, 182 ff., 278 ff., 285; chronology of, 60, 67, 92, 95, 125, 132; composition and style, 43, 55 ff., 65 ff., 92 ff., 108, 113, 120, 129, 139, 160, 182; source analysis, 64 ff., 66, 80, 83, 86, 92 ff., 128, 151, 160, 183; 'we' passages, 86, 113, 157, 278 ff., 288 ff.; 'speeches', 27, 38, 53, 82 ff., 92 ff., 154, 158 ff., ch. 9, 284; reviser of, 108, 113, 151, 288, 483; 'western' text, 288
Adar (twelfth month), 337
Adiabene, 5, 7, 8
Adonis, *see* Tammuz
advent (*parousia*), 34, 74, 116 ff., 220, 225, 237, 342, 346 ff., 362, 494
Africanus, 251, 411
Agabus, 67, 155
Agathopous, Rhaius, 447, 455
Agrippa I, 25, 77, 92, 125, 160
Agrippa II, 25, 77, 92, 164, 187 ff., 226 ff., 241, 251, 335, 410
Akiba, 426, 429, 482
Albinus, 188 ff.
Alexander of Ephesus, 139
Alexander the Great, 1 ff., 7
Alexander Jannaeus, 13, 22
Alexander, bishop of Rome, 475 ff.
Alexandra Salome, 13, 22
Alexandria, 2, 7 ff., 16, 20, 44, 68, 71, 129, 313 ff., 419 ff., 486
Alke, 449, 457
Alkimus (Jakin), 12, 22
allegorism, 20, 405, 489, 490
Alphaeus, *see* Clopas
Alphaeus, father of Levi or of James, 45
Amalek, 490
Amidah, 425
Amos, 98
Ampliatus, 149
Ananias of Damascus, 60
Ananias of Jerusalem, 41, 56
Ananias ben Nebediah, 92, 159, 186, 226 ff.
anathema, 89, 135
Andrew, 33, 45, 294, 307
Andronicus and Junia(s), 40, 149, 274
angel or spirit, angelic powers, 57, 76, 159, 282, 342, 393, 400 ff., 404
Annas I (Annanus), 27, 186 ff.
anomia (lawlessness), 248, 262 ff., 329 ff.
Antigonus II, 22, 25
Antioch (on the Orontes), 2, 4, 44, 435
Antioch, church of, 66 ff., ch. 4, 86 ff., 99, 104 ff., 314 ff., 420, 443 ff., ch. 25, 474
Antioch, legate in, 27, 59, 66, 72, 227
Antioch in Pisidia, *see* Little Antioch
Antiochus I, 2, 4
Antiochus III, 21
Antiochus IV (Epiphanes), 11, 21
Antipas, Herod, 25, 27, 30, 59, 70 ff., 80, 160
Antipas, martyr, 299
Antipater, 22, 24
Apamea, 5
Apion, 71
apocalyptic, in Jerusalem, 73 ff.; Thessalonian type, 73 ff., 115 ff.; Pauline sublimation of, 134, 138, 175 ff.; Johannine type, see *John, Revelation of*; Marcan type, *see* Little Apocalypse; Jewish type, 337 ff., see *Esdras II*, *Baruch*, Sibyl; of Matthew, see *Matthew*, *Gospel of*; sublimation of in John's Gospel, 362 ff.; *see also* Hermas and *Didache*
Character and language of, 74, 76, 113, 115 ff., 221 ff.; the writing of, 224, 384 ff.; historical and political implications, 73, 113, 118, 221 ff., chs. 12 and 18; *see also* temple; Caligula; Rome, government of; Nero myth
Apollonius of Tyana, 351 ff.

Apollos, 129 ff., 133, 139, 197, 313, 351
apologists, 120, 336
apostasia (apocalyptic), 118, 204, 264; *see* church, spiritual deterioration in
apostasies, 206, 371, 384, 430
apostles of Jesus, apostolate, mission and tradition of, 33, 38 ff., 45, 59, 61, 79, 83 ff., 88, 92, 135, 138, 179, 193, 195, 273, 275 ff., 319, 324, 374 ff., 400, 449, 452, 464, 471, 485, 494 ff.; *see also* The Twelve, *and* Jesus, disciples of
apostles, secondary type, 88, 106, 134, 141, 254, 274
Apostolic Constitutions, 491 ff.
apostolic literature, 273 ff., 286 ff., 386, 391 ff., 450, 459, 467 ff., 470, 473, 493; early quotations and usage, 279, 289, 312, 373, 384, *see also* gospels *and* epistles; New Testament, 391 ff.
apostolic staff, apostolic men, 81, 108 ff., 130, 152, 171 ff., 198 ff., 201 ff., 206, 272, ch. 14, 276, 377, 473; *see* evangelist
apostolic successors, 202, 206, ch. 14, 261, 271 ff.
Aquila, *see* Priscilla
Aquila of Sinope, 427, 429, 438 ff.
Arabia, 26, 68, 70, 413
Aramaic, 3, 7, 9, 15 ff., 47, 50, 78, 158, 211, 240, 254, 320, 336, 422
Arbela, 5
Arcadia, 393, 407
Archippus, 172, 174
Areopagus, 120
Aretas, 25, 59
Aristarchus, 139, 152, 156, 171
Aristeas, Letter of, 9, 17, 259, 491
Aristeas, Jewish author, 17
Aristides, apologist, 120
Aristion, 289, 294, 317
Aristobulus, Jewish author, 17 ff.
Aristobulus I, 22
Aristobulus II, 22
Aristobulus, of Rome, 149
Aristotle, 2, 7 ff.
Armageddon, 232
Arsacids, 2
Artemis, 126, 139
asceticism, 28, 40, 97, 104 ff., 150, 155, 174, 247 ff., 257, 262, 339, 413
Asia (Roman Province), 44, 109 ff., 126, 200
Asia Minor, Jews in, 4; high road across, 109 ff., 130
Asiarchs, 132, 140
Assouan papyri, 9
Asyncritus, 150
Athanasius, 420
'atheism', 181
atonement, day of (Tishri 10), 253, 371 ff.
'Atticus', proconsul, 417
Augustus, emperor, 21, 26, 70, 166

Babylon, 5 ff., 25, 242, 251; *see* Ctesiphon
Babylon, in apocalyptic, 202, 222, 233, 237 ff., 341 ff., 345
Babylonian ideas, 6 ff.
Balaam, 258, 299
baptism, 28, 55, 60, 64, 84, 87, 130, 175, 271, 309, 315, 371, 386, 412 f., 454, 489, 492 ff.
Barnabas, Epistle of, 404, 440, 483 ff., 486 ff., 498
Barnabas, Joseph, 41 ff., 46, 60, 67, 75, 78, 85, 89 f., 92, 108
Bartholomew, 45
Baruch, Apocalypse of, 259, 337 ff.
Basilides, 440
Beliar, 203, 416
beloved, as title of Christ, 203, 487, 489, 493
benedictions, Jewish, 267, 284, 497 ff.
Berea (Beroea), 110 ff., 114
Bernice, 25, 164, 241
Berosus (Berossus), 7 ff.
Bethlehem, 26
Bible, *see* scriptures
biblion, *biblos*, *see* papyrus
binding and loosing, 321
bishops, 44, 122, 153 ff., 172, 181 ff., 242, 256 ff., 265 ff., 271, 374 ff., 380 ff., 400, 418 ff., 448, 452, 474 ff., 494 ff.
Bithynia, 112 ff., 130, 200, 429 ff.
blood, abstention from, 100, 103 ff., 284, 492
Boanerges, 33
book-production, 212 ff.
building, imagery of, 35, 148, 179, 327, 399 ff., 407, 451

burials, Christian, 47, 196, 205; *see also* Priscilla, Domitilla
Burrhus, Roman official, 166, 457
Burrhus, deacon, 449

Caesar, appeal to, 63, 165; household of, 171, 181
Caesarea, 27, 49, 56 ff., ch. 3, 77, 128, 155 ff., ch. 8, 227, 239, 314, 410, 415
Caiaphas, 27, 58, 62, 186
calendar, 2, 4, 15, 17, 22 ff., 337, 359, 371, 455, 487 ff., 497
Caligula, emperor, 67 ff., 115, 118, 125, 166, 177, 343
catechism (commandments), 18, 101 ff., 118, 175, 179 ff., 201, 208, 403 ff., 412, 454, 481 ff., ch. 26, 492
catholic, catholicism, 451 ff., 464 ff., ch. 25, 494
Cenaculum, 41
Cenchreae, 144
Cerinthus, Cerinthian christology, 309 ff., 314, 357
Cestius, 227
Ceylon, 7
Chalcis, 25, 77, 92
Chaldaism, 6, 15, 321; *see* oriental syncretism, gnosis
Chaldee, 3; *see* Aramaic
charisma, 137, 262, 269, 272
chiliasm, *see* millennium
Chloe, 133
Chrestus (in Suetonius), 92, 99, 107
Christianism (Christianity), 452
Christians (the name), 67, 85, 165, 189, 193, 202, 435
christology, 29 ff., 32, 34, 36, 38, 174 ff., 176 ff., 181, 325, 329; christologies, 308, 309, 315, 356 ff., 423, 450, 453
church, local, unity and order, 123, 205 ff., ch. 14, 314, 358 ff., 374 ff., 380, 390, 444, 448, 465, 476 ff.
church at large, new Israel, *see* Diaspora, catholic, 144 ff., 179, 320, 327, 399 ff., 470, 474, 478 ff., 485, 493
church, spiritual deterioration in, 264, 299, 330, 371, 385 ff., 406, 496; see *anomia*, false teachers
Cilicia, 44, 57, 99, 109, 447
circumcision controversy, 54, 87 ff., 92, 108; *see* Jewish-Christian propaganda
Claudius, emperor, 55, 67, 107, 121, 125, 144, 166
Clemens, T. Flavius, 194, 377 ff.
Clement of Alexandria, 18, 299, 302, 305, 307, 392, 486, 491
Clement of Philippi, 153, 181 (perhaps identical with the following)
Clement of Rome, 122 ff., 182, 184, 195, 204, 207, 373 ff., 392 ff., 428, 475 ff.
Clement, Epistle of, 381 ff., 414
Clement, second Epistle of, so-called, 448
Clement in Syrian legend (apocryphal books of), 249, 314, 414, 416, 420
Cleodemus (Malchus), 7
Cleopas, 31, 50; *see* Clopas
Cletus (Anencletus), 207, 376, 475
Clopas (Cleopas? Alphaeus?), 31, 40
Cochabha, 151
Colossae, 168 ff., 292
Commagene, 5
Commandments (Mandata) of Hermas, 403 ff.
commandments given at baptism, 412, 454, 483 ff.; *see also* catechism
confirmation, 55, 130; *see* hands, laying on
Corinth, 110 ff., 121 ff., 133 ff., 373 ff., 379 ff., 476
Cornelius, 63
covenant, 488 ff., 500
creed-forms, 38, 138, 451, 464
Crescens, in Gaul, 196
Crescens of Smyrna, 457, 461 ff.
Crete, 197, 261 ff., 268 ff.
Crispus, 122, 134
Crocus, 449
cross, sign of, 205 ff.
Ctesiphon, 5, 436
Cumae, 393, 397
Cumanus, Ventidius, 92
Cyprus, Cypriot, 41, 66, 68 ff., 108, 110, 156, 436
Cyrene, 44, 66, 68, 80, 436
Cyril of Jerusalem, 501
Cyrus, 1

Damaris, 120
Damas, 450

Damascus, 58 ff., 68 ff.
Daniel, Book of, 15, 22, 32, 198, 203, 204, 346
David, in the gospel preaching, 24, 35, 38 ff., 67, 82 ff., 97 ff.; family of, 97 ff., 250 ff., 252, 334, 417, 453, 478; in liturgy, 493, 497 ff.
deaconesses (*ministrae*), 433; *see also* Phoebe
deacons, 44, 122, 148, 153, 181 ff., 257, 265 ff., 374 ff., 400, 420 ff., 473 ff., 492 ff.
dead, concern for the, 117, 347
Dead Sea Scrolls, 13, 28, 46 ff., 247, 482
Decapolis (Trachonitis), 48 ff., 70
dedication, festival of (Kislev 25), 12, 15, 22, 337
Demas, 171, 198
Demetrius (Jewish author), 17
Demetrius (silversmith), 139
Demetrius (in III John), 305
Demetrius of Alexandria, 420 ff.
Derbe, 85, 110 ff., 168
Diaspora (dispersion of Jews), 4 ff, 9 ff., 50, 101, 157, 200, 207, 238 ff., 254, 316, 478, 493
Didache, 274, 404, 466, 482 ff., 491 ff.
Didymus (Thomas), 45
Dio Cassius, 107, 378
Dionysius of Alexandria, 294, 363
Dionysius of Athens, 120
Dionysius of Corinth, 204, 381
Dionysus, 15
Diotrephes, 305
disciples, *see* Jesus
Docetics, 305, 308, 355, 423, 429, 442, 450, 456, 460 ff., 488
Domitian, 31, 239, 298, 312, 322 ff., ch. 18, 343 ff., 379, 428, 434
Domitilla, 378; cemetery of, 378
Dositheus, 29, 246
dreams, 60, 63, 75
Drusilla, 25, 160 ff.

Ebion, Ebionites, 191, 248, 411, 413 ff.
Ecclesiastes, Book of, 19
ecclesia, *kahal*, the church, 326
Ecclesiasticus, 326, 482
Edessa, 5, 6, 8
Edom, Edomites, 24, 98, 233 ff.
Egypt, 7 ff., 351; Jews in, 9, 11, 21, 436; Christianity in, *see* Alexandria
Egyptian prophet (in Acts), 156, 158
Eldad and Modat, Book of, 398
elder (presbyter), 78, 86, 92, 100, 153 ff., 181 ff., 256, 267 ff., 275, 374 ff., 380, 385, 420, 448, 460 ff., 471 ff., 473, 476
elder, the, 242, 290
elders in Asia Minor, 209, 290 ff., ch. 18
Eleazar, legendary high priest, 9
Eleazar, insurgent leader, 226 ff.
Eleazar the martyr, 16
elect, the, 195, 304, 385
Eliezer ben Hyrcanus, 227, 241, 426
Elijah, 2
Elizabeth, 31
Elkhasai, 411 ff., 440
Enoch, Book of, 16 ff., 32, 467
Epaenetus, 149
Epaphras, 171 ff.
Epaphroditus, 168, 180
Ephesus, 29; church of, 110 ff., 126 ff., 151, 199, ch. 14, 269, 298 ff., 450
Epictetus, 351, 394
Epicurus, 432
Epiphanes, *see* Antiochus IV
Epiphanius, 227, 249 ff., 411, 414, 418, 424, 437 ff., 477
episcopates, 256, 266, 452; *see also* bishops
episkopos, *see* bishops
epistles, production and dissemination, 99 ff., 201, 275 ff., 285 ff., 385, 462, 468, 473; *see also* writer's names quoted or referred to: 373, 383, 384, 450, 460, 469
eschatology, 14 ff., 29, 32, 116, 120, 180, 219 ff., 330 ff., 347 ff., 362
Esdras II (*Apocalypse of Ezra*), 259, 337 ff., 384, 440
Essenes, 13, 28, 247, 413
Esther, Book of, 13, 28, 337
eucharist, 34, 137, 175, 267, 450, 456, 466, 471, 475, 488 ff., 493 ff., 497 ff., 500, 501
Eunice, 109, 199
Euodia, 181
Euodius, 314
Euphrates, 66, 68, 78, 232, 344, 436 ff.
Eupolemos, 17

Eusebius, 18, 227, 294, 313, 418, 491
Eutychius, 419
evangelist, 57, 155, 179, 272
evil, conflict with, 74, 176ff., 180, 203, 413, 494; embodied in Roman Emperor, 73, 177, 203ff., 221, *see* Nero myth; visualized in the heavens, 176, 203, 415, *see* gnosis, planetary deities; sin and death, 176; powers of, *see* Beliar, Satan
exorcism, 131
Expositions, *see* Papias
Ezekiel, the prophet, 1, 15, 302, 346
Ezekiel, the tragic poet, 18
Ezra, 16, 241, 244
Ezra apocalypse, see *Esdras II*

Fadus, Cuspius, 77
'false teachers', Jewish type, 150, 154, 173ff., 197ff., 247ff., 255, ch. 14, 263ff., 271, 299, 329; anti-Jewish type, 299, 305, 308ff., 385, 496
famine of A.D. 45–46: 67, 75, 78
fasting, 81, 248; days of, 493; weeks of, 337, 400
Felicitas, martyr, 16
Felix, procurator, 25, 157ff., 163, 167
fermentum, 475
Festus, procurator, 163ff.
finance (money), 42, 118, 123, 139, 152, 160, 172, 180, 268ff., 496
first day of week (Lord's day, eighth day), 139, 153, 466, 496
first-fruits, 122, 149, 496
Flavian emperors, 239, 312: *see* Vespasian, Titus, Domitian
flesh in Christian theology, 357ff., 448, 450, 453, 488ff.; as evil, *see* gnostic themes
foods, clean and unclean, 62ff., 89ff., 136, 150, 492
forgiveness, *see* repentance
form-criticism, 212
fornication, 99ff., 103, 299
Fortunatus, 135, 381

Gaius of Corinth, 122, 134
Gaius of Doberium, 139, 152
Gaius of *III John*, 305
Gaius of Rome, 129
Galatia, 68, 80ff., 108, 110ff., 200
Galatian controversy, 83, 91ff.; *see* circumcision
Galatians, Epistle to, *see* Paul; compared with *Acts*, 60ff., 65, 78, 91, 105ff.
Galba, 231
Galilee, 12, 17, 24ff., 48ff., 253, 410
Gamaliel I, 27, 40, 43, 77, 158ff., 242
Gamaliel II, 241ff., 323, 410
Gaul, 25, 27, 71, 196ff.
gentile controversy 63ff., ch. 5; *see* circumcision
gentile converts become Israelites, 84ff., 87, 132, 158, 179, 192, 207ff., *see* God-fearers
Georgius Hamartolus, 369
Gerizim, 45ff., 54, 61
Gethsemane, 36
Gitta, 245
Glabrio, Manius Acilius, 377ff.
Glaucias, 421
God-fearers, gentile, 21, 87ff., 101, 132, 263, 481
gnosis, gnosticism, *see* heresy (for first stages); Samaritan, *see* Simon *and* Menander; Jewish type, 247ff., 401, *see* Hermas, Elkhasai *and* Ebionites; gentile types, *see* Cerinthus, Ophites, Marcion
gnostic rituals and liturgy, 230ff., 310
gnostic or spiritual man, 66, 68, 77, 82
gnostic themes, primal man, male emanation, 19, 247ff., 401, 403, 411, 419, 441, *see* God, son of *and* myth (for descent of the Christus); primal woman, female emanation, mother image, 19, 246ff., 401, 411, 422, 442
God Almighty, 222, 303, 319, 331, 388ff., 397, 466; the remote oriental deity, 246, 441, 449; the planetary deities, 246, 415; the creator as an adverse power, 246, 255, 415, 442; *see also* heavens
God-fearers, gentile, 21, 87ff., 101, 132, 263, 481
God, son of, 29, 36, 51, 59, 115ff., 214, 325, 356ff., 360ff., 489; *see also* Word of God, son of man, gnosis
golden rule, 288, 482

gospel, apostolic, 32, 37 ff., 38, 40, 51, 56, 63 ff., 82 ff., 92, 101, 120, 214, 224 ff., 324, 374, 464, 478 ff.
Gospel prologues, 280, 307
Gospels, written (*see* Matthew, Mark, etc.), also 161 ff., 209 ff., 214, 264, 277 ff., 367, 422 ff., 468 ff., 494; early quotation from or usage, 373, 383 ff., 392, 450, 469
grace, 59, 142 ff., 150
Gratus, Valerius, proconsul, 28
Greek language, etc. in Jerusalem, 5, 7, 10, 14, 47, 50, 210, 240 ff.

Hades, 416: *see* evil, powers of, *and* myth
Hadrian, emperor, 418, 437, 438
Haggai, 1
Hananel, high priest, 6
Hananiah of Alexandria, 49
hands, laying on, 44, 54 ff., 130, 197, 242, 269, 371, 478
hanukkah, *see* dedication festival
harvest symbolism, 225, 296, 497
hasidim, 12 ff.
Hasmonaeans, 1 ff., 23; *see* Maccabees
heavens, kingdom of, 320 ff., 327; heavenly powers, 174, 321, 453; *see also* evil, powers of, *and* planetary deities
Hebrew language, 3, 16 ff., 320
Hebrews, Epistle to, 313, 370 ff., 488 ff.
Hebrews, Gospel of, 422 ff.
Hegesippus, 31, 96 ff., 190, 247 ff., 336, 377, 381, 411, 417, 418, 422, 437, 476
Helen of Adiabene, 78
Hellenism, Jewish, ch. 1; *see also* Greek language, God-fearers, Diaspora; in Jerusalem, 43 ff., 47 ff., 69; in Caesaraea, 56 ff.; in Jerusalem church, 43 ff., 50; in the Diaspora, 101 ff., 134, 388 ff., 405; *see also* Judaism *and* synagogue worship
Heraclitus, 126
Herculaneum chapel, 205
heresies, 314; *see also* sects, parties, *and* gnosis
heresy, incipient, Jewish gnostic type, 173 ff., 247 ff.; anti-Jewish type, 255, 283 ff., 299, 305, see *anomia*, Docetics
Hermas, 57, 219, 224, 254, 340, 342, 377, 384 ff., ch. 21, 411, 474, 476
Hermes, 85, 134
Hermetic literature, 353 ff.
Herod Agrippa or Antipas, *see* Agrippa, Antipas
Herod the Great, 6, 14, 22 ff., 24 ff.
Herodias, 59, 70
Herodion, 149
Hezekiah of Galilee, 24 ff.
Hierapolis, 168, 254, 291 ff.
high priesthood, 10 ff., 25, 27, 62, 92, 163, 167, 186 (list), 191, ch. 12
Hillel the Elder (*za-ken*), 6, 33, 43, 241 ff., 483
Hippolytus, 411, 489, 497, 498
holiness, law of, 103 ff., 119; *see* Leviticus
Holy Spirit, in the church, 30, 37 ff., 55 ff., 63 ff., 80 ff., 84, 118 ff., 131, 361, 450; inspiration by (pneumatism, charismata), 37, 51, 55 ff., 63, 76, 80 ff., 112, 137, 308 ff., 342, 404 ff., 448, 450 ff., 496; *see also* angels, visions, apocalypse

Iconium, 85, 110 ff.
idols, idolatry, 119 ff., 135, 139; foods offered to, 100 ff., 103, 284, 299, 492
Ignatius, *Ignatius Epistles of*, 314 ff., 415, 440, 443 ff., 447 ff., ch. 24, 462, 466, 468 ff., 487 ff., 492, 497
Illyricum, 144
immersion, Jewish (*tebilah*), 104, 247 ff., 411 ff., 492
India, 7, 352, 410
Interpretations, *see* Papias
Iranian religious ideas, 6 ff., 14 ff., 410
Irenaeus, 291, 296, 298 ff., 302, 310, 315 ff.
Isaiah, 1
Isaiah, Ascension of, 177, 203 ff., 259, 264, 415 ff.
Iscariot, 33, 45
Ishmael ben Elishah, Rabbi, 426
Ishmael, high priest, 163, 186 ff.
Ishtar, 204, 416
Isis, 8, 20, 351
Italy, 370
Iturea, 25
Izates, 78

Jakin, *see* Alkimus
James, Epistle of, 157, 189, 254 ff., 377

James 'of Alphaeus', 49
James the Just, brother of the Lord, 31, 36ff., 60, 78, 89, 92ff., 96ff., 156ff., 422; martyrdom of, 190, 193, 248ff., tradition of, 244, 248ff., 478
James of Kefar Sama (or Sekanya), 243, 254
James, son of Zebedee, 31, 33, 45, 75
Jamnia, 48ff., 227, 231, 241ff., 426, 467
Jannaeus, Jannai, Jonathan, *see* Alexander Jannaeus
Jason of Cyrene, 16
Jeremiah, 1; *Epistle of*, 259
Jerome, 420, 422
Jerusalem, city of, 1, 11ff., 24ff., 68ff., ch. 12, 238ff., 340, 345ff., 437ff.
Jerusalem, church of, early years, 37–53; Paul's visit, 60; parties in, 52ff., 64, 81, 89, 99; prophets, 67, 73ff., 100, 155; persecution of Agrippa I, 75ff., famine, visit of Paul, 78ff.
Council of apostles and elders, ch. 5; epistle of council, 99ff., 102ff., 109ff., 119, 249ff., 284, 492; periodical councils, 127ff., 136; gentile churches, relation to, 78, 98, 127, 132ff., 139, 223, 238; Paul's last visit, ch. 8
In apocalyptic, 98n., 222, 223, 233ff., 339ff., 348, 402
Martyrdom of James the Just, 199ff., 248ff., persecutions, various, 42ff., 54, 59, 71, 188, 193; Pella, escape to, 227ff., 250; *see* Jewish Christians; return to Jerusalem, 418ff., 435ff., list of bishops, 190ff., 250ff., 417ff.
Jeshua (Jason), high priest, 11, 21
Jesus of Nazareth, family of, 39ff., 50, 97, 251; *see* David; disciples of, 30, 209, 243, 253ff., 294ff., 376; ministry, crucifixion and resurrection, 26, 29ff., 34, 36ff., 59, 138, 153; advent in glory, 34, 36, 38; *see* advent; temple, relations to, 34ff., 44; words of, *see* oral tradition, gospels, parables, apocalyptic
Jesus ben Ananus, 228
Jesus Justus, 171
Jewish-Christian propaganda in gentile churches, 87ff., 100, 141, 448; *see also under* 'false teachers'
Jewish Christians after the fall of Jerusalem, 191, 227, 231, ch. 13, 249ff., 251, 253, 417ff.
Johanan ben Zakkai, 43, 159, 227ff., 241ff., 323, 426
John the Baptist, 28ff., 31, 33, 130ff., 357
John the son of Zebedee, in Palestine, 31, 33, 45, 54, 78; in Asia Minor, 298, 302, 306, 366
John and the 'elders', ch. 17, 366; the elder in Papias, 294ff., 317; theory of two Johns, 295, 363, 366; his oral tradition, 209, 296, 317. Various traditions: through Polycarp, 297; through the *Revelation*, 298, 300; through Clement of Alexandria, 302; through Polycrates, 304; through the Epistles, 304ff., 308ff.; through the Gospel, 306ff., 365ff.; the 'beloved disciple', 306, 359, 364ff.
John and Cerinthus, 309; his school, 294, 304, 306, 310ff., 366ff., death of, 367ff.; in legend, the *Acts of John*, 368, and Philip of Side, etc., 368ff.
John, Acts of (apocryphal), 368
John, Gospel of, language and mode of thought, 350ff., 363ff.; Jews, relation to 354; docetism, relation to, 355; earlier literature, relation to, 353ff.; the Word of God, 356ff., 358ff.; the historical interest, 358; the liturgical structure, 359; discourses of Jesus, the Paraclete, 360ff.; comparison with the *Revelation*, 362ff.; the epilogue, 364ff.
John, Revelation of, the completed book, ch. 18; author and date, 298, 302, 341ff., 363ff.; the seven churches, 298ff., 342, 362; language and imagery, 301, 362; liturgy and worship, 303; the visions in Jerusalem, 73, 221ff., 236, 301; the call of the prophet, 223; the beast from the sea, 73, 221, 224, 232; the harlot city, 222, 233ff., 343ff.; the judgement on the temple, 237; the seven Caesars, 343ff.; the Nero myth, 344; the Word of God, 346ff.; millennial period, 348; new Jerusalem, 348
John of Gischala, 230ff., 240
Jonathan, the Maccabee, 12, 22

Jonathan the high priest, 62, 156, 163, 186
Joppa, 48 ff., 62
Jordan, 128
Joseph ben Cami, high priest, 92
Joseph the carpenter, 26, 31, 40
Josephus, 4, 13, 15, 18, 25 ff., 30, 43, 53, 72, 77, 94, 156, 158, 167, 187 ff.; reference to Christ, 189, 225 ff. (ch. 12), 229 ff., 240 ff., 335 ff.
Jubilees, *Book of*, 16 ff.
Judah the holy, Rabbi, 242
Judaism, Christianity continuous with, 51, 87 ff., 101, 179, 208, 238, 284 ff., 383 ff., 387, 390, 404, 465, 485, 490, 493 ff.
Judaism, rabbinic, 241 ff., 323, 467, 478; patriarchate, 241, 323, 478; reaction against among Christians, 323 ff., 440, 450, 493 ff., 496 ff.
Judas the Maccabee, 11, 22
Judas of Galilee, 26 ff.
Judas Iscariot, 33, 36, 45, 291, 297
Judas 'of James' (Theudas ?), 45
Judas the Jerusalem prophet, 100
Jude (Judas) the brother of the Lord, 31; grandsons of, 251, 334 ff., 377, 411
Jude, *Epistle of*, 254 ff., 264, 377
judgement, 29, 34, 35 ff., 160, 164, 189, 328
Judith, *Book of*, 16
Junia(s), 40, 149
justification, 54, 58 ff., 82, 89, 150
Justin Martyr, 192, 298, 315, 341, 416, 443, 486, 501
Justus, Titius, 123
Justus of Tiberias, 335
Justus, bishop of Jerusalem, 419
Juvenal, 479

Kedūshah, *see* sanctus
Kephas (Peter), 33, 45, 78
Kerioth or Karioth, 45
kerugma, *see* gospel
kingdom of God or of heaven, 30 ff., 36, 319, 320 ff., 327, 331
Kislev 25 (ninth month), 11 ff., 337
Klausner, J., 243

languages among Jews, 3, 5, 7, 14, 16; *see* Hebrew, Aramaic, Greek
Laodicea, 168 ff., 174, 292, 300
Laodiceans, *Epistle to*, 174, 178
last supper, 36, 498, 499
law of Moses and gospel, 21, 58 ff., 87 ff., 100 ff., 123, 150, 216, 372 ff., 387 ff.
Lebbaeus or Lebes, 46
Leontopolis, 11, 21
letters commendatory, 100, 129, 141, 274
Levi, 33, 45, 216
Leviticus, commandments of, 10 ff., 18, 103 ff., 119, 373, 482, 497
Libya, 44, 68
Linus, bishop of Rome, 200, 206, 376, 475
Little Antioch, 82 ff., 98 ff., 168, 199
Little Apocalypse (Mark xii), 74, 224 ff., 229, 232; in Luke, 229, 232; in Matthew 329 ff.
liturgy and worship, 175, 208, 263, 265 ff., 303 ff., 359 ff., 371 ff., 387 ff., 433, 451, 466, 487 f., 492 ff.; *see also* baptism, catechism, eucharist, etc.
'logia' (oracles), 317 ff.
Lois, 109, 199
Lord's day, *see* week
Lord's prayer, 217 (319), 493
lots, casting of, 230, 273
Lucius of Cyrene, 80
Luke the physician, 111 ff., 151 ff., ch. 8, 171, 206 ff., 278 ff.
Luke, *Gospel of*, 161, 278 ff., 281 ff.
Lydda, 48 ff., 62, 241, 426
Lydia, the country, 4, 300
Lydia, the woman, 114
Lysias, Claudius, 158 ff.
Lystra, 85, 109 ff., 168

Maccabaeans, Maccabees, 12 ff., 23 ff.
Maccabees, *Books of*, 15, 16, 337; *II Maccabees*, 259
Macedonia, 115 ff.
Machaerus, 30, 45 ff.
magi, magianism, 2, 6 ff., 57, 243, 321
magic, magician, 32, 57, 77, 81, 131, 174, 263, 413
Magnesia, 446, 540
Magnificat, 24, 282
Malachi, 493, 499
Manaen (Menahem?), 70, 80, 101

Mandaeans, 412
Manetho, 8
manuscripts, production of, 212 ff.; of the New Testament, Bezae (D), 130; Chester Beatty, 17; Vaticanus (B), 130
Maranatha, 493
Marcellus, procurator, 62
Marcion, 178, 307 ff., 423 ff., 440, 461 ff.; gospel of, 423 ff.
Mariamne, 25
Mark, John, 42, 50, 76, 80 ff., 108, 169, 171, 174, 183, 199, 202 ff., 206
Mark, Gospel of, 34 ff., 161, 209 ff., 277; last verses of, 217, 289, 313; *see also* Little Apocalypse
Marthana, Marthous, 412,
martyrs, martyrdoms, 16, 37, 45, 75, 180, 223, 333 ff., 347 ff., 352, 368, 398, 429, 432 ff., 445, 449, 454 ff., 458, 488
Martyrs, 'Acts' of, 16, 45, 191
Marullus, procurator, 62
Mary, the Virgin, 26, 31, 42, 252, 282, 453
Mary, mother of Mark, 42, 76
Mary, mother of Rufus, 149 ff.
Masada, 48, 226
Masbothaeans, Sebuai, 247, 411
Mattathias, 12, 22
Matthew, 23, 45, 243, 294, 317, 325
Matthew, Gospel of, Aramaic, 254, 317 ff., 422, 243 ff.
Matthew, Gospel of, Greek, ch. 17; Jewish-Christian sources, 215 ff., *and see above*; Petrine and Marcan sources, 320, 325 ff., authorship, structure, style, 316, 319 ff., 328 ff.; law, apocalypse, eschatology, 321 ff., 329 ff.; Pharisaism, relation to, 322 ff.; quoted in Ignatius, 452, 470, in *Didache*, 492 ff., 500
Matthias, 40, 46
Matthias, high priest, 187, 230 ff.
Maximus, an apostate, 398
Medes, 2
Mekilta, 487
Menahem (Menelaus), 11, 21
Menahem the Zealot, 226 ff.
Menander, of Ephesus or Pergamum, 8
Menander, the gnostic, 315
Mesopotamia, Jews in, 68, 435, 440
messiah or king, 21, 24, 30, 34 ff., 36, 38, 67, 74, 82 ff., 132, 192, 325, 334 ff., 372; political implications, 67, 84 ff., 114, 116, 140, *see* Rome, conflict with empire of; *see also* christology
Michael, 401, 407
Miletus, 153, 168
millennium (chiliasm), 296, 348, 363
minim, blessing of, 323, 423 ff.
ministry, 122, 132, 142, 146, 153, 155, 182 ff., 265 ff., 385 ff., 470 ff., 495; *see* apostles, bishops, elders, deacons
Mishnah, 33, 210, 242, 243 ff., 427
missionary journeys and reports, 62–5, 81–6, 92 ff., 127, 133, 151
Mithras, 6, 8
Mnason, 156
Montanus, Montanism, 291, 367
Moses, 17 ff., 354; *see also* law and gospel
Muratorian Fragment, 184, 305, 307, 392
Museum, the, 8
music and song, 175, 296, 303 ff., 450 ff.
Musonius Rufus, 333, 351
Myra, 168
Mysia, 112
mystery, language of (Paul), 73 ff., 134, 138, 142 ff., 174 ff. (*see* myth), 180, 338, 441, 416
mystery religions, 8, 134, 138
myth, mythological symbolism, 174, 176 ff., 180, 443; see also *Isaiah, Ascension of*, Hermas, gnosis; for descent of the Christus, 203 ff., 310 ff., 415 ff., 424, 453; *see* Nero myth, Ophites, evil, powers of

name in persecution, 202, 298, 400, 429, 433 ff.; in benedictions, 493 ff., 498
Narcissus of Jerusalem, 417 ff.
Narcissus of Rome, 149
Nazaraeans, Nazarenes, 42, 51 ff., 75, 244, 255, 323, 411
Nazareth, 48 ff., 251, 253
nazirites, 28 ff., 158, 253
Nebuchadnezzar, 1
Nehardea, 5
Nehemiah, 1
Nero, 125, 166 ff., 182, 187 ff., 194, 231, 333, 340, 343

Nero myth, 177, 203 ff., 340 ff., 344 ff.
Nero, persecution under, ch. 10, 428
Nerva, 334, 379
Nicolaitans, 299
Nicolas of Antioch, 144, 299
Nisan (first month), 14 or 15th of, 34 ff., 158; *see* passover
Nisibis, 5
Noah, Book of, 17
notzrim, 244, 233; *see* Nazaraeans, 425
Nymphas, 174

Onesimus, bishop, 449, 471
Onesimus, slave, 172
Onesiphorus, 198
Onias III, 4, 21
Onias IV, 11, 13, 21
Ophel, mount Zion, 47, 240, 438
Ophites, 255, 416
oral tradition, 38 ff., 51, 136 ff., 175, 210, 243, 263 ff., 273, 277, 296, 371, 383, 403, 459, 469
Origen, 412, 422
Orontes, 4, 479
Orosius, 107
Osrhoene, 5
Otho, M. Salvius, 187, 231

pais, servant or child, 51, 499 ff.
Pamphylia, 68, 82
Papias, *Interpretations* or *Expositions*, 209 291 ff., 298, 307, 317 ff., 367, 368 ff.
papyrus, 8
Parables of Hermas, 360, 393, 403 ff., 406 ff., 443, 451
parables of Jesus, 219, 266, 281, 319, 330
Paraclete, 361
Paradise, 73
parchment (*pergamena*), 8
Parthia, 2, 7, 24, 68, 71 ff., 78, 340 ff., 410, 435, 440
parties in the church, 'sects', 64, 134, 150, 213, 380, 448, 456; *see also under* Jerusalem church *and* sects
passover, feast of (Nisan 14), 34 ff., 75, 136 ff., 152, 207, 356, 359, 371, 475, 488
Pastoral Epistles, *see* Paul
pastors, *see* shepherd

Patara, 155, 168
Patmos, island, 292, 342 ff.
Patriarchs, Testaments of the Twelve, 16 ff., 404, 407, 467
Paul, early history, 38 ff., 57 ff., 257; Roman citizen, 114, 159, 163 ff., at Antioch, 67, 73, 78; visit to Jerusalem, 75, 78 ff.
Mission to Galatia, 80 ff.; circumcision controversy, 87 ff.; *Galatians, Epistle to*, 60 ff., 81, 84, 90 ff., 145, 150; Jerusalem council, ch. 5
Galatian and Phrygian journey, 108 ff.; Macedonia and Achaia, ch. 6; *Thessalonians, Epistle to*, 73 ff., 145, 201; visit to Palestine and Syria, 127 ff; in Ephesus, ch. 7; theory of imprisonment in Ephesus, 149, 161; *Corinthians, Epistle to*, 143 ff, 146; production and dissemination of epistles 146, 178; *Romans, Epistle to*, 143 ff.; pilgrimage to Jerusalem, chs. 8 and 9; imprisonment in Caesarea, ch. 9
Imprisonment in Rome, ch. 10; imprisonment, epistles of, 161, 171 ff.; *Philemon Epistle to*, 171 ff.; *Colossians, Epistle to*, 173 ff.; *Ephesians, Epistle to*, 177 ff., 415; *Philippians, Epistle to*, 180 ff.; imprisonment, release from (?), 181 ff., 185; Spain, journey to (?), 145, 148, 184
Pastoral Epistles, 185, 196 ff., ch. 14; martyrdom of, 195 ff., 261; successors of, ch. 14; Pauline schools, hypothetical 283 ff., 429; collection of epistles, 286
Paul, Acts of, apocryphal, 85
Paul, nephew of, 159
pavement, in Jerusalem, 358
Pella, 48 ff., 227 ff., 231, 250 ff., 411, 418, 438 ff.
pentecost, feast of (Siwan 6), 37, 127 ff., 139, 142, 156, 371
Perga, 82
Pergamum, 8, 168, 292, 299
persecutions, in Alexandria, of Jews, 71; in Jerusalem, of Christians, *see* Jerusalem; in the Roman Empire, *see* Rome, conflict with; under Nero, ch. 10, 428; under Domitian, 298 ff., 332 ff.,

persecutions (*cont.*)
344, 377ff., 400, 429ff.; under Trajan, 430ff., ch. 24
Persian (Iranian) religious ideas, 6ff., 14ff., 441; *see* gnosis; syncretism, oriental
Peter, one of the Twelve, 33, 45; in the Jerusalem church, 36ff; in Samaria 61ff., journey to Caesarea and report, 62ff.; imprisoned by Agrippa, 75ff., at Antioch, 89; at Jerusalem council, ch. 5; subsequent travels (Asia Minor? Rome?), 106, 130, 163; *Epistle of*, 130, 200ff., 207ff., 416, 429ff., 435, 462; martyrdom of, 195ff., 202, 364; Mark, relation to, 202, 206, 209, 215, 218, 317; tradition of, 34, 213ff, 292, 317, 324ff.; in later legend, 314, 414, 420; *see* Clement
Peter, Second Epistle of, 200, 254, 259
Peter and Paul, joint tradition of, 93, 101, 106, 195ff., 206ff., 213, 238, 283, 315, 370, 383, 449, 452
Petronius, 72
Phanni (Phineas?), 186, 230ff.
Pharisees, Pharisaism, 13ff., 16, 24, 26ff., 32, 42ff., 50, 57, 189, 216, 238, 241, *see* Rabbis, rabbinic schools; in Jerusalem church, 92, 99
Pheroras, 26
Philadelphia, 88, 293, 300, 448, 455, 471
Philemon, 172, 174
Philip the apostle, 45, 169, 254, 291; daughters of, 291ff.
Philip the evangelist, 44, 54ff., 155ff., 291; daughters of, 155, 291
Philip, Herod, 25, 70
Philip of Side, 334, 368ff.
Philippi, 110ff., 114, 152ff., 180ff., 457ff., 472ff.
Philo 'the Elder', 18
Philo the philospher, 26ff., 71, 77, 247, 351
Philologus, etc., 151
philosophers, 332ff., 351ff.; *see also* Plato, Aristotle, Stoicism
Philostratus, 351
Phocylides, pseudo-, 18, 482
Phoebe, 144, 148
Phoenicia, 8, 66, 68ff., 92
phoenix, 428
Phrygia, 2, 4, 68, 88, 112, 172, 300ff.
Pilate, Pontius, 27ff., 36, 47, 61ff., 192, 193
Pirke Aboth, 241, 492
Pius, bishop of Rome, 392
planetary deities, 6ff., 176, 246, 321, 415; *see* Chaldaism, gnosis, etc.
Plato, Platonism, 7, 20, 333, 351
Pliny the elder, 428ff.
Pliny the younger, 247, 428ff.
Plutarch, 351
'pneumatism', *see* Holy Spirit
Polybius, 450
Polycarp, 297, 299, 423, 445ff., ch. 25, 445, 449; *Epistle of*, 457ff., 459ff.; theory of two epistles, 461ff.
Polycrates, 291, 304
Pompey the Great, 24
Pontus, 68, 130, 200, 429ff.
Poppaea, 187, 231
Praxedis, 477
presbyter, *see* elder
presbytery, 262, 269
Prisca, Priscilla, 111, 121, 127, 129, 144, 149, 200
Priscilla, in Roman tradition, cemetery of, 378ff., 477
priesthood in the church, 124, 375, 448, 496ff.
Proclus, the Montanist, 291
procurators, 27, 62, 77, 156, 163, 188, 226
prophets, Jewish, 228ff.
prophets, Christian, 61, 67ff., 72ff., 80ff., 115ff., 137, 155, 179, 264, 274, 381, 384ff., 392ff., 398, 409, 492ff., 496ff.
Proto-Luke, theory of, 162
Proverbs, Book of, 19
pseudonymity, 185, 259ff., 276, 286ff.
pseudonymous literature, 200, 259, 336
Ptolemais, 48, 72, 155
Ptolemy I, 2, 7ff.
Ptolemy II, 2, 8ff.
Ptolemy VI, 11, 17, 21
Pudens, 200, 387
Pudentiana, 477

'Q', gospel source, 161ff., 211ff.
Quietus, Lusius, 435ff.
Qumran, 46, 247

Rabbis, rabbinic schools, 33, 51, 215, 231, 322 ff., 478
Red Sea, 7
renunciations, 105
repentance and forgiveness (church discipline), 331, 371 ff., 382, 385 ff., 387, 395, 400, 411, 456, 460, 466
resurrection of the dead, 117, 138, 142, 199, 204, 315
resurrection of Jesus, 37 ff., 51, 116, 138, 423, *see* gospel apostolic
Rhoda, 76, 394 ff.
Rome, Christians in, 55, 98, 106, 111, 121, 139, 194; church of, 144, 148 ff., 170, 193 ff., ch. 11, 376 ff., ch. 20, 392, 452, 454, 474 ff., 479 ff.
Rome, empire and government of, *see* persecutions; conflict with, prior to persecution, 67, 85, 114, 124, 126, 132, 140, 160, 176, 182, 192; on submission to civil power, 15, 151, 177, 208, 384; as embodiment of evil, 73 ff., 115 ff., 118, 176 ff., 203, 346, *see* apocalyptic, Nero myth
Rufus, 149, 206
Rufus the martyr, 445, 457, 460

Sabazius, 5
sabbath, 448
Sabinus, F., 194
Sadducees, 13 ff., 27, 42, 245
Salome (Alexandra), *see* Alexandra
Salome (the dancer), 25, 160
Salome, sister of Herod the Great, 26
Salome, wife of Zebedee, 31
Samaria, Samaritans, 12 ff., 27, 29, 45 ff., 54 ff., 61, 92, 244, 315, 357, 416
Samosata, 5
sanctus (in liturgy), 303, 389
sanhedrin, 14, 27, 42, 50, 92, 159, 188, 241, 411
Sardis, 292
Satan, 118, 135, 461; *see* evil, powers of
Satornil, 441 ff.
Saul of Tarsus, 40, 57, 85; *see* Paul
Scaeva, 131
schism, 380, 448, 456, 461, 464; *see* parties, sects
scriptures, Hebrew; 3, 9 ff., 52 ff., 54, 101, 129, 137, 262, 323, 372, 425, 439, 451, 467, 490
sects, Jewish, 13, 28, 38, 55, 241, 247 ff., 250, 411 ff., 417, 437; *see also* heresies
Secundus, 152
Seleucia in Mesopotamia, 5
Seleucids, Seleucid era, 2, 4 ff., 6, 11, 19, 23 ff.
Seleucus I, Nicator, 2, 4
semikah (laying on of hands), 120, 166, 187, 333
Seneca, 120, 166, 187, 333
Sennacherib, 1
Sepphoris, 48 ff., 227
Septuagint (LXX), 2, 8 ff., 16, 98, 427
Serapis, 8
Sergius Paulus, 8
serpent, 255, 490
servant, see *pais*
seven, the, 43 ff.
Severus of Antioch, 420
Shammai, 33, 241, 326
Shechem, 12, 49, 54
Shelom Zion, *see* Alexandra Salome
Shepherd (Angel), 403, 407
shepherd (pastors) 154, 179, 209, 470 ff.
Sibyl, *Sibylline Oracles*, 188 ff., 316, 321, 340 ff., 397, 416
Sicarius, 33, 45, 163, 226 ff.
Silas, Silvanus, 46, 72 ff., 100, 109 ff., ch. 6, 160, 201, 206
Simeon, son of Gamaliel I, 159
Simeon, son of Gamaliel II, 242
Similitudines, see *Parables*
Simon the high priest, 11, 13
Simon the Maccabee, 112
Simon Magus, 29, 55 ff., 245 ff.; legend of 414 ff.; *see also* gnosis
Simon Peter, 33; *see* Peter
Simon the tanner, 62
Simon the Zealot, or Cananean, 45, 77
Simon ben Geiora, 227, 240
Simon, son of Clopas, *see* Symeon
Sinope, 427, 429
Siwan (third month) 6, *see* pentecost; 37 43 ff.
Sixtus, *see* Xystus
slaves, 172, 208, 394, 433
Smyrna, 68, 168, 292, 297, 299, 449 ff., 455 ff.
Solomon, *Proverbs of*, 19

Solomon, Psalms of, 24
Solomon, Song of (Canticles), 337, 408, 426
Solomon, Wisdom of, 19 ff., 442, 467
son of man, 14 ff., 17, 30 ff., 34, 36, 44, 74, 216, 220, 237, 325, 331
Sopater (Sosipater?), 124, 135, 146
Sosthenes, 124, 135, 146
Spain, 145, 148, 184
Stephanas, 122 ff., 134, 146, 476
Stephen, 43 ff., 50, 53
Stoicism, 7, 16, 20, 57, 120, 126, 135, 166, 333
stone symbolism, 327, 489
strangers and pilgrims, 119
successions, 97, 252, 478
Suetonius, 107, 332, 429
Sunday, *see* first day of week
Symeon, son of Clopas, 31, 40, 190 ff., 249 ff., 411, 417 ff.
Symeon the Black (Niger), 80
Symphorosa, 16
synagogue liturgy and order, 101, 263, 371 ff.; worship, 303 ff., 323, 389 ff., 424 ff., 438; order and ministry, 303, 375 ff., 465 ff., 467 ff., 477 ff.
synagogues, 15, 21, 44, 47, 68 ff., 82, 88, 90, 121, 131 ff., 388
syncretism, oriental, 3, 5 ff., 14 ff., 28, 134
Syntyche, 18
Synzygus, 180
Syria, Syrian religious ideas, 4, 6 ff., 410, 452, 479
Syrian Christianity, 100, 104 ff., 314, 440, 450 ff., 495; *see also* Antioch, church of

Taanit, 490
tabernacles, festival of, Tishri 15–22: 15, 35
Tacitus, 72, 193, 332, 428, 433, 479
Tammuz (Adonis), 6, 8, 339, 407
Tammuz (fourth month), fast of, 235, 337, 487
tanna, 242, 274; *see* Rabbis, teachers
Tarsus, 5, 57, 67 ff., 168
teachers (teaching), 179, 262, 267 ff., 274 ff., 400, 409, 474, 480, 492 ff.
tebilah, *see* immersion
temple, in Egypt, *see* Leontopolis
temple, in Jerusalem; destructions and desecrations of, 11, 21 ff., 24 ff., 72, ch. 12, 225, 228, 233, 236; Jesus and the temple, 34 ff., 44; in Christian apocalyptic, 35, 44, 73, 225, 228, 233, 236
temple, in Samaria, 12, 49
temple, spiritual, 119, 135, 208, 402; *see also* Jerusalem in apocalyptic, *and* building, imagery of
Tertius, 147
Tertullian, 302, 377, 414, 424, 489
Tertullus, 159
Testaments, see *Patriarchs*
testimonies, books of, 53, 91, 252 ff., 373, 485 ff., 487 ff., 490
tetrarch, 25, 27
textual variations and criticism, 287, 289
Thaddaeus, Theudas, 43, 243 ff.
Thebuthis, 250
Theodas, 421
Theodotion, 47
Theodotus, Samaritan poet, 18
Theophilus of Antioch, 414
Theophilus, high priest, 62, 186
Theophilus, Luke's patron, 278 ff.
Therapeutae, 247
Thessalonica, 110 ff., 114
Theudas the apostle, *see* Thaddaeus
Theudas the rebel, 27, 77
third heaven, 73
Thomas, Didymus, 45, 293
Thyatira, 48 ff., 63, 72
Tiberius, emperor, 36, 62, 70, 166
Timothy, 109 ff., ch. 6, 132, 142, 171, 199, 206, ch. 14, 261 ff., 370; Epistle to, *see* Paul
Titus, 78 ff., 130, 141 ff., 197 ff., ch. 14, 261 ff., 268 ff.; *Epistle to*, *see* Paul
Titus, emperor, 234 ff., 239 ff., 312, 343 ff., 438; arch of, 240
Tobit, Book of, 16, 337, 483
tower, vision of (Hermas), 400, 407 ff.
Trachonitis, 25
Trajan, emperor, 411, 428 ff.; *Rescript* of, 434; wars of, 435 ff., 440, 445
Tralles, 446, 450

Transjordania (Arabia, Trachonitis), 29, 247, 251
Troas, 110, 112, 152, 197, 450 ff.
Trophimus, 152, 156, 158
Tryphaena, etc., 150
Trypho, Dialogue with, 486
Two Ways (catechism), 404, 482 ff., 490, 492
Twelve, the, 33, 39 ff., 45 (list of), 61, 203, 215, 221, 273, 326, 415
Tychicus, 152, 171 ff., 197 ff., 261
Tyrannus, 131
Tyre, 155

Valens, 457, 460 ff., 473
Vatican Hill, 192
Victor of Capua, 369
Ventidius, *see* Cumanus
Vespasian, emperor, 182, 190, 229, 239 ff., 250, 312
Vesuvius, eruption of, 341
Virgil, 393
vision or mystery, language of, 30, 73 ff., 76, 115 ff., 117, 328, 337, 387, 390, 393 ff.; in Paul, 138, 173, 180, 363 ff.; in John, 349, 354, 362 ff., 364 ff.; *see* gnosis, myth, apocalypse
visions, 63, 73, 308 ff., 337 ff., 399 ff., 410 ff.
Visions of Hermas, 392 ff., 403; Rhoda, dialogue with, 394 ff.; elder lady, 396; tower building, 399; monster, 400; bride, 400, 402
Vitellius, emperor, 232

War, Jewish, 192, 226 ff., ch. 12
week, 7; *see* fasting, first day
widows, 43 ff., 267 ff.
Wisdom of God, 19, 401, 442
woman, seen in vision, mother or bride, 388 ff., 343, 384 ff., 396 ff., 400, 408, 422, 442
women in the church, 114, 120, 133, 137, 162, 181, 208, 275
Word of God, 19, 223, 247, 306, 346 ff., 353 ff., 357, 401
worship of God, 175, 208, 267, 303, 387 ff., 390; *see* liturgy *and* eucharist

Xystus, 475

Zachariah, son of Baruch, 231
Zacharias, 31
Zaddik, 13
Zadduk, 26
Zadok, 11 ff., 25, 27, 54
Zadokite, 12 ff., 482
za-ken (elder), 242, *see* Hillel
Zarvan, 6
Zealots, 26, 33, 45, 77, 226 ff.
Zebedee, 31
Zechariah, 1, 15
Zeus, 6, 11, 22, 85
Zion mount (Ophel), 47, 49, 438
Zoroaster (Zarathustra), Zoroastrian, 6; *see* Persia, magi, gnosis
Zosimus, 445, 457, 460